PASCAL

5th Edition

Elliot B. Koffman

Addison-Wesley Publishing Company

Reading, Massachusetts • Menlo Park, California • New York • Don Mills, Ontario
Wokingham, England • Amsterdam • Bonn • Sydney • Singapore • Tokyo
Madrid • San Juan • Milan • Paris

Senior Editor: Lynne Doran Cote
Development Editors: Elizabeth Zayatz, Marjorie Singer-Anderson
Editorial Assistant: Maite Suarez-Rivas
Production Services: Anita Wagner
Senior Production Supervisor: John Walker
Marketing Manager: Tom Ziolkowski
Composition: Compset, Inc.
Illustration: Rolin Graphics
Text Designer: Darci Mehal, Aureo Design
Cover Designer: Trudi Gershenov
Cover Design Supervisor: Peter Blaiwas
Senior Manufacturing Manager: Roy Logan

Library of Congress Cataloging-in-Publication Data
Koffman, Elliot B.
    Pascal / Elliot B. Koffman — 5th ed.
      p. cm.
    Includes index.
    ISBN 0-201-52674-3
    1. Pascal (Computer program language)   I. Title.
  QA76.73.P2K624   1994
  005.13'3—dc20   94-34314
                                CIP

Reprinted with corrections November, 1995

ISBN 0-201-52674-3

  3 4 5 6 7 8 9 10 - DOC - 9998979695

PREFACE

This textbook is intended for a first course in problem solving and program design using Pascal. It assumes no prior knowledge of computers or programming, and for most of its material, high school algebra is sufficient mathematics background. A limited knowledge of discrete mathematics, however, is desirable for certain sections.

This edition, like its predecessors, closely follows the recommendations of the ACM Computing Curricula Task Force for CS1[1] and CS2[2] and the ACM/IEEE-CS Joint Curriculum Task Force.[3] We emphasize problem solving, abstraction, and software engineering throughout the text.

In preparing this revision, we have made every effort to simplify the presentation wherever possible, striving for shorter, more focused chapters. For example, we have reorganized the coverage of arrays and records into a three-chapter sequence: one-dimensional arrays (Chapter 10), multidimensional arrays (Chapter 11), and records (Chapter 12).

Problem Solving

The connection between good problem-solving skills and effective software development is established early in Chapter 1 (Overview of Computers and Programming). The software development method, introduced in Chapter 2 (Problem Solving and Pascal), is used to solve the first case study and is applied consistently to all the case studies of the text.

Chapter 3 (Functions and Procedures) continues the emphasis on problem solving by discussing top-down design, divide-and-conquer, solution by analogy, and generalization of a solution. An important section of this chapter demonstrates how a Pascal program can be derived by editing the documentation that results from systematically following the software development method.

Software Engineering

The text covers many aspects of software engineering. Discussions of program style issues appear throughout in special displays. The concept of a program as a sequence of control structures is introduced early in Chapter 4 (Selection Control Structures: if and case Statements). Several chapters include sections that discuss algorithm tracing, debugging, and testing.

[1]Recommended Curriculum for CS1, E. Koffman, P. Miller, and C. Wardle, *Communications of the ACM* 27, 10 (October 1984), 998–1001.
[2]Recommended Curriculum for CS2, E. Koffman, D. Stemple, and C. Wardle, *Communications of the ACM* 28, 8 (August 1985), 815–818.
[3]*Computing Curricula 1991, Report of the ACM/IEEE-CS Joint Curriculum Task Force,* A.B. Tucker (editor), 1991, ACM Press and IEEE Computer Society Press.

Chapter 9 (Software Engineering) is a complete unit on software engineering. This chapter discusses the system/software life cycle (SLC), prototyping, and programming teams. The in-depth coverage of all phases of the SLC includes more discussion of informal techniques for program testing (e.g., glass box versus black box testing, integration testing, structured walkthroughs) and formal methods for program verification as well as a discussion of loop invariants. This chapter also reviews procedural abstraction and introduces data abstraction. Chapter 9 concludes with a discussion of professional ethics.

Procedural Abstraction

Although there is no universal agreement on when to introduce procedures and procedure parameters, most educators do agree on the following points: Procedures should be introduced as early as feasible, procedures should never process global variables (side effects), and procedure parameters are a difficult concept for students to understand. The approach taken in the text is to discuss the importance of program modularization and reusability in Chapter 3 by introducing the standard functions, structure charts, and procedures without parameters. The chapter motivates the use of procedures as program building blocks by showing some applications of procedures without parameters (for example, by displaying long lists of user instructions and drawing diagrams). Chapter 3 then discusses, in Section 3.5, the need for parameters and the limitations of procedures without parameters, thereby providing a foundation for the later study of parameters.

Chapter 6 (Modular Programming) completes the study of procedures and functions, covering all aspects of parameter lists. The chapter begins by discussing procedures with only value parameters, then value and variable parameters, and finally functions. An optional section at the end of the chapter introduces recursive functions.

Some instructors prefer to cover procedures with and without parameters together. To this end, you can easily rearrange the sequence of topic coverage. If you want to wait until Chapter 6 to cover procedures with and without parameters, defer Sections 3.4 and 3.5 until then. Conversely, if you want to cover procedure parameters earlier, cover Section 6.1 (introduction to parameter lists) right after Chapter 3 and cover Sections 6.2 and 6.3 (variable parameters, syntax of parameter lists) after completing the first three sections of Chapter 4 (control structures, Boolean expressions, and the if statement).

Data Abstraction and ADTs

The software engineering chapter (Chapter 9) introduces data abstraction, providing the first example of an abstract data type (ADT). Data abstraction and ADTs are used in the advanced topics portion of the textbook, starting in Chapter 12. We show how to implement ADTs as VAX Pascal modules in Appendix D and as Turbo Pascal units in Appendix E.

Interviews with Computer Scientists

A popular feature of the last edition was a collection of interviews with notable computer scientists (Adele Goldberg, David Patterson, and Patrick Winston, among others), which were placed throughout the text. These interviews alert beginning students to the breadth of the subject area, providing them with a description of issues of concern in several fields of computer science (for example, artificial intelligence, operating systems, databases, user interfaces) and some idea of the background preparation needed for success in these fields. We have updated these interviews and provided several new ones.

Coverage of Theoretical Concepts

This edition covers theoretical topics recommended by the curriculum committee report. An optional section in Chapter 7 introduces numerical computation and iterative approximations. Chapter 9 provides a discussion of program verification, focusing on assertions and loop invariants. Chapter 10 introduces searching and sorting of an array followed by a discussion of algorithm analysis and Big-O notation.

Pedagogical Features

We employ several pedagogical features to enhance the usefulness of this book as a teaching tool. Discussion of some of these features follows. Approximately one-third of all exercises, review questions, and programming projects are new to this edition.

End-of-Section Exercises: Most sections end with a number of self-check exercises, including exercises that require analysis of program fragments as well as short programming exercises. Answers to odd-numbered self-check exercises appear at the back of the book; answers to the rest of the exercises are provided in the Instructor's Manual.

End-of-Chapter Exercises: Each chapter ends with a set of quick-check exercises and answers. Immediately following are chapter review questions, whose solutions appear in the Instructor's Manual.

End-of-Chapter Projects: Most end-of-chapter projects include one or two special programming project pairs in which the second of the pair requires a modification to the solution of the first project. Solutions to the first project in each pair are available from Addison-Wesley. All project solutions appear in the Instructor's Manual.

Examples and Case Studies: The text contains a large number and variety of programming examples. Whenever possible, examples contain complete programs or procedures rather than incomplete program fragments. Each chapter contains one or more substantial case studies that are solved following the software development method.

Syntax Displays: The syntax displays describe the syntax and semantics of each new Pascal feature and then provide examples. Several syntax diagrams appear in the body of the text; an appendix contains a complete collection of syntax diagrams.

Program Style Displays: The program style displays discuss issues of good programming style.

Error Discussions and Chapter Review: Each chapter ends with a section that discusses common programming errors. Chapter reviews include a table of new Pascal constructs.

Coverage of Advanced Topics

The material in Chapters 1 through 12 normally will be covered in the first semester of a course in programming methods. The book contains five additional chapters that cover advanced topics normally studied in the second semester or in the first semester of an accelerated course. This material may be used as a reference for students continuing their study of computer science and, in some cases, may be used as the primary text for a second-semester course. There is certainly sufficient material for a two-quarter sequence. Advanced topics covered include:

Recursion (Chapter 13)
Sets (Chapter 14)
External data structures: files (Chapter 15)
Pointers and linked lists (Chapter 16)
Dynamic data structures (Chapter 17)

Appendixes and Supplements

Appendixes and Pascal Compilers: The text concludes with separate appendixes covering Pascal language elements, syntax diagrams, and character codes. The appendixes describe how to use VAX Pascal modules and Turbo Pascal units to implement abstract data types, and how to use three Pascal compilers for personal computers (Dr. Pascal™, PcPix™—available free to users of this book—and Turbo Pascal™). There is also an appendix containing a program that incorporates most Pascal language constructs.

Directory: CHAP2
File: METRIC.PAS

Program Files: For case studies, all procedures and functions are incorporated in a single program file. Also available are files containing solutions to selected programming projects. These solutions serve as the starting point for follow-on projects. These files can be accessed via `ftp` from Addison-Wesley and loaded into the Turbo Pascal environment. An icon like the one in the margin appears alongside each program module or project indicating the name of the disk directory (e.g., `CHAP2`) and file (e.g., `METRIC.PAS`) containing the program.

To access these files, log in (using `anonymous` as your log-in id) to `ftp aw.com`. The files are located two subdirectories down from the main directory. Change directories following the path `aw.computer.science/Pas-`

`cal5e`. Those unfamiliar with `ftp` procedures can refer to the explicit instructions included in the Instructor's Manual.

Instructor's Manual: An Instructor's Manual is available through your Addison-Wesley sales representative. Use reference number 0–201–93389–6 when ordering. All material in the Instructor's Manual, plus test questions, solutions to programming projects, and transparency masters are available on-line. For more information, send mail to pascal5e@aw.com with the following line as the only text of the message:

`send information`

Acknowledgments

The principal reviewers were most essential in suggesting improvements and finding errors. They include:

Martha Dinwiddie
University of Dallas—Texas

Michael Doran
University of Southern Alabama

Deborah Dunn
Texas A & M University

Mary Lou Hines
University of Missouri—Kansas City

Van Howbert
Colorado State University

Ivan Liss
Radford University

Charles Owen
Dartmouth College

Wayne Smith
Mississippi State University

Tim Thurman
University of Kansas

In addition to reviewing the manuscript, Charles Owen, Dartmouth College, contributed many exercises and projects new to this edition. Also, I would like to acknowledge the contributions of James C. Pleasant, Tennessee State University, to the section on program verification.

We are also grateful to the many teachers who participated in telephone interviews or completed course surveys for Addison-Wesley's market research department. The information this research provided helped to shape the book's organization and pedagogy. They include:

Stephen Allan
Utah State University

Taylor Binkley
Georgia State University

Elvira Caldwell
Winston-Salem State University

Brad Chilton
Tartleton State University

Harry Edwards
University of Michigan-Flint

Lewis Hall
Riverside Community College

Lawrence J. Henschen
Northwestern University

Dennis Higgins
SUNY—Oneonta

Arthur Jackman
Dean College

Sandria Kerr
Winston-Salem State University

Maria C. Kolatis
County College of Morris

Barbara Lacey
Onendaga Community College

Stephen G. Landry
Seton Hall University

Phillip La Plante
Farleigh-Dickinson University

Dale Magoun
Northeast Louisiana University

Dolores Malecka
Chestnut Hill College

Mary Alice Muraski
University of Wisconsin—River Falls

John Pagliarulo
Rockland Community College

Sue Pilgreen
McNeese State University

James Ramey
Francis Marion University

Carl Richards
National University

James Roberts
Charleston Southern University

Becky Rutherford
Southern College of Tech

D'anna Shaver
Tarrant Co. Junior College

Daniel Spiegel
Wright State University

Ron Stearns
Miami-Dade Community College

Bill Taylor
Camden County College

Barbara Bernal Thomas
Southern College of Tech

David Thomas
Texas A&M University—Corpus Christi

Geneva Whitefield
Mountain View College

Marie Wilde
Cedar Crest College

Dawn Wilkins
Vanderbilt University

Mark Williams
Albuquerque Tech

I would like to thank three Temple University students for their valuable contributions. Christian J. Polizzi tested and made corrections to all the programs, proofread and indexed the text, and also prepared solutions to exercises. Donna Chrupcala prepared solutions to exercises and made many improvements to exercises. Bill Jones provided several suggestions for graphics examples. Also, I would like to thank my daughter, Robin Koffman, computer science teacher at Haverford School, Haverford, Pennsylvania, for carefully proofreading the page proofs.

The personnel at Addison-Wesley responsible for the production of this book worked diligently to meet a very demanding schedule. My editor, Lynne Doran Cote, was closely involved in all phases of this project. She was ably assisted by Maite Suarez-Rivas, who did an excellent job of coordinating the writing and reviewing process and trying to keep me on a very tight schedule. The development editors, Elizabeth Zayatz and Marjorie Singer-Anderson, provided valuable suggestions for improving the textbook. John Walker supervised the production of the book, while Anita Wagner coordinated the conversion of the manuscript to a finished book. I am grateful to all of them for their fine work.

Philadelphia, PA   E.B.K.

C O N T E N T S

CHAPTER ONE

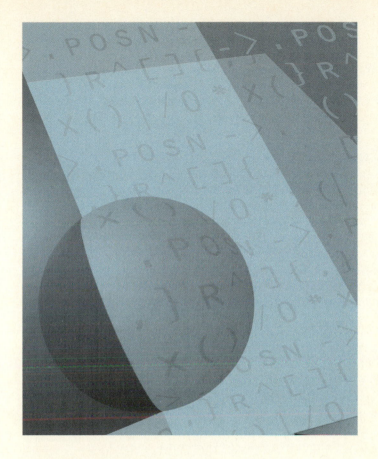

Overview of Computers and Programming

Since the 1940s, the computer has dramatically changed the way we live and how we do business. Today computers provide instructional material in school, print transcripts, prepare bills and paychecks, reserve airline and concert tickets, allow us to bank and shop conveniently, and help us write term papers and even books.

Although we often are led to believe otherwise, computers cannot reason as we do. Basically, computers are devices for performing computations at incredible speeds (more than one million operations per second) and with great accuracy. To accomplish anything useful, however, a computer must be provided with a program, that is, a list of instructions to perform. Programs are usually written in special computer programming languages such as Pascal, which is the subject of this book.

In this chapter, we introduce you to the computer and its components and then present an overview of programming languages. We describe how the computer processes Pascal programs. Finally, we describe how to interact with a computer's operating system.

1.1 Electronic Computers Then and Now

In our everyday life, we come in contact with computers frequently, some of us using computers for word processing or even having studied programming in high school. But it wasn't always this way. Not so long ago, most people considered computers to be mysterious devices whose secrets were known only by a few computer wizards.

The first electronic computer was designed in the late 1930s by Dr. John Atanasoff at Iowa State University. Atanasoff designed his computer to assist graduate students in nuclear physics with their mathematical computations.

The first large-scale, general-purpose electronic digital computer, called the ENIAC, was completed in 1946 at the University of Pennsylvania with funding from the U.S. Army. Weighing 30 tons and occupying a 30-by-50-foot space, the ENIAC was used to compute ballistics tables, predict the weather, and make atomic energy calculations.

These early computers used vacuum tubes as their basic electronic component. Technological advances in the design and manufacture of electronic components led to new generations of computers that were considerably smaller, faster, and less expensive than previous ones.

computer chip
the electronic component that comprises a computer processor

Using today's technology, a computer processor can be packaged in a single electronic component called a **computer chip,** which is about the size of a postage stamp. Their affordability and small size enable computer chips to be installed in watches, pocket calculators, cameras, home appliances, automobiles, and, of course, computers.

Today, a common sight in offices and homes is a personal computer, which can cost less than $2000 and sit on a desk, and yet has as much computational power as one that 15 years ago cost more than $100,000 and filled a 9-by-12-foot room. Even smaller computers can fit inside a briefcase (Fig. 1.1a) or your hand (Fig. 1.1b).

Modern-day computers are categorized according to their size and performance. *Microcomputers,* shown in Fig. 1.1, are used by a single person at a time. The largest microcomputers are called *workstations* (Fig. 1.1c). Businesses and research laboratories also use larger and faster computers, called *minicomputers* and *mainframes,* which can be used by many people simultaneously. *Supercomputers,* the most powerful mainframe computers, can perform in seconds computations that might take hours or even days on other computers.

Figure 1.1
(a) Notebook Computer. (b) Palmtop Computer. (c) Workstation.

(a)

(b)

(c)

hardware
the actual computer equipment
software
the set of programs associated with a computer
program
a list of instructions that enable a computer to perform a specific task
binary number
a number whose digits are 0 and 1

A computer system consists of two major components: hardware and software. **Hardware** is the equipment used to perform the necessary computations and includes the central processing unit (CPU), monitor, keyboard, and printer. The **software** is the **programs** that enable us to solve problems with a computer by providing it with lists of instructions to perform.

Programming a computer has undergone significant changes over the years. Initially, the task was very difficult, requiring programmers to write their program instructions as long **binary numbers** (sequences of 0s and 1s). Today's programming languages such as Pascal make programming much easier.

Exercises for Section 1.1

Self-Check

1. Is a computer program a piece of hardware or is it software?
2. Which do you think is the major source of computer errors, faulty computer hardware or incorrect software?

1.2   Introduction to Computer Hardware

Despite significant variations in cost, size, and capabilities, modern computers resemble one another in many basic ways. Essentially, most consist of the following components:

▶ Main memory
▶ Secondary memory, which includes storage devices such as hard disks and floppy disks
▶ The central processor unit
▶ Input devices, such as keyboards and mouses
▶ Output devices, such as monitors and printers

Figure 1.2 shows how these components interact in a computer, with the arrows pointing in the direction of information flow. The program must first be transferred from *secondary memory* to *main memory* before it can be executed. Normally the person using a program (the *program user*) must supply some data to be processed. These data are entered through an *input device* and are stored in the computer's *main memory,* where they can be accessed and manipulated by the *central processor unit*. The results of this manipulation are then stored back in *main memory*. Finally, the information in main memory can be displayed through an *output device*. In the remainder of this section, we describe these components in more detail.

Memory

Memory is an essential component in any computer. Before discussing the types of memory—main and secondary—let's look at what it consists of and how the computer works with it.

Figure 1.2
Components of
a Computer

Anatomy of Memory

memory cell
an individual storage location in memory

address of a memory cell
the relative position of a memory cell in the computer's main memory

contents of a memory cell
the information stored in a memory cell, either a program instruction or data

Imagine the memory of a computer as an ordered sequence of storage locations called **memory cells** (see Fig. 1.3). To store and access information, the computer must have some way of identifying the individual memory cells. Therefore each memory cell has a unique **address** that indicates its relative position in memory. Figure 1.3 shows a computer memory consisting of 1000 memory cells with addresses 0 through 999. Most computers, however, have millions of individual memory cells, each with its own address.

The data stored in a memory cell are called the **contents** of the cell. Every memory cell always has some contents, although we may have no idea what they are. In Fig. 1.3, the contents of memory cell 3 are the number −26 and the contents of memory cell 4 are the letter H.

stored program concept
storing program instructions in main memory prior to execution

Although not shown in Fig. 1.3, a memory cell can also contain a program instruction. The ability to store programs as well as data is called the **stored program concept**: A program's instructions must be stored in main memory before they can be executed. We can change the computer's operation by storing a different program in memory.

Bytes and Bits

byte
the amount of storage required to store a single character

A memory cell is actually a grouping of smaller units called bytes. A **byte** is the amount of storage required to store a single character, such as the letter H used in Fig. 1.3. The number of bytes a memory cell can contain varies

Figure 1.3
1000 Memory Cells in
Main Memory

from computer to computer. A byte is composed of even smaller units of storage called bits (see Fig. 1.4). The term **bit**, deriving from the words **bi**nary digi**t**, is the smallest element a computer can deal with. Binary refers to a number system based on two numbers, 0 and 1, and so a bit is either a 0 or a 1. Generally there are eight bits to a byte.

bit
a **bi**nary digi**t**; a 0 or a 1

Storage and Retrieval of Information in Memory

Each value in memory is represented by a particular pattern of 0s and 1s. A computer can either store a value or retrieve a value. To **store** a value, the computer sets each bit of a selected memory cell to either 0 or 1, destroying the previous contents of the cell in the process. To **retrieve** a value from a memory cell, the computer copies the pattern of 0s and 1s stored in that cell to another storage area for processing; the copy operation does not destroy the contents of the cell whose value is retrieved. This process is the same regardless of the kind of information—character, number, or program instruction—to be stored or retrieved.

data storage
setting the individual bits of a memory cell to 0 or 1, destroying its previous contents
data retrieval
copying the contents of a particular memory cell to another storage area

Figure 1.4
Relationship Between a
Byte and a Bit

Main Memory

random access memory (RAM)

the part of main memory that temporarily stores programs, data, and results

read-only memory (ROM)

the part of main memory that permanently stores programs or data

volatile memory

memory whose contents disappear when the computer is switched off

Main memory stores programs, data, and results. Most computers have two types of main memory: **random access memory (RAM)**, which offers temporary storage of programs and data, and **read-only memory (ROM)**, which stores programs or data permanently. RAM temporarily stores programs while they are being executed (carried out) by the computer. It also temporarily stores such data as numbers, names, and even pictures while a program is manipulating them. RAM is usually **volatile memory**, which means that everything in RAM will be lost when the computer is switched off.

ROM, on the other hand, stores information permanently within the computer. The computer can retrieve (or read), but cannot store (or write), information in ROM, hence its name, read-only. Because ROM is not volatile, the data stored there do not disappear when the computer is switched off. ROM stores the instructions needed to get the computer running when you first switch it on. In most computers, RAM memory capacity is much greater than ROM memory and RAM can often be increased (up to a specified maximum), whereas the amount of ROM is usually fixed. When we refer to main memory in this text, we mean RAM because that is the part of main memory that is normally accessible to the Pascal programmer.

Secondary Memory and Secondary Storage Devices

disk drive

a device used to store and retrieve information on a **disk**

hard disk

a disk with drive that is built into the computer and normally cannot be removed

floppy disk

a personal, portable disk that can be used with different computers

file

a collection of related information stored on a disk

Secondary memory, through secondary storage devices, provides semipermanent data storage capability. A common secondary storage device is a **disk drive**, which stores and retrieves data and programs on a storage medium called a **disk**. A disk is considered semipermanent instead of permanent because its contents can be changed, rather like a cassette tape that contains music that can be played over and over, but that can be erased and recorded over.

There are two kinds of disks: **hard** (also called fixed) and **floppy**. Most computers contain one hard disk that cannot be removed from its disk drive and so provides a storage area to be shared by all users of the computer. Normally the programs that are needed to operate the computer system are stored on its hard disk. Each computer user can have one or more floppy disks that can be inserted into a computer's floppy disk drive. A floppy disk is a plastic sheet with a diameter of 3.5 or 5.25 inches housed in a thin square container. These floppy disks can store an individual user's programs and personal data.

A hard disk can store much more data, and can be accessed by the CPU much more quickly, than can a single floppy disk. Each user, however, can have an unlimited number of floppy disks. Unlike a hard disk, a floppy disk is portable, which means it can be used with many different computers as long as they are all compatible.

Information stored on a disk is organized into separate collections called **files**. One file may contain a Pascal program. Another file may contain the data to be processed by that program (a *data file*). A third file could contain the results generated by a program (an *output file*).

An increasingly common secondary storage device is a CD-ROM drive. This drive accesses information stored on plastic disks that resemble the CDs used in a CD player. The ROM in CD-ROM indicates that currently most drives can only read the data stored on a CD and cannot write new information to the CD.

Comparison of Main and Secondary Memory

Because the computer processor can manipulate data only in main memory, data stored in secondary memory, including program instructions, must be transferred into main memory before they can be processed. For this reason, the computer manipulates data and instructions already in main memory much faster than those in secondary memory.

A fixed disk has much more storage capacity than does main memory. On most computers, you can increase the size of main memory by installing additional memory chips. You can also increase the size of secondary memory, by purchasing additional floppy disks or installing another fixed disk. However, main memory is considerably more expensive than secondary memory. Furthermore, data in main memory are volatile and disappear when you switch off the computer, whereas data in secondary memory are semipermanent and do not disappear when the computer is switched off. Therefore store all your programs as files in secondary memory, and transfer a program file into main memory when you want it executed.

Central Processor Unit

central processor unit (CPU)
coordinates all computer operations and performs arithmetic and logical operations on data

The **central processor unit (CPU)** has two roles: coordinating all computer operations and performing arithmetic and logical operations on data. The CPU follows the instructions contained in a computer program to determine which operations should be carried out and in what order. It then transmits coordinating control signals to the other computer components. For example, if the instruction requires reading a data item, the CPU sends the necessary control signals to the input device.

fetching an instruction
retrieving an instruction from main memory

To process a program stored in main memory, the CPU retrieves each instruction in sequence (called **fetching an instruction**), interprets the instruction to determine what should be done, and then retrieves any data needed to carry out that instruction. Next, the CPU performs the actual manipulation, or processing, of the data it retrieved. The CPU stores the results in main memory.

The CPU can perform such arithmetic operations as addition, subtraction, multiplication, and division. The CPU also can compare the contents of two memory cells (for example, Which contains the larger value? Are the values equal?) and make decisions based on the results of that comparison.

Input/Output Devices

input/output devices
devices used for reading data (inputs) from the program user or displaying or writing results (outputs)

cursor
a moving place marker that appears on the monitor

function keys
special keyboard keys used to select a particular operation; the operation selected depends on the program being used

mouse
an input device that moves its cursor on the computer screen to select an operation

We use **input/output (I/O) devices** to communicate with the computer. Specifically, they allow us to enter data for a computation and to observe the results of that computation.

You will be using a *keyboard* (see Fig. 1.5) as an input device and a *monitor* (display screen) as an output device. When you press a letter or digit key on a keyboard, that character is sent to main memory and is also displayed on the monitor at the position of the **cursor**, a moving place marker (normally a blinking underscore symbol). A computer keyboard resembles a typewriter keyboard except for some extra keys for performing special functions. For example, on the computer keyboard shown in Fig. 1.5, the 12 keys in the top row labeled F1 through F12 are **function keys**. The activity performed when you press a function key depends on the program currently being executed; that is, pressing F1 in one program will usually not produce the same results as pressing F1 in another program. Other special keys enable you to delete characters, move the cursor, and "enter" a line of data you typed at the keyboard (see the highlighted parts of Fig. 1.5).

Another common input device is a mouse. A **mouse** is a hand-held device used to select an operation. When you move the mouse around on your desktop, a rubber ball attached to the mouse rotates and simultaneously moves the *mouse cursor* (normally a small rectangle or an arrow) displayed on the monitor's screen. You select an operation by moving the mouse cursor to a word or picture that represents the computer operation you wish to perform and then pressing or clicking a mouse button to activate the operation selected.

Figure 1.5
Keyboard for IBM-Type Computers

A monitor provides a temporary display of the information that appears on its screen. Once the image disappears from the monitor screen, it is lost. If you want *hard copy* (a printed version) of some information, you must send that information to an output device called a **printer**.

printer
an output device that produces a hard copy of information sent to it

Computer Networks

computer network
a group of interconnected computers

file server
the computer in a network that controls access to the shared disk

Until now we have talked about the components of individual computers. Often several computers are interconnected as a **computer network**, so each computer user can access a large hard disk and high-quality printers. The computer that controls access to the shared disk is called the **file server**. Each computer in the network also has its own keyboard, monitor, and disk drives. Many computer laboratories arrange their computer hardware in a network.

Exercises for Section 1.2

Self-Check

1. If a computer were instructed to sum the contents of memory cells 2 and 999 in Fig. 1.3 and store the result in cell 0, what would be the contents of cells 0, 2, and 999?
2. One bit can have two values, 0 or 1. A combination of 2 bits can have 4 values: 00, 01, 10, 11. List all of the values you can form with a combination of 3 bits. Do the same for 4 bits.
3. List the following in order of smallest to largest: byte, bit, main memory, memory cell, secondary memory.

1.3 Problem Solving and Programming

Because it cannot think, a computer requires a program to do any useful work. Computer programming involves much more than simply writing a list of instructions. Problem solving is a crucial component of programming and requires a good deal of preplanning. Before writing a program to solve a particular problem, you must consider carefully all aspects of the problem and then develop and organize its solution.

Like most programming students, you will probably spend a great deal of time entering your programs into the computer. Later you will spend more time removing the errors that inevitably will be present in your programs. So resist the temptation to rush to the computer and start entering your program as soon as you have some idea of how to write it. Instead, think carefully about the problem and its solution before writing any program instructions. When you have a potential solution in mind, plan it out beforehand, using either paper and pencil or a word processor, and modify the solution if necessary before you write the program in a programming language.

desk check
a step-by-step simulation of a solution plan

You should **desk check** your solution plan by carefully performing each step much as the computer would. To desk check a solution plan, simulate

Figure 1.6
Programming Strategy

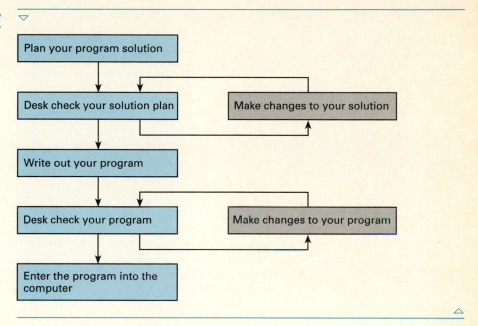

the result of each step using sample data that are easy to manipulate (for example, small whole numbers). Then compare your results with the expected results, and make any necessary corrections to the solution plan.

At this point, you can write your solution plan as a program. You should also desk check your program before you enter it into the computer. A few extra minutes spent evaluating the solution plan and program using the process summarized in Fig. 1.6 often saves hours of frustration later.

In this text, we stress a methodology for problem solving that has proved useful in helping students learn to program. We describe this technique and show you how to apply it in Section 2.1.

Exercise for Section 1.3 **Self-Check**

1. If a computer can execute your program quickly and efficiently, what is the purpose of desk checking the program?

1.4 Overview of Programming Languages

We use programming languages to write computer programs. Although there are many different programming languages, the most commonly used today are called high-level languages. To understand the advantage of high-level languages, we must first understand how a computer communicates.

Machine Language

machine language
a computer's native language with instructions that are binary numbers

The native tongue of a computer is **machine language**. Each machine language instruction is a binary string of 0s and 1s that specifies an operation and identifies the memory cells involved in that operation. For example, if we wanted to represent the algebraic formula

cost = price + tax

in a machine language program, we might need a sequence of instructions such as

```
0010 0000 0000 0100
0100 0000 0000 0101
0011 0000 0000 0110
```

In each machine language instruction, the operation to be performed and the address of the data to be manipulated are written as binary numbers. Although the computer would have no difficulty understanding the three preceding machine language instructions, they are unintelligible to most people.

High-Level Languages

high-level language
a programming language whose instructions resemble everyday language

When writing programs in a **high-level language**, we use instructions that resemble everyday language. In Pascal, we would use the statement

```
Cost := Price + Tax
```

which closely resembles the original formula. This statement means "Add the value of Price to the value of Tax and store the result as Cost." When writing a program in a high-level language, we can reference data that are stored in memory using descriptive names—for example, Price, Cost, Tax—rather than numeric memory cell addresses. We can also use familiar symbols (such as +) to describe operations we want performed.

language standard
a description of the syntax and meaning of each high-level language instruction

A high-level language has a **language standard** that describes the grammatical form (syntax) of the language. Every high-level language instruction must conform to the syntax rules specified in the language standard. These rules are very precise—they make no allowances for instructions that are *almost* correct. Programs that conform to these rules are *portable,* which means that they can be used without modification on many types of computers. A machine language program, on the other hand, can be used on only one type of computer.

application software
programs written for a computer user

system software
programs written for the computer system

Common high-level languages include Pascal, Fortran, BASIC, COBOL, C, and C++. Although each of these languages was designed for a specific purpose (see Table 1.1), all are used to write a variety of **application software**—software that performs tasks for the computer user. The languages C and C++ are frequently used to write **system software**—software that performs tasks required for the operation of the computer system.

Table 1.1
Common High-Level
Languages

High-Level Language	Original Purpose
Pascal	For teaching students to program in a careful, disciplined way
Fortran (**For**mula **tran**slation)	For engineering and scientific applications
BASIC	Simple language intended for student use in schoolwork
COBOL	For performing business data processing
C	For writing system software
C++	Extension of C that supports object-oriented programming

Relationship Between High-Level and Machine Language

source program
the high-level language program being translated

object program
the machine-language translation of a source program

Because a computer understands only programs written in machine language, each instruction in a high-level language program must first be translated into machine language before it can be executed. The original high-level language program is called the **source program**; the machine-language translation is called the **object program**. The next section discusses the steps required to process a high-level language program.

Exercises for Section 1.4

Self-Check

1. What do you think these four high-level language statements mean? Assume that the symbol ; separates the statements.

   X := A + B + C;   X := Y / Z;   D := C - B + A;   Z := Z + 1

2. List two reasons why it would be preferable to write a program in Pascal rather than machine language.

1.5 Processing a High-Level Language Program

Before the computer can execute a high-level language program, the programmer must enter the source program into the computer and the computer must store it in executable form in memory. Several system programs assist with this task. We describe the role of these programs next and summarize the process in Fig. 1.7.

Steps for Preparing a Program for Execution

editor
a program used to enter source programs and save source files

1. Use the **editor** program to enter each line of the source program into memory and to save it on disk as a source file.

compiler

a program that translates a high-level language program into machine language

syntax error

an error in the grammatical form of a line in a high-level language program

linker/loader

a program that combines (**links**) an object program with other object files and stores (**loads**) the final machine language program in memory

executable file

a disk file containing a ready-to-execute machine language program

2. Use a **compiler** program to translate the source program into machine language. If there are any **syntax errors** (errors in grammar), the compiler displays these errors on the monitor. Use the editor program to correct the errors by editing and resaving the source program.

3. When the source program is error free, the compiler saves its machine-language translation as an object program.

4. The **linker/loader** program combines your object program with additional object files that may be needed for your program to execute (for example, programs for input and output) and stores the final machine language program in memory, ready for execution. The linker/loader can also save the final machine language program as an **executable file** on disk. Often the linker/loader is written as two separate system programs.

Executing a Program

To execute a machine language program, the CPU must examine each program instruction in memory and send out the command signals required to carry out the instruction. Although the instructions normally are executed in sequence, as we will discuss later, it is possible to have the CPU skip over some instructions or execute some instructions more than once.

During execution, data can be entered into memory and manipulated in some specified way. Special program instructions are used for entering or

Figure 1.7
Preparing a Program for Execution

input data
the data values that are read by a program

program output
the lines displayed by a program

reading a program's data (called **input data**) into memory. After the input data have been processed, instructions for displaying or printing values in memory can be executed to display the program results. The lines displayed by a program are called the **program output**.

Let's use the situation described in Fig. 1.8—executing a payroll program stored in memory—as an example. The first step of the program enters into memory data that describe the employee's hours and pay rate. In step 2, the program manipulates the employee data and stores the results of the computations in memory. In the final step, the computational results are displayed as payroll reports or employee payroll checks.

Exercises for Section 1.5 — Self-Check

1. Would a syntax error be found in a source program or an object program? What system program would find a syntax error if one existed? What system program would you use to correct it?
2. Explain the differences among the source program, the object program, and an executable program. Which do you create, and which does the compiler create? Which does the linker/loader create?

Figure 1.8
Flow of Information During Program Execution

1.6   Using an Operating System

The mechanics of entering a program as a source file and translating and executing it differ from system to system. Although we cannot give specific details for a particular computer system, we describe the general process in this section.

Operating Systems

Some of you will be using a *time-shared computer*. Universities often use time-shared computers for instructional purposes. In a time-share environment, many users are connected by terminals to one central computer, and all users share the central facilities.

Others of you will be using a personal computer, which is a smaller, desktop computer used by one individual at a time. Regardless of what type of computer you use, you will need to interact with a supervisory program, called the *operating system*, within the computer. In time-shared computers, the operating system allocates the central resources among many users. Some operating system tasks are as follows:

▶   validating user identification and account number (time-shared system)
▶   making the editor, compiler, or linker programs available to users
▶   allocating memory and processor time
▶   providing input and output facilities
▶   retrieving needed files
▶   saving new files

The operating system for a personal computer performs all but the first task.

Each computer has its own special *control language* for communicating with its operating system. Although space does not allow us to provide the details here, we will discuss the general process for time-shared computers. Your instructor will provide the specific commands for your system. Appendixes F and G describe Dr. Pascal and Turbo Pascal, two popular systems for personal computers.

Logging On

Before you can use a time-shared computer, you must *log on*, or connect, to the computer. To log on, you enter your account name and password (given to you by your instructor). For security reasons, your password is not displayed. Figure 1.9 demonstrates this process for the Digital Equipment Corporation VAX computer. The computer user enters the characters that are in color; the other characters are those that the operating system displays. The time-shared operating system shown (VMS Version 5.1) displays the symbol $ as a prompt.

Figure 1.9

Logging On to a Computer

```
Username: Koffman
Password: Mad127EK

            CIS Department Vax-11/780 VMS V5.1

    Last interactive login on Friday, 28-April-1995 10:20

$
```

Creating a Program or File

Once you have gained access to the computer, you can begin to create your program. In most cases, you will use a special program called an *editor* to enter your Pascal program. After accessing the editor, you can start to enter a new Pascal program. If you want a record of the program once it is entered, you must save it as a permanent file on disk; otherwise, your program will disappear when your session with the editor is over. Follow these steps to create and save a program file:

1. Access the editor program and indicate that you are creating a new file.
2. Enter each line of the program file.
3. Name your program file (if not named in step 1) and save it as a permanent file in secondary memory.
4. Exit from the editor.

Once you have created your program and you are satisfied that each line is entered correctly, you can attempt to compile, link, and execute the program. On some systems, you must give three separate commands; on other systems, one command, such as RUN, initiates this sequence of operations.

If your program will not compile because it contains syntax errors, you must edit, or correct, the program. Follow these steps to correct and reexecute a program file:

1. Reaccess the editor program and retrieve your program file.
2. Correct the statements containing syntax errors.
3. Save your edited program file.
4. Compile, link, and execute the new program file.

CHAPTER REVIEW

1. The basic components of a computer are main and secondary memory, the CPU, and input and output devices.
2. Main memory is organized into individual storage locations called memory cells.
   ▶ Each memory cell has a unique address.
   ▶ A memory cell is a collection of bytes; a byte is a collection of 8 bits.
   ▶ A memory cell is never empty, but its initial contents may be meaningless to your program.

▶ The current contents of a memory cell are destroyed whenever new information is stored in that cell.

▶ Programs *must* be loaded into the memory of the computer before they can be executed.

▶ Data cannot be manipulated by the computer until they are first stored in memory.

3. Information in secondary memory is organized into files: program files and data files. Secondary memory stores information in semipermanent form and is less expensive than main memory.

4. A computer cannot think for itself; you must use a programming language to instruct it in a precise and unambiguous manner to perform a task.

5. Programming a computer can be fun—if you are patient, organized, and careful.

6. Two categories of programming languages are machine language (meaningful to the computer) and high-level language (meaningful to the programmer). Several system programs are used to prepare a high-level language program for execution, and an editor enters a high-level language program into memory. A compiler translates a high-level language program (the source program) into machine language (the object program). The linker/loader links this object program to other object files, creating an executable program, and loads the executable program into memory.

7. Through the operating system, you can issue commands to the computer and manage files.

Quick-Check Exercises

1. The _____ translates a(n) _____ language program into _____.

2. A(n) _____ provides access to system programs for editing, compiling, and so on.

3. Specify the correct order for these operations: execution, translation, linking/loading.

4. A high-level language program is saved on disk as a(n) _____ file or a(n) _____ file.

5. The _____ finds syntax errors in the _____ file.

6. Before linking, a machine language program is saved on disk as a(n) _____ file.

7. After linking, a machine language program is saved on disk as a(n) _____ file.

8. Computer programs are _____ components of a computer system while a disk drive is _____.

9. In a high-level language, you can reference data using _____ rather than memory cell addresses.

10. Determine whether each of the following characteristics applies to main memory or secondary memory:

a. Faster to access
b. Volatile
c. May be extended without limit
d. Less expensive
e. Used to store files
f. Central processor accesses it to obtain the next machine language instruction for execution
g. Provides semipermanent data storage

Answers to Quick-Check Exercises

1. compiler, high-level (or source program), machine language (or object program)
2. operating system
3. translation, linking/loading, execution
4. source, program
5. compiler, source program
6. object
7. executable
8. software, hardware
9. descriptive names
10. main (a, b, f), secondary (c, d, e, g)

Review Questions

1. List at least three kinds of information stored in a computer.
2. List two functions of the CPU.
3. List two input devices, two output devices, and two secondary storage devices.
4. Draw the process that should be used to evaluate a proposed solution to a problem.
5. Why are there two categories of programming languages?
6. What is a syntax error?
7. What processes are needed to transform a Pascal program to a machine language program that is ready for execution?
8. Explain the relationship between memory cells, bytes, and bits.
9. Name two operating systems for IBM compatible computers. Which are you using?
10. Name three high-level languages, and describe their original usage.
11. What are the differences between RAM and ROM?

INTERVIEW

▼

David A. Patterson

David A. Patterson is a professor of computer science at the University of California, Berkeley. An author and active consultant, Patterson led the design and implementation of RISC I, a 45,000-transistor microprocessor that was likely the first Reduced Instruction Set Computer. He is currently working on developing input/output systems to match the increasingly higher performance of new processors.

▼ **Looking back on your own experience as a student, what influenced you to choose computer science as a profession? Why computer architecture?**

▲ I was a mathematics major as an undergraduate, and the math class I was planning to take was canceled. I took a computer class instead. I found I loved the reality of the problem solving and the rapid change of ideas in computer science more than the abstraction and stability of higher mathematics. Serendipity played a role in my choice of computer architecture as well. As a graduate research assistant in computer software, I became the father of two sons about the time the research grant ran out. While I finished my Ph.D., my adviser helped get me a job at Hughes Aircraft Company, where we designed computers. Hence I learned software in academia and hardware in industry. My dissertation combined hardware and software, leaving my options open when I got a "real" job. U.C. Berkeley wanted me to work in computer architecture, so my path was set.

▼ **What are your impressions of the state of computer architecture education today? Do you think students majoring in computer science receive enough of a background in architecture?**

▲ Computer architecture education today is in the middle of a revolution—from a more historical or descriptive list of possible problem solutions to a foundation that teaches how to evaluate quantitatively the cost/performance of different options in different situations. I believe this is a transition that all systems fields will need to go through if computer science is to mature as a discipline. Obviously, it is better to learn the quantitative approach.

▼ **Where do you see the exciting research being done in computer architecture today?**

▲ The processor-centric approach to doing research in computer architecture is now reaping the harvest of neglect: computers are becoming input/output bound. Hence I believe the most exciting areas in computer architecture today revolve around I/O, particularly communication and storage. The possibility of using fast networks to allow thousands of desktop computers to act in concert as a supercomputer could change the industry. Taking advantage of the advances in magnetic tape (such as those used in video cameras) or optical disks (like those used in CD players) offers the opportunity to store 1000 times the data we can today. Such a large quantitative change will bring about a qualitative change in our society. For example, all books on a college campus could be stored on-line, requiring the same space and cost as a minicomputer. Imagine what would happen if any student with a TV screen and a telephone could get any book in several seconds!

My thesis is that a factor-of-1000 increase in the storage capacity available on most local area networks will have a much greater impact than a factor-of-1000 increase in processing speed for a gaggle of scientists.

▼ **The complexity of architecture seems to be ever increasing. What do you think fuels the need for more powerful and efficient machines?**

▲ Architecture complexity goes in cycles, and we recently just reset to simplicity as a result of the Reduced Instruction Set Computer (RISC) movement. Complexity comes from the desire to get greater performance from a mature technology. As new technologies emerge, the rewards of simplicity inspire the return to simpler styles of computers.

▼ **Do you think the much discussed international competition (the United States versus Japan, for example) in the creation of supercomputers is overblown?**

▲ The international competition over the lead in traditional supercomputers is, to my way of thinking, like a competition to produce the world's fastest car. Even though it may be possible to build a few exotic cars that go as fast as a slow jet, it is clear that jets offer much greater speed and distance. The jets of computer architecture are parallel computers, with the effective top speed being a function of the number of processors you buy and the parallelism of the problem being stored. This is clearly the important competition, although not everyone may realize it.

The opportunity to become technological heroes is available for people who know their three A's: architecture, algorithms, and applications. These will be the people who can take advantage of the potential of parallel computers to solve problems important to society hundreds or thousands of times faster than today's most expensive computer.

▼ **What major developments do you foresee occurring in architecture in the 1990s?**

▲ Massively parallel computers will be established as the fastest computers in the land in the 1990s, washing away traditional supercomputers built by Cray, Convex, and NEC. For example, I believe we have already crossed the "teraflops threshold." A teraflops computer can calculate 10^{12} ("tera") **f**loating-point arithmetic **o**perations **p**er **s**econd ("FLOPS"), which is about 1000 times faster than today's supercomputers. Suppose you had an important computation that takes 10^{17} operations today and you have the choice of buying today's supercomputer and dedicating it to that computation or waiting and buying a teraflops machine and then starting the computation. Crossing the "teraflops threshold" means you get your answer sooner if you wait for the teraflops machine than if you started today. My view is that we have already crossed that threshold.

Terabytes (10^{12} bytes) are the flip side of teraflops—computers that will be connected to hundreds of terabytes via high-speed networks. If copyrights and royalties can be resolved to the benefit of authors, publishers, and society, this technology will revolutionize the availability of information in all forms: books, libraries, magazines, mail, newspapers, and so on.

CHAPTER TWO

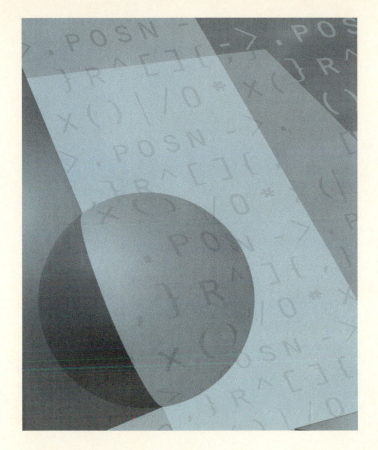

Problem Solving and Pascal

Programming is a problem-solving activity. If you are a good problem solver, you have the potential to become a good programmer. One goal of this book is to help you improve your problem-solving ability. To this end, we introduce in Section 2.1 a systematic approach to solving programming problems called the software development method and show you how to apply it in Section 2.2.

This chapter introduces Pascal, a high-level programming language developed in 1971 by Nicklaus Wirth of Zurich, Switzerland. Currently, Pascal is the most popular programming language for teaching programming concepts, partly because its syntax is relatively easy to learn. Another reason for Pascal's popularity is the availability of efficient Pascal compilers for most computers.

Pascal facilitates the writing of *structured programs*—programs that are easy to read, understand, and keep in good working order. Pascal is popular in industry because structured programming is standard programming practice. Another good reason for studying Pascal is that it is the basis for the design of the programming language Ada, the official language approved by the Department of Defense for software development.

To ensure that a Pascal program written on one computer executes on another, the coded instructions must conform to the Pascal language standard, which describes all Pascal language constructs and their syntax. This text follows the standard for Pascal approved by the American National Standards Institute (ANSI) and the International Standards Organization (ISO).

This chapter describes the sections of a Pascal program and the types of data that can be processed by Pascal. It also describes Pascal statements for performing computations, for entering data, and for displaying results.

2.1   The Software Development Method

Problem-solving methods are covered in many subject areas. For example, business students learn to solve problems with a *systems approach,* engineering and science students the *engineering and scientific method,* and programmers the *software development method.*

Software Development Method

1. Specify the problem requirements.
2. Analyze the problem.
3. Design the algorithm to solve the problem.
4. Implement the algorithm.
5. Test and verify the completed program.
6. Maintain and update the program.

PROBLEM ▼

Specifying the problem requirements forces you to state the problem clearly and unambiguously and to gain a clear understanding of what is required for its solution. Your objective is to eliminate unimportant aspects and zero in on the root problem. This may not be as easy as it sounds. You may find you need more information from the person who posed the problem.

ANALYSIS ▼

Analyzing the problem involves identifying the problem (a) *inputs,* that is, the data you have to work with; (b) *outputs,* the desired results; and (c) any additional requirements or constraints on the solution. At this stage, you should also determine the required format in which the results should be displayed (for example, as a table with specific column headings) and develop a list of problem variables and their relationships. These relationships may be expressed as formulas.

If steps 1 and 2 are not done properly, you will solve the wrong problem. Read the problem statement carefully, first to obtain a clear idea of the problem and second to determine the inputs and outputs. You may find it helpful to underline phrases in the problem statement that identify the inputs and outputs, as in the following problem statement:

Determine the <u>total cost of apples</u> given the number of <u>pounds of apples purchased</u> and the <u>cost per pound of apples</u>.

Next, summarize the information contained in the underlined phrases:

Problem Inputs

quantity of apples purchased (in pounds)
cost per pound of apples (in dollars per pound)

Problem Output

total cost of apples (in dollars)

Once you know the problem inputs and outputs, develop a list of formulas that specify relationships between them. The general formula

total cost = unit cost × number of units

computes the total cost of any item purchased. Substituting the variables for our particular problem yields the formula

total cost of apples = cost per pound × pounds of apples

In some situations, you may have to make certain assumptions or simplifications to derive these relationships. This process of extracting the essential problem variables and their relationships from the problem statement is called **abstraction.**

abstraction
the process of extracting the essential variables and relationships of a problem

DESIGN ▼

Designing the algorithm to solve the problem requires you to write step-by-step procedures—the **algorithm**—and then verify that the algorithm solves the problem as intended. Writing the algorithm is often the most difficult part of the problem-solving process. Don't attempt to solve every detail of the

algorithm
a recipe, or list of steps, for solving a problem

top-down design

breaking a problem into its major subproblems and solving it by solving the subproblems

problem initially; instead, discipline yourself to use top-down design. In **top-down design** (also called *divide and conquer*), you first list the major steps, or subproblems, that need to be solved, then solve the original problem by solving each of its subproblems. Most computer algorithms consist of at least the following subproblems.

Algorithm for a Programming Problem

1. Read the data.
2. Perform the computations.
3. Display the results.

algorithm refinement

a detailed list of steps needed to solve a particular step in the original algorithm

Once you know the subproblems, you can attack each one individually. For example, the *perform the computations* step may need to be broken down into a more detailed list of steps called **algorithm refinements**.

You may be familiar with top-down design if you use outlines when writing term papers. Your first step is to create an outline of the major topics, which you then refine by filling in subtopics for each major topic. Once the outline is complete, you begin writing the text for each subtopic.

desk checking

the step-by-step simulation of the computer execution of an algorithm

Desk checking is an important but often overlooked part of algorithm design. To **desk check** an algorithm, carefully perform each algorithm step (or its refinements) just as a computer would and verify that the algorithm works as intended. You'll save time and effort if you locate algorithm errors early in the problem-solving process.

IMPLEMENTATION ▼

Implementing the algorithm (step 4 in the software development method) involves writing the algorithm as a program. You must convert each algorithm step into one or more statements in a programming language.

structured program

a program that is easy to read, understand, and maintain

Structured programming is a disciplined approach to programming that results in programs that are easy to read and understand and less likely to contain errors. The emphasis is on following accepted program style guidelines (which will be stressed in this book) to write code that is clear and readable. Obscure tricks and programming shortcuts are strongly discouraged. Government organizations and industry are strong advocates of structured programming because structured programs are much easier to design in the beginning and easier to maintain over the long term.

TESTING ▼

Testing and verifying the program requires testing the completed program to verify that it works as desired. Don't rely on just one test case—run the program several times using different sets of data, making sure that it works correctly for every situation provided for in the algorithm.

MAINTENANCE ▼

Maintaining and updating the program involves modifying a program to remove previously undetected errors and to keep it up to date as government regulations or company policies change. Many organizations maintain a program for five years or more, often after the programmers who originally coded it have left or moved on to other positions.

Exercises for Section 2.1   **Self-Check**

1. List the steps of the software development method.
2. In which phase is the algorithm developed? In which phase do you identify the problem inputs and outputs?

2.2   Applying the Software Development Method

Throughout this book, we use the first five steps of the software development method to solve programming problems. These problems, presented as case studies, begin with a *problem statement*. As part of the problem *analysis,* we identify the data requirements for the problem, indicating the problem inputs and the desired outputs. Next, we *design* and refine the initial algorithm. Finally, we *implement* the algorithm as a Pascal program. We also provide a sample run of the program and discuss how to *test* the program.

We walk you through a sample case study next. This example includes a running commentary on the process that you can apply when solving other problems.

CASE STUDY   **Converting Units of Measurement**

PROBLEM ▼

You work in a store that sells imported fabric. Most of the fabric you buy is measured in square meters, but your customers want to know the equivalent amount in square yards. Write a program to perform this conversion.

ANALYSIS ▼

The first step in solving this problem is to determine what you are asked to do. You must convert from one system of measurement to another, but are you supposed to convert from square meters to square yards, or vice versa? The problem states that you buy <u>fabric measured in square meters</u>, so the problem input is *fabric size in square meters*. Your customers want to know the <u>equivalent amount in square yards</u>, so the problem output is *fabric size in square yards*. To write the program, you need to know the relationship between square meters and square yards. Consulting a metric table shows that 1 square meter equals 1.196 square yards.

The data requirements and relevant formulas are listed next. `SqMeters` identifies the memory cell that will contain the problem input. `SqYards` identifies the memory cell that will contain the program result, or the problem output.

Data Requirements

Problem Input

`SqMeters {the fabric size in square meters}`

Problem Output

`SqYards {the fabric size in square yards}`

Relevant Formula

1 square meter = 1.196 square yards

DESIGN ▼

Next, formulate the algorithm that solves the problem. Begin by listing the three major steps, or subproblems, of the algorithm.

Algorithm

1. Read the fabric size in square meters.
2. Convert the fabric size to square yards.
3. Display the fabric size in square yards.

Now decide whether any steps of the algorithm need refinement or whether they are perfectly clear as stated. Step 1 (reading data) and step 3 (displaying a value) are basic steps and require no refinement. Step 2 is fairly straightforward, but some detail might help.

Step 2 Refinement

2.1 The fabric size in square yards is 1.196 times the fabric size in square meters.

The complete algorithm with refinements is listed next to show how it all fits together. The algorithm resembles an outline for a term paper. The refinement of step 2 is numbered as step 2.1 and is indented under step 2.

Algorithm with Refinements

1. Read the fabric size in square meters.

2. Convert the fabric size to square yards.
   2.1 The fabric size in square yards is 1.196 times the fabric size in square meters.
3. Display the fabric size in square yards.

Let's desk check the algorithm before going further. If step 1 reads in a fabric size of 2.00 square meters, step 2.1 would convert it to 1.196 × 2.00, or 2.392 square yards. This correct result would be displayed by step 3.

IMPLEMENTATION ▼

To implement the solution, you must write the algorithm as a Pascal program. Begin by telling the Pascal compiler about the problem data requirements, that is, what memory cell names you are using and what kind of data will be stored in each memory cell. Then convert each algorithm step into one or more Pascal statements. If an algorithm step has been refined, you must convert the refinements, not the original step, into Pascal statements.

Figure 2.1 shows the Pascal program along with a sample run. For easy identification, the input data typed in by the program user is in color in

Figure 2.1
Metric Conversion
Program

Directory: CHAP2
File: METRIC.PAS

```pascal
program Metric (Input, Output);
{Converts square meters to square yards.}

   const
     MetersToYards = 1.196; {conversion constant}

   var
     SqMeters,          {input - fabric size in meters}
     SqYards : Real;    {output - fabric size in yards}

begin
  {Read the fabric size in square meters.}
  WriteLn ('Enter the fabric size in square meters> ');
  ReadLn (SqMeters);

  {Convert the fabric size to square yards.}
  SqYards := MetersToYards * SqMeters;

  {Display the fabric size in square yards.}
  WriteLn ('The fabric size in square yards is ', SqYards)
end.
```

Sample Run

```
Enter the fabric size in square meters>
2.00
The fabric size in square yards is 2.392000E+00
```

the sample run. Don't worry about understanding the details of this program yet. We explain the program in the next several sections.

TESTING ▼

How do you know the sample run is correct? You should always examine program results carefully to make sure that they make sense. In this run, a fabric size of 2.00 square meters is converted to 2.392 square yards, as it should be. To verify that the program works properly, enter a few more test values of square meters. You needn't try more than a few test cases to verify that a simple program like this is correct.

....

Exercises for Section 2.2   *Self-Check*

1. Change the algorithm for the metric conversion program to convert fabric size in square yards to fabric size in square meters.
2. List the data requirements, formulas, and algorithm for a program that converts a weight from pounds to kilograms.

2.3   Overview of Pascal, Reserved Words, and Identifiers

One advantage of Pascal is that it lets us write programs that resemble everyday English. Even though you do not yet know how to write your own programs, you can probably read and understand the program in Fig. 2.1. Figure 2.2 repeats Fig. 2.1 with the basic features of Pascal highlighted. We identify them briefly next, and explain them in detail in Sections 2.4 through 2.6.

A Pascal program has two parts: the declaration part and the program body. The **declaration part** tells the compiler which memory cells are needed in the program. To create this part of the program, the programmer uses the problem data requirements identified during problem analysis. The **program body** begins with the line `begin` and contains statements (derived from the algorithm) that are translated into machine language and later executed. Certain words in the program, such as `begin` and `end`, are **reserved words**, which have special meaning to the Pascal compiler.

The lines that contain text enclosed in braces are *comments*. Comments provide supplementary information to the person reading the program, but they are ignored by the Pascal compiler.

Finally, the program contains *punctuation* and *special symbols* ($*$, $=$, $:=$). Commas separate items in a list, and a semicolon appears at the end of several lines. The last line ends with a period.

declaration part
the part of a program that tells the compiler the names of memory cells in a program

program body
the executable statements in a program

reserved word
a word that has special meaning in Pascal

Figure 2.2
Pascal Language Elements in Metric Conversion Program

After learning more about each feature, you will be able to write your own simple programs, such as the metric conversion program.

Each line of Fig. 2.2 contains one or more words, some written in all lowercase characters and some written in mixed upper- and lowercase. The words in lowercase are reserved words and have special meaning to the Pascal compiler. Table 2.1 describes the reserved words in Fig. 2.2.

Table 2.1
Reserved Words in Fig. 2.2

Reserved Word	Meaning
program	The first word of a Pascal program
const	Precedes the list of constants
var	Precedes the list of variables
begin	Starts the program body
end	The last word of a Pascal program

Standard Identifiers

standard identifier

a word having special meaning but one that a programmer may redefine

The other words in Fig. 2.2 are identifiers that come in two varieties: standard and user-defined. Like reserved words, **standard identifiers** have special meaning in Pascal. Some standard identifiers represent names of predefined operations (e.g., ReadLn for **Read** a **Lin**e, WriteLn for **Write** a **Lin**e), and others name the predefined data types (e.g., Real for real number). Unlike reserved words, standard identifiers can be redefined and used by the programmer for other purposes—however, we don't recommend this practice. If you redefine a standard identifier, Pascal will no longer be able to use it for its original purpose. Appendix A lists all of Pascal's reserved words and standard identifiers.

User-Defined Identifiers

We choose our own identifiers (called user-defined identifiers) to name memory cells that will hold data and program results, to name operations that we define (more on this in Chapter 3), and to specify the name of a Pascal program. The first user-defined identifier in Fig. 2.2, Metric, specifies the program name and appears in the program heading

```
program Metric (Input, Output);
```

You have some freedom in selecting identifiers. The syntax rules and some valid identifiers follow. Table 2.2 shows some invalid identifiers.

Syntax Rules for Identifiers

1. An identifier must always begin with a letter.
2. An identifier must consist only of a combination of letters and digits.
3. A Pascal reserved word cannot be used as an identifier.

Valid Identifiers

```
Letter1, Letter2, Inches, Cent, CentPerInch, Hello, Variable
```

Table 2.2
Invalid Identifiers

Invalid Identifier	Reason Invalid
1Letter	Begins with a number
const	Reserved word
var	Reserved word
Two*Four	Character * not allowed
Joe's	Character ' not allowed

The maximum length of an identifier is system dependent, and some compilers will ignore all characters past a certain length. For example, if the maximum is eight, you cannot declare both `Consonant1` and `Consonant2` as identifiers. They are considered the same identifier because they begin with the same eight characters.

The category of each identifier appearing in Fig. 2.2 is listed in Table 2.3.

Table 2.3
Reserved Words and
Identifiers in Fig. 2.2

Reserved Words	Standard Identifiers	User-Defined Identifiers
program, var, const, begin, end	Real, ReadLn, WriteLn, Input, Output	Metric, MetersToYards, SqMeters, SqYards

Syntax Display for Program Heading

For each new Pascal construct introduced in this book, we provide a syntax display that describes and explains its syntax and shows examples of its use. In the following syntax display, the italicized element, *pname*, is discussed in the interpretation section.

SYNTAX DISPLAY

Program Heading

Form: program *pname* (Input, Output);
Example: program Hello (Input, Output);
Interpretation: The program name is specified by *pname*. The input data will be read from the system Input (the keyboard); the output results will be written to the system Output (the screen).

Program Style

The Use of Uppercase and Lowercase in Pascal Programs

We discuss program style throughout the text in displays like this one. A program that "looks good" is easier to read and understand than one that is sloppy. Most programs will be examined or studied by someone other than the original programmers. In the real world, only about 25% of the time spent on a particular program is devoted to its original design or coding; the remaining 75% is spent on maintenance (i.e., updating and modifying the program). A program that is neatly stated and whose meaning is clear makes everyone's job simpler.

In the programs in this text, reserved words always appear in lowercase and identifiers are in mixed uppercase and lowercase. The first letter of each identifier is capitalized. If an identifier consists of two or more "words" run on together (e.g., `MetersToYards`), the first letter of each word is capitalized. We recommend that you follow this convention in your programs to simplify distinguishing reserved words from other identifiers.

The Pascal compiler does not differentiate between uppercase and lowercase. This means that you could write the reserved word `const` as `CONST` or the standard identifier `ReadLn` as `READLN`. However, according to our convention, `const` and `ReadLn` are the preferred forms.

Because standard identifiers have special meanings just like reserved words, many computer scientists write standard identifiers in the same way as reserved words (i.e., all lowercase). If your instructor prefers this convention, you should write the standard identifier `ReadLn` as `readln`.

Program Style

Choosing Identifier Names

Pick a meaningful name for a user-defined identifier so that its use is easy to understand. For example, the identifier `Salary` would be a good name for a variable used to store a person's salary, whereas the identifier `S` or `Bagel` would be a bad choice.

It is difficult to form meaningful names with fewer than three letters. On the other hand, typing errors become more likely when identifiers are too long. A reasonable rule of thumb is to use names having 3 to 10 characters.

If you mistype an identifier, the compiler detects the mistake as a syntax error and displays an `undefined identifier` error message during program translation. Because mistyped identifiers sometimes resemble other identifiers, avoid picking similar names. Don't choose two names that are identical except for their case, because the compiler will not distinguish between them.

Exercises for Section 2.3

Self-Check

1. What are the two parts of a Pascal program?
2. Why shouldn't you use a standard identifier as the name of a memory cell in a program? Can you use a reserved word instead?
3. Which of the following identifiers are (a) Pascal reserved words, (b) standard identifiers, (c) valid identifiers, and (d) invalid identifiers?

    ```
    end          ReadLn       Bill      program     Sue's
    Rate         Start        begin     const       XYZ123
    123XYZ       ThisIsALongOne         Y=Z         Prog#2      'MaxScores'
    ```

2.4 # Data Types and Declarations

declaration part
the program part that communicates to the compiler the identifiers in the program, the usage of each identifier, and the kind of information stored in each identifier that names a memory cell

The **declaration part** of a Pascal program communicates to the Pascal compiler the names of all user-defined identifiers that can appear in the program and the usage of each identifier. It also tells the compiler what kind of information will be stored in each memory cell.

Data Types

data type
a set of values and operations that can be performed on those values

How a particular value is represented in memory is determined by the **data type** of that value. There are four predefined data types: Real (for real numbers), Integer (for integers), Char (for single character values), and Boolean (for values of True and False). Each data type has its own set of values and operations that can be performed on those values. We introduce these data types in this section and elaborate on them in Chapter 7.

A value can be written within a line of a Pascal program (in-line) or typed in as a data item to be read by the program. A value that appears in-line in a program is called a **literal**.

literal
a value that appears in-line in a program

Integer Data Type

In mathematics, integers are positive or negative whole numbers and a number without a sign is assumed to be positive. The Integer data type is used to represent integers in Pascal.

Because of the finite size of a memory cell, not all integers can be represented. Although the range of integers is system dependent, there is a predefined constant named MaxInt whose value represents the largest positive integer. On many computers including personal computers, MaxInt has the value 32767. An integer cannot contain a comma. Some valid integers are

```
-10500    435    15    -25
```

We can read and display integers, perform the common arithmetic operations (add, subtract, multiply, and divide), and compare two integers.

Real Data Type

A real number has an integral part and a fractional part and separates them with a decimal point. In Pascal, the Real data type is used to represent real numbers and a Real literal must always begin and end with a digit. Therefore the fraction -.25 and the whole number 64. must be written in Pascal as the real literals -0.25 and 64.0, respectively.

We can use scientific notation to represent very large and very small values. In normal scientific notation, for example, the real number 1.23×10^5 is equivalent to 123000.0 where the exponent 5 means "move the decimal point 5 places to the right." In Pascal scientific notation, we write this number as 1.23E5 or 1.23E+5. If the exponent has a minus sign, the decimal point is moved to the left (e.g., 0.34E-4 is equivalent to 0.000034). Table 2.4 lists some valid and invalid real numbers. The last line shows that we can write a Real literal in Pascal scientific notation without a decimal point.

Table 2.4
Valid and Invalid
Real Literals

Valid Real Literals	Invalid Real Literals
3.14159	150 (no decimal point)
0.005	.12345 (no digit before decimal point)
12345.0	16. (no digit after decimal point)
15.0E-04 (value is 0.0015)	-15E-0.3 (0.3 invalid exponent)
2.345E2 (value is 234.5)	12.5E.3 (.3 invalid exponent)
1.15E-3 (value is 0.00115)	.123E3 (no digit before decimal point)
12E+5 (value is 1200000.0)	12,500.34 (comma not allowed)

We can read and display real numbers, perform the common arithmetic operations (add, subtract, multiply, and divide), and compare them.

Char Data Type

Data type Char represents an individual character value—a letter, a digit, or a special symbol. Each type Char literal is enclosed in apostrophes (single quotes), as shown here.

'A' 'z' '2' '9' '*' ':' '"' ' '

The next to last literal represents the character " ; the last literal represents the blank character, which is typed by pressing the apostrophe key, the space bar, and the apostrophe key.

Although a type Char literal in a program requires apostrophes, a type Char data value should not have them. Thus, for example, when entering the letter z as a character data item to be read by a program, press the z key instead of the sequence 'z'.

We cannot perform arithmetic operations on type Char data. This means that '3' + '5' is invalid in Pascal. However, we can compare characters and read and display them.

Boolean Data Type

Unlike the other data types, the Boolean* data type has just two possible values: `True` and `False`. We can use this data type to represent conditional values so that a program can make decisions. We can display Boolean data but we cannot read a Boolean data item.

Purpose of Data Types

The use of different data types enables the compiler to know which operations are valid for each memory cell used in a program. If you try to manipulate a value in memory in an incorrect way (for example, add two character values), the Pascal compiler displays an error message telling you that this is an incorrect operation. Similarly, if you try to store the wrong kind of value in a memory cell (for example, a real number in a memory cell that is type `Integer`), you get an error message. Detecting these errors keeps the computer from performing operations that make no sense. In the next section, we discuss how to tell the Pascal compiler the data type of each memory cell.

Declarations

We tell the Pascal compiler the names of memory cells used in a program and the kind of information stored in these cells through constant declarations and variable declarations.

Constant Declarations

The constant declaration

```
const
   MetersToYards = 1.196;
```

constant
a memory cell whose value cannot change

specifies that the identifier `MetersToYards` is the name of a memory cell that always contains the real number `1.196`; the identifier `MetersToYards` is called a **constant**. Pascal determines the data type of `MetersToYards` (type is `Real`) from the form of the literal (`1.196`) it represents. Use constants only to identify data values that never change (e.g., the number of square yards in a square meter is always `1.196`). You cannot write instructions that attempt to change the value of a constant.

EXAMPLE 2.1 ▼

The constant declaration

---

*The Boolean data type is named after the English mathematician George Boole (1815–1864), the inventor of a two-valued algebra.

```
const
   MyLargeInteger = 9999;              {value is 9999}
   MySmallInteger = -MyLargeInteger;   {value is -9999}
   Star = '*';                         {value is symbol *}
   FirstMonth = 'January';             {value is string
                                        'January'}
```

declares four constants of different types. The value of the second constant, `MySmallInteger`, is based on the first constant, `MyLargeInteger`. The third constant, `Star`, has a type `Char` value. The fourth constant, `FirstMonth`, has a `string` value, where a **string** is a sequence of characters enclosed in apostrophes. ▲

string
a sequence of characters
enclosed in apostrophes

In standard Pascal, constants can have string values, but variables can't. String literals often appear in instructions used to display information.

Constant Declaration

Form: `const`
                 constant = *value*;
Example: `const`
                 `Pi = 3.14159;`
Interpretation: The specified *value* is associated with the identifier *constant* and cannot be changed. The *value* can be a literal or a previously defined constant; a numeric *value* can have a sign. More than one constant declaration may follow the word `const`, with a semicolon appearing at the end of each constant declaration.

Variable Declarations

The memory cells used for storing a program's input data and its computational results are called **variables** because the values stored in them can change (and usually do) as the program executes. The variable declaration

variable
a memory cell whose value
can change

```
var
   SqMeters,        {input - fabric size in meters}
   SqYards : Real; {output - fabric size in yards}
```

in Fig. 2.1 gives the names of two variables (SqMeters, SqYards) used to store real numbers. Note that Pascal ignores the comments in braces describing the usage of each variable.

In a variable declaration, the identifier (e.g., `Real`) after the symbol : tells the Pascal compiler the type of data (e.g., a real number) stored in a particular variable. You can declare variables for any data type.

Variable Declaration

Form: `var`
                 variable list : *data type*;

Example: var
    X, Y   : Real;
    Me, You : Integer;
Interpretation: A memory cell is allocated for each variable in the *variable list*. The data type (Real, Integer, etc.) of each variable is specified between the colon and the semicolon. Commas separate the variables in *variable list*. The word var should appear only once, but it can be followed by multiple variable lists and associated data types, each ending with a semicolon.

Exercises for Section 2.4

Self-Check

1. a. Write the following numbers in normal decimal notation:

    103E-4 1.2345E+6 123.45E+3

   b. Write the following numbers in Pascal scientific notation:

    1300 123.45 0.00426

2. Indicate which of the following literal values are legal in Pascal and which are not. Identify the data type of each valid literal value.

    15 'XYZ' '*' $25.123 15. -999 .123 'x'
    "X" '9' '-5' True 'True'

3. Why should the value of pi (3.14159) be stored in a constant?
4. What would be the best variable type for the area of a circle in square inches? How about the number of cars passing through an intersection in an hour? Your name? The first letter of your last name?

Programming

1. Write the program heading and declarations for a program named Mine that has the constant Pi (3.14159), variables Radius, Area, and Circumf defined as Real, and variable NumCirc as an Integer.

2.5 Executable Statements

The executable statements follow the declaration part, after the reserved word begin. They are the Pascal statements used to write or code the algorithm and its refinements. The Pascal compiler translates the executable statements into machine language; the computer executes the machine language version of these statements when we run the program.

Programs in Memory

Before examining the executable statements in the metric conversion program (Fig. 2.1), let's see what computer memory looks like before and after that program executes. Figure 2.3(a) shows the program loaded into memory and

Figure 2.3
Memory Before and After
Execution of a Program

a. Memory Before Execution   b. Memory After Execution

the program memory area before the program executes. The question marks in memory cells `SqMeters` and `SqYards` indicate that the values of these cells are undefined before program execution begins. During program execution, the data value 2.00 is read into the variable `SqMeters`. After the program executes, the variables are defined as shown in Fig. 2.3(b). We will see why next.

Assignment Statements

assignment statement
an instruction that stores a value or a computational result in a variable

An **assignment statement** stores a value or a computational result in a variable and is used to perform most arithmetic operations in a program. The assignment statement

```
SqYards := MetersToYards * SqMeters
```

in Fig. 2.1 assigns a value to the variable `SqYards`. The value assigned is the result of the multiplication (* means multiply) of the constant `MetersToYards` by the variable `SqMeters`. The memory cells for `MetersToYards` and `SqMeters` must both contain valid information (in this case, real numbers) before the assignment statement is executed. Figure 2.4 shows the contents of memory before and after the assignment statement executes; only the value of `SqYards` is changed. In Pascal the symbol `:=` is the assignment operator. Read it as "becomes," "gets," or "takes the value of" rather than "equals." The `:` and the `=` must be adjacent with no intervening space.

SYNTAX DISPLAY

Assignment Statement

Form: *variable* `:=` *expression*
Example: `X := Y + Z + 2.0`

Figure 2.4
Effect of SqYards :=
MetersToYards * SqMeters

Interpretation: The *variable* before the assignment operator is assigned the value of the *expression* after it, and in the process, the previous value of *variable* is destroyed. The *expression* can be a variable, a constant, a literal, or a combination of these connected by appropriate operators (for example, +, -, /, and *). The data type of *expression* and *variable* must be the same except that *expression* can be type `Integer` when *variable* is type `Real`.

EXAMPLE 2.2 ▼

In Pascal, you can write assignment statements of the form

```
Sum := Sum + Item
```

where the variable `Sum` appears on both sides of the assignment operator. This is obviously not an algebraic equation, but it does illustrate a common programming practice: This statement instructs the computer to add the current value of `Sum` to the value of `Item`; the result is then stored back into `Sum`. The previous value of `Sum` is destroyed in the process, as illustrated in Fig. 2.5. The value of `Item`, however, is unchanged. ▲

Figure 2.5
Effect of Sum :=
Sum + Item

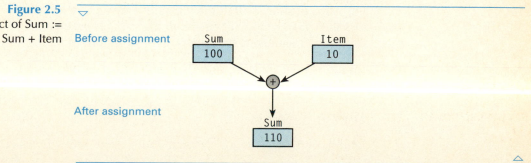

EXAMPLE 2.3 ▼

You can also write assignment statements that assign the value of a single variable or constant to a variable. If X and NewX are type Real variables, the statement

```
NewX := X
```

copies the value of variable X into variable NewX. The statement

```
NewX := -X
```

instructs the computer to get the value of X, negate that value, and store the result in NewX. For example, if X is 3.5, NewX is -3.5. Neither of these assignment statements changes the value of X.   ▲

    Section 2.7 continues the discussion of type Integer and Real expressions and operators. Next, we show some assignment statements involving other data types.

EXAMPLE 2.4 ▼

Assume Ch is type Char, BoolVar is type Boolean, and Count is type Integer for the following assignment statements, all valid in Pascal. Note that Pascal requires you to insert a semicolon between executable statements.

```
Ch := 'C';
BoolVar := True;
Count := 5
```

Next, we show memory after these statements execute. Note that the apostrophes are not stored with character data and that the Boolean value True is stored in BoolVar.

```
Ch    BoolVar   Count
 C     True      5
```

Because Pascal represents the values of each data type differently, the value being assigned must be *assignment compatible* with the variable receiving it. For now, this means that the variable and value must be the same type, unless the value is type Integer and the variable receiving it is type Real. The following assignment statements are invalid for the reasons given:

```
Ch := 5;                 {invalid assignment of integer to
                            type Char variable}
Ch := 'Hi';              {invalid assignment of string to
                            type Char variable}
BoolVar := 'False';      {invalid assignment of string to
                            type Boolean variable}
Count := 5.0             {invalid assignment of Real value to
                            type Integer variable}  ▲
```

Input/Output Operations and Procedures

Data can be stored in memory in three ways: associated with a constant, assigned to a variable, or read into a variable. We have discussed the first two methods. You would use the third method, reading data into a variable, if you wanted a program to manipulate different data each time it executes. Reading data into memory is called an **input operation**. As it executes, a program performs computations and stores the results in memory. These program results can be displayed to the program user by an **output operation**.

All input/output operations in Pascal are performed by special program units called **input/output procedures**. The input/output procedures are supplied as part of the Pascal compiler, and their names are standard identifiers (for example, ReadLn and WriteLn). In Pascal, a **procedure call statement** is used to call or activate a procedure. Calling a procedure is analogous to asking a friend to perform an urgent task. You tell your friend what to do (but not how to do it) and wait for your friend to report back that the task is finished. After hearing from your friend, you can go on and do something else.

input operation
an instruction that reads data into memory
output operation
an instruction that displays information stored in memory
input/output procedure
a Pascal procedure that performs an input or output operation
procedure call statement
an instruction that calls or activates a procedure

The WriteLn Procedure

To see the results of a program execution, we must have a way to specify what variable values should be displayed. In Fig. 2.1 the procedure call statement

```
WriteLn ('The fabric size in square yards is ', SqYards)
```

calls procedure WriteLn to display a line of program output containing two items: the string literal 'The fabric size ... is ' and the value of Sq-Yards. For the string literal, the characters inside the apostrophes are printed but the apostrophes are not. The WriteLn procedure displays the line

```
The fabric size in square yards is 2.392000E+00
```

Unless directed otherwise, Pascal scientific notation is used to display a real value (2.392000E+00 is 2.392).

WriteLn Without an Output List

The statements

```
WriteLn ('The fabric size in square yards is ', SqYards);
WriteLn;
WriteLn ('Metric conversion completed')
```

would display the lines

```
The fabric size in square yards is 2.392000E+00

Metric conversion completed
```

Because the second `WriteLn` has no output list, the blank line you see in the middle of the program output occurs. Execution of a `WriteLn` always causes the cursor to advance to the next line, creating a blank line if nothing is printed on the current line.

SYNTAX DISPLAY

WriteLn Procedure

Form: `WriteLn (output list)`
            `WriteLn`
Example: `WriteLn ('My height in inches is ', Height)`
Interpretation: The `WriteLn` procedure displays the value of each variable or constant in the order in which it appears in the *output list* and then advances the cursor to the next line. A string literal is printed without the apostrophes. If there is no *output list,* the cursor advances to the first column of the next line.

The Write Procedure

Pascal provides a second output procedure, `Write`, that is similar to `WriteLn` in all respects except that the cursor does not advance to the start of the next line after the output list is displayed. The statement pair

```
Write ('The fabric size in square yards is ');
WriteLn (SqYards)
```

would display the same output line as the single statement

```
WriteLn ('The fabric size in square yards is ', SqYards)
```

It is generally more convenient to use the latter form.

SYNTAX DISPLAY

Write Procedure

Form: `Write (output list)`
Example: `Write ('My height in inches is ', Height, ' and my ')`
Interpretation: Displays the value of each variable or constant in its output list. A string literal is displayed without the apostrophes. The cursor does not advance to the next line after the output is displayed.

Program Style

Guidelines for Write Versus WriteLn

Generally, the `WriteLn` procedure is used to display program results, but very long output lists can be split and displayed piecemeal. In this case, use the `Write` procedure to display all but the last part of the output list and use the `WriteLn` procedure to display only the last part of the output list, as shown here:

```
Write ('This line displays ');
Write ('the value of X (', X, ') and ');
WriteLn ('the value of Y (', Y, ').')
```

The output lists for the second and third lines contain a string, a variable, and a string. If X is 55 and Y is 7, the three statements print

```
This line displays the value of X (55) and the value of Y (7).
```

The ReadLn Procedure

When input data are needed, use the `Write` procedure to display a prompting message, or prompt, that tells the program user what data to enter. The `Write` statement

```
Write ('Enter the fabric size in square meters >');
ReadLn (SqMeters)
```

displays a prompt for square meters (a numeric value) in the form of a string literal and advances the cursor to the screen position just after the symbol >. The program user can then type in the data value requested, and the `ReadLn` procedure will process the input.

The statement

```
ReadLn (SqMeters)
```

calls procedure `ReadLn` (pronounced "read line") to read data into the variable `SqMeters`. Where does procedure `ReadLn` get the data it stores in the variable `SqMeters`? It reads the data from the standard input device (called `Input` by Pascal). In most cases the standard input device is the keyboard; consequently, the computer will attempt to store in `SqMeters` whatever data the program user types at the keyboard. Since `SqMeters` is declared as type `Real`, the input operation will proceed without error only if the program user types in a number. The effect of the `ReadLn` operation is shown in Fig. 2.6.

Whenever `ReadLn` executes, the program pauses until the required data are entered and the Return key is pressed. If an incorrect data character is typed, the program user can press the backspace key ($\leftarrow$) to edit the data. However, once the Return key is pressed, the data are read exactly as typed in and it is too late to correct any data entry errors.

`ReadLn` can also read data values for the other predefined data types, except for type `Boolean`. The number of characters read by the `ReadLn` proce-

Figure 2.6
Effect of ReadLn (SqMeters)

dure depends on the type of variable receiving data. Table 2.5 shows some examples of ReadLn with a single input variable. Assume that the Return key is pressed after the last character shown in the column labeled "Data Line." Remember, when typing in character data in a program, do not enclose those characters in apostrophes.

Table 2.5
Rules for Reading Data

Type of *invar*	Effect of ReadLn (*invar*)	Example	
		Data Line	*Effect*
Char	Reads next data character.	XYZ	Stores X in *invar*.
Integer	Skips leading blanks— reads all characters through next blank, control character, or Return. Characters read must form an integer value.	35 55	Stores 35 in *invar*.
Real	Skips leading blanks— reads all characters through next blank, control character, or Return. Characters read must form a real or integer value.	1.54	Stores 1.54 in *invar*.

What happens to the extra data characters in the data lines shown in Table 2.5 (for example, YZ in the first data line and 55 in the second)? These characters are processed by ReadLn but are not stored in memory.

SYNTAX DISPLAY

The ReadLn Procedure

Form: ReadLn (*input list*)
               ReadLn

Example: ReadLn (Age, NumDepend)

Interpretation: The ReadLn procedure reads into memory the data the program user types at the keyboard during program execution. The program user must enter one data item for each variable specified in the *input list* and then press the Return key. Commas separate the variable names in the *input list*.

The order of the data must correspond to the order of the variables in the *input list*. Insert one or more blank characters between consecutive numeric data items. Do not use commas within or between numeric values. Do not insert any blanks between consecutive character data items unless the blank character is one of the data items to be read and stored. Any extra data characters at the end of the line are processed but ignored (i.e., not stored in memory). If there is no *input list* (second form line), all data characters through the Return key are processed but ignored.

The Read Procedure

In Chapter 8, we will discuss another way to enter data, the Read procedure. The main difference between Read and ReadLn is that any extra characters on a data line after a Read operation are not read until the next Read or ReadLn operation. A ReadLn operation, in contrast, processes all characters on a data line, ignoring any extra characters at the end of the line.

Reading Multiple Data Items

Most of the time ReadLn will read one data item at a time, although it is possible for a single ReadLn to read multiple data values. This is most often done with type Char variables.

EXAMPLE 2.5 ▼

Assuming Ch1, Ch2, and Ch3 are type Char variables, the statement

```
ReadLn (Ch1, Ch2, Ch3)
```

reads and stores three data characters, storing the first in Ch1, the second in Ch2, and the third in Ch3. Entering the data characters EBK results in

Ch1   Ch2   Ch3

Unless you intend to store a blank data character in memory, do not press the space bar between the data characters, as it would count as one of the three characters read and stored. For example, if you enter E B K, the three characters stored would be E, a blank, and B. The next blank and K would be processed but not stored. ▲

Exercises for Section 2.5   **Self-Check**

1. Show the output displayed by the following program lines when the data entered are 5 and 7:

```
WriteLn ('Enter two integers> ');
ReadLn (M, N);                    {data line is: 5 7 }
M := M + 5;
N := 3 + N;
WriteLn ('M = ', M);
WriteLn ('N = ', N)
```

2. Show the output displayed by the following lines:

```
Write ('My name is: ');
WriteLn ('Doe, Jane');
WriteLn;
Write ('I live in ');
Write ('Ann Arbor, MI ');
WriteLn ('and my zip code is ', 48109)
```

3. Indicate whether each of the following assignments is valid or invalid and indicate the result of each valid assignment. Assume R is type Real, I is type Integer, B is type Boolean, and C is type Char.

   a. R := 3.5 + 5.0   f. C := '5'
   b. I := 2 * 5   g. C := 'I'
   c. C := 'My name'   h. R := I
   d. C := I   i. I := R
   e. B := Boolean   j. R := 10 + I

Programming

1. Write statements that ask the user to enter three numbers and then read the three user responses into First, Second, and Third.
2. a. Write a statement that displays the following line with the value of X at the end:

   ```
   The value of X is _____.
   ```

   b. Assuming Radius and Area are Real variables containing the radius and area of a circle, write a statement that will display this information in the form:

   ```
   The area of a circle with radius _____ is _____.
   ```

3. Write a program that asks the user to enter the radius of a circle and then computes and displays the circle's area. Use the formula

   Area = Pi × Radius × Radius

   where *Pi* is the constant 3.14159.

2.6 General Form of a Pascal Program

Now that we have discussed the individual statements that can appear in Pascal programs, we will review the rules for combining them into programs. We will also cover the use of punctuation, spacing, and comments in a program.

As shown in Fig. 2.7, each program begins with a heading that specifies the name of the program. Next comes the declaration part, in which you declare every identifier used in the program except for standard identifiers. All

Figure 2.7

The General Form of a
Pascal Program

```
program Name (Input, Output);
   const
      constant = value;
              .
              .
              .
      constant = value;

   var
      variable list : type;
              .
              .
              .
      variable list : type;

begin
   statement;
         .
         .
         .
   statement
end.
```

Declaration part

Program body

constant declarations follow `const`, and all variable declarations follow `var`. More than one constant may be declared, and there may be more than one variable list. Commas separate identifiers in a variable list; the semicolon terminates each declaration.

The reserved word `begin` signals the start of the program body. The program body contains statements that are translated into machine language and eventually executed. The statements we have looked at so far perform computations and input/output operations. The last line in a program is `end.`.

Semicolons separate Pascal statements. Because a semicolon is not needed before the first statement in a sequence or after the last statement, a semicolon should not appear after the reserved word `begin`. Although we don't recommend it, you can type in a semicolon after the last statement in a program. If present, this semicolon has the effect of inserting an "empty statement" between the last actual statement and the program terminator (`end.`).

Pascal ignores line breaks, so a Pascal statement can extend over more than one line. For example, the variable and constant declarations in Fig. 2.1 start on one line and finish on the next. A statement that extends over more than one line cannot be split in the middle of an identifier, a reserved word, or a literal.

Also, we can write more than one statement on a line. For example, the line

```
WriteLn ('Enter two letters> ');  ReadLn (Letter1, Letter2)
```

contains a statement that displays a prompt message and a statement that reads the data requested. A semicolon separates the two statements; another semicolon should occur at the end of the line if more statements follow. We recommend that you place only one statement on a line because it improves readability and simplifies program maintenance.

Spaces in Programs

The consistent and careful use of blank spaces can improve the style of a program. A blank space is required between words in a program line.

The compiler ignores extra blanks between words and symbols, but you may insert space to improve the readability and style of a program. You should always leave a blank space after a comma and before and after operators such as `*`, `-`, and `:=`. Remember to indent each line of a program except for the first and last lines and the line `begin` and to write the reserved words `const`, `var`, and `begin` on lines by themselves so they stand out. All lines except the first and last lines of the program and the line `begin` are indented two or more spaces. Finally, use blank lines between sections of the program.

Although stylistic issues have no effect whatever on the meaning of the program as far as the computer is concerned, they can make it easier for people to read and understand the program. Take care, however, not to insert blank spaces where they do not belong. For example, there cannot be a space between the characters `:` and `=` when they form the assignment operator `:=`. Also, an identifier such as `StartSalary` cannot be written as two words, `Start Salary`.

Comments in Programs

program documentation
information (comments) that enhances the readability of a program

Programmers make a program more readable by using comments to describe the purpose of the program, the use of identifiers, and the purpose of each program step. Comments are part of the **program documentation** because they help others read and understand the program. The compiler, however, ignores comments and does not translate them into machine language.

A comment can appear by itself on a program line, at the end of a line following a statement, or embedded in a statement. In the following variable declarations, the first comment is embedded in the declaration, while the second one follows the declaration. We document most variables in this way.

```
var
  SqMeters,            {input - fabric size in meters}
  SqYards   : Real;    {output - fabric size in yards}
```

SYNTAX DISPLAY

Comments

Form: {*comment*}

Example: {This is a comment}
        (* and so is this *)

Interpretation: A left curly brace indicates the start of a comment; a right curly brace indicates the end of a comment. Also (* and *) can mark the beginning and the end, respectively, of a comment. Comments are listed with the program but are otherwise ignored by the Pascal compiler.

Note: Standard Pascal does not allow comments to be nested inside one another.

Program Style

Using Comments

Each program should begin with a header section that consists of a series of comments specifying

▶ the programmer's name
▶ the date of the current version
▶ a brief description of what the program does

When writing programs for a class assignment, you should also list the class identification and your instructor's name. For example:

```
program Metric (Input, Output);
{
 Programmer: William Bell      Date completed: May 9, 1995
 Instructor: Janet Joseph      Class: CS1
 This program reads a value in square meters and converts it
 to square yards.
}
```

Before implementing each step in the initial algorithm, you should write a comment that summarizes the purpose of the algorithm step. This comment should describe what the step does rather than simply restate the step in English. For example, the comment

```
{Convert the fabric size to square yards}
SqYards := MetersToYards * SqMeters;
```

is more descriptive and hence preferable to

```
{Multiply MetersToYards by SqMeters, save result in SqYards.}
SqYards := MetersToYards * SqMeters;
```

Exercises for Section 2.6

Self-Check

1. Change these comments so they are syntactically correct:

   {This is a comment?*)

```
(*How about this {it seems like a comment} doesn't it*)
```

2. What is the purpose of a semicolon in the program body?
3. Correct the syntax errors in the following program and rewrite it so it follows our style conventions. What does each statement of your corrected program do? What values are printed?

```
program SMALL  VAR X, Y, X, real;
BEGIN Y = 15.0
Z := -Y + 3.5;  Y + z =: x;
writeln (x; Y; z);  end;
```

Programming

1. Write a program that stores the values 'X', 76.1, and 'MyDog' (a constant) in separate memory cells. Your program should read the first two values as data items and display all three for the user when done.

2.7 Arithmetic Expressions

To solve most programming problems, you need to write arithmetic expressions that manipulate type Integer and Real data. This section describes the operators used in arithmetic expressions and the rules for writing and evaluating these expressions.

Table 2.6 shows all the arithmetic operators. Each operator manipulates two *operands,* which may be constants, variables, or other arithmetic expressions. The operators +, −, *, and / may be used with type Integer or Real operands. As shown in the last column, for operators +, −, and * the data type of the result is the same as the data type of its operands. The real divi-

Table 2.6
Arithmetic Operators

Arithmetic Operator	Meaning	Example
+	Addition	5 + 2 is 7 5.0 + 2.0 is 7.0
−	Subtraction	5 - 2 is 3 5.0 - 2.0 is 3.0
*	Multiplication	5 * 2 is 10 5.0 * 2.0 is 10.0
/	Real division	5.0 / 2.0 is 2.5 5 / 2 is 2.5
div	Integer division	5 div 2 is 2
mod	Modulus operator	5 mod 2 is 1

sion operator (/) always yields a real number as its result, so the expression X / 2 always yields a type Real result even when X is type Integer. For example, if X is 4, the value of X / 2 is the real number 2.0. The last two operators, div and mod, can be used only with integers.

Operators div and mod

The integer division operator, div, computes the integral part of the result of dividing its first operand by its second. For example, the value of 7 / 2 is 3.5, but the value of 7 div 2 is the integral part of this result, or 3. Similarly, the value of 299 / 100 is 2.99, but the value of 299 div 100 is the integral part of this result, or 2. Both operands of div must be integers, and the div operation is undefined when the divisor (the second operand) is zero. Table 2.7 shows some examples of the div operator.

Table 2.7
Examples of the div Operator

3 div 15 = 0	3 div -15 = 0
15 div 3 = 5	15 div -3 = -5
16 div 3 = 5	16 div -3 = -5
17 div 3 = 5	-17 div 3 = -5
18 div 3 = 6	-18 div 3 = -6

Although mathematically equivalent, the results of the expressions 6 / 2 and 6 div 2 are not the same in Pascal. The value of 6 / 2 is the real number 3.0, but the value of 6 div 2 is the integer 3.

The modulus operator, mod, returns the integer remainder of the result of dividing its first operand by its second. For example, the value of 7 mod 2 is 1 because the integer remainder is 1.

You can use long division to determine the result of a div or mod operation. The following calculation on the left shows the effect of dividing 7 by 2 by long division: We get a quotient of 3 (7 div 2 is 3) and a remainder of 1 (7 mod 2 is 1). The calculation on the right shows that 299 div 100 is 2 (quotient) and that 299 mod 100 is 99 (remainder).

```
7 div 2                          299 div 100
  ↓                                   ↓
  3 R1  ← 7 mod 2                     2 R99  ← 299 mod 100
2 7                            100 299
  6                                200
  1                                 99
```

The magnitude of M mod N must always be less than the divisor N, so if M is positive, the value of M mod 100 must be between 0 and 99. The mod operation is undefined when N is zero. Table 2.8 shows some examples of the mod operator. By comparing the second and third columns, you can see that -M mod N is equivalent to -(M mod N).

Table 2.8
Examples of the
mod Operator

3 mod 5 = 3	5 mod 3 = 2	-5 mod 3 = -2
4 mod 5 = 4	5 mod 4 = 1	-5 mod 4 = -1
5 mod 5 = 0	15 mod 5 = 0	-15 mod 5 = 0
6 mod 5 = 1	15 mod 6 = 3	-15 mod 6 = -3
7 mod 5 = 2	15 mod 7 = 1	-15 mod -7 = -1
8 mod 5 = 3	15 mod 8 = 7	15 mod 0 is undefined

EXAMPLE 2.6 ▼

If you have P people and B identical boats, the expression

P div B

tells you how many people to put in each boat. Notice that P / B may give the wrong answer. For example, if P is 18 and B is 4, 18 div 4 is 4 (correct), but 18 / 4 is 4.5 (incorrect). The formula

P mod B

tells you how many people would be left over (18 mod 4 is 2). ▲

Data Type of an Arithmetic Expression

We indicated earlier that a type Integer expression could be assigned to a type Real variable, but not vice versa. How does Pascal determine the data type of an arithmetic expression? The following rule applies:

An expression is type Integer if all of its operands are type Integer and none of its operators is /; otherwise, the expression is type Real.

This rule is based on two properties of arithmetic operators:

▶ The operator / always yields a Real result.
▶ If an operator has one Real operand and one Integer operand, the operator yields a Real result (for example, 5 + 2.0 is 7.0, not 7).

mixed-type expression
an expression that has type
Real and Integer operands
and always evaluates to a
Real result

A **mixed-type expression** has both Integer and Real operands. According to the preceding rule, a mixed-type expression must be type Real. It is a good programming practice to avoid writing mixed-type expressions.

Mixed-Type Assignment Statements

When an assignment statement is executed, the expression is first evaluated and then the result is assigned to the variable preceding the assignment operator (:=). Either a type `Real` or a type `Integer` expression may be assigned to a type `Real` variable. Thus, if `M` and `N` are type `Integer` and `X` and `Y` are type `Real`, all the following assignment statements are valid:

```
M := 3;
N := 2;
X := M / N;     {assigns 1.5 to X}
Y := M + N      {assigns 5.0 to Y}
```

In the last statement, the expression `M + N` evaluates to the integer 5 and this value is converted to its type `Real` equivalent (`5.0`) before it is stored in `Y`. Notice that the type conversion is done after the two integer values are summed, not before (i.e., `3` and `2` are summed, not `3.0` and `2.0`). This is an example of a **mixed-type assignment** statement because the variable being assigned and the expression have different data types.

mixed-type assignment
assignment of an expression of one type to a variable of a different type

Pascal does not allow a type `Real` expression to be assigned to a type `Integer` variable, because the fractional part of the expression cannot be represented and so will be lost. This means that the following mixed-type assignment statements are invalid if `Count` is type `Integer`:

```
Count := 3.5;           {invalid assignment of real value to
                          Integer variable}
Count := Count + 1.0;   {invalid; 1.0 is Real, so result is
                          Real}
Count := Count / 2;     {invalid; result of division is
                          Real}
```

Expressions with Multiple Operators

In our examples so far, most expressions have had a single operator; however, expressions with multiple operators are common. To understand and write expressions with multiple operators, we must know the Pascal rules for evaluating expressions. For example, in the expression `10 + 5 / 2`, is + performed before /, or vice versa? In the expression `10 / 5 * 2`, is / performed before *, or vice versa? Verify for yourself that the order of evaluation does make a difference. In both expressions, the / operator is evaluated first. The reasons are explained in the Pascal rules for expression evaluation, which are based on familiar algebraic rules.

Rules for Evaluating Expressions

a. *Parentheses rule:* All expressions in parentheses must be evaluated separately. Nested parenthesized expressions must be evaluated from the inside out, with the innermost expression evaluated first.

b. *Operator precedence rule:* Operators in the same expression are evaluated in the following order.

```
*,/,div,mod      first
+,-              last
```

c. *Left associative rule:* Operators in the same expression and at the same precedence level (such as + and -) are evaluated left to right.

These rules will help you understand how Pascal evaluates expressions. Use parentheses as needed to specify the order of evaluation. For complicated expressions, it is a good idea to use extra parentheses to document clearly the order of operator evaluation. For example, the expression

```
X * Y * Z + A / B - C * D
```

can be written in a more readable form using parentheses:

```
(X * Y * Z ) + (A / B) - (C * D)
```

EXAMPLE 2.7 ▼

The formula for the area of a circle

$$a = \pi r^2$$

can be written in Pascal as

```
Area := Pi * Radius * Radius
```

where `Pi` is the constant `3.14159`. Figure 2.8 shows the evaluation tree for this formula. In this tree, read from top to bottom, arrows connect each operand with its operator. The order of operator evaluation is shown by the number to the left of each operator; the letter to the right of the operator indicates which evaluation rule applies.   ▲

Figure 2.8
Evaluation Tree for Area :=
Pi * Radius * Radius

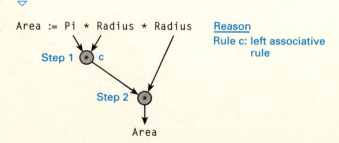

EXAMPLE 2.8 ▼

The formula for the average velocity, v, of a particle traveling on a line between points p_1 and p_2 in time t_1 to t_2 is

$$v = \frac{p_2 - p_1}{t_2 - t_1}$$

This formula can be written and evaluated in Pascal as shown in Fig. 2.9.   ▲

EXAMPLE 2.9 ▼

Consider the expression

```
Z - (A + B div 2 ) + W * Y
```

containing Integer variables only. The parenthesized expression (A + B div 2) is evaluated first (rule a) beginning with B div 2 (rule b). Once the value of B div 2 is determined, it can be added to A to obtain the value of (A + B div 2). Next, the multiplication operation is performed (rule b) and the value for W * Y is determined. Then, the value of (A + B div 2) is subtracted from Z (rule c). Finally, the result is added to W * Y. The evaluation tree for this expression is shown in Fig. 2.10.   ▲

Writing Mathematical Formulas in Pascal

You may encounter two problems in writing a mathematical formula in Pascal. The first concerns multiplication, which often is implied in a formula by writing the two multiplicands next to each other, for example, $a = bc$. In Pascal, however, you must always use the * operator to indicate multiplication, as in

```
A := B * C
```

The other difficulty arises in formulas using division, in which we normally write the numerator and the denominator on separate lines:

Figure 2.9
Evaluation Tree for V :=
(P2 − P1) / (T2 − T1)

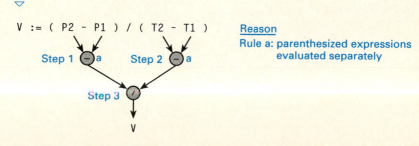

Figure 2.10
Evaluation Tree for
Z − (A + B div 2) + W * Y

Reason
Step 1: div before +
Step 2: parenthesized expressions
       evaluated separately
Step 3: * before − and +
Step 4: left associative rule

$$m = \frac{y - b}{x - a}$$

In Pascal, however, the numerator and denominator must be placed on the same line. Consequently, parentheses often are needed to separate the numerator from the denominator and to indicate clearly the order of evaluation of the operators in the expression. Thus the preceding formula would be written in Pascal as

```
M := (Y - B) / (X - A)
```

Table 2.9 gives other examples of mathematical formulas rewritten in Pascal. The points illustrated in Table 2.9 can be summarized as follows:

▶ Always specify multiplication explicitly by using the operator * where needed (formulas 1 and 4).

Table 2.9
Mathematical Formulas as
Pascal Expressions

Mathematical Formula	Pascal Expression
1. $b^2 - 4ac$	B * B - 4 * A * C
2. $a + b - c$	A + B - C
3. $\dfrac{a + b}{c + d}$	(A + B) / (C + D)
4. $\dfrac{1}{1 + x^2}$	1 / (1 + X * X)
5. $a \times -(b + c)$	A * (-(B + C))

> ▶ Use parentheses when required to control the order of operator evaluation (formulas 3 and 4).
> ▶ Never write two arithmetic operators in succession; they must be separated by an operand or an open parenthesis (formula 5).

Unary Minus

The fifth Pascal expression in Table 2.9 uses a unary minus to negate the value of (B + C) before performing the multiplication. The unary minus has only one operand and has the same precedence as the subtraction operator.

Mixed-Type Expressions with div and mod

You must be very careful when using div and mod in a mixed-type expression or with the real division operator /. The expression

```
7 div 2 / 3.0
```

is valid and evaluates to 1.0 as shown in Fig. 2.11. However, the expression

```
7 / 2 div 3
```

is invalid because 7 / 2 is 3.5 (/ yields a Real result) and 3.5 cannot be an operand of div.

The following case study demonstrates the manipulation of type Integer data.

CASE STUDY ## Evaluating Coins

PROBLEM ▼

Your little sister, who has been saving nickels and pennies, is tired of lugging her piggy bank when she goes shopping. She wants to exchange the

Figure 2.11
Evaluation Tree for
7 div 2 / 3.0

coins for dollar bills and change, so she needs to know the value of her coins in dollars and cents.

ANALYSIS ▼

To solve this problem, you need a count of nickels and a count of pennies in the collection. From those counts, determine the total value of the coins in cents. Once you have that figure, you can do an integer division using 100 as the divisor to get the dollar value; the remainder of this division will be the loose change that she should receive. In the data requirements, list the total value in cents (TotalCents) as a program variable, because it is needed as part of the computation process but is not a required problem output.

Data Requirements

Problem Inputs

```
Nickels : Integer   {the count of nickels}
Pennies : Integer   {the count of pennies}
```

Problem Outputs

```
Dollars : Integer   {the number of dollars she should receive}
Change : Integer    {the loose change she should receive}
```

Additional Program Variables

```
TotalCents : Integer   {the total number of cents}
```

Relevant Formulas

1 dollar = 100 pennies
1 nickel = 5 pennies

DESIGN ▼

The algorithm is straightforward.

Initial Algorithm

1. Read in the count of nickels and pennies.
2. Compute the total value in cents.
3. Find the value in dollars and loose change.
4. Display the value in dollars and loose change.

Steps 2 and 3 may need refinement. Their refinements follow.

Step 2 Refinement

2.1 TotalCents is the value of Nickels in cents plus Pennies.

Step 3 Refinement

3.1 Dollars is the integer quotient of TotalCents and 100.
3.2 Change is the integer remainder of TotalCents and 100.

IMPLEMENTATION ▼

The program is shown in Fig. 2.12. The statement

```
TotalCents := 5 * Nickels + Pennies;
```

implements algorithm step 2.1. The statements

```
Dollars := TotalCents div 100;
Change := TotalCents mod 100;
```

use the mod and div operators to implement algorithm steps 3.1 and 3.2.

Figure 2.12
Finding the Value of Coins

Directory: CHAP2
File: COINS.PAS

```
program Coins (Input, Output);
{Determines the value of a coin collection.}

   var
     Pennies,                      {input - count of pennies}
     Nickels,                      {input - count of nickels}
     Dollars,                      {output - number of dollars}
     Change,                       {output - loose change}
     TotalCents : Integer;    {total cents}

begin
  {Read in the count of nickels and pennies.}
  Write ('Number of nickels> ');
  ReadLn (Nickels);
  Write ('Number of pennies> ');
  ReadLn (Pennies);

  {Compute the total value in cents.}
  TotalCents := 5 * Nickels + Pennies;

  {Find the value in dollars and change.}
  Dollars := TotalCents div 100;
  Change := TotalCents mod 100;

  {Display the value in dollars and change.}
  WriteLn;
  Write ('Your coins are worth ', Dollars, ' dollars');
  WriteLn (' and ', Change, ' cents.')
end.
```

Sample Run

```
Number of nickels> 30
Number of pennies> 77

Your coins are worth        2 dollars and        27 cents.
```

TESTING ▼

To test this program, try running it with a combination of nickels and pennies that yields an exact dollar amount with no change left over. For example, 35 nickels and 25 pennies should yield a value of 2 dollars and no cents. Then increase and decrease the amount of pennies by one (26 and 24 pennies) to make sure that these cases are also handled properly.

....

Exercises for Section 2.7   **Self-Check**

1. a. Evaluate the following expressions with 7 and 22 as operands.

    ```
    22 div 7    7 div 22    22 mod 7    7 mod 22
    ```

    Repeat the exercise for these pairs of integers:
    b. 15, 16   c. 3, 23   d. -4, 16

2. Given the declarations

    ```
    const
      Pi = 3.14159;
      MaxI = 1000;

    var
      X, Y : Real;
      A, B, I : Integer;
    ```

    indicate which statements are valid and find the value of each valid statement. Also indicate which statements are invalid and explain why. Assume that A is 3, B is 4, and Y is -1.0.

    a. I := A mod B
    b. I := (990 - MaxI) div A
    c. I := A mod Y
    d. X := Pi * Y
    e. I := A / B
    f. X := A / B
    g. X := A mod (A / B)
    h. I := B div 0
    i. I := A mod (990 - MaxI)
    j. I := (MaxI - 990) div A
    k. X := A / Y
    l. I := Pi * A
    m. X := Pi div Y
    n. X := A div B
    o. I := (MaxI - 990) mod A
    p. I := A mod 0
    q. I := A mod (MaxI - 990)

3. Draw evaluation trees for the following expressions. What is the value of the last one?

    ```
    1.8 * Celsius + 32.0
    (Salary - 5000.00) * 0.20 + 1425.00
    10 mod 4 + 1 div 2
    ```

4. Write an assignment statement to implement the following equation in Pascal:

    $$q = \frac{kA(T_1 - T_2)}{L}$$

5. Assume that you have the following variable declarations:

```
var
   Color, Lime, Straw, Red, Orange : Integer;
   White, Green, Blue, Purple, Crayon : Real;
```

Evaluate each of the following statements given these values: `Color` is 2, `Crayon` is `-1.3`, `Straw` is 1, `Red` is 3, `Purple` is `0.2E+1`.

a. `White := Color * 2.5 / Purple`
b. `Green := Color / Purple`
c. `Orange := Color div Red`
d. `Blue := (Color + Straw) / (Crayon + 0.3)`
e. `Lime := Red div Color + Red mod Color`
f. `Purple := Straw / Red * Color`

6. Let A, B, C, and X be the names of four type `Real` variables, and let I, J, and K be the names of three type `Integer` variables. Each of the following statements contains a violation of the rules for forming arithmetic expressions. Rewrite each statement so it is consistent with the rules.

a. `X := 4.0 A * C` d. `K := 3(I + J)`
b. `A := AC` e. `X := 5A / BC`
c. `I := 2 * -J` f. `I := 5J3`

Programming

1. Extend the program in Fig. 2.12 to handle dimes and quarters as well as nickels and pennies.

2.8 Formatting Program Output

Pascal displays all real numbers in scientific notation unless we instruct it to do otherwise. This section explains how to specify the format or appearance of your output.

Formatting Integer Values

It is fairly easy to specify the format of an `Integer` variable or value displayed by a Pascal program. You simply add the symbols :*fw* after the variable or value, where *fw* specifies the **field width**, or number of digits to be displayed. The lines

field width
the number of characters used
to display a value

```
Write ('Your coins are worth ', Dollars :1, ' dollars');
WriteLn (' and ', Change :2, ' cents.')
```

indicate that one digit will be used to display the value of `Dollars` and two digits will be used to display the value of `Change` (a number between 0 and 99). If `Dollars` is 7 and `Change` is 8, the program output would be

```
Your coins are worth 7 dollars and  8 cents.
```

In this line, notice that there is an extra space before the value of Change (value is 8). The reason is that the format specification :2 allows space for two digits to be displayed. If the value of Change is between 0 and 9, a single digit is displayed right-justified, preceded by one blank space. We can use the format symbols :2 to display any output value between -9 and 99. For negative numbers, you must include the minus sign in the count of digits displayed.

Table 2.10 shows how two integer values are displayed using different format specifications. In this table, the character □ represents a blank character. The next-to-last line shows that Pascal expands the field width if it is too small for the integer value displayed. You can use the format specification :1 to display any integer value without leading blanks. The last line shows the field width specification may be a variable (or even an expression) that has an integer value.

Value	Format	Displayed Output	Value	Format	Displayed Output
234	:4	□234	-234	:4	-234
234	:5	□□234	-234	:5	□-234
234	:6	□□□234	-234	:6	□□-234
234	:1	234	-234	:1	-234
234	:Len	□□234 (if Len is 5)	-234	:Len	□-234 (if Len is 5)

Formatting Real Values

To describe the format specification for a type Real variable or value, we must indicate both the total *field width* needed and the desired number of *decimal places* after the variable or value (:*fw* :*dp*). The total field width should be large enough to accommodate all digits before and after the decimal point. We should also include a display column for the decimal point and for a minus sign if the number can be negative.

If X is a type Real variable whose value will be between -99.9 and 999.9, we could use the output list item X :5:1 to display the value of X to an accuracy of one decimal place. Table 2.11 shows different values of X displayed using this format specification. The values displayed are rounded to one decimal place, and all values are displayed right-justified in five columns.

Table 2.11
Displaying X Using Format
Specification :5 :1

Value of X	Displayed Output	Value of X	Displayed Output
99.42	-99.4	-25.55	-25.6
0.123	□□0.1	99.999	100.0
-9.53	□-9.5	999.43	999.4

Table 2.12 shows some real values displayed using other format specifications. The next-to-last line shows that Pascal expands the field width if it is too small for the real value displayed. You can use format specifications 3:1 and 4:2 to display any real value without leading blanks. The last line shows that you can use a format specification of the form :*n* for real values. In this case, the real value is displayed in scientific notation using a field width of *n*.

Table 2.12
Formatting Real Values

Value	Format	Displayed Output	Value	Format	Displayed Output
3.14159	:5:2	□3.14	3.14159	:4:2	3.14
3.14159	:4:2	3.14	3.14159	:5:1	□□3.1
3.14159	:5:3	3.142	3.14159	:8:5	□3.14159
0.1234	:4:2	0.12	-0.006	:4:2	-0.01
-0.006	:8:3	□□-0.006	-0.006	:8:5	-0.00600
25.876	:3:1	25.9	-124.3123	:4:2	-124.31
-0.006	:9	-6.00E-03	-3.14159	:9	-3.14E+00

Program Style

Eliminating Leading Blanks

As shown in Tables 2.10 through 2.12, a number that requires fewer display columns than are specified by the format field width is displayed with leading blanks. To eliminate extra leading blanks, choose a format that will display the smallest value expected. If the actual value requires more display columns, the field width will expand to accommodate it. Thus a format of :1 displays any integer value without leading blanks (for example, 29397 :1 is displayed as 29397). A format of :3:1 displays any real number to an accuracy of one decimal place without leading blanks (for example, 99397.567 :3:1 is displayed as 99397.6); similarly, a format of :4:2 displays any real number to an accuracy of two decimal places without leading blanks.

Formatting Strings

A string value is always displayed right-justified in its field. Therefore blank spaces will precede a string if the field in which it is displayed is wider than the string. If the field width is too small for a string value, the number of characters displayed is equal to the field width, so not all characters will be displayed. Table 2.13 illustrates these points.

Table 2.13
Displaying String Values
Using Formats

String	Format	Displayed Output
'*'	:1	*
'*'	:2	□*
'*'	:3	□□*
'ACES'	:1	A
'ACES'	:2	AC
'ACES'	:3	ACE
'ACES'	:4	ACES
'ACES'	:5	□ACES

EXAMPLE 2.10 ▼

The statements

```
Quantity := 15;
Cost := 55.0;
Delivered := True;
WriteLn (Quantity :5, '$' :5, Cost :8:2, Delivered :10)
```

display an integer (value of Quantity), a character ($), a real number (value of Cost), and a Boolean value (Delivered). The output line displayed would be

□□□15□□□□$□□□55.00□□□□□□True

where the symbol □ denotes a blank. The integer 15 is preceded by 3 blanks, the character $ by 4 blanks, the real number 55.00 by 3 blanks, and the Boolean value True by 6 blanks. You may prefer to remove the spaces between the $ character and the number 55.00. You can accomplish this by changing the third output list item to `Cost :5:2`. ▲

Exercises for Section 2.8

Self-Check

1. Show the output lines for the following statements:

```
Write (-99 :4);
WriteLn ('Bottles' :8);
WriteLn (-99 :4, -99 :8)
```

2. Show how the value -15.564 (stored in X) would be displayed using these formats:

```
X :8:4    X :8:3    X :8:2    X :8:1    X :8:0    X :8
```

3. What is the output of the following sequence of program statements assuming I is an integer? Use the symbol □ to denote a blank space.

```
I := 1;
WriteLn (I : 5, ' ', I :1, I : 5);
I := I * 10;
WriteLn (I : 5, ' ', I :1, I : 5);
I := I * 10;
WriteLn (I : 5, ' ', I :1, I : 5);
I := I * 10;
WriteLn (I : 5, ' ', I :1, I : 5)
```

4. Assuming X (type Real) is 12.335 and I (type Integer) is 100, show the output lines for the following statements:

```
WriteLn ('X is ' :10, X :6:2, 'I is ' :4, I :5);
Write ('I is ' :10, I :1);
WriteLn ('X is ' :10, X :2:1)
```

Programming

1. A researcher wants to display a table of readings from an experiment. Each line will contain an integer from 1 to 1000, to indicate the reading number (value of Reading), and the pressure amount (value of Pressure), which is always less than 100 pounds. Give a WriteLn statement that will display outputs in the form

   `RRRR□□□□□PP.PPP`

   where each R is a digit of the reading value, each P is a digit of the pressure value, and each □ is a space.

2. Write a series of statements that will display a three-line heading consisting of your name, your school, and its city and state. Each line should be approximately centered on the computer screen.

2.9 Interactive Mode, Batch Mode, and Data Files (Optional)

There are two basic modes of computer operation: batch mode and interactive mode. The programs that we have written so far are intended to be run in interactive mode. In *interactive mode*, the program user can interact with the program and enter data while the program is executing. In *batch mode*, all data must be supplied beforehand, and the program user cannot interact with the program while it is executing. Batch mode is optional on most computers.

If you use batch mode, you must prepare a batch data file before you execute your program. On a time-shared system or a personal computer, a batch data file is created and saved in the same way as a program file or a source file.

Input Redirection

Figures 2.13 and 2.14 show two versions of the metric conversion program rewritten as batch programs. In Fig. 2.13, we assume that the system file Input is associated with a batch data file instead of the keyboard. In most systems, this can be done relatively easily through *input-output redirection* using operating system commands. For example, in the UNIX and MS-DOS operating systems, you could instruct your program to take its input from file MyData instead of the keyboard by placing the symbols <MyData at the end

Figure 2.13
Batch Version of Metric
Conversion Program

Directory: CHAP2
File: METRICBA.PAS

```pascal
program MetricBatch (Input, Output);
{Converts square meters to square yards.}

  const
    MetersToYards = 1.196;      {conversion constant}

  var
    SqMeters,                   {input - fabric size in meters}
    SqYards   : Real;           {output - fabric size in yards}

begin
  {Read the fabric size in square meters.}
  ReadLn (SqMeters);
  WriteLn ('The fabric size in square meters is ', SqMeters :3:1);
```

▷ ▷ ▷ ▷ ▷ ▷

```
{Convert the fabric size to square yards.}
SqYards := MetersToYards * SqMeters;

{Display the fabric size in square yards.}
 WriteLn ('The fabric size in square yards is ', SqYards :4:2)
end.
```

Sample Run

```
The fabric size in square meters is 2.0
The fabric size in square yards is 2.39
```

of the command line that causes your compiled and linked program to execute. If you normally used the command line

```
MetricBa
```

to execute this program, your new command line would be

```
MetricBa <MyData
```

Program Style

Echo Prints Versus Prompts

In Fig. 2.13, the statement

```
ReadLn (SqMeters);
```

reads the value of `SqMeters` from the first (and only) line of the data file. Because the program input comes from a data file, there is no need to precede this statement with a prompt. Instead we follow the `ReadLn` with the statement

```
WriteLn ('Fabric size in square meters is ', SqMeters :3:1);
```

which *echo prints*, or displays, the value just read into `SqMeters`. This statement provides a record of the data manipulated by the program; without it, we would have no easy way of knowing what value was read. Whenever you convert an interactive program to a batch program, make sure you replace each prompt with an echo print that follows the `ReadLn` statement.

Output Redirection

You can also redirect program output to a disk file instead of to the screen. Then you could send the output file to the printer (using an operating system command) to obtain a hard copy of the program output. In UNIX or MS-DOS, you would use `>MyOutput` to redirect output from the screen to the file MyOutput. These symbols should also be placed on the command line, which causes your program to execute. The command line

```
MetricBa >MyOutput
```

executes the compiled and linked code for the metric conversion program, reading program input from the keyboard and writing program output to the file MyOutput. However, it would be difficult to interact with this program because all program output, including any prompts, are sent to the output file. It would be better to use the command line

```
MetricBa <MyData >MyOutput
```

which reads program input from the data file MyData and sends program output to the output file MyOutput.

Preview of Text Files

This section previews the use of text files as data files in Pascal. There is a complete treatment of this topic in Chapter 8. Skip this section if you will not be using data files until then.

A batch program reads its data from a data file that is created and saved beforehand with an editor program. The process used to create a text file is the same as that used to create a program file. The metric conversion program in Fig. 2.14 reads its data from the data file InData instead of the system file Input.

In Fig. 2.14, the program heading

```
program MetricFile (InData, Output);
```

identifies InData as the name of the data file instead of the system file Input. The declaration

```
var
   InData : Text;    {input - data file}
```

indicates that InData has data type Text (a standard identifier) and is, therefore, a text file. The statement

```
Reset (InData);
```

prepares the file InData so that it can be read. Finally, the statement

```
ReadLn (InData, SqMeters);
```

reads a data value from the first (and only) line of the file InData. The sample output shown in Fig. 2.14 is generated when the file InData contains the line

```
2.0
```

Figure 2.14
Metric Conversion Program
Using the File InData

Directory: CHAP2
File: METRICFI.PAS

```pascal
program MetricFile (InData, Output);
{Converts square meters to square yards.}

   const
      MetersToYards = 1.196;      {conversion constant}

   var
      InData : Text;              {input - data file}
      SqMeters,                   {input - fabric size in meters}
      SqYard   : Real;            {output - fabric size in yards}

begin
   {Read the fabric size in square meters.}
   Reset (InData);
   ReadLn (InData, SqMeters);
   WriteLn ('The fabric size in square meters is ', SqMeters :3:1);

   {Convert the fabric size to square yards.}
   SqYards := MetersToYards * SqMeters;

   {Display the fabric size in square yards.}
   WriteLn ('The fabric size in square yards is ', SqYards :4:2)
end.
```

Sample Run

```
The fabric size in square meters is 2.0
The fabric size in square yards is 2.39
```

Internal and External File Names

The program in Fig. 2.14 uses InData as the name of the data file being processed. InData is called the *internal name* of the data file. The data file may be stored under a different name on disk (its *external name*). The Pascal system does not know the file's external name unless you specify it. Specifying a file's external name is system dependent; check with your instructor.

Some systems allow the use of an extended form of the Reset procedure. On these systems, the procedure call statement

```
Reset (InData, 'DataFile'); {prepare external file 'DataFile'}
```

may associate the internal name InData with the external name DataFile.

Self-Check

1. Explain the difference in placement of WriteLn statements used to display prompts and WriteLn statements used to echo data. Which are used in interactive programs? In batch programs?
2. How are input data provided to an interactive program? To a batch program?

Programming

1. Rewrite the program in Fig. 2.12 as a batch program. Assume data are read from the file InData.
2. Redo Programming Exercise 1, this time assuming that the data are read from the file MyData.

2.10   Debugging and Programming Errors

Beginning programmers soon discover that a program rarely runs correctly the first time it executes. Murphy's Law, "If something can go wrong, it will," seems to have been written with the computer program in mind. In fact, errors are so common that they have their own special name—*bugs*—and the process of correcting them is called **debugging** a program. (According to computer folklore, the first hardware error was caused by a large insect found inside a computer component.) To alert you to potential problems, we will provide a section on common programming errors at the end of each chapter.

debugging
removing errors from a program

When the compiler detects an error, the computer displays an error message indicating that you have made a mistake and what the likely cause of the error might be. Unfortunately, error messages are often difficult to interpret and are sometimes misleading. As you gain experience, you will become more proficient at locating and correcting errors.

Three kinds of errors—syntax errors, run-time errors, and logic errors—can occur, as discussed in the following sections.

Syntax Errors

syntax error
a violation of the Pascal grammar rules, detected during program translation

A **syntax error** occurs when your code violates one or more grammar rules of Pascal and is detected and displayed by the compiler as it attempts to translate your program. If a statement has a syntax error, it cannot be translated and your program will not be executed.

Figure 2.15 shows a compiler listing of the metric conversion program with errors introduced. A *compiler listing* is a listing printed by the compiler during program translation that shows each line of the source program (preceded by a line number) and any syntax errors detected by the compiler. For this particular compiler, errors are indicated by five asterisks and are summa-

Figure 2.15
Compiler Listing of a
Program with Syntax Errors

```
 1 program Metric (Input, Output)
 2 {Converts square meters to square yards.}
 3
 4   const
*****        ^14
 5     MetersToYards : 1.196;            {conversion constant}
*****                     ^16,50
 6
 7   var
 8     SqMeter : Real;        {input - fabric size in meters}
 9
10 begin
11   {Read the fabric size in square meters.}
12   WriteLn ('Enter the fabric size in square meters> ')
13   ReadLn (SqMeters);
*****        ^6
14
15   {Convert the fabric size to square yards.}
16   MetersToYards * SqMeters := SqYards;
*****              ^59             ^104
17
18   {Display the fabric size in square yards.}
19   WriteLn ('The fabric size in square yards is ', SqYards)
*****                                              ^104
20 end.
```

```
  6:  illegal symbol
 14:  ";" expected
 16:  "=" expected
 50:  error in constant
 59:  error in variable
104: identifier not declared
```

rized at the bottom of the compiler listing. The program contains the following syntax errors:

▶ missing semicolon after the program heading (line 1)
▶ use of : instead of = in the constant declaration (line 5)
▶ missing semicolon after the WriteLn statement (line 12)
▶ assignment statement with transposed variable and expression part (line 16)
▶ missing declaration for variable SqYards (lines 16 and 19)

The actual formats of the listing and the errors messages produced by your compiler may differ from those in Fig. 2.15. In this listing, whenever an error is detected, the compiler prints a line with five asterisks, a caret symbol (^), and one or more numbers. The caret points to the position where the error was detected in the line above. Each number is a preassigned code for an error; the codes and their meanings are listed following the program.

To understand how this works, look at the first error in the program, which was detected after the reserved word `const` in line 4 was processed by the compiler. At this point the compiler recognized that a semicolon is missing (after the program heading) and indicated this by printing error code 14 (`";" expected`). In this case, the position of the caret is misleading, because the compiler could not detect the error until it started to process the constant declaration. There is also a missing semicolon after line 12; however, the compiler prints error code 6 (`illegal symbol`) after it processes the standard identifier `ReadLn` in line 13.

Two error codes are printed after line 5 to indicate an incorrect symbol (`:` instead of `=`). The transposed assignment statement in line 16 is detected as error code 59 (`error in variable`); the compiler is looking for the variable in the assignment statement and detects an error when it reaches an asterisk.

An `identifier not declared` syntax error occurs if the compiler cannot find the declaration for an identifier referenced in the program body. This can happen because the programmer forgot the declaration or mistyped the name of the identifier. In Fig. 2.15 omission of the declaration for the variable `SqYards` causes the display of error code 104 (`identifier not declared`) after lines 16 and 19.

One syntax error often leads to the generation of multiple error messages. For example, forgetting to declare variable `SqYards` will cause an error message to be printed each time `SqYards` is used in the program. For this reason, it is often a good idea to concentrate initially on correcting the errors in the declaration part of the program and then to recompile rather than attempting to fix all the errors at once. Many later errors will disappear once the declarations are correct.

Syntax errors are often caused by the *improper use of apostrophes with strings*. Always use an apostrophe, not a double quotation mark, to begin and end a string. Also, a string must begin and end on the same line.

Another common syntax error is a missing apostrophe or an extra apostrophe in a string. If an apostrophe is missing at the end, the compiler will assume that whatever follows is part of the string.

The following string contains an extra apostrophe:

```
WriteLn ('Enter Joe's nickname:');
```

The compiler will assume that the apostrophe used to indicate possession (`Joe's`) is terminating the string. This string must be entered as

```
WriteLn ('Enter Joe''s nickname:');
```

Two consecutive apostrophes inside a string indicate an apostrophe as a punctuation mark.

Two common errors made by beginning programmers are forgetting to declare (or misspelling) identifier names and omitting semicolons. Both errors are easily discovered by careful desk checking.

Improper use of a Pascal data type often causes a syntax error. Two examples follow:

▶ Use of arithmetic operators with character or string data
▶ Assigning a value of one type to a variable of another type (exception: an `Integer` value can be assigned to a type `Real` variable)

When using comments, you must enclose them in { and } or (* and *). If the opening { is missing, the compiler will attempt to process the comment as a Pascal statement, which should cause a syntax error. If the closing } is missing, the comment will simply be extended to include the program statements that follow it. If the comment is not terminated, the rest of the program will be included in the comment, and a syntax error such as `incomplete program` will be printed.

Run-Time Errors

run-time error

an attempt to perform an invalid operation, detected during program execution

Run-time errors are detected and displayed by the computer during the execution of a program. A run-time error occurs when the program directs the computer to perform an invalid operation, such as dividing a number by zero or manipulating undefined or invalid data.

The program in Fig. 2.16 compiles successfully but contains no statement assigning a value to the variable X before the assignment statement

```
Z := Y / X;
```

executes, causing a run-time error. If your Pascal compiler assigns the default value 0.0 to X, the error message `Division by Zero` is displayed, indicating an *attempt to divide by zero,* an invalid operation. You should insert

Figure 2.16
Program with a
Run-Time Error

```
program TestError (Input, Output);

   var
      X, Y, Z : Real;

begin
   Y := 5.0;
   Z := Y / X;
   WriteLn (X, Y, Z)
end.
```

a statement that assigns a nonzero value to X; it is poor programming practice to allow the compiler to assign default values to your variables.

Data entry errors are common run-time errors caused by reading data of the wrong type into a variable—for example, reading a real number or a character into a type Integer variable. Another common run-time error is **arithmetic overflow**. This error occurs when a program attempts to store a value that is too large in a variable.

arithmetic overflow

a run-time error caused by an attempt to store a value in a variable that is too large

Logic Errors

logic error

an error caused by following a faulty algorithm

Logic errors occur when a program follows a faulty algorithm. Because logic errors usually do not cause run-time errors and do not display error messages, they are very difficult to detect. The only sign of a logic error may be incorrect program output. You can detect logic errors by testing the program thoroughly, comparing its output to calculated results. You can prevent logic errors by carefully desk checking the algorithm and the program before you type it in.

Because debugging can be time-consuming, plan your program solutions carefully and desk check them to eliminate bugs early. If you are unsure of the syntax for a particular statement, look it up in the text or in Appendix H. Following this approach will save time and avoid trouble.

CHAPTER REVIEW

1. Follow the first five steps of the software development method to solve programming problems: (1) specify the problem, (2) analyze the problem, (3) design the algorithm, (4) implement the program, and (5) test and verify the solution. Use structured programming techniques to write error-free code that is easy to read and maintain.
2. Every Pascal program has a declaration part and a program body.
3. Within the declaration part, you must declare each identifier and its use unless the identifier is a standard identifier in which case its meaning is predefined. All identifiers begin with a letter and consist only of letters and digits. A reserved word cannot be used as an identifier.
   ▶ Declare as a constant a memory cell used to store a value that cannot change.
   ▶ Declare as a variable a memory cell used to store a data value or a program result.
4. Pascal's data types enable the compiler to determine how to store a particular value in memory and what operations can be performed on that value. The four standard data types are Integer, Real, Char, and Boolean. The data type of each variable must be declared; Pascal determines the data type of a constant from its value.
5. The program body consists of the executable statements, which are translated into machine language. Assignment statements perform computations and store results in memory, Write/WriteLn statements display values stored in memory, and ReadLn statements read data values into memory.

Summary of New Pascal Constructs

Construct	Effect
Program Heading	
`program Payroll` `    (Input, Output);`	Identifies `Payroll` as the name of the program.
Constant Declaration	

`const`
`  Tax = 25.00;`
`  Star = '*';`
	Associates the constant `Tax` with the real value `25.00` and the constant `Star` with the type `Char` value `'*'`.

Variable Declaration	

`var`
`  X, Y, Z : Real;`
`  Me, It : Integer;`
	Allocates memory cells named `X`, `Y`, and `Z` for storage of real numbers and `Me` and `It` for storage of integers.

Assignment Statement	
`Distance := Speed * Time`	Assigns the product of `Speed` and `Time` as the value of `Distance`.
ReadLn Procedure	
`ReadLn (Hours, Rate)`	Enters data into the variables `Hours` and `Rate`.
Write Procedure	
`Write ('Net = ', Net :4:2)`	Displays the string `'Net = '` followed by the value of `Net` printed in a field of four columns and rounded to two decimal places.
WriteLn Procedure	
`WriteLn (X, Y)`	Prints the values of `X` and `Y` and advances the cursor to the next line.

Quick-Check Exercises

1. What value is assigned to X by the following statement?

   `X := 25.0 * 3.0 / 2.5`

2. What value is assigned to X by the following statement, assuming X is `10.0`?

   `X := X - 20.0`

3. Show the exact form of the output line displayed when X is 3.456 and N is 890:

```
WriteLn ('Some numbers are ', X :3:1, '*', X :6:3,
         N : 4, '*', N : 1);
```

4. In the following expression, what operator will be evaluated first: A + B / C * D?

5. Indicate which data type you would use to represent the following items: number of children at school, a letter grade on an exam, the average number of school days absent each year.

6. In which step of the software development method are the problem inputs and outputs identified?

7. How does `WriteLn` differ in its effect from `Write`?

8. If procedure `ReadLn` is reading two numbers from a data line, what character is typed in after the first number? What is typed in after the second number?

9. In Pascal, `begin` is a _____ .

10. How does the computer determine how many and what kind of data values to read when a `ReadLn` operation is performed?

11. What is the syntactic purpose of the semicolon in the body of a Pascal program?

Answers to Quick-Check Exercises

1. `30.0`
2. `-10.0`
3. `Some numbers are 3.5* 3.456 890*890`
4. `/`
5. `Integer,Character,Real`
6. Analysis
7. `WriteLn` causes subsequent output to be displayed on the next line; `Write` causes subsequent output to be displayed on the same line.
8. A blank, the Return key
9. reserved word
10. By the number of variables in the input list and their data types
11. It separates two executable statements.

Review Questions

1. What kind of information should be specified in the comments that appear at the beginning of a program?

2. Check the variables that are syntactically correct:

Income ___	Two fold ___	Hours*Rate ___	MyProgram ___
1time ___	C3PO ___	ReadLn ___	program ___
const ___	Income#1 ___	var ___	Program ___
Tom's ___	item ___	variable ___	Pi ___

3. What is illegal about the following declarations and statement?

    ```
    const
      Pi = 3.14159;

    var
      C, R : Real;

    begin
      Pi := C / (2 * R * R)
    ```

4. List and define the rules for order of evaluation of arithmetic expressions.
5. If the average size of a family is `2.8` and this value is stored in the variable `FamilySize`, provide the Pascal statement to display this fact in a readable way (leave the cursor on the same line).
6. Which of the following expressions evaluate to the same value?
    a. `A + B * C`   b. `(A + B) * C`   c. `A + (B * C)`
7. List the four standard data types.
8. Assuming `A` and `B` are integer variables, what are the types of the following expressions?
    a. `A div B`   b. `A mod B`   c. `A * B`   d. `A / B`
9. Differentiate among syntax errors, run-time errors, and logic errors.

Programming Projects

1. Write a program to convert a temperature in degrees Fahrenheit to degrees Celsius.

    Problem input
    ```
    Fahrenheit : Integer {temperature in degrees Fahrenheit}
    ```

    Problem output
    ```
    Celsius : Real {temperature in degrees Celsius}
    ```

    Relevant formula
    ```
    Celsius = (5.0 / 9.0) × (Fahrenheit - 32.0)
    ```

2. Write a program to read two data items and print their sum, difference, product, and quotient.

    Problem inputs
    ```
    X, Y : Integer {two items}
    ```

    Problem outputs
    ```
    Sum : Integer {sum of X and Y}
    Difference : Integer {difference of X and Y}
    Product : Integer {product of X and Y}
    Quotient : Real {quotient of X divided by Y}
    ```

3. Write a program to read in the weight (in pounds) of an object and then compute and print the weight in kilograms and grams. (*Hint:* 1 pound is equal to 0.453592 kilogram and 453.59237 grams.)

4. Write a program that prints your first initial as a block letter. (*Hint:* Use a 6 × 6 grid for the letter and read in six strings, each representing a different row of

the grid and consisting of asterisks (symbol *) interspersed with blanks. For example, if E is your first initial, the first string would consist of six asterisks and the second string would begin with one or two asterisks and the rest blanks. After reading the six strings, display them in sequence to show the block letter.

5. Write a program that reads in the number of years ago that a dinosaur lived and then computes the number of months, days, and seconds ago that the dinosaur lived. (Use 365.25 days per year.) Test your program with a triceratops that lived 145 million years ago, and a brontosaurus that lived 182 million years ago.

6. Write a program that reads in the length and the width of a rectangular yard and the length and the width of a rectangular house situated in the yard. Your program should compute the time required (in minutes) to cut the grass at the rate of 2.3 square meters a second.

7. Arnie likes to jog in the morning. As he jogs, he counts the number of strides he makes during the first minute and during the last minute of his jogging. Arnie then averages these two and calls this the average number of strides he makes in a minute when he jogs. Write a program that accepts these averages and the total time Arnie spends jogging in hours and minutes and then outputs the distance Arnie has jogged in miles. Assume Arnie's stride to be 2.5 feet. (There are 5280 feet in a mile.)

8. Write a program that inputs a number of seconds up to 18,000 (5 hours) and outputs the hours, minutes, and seconds equivalent.

9. The Pythagorean theorem states that the sum of the squares of the sides of a right triangle is equal to the square of the hypotenuse. For example, if two sides of a right triangle have lengths 3 and 4, then the hypotenuse must have a length of 5. The integers 3, 4, and 5 together form a Pythagorean triple. There are an infinite number of such triples. Given two positive integers, m and n, where $m > n$, a Pythagorean triple can be generated by the following formulas:

$side1 = m^2 - n^2$

$side2 = 2m\,n$

$hypotenuse = m^2 + n^2$

Write a program that reads in values for m and n and prints the values of the Pythagorean triple generated by these formulas.

▼ **What was the impetus to developing your own software company?**

▲ I was lucky—twice—to be in the right place at the right time: in Zurich to study under Niklaus Wirth, one of the most influential computer scientists of the last decade, and then discovering the Micral and programming on it. The Micral was the first computer I ever used, and it has since been recognized by the Boston Computer Museum as the first personal computer.

I never really planned to start a company. I moved to Silicon Valley to work in high tech, but I couldn't get a legitimate job because I didn't have a green card. It was the decision to market the Pascal we had written that launched Borland. We placed an ad in *Byte* for our first product, Turbo Pascal, and pulled in $500,000 in orders. I was amazed!

▼ **What role has Turbo Pascal taken in helping to redefine the way that people use Pascal? What do you see as major advantages of Turbo Pascal over standard Pascal?**

▲ Back in 1983, Turbo Pascal went beyond what Jensen and Wirth originally defined for the language. Since then, Turbo Pascal has advanced even further, with enhancements for structured and object-oriented programming.

Throughout the eighties, Pascal was the ideal language for learning structured programming. In the nineties, Turbo Pascal has become the standard for learning object-oriented programming. Turbo Pascal's unit feature lets programmers create libraries of reusable procedures and abstract data types. Using it, they can create the reusable objects and truly modular programs that are so important in software engineering today. Whether a student is planning to become a dedicated software engineer or not, Pascal is the perfect training ground for developing object-oriented programming skills.

▼ **How do you explain the success of Turbo Pascal? Where is it primarily used?**

▲ At one time, Pascal was considered to be only a learning language. With over two million users today, however, it has become recognized as an important commercial tool. It is used by corporations throughout the world to create mission-critical applications, and there are more proponents of it every day. Turbo Pascal is used for a wide variety of applications, ranging from commercial and complex business and scientific applications to vertical market applications. Turbo Pascal has always appealed to programmers who want to work smarter, not harder.

Working smarter is possible because Pascal is a structured language that allows you to specify more clearly the code that you write. It allows users to solve problems in a more structured fashion. Turbo Pascal's integrated programming environment also makes it easier to work smarter. Programmers can write, compile, run, and debug programs without exiting to the operating system. This not only saves time, but the environment also gives programmers tools for accomplishing these tasks efficiently.

For the same reasons, Turbo Pascal is a fantastic learning aid for students, too. To program in Pascal, the student must adhere to structured programming methods, and these lessons become lifelong habits.

INTERVIEW
▼

Philippe Kahn

Philippe Kahn is chairman, president, and CEO of Borland International, Inc. Kahn holds a doctorate in mathematical sciences and taught at the university level in his native France before setting out with close colleagues to build a compiler based on the Pascal programming language. The result was Turbo Pascal, destined to become the number one programming language in the world. In 1983, Kahn came to the United States and founded Borland International to market this product. Kahn remains closely involved with product development and marketing at Borland today.

Whether a student wishes later to become a dedicated programmer or not, the logic and problem-solving skills learned during the process are invaluable.

▼ **Your two biggest language products are Turbo Pascal and C++. How do you see their interrelationship and development in the future?**

▲ Turbo Pascal is an applications programming language, while C is a systems language. That is, they are both modern and powerful languages, but Turbo Pascal is designed for higher-level applications programming—writing programs to solve specific problems. Borland C++ is more frequently used to create the systems within which applications programs run. Both products will continue to be improved. As the leader in language tools, we continually add new features and functionality to our products.

▼ **How do you see the changing role of programmer in the future as application packages such as Paradox and Quattro become more widely used?**

▲ Although prepackaged software is a valuable resource for corporations, companies will always have a need for mission-critical applications that are customized for particular applications. That's where products such as Turbo Pascal and Borland C++ come in.

▼ **Do you have any advice for students who are currently learning Turbo Pascal and/or anyone entering the field of computer science?**

▲ Stick with it! U.S. industry needs more engineering and science majors, and the future of our competitiveness is dependent upon you. You should learn all you can about object-oriented programming—that's the wave of the future.

CHAPTER THREE

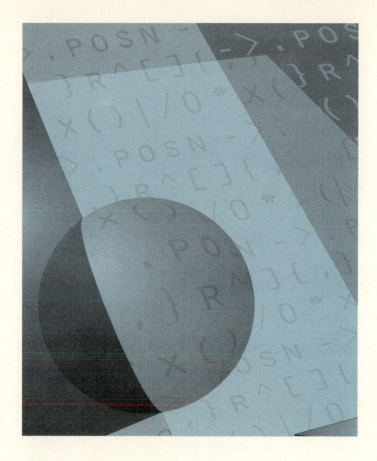

Functions and Procedures

Programmers who use the software development method to solve problems seldom tackle each new program as a unique event. Information contained in the problem statement and amassed during the analysis and design phases helps the programmer plan and complete the program. Programmers also use segments of earlier program solutions as building blocks to construct new programs.

In Section 3.2, we demonstrate how to tap existing information and code in the form of predefined functions to write programs. In addition to using existing information, programmers can use top-down design techniques to simplify the development of algorithms and the structure of the resulting programs. To apply top-down design, the programmer starts with the broadest statement of the problem solution and works down to more detailed subproblems. In Sections 3.3–3.5, we demonstrate top-down design and emphasize the role of modular programming using procedures.

3.1 Building Programs from Existing Information

Programmers seldom start off with a blank slate (or empty screen) when they develop a program. Often some—or all—of the solution can be developed from information that already exists or from the solution to another problem, as we demonstrate for the metric conversion program.

Carefully following the software development method generates important system documentation before you even begin to code a program. Such documentation, consisting of a description of a problem's data requirements (developed during the analysis phase) and its solution algorithm (developed during the design phase), summarizes your intentions and thought processes.

You can use this documentation as a starting point in coding your program. For example, you would begin by duplicating the problem data requirements in the program declaration part (Fig. 3.1), then edit those lines to conform to the Pascal syntax for constant and variable declarations, thereby completing the declaration part of the program (Fig. 3.2). This approach is especially helpful if the documentation was created with a word processor and is in a file that you can edit.

To develop the program body, first use the initial algorithm and its refinements as program comments. The comments describe each algorithm step and provide program documentation that guides your Pascal code. Figure 3.2 shows how the program will look at this point. After the comments are in place in the program body, you can begin to write the Pascal statements. Place the

Figure 3.1
The Declaration Part
Before Editing

```
program Metric (Input, Output);
{Converts square meters to square yards}

relevant formula
    1 square meter = 1.196 square yards

problem input
    SqMeters {the fabric size in square meters}

problem output
    SqYards {the fabric size in square yards}

begin

end.
```

```
program Metric (Input, Output);
{Converts square meters to square yards}

    const
        MetersToYards = 1.196; {conversion constant}

    var
        SqMeters,          {input - fabric size in meters}
        SqYards : Real;    {output - fabric size in yards}
begin
    {1.   Read the fabric size in square meters.}

    {2.   Convert the fabric size to square yards.}
          {2.1  Size in sq. yards is 1.196 * size in sq. meters.}

    {3.   Display the fabric size in square yards.}

end.
```

Pascal code for an unrefined step directly under that step. For a refined step, either edit the refinement to convert it from English to Pascal or replace it with Pascal code (Fig. 2.1). We illustrate this entire process in the next case study.

CASE STUDY

Finding the Area and Circumference of a Circle

PROBLEM ▼

Read in the radius of a circle and compute and print the circle's area and circumference.

ANALYSIS ▼

Clearly, the problem input is the circle's radius. Two outputs are requested: the circle's area and circumference. These variables should be type `Real` because the inputs and outputs may contain fractional parts. The geometric relationships between a circle's radius and its area and circumference are listed next, along with the data requirements.

Data Requirements

Problem Constant

`Pi = 3.14159;`

Problem Input

`Radius : Real {radius of a circle}`

Problem Outputs

```
Area : Real {area of a circle}
Circum : Real {circumference of a circle}
```

Relevant Formulas

area of a circle = $\pi \times radius^2$
circumference of a circle = $2\pi \times radius$

DESIGN ▼

After identifying the problem inputs and outputs, list the steps necessary to solve the problem. Pay close attention to the order of the steps.

Initial Algorithm

1. Read the circle radius.
2. Find the area.
3. Find the circumference.
4. Print the area and the circumference.

Algorithm Refinements

Next, refine any steps that lack an obvious solution (steps 2 and 3).

Step 2 Refinement

2.1 Assign `Pi * Radius * Radius` to `Area`.

Step 3 Refinement

3.1 Assign `2 * Pi * Radius` to `Circum`.

IMPLEMENTATION ▼

Figure 3.3 shows the Pascal program so far. The program body consists of the initial algorithm and its refinements.

Figure 3.3
Outline of Program Circle

```
program Circle (Input, Output);
{Finds and prints the area and circumference of a circle}

   const
     Pi = 3.14159;

   var
     Radius,          {input - radius of a circle}
     Area,            {output - area of a circle}
     Circum : Real;   {output - circumference of a circle}
```

▷ ▷ ▷ ▷ ▷ ▷

```
begin
  {1.  Read the circle radius.}

  {2.  Find the area.}
       {2.1 Assign Pi * Radius * Radius to Area.}

  {3.  Find the circumference.}
       {3.1 Assign 2 * Pi * Radius to Circum.}

  {4.  Print the area and circumference.}
end.
```

To write the final program, convert the refinements (steps 2.1 and 3.1) to Pascal, write Pascal code for the unrefined steps (steps 1 and 4), and delete the step numbers from the comments. Figure 3.4 shows the final program.

Figure 3.4
Finding the Area and
Circumference of a Circle

Directory: CHAP3
File: CIRCLE.PAS

```
program Circle (Input, Output);
{Finds and prints the area and circumference of a circle}

   const
     Pi = 3.14159;

   var
     Radius,            {input - radius of a circle}
     Area,              {output - area of a circle}
     Circum : Real;     {output - circumference of a circle}

begin
  {Read the circle radius.}
  Write ('Enter radius> ');
  ReadLn (Radius);

  {Find the area.}
  Area := Pi * Radius * Radius;

  {Find the circumference.}
  Circum := 2.0 * Pi * Radius;

  {Print the area and circumference.}
  WriteLn ('The area is ', Area :4:2);
  WriteLn ('The circumference is ', Circum :4:2)
end.
```

Sample Run

```
Enter radius> 5.0
The area is 78.54
The circumference is 31.42
```

TESTING ▼

The sample output in Fig. 3.4 provides a good test of the solution because it is relatively easy to compute by hand the area and the circumference for a radius value of 5.0. The radius squared is 25.0 and `Pi` is approximately 3, so the value of the area appears to be correct. The circumference should be 10 times `Pi`, which is also an easy number to compute by hand.

CASE STUDY   **Finding the Most Pizza for Your Money**

Another way in which programmers use existing information is by *extending the solution for one problem to solve another*. For example, you can easily solve the next problem by building on the solution to the previous one.

PROBLEM ▼

You and your college roommates frequently order a late-night pizza snack from the many pizzerias in the area that deliver. Since you are on a tight budget, you want to know which pizza is the best value.

ANALYSIS ▼

To find which pizza is the best value, you must be able to compare pizza costs. One way to make this comparison is to compute the *unit price* of each pizza by dividing the total price of each pizza by a measure of its quantity. A good measure of quantity would be the pizza weight, but pizzas are not sold by weight—they are sold by size (diameter) measured in inches. Consequently, the best you can do is to use some meaningful measure of quantity based on pizza diameter. One such measure is pizza area. Using pizza area, you can define the unit price of a pizza as its price divided by its area.

The following data requirements list a pizza's size and price as problem inputs. Although the problem statement does not ask you to display the pizza's area, we are listing it as a problem output because the pizza's area will give you some idea of how many friends you can invite to share your pizza. The radius (half the diameter) is listed as a program variable because you need it to compute the pizza's area, but it is not a problem input or output.

Data Requirements

Problem Constant

`Pi = 3.14159;`

Problem Inputs

```
Diameter : Real     {diameter or size of a pizza}
Price : Real        {price of a pizza}
```

Problem Outputs

```
UnitPrice : Real      {unit cost of a pizza}
Area : Real           {area of a pizza}
```

Program Variables

```
Radius : Real         {radius of a pizza}
```

Relevant Formulas

area of a circle $= \pi \times radius^2$
radius of a circle $= diameter / 2$
unit price $= total\ price / area$

DESIGN ▼

The initial algorithm here is similar to that of the previous case study. The step that computes the circle's circumference (step 3) has been replaced with one that computes the pizza's unit price.

Initial Algorithm

1. Read in the pizza's diameter and price.
2. Compute the pizza's area.
3. Compute the pizza's unit price.
4. Display the unit price and area.

The algorithm refinements follow. Step 2 requires refinement because you must compute the pizza's radius before you can compute its area.

Step 2 Refinement

2.1 Assign `Diameter / 2` to `Radius`.
2.2 Assign `Pi * Radius * Radius` to `Area`.

Step 3 Refinement

3.1 Assign `Price / Area` to `UnitPrice`.

IMPLEMENTATION ▼

To write this program, edit the data requirements to develop the program declaration part and use the initial algorithm with refinements as a starting point for the program body. Figure 3.5 shows the Pascal program.

TESTING ▼

To test this program, run it with a few pizza sizes. You can verify that the program is working correctly by multiplying the unit price by the area. The product should equal the price of the pizza.

Figure 3.5
Pizza Program

Directory: CHAP3
File: PIZZA.PAS

```
program Pizza (Input, Output);
{Computes the unit price of a pizza}

   const
     Pi = 3.14159;

   var
     Diameter,          {input - diameter or size of a pizza}
     Price,             {input - price of a pizza}
     UnitPrice,         {output - unit cost of pizza}
     Area,              {output - area of a pizza}
     Radius : Real;     {radius of a pizza}

begin
  {Read in the pizza diameter and price.}
  Write ('Diameter of pizza in inches> ');
  ReadLn (Diameter);
  Write ('Price of pizza $');
  ReadLn (Price);

  {Compute the pizza area.}
  Radius := Diameter / 2;
  Area := Pi * Radius * Radius;

  {Compute the pizza unit price.}
  UnitPrice := Price / Area;

  {Display the area and unit price.}
  WriteLn;
  Write ('The pizza unit price is $', UnitPrice :4:2);
  WriteLn (' per square inch.');
  WriteLn ('The area is ', Area :3:1, ' square inches.')
end.
```

Sample Run

```
Diameter of pizza in inches> 9.0
Price of pizza $7.45

The pizza unit price is $0.12 per square inch.
The area is 63.6 square inches.
```

Exercises for Section 3.1   *Self-Check*

1. Describe the problem inputs and outputs and write the algorithm for a program that computes an employee's gross salary given the hours worked and the hourly rate.

2. Write a preliminary version of the program from your solution to Exercise 1. Show the declaration part of the program and the program comments corresponding to the algorithm and its refinements.

3. What changes should you make to extend the payroll algorithm in Exercise 1 to include overtime hours to be paid at 1.5 times an employee's normal hourly rate when computing his or her gross salary? Assume that overtime hours are entered separately.

Programming

1. Add refinements to the program outline that follows and write the final Pascal program:

```
program SumAndAverage (Input, Output);
{Finds and prints the sum and average of two numbers}

   var
      One, Two,        {input - numbers to process}
      Sum,             {output - sum of One and Two}
      Average : Real;  {output - average of One and Two}

begin
   {1. Read two numbers.}
   {2. Compute sum of numbers.}
   {3. Compute average of numbers.}
   {4. Print sum and average.}
end.
```

2. Write a complete Pascal program for Self-Check Exercise 1.
3. Write a complete Pascal program for the revised payroll algorithm developed in Self-Check Exercise 3.

3.2 Functions

Functions and Reusability

A primary goal of structured programming is to write error-free code. One way to do so, called *reusability,* is to reuse whenever possible code that has already been written and tested. Stated more simply, "Why reinvent the wheel?" Pascal promotes reusability by providing many predefined functions for performing mathematical computations. A **function** is a separate module of code that computes a single result.

> **function**
> a separate module of code that computes a single result

Consider, for example, the Pascal function named Sqrt, which performs the square root computation. The expression part of the assignment statement,

$$Y := Sqrt(X)$$

Function designator — Sqrt(X)

Function name — Sqrt

Function argument — X

> **function argument**
> a value passed into a function
>
> **function designator**
> the part of an expression that activates a function and passes arguments to the function

activates the code for function Sqrt, passing the **argument** X to the function. A function is activated by a **function designator** (Sqrt(X)) that is part of an expression. After the function executes, the function result is substituted for the function designator in the expression. If X is 16.0, the assignment statement is evaluated as follows:

1. X is 16.0, so function Sqrt computes the square root of 16.0, or 4.0.
2. The function result, 4.0, is assigned to Y.

A function can be thought of as a "black box" that is passed one or more input values and automatically returns a single output value. Figure 3.6 illustrates this process for the call to function Sqrt. The value of X (16.0) is the function input, and the function result, or output, is the square root of 16.0 (result is 4.0).

As another example, if W is 9.0, the assignment statement

```
Z := 5.7 + Sqrt(W)
```

is evaluated as follows:

1. W is 9.0, so function Sqrt computes the square root of 9.0, or 3.0.
2. The values 5.7 and 3.0 are added together.
3. The sum, 8.7, is stored in Z.

EXAMPLE 3.1 ▼

The program in Fig. 3.7 displays the square root of two numbers provided as input data (First and Second) and the square root of their sum. To do so, it must call the Pascal function Sqrt three times:

```
Answer := Sqrt(First);
Answer := Sqrt(Second);
Answer := Sqrt(First + Second);
```

For the first two calls, the function arguments are variables (First and Second). The third call shows that a function argument can also be an expression (First + Second). For all three calls, the result returned by function Sqrt is assigned to variable Answer.

If you look closely at the program in Fig. 3.7, you will see that each statement contains a call to a Pascal procedure (Write, WriteLn, ReadLn) or a Pascal function (Sqrt)—we have used Pascal's predefined procedures and functions as building blocks to construct a new program. ▲

Figure 3.6
Function Sqrt as a
"Black Box"

Figure 3.7
Program SquareRoots

**Directory: CHAP3
File: SQUARERO.PAS**

```
program SquareRoots (Input, Output);
{Performs three square root computations}

   var
     First, Second,           {input - two data values}
     Answer : Real;           {output - a square root value}
begin
   {Get first number and display its square root.}
   Write ('Enter the first number> ');
   ReadLn (First);
   Answer := Sqrt(First);
   WriteLn ('The square root of the first number is ',
           Answer :4:2);

   {Get second number and display its square root.}
   Write ('Enter the second number> ');
   ReadLn (Second);
   Answer := Sqrt(Second);
   WriteLn ('The square root of the second number is ',
           Answer :4:2);

   {Display the square root of the sum of both numbers.}
   Answer := Sqrt(First + Second);
   WriteLn ('The square root of the sum of both numbers is ',
           Answer :4:2)
end.
```

Sample Run

```
Enter the first number> 9.0
The square root of the first number is 3.00
Enter the second number> 16.0
The square root of the second number is 4.00
The square root of the sum of both numbers is 5.00
```

Program Style

Use of Color to Highlight New Constructs

In Fig. 3.7, program lines that illustrate new constructs are in color so that you can find them easily. We will continue to use color for this purpose in figures that contain programs.

Standard Pascal Functions

Table 3.1 lists the names and descriptions of some of Pascal's predefined functions. Except for Abs, Round, Sqr, and Trunc, each function in Table 3.1

returns a Real value regardless of its argument type (Real or Integer). The type of the result returned by Abs or Sqr is the same as the type of its argument.

Table 3.1
Standard Functions

Function	Purpose	Argument	Result
Abs(X)	Returns the absolute value of X	Real or Integer	Same as argument
ArcTan(X)	Returns the angle y in radians satisfying $X = \tan(y)$, where $-\pi/2 < y < \pi/2$	Real or Integer	Real (radians)
Cos(X)	Returns the cosine of angle X	Real or Integer (radians)	Real
Exp(X)	Returns e^X, where $e = 2.71828\ldots$	Real or Integer	Real
Ln(X)	Returns the natural logarithm of X for $X > 0.0$	Real or Integer	Real
Round(X)	Returns the closest integer value to X	Real	Integer
Sin(X)	Returns the sine of angle X	Real or Integer (radians)	Real
Sqr(X)	Returns the square of X	Real or Integer	Same as argument
Sqrt(X)	Returns the positive square root of X for $X > 0.0$	Real or Integer	Real
Trunc(X)	Returns the integral part of X	Real	Integer

The functions Round and Trunc require type Real arguments and return type Integer values. These functions determine the integral part of a real-valued expression. Consequently, the expressions

```
Trunc(1.5 * Gross);
Round(Cents / 100)
```

have Integer values and may be assigned to Integer variables. Trunc simply *truncates,* or removes, the fractional part of its argument; Round *rounds* its argument to the nearest whole number. For example, Trunc(17.5) is

17, while `Round(17.5)` is 18; `Trunc(-3.8)` is -3, while `Round(-3.8)` is -4.

Most of the functions in Table 3.1 perform common mathematical computations. The arguments for `Ln` and `Sqrt` must be positive. The arguments for `Sin` and `Cos` must be expressed in radians, not degrees. `ArcTan` expresses its results in radians.

EXAMPLE 3.2 ▼

We can use the Pascal functions `Sqr` and `Sqrt` to compute the roots of a quadratic equation in X of the form

$AX^2 + BX + C = 0$

The two roots are defined as

$$Root_1 = \frac{-B + \sqrt{B^2 - 4AC}}{2A} \qquad Root_2 = \frac{-B - \sqrt{B^2 - 4AC}}{2A}$$

when the *discriminant* $(B^2 - 4AC)$ is greater than zero. If we assume that this is the case, we can use the following assignment statements to assign values to `Root1` and `Root2`:

```
{Compute two roots, Root1 and Root2, for Disc > 0.0.}
Disc := Sqr(B) - 4 * A * C ;
Root1 := (-B + Sqrt(Disc)) / (2 * A);
Root2 := (-B - Sqrt(Disc)) / (2 * A)   ▲
```

EXAMPLE 3.3 ▼

If we know the length of two sides (B and C) of a triangle and the angle between them in degrees (*Alpha*) (see Fig. 3.8), we can compute the length of the third side (A) by using the formula

$A^2 = B^2 + C^2 - 2BC \cos Alpha$

To use Pascal's cosine function (`Cos`), we must express its argument angle in radians instead of degrees. To convert an angle from degrees to radians, we

Figure 3.8
Triangle with Unknown
Side *A*

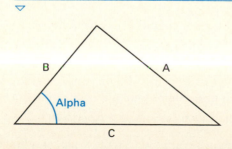

multiply the angle by $\pi/180$. If we assume that `Pi` is the constant π, the following Pascal assignment statement computes the unknown side length:

```
A := Sqrt(Sqr(B) + Sqr(C) - 2 * B * C * Cos(Alpha * Pi/180.0))
```
▲

EXAMPLE 3.4 ▼

Since Pascal has no exponentiation operator, it is not possible to write u^v directly when u and v are type `Real`. However, the theory of logarithms tells us that

$\ln(u^v) = v \times \ln(u)$

and

$z = e^{\ln(z)}$

where e is 2.71828 . . . . So if we substitute u^v for z in the preceding equation, we get

$u^v = e^{\ln(u^v)} = e^{(v \times \ln(u))}$

This formula can be implemented in Pascal as

```
UToPowerV := Exp(v * Ln(u))
```
▲

A Look at Where We Are Heading

Pascal also allows us to write our own functions. Let's assume that we have already written functions `FindArea` and `FindCircum`:

▶ Function `FindArea(R)` returns the area of a circle with radius R.
▶ Function `FindCircum(R)` returns the circumference of a circle with radius R.

We can reuse these functions in two programs shown earlier in this chapter (see Figs. 3.4 and 3.5). The program in Fig. 3.4 displays the area and the circumference of a circle whose radius is provided as input data; Fig. 3.9 shows a revised program that uses the two functions `FindArea` and `FindCircum`. In Fig. 3.9, the expression part for each of the two assignment statements

```
Area := FindArea(Radius);
Circum := FindCircum(Radius);
```

is a function designator with argument `Radius` (the circle radius). The result returned by each function execution is stored in an output variable for the program (`Area` or `Circum`). To run this program, we need to complete the functions and insert them right after the comment

```
{Insert functions FindArea and FindCircum here.}
```

Section 6.5 shows you how to write your own functions.

Figure 3.9
Finding Area and
Circumference with
Functions

Directory: CHAP3
File: CIRCLEFU.PAS

```
program CircleFunction (Input, Output);
{Finds area and circumference of a circle using functions}

   var
      Radius,            {input - radius of a circle}
      Area,              {output - area of a circle}
      Circum : Real;     {output - circumference of a circle}

   {Insert functions FindArea and FindCircum here.}

begin
   {Read the circle radius.}
   Write ('Enter radius> ');
   ReadLn (Radius);

   {Find the area.}
   Area := FindArea(Radius);

   {Find the circumference.}
   Circum := FindCircum(Radius);

   {Print the area and circumference.}
   WriteLn ('The area is ', Area :4:2);
   WriteLn ('The circumference is ', Circum :4:2)
end.
```

Besides the advantage of reusing "tried and true" code, using these two functions frees us from the details of computing a circle's area or circumference when we write the main program. This is one way we can manage and reduce the complexity of writing programs.

Exercises for Section 3.2

Self-Check

1. Rewrite the following mathematical expressions using Pascal functions:
   a. $\sqrt{U + V \times W^2}$ c. $\sqrt{(X - Y)^3}$
   b. $\log_n (X^Y)$ d. $|XY - W/Z|$
2. Evaluate the following function designators and indicate the type of the result:
   a. Trunc(-15.8)   e. Sqrt(Abs(Round(-15.8)))
   b. Round(-15.8)   f. Round(3.5)
   c. Round(6.8) * Sqr (3)   g. Sqr(3.0)
   d. Trunc(-15.8) * Sqr(3) h. Trunc(22.1) * Sqr(3)

Programming

1. Write statements that read values into X and Y and compute and display the absolute difference (e.g., if X is 9 and Y is 7, the absolute difference is 2).

2. Using the Round function, write a Pascal statement to round any real value *X* to the nearest two decimal places. *Hint:* You will have to multiply the value by 100 before rounding, round the result, and then divide by 100.

3. Write a complete Pascal program that prompts the user for the Cartesian coordinates of two points, (*X1, Y1*) and (*X2, Y2*), and displays the distance between them computed by using the following formula:

$$distance = \sqrt{(X1 - X2)^2 + (Y1 - Y2)^2}$$

3.3   Top-Down Design and Structure Charts

top-down design
a problem-solving method in which you first break a problem up into its major subproblems and then solve the subproblems to derive the solution to the original problem

structure chart
a documentation tool that shows the relationships among the subproblems of a problem

Often the algorithm needed to solve a problem is more complex than those we have seen so far and the programmer has to break up the problem into subproblems to develop the program solution. In attempting to solve a subproblem at one level, we introduce new subproblems at lower levels. This process, called **top-down design**, proceeds from the original problem at the top level to the subproblems at each lower level. The splitting of a problem into its related subproblems is analogous to the process of refining an algorithm. The following case study introduces a documentation tool—the **structure chart**—that will help you to keep track of the relationships among subproblems.

CASE STUDY   Drawing Simple Diagrams

PROBLEM ▼

You want to draw some simple diagrams on your printer or screen. Two examples are the house and the female stick figure in Fig. 3.10.

Figure 3.10
House and Stick Figure

ANALYSIS ▼

The house is formed by displaying a triangle without its base on top of a rectangle. The stick figure consists of a circular shape, a triangle, and a triangle without its base. We can draw both figures with these four basic components:

▶ A circle
▶ A baseline
▶ Parallel lines
▶ Intersecting lines

DESIGN ▼

To create the stick figure, you can divide the problem into three subproblems.

Initial Algorithm

1. Draw a circle.
2. Draw a triangle.
3. Draw intersecting lines.

Algorithm Refinements

Because a triangle is not a basic component, you must refine step 2, generating the following subproblems:

Step 2 Refinement

2.1 Draw intersecting lines.
2.2 Draw a base.

You can use a structure chart to show the relationship between the original problem and its subproblems, as in Fig. 3.11, where the original problem (level 0) is in the darker color and its three subordinate subproblems are shown at level 1. The subproblem *Draw a Triangle* is also in color because it has its own subproblems (shown at level 2).

The subproblems appear in both the algorithm and the structure chart. The algorithm, not the structure chart, shows the order in which you carry out each step to solve the problem. The structure chart simply illustrates the subordination of subproblems to each other and to the original subproblem.

....

Exercises for Section 3.3   ***Self-Check***

1. In which phase of the software development method do you apply top-down design to break the problem into suitable subproblems?
2. Draw the structure chart for the problem of drawing the house shown in Fig. 3.10.

Figure 3.11
Structure Chart for
Drawing a Stick Figure

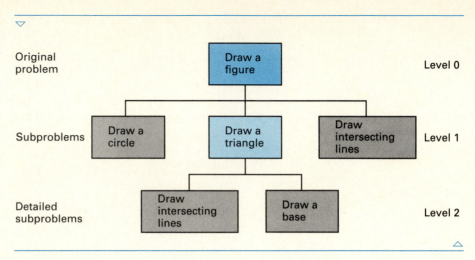

3.4 Procedures

procedure
a separate program module
solving a particular sub-
problem

Programmers often use procedures to implement top-down design in their programs. A **procedure,** like a function, is a separate program unit or module containing a group of program statements that solves a particular subproblem. Often a programmer will write one procedure for each subproblem in the structure chart. Procedures are more general than functions because they can return any number of results.

Chapter 2 introduced three procedures supplied by the Pascal compiler: ReadLn, Write, and WriteLn. Recall that you activated each of these procedures with a **procedure call statement.** In this section, you will learn to write and call your own procedures.

procedure call statement
an instruction that calls or
activates a procedure

As an example of top-down design with procedures, you could use the program body in Fig. 3.12 to draw a stick figure. The three algorithm steps are coded as calls to three Pascal procedures. For example, the statement

```
DrawTriangle;          {Draw a triangle.}
```

calls a procedure (DrawTriangle) to implement the algorithm step *Draw a Triangle*.

Figure 3.12
Program Body to Draw a
Stick Figure

```
begin {StickFigure}
    DrawCircle;          {Draw a circle.}
    DrawTriangle;        {Draw a triangle.}
    DrawIntersect        {Draw intersecting lines.}
end. {StickFigure}
```

A procedure is an independent program unit whose form is very similar to that of a program. A procedure begins with a *procedure heading,* which consists of the word `procedure` followed by the procedure name (an identifier) and a semicolon. The *declaration part* is optional and is needed only when the procedure has its own constants and variables. Each procedure has a *procedure body,* which starts with `begin` and ends with `end;`.

A procedure name is a user-defined identifier, so its usage must be declared in the declaration part of the program unit that calls it. You use a *procedure declaration* to declare a procedure.

SYNTAX DISPLAY

Procedure Declaration

Form:
```
procedure pname;
declaration part
begin
    procedure body
end;
```
Example:
```
procedure Skip3Lines;
{Skips three lines}

begin {Skip3Lines}
    WriteLn;
    WriteLn;
    WriteLn
end; {Skip3Lines}
```
Interpretation: The user-defined identifier *pname* is declared to be the name of a procedure. Any identifiers declared in the *declaration part* are defined only during the execution of the procedure and can be referenced only within the procedure. The *procedure body* describes the data manipulation performed when the procedure is activated through a procedure call statement.

SYNTAX DISPLAY

Procedure Call Statement

Form: *pname*
Example: `DrawCircle`
Interpretation: The procedure call statement initiates the execution of procedure *pname.* After *pname* has finished executing, the program statement that follows the procedure call will be executed.

EXAMPLE 3.5 ▼

Figure 3.13 shows the declaration for procedure `DrawCircle`. The procedure body contains the three `WriteLn` statements that cause the computer to draw a circular shape. The procedure call statement

Figure 3.13
Procedure DrawCircle

```
procedure DrawCircle;  ←———    Procedure heading
{Draws a circle}

begin  {DrawCircle}
  WriteLn ('   *   ');
  WriteLn (' *   *');            Procedure body
  WriteLn (' * * ')
end; {DrawCircle}
```

```
DrawCircle
```

causes these `WriteLn` statements to execute. ▲

The structure chart in Fig. 3.11 shows that the subproblem *Draw a Triangle* (level 1) depends on the solutions to its subordinate subproblems *Draw Intersecting Lines* and *Draw a Base* (both level 2). Figure 3.14 shows how to use top-down design to code procedure `DrawTriangle`. Instead of using `WriteLn` statements to display a triangular pattern, the body of procedure `DrawTriangle` calls procedures `DrawIntersect` and `DrawBase` to draw a triangle.

Placement of Procedure Declarations in a Program

Figure 3.12 showed the program body for the stick figure program. In the declaration part, you must declare the three procedures that are called in the program. The procedure declarations must follow the variable declarations.

The relative order of the procedure declarations does not affect their order of execution; that is determined by the order of execution of the procedure call statements. However, each procedure must be declared before you can write a procedure call statement that activates it. For this reason, you must declare the two procedures that are called by `DrawTriangle` (`DrawIntersect` and `DrawBase`) before `DrawTriangle`. That is the only restriction.

Figure 3.14
Procedure DrawTriangle

```
procedure DrawTriangle;  ←———    Procedure heading
{Draws a triangle}

begin {DrawTriangle}
   DrawIntersect;          ←———    Procedure body
   DrawBase
end; {DrawTriangle}
```

main program
the program body in a program with procedures

Figure 3.15 shows the completed stick figure program. To help you identify each procedure, its first and last lines are in color. In a program that uses
procedures, we refer to the program body as the **main program**.

Figure 3.15
Stick Figure Program

Directory: CHAP3
File: STICKFIG.PAS

```
program StickFigure (Input, Output);
{Displays a stick figure}

  procedure DrawCircle;
  {Draws a circle}

  begin  {DrawCircle}
    WriteLn ('   *   ');
    WriteLn (' *   *');
    WriteLn ('  * * ')
  end; {DrawCircle}

  procedure DrawIntersect;
  {Draws intersecting lines}

  begin  {DrawIntersect}
    WriteLn (' / \ ');
    WriteLn (' /   \ ');
    WriteLn ('/     \')
  end; {DrawIntersect}

  procedure DrawBase;
  {Draws a base}

  begin  {DrawBase}
    WriteLn ('-------')
  end; {DrawBase}

  procedure DrawTriangle;
  {Draws a triangle}

  begin  {DrawTriangle}
    DrawIntersect;
    DrawBase
  end; {DrawTriangle}

begin {StickFigure}
  DrawCircle;          {Draw a circle.}
  DrawTriangle;        {Draw a triangle.}
  DrawIntersect        {Draw intersecting lines.}
end. {StickFigure}
```

Program Style

Use of Comments in a Program with Procedures

Figure 3.15 includes several comments. Each procedure begins with a comment that describes its purpose. The `begin` and `end` that bracket each procedure body and the main program body are followed by a comment identifying that procedure or program.

Order of Execution of Procedures and Main Program

Because procedures appear in the declaration part of the program, which precedes the main program, the compiler translates the procedure declarations before it translates the main program. During translation, the compiler inserts a statement at the end of the procedure that causes a *return* from the procedure back to the statement that called it.

Figure 3.16 shows the main program and procedure `DrawCircle` of the stick figure program in separate areas of memory. Although the Pascal statements are shown in Fig. 3.16, it is actually the object code corresponding to each statement that is stored in memory.

When we run the program, the first statement in the main program is the first statement executed (the call to `DrawCircle` in Fig. 3.16). When the computer executes a procedure call statement, it transfers control to the referenced procedure (indicated by the colored line in Fig. 3.16). The computer allocates any memory that may be needed for constants and variables declared in the procedure and then performs the statements in the procedure body. After the last statement in procedure `DrawCircle` is executed, control returns to the main program (indicated by the black line in Fig. 3.16) and the computer releases any memory that was allocated to the procedure. After the return to the program, the next statement is executed (the call to `DrawTriangle`).

Figure 3.16
Flow of Control Between
the Main Program and
a Procedure

Advantages of Using Procedures

There are many advantages to using procedures. Their availability changes how an individual programmer organizes the solution to a programming problem. For a team of programmers working together on a large program, procedures simplify the apportioning of programming tasks; each programmer will be responsible for a particular set of procedures. Finally, they simplify programming tasks, as existing procedures can be used as the building blocks for new programs.

Procedural Abstraction

procedural abstraction
a programming technique in which a main program consists of a sequence of procedure calls and each procedure is implemented as a separate program module

Procedures allow us to remove from the main program the code that provides the detailed solution to a subproblem. Because these details are provided in the procedures and not in the main program, we can write the main program as a sequence of procedure call statements as soon as we have specified the initial algorithm and before we refine any of the steps. We should delay writing the procedure for an algorithm step until we have finished refining that step. With this approach to program design, called **procedural abstraction,** we defer implementation details until we are ready to write an individual procedure module. Focusing on one procedure at a time is much easier than trying to write the complete program all at once.

Reuse of Procedures

Another advantage of using procedures is that they can be executed more than once in a program. For example, procedure `DrawIntersect` is called twice in Fig. 3.15 (once by `DrawTriangle` and once by the main program). Each time `DrawIntersect` is called, the list of output statements shown in Fig. 3.15 is executed and a pair of intersecting lines is drawn. Without procedures, the `WriteLn` statements that draw the lines would have to be listed twice in the main program, thereby increasing the main program's length and the chance of error.

Finally, once you have written and tested a procedure, you can use it in other programs or procedures. For example, the procedures in program `StickFigure` could easily be used in programs that draw other diagrams.

Exercises for Section 3.4   Self-Check

1. Assume that you have procedures `PrintM` and `PrintO`, each of which draws a large block letter (for example, `PrintO` draws a block letter O). Why would the following program body be more efficient using these procedures than if it did not use procedures at all?

```
begin {Main}
   PrintM;
   PrintO;
   PrintM
end. {Main}
```

2.   Draw a structure chart for a program with three procedures that displays HI HO in block letters.

Programming

1.   Write procedure DrawParallel that draws parallel lines and a procedure DrawRectangle that uses DrawParallel and DrawBase to draw a rectangle.
2.   Write the main program and procedures for the problem described in Self-Check Exercise 2.
3.   You have written a very good program called GreatProgram and you want all users to know you wrote it. Write a procedure called Credits that is executed upon program start and that tells the program name and its creator.

3.5   Procedures as Program Building Blocks

Programmers use procedures like building blocks to construct large programs. Procedures are more like Lego® blocks (Fig. 3.17) than the smooth-sided wooden blocks you might have used as a young child to demonstrate your potential as a budding architect. Your first blocks were big and did not link together, so buildings over a certain size would topple over. Legos, in contrast, have one surface with little protrusions and one surface with little cups. By placing the protrusions into the cups, you can build rather elaborate structures.

What does this have to do with programming? Procedures DrawCircle and DrawParallel are like simple wooden blocks. You can write some cute little programs with these procedures, but they are not particularly useful. To construct more interesting programs, we must provide procedures with protrusions and cups so they can be easily interconnected.

Figure 3.17
Lego® Blocks

procedure parameters
information passed between a procedure and the program unit that calls it
procedure inputs
values passed into a procedure by the calling program unit
procedure outputs
results returned to the calling program unit by a procedure

The parameters of a procedure provide the linkage between a procedure and the main program or between two or more procedures. The **parameters** of a procedure receive values (**procedure inputs**) passed into the procedure from the calling module or they return results (**procedure outputs**) computed by the procedure back to the calling module. Figure 3.18 is a diagram of a procedure with inputs and outputs.

You have already encountered parameters in working with the WriteLn and ReadLn procedures. The procedure call statement

```
WriteLn ('The area is ', Area :4:2)
```

↑   ↑
Procedure   Parameter
name   list

consists of two parts: the name of the Pascal procedure being called, WriteLn, and a parameter list enclosed in parentheses (containing two parameters, a string and a variable name, separated by a comma). Because it has a parameter list, procedure WriteLn is more versatile and hence more useful than procedure DrawCircle. Procedure DrawCircle can display only a circle shape, whereas procedure WriteLn can display whatever we want it to.

Chapter 6 discusses parameters in more detail. For the time being, we will restrict our use to procedures without parameters, to display lengthy messages or instructions to program users. We also will continue to use the Pascal ReadLn, Write, and WriteLn procedures for data entry and display. To learn more about procedure parameters, skip ahead to Section 6.1.

EXAMPLE 3.6: Displaying User Instructions ▼

Let's write a procedure that displays instructions to a user of the program that computes the area and the circumference of a circle (see Fig. 3.4). This simple procedure demonstrates one of the benefits of separating the statements that display user instructions from the main program body: Editing these instructions is simplified when they are separate from the code that performs the calculations.

Figure 3.18
Procedure with Inputs and Outputs

Figure 3.19
Procedure Instruct

Directory: CHAP3
File: INSTRUCT.PAS

```pascal
procedure Instruct;
{Displays instructions to a user of program Circle}

begin {Instruct}
  WriteLn ('This program computes the area');
  WriteLn ('and circumference of a circle.');
  WriteLn;
  WriteLn ('To use this program, enter the radius of');
  WriteLn ('the circle after the prompt: Enter radius> ');
  WriteLn;
  WriteLn ('The circumference will be computed in the');
  WriteLn ('same units of measurement as the radius.');
  WriteLn ('The area will be computed in the same ',
           'units squared');
  WriteLn
end; {Instruct}
```

If you place procedure `Instruct` (see Fig. 3.19) in the declaration part of the original program, you can begin the revised main program with the procedure call statement

```pascal
Instruct;
```

The rest of the main program consists of the executable statements shown earlier. Figure 3.20 shows the output displayed by calling procedure `Instruct`. ▲

Exercises for Section 3.5

Self-Check

1. How does the use of procedure parameters make it possible to write larger, more useful programs?
2. Why are the parameters for `WriteLn` considered procedure inputs and the parameters for `ReadLn` considered procedure outputs?

Figure 3.20
Output Displayed by
Procedure Instruct

```
This program computes the area
and circumference of a circle.

To use this program, enter the radius of
the circle after the prompt: Enter radius>

The circumference will be computed in the
same units of measurement as the radius.
The area will be computed in the same units squared
```

Programming

1. Show the revised program `Circle` with a call to `Instruct`.
2. Write a procedure like `Instruct` for the pizza program in Fig. 3.5, and show where to call it.

3.6 Common Programming Errors

Remember to declare each procedure used in a program. Procedure declarations *must* precede procedure calls and are found in the declaration part of a program just after the variable declarations. If procedure A calls procedure B, you must declare procedure B first.

Syntax or run-time errors can occur when you use Pascal's predefined functions, so make sure that each function argument is the correct type. For example, the arguments for functions `Round` and `Trunc` should be type `Real`. If the argument for function `Sqrt` or `Ln` is negative, a run-time error will occur.

CHAPTER REVIEW

1. Develop your program solutions from existing information. Use the system documentation derived from applying the software development method as the initial framework for the program. Edit the data requirements to obtain the declaration part, then use the refined algorithm as the starting point for the program body.
2. If a new problem is an extension of a previous one, modify the previous program rather than start from scratch.
3. Pascal's predefined functions can simplify mathematical computations. Write a function designator (consisting of the function name and argument list) in an expression to activate a function.
4. Use a structure chart to show subordinate relationships between subproblems.
5. Utilize modular programming by writing separate procedures to implement the different subproblems in a structure chart. Your main program will contain procedure call statements that activate the procedures listed in the declaration part.

Summary of New Pascal Constructs

Construct	Effect
Procedure Declaration	

`procedure Display;`
`{Prints 3 lines}`
`   const`
`      Star = '*';`
	Procedure `Display` is declared and can be called to print three lines with an asterisk. The constant `Star` is defined only when `Display` is executing.

Construct	Effect
| ```
begin {Display}
  WriteLn (Star);
  WriteLn (Star);
  WriteLn (Star)
end; {Display}
``` | |

Procedure Call Statement

| ```
Display
``` | Procedure Display is called and begins execution. |

Function Designator

| ```
Z := Sqrt(X + Y)
``` | Function Sqrt computes the square root of the expression X + Y, which is assigned to Z. |

Quick-Check Exercises

1. Developing a program from its documentation means that every statement in the program has a comment. True or false?
2. The principle of reusability states that every procedure in your program must be used more than once. True or false?
3. Write this equation as a Pascal statement using functions Exp, Ln, and Sqr:

$$y = (e^n \ln b)^2$$

4. Top-down design means writing the Pascal declaration section first, then the program body. True or false?
5. Each procedure is executed in the order in which it is declared in the main program. True or false?
6. What syntax is required in a Pascal program to invoke a procedure?
7. List the order of the declarations in a standard Pascal program.
8. What is a procedure parameter?
9. Explain how a structure chart differs from an algorithm.
10. A procedure can have inputs, outputs, or both. True or false?
11. What does the following procedure do?

```
procedure Nonsense;
begin {Nonsense}
  WriteLn ('*****');
  WriteLn ('*   *');
  WriteLn ('*****')
end; {Nonsense}
```

12. What does the following program body do?

```
begin
  Nonsense;
  Nonsense;
  Nonsense
end.
```
```

Answers to Quick-Check Exercises

1. False
2. False
3. `Y := Sqr(Exp(N * Ln(B)));`
4. False
5. False
6. A procedure call statement
7. Constants, variables, procedures
8. Parameters are used to receive information from the calling program unit or to pass results back to the calling program unit.
9. A structure chart shows the subordinate relationships between subproblems; an algorithm lists the sequence in which subproblems are performed.
10. True
11. It displays a rectangle.
12. It displays three rectangles on top of each other.

Review Questions

1. Define top-down design and structure charts.
2. In which section of a Pascal program should a procedure be declared? Where in the program can the procedure by called?
3. What are three advantages of using procedures?
4. When is a procedure executed, and where must it appear in the main program?
5. Is the use of procedures a more efficient use of the programmer's time or of the computer's time? Why?
6. How do functions differ from procedures?
7. Write a program that prompts the user for the two legs of a right triangle and makes use of the Sqr and Sqrt functions and the Pythagorean theorem to compute the length of the hypotenuse.
8. Write a program that draws a rectangle made up of asterisks. Use two procedures: `DrawSides` and `DrawLine`.

Programming Projects

Directory: CHAP3
File: PROJ1.PAS

1. Write two procedures, one that displays a triangle and one that displays a rectangle. Use these procedures to write a complete Pascal program from the following outline:

```
program StackHouses (Input, Output);
begin
   {1. Draw triangle.}
   {2. Draw rectangle.}
   {3. Print 2 blank lines.}
   {4. Draw triangle.}
   {5. Draw rectangle.}
end;
```

2. Add the procedures from Fig. 3.15 to the ones for Programming Project 1. Use these procedures in a program that draws a rocket ship (triangle over rectangles

over intersecting lines), a male stick figure (circle over rectangle over intersecting lines), and a female stick figure standing on the head of a male stick figure. Write procedure `Skip5Lines` and call it to place five blank lines between each drawing.

3. Write a computer program that computes the duration of a projectile's flight and its height above the ground when it reaches the target. As part of your solution, write and call a procedure that displays instructions to the program user.

Problem constant
```
G = 32.17              {gravitational constant}
```

Problem input
```
Theta    : Real        {input - angle (radians) of elevation}
Distance : Real        {input - distance (ft) to target}
Velocity : Real        {input - projectile velocity (ft/sec)}
```

Problem output
```
Time     : Real        {output - time (sec) of flight}
Height   : Real        {output - height at impact}
```

Relevant formulas
  $time = distance/(velocity \times cos\ Theta)$
  $height = velocity \times sin\ Theta \times time - (g \times time^2)/2$

4. Four track stars have completed the mile race at the Penn Relays. Write a program that will read in each of their race times (listed here) in minutes (`Minutes`) and seconds (`Seconds`) and compute and print the speed in feet per second (`FPS`) and in meters per second (`MPS`). (*Hint:* There are 5280 feet in one mile, and one kilometer equals 3282 feet.) Write and call a procedure that displays instructions to the program user.

Minutes	Seconds
3	52.83
3	59.83
4	00.03
4	16.22

5. In shopping for a new house, you must consider several factors. In this problem, the initial cost of the house, the estimated annual fuel costs, and the annual tax rate are available. Write a program that will determine the total cost of a house after a five-year period for each of the following sets of data. You should be able to inspect your program output to determine the best buy.

Initial House Cost	Annual Fuel Cost	Tax Rate
$67,000	$2300	0.025
$62,000	$2500	0.025
$75,000	$1850	0.020

To calculate the house cost, add the initial house cost to the fuel cost for five years, then add the taxes for five years. Taxes for one year are computed by multiplying the tax rate by the initial cost. Write and call a procedure that displays instructions to the program user.

6. The first two verses of the song "99 bottles of beer on the wall" are:

99 bottles of beer on the wall.
99 bottles of beer.
Take one down and pass it around.
98 bottles of beer on the wall.

98 bottles of beer on the wall.
98 bottles of beer.
Take one down and pass it around.
97 bottles of beer on the wall.

Write a program that will print the first five verses of this song. Use procedures to minimize duplication of `WriteLn` statements.

INTERVIEW

James D. Foley

James Foley is a professor of computer science and director of the new Graphics, Visualization, and Usability Center in the College of Computing at Georgia Institute of Technology. His interests include user interfaces and interactive computer graphics; his research focuses on building UIDE, the User Interface Design Environment.

▼ **How would you define "human–computer interaction"? Why is it important?**

▲ I would define it by analogy to person-to-person communication. People communicate back and forth using a combination of words, gestures, and facial expressions to represent information that they want to convey to each other. Human–computer interaction addresses the ways in which humans and computers communicate. We have to tell the computer what we want and the computer has to tell us what information it has. Human–computer interaction looks at the language that encompasses this two-way communication: from the person to the computer and from the computer to the person.

The challenge is to design a language that makes it easy for the person to communicate to the computer and that enables the computer to respond in a form most understandable to people. Graphics plays an important part because graphical representations are often more understandable—that is, you can get information out of a chart of data, for example, more quickly than from a column of data.

Computer–human interaction is important in both an economic sense and a broader sense. In an economic sense, it is really the last frontier in the growth of the computer industry. The only thing keeping the computer industry growing is being able to do more and more things with computers. To get computers in the hands of more and more people, we need to find new forms of human–computer communication that will enable and facilitate new types of work.

In a broader sense, human–computer interaction strives to expand people's capabilities and intellectual leverage, so people can do their jobs more quickly, concentrate on the intellectually fulfilling parts of a job, and have access to more information more quickly.

▼ **What has influenced you the most in your own work?**

▲ I started out in graphics and came to realize that graphics was only an enabler—an important enabler, and one where research issues are plentiful—but the experience of building interactive computer graphics systems and seeing the power they brought to people got me interested in human–computer interaction, as well as continuing my interest in computer graphics.

▼ **It seems the most dramatic achievements in computer science have occurred in the area of graphics. Can the gains made in the 1980s be matched in the 1990s, or has this field matured to the point where achievements will be more evolutionary than revolutionary?**

▲ Yes, the achievements will be more evolutionary than revolutionary. As you go from year to year now, the gains in realism are smaller than they used to be because we've done all the easy things. Making pictures more and more realistic is essentially becoming a matter of dealing with mathematical formulations of physics, of how light interacts with surfaces, and of modeling of objects. We know how to model things that are geometrically shaped and to some extent those that are probabilistically or randomly shaped, like the branching patterns of trees, and we're making progress on doing things that don't have nice mathematical formulations.

A question that I and others keep asking is, How realistic is realistic enough? We sometimes get preoccupied with making pictures more and more realistic, but we may not always need the picture to be completely realistic. In fact, some studies have shown that realistic detail can sometimes get in the way of the message to be conveyed. I think the biggest growth for graphics is not in making pictures more and more realistic but in finding creative new ways in which graphics can be used to leverage productivity.

▼ **For someone electing to concentrate in the area of graphics, how important is it to understand the underlying hardware principles?**

▲ It depends on what you want to do. It's analogous to whether you want to be a race car driver or an automobile designer. If you're the race car driver, that would correspond to trying to get the most you can out of the current technology. You need to understand some of the underlying hardware in order to make it work as well as possible—which operations are fast and which are slow, how to organize the data so that access speeds are maximized, and so on. If you want to be an automobile designer, you need to understand the hardware very well. I think most people who study graphics are in the race car driver category.

▼ **What exciting things are being done today in the area of user interfaces?**

▲ Exciting things are going on in the area of virtual realities, creating 3D environments that appear to be real, that behave realistically, and with which you interact realistically. Speech recognition is another exciting area, as are the gesture-based interfaces, or what's now called "pen computing." Pen computing allow users to use a stylus on a liquid crystal display as they would write on a piece of paper. All three developments are making the way we interact with computers more like the way we interact with the real world, so we need to learn less about the system to transfer the skills and knowledge we use in the real world into working with the computer.

▼ **What advice do you have for students who want to work in human–computer interaction?**

▲ If you want to study human–computer interaction, there are two computing systems that you have to understand: the one on the desk and the one in your head. You need to understand the input/output channels for the human processor, as it is sometimes called—the eyes, ears, hands, and fingers—and you need to understand these capabilities as well as the capabilities of the computer. That means studying psychology, particularly cognitive psychology and perceptual psychology, and human factors. I like to compare people who get involved in human–computer interaction to the "Renaissance man," because to do a good job of designing computer interfaces you have to have a breadth of understanding beyond computer science, understanding both the human processor and the application area for which you are designing, and be open to learning about a new discipline.

CHAPTER FOUR

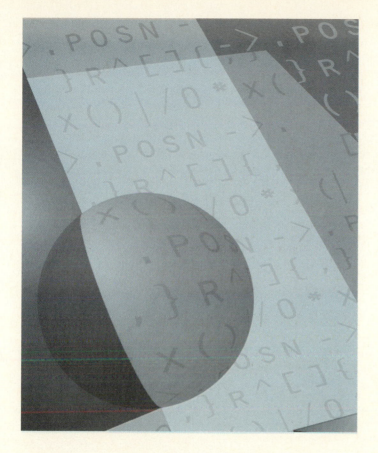

Selection Structures: if and case Statements

This chapter begins your study of statements that control the flow of program execution. You will learn to use Pascal if and case statements to select one statement to execute from many alternatives. First, the chapter discusses Boolean expressions because the if statement relies on them.

The case studies in this chapter extend your problem-solving abilities by introducing the techniques of solution by analogy and hand-tracing the execution of an algorithm. The chapter also introduces visual techniques to identify the data flow in structure charts and to represent Pascal constructs (language elements) in syntax diagrams.

4.1   Control Structures

control structures

combinations of individual in-structions into a single logical unit with one entry point and one exit point

Structured programming utilizes **control structures** to control the flow of execution in a program or procedure. The Pascal control structures enable us to combine individual instructions into a single logical unit with one entry point and one exit point. We can then write a program as a sequence of control structures rather than as a sequence of individual instructions (Fig. 4.1).

Instructions are organized into three kinds of control structures to control execution flow: sequence, selection, and repetition. Until now we have been using only sequential flow. A **compound statement,** written as a group of statements bracketed by begin and end, is used to specify sequential flow:

compound statement

a group of statements brack-eted by begin and end that are executed sequentially

```
begin
    statement₁;
    statement₂;
        .
        .
        .
    statementₙ
end
```

Control flows from *statement₁* to *statement₂*, and so on. You have been using compound statements all along—a program or procedure body consists of a single compound statement.

Figure 4.1

A Program as a Sequence of Three Control Structures

This chapter describes the Pascal control structures for selection. Some problem solutions require that choices be made between alternative steps, for which Pascal statements may or may not be executed, depending on the input data. A **selection control structure** chooses which alternative to execute.

selection control structure
a control structure that chooses among alternative program statements

4.2 Boolean Expressions

A program chooses among alternative steps by testing the value of key variables. For example, since different tax rates apply to various salary levels, an income tax program must select the rate appropriate for each worker's salary by comparing the salary value to the maximum salary for a particular income tax bracket. In Pascal, Boolean expresssons, or *conditions,* perform such comparisons. Each Boolean expression has two possible values, `True` or `False`, where `True` indicates a successful test and `False` indicates an unsuccessful test.

Boolean Variables and Constants

The simplest Boolean expression is a Boolean variable or constant. The statement

```
const
  LeapYear = True;
```

specifies that the Boolean constant `LeapYear` has the value `True`; the statement

```
var
  Switch, Flag : Boolean;
```

declares `Switch` and `Flag` to be Boolean variables—variables that may be assigned only the values `True` and `False`. Given these declarations, all these assignment statements are valid:

```
Switch := True;          {Switch gets True}
Flag := False;           {Flag gets False}
Switch := Flag           {Switch gets value of Flag}
```

After these statements execute, both `Flag` and `Switch` have the value `False`.

Boolean Expressions with Relational Operators

Boolean expressions that perform comparisons have one of these forms:

variable   *relational-operator*   *variable*
variable   *relational-operator*   *constant*

Relational operators are the following symbols:

< (less than)   > (greater than)
<= (less than or equal) >= (greater than or equal)
= (equal)   <> (not equal)

The items being compared, or operands, are often two variables or a variable and a constant. If I is type `Integer`, the condition `I < 3` is true when I is negative or 0, 1, or 2.

The two operands of a relational operator must be the same data type (both type `Integer`, `Real`, `Char`, or `Boolean`), or one may be type `Real` and the other type `Integer`. If I is type `Integer`, the condition `I < '3'` causes a `type mismatch` syntax error because `'3'` is a type `Char` literal.

EXAMPLE 4.1 ▼

An individual's tax rate depends on his or her salary. Single persons who earn less than $18,550 are taxed at a rate of 15%, and those who earn between $18,550 and $44,900 pay 15% of the first $18,550 earned and 28% of the rest. If taxable income is stored in the type `Real` variable `Income`, the Boolean expression corresponding to the question "Is annual income less than $18,550?" is

```
Income < 18550.00
```

This expression evaluates to `True` when the answer is yes, and to `False` when the answer is no.   ▲

EXAMPLE 4.2 ▼

Table 4.1 lists the relational operators and some sample conditions. Each condition is evaluated assuming the variables have the following values:

X	Power	MaxPow	Y	Item	MinItem	MomOrDad	Num	Sentinel
-5	1024	1024	7	1.5	-999.0	M	999	999	▲

Table 4.1
Pascal Relational Operators and Sample Conditions

Operator	Condition	Meaning	Boolean Value
<=	X <= 0	X less than or equal to 0	True
<	Power < MaxPow	Power less than MaxPow	False
>=	X >= Y	X greater than or equal to Y	False
>	Item > MinItem	Item greater than MinItem	True
=	MomOrDad = 'M'	MomOrDad equal to 'M'	True
<>	Num <> Sentinel	Num not equal to Sentinel	False

Boolean Operators

We can form more complicated Boolean expressions by using the three Boolean operators—and, or, not—which require type Boolean operands. Two examples of Boolean expressions formed with these operators are

```
(Salary < MinimumSalary) or (Dependents > 5)
(Temperature > 90.0) and (Humidity > 0.90)
```

The first Boolean expression determines whether an employee is eligible for special scholarship funds. It evaluates to True if *either* condition in parentheses is true. The second Boolean expression describes an unbearable summer day, with temperature and humidity both in the nineties. The expression evaluates to True only when *both* conditions are true.

Boolean variables are Boolean expressions, so they also can be operands of Boolean operators. The Boolean expression

```
WinningRecord and (not Probation)
```

manipulates two Boolean variables (WinningRecord, Probation). A college team for which this expression is true has a winning record and is not on probation so it may be eligible for the postseason tournament. Note that although the expression

```
(WinningRecord = True) and (Probation = False)
```

is logically equivalent to the prior one, the prior one is preferred because it is more concise and more readable.

Table 4.2 shows that the and operator yields a true result only when both its operands are true. Table 4.3 shows that the or operator yields a false result only when both its operands are false. The not operator has a single

Table 4.2
The and Operator

operand1	operand 2	operand1 and operand 2
true	true	true
true	false	false
false	true	false
false	false	false

Table 4.3
The or Operator

operand1	operand2	operand1 or operand2
true	true	true
true	false	true
false	true	true
false	false	false

logical complement (negation)
the logical complement of True is False and vice versa.

operand; Table 4.4 shows that the `not` operator yields the logical **complement,** or **negation,** of its operand (that is, if `Switch` is `True`, `not Switch` is `False` and vice versa).

Table 4.4
The not Operator

operand1	`not` **operand1**
true	false
false	true

An operator's precedence determines its order of evaluation. Table 4.5 shows the precedence of all Pascal operators, including the relational operators. The `not` operator has the highest precedence, followed by the multiplicative operators (including `and`), the additive operators (including `or`), and last, the relational operators.

Table 4.5
Operator Precedence

Operator	**Precedence**
`not`	Highest (evaluated first)
`*, /, div, mod, and`	
`+, -, or`	
`<, <= , = , <>, >= , >`	Lowest (evaluated last)

Because relational operators have the lowest precedence, you may need to place parentheses in expressions using them to prevent syntax errors. To illustrate, the Pascal compiler interprets the expression

`X < Min + Max`

correctly as

`X < (Min + Max)`

because + has higher precedence than <. However, the expression

`Min <= X and X <= Max     {incorrect Boolean expression}`

causes the syntax error `type mismatch` because the Pascal compiler interprets it as

`Min <= (X and X) <= Max     {incorrect Boolean expression}`

since and has higher precedence than <=. This is an error because the type `Real` variable X cannot be an operand of the Boolean operator and. Adding parentheses avoids a syntax error:

`(Min <= X) and (X <= Max)`

EXAMPLE 4.3 ▼

Expressions 1 to 4 contain different operands and operators. Each expression's value in the comment assumes X, Y, and Z are type Real, Flag is type Boolean, and the variables have the values:

X	Y	Z	Flag
3.0	4.0	2.0	False

```
1.  not Flag                              {not False is True}
2.  (X + Y / Z) <= 3.5                     {5.0 <= 3.5 is False}
3.  (not Flag) or ((Y + Z) >= (X - Z))    {True or True is True}
4.  not (Flag or ((Y + Z) >= (X - Z)))    {not (False or True) is
                                            False}
```

Figure 4.2 shows the evaluation tree for expression 3.   ▲

Writing English Conditions in Pascal

To solve programming problems, we must convert conditions expressed in English to Pascal. Many algorithm steps test whether a variable's value is within a specified range of values. For example, if Min represents the lower bound of a range of values and Max represents the upper bound (Min is less than Max), the expression

```
(Min <= X) and (X <= Max)
```

Figure 4.2
Evaluation Tree
for (not Flag)
or ((Y + Z) >= (X – Z))

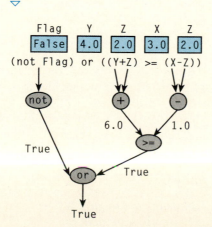

Figure 4.3
Range of True Values for
(Min <= X) and (X <= Max)

tests whether X lies within the range Min through Max, inclusive. In Fig. 4.3 this range is shaded. The expression is true if X lies within this range and false if X is outside the range.

EXAMPLE 4.4 ▼

Pascal expressions 1 to 5 implement an English condition shown in the comment on the right. The comments also show the evaluation of each expression assuming X is 3.0, Y is 4.0, and Z is 2.0.

1. (Z > X) or (Z > Y)   {Z is greater than X or Y –
                                False or False is False}

2. (X = 1.0) or (X = 3.0)   {X equals 1.0 or 3.0 –
                                False or True is True}

3. (X > Z) and (Y > Z)   {X and Y are greater than Z –
                                True and True is True}

4. (Z <= X) and (X <= Y)   {X is in the range from Z to
                                Y – True and True is True}

5. (X < Z) or (X > Y)   {X is outside the range Z to
                                Y – False or False is False}

Expression 1 is the Pascal code for the English condition "Z greater than X or Y". You may be tempted to write this condition as

Z > X or Y

but this expression is invalid because Pascal evaluates X or Y first and the type Real variables X and Y cannot be operands of the Boolean operator or.

Expression 4 is the Pascal code for the relationship Z <= X <= Y. The boundary values, 2.0 and 4.0, are included in the range of X values that yield a result of True.

Expression 5 is true if X lies outside the range bounded by Z and Y. In Fig. 4.4 the shaded areas represent the values of X that yield a True result. Both Y and Z are excluded from the set of values that yield a True result.   ▲

Boolean Assignment

You can write statements to assign a Boolean value to a Boolean variable. If Same is type Boolean, the statement

Figure 4.4
Range of True Values for
(X < Z) or (X > Y)

Same := True

assigns the value True to Same. Since assignment statements have the general form

variable := expression

you can use the statement

Same := (X = Y)

to assign the value of the Boolean expression (X = Y) to Same. The value of Same is True when X and Y are equal; otherwise, Same is False.

EXAMPLE 4.5 ▼

The following assignment statements assign values to two Boolean variables, InRange and IsLetter. InRange gets True if the value of N is in the range -10 through 10; IsLetter gets True if Ch is an uppercase or a lowercase letter.

```
InRange := (N > -10) and (N < 10);
IsLetter := (('A' <= Ch) and (Ch <= 'Z')) or
            (('a' <= Ch) and (Ch <= 'z'))
```

The expression in the first assignment statement is True if N satisfies both the conditions listed (N is greater than -10 and N is less than 10); otherwise, the expression is False. The expression in the second assignment statement uses the Boolean operators and, or. The subexpression on the first line is True if Ch is an uppercase letter; the subexpression on the second line is True if Ch is a lowercase letter. Consequently, IsLetter gets True if Ch is a letter; otherwise, IsLetter gets False. ▲

EXAMPLE 4.6 ▼

The next statement assigns the value True to IsEven (type Boolean) if 2 is a divisor of N (type Integer):

```
IsEven := (N mod 2 = 0)
```

Because all even numbers are divisible by 2, the value assigned to IsEven indicates whether N is even (IsEven is True) or odd (IsEven is False). ▲

Writing Boolean Values

Most Boolean expressions appear in control structures, where they determine the sequence in which Pascal statements execute. Because programs do not process Boolean data in the same way that they process numerical data, your programs will rarely read Boolean values as input data or display Boolean values as program results. If necessary, you can display the value of a Boolean variable with procedure `Write` or `WriteLn`, but you cannot use procedure `ReadLn` to read in a Boolean variable. If `Switch` is `False`, the statement

```
WriteLn ('Value of Switch is ', Switch)
```

displays the line

```
Value of Switch is FALSE
```

Exercises for Section 4.2

Self-Check

1. Which of the following Boolean expressions is incorrect and why? Assume X and Y are `Real` and P, Q, and R are `Boolean`.
   a. `X < 5.1 and Y > 22.3`   b. `P and Q or Q and R`
2. Draw evaluation trees for the following expressions:
   a. `A = (B + A - B)`
   b. `(C = (A + B)) or not Flag`
   c. `(A <> 7) and (C >= 6) or Flag`
   d. `not (B <= 12) and (A mod 2 = 0)`
   e. `not ((A > 5) or (C < ( A + B)))`
3. Evaluate each expression in Exercise 2 if A is 5, B is 10, C is 15, and `Flag` is `True`.

Programming

1. Write a Boolean expression for each of the following relationships.
   a. `Age` is from 18 to 21 inclusive.
   b. `Water` is less than `1.5` and is greater than `0.1`.
   c. `Year` is divisible by 4. (*Hint:* Use mod.)
   d. `Speed` is not greater than 55.
2. Write Boolean assignment statements for the following.
   a. Assign a value of `True` to `Between` if N is in the range `-K` to `+K`, inclusive; otherwise, assign a value of `False`.
   b. Assign a value of `True` to `Uppercase` if `Ch` is an uppercase letter; otherwise, assign a value of `False`.
   c. Assign a value of `True` to `Divisor` if M is a divisor of N; otherwise, assign a value of `False`.

4.3 The if Statement

In Pascal, the primary selection control structure consists of an `if` statement, which always contains a Boolean expression. The `if` statements determine which of several alternative code fragments executes in a particular situation. The if statements in this section select among one or two alternatives.

if Statement with Two Alternatives

The if statement

```
if Gross > 100.00 then
   Net := Gross - Tax
else
   Net := Gross
```

selects one of the two assignment statements. It either selects the statement following then if the Boolean expression is true (i.e., Gross is greater than 100.00), or it selects the statement following else if the Boolean expression is false (i.e., Gross is not greater than 100.00).

flowchart
a diagram that shows the step-by-step execution of a control structure or a program fragment

Figure 4.5(a) is a flowchart of the preceding if statement. In a **flowchart,** boxes and arrows diagram the step-by-step execution of a control structure or program fragment. A diamond-shaped box in a flowchart represents a decision, for which there is always one path in and two paths out (labeled True and False). A rectangular box represents an assignment statement or a process.

Figure 4.5(a) shows that the condition (Gross > 100.00) is evaluated first. If the condition is true, program control follows the arrow labeled True and the assignment statement in the right rectangle is executed. If the condition is false, program control follows the arrow labeled False and the assignment statement in the left rectangle is executed. The flowchart also shows that after the execution of either assignment statement, control goes to the next statement in the program.

Figure 4.5
Flowcharts of if Statements with (a) Two Alternatives and (b) One Alternative

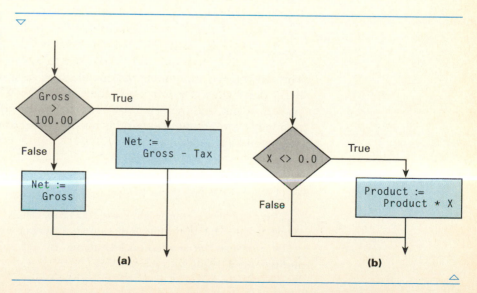

(a)   (b)

if Statement with One Alternative

The if statement in the last section has two alternatives but executes only one for a given value of Gross. You also can write if statements with a single alternative that executes only when the condition is true.

The if statement diagrammed in Fig. 4.5(b),

```
{Multiply Product by a non zero X only}
if X <> 0.0 then
  Product := Product * X
```

has one alternative, which is executed only when X is not equal to 0. It causes Product to be multiplied by X and the new value to be saved in Product, replacing the old value. If X is equal to 0, the multiplication is not performed.

A Comparison of One- and Two-Alternative if Statements

To differentiate between one- and two-alternative if statements, programmers often refer to an if statement with two alternatives as an if-then-else and an if statement with one alternative as an if-then.

EXAMPLE 4.7 ▼

The if statement

```
if MomOrDad = 'M' then
  WriteLn ('Hi Mom')
else
  WriteLn ('Hi Dad')
```

has two alternatives. It displays either 'Hi Mom' or 'Hi Dad', depending on the character stored in the variable MomOrDad (type Char).   ▲

EXAMPLE 4.8 ▼

The following if statement has one alternative: It displays the message 'Hi Mom' only when MomOrDad has the value 'M'. Whether 'Hi Mom' is displayed or not, the message 'Hi Dad' is always displayed. The semicolon terminates the if statement and is needed to separate the if statement from the second WriteLn.

```
if MomOrDad = 'M' then
  WriteLn ('Hi Mom');
WriteLn ('Hi Dad')
```

The next if statement is incorrect because there is a semicolon before the word else. The compiler will detect a syntax error when it reaches the else, because the semicolon terminates the if statement and a new statement cannot begin with else.

```
if MomOrDad = 'M' then
   WriteLn ('Hi Mom');
else                          {error - new statement begins with else}
   WriteLn ('Hi Dad')  ▲
```

SYNTAX DISPLAY

▌ **if Statement (One Alternative)**

Form: if *condition* then
                  statement$_T$

Example: if X > 0.0 then
                  PosProd := PosProd * X

Interpretation: If *condition* evaluates to True, then *statement$_T$* (the true task) is executed; otherwise, *statement$_T$* is skipped.

SYNTAX DISPLAY

▌ **if Statement (Two Alternatives)**

Form: if *condition* then
                  statement$_T$
              else
                  statement$_F$

Example: if X >= 0.0 then
                  Write ('Positive')
              else
                  Write ('Negative')

Interpretation: If *condition* evaluates to True, then *statement$_T$* (the true task) is executed and *statement$_F$* is skipped; otherwise, *statement$_T$* is skipped and *statement$_F$* (the false task) is executed.

Program Style

Format of the if Statement

All if statement examples in this text indent *statement$_T$* and *statement$_F$*. The word else is typed on a separate line, aligned with the word if. The format of the if statement makes its meaning apparent and is used solely to improve program readability; the format makes no difference to the compiler.

Exercises for Section 4.3   **Self-Check**

1. What do these statements display?
    a.   if 12 < 12 then
             WriteLn ('Less')
         else
             WriteLn ('Not less')
    b.   Var1 := 25.12;
         Var2 := 15.00;
         if Var1 <= Var2 then
           WriteLn ('Less or equal')
         else
           WriteLn ('Greater than')

2. What value is assigned to X when Y is 15.0?
    a. ```
        X := 25.0;
        if Y <> (X - 10.0) then
            X := X - 10.0
        else
            X := X / 2.0
        ```
    b.  ```
        if (Y < 15.0) and (Y >= 0.0) then
            X := 5 * Y
        else
            X := 2 * Y
        ```

Programming

1. Write Pascal statements to carry out the following steps.
    a. If Item is nonzero, then multiply Product by Item and save the result in Product; otherwise, skip the multiplication. In either case, print the value of Product.
    b. Store the absolute difference of X and Y in Y, where the absolute difference is (X - Y) or (Y - X), whichever is positive. Do not use the Abs function in your solution.
    c. If X is 0, add 1 to ZeroCount. If X is negative, add X to MinusSum. If X is greater than 0, add X to PlusSum.

4.4 Syntax Diagrams

syntax diagram
a graphical representation
of the syntax of a Pascal
construct

In addition to syntax displays, we can use **syntax diagrams** to describe Pascal constructs. Syntax diagrams are sometimes called railroad diagrams because they resemble track layout diagrams for a model railroad.

To learn how to read syntax diagrams, study the syntax diagram for *program* (Fig. 4.6). The diagram consists of a group of syntactic elements connected by arrows, with the category of each syntactic element indicated by its shape:

▶   Reserved words appear in gray ovals.
▶   Special symbols (punctuation marks and operators) appear in gray circles.
▶   Syntactic elements with their own syntax diagrams appear in colored rectangles.

Figure 4.6
Syntax Diagram for
program

Trace through the syntax diagram in Fig. 4.6 following the arrows, starting at the leftmost arrow (into `program`) and exiting at the rightmost arrow (out of the symbol .). From the top row, notice that a Pascal program begins with the reserved word `program` followed by an *identifier, program parameters,* and the symbol ; . The program header

```
program First (Input, Output);
```

satisfies this part of the syntax diagram because `First` is an *identifier* and (`Input, Output`) are *program parameters*. The rest of the syntax diagram for *program* indicates that the symbol ; should be followed by the syntactic elements *declaration part, body,* and the . symbol.

The syntax diagram for *identifier* (Fig. 4.7) shows that an identifier may be a single letter (A–Z, a–z). We determine this by tracing the horizontal arrow at the top of the diagram from left to right. By tracing through the loops in the diagram, we see that the initial letter may be followed by one or more letters or digits (0–9) (for example, `R2D2, First`). This corresponds to our earlier definition of *identifier* (see Section 2.3).

The syntax diagrams for the syntactic elements *declaration part* and *body* complete the description of the syntactic element *program*. The diagram for *declaration part* is in Appendix B, along with the other syntactic elements of Pascal. The syntax diagram for *body* (Fig. 4.8) shows that a program *body* is a *compound statement,* or a sequence of one or more *statement* elements separated by semicolons and bracketed by `begin` and `end`.

Figure 4.9 shows the syntax diagram for an `if` statement. The arrow out of the *statement* element on the top row splits in two, with the arrow pointing to the right defining an `if` statement with one alternative (`if-then`). The arrow pointing down and to the left passes through the reserved word `else`, defining an `if` statement with two alternatives (`if-then-else`). The statement following the word `then` or `else` may be a single executable statement or a compound statement. Examples of such statements include assignment statements, procedure call statements, and other `if` statements.

Figure 4.7
Syntax Diagram for *identifier*

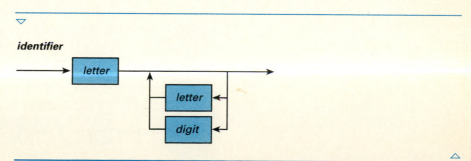

identifier

Figure 4.8
Syntax Diagrams for *body*
and *compound statement*

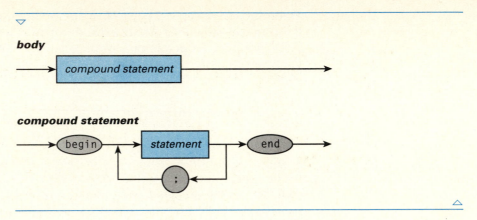

By comparing a program statement to its corresponding syntax diagram, you can verify that the statement is correct. If a syntax error occurs during debugging, you can refer to the appropriate syntax diagram to determine the correct form of the element that caused the problem. Appendix B contains all Pascal syntax diagrams.

Exercises for Section 4.4   **Self-Check**

1. Which of these identifiers satisfy the syntax diagram that follows?

    ```
    Ace  R2D2  R245  A23B  A1c  B34d5c  A23cd
    ```

2. Draw a syntax diagram to describe `Real`-like numeric literals that begin with a digit, end with a digit, and contain a single decimal point somewhere in between.

Figure 4.9
Syntax Diagram for an if
Statement

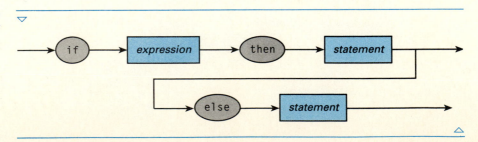

3. Modify the syntax diagram for *identifier* to show that an identifier may start with the underscore symbol or a letter.

4.5 if Statements with Compound Statements

Some `if` statements have compound statements following `then` or `else`. When the reserved word `begin` follows `then` or `else`, the Pascal compiler translates the statements between the `begin` and the `end` as a compound statement.

EXAMPLE 4.9 ▼

In many programming problems, you must order a pair of data values in memory so that the smaller value is stored in one variable (say, X) and the larger value in another (say, Y). The `if` statement in Fig. 4.10 rearranges any two values stored in X and Y so that the smaller number is in X and the larger number is in Y. If the two numbers are already in the proper order, the compound statement is not executed. Variables X, Y, and Temp should all be the same data type. Although the values of X and Y are being switched, an additional variable, Temp, is needed to store a copy of one of these values.

Table 4.6 simulates the execution of this `if` statement when X is 12.5 and Y is 5.0. The table shows that Temp is initially undefined (indicated by ?). Each line shows the part of the `if` statement that is being executed, followed by its effect. If any variable gets a new value, its new value is shown on that line. If no new value is shown, the variable retains its previous value. The last value stored in X is 5.0, and the last value stored in Y is 12.5. ▲

Table 4.6
Step-by-Step Simulation of
if Statement

Statement Part	X	Y	Temp	Effect
	12.5	5.0	?	
`if X > Y then`				12.5 > 5.0 is true
`Temp := X;`			12.5	Stores old X in Temp
`X := Y;`	5.0			Stores old Y in X
`Y := Temp`		12.5		Stores old X in Y

Figure 4.10
if Statement to Order
X and Y

```
if X > Y then
   begin {switch X and Y}
      Temp := X;                {Stores old X in Temp}
      X := Y;                   {Stores old Y in X}
      Y := Temp                 {Stores old X in Y}
   end {if}
```

EXAMPLE 4.10 ▼

As manager of a clothing boutique, you keep records of your checking transactions. When `TransType` is `'C'` in the next `if` statement, the compound statement following `then` processes a transaction (`TransAmount`) that represents a check you wrote to pay for goods received; otherwise, the compound statement following `else` processes a deposit made into your checking account. Both compound statements display an appropriate message and update the account balance (`Balance`).

```
if TransType = 'C' then
  begin {check}
    Write ('Check for $', TransAmount :4:2);
    Balance := Balance - TransAmount        {Deduct check.}
  end {check}
else
  begin  {deposit}
    Write ('Deposit of $', TransAmount :4:2);
    Balance := Balance + TransAmount        {Add deposit.}
  end {deposit and if}
```

The semicolons in the `if` statement separate the individual statements in each alternative. A common error would be to insert a semicolon after the first end (`end; {check}`), causing the `if` to separate into two statements. Because the second statement can't begin with `else`, the compiler would display an `unexpected symbol` error message.   ▲

Semicolons are required between the individual statements within a compound statement, but they should not appear before or after the reserved words `then`, `else`, or `begin`. A semicolon may appear after an `end` that terminates the entire `if` statement.

Program Style

Writing if Statements with Compound True or False Statements

Each `if` statement in this section contains at least one compound statement bracketed by `begin` and `end`. To improve our ability to read and understand the `if` statement, each compound statement is indented; indentation is ignored by the Pascal compiler.

The comment after each `end` helps to associate the `end` with its corresponding `begin`. The comments are not required but are included to improve program readability.

Exercises for Section 4.5   **Self-Check**

1. Insert semicolons where needed to avoid syntax errors and indent to improve readability:

```
{incorrect if statement}
if X > Y then
begin
X := X + 10.0
WriteLn ('X Bigger')
end
else
WriteLn ('X Smaller')
WriteLn ('Y is ', Y)
```

2. Explain why the program will not compile if you remove the bracketing `begin` and `end`.

3. What is the effect of placing a bracketing `begin` and `end` around the last two lines in Exercise 1?

4. Find the syntax error and logic error in the `if` statement:

```
if Num1 < 0 then
   begin
      Product := Num1 * Num2 * Num3;
      WriteLn ('Product is ', Product :1)
   end;
else
   Sum := Num1 + Num2 + Num3;
   WriteLn ('Sum is ', Sum :1)
```

5. What syntax diagrams would you use to validate the following `if` statement? Provide the label of every syntax diagram that describes an element of this statement.

```
if X > 0 then
   begin
      X := 25.0;
      WriteLn ('Positive')
   end
```

Programming

1. Write an `if` statement that, given two real values X and Y, will negate the two values if both are negative or both are positive.

2. Write an interactive program that computes the area of a rectangle (*area = base × height*) or a triangle (*area = 1/2 × base × height*) after prompting the user to type the first character of the figure name (R or T).

4.6   Decision Steps in Algorithms

decision step

an algorithm step that selects one of several actions

Algorithm steps that select from a choice of actions are called **decision steps.** The algorithm in the following payroll problem contains decision steps that are coded as Pascal `if` statements to compute an employee's gross pay and net pay.

Payroll Problem

PROBLEM ▼

Your company pays its employees time and a half for all hours worked over 40 hours a week. Employees who earn more than $100.00 a week pay union dues of $25 per week. Write a program to compute an employee's gross pay and net pay.

ANALYSIS ▼

You first must read the hours worked and the hourly rate for an employee (the problem inputs). After reading these data, compute gross pay. Employees who work 40 hours or less are to be paid the same rate for all hours worked. Those who work more than 40 hours are to be paid one rate for the first 40 hours and 1.5 times that rate for the overtime hours. Compute net pay by subtracting any union dues from gross pay.

Data Requirements

Problem Constants

```
MaxNoOvertime = 40.0      {maximum hours without overtime pay}
BonusRate = 1.5           {time and a half for overtime}
MaxNoDues = 100.00        {maximum salary without union dues}
Dues = 25.00              {union dues}
```

Problem Inputs

```
Hours : Real      {hours worked}
Rate : Real       {hourly rate}
```

Problem Outputs

```
Gross : Real      {gross pay}
Net : Real        {net pay}
```

Relevant Formulas

gross pay = *hours worked* × *hourly rate*
gross pay = 40 × *hourly rate* + 1.5 × *overtime hours* × *hourly rate*
net pay = *gross pay* − *union dues*

Two formulas are listed for gross pay: the first for the employee who receives no overtime pay, the second for the employee eligible for overtime pay.

DESIGN ▼

The structure chart (Fig. 4.11) for this problem contains data flow information showing the inputs and outputs of each algorithm step. The structure chart shows that step 2, *Enter data,* provides values for Hours and Rate as

Figure 4.11
Structure Chart
for Payroll Problem

its outputs (data flow arrow points up). Similarly, the step *Compute gross pay* uses Hours and Rate as its inputs (data flow arrow points down) and provides Gross as its output.

Initial Algorithm

1. Display user instructions.
2. Enter hours worked and hourly rate.
3. Compute gross pay.
4. Compute net pay.
5. Display gross and net pay.

Algorithm Refinements

Refine algorithm steps 3 and 4 as decision steps.

Step 3 Refinement

3.1 if no overtime then
  3.2 Compute gross pay without overtime pay.
else
  3.3 Compute gross pay with overtime pay.

Step 4 Refinement

4.1 if no union dues then
  4.2 Net gets Gross
else
  4.3 Net gets Gross - Dues

pseudocode
a combination of English phrases and Pascal constructs to describe algorithm steps

These decision steps are expressed in **pseudocode,** which is a mixture of English and Pascal used to describe algorithm steps. The pseudocode uses indentation and the reserved words if, then, and else to show the logical structure of each step. Each decision step has a condition (following if) that can be written in English or Pascal, as can the sequentially numbered True and False tasks.

IMPLEMENTATION ▼

The program (Fig. 4.12) begins by calling procedure InstructPay to display the user instructions (the first ten lines of program output). After the input data are read, the if statement

```
{Compute gross pay.}
if Hours <= MaxNoOvertime then
  Gross := Hours * Rate                        {no overtime pay}
else
  Gross := MaxNoOvertime * Rate +
           BonusRate * (Hours - MaxNoOvertime) * Rate;
                                                    {overtime}
```

implements step 3. The first comment on the right is embedded in the if statement. The semicolon in the next-to-last line separates the if statement from the next if statement.

TESTING ▼

To test this program, run it with several data sets that yield all possible combinations of values for the two if statement conditions (True/True, True/False, False/True, False/False). As an example, to get the condition values True/True, hours worked should be less than 40 and gross pay should be less than $100.00. Also test the program with a data set for which hours worked is exactly 40 and one for which gross pay is exactly $100.00.

Figure 4.12
Program for
Payroll Problem

Directory: CHAP4
File: PAYROLL.PAS

▽

```
program Payroll (Input, Output);
{
 Computes and prints gross pay and net pay given an hourly
 rate and number of hours worked. Overtime pay is included in
 the gross pay computation. The employee's net pay includes
 a possible deduction for union dues.
}
```

▷ ▷ ▷ ▷ ▷ ▷

```
const
  MaxNoOvertime = 40;      {maximum hours without overtime pay}
  BonusRate = 1.5;         {time and a half for overtime}
  MaxNoDues = 100.00;      {maximum salary without union dues}
  Dues = 25.00;            {union dues}

var
  Hours, Rate,             {inputs - hours worked, hourly rate}
  Gross, Net : Real;       {outputs - gross pay, net pay}

procedure InstructPay;
{Displays user instructions}

begin {InstructPay}
  WriteLn ('This program computes gross and net pay.');
  WriteLn ('Employees who work more than ', MaxNoOvertime :1);
  WriteLn ('hours receive overtime pay for the excess hours.');
  WriteLn ('Union dues of $', Dues :4:2, ' are deducted');
  WriteLn ('for an employee who earns more than $', MaxNoDues :4:2);
  WriteLn;
  WriteLn ('Enter hours worked and hourly rate');
  WriteLn ('on separate lines after the prompts.');
  WriteLn ('Press Enter after typing each number.');
  WriteLn
end; {InstructPay}

begin {Payroll}
  InstructPay;                {Display user instructions.}

  {Enter Hours and Rate.}
  Write ('Hours worked> ');
  ReadLn (Hours);
  Write ('Hourly rate> ');
  ReadLn (Rate);

  {Compute gross pay.}
  if Hours <= MaxNoOvertime then
    Gross := Hours * Rate                                        {no overtime pay}
  else
    Gross := MaxNoOvertime * Rate +
             BonusRate * (Hours - MaxNoOvertime) * Rate;         {overtime}

  {Compute net pay.}
  if Gross <= MaxNoDues then
    Net := Gross                {Deduct no dues.}
  else
    Net := Gross - Dues;        {Deduct union dues.}

  {Print Gross and Net.}
  WriteLn ('Gross pay is $', Gross :4:2);
  WriteLn ('Net pay is $', Net :4:2)
end.    {Payroll}
```

Sample Run

```
This program computes gross and net pay.
```

▷ ▷ ▷ ▷ ▷ ▷

```
Employees who work more than 40
hours receive overtime pay for the excess hours.
Union dues of $25.00 are deducted
for an employee who earns more than $100.00

Enter hours worked and hourly rate
on separate lines after the prompts.
Press Enter after typing each number.

Hours worked> 40.0
Hourly rate> 5.0
Gross pay is $200.00
Net pay is $175.00
```

Program Style

Using Constants to Enhance Readability and Maintenance

The constants MaxNoOvertime and BonusRate appear in the if statement in Fig. 4.12. We could just as easily have placed the literals 40 and 1.5 directly in the if statement:

```
{Compute gross pay.}
if Hours <= 40 then
  Gross := Hours * Rate            {no overtime pay}
else
  Gross := 40 * Rate +
           1.5 * (Hours - 40) * Rate;   {overtime pay}
```

However, using constants rather than literals has two advantages. First, the original if statement is easier to understand because it includes the descriptive names MaxNoOvertime and BonusRate rather than numbers, which have no intrinsic meaning. Second, a program written with constants is much easier to maintain than one written with literals. For example, to change the bonus for overtime to double pay instead of time and a half, you need to change only the constant declaration for BonusRate to 2.0. However, if you had inserted the literal 1.5 directly in the if statement, you would have to change the if statement and any other statements that manipulate that literal.

Note that the constants also appear in WriteLn statements in procedure InstructPay. It is perfectly permissible to reference program constants in a procedure body.

Using Data Flow Information in Structure Charts

In Fig. 4.11, the data flow information in the structure chart showed the inputs and outputs of each individual algorithm step. Data flow information is an important part of system documentation because it shows which program variables are processed by each step and the manner in which those variables are processed. If a step gives a new value to a variable, then that variable is considered an *output of the step.* If a step displays a variable's value or uses a variable in a computation without changing its value, the variable is considered an *input to the step*. For example, the step *Compute net pay* processes variables `Gross` and `Net`, using the value of `Gross` (its *input*) to compute `Net` (its *output*).

Figure 4.11 shows that a variable may have different roles for different subproblems in the algorithm. For example, in the context of the original problem statement, `Hours` and `Rate` are problem *inputs* (data supplied by the program user). In the context of the subproblem *Enter data,* however, where the task is to deliver values for `Hours` and `Rate` to the main program, they are considered *outputs*. In the context of the subproblem *Compute gross pay,* where the subproblem's task is to use `Hours` and `Rate` to compute `Gross`, they are *inputs* to this step. In the same way, the role of the variables `Gross` and `Net` changes as we go from step to step in the problem.

Solution by Analogy

solution by analogy
solving a new problem by adapting the solution to a similar problem

Sometimes a new problem is simply an old one presented in a new guise. Each time you face a problem, determine whether you have solved a similar one in the past and, if so, adapt the earlier solution. This problem-solving strategy—**solution by analogy**—requires a careful reading of the problem statement to recognize requirements that may be similar to those of earlier problems.

CASE STUDY   ## Computing Insurance Dividends

PROBLEM ▼

An insurance company sends annual dividend checks to its policyholders. The basic dividend rate is a fixed percentage (4.5%—0.045 in Pascal) of the policyholder's paid premium. If the policyholder has made no claims, the dividend rate for that policy is increased by a bonus rate (0.5%—0.005 in Pascal). Write a program to compute dividends.

ANALYSIS ▼

This problem is similar to the payroll problem. Just as there was a bonus pay rate for workers with overtime hours, there is a bonus dividend for policy-holders with no claims. Begin by reading in the input data (the number of claims and the premium), then use a decision step to select either the basic dividend computation or the computation with a bonus dividend.

Data Requirements

Problem Constants

```
BasicRate = 0.045        {the basic dividend rate of 4.5%}
BonusRate = 0.005        {the bonus dividend rate of 0.5%}
```

Problem Inputs

```
Premium : Real              {premium amount}
NumClaims : Integer         {number of claims}
```

Problem Output

```
Dividend : Real             {dividend amount}
```

DESIGN ▼

The initial algorithm follows.

Initial Algorithm

1. Display user instructions.
2. Enter premium amount and number of claims.
3. Compute dividend including any bonus dividend.
4. Display dividend.

Algorithm Refinements

The refinement of step 3 is similar to the refinement of step 3 in the payroll problem.

Step 3 Refinement

3.1 if no claims then
     3.2 Compute dividend including a bonus dividend.
   else
     3.3 Compute dividend as the basic dividend.

IMPLEMENTATION AND TESTING ▼

We leave the program coding as a programming exercise. The if statement

```
{Compute dividend including any bonus dividend.}
if NumClaims = 0 then
  Dividend := Premium * BasicRate +    {basic dividend}
              Premium * BonusRate;     {bonus dividend}
else
  Dividend := Premium * BasicRate      {basic dividend}
```

implements algorithm step 3.

....

Exercises for Section 4.6   **Self-Check**

1. Change the refinement of step 4 of the payroll problem so that it uses a decision step with one alternative. *Hint:* Assign Gross to Net before the decision step, and use the decision step to change Net when necessary.
2. Predict the payroll program output when

   a.   Hours is 30.0, Rate is 5.00.
   b.   Hours is 20.0, Rate is 4.00.
   c.   Hours is 50.0, Rate is 2.00.
   d.   Hours is 50.0, Rate is 6.00.

3. Revise the pizza problem from Section 3.1 so that the user can compute the unit price of either a circular or a square pizza. Give the algorithm with refinements. Draw a structure chart with data flow information for the new pizza problem showing the relationship between the main program and its subproblems. Discuss how the role of the variable that represents pizza area (a problem output) changes for each subproblem.

Programming

1. Modify the program for the payroll problem to deduct union dues of 10% for gross salary over $100.00 and 5% otherwise. Also, deduct a 3% city wage tax for all employees.
2. Provide the structure chart and complete program for computing insurance company dividends.

4.7   Hand-Tracing an Algorithm

A critical step in algorithm design is to verify the algorithm's accuracy before you spend extensive time coding it. These few extra minutes often save hours of coding and testing time.

hand trace (desk check)
step-by-step simulation of an algorithm's execution

A **hand trace,** or **desk check,** is a careful, step-by-step simulation on paper of how a computer would execute an algorithm. The results should show the effect of each step's execution using data that are relatively easy to process by hand. In Section 4.5, we simulated the execution of an if statement that switches the values of two variables. Now we will trace the execution of the refined algorithm for the payroll problem solved in Section 4.6.

Refined Algorithm

1. Display user instructions.
2. Enter hours worked and hourly rate.
3. Compute gross pay.
    3.1 if no overtime then
            3.2 Compute gross pay without overtime pay.
        else
            3.3 Compute gross pay with overtime pay.
4. Compute net pay.
    4.1 if no union dues then
            4.2 Net gets Gross
        else
            4.3 Net gets Gross - Dues
5. Display gross and net pay.

Table 4.7 is a hand trace of steps 2 through 5 of the algorithm. Each step is listed at the left in the order of its execution, and the effect of each step is given in the last column. If a step changes the value of a variable, then the table shows the new value. If no new value is shown, the variable retains its previous value. For example, the table shows that the step

2.   Enter hours worked and hourly rate.

stores the data values 30.0 and 10.00 in the variables Hours and Rate, respectively; Gross and Net are still undefined (indicated by ? in the first table row).

Table 4.7

Trace of Algorithm for
Payroll Problem

Algorithm Step	Hours	Rate	Gross	Net	Effect
	?	?	?	?	
2. Enter hours and rate	30.0	10.00			Reads the data
3.1 if no overtime then					Hours <= 40 is true
3.2 Gross gets Hours * Rate			300.0		Compute gross with no overtime
4.1 if no union dues then					Gross <= 100.00 is false
4.3 Net gets Gross - Dues				275.0	Deduct union dues
5. Display Gross and Net					Displays 300.00 and 275.00

The trace in Table 4.7 shows that 300.0 and 275.0 are stored in Gross and Net, respectively, and displayed. To verify that the algorithm is correct, you must select other data that cause the two conditions to evaluate to different combinations of their values. Since there are two conditions and each has two possible values (True or False), there are two times two, or four, different combinations that should be tried. (What are they?) An exhaustive hand trace of the algorithm would show that it works for all combinations.

Besides the four cases already discussed, you should verify that the algorithm works correctly for unusual data. For example, what would happen if Hours were 40.0 (value of MaxNoOvertime) or if Gross were 100.0 (value of MaxNoDues)? Would the algorithm still provide the correct result? To complete the hand trace, you should show that the algorithm handles these special situations properly.

Take care when tracing each case, making sure to execute the algorithm exactly as the computer would. Often programmers assume how a particular step will be executed and don't explicitly test each condition and trace each step. A trace performed in this way is of little value.

Exercises for Section 4.7   **Self-Check**

1. Provide sample data that cause the first condition in the payroll problem to be false and the second to be true, and trace the execution for these data.
2. If `Hours = MaxHours` and `Gross = MaxNoDues`, which assignment steps in the algorithm would be performed? Provide a trace.

4.8   Nested if Statements and Multiple-Alternative Decisions

nested if statement
an if statement with another if statement as its true task or its false task

Until now we have used if statements to code decisions with one or two alternatives. In this section, we will use **nested if statements** (one if statement inside another) to code decisions with multiple alternatives.

EXAMPLE 4.11 ▼

The following nested if statement has three alternatives. It increases one of three variables (NumPos, NumNeg, or NumZero) by 1, depending on whether X is greater than zero, less than zero, or equal to zero, respectively. The boxes show the logical structure of the nested if statement: The second if statement is the false task (following else) of the first if statement.

```
{increment NumPos, NumNeg, or NumZero depending on X}
if X > 0 then
   NumPos := NumPos + 1
else
   if X < 0 then
      NumNeg := NumNeg + 1
   else {X = 0}
      NumZero := NumZero + 1
```

The execution of the nested if statement proceeds as follows: The first condition (X > 0) is tested; if it is true, NumPos is incremented and the rest of the if statement is skipped. If the first condition is false, the second condition (X < 0) is tested; if it is true, NumNeg is incremented; otherwise, NumZero is incremented. It is important to realize that the second condition is tested *only* when the first condition is false.

Table 4.8 traces the execution of this statement when X is -7. Because X > 0 is false, the second condition (X < 0) is tested.   ▲

Table 4.8

Trace of if Statement in
Example 4.11 for X = –7

Statement Part	Effect
if X > 0 then	-7 > 0 is false.
if X < 0 then	-7 < 0 is true;
NumNeg := NumNeg + 1	add 1 to NumNeg.

Comparison of Nested if and Sequence of ifs

Beginning programmers sometimes prefer to use a sequence of if statements rather than a single nested if statement. The nested if statement for Example 4.11 is logically equivalent to this sequence of if statements:

```
if X > 0 then
  NumPos := NumPos + 1;
if X < 0 then
  NumNeg := NumNeg + 1;
if X = 0 then
  NumZero := NumZero + 1
```

The nested if statement is more readable and more efficient, however, because the sequence doesn't clearly show that one and only one of the three assignment statements is executed for a particular X as the nested if does. With respect to efficiency, the nested if statement executes more quickly when X is positive because the first condition (X > 0) is true, so the part of the if statement following the first else is skipped. In contrast, all three conditions are always tested in the sequence of if statements. When X is negative, two conditions are tested in the nested if versus three in the sequence of if statements.

Pascal Rule for Matching else with if

The use of indentation conveys the logical structure of a nested if statement. The indentation in Example 4.11 clearly shows an if-then-else statement with a second if-then-else statement as its false task. The Pascal compiler disregards this indentation, however, and uses its own rule for matching each else with its corresponding if: Pascal matches each else with the closest preceding if that is not matched with a closer else. This rule is analogous to the rule for matching left and right parentheses in an expression, in that an if is like a left parenthesis and an else is like a right parenthesis.

EXAMPLE 4.12 ▼

In the nested if statement

```
{if-then-else as true task of an if-then}
if X > 0 then
   if Y > X then
      WriteLn ('Y > X > 0')
   else
      WriteLn ('(X > 0) and (Y <= X)')
```

Pascal matches the else with the second if. Therefore Pascal translates this statement as an if-then statement whose true task (following then) is an if-then-else statement.

 If you want the else to go with the first if, not the second, then you must place a begin-end bracket around the inner if-then statement:

```
{if-then as true task of if-then-else}
if X > 0 then
   begin
      if Y > X then
         WriteLn ('Y > X > 0')
   end
else
   WriteLn ('X <= 0')
```

Pascal translates this statement as an if-then-else statement whose true task is an if-then statement. ▲

Multiple-Alternative Decision Form of Nested if

multiple-alternative decision
a nested if statement in which each false task (except possibly the last) is an if-then-else statement

Nested if statements can become quite complex. If there are more than three alternatives and indentation is not consistent, it may be difficult to determine the logical structure of the if statement. In situations like Example 4.11 in which each false task (except possibly the last) is followed by an if-then-else statement, you can code the nested if as the **multiple-alternative decision** described in the next display.

SYNTAX DISPLAY

Multiple-Alternative Decision

Form:
```
if condition₁ then
      statement₁
   else if condition₂ then
      statement₂
   else if condition₃ then
      statement₃
```

```
              .
              .
              .
         else if condition_n then
              statement_n
         else
              statement_e
```

Example: `{increment NumPos, NumNeg, NumZero depending on X}`
```
         if X > 0 then
              NumPos := NumPos + 1
         else if X < 0 then
              NumNeg := NumNeg + 1
         else {X = 0}
              NumZero := NumZero + 1
```

Interpretation: The *conditions* in a multiple-alternative decision are evaluated in sequence until a true *condition* is reached. If a *condition* is true, the *statement* following it is executed and the rest of the multiple-alternative decision is skipped. If a *condition* is false, the *statement* following it is skipped and the next *condition* is tested. If all *conditions* are false, the *statement_e* following the last `else` is executed.

Note: It is not necessary to have an `else` *statement_e*. In this case, nothing happens if all *conditions* are false.

EXAMPLE 4.13 ▼

Suppose you want to assign letter grades based on exam scores.

Exam Score	Grade Assigned
90 and above	A
80 – 89	B
70 – 79	C
60 – 69	D
below 60	F

The following multiple-alternative decision displays the letter grade assigned according to this table. For an exam score of 85, the first true condition is `Score >= 80`, so B would be displayed and program control would pass to the `WriteLn` statement after the multiple-alternative decision.

```
if Score >= 90 then
   Write ('A')
else if Score >= 80 then
   Write ('B')
else if Score >= 70 then
   Write ('C')
```

```
else if Score >= 60 then
   Write ('D')
else
   Write ('F');
WriteLn (' is the exam grade - score is ', Score)  ▲
```

Program Style

Writing a Multiple-Alternative Decision

In the multiple-alternative decision, the reserved words `else if` and the next condition appear on the same line. All the words `else` align, and each task is indented under the condition that controls its execution.

Order of Conditions in a Multiple-Alternative Decision

When more than one condition in a multiple-alternative decision is true, only the task following the first true condition executes. Therefore the order of the conditions can affect the outcome.

The following multiple-alternative decision assigns grades incorrectly. All passing exam scores (60 or above) would be categorized as a grade of D because the first condition would be true and the rest would be skipped. The most restrictive condition (`Score >= 90`) should come first.

```
{incorrect grade assignment}
if Score >= 60 then
   Write ('D')
else if Score >= 70 then
   Write ('C')
else if Score >= 80 then
   Write ('B')
else if Score >= 90 then
   Write ('A')
else
   Write ('F')
```

EXAMPLE 4.14 ▼

You could use a multiple-alternative decision to implement a *decision table* that describes several ranges of values for a particular variable and the outcome for each range. For instance, let's say you are an accountant setting up a payroll system based on Table 4.9, which shows five different ranges for salaries up to $15,000.00. Each table line shows the base tax amount (column 2) and tax percentage (column 3) for a particular salary range (column 1). Given a person's salary, you can calculate the tax due by adding the base tax to the product of the percentage times the excess salary over the minimum salary for that range. For example, the second line of the table specifies that the tax due on a salary of $2000.00 is $225.00 plus 16% of the excess

Table 4.9
Decision Table for
Example 4.14

Salary Range	Base Tax	Percentage of Excess
0.00 – 1499.99	0.00	15%
1500.00 – 2999.99	225.00	16%
3000.00 – 4999.99	465.00	18%
5000.00 – 7999.99	825.00	20%
8000.00 – 15,000.00	1425.00	25%

salary over $1500.00 (i.e., 16% of $500.00, or $80.00). Therefore the total tax due is $225.00 plus $80.00, or $305.00.

The if statement in Fig. 4.13 implements the tax table. If the value of Salary is within the table range (0.00 to 15000.00), exactly one of the statements assigning a value to Tax will execute. Table 4.10 shows a hand trace of the if statement when Salary is 2000.00. Verify for yourself that the value assigned to Tax, 305.00, is correct. ▲

Table 4.10
Trace of if Statement in Fig.
4.13 for Salary = $2000.00

Statement Part	Salary	Tax	Effect
	2000.00	?	
if Salary < 0.0			2000.0 < 0.0 is false.
else if Salary < 1500.00			2000.0 < 1500.0 is false.
else if Salary < 3000.00			2000.0 < 3000.0 is true.
Tax := (Salary - 1500.00)			Evaluates to 500.00.
* 0.16			Evaluates to 80.00.
+ 225.00		305.00	Evaluates to 305.00.

Figure 4.13
if Statement for Table 4.9

```
if Salary < 0.00 then
   WriteLn ('Error! Negative salary $', Salary :10:2)
else if Salary < 1500.00 then              {first range}
   Tax := 0.15 * Salary
else if Salary < 3000.00 then              {second range}
   Tax := (Salary - 1500.00) * 0.16 + 225.0
else if Salary < 5000.00 then              {third range}
   Tax := (Salary - 3000.00) * 0.18 + 465.00
```

▷ ▷ ▷ ▷ ▷ ▷

```
else if Salary < 8000.00 then                    {fourth range}
   Tax := (Salary - 5000.00) * 0.20 + 825.00
else if Salary <= 15000.00 then                  {fifth range}
   Tax := (Salary - 8000.00) * 0.25 + 1425.00
else
   WriteLn ('Error! Too large salary $', Salary :10:2)
```

△

Program Style

Validating the Value of Variables

If you validate the value of a variable before using it in a computation, you can avoid processing invalid or meaningless data. Instead of computing an incorrect tax amount, the if statement in Fig. 4.13 prints an error message if the value of Salary is outside the range covered by the table (0.0 to 15000.00). The first condition detects negative salaries; an error message is displayed if Salary is less than zero. All conditions evaluate to False if Salary is greater than 15000.00, so the task following else displays an error message.

Nested if Statements with More Than One Variable

In most of our examples, the use of nested if statements to test the value of a single variable has enabled us to write each nested if statement as a multiple-alternative decision. When several variables are involved, we cannot always use a multiple-alternative decision. Example 4.15 contains a situation in which we can use a nested if statement as a "filter" to select data that satisfy several different criteria.

EXAMPLE 4.15 ▼

The Department of Defense would like a program that identifies single males between the ages of 18 and 26, inclusive. One approach uses a nest of if-then statements whose conditions test the next criterion only if all previous criteria tested were satisfied. In the following nest of if-then statements, assume that all variables have initial values and that the Boolean variable Single has been set previously to indicate whether the individual is single (Single is True). Recall that the condition Single is preferable to Single = True. The WriteLn statement executes only when all conditions are true.

```
{Display message if all criteria are met.}
if Single then
   if Gender = 'M' then
      if (Age >= 18) and (Age <= 26) then
         WriteLn ('Current person satisfies the criteria.')
```

Another approach to solving this problem is to write a Boolean expression that combines all the individual conditions that must be true using the and operator. This expression appears on the right side of the following

Boolean assignment. The if statement following the Boolean assignment displays an appropriate message based on the value assigned to AllMet.

```
{Set AllMet to True if all criteria are met.}
AllMet := Single and (Gender = 'M') and
            (Age >= 18) and (Age <= 26);

{Display the result of the filtering operation.}
if AllMet then
  WriteLn ('Current person satisfies the criteria.')
else
  WriteLn ('All criteria are not satisfied.')  ▲
```

EXAMPLE 4.16 ▼

In a discussion about your options for college, your parents tell you that you may apply to your first-choice school if your SAT scores are above 1300 and you earn more than $2000 over the summer. If your SAT scores are not over 1300 but you still earn over $2000, then your parents suggest you apply to their alma mater and live at the dorm. If you cannot earn the necessary $2000, your parents want you to commute to a local college. The following nested if statement summarizes this decision process:

```
if Earnings > 2000.00 then
  if SAT > 1300 then
    WriteLn ('Apply to first-choice college')
  else
    WriteLn ('Apply to parents alma mater')
else
  WriteLn ('Apply to local college')
```

The first WriteLn executes when both conditions are True; the second WriteLn executes when the first condition is True and the second is False; the third WriteLn executes when the first condition is False.

We could also use the following multiple-alternative decision to implement this decision:

```
if (Earnings > 2000.00) and (SAT > 1300) then
  WriteLn ('Apply to first-choice college')
else if Earnings > 2000.00 then
  WriteLn ('Apply to parents alma mater')
else
  WriteLn ('Apply to local college')
```

The first WriteLn executes when both summer earnings and SAT scores are sufficient. Because the condition following else if is tested only when the first condition fails, it can be True only when earnings are sufficient but SAT scores are not. Note that it is not necessary to test the value of SAT in that condition. The third WriteLn executes when summer earnings are insufficient. ▲

Figure 4.14
Evaluation Tree for Flag or
((Y + Z) >= (X – Z))

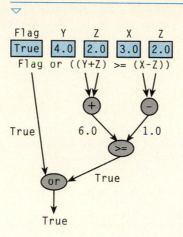

Short-Circuit Evaluation of Boolean Expressions (Non-Standard)

short-circuit evaluation

evaluating only as much of a Boolean expression as is necessary to determine its value

When evaluating Boolean expressions, some compilers employ a technique called **short-circuit evaluation.** A compiler using this technique stops evaluating a Boolean expression as soon as its value can be determined. For example, if the value of Flag is True, the expression in Fig. 4.14 must evaluate to True regardless of the value of the parenthesized expression following or (that is, True or (. . .) must always be True). Consequently, there is no need to evaluate the parenthesized expression following or when Flag is True. Similarly, we can show that False and (. . .) must always be False, so there is no need to evaluate the parenthesized expression following the and operator.

Standard Pascal does not use short-circuit evaluation. This can lead to execution errors, as shown next.

EXAMPLE 4.17 ▼

If X is zero, the if condition

```
if (X <> 0.0) and (Y / X > 5.0) then
```

is False because (X <> 0.0) is False, so False and (. . .) must be False. Consequently, there is no need to evaluate (Y / X > 5.0) when X is zero. However, Pascal does evaluate this expression, causing a division by zero run-time error.

To prevent this run-time error, the if condition should be split:

```
if (X <> 0.0) then
  if (Y / X > 5.0) then
```

The first condition guards the second and prevents the latter from being evaluated when X is zero. The result of evaluating these conditions is the same for short-circuit or complete evaluation. ▲

Be wary of short-circuit evaluation and avoid writing Boolean expressions that rely on it.

Exercises for Section 4.8

Self-Check

1. Trace the execution of the nested if statement in Example 4.14 when Salary is 13500.00.
2. In Example 4.16, how many comparisons are required to execute the first if statement? What about the second? Which if statement is more efficient?
3. Evaluate the following expressions, with and without short-circuit evaluation, if X is 6 and Y is 7.

   a. (X > 5) and (Y div X <= 10)
   b. (X <= 10) or (X / (Y - 7) > 3)

Programming

1. Rewrite the if statement for Example 4.13 using only the relational operator < in all conditions. Test for a failing grade first.
2. Implement the following decision table using a nested if statement. Assume that the grade point average is within the range 0.0 through 4.0.

Grade Point Average	Transcript Message
0.0 – 0.99	Failed semester—registration suspended
1.0 – 1.99	On probation for next semester
2.0 – 2.99	(No message)
3.0 – 3.49	Dean's list for semester
3.5 – 4.0	Highest honors for semester

4.9 The case Statement

In addition to the if statement, the case statement can be used in Pascal to select one of several alternatives. The case statement is especially useful when selection is based on the value of a single variable or a simple expression (called the *case selector*). The case selector must be an **ordinal data type,** or a data type whose values may all be listed. Data types Integer, Boolean, and Char are ordinal types, but data type Real is not. (If you tried to list the real numbers between 3.1 and 3.2 as 3.11, 3.12, 3.13, . . . , you would be leaving out 3.111, 3.112, 3.113, ...)

ordinal data type

a data type having a finite set of values that can always be listed in order from the first to the last

EXAMPLE 4.18 ▼

The case statement

```
case MomOrDad of
  'M', 'm' : WriteLn ('Hello Mom - Happy Mother''s Day');
  'D', 'd' : WriteLn ('Hello Dad - Happy Father''s Day')
end; {case}
```

behaves the same way as the following if statement when the character stored in MomOrDad is one of the four letters listed (M, m, D, or d):

```
if (MomOrDad = 'M') or (MomOrDad = 'm') then
  WriteLn ('Hello Mom - Happy Mother''s Day')
else if (MomOrDad = 'D') or (MomOrDad = 'd') then
  WriteLn ('Hello Dad - Happy Father''s Day')
```

The message displayed by the case statement depends on the value of the case selector MomOrDad (type Char). If the case selector value is 'M' or 'm', the first message is displayed. If the case selector value is 'D' or 'd', the second message is displayed. The lists 'M', 'm' and 'D', 'd' are called *case labels*. ▲

EXAMPLE 4.19 ▼

The following case statement computes the gross pay a worker earns on a particular day, where the value of DayNumber indicates whether the day is a Saturday (DayNumber is 7), a Sunday (DayNumber is 1), or a weekday (DayNumber is 2 through 6). The worker is paid time and a half for weekend work. Of course, the values of DayNumber, DailyRate, and Hours must be defined before the case statement executes.

```
{Compute gross pay for a particular day}
case DayNumber of
  1, 7          : Gross := Hours * 1.5 * DailyRate;
  2, 3, 4, 5, 6 : Gross := Hours * DailyRate
end; {case} ▲
```

One common error is using a string such as 'Saturday' or 'Sunday' as a case label. This causes a syntax error such as ordinal expression expected. Remember that only ordinal values (i.e., single characters, integers, or Boolean values) may appear in case labels.

We describe the case statement next and diagram it in Fig. 4.15.

SYNTAX DISPLAY

case Statement

Form: case *selector* of
                  label₁ : *statement₁*;
                  label₂ : *statement₂*;

```
                            .
                            .
                            .
                label  :  statement
                     n             n
              end {case}
Example: case N of
              1, 2 : begin
                       Write ('1, 2, ');
                       WriteLn ('Buckle my shoe')
                     end; {1, 2}
              3, 4 : WriteLn ('3, 4, Shut the door');
              5, 6 : WriteLn ('5, 6, Pick up sticks')
              end {case}
```

Interpretation: The *selector* expression is evaluated and compared to each *label,* which is a list of one or more possible values for the *selector*. Only one *statement* is executed; if the *selector* value is listed in *label$_i$*, then *statement$_i$* is executed. Control is then passed to the first statement after end {case}. Each *statement* may be a single or a compound Pascal statement.

Note 1: A case expression out of range run-time error occurs when the *selector* value fails to match any *label*.

Note 2: A particular *selector* value may appear in, at most, one *label*.

Note 3: The type of each *selector* value must correspond to the type of the *selector* expression.

Note 4: Any ordinal data type is permitted as the *selector* type.

Figure 4.15
Syntax Diagrams for case
Statement and case Label

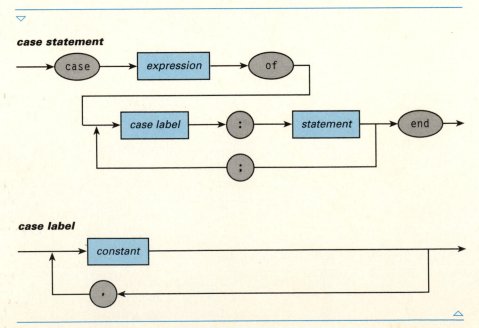

If no action is to be performed for a particular case *label*, the semicolon is placed right after the colon. Each *statement,* except the last, should be followed by a semicolon; the last *statement* is followed by the word `end`. There is no corresponding `begin` for a `case` statement.

Guarding a case Statement

guarded `case` statement
a `case` statement that executes only for valid values of the *selector*

Programmers often **guard a `case` statement** with an `if` statement to prevent the occurrence of a `case expression out of range` error caused by the program user entering a value that is not listed in a `case` label. In the next program fragment, the `if` statement guards the `case` statement nested inside it. The `case` statement executes only when the value of `DayNumber` is in the range 1 through 7, as required; an error message is printed when `DayNumber` is invalid. Note that no semicolon follows the `end {case}`. (Why?)

```
{Compute gross pay for a particular day.}
if (DayNumber >= 1) and (DayNumber <= 7) then
   case DayNumber of
     1, 7           : Gross := Hours * 1.5 * DailyRate;
     2, 3, 4, 5, 6 : Gross := Hours * DailyRate
   end {case}
else
   WriteLn ('invalid day number.')
```

otherwise or else Clause (Non-Standard)

Instead of guarding a `case` statement, some compilers allow the use of an `otherwise` or `else` clause, which can display an error message or take some corrective action if the `case` selector has an unexpected data value. In the next `case` statement, the `otherwise` clause displays the error message `invalid day number` if an unexpected value is stored in `DayNumber`. The `otherwise` clause cannot be used in standard Pascal.

```
{Compute gross pay for a particular day}
case DayNumber of
  1, 7           : Gross := Hours * 1.5 * DailyRate;
  2, 3, 4, 5, 6 : Gross := Hours * DailyRate
otherwise
   WriteLn ('invalid day number.')
end {case}
```

Comparison of Nested if and case

Nested `if` statements, which are more general than a `case` statement, can be used to implement any multiple-alternative decision. A `case` statement, however, is more readable and should be used whenever practical. Remember not to use type `Real` values or strings as case labels.

Use the `case` statement when each case label contains a reasonably sized list of values (10 or fewer). When the number of values in a case selector is large or there are large gaps in those values, however, use a nested `if` statement.

Program Style

Type Boolean case Selectors

Although `case` statements may contain type `Boolean` case selectors, this rarely happens. The following `case` and `if` statements are equivalent, but the `if` statement is preferable:

```
case X = Y of                              if X = Y then
  True : WriteLn ('Equal');                  WriteLn ('Equal')
  False : WriteLn ('Unequal')              else
end {case}                                   WriteLn ('Unequal')
```

Exercises for Section 4.9   **Self-Check**

1. Write an `if` statement that corresponds to the following `case`:

    ```
    case X of
      2 : WriteLn ('Snake Eyes!');
      7, 11 : WriteLn ('Win!')
    end {case}
    ```

2. Write a `case` statement that corresponds to the following `if`:

    ```
    if (Grade >= 'A') and (Grade <= 'C') then
      WriteLn ('Passing')
    else if (Grade = 'D') or (Grade = 'F') then
      WriteLn ('No credit')
    else
      WriteLn ('Invalid grade')
    ```

3. Can the nested `if` statements in Section 4.8 be rewritten using `case` statements? If not, why not?

Programming

1. Write a `case` statement that prints a message indicating whether `NextCh` (type `Char`) is an operator symbol (+, -, *, =, <, >, /), a punctuation mark (comma, semicolon, parenthesis, brace, bracket), or a digit. Your statement should print the category selected.
2. Write a nested `if` statement that is equivalent to the `case` statement described in Programming Exercise 1.
3. Guard the `case` statement described in Programming Exercise 1.

4.10 Common Programming Errors

The Boolean operators, `and`, `or`, and `not`, can be used only with Boolean expressions. In the expression

```
Flag and (X = Y)
```

the variable `Flag` must be type `Boolean`. The expression would be invalid without the parentheses unless `X` and `Y` were also type `Boolean`. In this case, `Flag and X` would be evaluated first because `and` has higher precedence than `=`.

Be careful when using semicolons inside an `if` statement. Use them only to separate the statements of a compound statement within an `if` statement, and place a semicolon after the `if` statement when more statements follow. Never use semicolons before or after the reserved words `then` or `else` in an `if` statement. If you use a semicolon just before `else`, the compiler will terminate the `if` statement and incorrectly assume that the `else` begins a new statement.

Don't forget to bracket a compound statement used as a true task or a false task with `begin` and `end`. If the `begin-end` bracket is missing, only the first statement will be considered part of the task, which can lead to a syntax error. In the following example, the missing `begin-end` bracket around the true task causes the compiler to assume that the semicolon after the assignment statement terminates the `if` statement. As a result, you get a `; expected` syntax error when `else` is reached. If you then insert a semicolon at the end of the first `WriteLn` statement, you will get an `error in statement` syntax error because a statement cannot begin with `else`.

```
{if with missing begin - end}
if X > 0 then
  Sum := Sum + X;
  WriteLn ('X is positive')
else
  WriteLn ('X is not positive')
```

When writing a nested `if` statement, try to select the conditions in such a way that you can use the multiple-alternative format shown in Section 4.8. If more than one condition may be true at the same time, place the most restrictive condition first.

Remember that the Pascal compiler matches each `else` with the closest unmatched `if`. If careless, you may get an unexpected pairing that, while perhaps not causing a syntax error, will affect the outcome.

In `case` statements, make sure the case selector and labels are of the same ordinal type (`Integer`, `Char`, or `Boolean`, but not `Real` or a string). Remember that no value may appear in more than one case label. Guard the `case` with an `if` statement to prevent a run-time error when the selector value is not listed in a case label. Don't forget to terminate a `case` statement with an `end {case}`; there is no matching `begin`.

CHAPTER REVIEW

1. Use control structures to control the flow of execution through a program. The compound statement is a control structure for sequential execution.
2. Boolean expressions appear in if statements and can be written
   ▶ using Boolean variables or constants
   ▶ using the relational operators (<, <=, >, >=, =, <>), to compare variables and constants of the same data type
   ▶ using the logical operators (and, or, not) with Boolean operands
3. Use selection control structures to represent decisions in an algorithm, and write them in algorithms using pseudocode. We use the if statement to code decision steps in Pascal.
4. Syntax diagrams describe the syntax of Pascal. To avoid syntax errors when you are unsure of the form of a statement, refer to the appropriate syntax diagrams (see Appendix B). If the compiler detects a syntax error that you don't understand, refer to the syntax diagram to determine the cause of the error.
5. Data flow information in a structure chart indicates whether a variable processed by a subproblem is used as an input or an output, or as both. An input provides data that are manipulated by the subproblem, and an output returns a value read or computed by the subproblem. The same variable can be an input to one subproblem and an output from another.
6. Solution by analogy is a problem-solving technique in which you solve a new problem by applying logic similar to that used in an earlier solution.
7. A hand trace of an algorithm verifies whether it is correct. You can discover errors in logic by carefully hand-tracing an algorithm. Hand-tracing an algorithm before coding it as a program will save you time in the long run.
8. Nested if statements are commonly used in Pascal to represent decisions with multiple alternatives. Programmers use indentation and the multiple-alternative decision form to enhance readability of nested if statements.
9. A second selection structure, the case statement, implements decisions with several alternatives, depending on the value of a variable or expression (the *case selector*). The *case selector* can be type Integer, Char, or Boolean, but not type Real or a string.

Summary of New Pascal Constructs

Construct	Effect
Compound Statement	

```begin {group}```
``` Write ('Enter X> ');```
``` ReadLn (X);```
``` Positive := Abs(X);```
``` Root := Sqrt(Positive)```
```end {group}```
	The statements in the compound statement are executed in sequence.

Construct	Effect

Construct

Effect

if *Statement*

One Alternative

```
if X <> 0.0 then
   Product := Product * X
```

Multiplies `Product` by `X` only if `X` is nonzero.

Two Alternatives

```
if X >= 0.0 then
   WriteLn (X, ' positive')
else
   WriteLn (X, ' negative')
```

If `X` is greater than or equal to 0.0, displays `X` followed by `positive`; otherwise, displays `X` followed by `negative`.

Several Alternatives

```
if X < 0.0 then
   begin
      WriteLn ('negative');
      Sign := '-'
   end
else if X = 0.0 then
   begin
      WriteLn ('zero');
      Sign := '0'
   end
else
   begin
      WriteLn ('positive');
      Sign := '+'
   end
```

One of three messages is printed, depending on whether `X` is negative, positive, or zero. `Sign` (type `Char`) stores the sign of `X`.

case *Statement*

```
case NextCh of
   'A', 'a' : WriteLn ('Excellent');
   'B', 'b' : WriteLn ('Good');
   'C', 'c' : WriteLn ('O.K.');
   'D', 'd', 'F', 'f' :
      begin
         Write ('Poor, student');
         WriteLn (' on probation')
      end
end {case}
```

Displays one of four messages based on the value of `NextCh` (type `Char`). If `NextCh` is `'D'`, `'d'` or `'F'`, `'f'`, the student is put on probation.

Quick-Check Exercises

1. An `if` statement is a control statement for _____.
2. What is a compound statement?
3. A `case` statement is often used instead of _____.
4. Why would the following statement fail in some Pascal implementations but not fail in others? Assume `I` and `J` are integer variables.

```
if (I > 0) and (J div I = 0) then
   WriteLn ('I is a factor of J')
```

5. The relational operator `<>` means _____.
6. What operator has the highest precedence? Name four that have the lowest precedence.
7. What is the purpose of a syntax diagram?
8. Correct the syntax errors in the following statement:

```
if X > 25.0 then
   begin
      Y := X - 25.0;
   else
      Y := X
   end {if}
```

9. What value is assigned to `Fee` by each of the following `if` statements when `Speed` is 75? Is the one on the left or the one on the right correct?

```
if Speed > 35 then         if Speed > 75 then
   Fee := 20.0                Fee := 60.0
else if Speed > 50 then    else if Speed > 50 then
   Fee := 40.00               Fee := 40.00
else if Speed > 75 then    else if Speed > 35 then
   Fee := 60.00               Fee := 20.00
```

10. What output line(s) are displayed by the following statements when `Grade` is `'I'`? When `Grade` is `'B'`? When `Grade` is `'b'`?

```
case Grade of
   'A' : Points := 4;
   'B' : Points := 3;
   'C' : Points := 2;
   'D' : Points := 1;
   'E', 'I' ,'W' : Points := 0
end; {case}

if ('A' <= Grade) and (Grade <= 'D') then
   WriteLn ('Passed, points earned = ', Points)
else
   WriteLn ('No points earned')
```

11. Explain the difference between the statements on the left and the statements on the right. For each, what is the final value of X if the initial value of X is 1?

```
if X >= 1 then          if X >= 1 then
   X := X + 1               X := X + 1;
else if X >= 0 then     if X >= 0 then
   X := X + 2               X := X + 2
```

Answers to Quick-Check Exercises

1. selection or decision making
2. One or more statements bracketed by `begin` and `end`
3. a nested `if` statement or a multiple-alternative decision
4. This statement would fail when I is 0 if short-circuit evaluation is not used.
5. not equal
6. `not; <, <=, >, >=, =, <>`
7. To check the syntax of a Pascal construct
8. Remove `begin` and `end` and the semicolon.
9. `20.00` (first condition is true), `40.00`; `40.00` is correct
10. When `Grade` is `'I'`: `No points earned`. When `Grade` is `'B'`: `Passed, points earned = 3`. When `Grade` is `'b'`: `A case expression out of range` run-time error occurs.
11. A nested `if` statement is on the left; a sequence of `if` statements is on the right. X becomes 2 on the left; X becomes 4 on the right.

Review Questions

1. Why are the relational operators placed in parentheses when the `and` or `or` operators are used?
2. How does a relational operator differ from a Boolean operator?
3. What is short-circuit Boolean evaluation? Why should its use be discouraged?
4. Trace the following program fragment and indicate which procedure will be called if a data value of `27.34` is entered:

```
WriteLn ('Enter a temperature> ');
ReadLn (Temp);
if Temp > 32.0 then
   NotFreezing
else
   IceForming
```

5. Write a nested `if` statement to display a message that indicates the educational level of a student based on his or her number of years of schooling: `0—None, 1 through 5—Elementary School, 6 through 8—Middle School, 9 through 12—High School, > 12—College`. Print a message to indicate bad data as well.
6. Redo Review Question 5 using a `case` statement.

7. Given the following syntax diagram, which of the following words are valid?

   pear   bread   drear   deaden   dad   drab

words

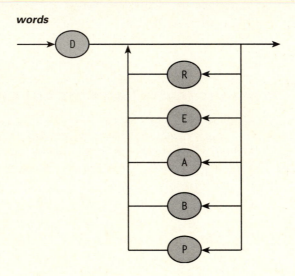

8. Write a guarded `case` statement to select an operation based on the value of `Inventory`. Increment `TotalPaper` by `PaperOrder` if `Inventory` is `'B'` or `'C'`; increment `TotalRibbon` by 1 if `Inventory` is `'E'`, `'F'`, or `'D'`; increment `TotalLabel` by `LabelOrder` if `Inventory` is `'A'` or `'X'`. Do nothing if `Inventory` is `'M'`.

9. Write the six pairs of words that satisfy the syntax diagram for *thing*.

thing   **stuff**

10. What is solution by analogy?

Programming Projects

1. Write procedures to draw a circle, square, and triangle. Then write a program that reads a letter C, S, or T and, depending on the letter chosen, draws either a circle, square, or triangle.

2. Write a program that reads in four words and displays them in increasing alphabetical sequence and also in decreasing alphabetical sequence.

3. While spending the summer as a surveyor's assistant, you decide to write a program that transforms compass headings in degrees (0 to 360) to compass bearings. A compass bearing consists of three items: the direction you face (north or south), an angle between 0 and 90 degrees, and the direction you turn before walking (east or west). For example, to get the bearing for a compass heading of 110.0 degrees, you would first face due south (180 degrees) and then turn 70.0 degrees east (180.0 –70.0 is 110.0). Therefore, the bearing is south 70.0 degrees east. Be sure to check the input for invalid compass headings.

4. Write a program that reads in a room number, its capacity, and the size of the class enrolled so far and prints an output line showing the classroom number, capacity, number of seats filled, number of seats available, and a message indicating whether the class is filled. Call a procedure to display the following heading before the output line:

```
Room    Capacity    Enrollment    Empty seats    Filled/
                                                  Not filled
```

Display each part of the output line under the appropriate heading. Test your program with the following classroom data:

Room	Capacity	Enrollment
426	25	25
327	18	14
420	20	15
317	100	90

5. Write a program that determines the additional state tax owed by an employee. The state charges a 4% tax on net income. Determine net income by subtracting a $500 allowance for each dependent from gross income. Your program will read gross income, number of dependents, and tax amount already deducted. It will then compute the actual tax owed and print the difference between tax owed and tax deducted followed by the message 'SEND CHECK' or 'REFUND', depending on whether the difference is positive or negative.

6. Write a program to control a bread machine. Allow the user to input the type of bread as W for white and S for sweet. Ask the user whether the loaf size is double and whether the baking is manual. The program should fail if the user inputs are invalid. The following table details the time chart for the machine for each bread type. Print a statement for each step. If the loaf size is double, increase the baking time by 50%. If baking is manual, stop after the loaf shaping cycle and instruct the user to remove the dough for manual baking. Use a procedure to print program instructions.

Bread Time Chart

Operation	White Bread	Sweet Bread
Primary kneading	15 min	20 min
Primary rising	60 min	60 min
Secondary kneading	18 min	33 min
Secondary rising	20 min	30 min
Loaf shaping	2 sec	2 sec
Final rising	75 min	75 min
Baking	45 min	35 min
Cooling	30 min	30 min

7. Write a program that determines the day number (1 to 366) in a year for a date that is provided as input data. As an example, January 1, 1994, is day 1; December 31, 1993, is day 365; December 31, 1996, is day 366 since 1996 is a leap year. A year is a leap year if it is divisible by 4, except that any year divisible by 100 is a leap year only if it is divisible by 400. Your program should accept the month, day, and year as integers.

▼ You studied psychology and semiotics as an undergraduate and earned your Ph.D. in cognitive psychology. What attracted you to the computer science industry?

▲ While in graduate school at Stanford, I studied ordinary conversation—how people work together to make sure they are understanding each other throughout a conversation. Some of my research involved observing how people communicate through various media. I became interested in how people interact with computers and signed on to a project that attempted to add a speech interface to a medical expert system. Using this prototype, a doctor could speak to the computer and report the results of a patient's visit. The goal of the project was to gain insight into how doctors adapted their speech to match the computer's capabilities. This was my first exposure to a more applied setting and I found it very gratifying to work on a tangible tool that would be used by real people.

My work continues to revolve around how computers can enhance human communication. I work in the Collaborative Computing (COCO) group at SunSoft, which designs, develops, and studies the use of video-based tools that enable people to communicate face-to-face from different locations. I bring to the group an understanding of how people cooperate in a conversation as well as experience studying groups to learn how they approach tasks we want to support on the computer.

▼ What applications is the group currently developing? How will these tools be used and by whom?

▲ The COCO group builds proof-of-concept prototypes that use video to enable people to collaborate across distance. We have two projects in development. *Forum* allows users to give interactive presentations or classes over the network. Using Forum, the audience sits at their desktops and receives live video and audio of the presenter as well as slides. The presenter can draw or write on these slides, and the marks are seen by the audience. The audience can interact with the presenter by speaking, sending in written comments, or by responding anonymously to yes/no and multiple-choice questions. (For example, a speaker might ask, "How many of you think the term *multimedia* has become a meaningless buzzword?" and she would see a bar chart indicating how many people were voting yes or no.) Audience members can also interact with each other via short text messages that can be sent back and forth throughout the presentation.

The other project we are working on, *Montage*, expands on basic video-conferencing tools by building in support for the "pre-interaction coordination" that goes on among people who are colocated. For example, when you want to speak to someone nearby, you might walk down the hall to check if they are in. If they're not you might leave a note indicating that you are looking for them. If they're on the phone, you might signal that you would like to talk to them when they are done. Montage seeks to provide these capabilities for people who are distributed across distance. It allows you to quickly and unobtrusively "glance" into someone's office. If they are not there, you can leave an electronic "stickup" message, check their calendar, or send e-mail. If they are there, you can see whether it is a good time to interact, and if so, enter into a full video conference.

INTERVIEW
▼

Ellen Isaacs

Ellen Isaacs received her Ph.D. in 1989 from Stanford University. She has since authored a number of papers which address the development of video applications and presented "What Video Can and Can't Do for Collaboration" at ACM's 1993 Multimedia Conference. As a human-interface engineer in the Collaborative Computing group at SunSoft, Ellen Isaacs applies her knowledge of human communication skills to the design and development of video software for desktop computers.

▼ **Do you foresee any technical or cultural obstacles in implementing video conferencing on a large scale?**

▲ There are several obstacles to be overcome before such video-based tools are widely used, some technical and some social. I'm not an expert on the technical issues, but at the very least, the cost of video processing hardware needs to come down and high bandwidth networks need to become more widely available; both of these are starting to happen. Perhaps the biggest technical obstacle to software developers is the lack of interoperability. This term refers to the ability to run software (in this case, video-conferencing software) on numerous hardware platforms. Even within a single company, you cannot expect everyone to work on the same type of computer. Most large companies have some combination of PCs, Macs, UNIX boxes, and mainframes, all from different manufacturers. When you start talking about cross-company communication or communication into the home, it becomes essential to handle video connectivity across different platforms.

From a user point of view, the biggest obstacle to ubiquitous video conferencing is the privacy issue. I think we as researchers have already learned quite a bit about handling many of the practical issues surrounding privacy, but it will take a while until people feel that they have control over their privacy. For example, Montage permits only reciprocal audio and video. This means no one can watch or listen to you without your being able to see and hear them. Montage also provides varying levels of access. It permits the equivalent of closing your door but still allowing knocking, as well as completely locking visual access. These functions let people use their existing social mechanisms to keep from invading others' privacy. Montage was field-tested on a group of marketers and engineers. Some of the participants were extremely apprehensive about signing on. But once they started using Montage, they quickly became more comfortable with it. Soon enough, most ended up using the access modes to give *more* information about their whereabouts when they weren't in their offices.

▼ **What guidelines do you apply in designing and developing user interfaces for these video tools?**

▲ The best user interface feels invisible to the user. I think video, as well as audio and animation, provides an opportunity to reduce the amount of work required by the rest of the user interface. If you can build upon people's sophisticated skills in dealing with sounds and both static and moving images, you can reduce the amount of buttons, menus, and other artificial devices to manipulate an application. In addition, video conferencing (or any tool for that matter) needs to do a better job of integrating itself with other desktop tools. Users need the ability to quickly call up an image, share a text editor, or check e-mail messages whenever the need should arise during a video conference. If it takes too long or is too tedious to access another application, people are less likely to use the tools when they need them. On the whole, I think the key to designing good multimedia applications is to use the media as tools to enhance users' tasks rather than just showcasing multimedia technology for its own sake.

CHAPTER FIVE

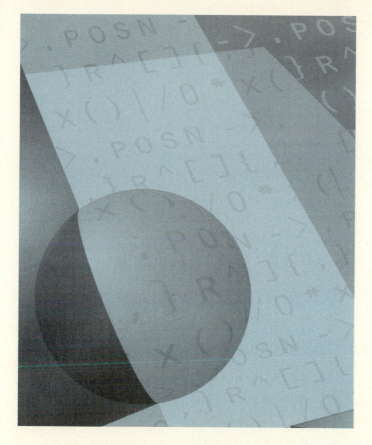

Repetition: while, for, and repeat Statements

loop
the repetition of steps in a program

In the programs studied so far, the statements in the program body execute only once. In most commercial software, however, a process can be repeated many times. For example, in an editor, the user can repeat the process of moving the cursor to a program line and editing a line as often as necessary.

Repetition, you'll recall, is the third type of program control structure (*sequence, selection, repetition*), and the repetition of steps in a program is called a **loop.** In this chapter, we describe the three Pascal loop-control statements—while, for, and repeat—and the advantages of each and we explain when to use each one. Like if statements, loops can be nested, and this chapter demonstrates how to write and use nested loops in your programs.

5.1 The while Statement

loop body
the instructions that are
repeated in the loop

Our study of loops begins with the most versatile loop-control statement, the while statement. The program fragment in Fig. 5.1 computes and displays the weekly pay for each of seven employees, assuming no overtime pay. The instructions that are repeated, called the **loop body,** follow the word do. The loop body is the compound statement bracketed by begin and end; {while} consisting of instructions that read an employee's payroll data and compute and display that employee's gross pay. After seven weekly pay amounts are displayed, the statement following the loop body executes and displays the message All employees processed.

The three lines in color in Fig. 5.1 control the looping process. The first statement,

```
CountEmp := 0;          {no employees processed yet}
```

stores an initial value of 0 in the variable CountEmp, which represents the count of employees processed so far. The next line evaluates the Boolean expression CountEmp < 7. If it is true, the loop body is executed, causing the program to read a new pair of data values and to compute and display a new pay amount. The last instruction in the loop body,

```
CountEmp := CountEmp + 1     {increment CountEmp}
```

adds 1 to the value of CountEmp. After the last instruction in the loop body has been executed, control returns to the line beginning with while, and the Boolean expression CountEmp < 7 is reevaluated for the next value of CountEmp.

The loop body is executed once for each value of CountEmp from 0 to 6. Eventually, CountEmp becomes 7, at which time the Boolean expression

Figure 5.1
Loop to Process Seven
Employees

```
CountEmp := 0;                    {no employees processed yet}
while CountEmp < 7 do             {test value of CountEmp}
      begin
        Write ('Hours> ');
        ReadLn (Hours);
Loop    Write ('Rate> $');
body    ReadLn (Rate);
        Pay := Hours * Rate;
        WriteLn ('Weekly pay is $', Pay :4:2);
        CountEmp := CountEmp + 1     {increment CountEmp}
      end; {while}

WriteLn ('All employees processed');
```

evaluates to False. At this point, the loop is exited and control transfers to the WriteLn statement following the loop body.

loop-repetition condition
the condition following while that controls loop repetition

The Boolean expression after the reserved word while, called the **loop-repetition condition,** is evaluated before each repetition of the loop body. The loop body is repeated when this condition is true, and exited when this condition is false. The flowchart of the while loop in Fig. 5.2 illustrates this execution. The condition in the diamond-shaped box is evaluated first. If it is true, the loop body is executed and the process is repeated until the condition becomes false. At that point, the while loop is exited.

Make sure you understand the difference between the while statement in Fig. 5.1 and the if statement

```
if CountEmp < 7 then
  begin
    . . .
  end; {if}
```

The compound statement after the reserved word then executes at most one time. In a while statement, the compound statement after the reserved word do may execute more than once.

loop-control variable
the variable whose value controls loop repetition

The variable CountEmp in Fig. 5.1 is called the **loop-control variable** because its value determines whether the loop body is repeated. The loop-control variable CountEmp must be *initialized, tested,* and *updated* for the loop to execute properly:

▶   *Initialization.* CountEmp is set to an initial value of 0 (*initialized to* 0) before the while statement is reached.
▶   *Testing.* CountEmp is tested before the start of each loop repetition (called an *iteration* or a *pass*).
▶   *Updating.* CountEmp is updated (its value increased by 1) during each iteration.

Similar steps must be performed for every while loop. Without the initialization, the initial test of CountEmp would be meaningless. The updating step ensures that the program progresses toward the final goal (CountEmp >= 7)

Figure 5.2
Flowchart of a while Loop

infinite loop
a loop that executes forever

counting loop
a loop whose required number of iterations can be determined before loop execution begins

counter
the loop-control variable for a counting loop

during each repetition of the loop. If the loop control variable were not updated, the loop would execute "forever." Such a loop is called an **infinite loop.**

The `while` loop in Fig. 5.1 is called a **counting loop** (or **counter-controlled loop**) because its repetition is controlled by a **counter** variable, whose value represents the number of loop iterations performed so far. We use a counting loop when we can determine prior to loop execution exactly how many loop repetitions are needed to solve our problem. The `while` condition should compare the counter to the number of loop repetitions needed. We describe the `while` statement syntax next and diagram it in Fig. 5.3.

SYNTAX DISPLAY

The while Statement

Form: `while` *expression* `do`
        statement

Example: `{Display N asterisks.}`
        `CountStar := 0;`
        `while CountStar < N do`
          `begin`
            `Write ('*');`
            `CountStar := CountStar + 1`
          `end {while}`

Interpretation: The *expression* (loop repetition condition) is tested; if it is true, *statement* (the loop body) is executed and *expression* is retested. *statement* is repeated as long as *expression* is true. When *expression* is tested and found to be false, the loop is exited, and the next program statement after the `while` statement is executed.

Note: If *expression* evaluates to false the first time it is tested, *statement* is not executed.

Position semicolons in a `while` statement carefully. Do not put a semicolon after the word `do`, or the Pascal compiler will execute what it assumes is an *empty statement* as your loop body. Such a "statement" will do nothing forever or until your patience or time expires.

Program Style

Formatting the while Statement

For clarity, indent the body of a `while` loop. If the loop body is a compound statement, bracket it with `begin` - `end {while}`.

Figure 5.3
Syntax Diagram for while Statement

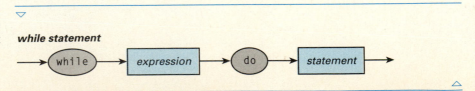

while statement

Exercises for Section 5.1   **Self-Check**

1. How many times is the following loop body repeated? What is printed during each repetition of the loop body and after exit?

```
X := 3;
Count := 0;
while Count < 3 do
  begin
    X := X * X;
    WriteLn (X);
    Count := Count + 1
  end; {while}

WriteLn {Count}
```

2. Answer Exercise 1, assuming the last statement in the loop body is

```
Count := Count + 2
```

3. Answer Exercise 1, this time omitting the last statement in the loop body.

Programming

1. Write a `while` loop that displays each integer from 1 to 5 on a separate line together with its square.
2. Write a `while` loop that displays each integer from 4 down to -6 on a separate line. Display the values in the sequence 4, 2, 0, and so on.

5.2 Using Loops to Accumulate a Sum

Loops often accumulate a sum by repeating an addition operation, as demonstrated in Example 5.1.

EXAMPLE 5.1 ▼

The program in Fig. 5.4 has a `while` loop similar to the loop in Fig. 5.1. Besides displaying each employee's weekly pay, it computes and displays the company's total payroll (`TotalPay`). Prior to loop execution, the statements

```
TotalPay := 0.0;
CountEmp := 0;                {Start with first employee.}
```

accumulator

a variable used to store a value being computed in increments during the execution of a loop

initialize both `TotalPay` and `CountEmp` to 0, where `CountEmp` is the counter variable and `TotalPay` is an **accumulator** variable (it accumulates the total payroll value). Initializing `TotalPay` to 0 is critical; omitting this step will cause the final total to be off by whatever value happens to be stored in `TotalPay` when the program begins execution.

In the loop body, the assignment statement

```
TotalPay := TotalPay + Pay;              {Add next pay.}
```

Figure 5.4
Program to Compute
Payroll

Directory: CHAP5
File: PAYROLL.PAS

```pascal
program Payroll (Input, Output);
{Computes the payroll for a company}

  var
    NumberEmp,                  {input - number of employees}
    CountEmp : Integer;         {current employee}
    Hours,                      {input - hours worked}
    Rate,                       {input - hourly rate}
    Pay,                        {output - weekly pay}
    TotalPay : Real;            {output - company payroll}

begin {Payroll}
  {Enter number of employees.}
  Write ('Enter number of employees> ');
  ReadLn (NumberEmp);

  {Compute each employee's pay and add it to the payroll.}
  TotalPay := 0.0;
  CountEmp := 0;                      {Start with first employee.}
  while CountEmp < NumberEmp do
    begin
      Write ('Hours> ');
      ReadLn (Hours);
      Write ('Rate> $');
      ReadLn (Rate);
      Pay := Hours * Rate;
      WriteLn ('Pay is $', Pay :4:2);
      WriteLn;
      TotalPay := TotalPay + Pay;            {Add next pay.}
      CountEmp := CountEmp + 1
    end; {while}

  WriteLn ('All employees processed');
  WriteLn ('Total payroll is $', TotalPay :4:2)
end. {Payroll}
```

Sample Run

```
Enter number of employees> 3
Hours> 5
Rate> $4.00
Pay is $20.00

Hours> 6
Rate> $5.00
Pay is $30.00

Hours> 1.5
Rate> $10.00
Pay is $15.00

All employees processed
Total payroll is $65.00
```

Figure 5.5
Accumulating a Sum

adds the current value of Pay to the sum being accumulated in TotalPay, thereby increasing the value of TotalPay with each loop iteration. Figure 5.5 traces the effect of repeating this statement for the three values of Pay shown in the sample run. Recall that iteration means a pass through the loop. ▲

Program Style

Writing General Loops

Because the loop in Fig. 5.1 uses the loop repetition condition CountEmp < 7, it processes exactly 7 employees. The more general loop in Fig. 5.4 uses the loop repetition condition CountEmp < NumberEmp, so it can process any number of employees. The number of employees to be processed in the latter loop must be read into variable NumberEmp before the while statement executes.

Exercises for Section 5.2

Self-Check

1. What output values are displayed by the following while loop for a data value of 5?

```
WriteLn ('Enter an integer> ');
ReadLn (X);
Product := 1;
Count := 0;
```

```
while Count < 4 do
   begin
      WriteLn (Product);
      Product := Product * X;
      Count := Count + 1
   end; {while}
```

2. What values are displayed if the call to `WriteLn` comes at the end of the loop instead of at the beginning?

3. What mathematical operation does the following segment compute?

```
Write ('Enter X> ');
ReadLn (X);
Write ('Enter Y> ');
ReadLn (Y);
Product := 1;
while Y > 0 do
   begin
      Product := Product * X;
      Y := Y - 1
   end; {while}
WriteLn ('Result = ', Product)
```

4. How would you modify the program in Fig. 5.4 to display the average employee salary, in addition to the total payroll amount?

Programming

1. When Robin's new baby was born, she opened a savings account with $1000.00. On each birthday, starting with the first, the bank added an additional 4.5% of the balance and Robin added another $500.00 to the account. Write a loop that will determine how much money was in the account on the child's 18th birthday.

5.3 Event-Controlled Loops

Programmers use two kinds of loops: counter-controlled loops and event-controlled loops (or conditional loops). In the former, the loop body repeats a specified number of times. In an **event-controlled loop,** loop repetition stops when a particular event occurs.

event-controlled loop
a loop whose repetition stops when a particular event occurs

For example, if faced with a pile of bills when sitting down to write monthly checks, you might not know how many checks to write. However, if you wanted to pay as many bills as possible, you could pay them in order by amount (smallest bill first) and stop writing checks when the event "account is overdrawn" occurs. In other words, you would continue writing checks as long as your account was not overdrawn, as indicated by the following pseudocode description:

```
while account is not overdrawn do
   begin
      Read the next bill
      Pay the bill if there are sufficient funds
      Update the balance
   end
```

The actual number of loop repetitions performed would depend on the amount of your initial checking account balance and the amount owed on each bill.

EXAMPLE 5.2 ▼

The program in Fig. 5.6 uses the preceding algorithm to pay bills, assuming that the total amount owed exceeds the initial checking account balance. The `while` loop reads each bill and processes it, and the `if` statement nested inside the loop determines whether to pay the bill by comparing the current account balance to the bill amount. If `Balance >= Bill` is true, the bill is paid; otherwise it is not paid and the last positive value of balance is displayed instead.

Figure 5.6
Paying Monthly Bills

Directory: CHAP5
File: PAYBILLS.PAS

```
program PayBills (Input, Output);
{
   Authorizes payment of each bill as long as there are
   sufficient funds in the checking account. Assumes bills
   are entered in order starting with the smallest and the total
   amount owed exceeds the initial account balance.
}
   var
      Bill,                {input - amount of bill}
      InitBal,             {input - starting balance}
      Balance : Real;      {output - current account balance}

begin {PayBills}
   Write ('Enter initial account balance> $');
   ReadLn (InitBal);

   {
    Pay each bill as long as the account is not overdrawn.
    Decrease the balance by the bill amount after each bill is
    processed.
   }
   Balance := InitBal;
   while Balance >= 0.0 do
      begin
         WriteLn;                          {Skip a line.}
```

▷ ▷ ▷ ▷ ▷

```
      Write ('Enter amount owed> $');
      ReadLn (Bill);
      if Balance >= Bill then
        WriteLn ('Issue check for $', Bill :3:2)
      else
        WriteLn ('No check issued -- ',
                 'Account balance is only $', Balance :3:2);
        Balance := Balance - Bill        {Update balance.}
    end; {while}

  WriteLn ('Insufficient funds to pay any more bills!')
end. {PayBills}
```

Sample Run

```
Enter initial account balance> $120.00

Enter amount owed> $65.00
Issue check for $65.00

Enter amount owed> $70.00
No check issued -- Account balance is only $55.00
Insufficient funds to pay any more bills!
```

Table 5.1 traces the execution of the program for the data shown in the sample run. During the first loop iteration, the if statement displays instructions for writing a check. During the second iteration, the if statement displays the last positive account balance. The next execution of the statement

```
Balance := Balance - Bill          {Update balance.}
```

assigns a negative value to Balance, so the loop would be exited when its repetition condition is retested. ▲

Table 5.1
Trace of Program
in Fig. 5.6

Statement	InitBal	Balance	Bill	Effect
ReadLn (InitBal)	120.00	?	?	Enter start balance
Balance := InitBal;		120.00		Initialize Balance
while Balance >= 0.0 do				120.00 >= 0.0 is true

	Statement	InitBal	Balance	Bill	Effect
Table 5.1 Trace of Program in Fig. 5.6 (*continued*)	ReadLn (Bill);			65.00	Enter first bill
	if Balance >= Bill then				120.00 >= 65.00 is true
	WriteLn ('Issue check ...				Pay the bill
	Balance := Balance - Bill		55.00		Reduce Balance
	while Balance >= 0.0 do				55.00 >= 0.0 is true
	ReadLn (Bill)			70.00	Enter second bill
	if Balance >= Bill then				55.00 >= 70.00 is false
	WriteLn ('No check ...				Display Balance
	Balance := Balance - Bill		-15.00		Reduce Balance
	while Balance >= 0.0 do				-15.00 >= 0.0 is false, exit loop
	WriteLn ('Insufficient...				Display final message

Just like the counter in a counting loop, the loop-control variable `Balance` for an event-controlled loop must be *initialized, tested,* and *updated* for the loop to execute properly.

▶ *Initialization.* `Balance` is initialized to `InitBal` before the loop is reached.
▶ *Testing.* `Balance` is tested before each execution of the loop body.
▶ *Updating.* `Balance` is updated (reduced by the value of `Bill`) during each literation.

Remember to include similar steps in *every* loop that you write.

Checking Zero-Iteration Loops

zero-iteration loop
a loop whose body is not executed

Although we expect a loop body to be repeated, in some cases it will never execute (called a **zero-iteration loop**). The loop body will not execute if the loop-repetition condition evaluates to false when first tested. Because the loop initialization step is always performed, even for zero-iteration loops, it should always be written to ensure that a program with a zero-iteration loop generates meaningful results.

The bill-paying program of Fig. 5.6 has a zero-iteration loop when the initial account balance is negative. If InitBal is -120.00, the loop initialization step would assign -120.00 to Balance, the loop would be skipped, and the statements following the loop would execute. The program output would be:

```
Enter initial account balance >$-120.00
Insufficient funds to pay any more bills!
```

Exercises for Section 5.3 **Self-Check**

1. What is the least number of times that the body of a while loop can be executed?
2. When would the output of the following segment be erroneous? How could it be fixed?

    ```
    Total := 0;
    Write ('Enter number of items> ');
    ReadLn (Num);
    Count := 0;
    while Count < Num do
      begin
        Write ('Enter a value> ');
        ReadLn (Value);
        Last := Value
      end; {while}
    WriteLn ('The last value entered was ', Last)
    ```

3. Trace the program in Fig. 5.6 for the following data: 150.00, 75.00, 50.00, 25.00, 30.00.
4. a. How would you modify the loop in Fig. 5.6 so that it also determines the number of bills paid (CountBills)?
    b. How would you modify the loop in Fig. 5.6 if it is possible for all bills to be paid before the account becomes overdrawn? Assume that the number of bills to pay (NumberBills) as well as the initial account balance are provided as data.
        Hint: Use the loop repetition condition (Balance >= 0.0) and (CountBills < NumberBills).

Programming

1. There are 9870 people in a town whose population increases by 10% each year. Write a loop that determines how many years (CountYears) it would take for the population to exceed 30,000.

5.4 Loop Design

It is one thing to analyze the operation of a loop and another to design your own loops. Loop design can be approached in two ways. One method analyzes the requirements for a new loop to determine the needed initialization, testing, and updating of the loop-control variable. The second method develops templates for frequently recurring loop forms and uses a template as the basis for a new loop.

Analyzing Loop Requirements

To gain some insight into the design of the loop needed for the bill paying program, let's study the comment in Fig. 5.6 that summarizes the goals of the loop:

```
{
 Pay each bill as long as the account is not overdrawn. Decrease
 the balance by the bill amount after each bill is processed.
}
```

To accomplish these goals, we must focus on loop control and loop processing. Focusing on loop control means making sure that the loop exit occurs when it should; focusing on loop processing means making sure that the loop body performs the required operations.

To formulate the necessary loop-control and loop-processing steps, we start by listing what we know about the loop. In this example, if `Balance` is the loop-control variable, we can make four observations:

1. `Balance` must be equal to `InitBal` just before the loop begins.
2. We pay the current bill if the account has sufficient funds.
3. `Balance` during the next pass must be less than `Balance` during the current pass by the amount of the current bill.
4. We stop paying bills when `Balance` becomes negative.

Requirement 1 tells us which initialization must be performed. Requirement 2 tells us when to pay the current bill (if `Balance >= Bill` is true). Requirement 3 tells us how to update `Balance` within the loop body (`Balance := Balance - Bill`). Requirement 4 tells us that the loop should be exited when the first bill to make `Balance` negative is processed. These requirements form the basis for the following algorithm design. The loop-repetition condition, `Balance >= 0.0`, is the opposite of the loop-exit condition, `Balance < 0.0`.

1. Initialize `Balance` to `InitBal`.
2. while `Balance >= 0.0` do
   begin

3. Read the data for the current bill.
4. Display the check-writing information if the bill can be paid.
5. `Balance := Balance - Bill`
    `end {while}`

One common way to generate output from a loop is to arrange it in a table. In the next example, we analyze loop requirements to produce a table of values.

EXAMPLE 5.3: Designing a Loop to Display a Table of Values ▼

Your physics professor wants you to write a program that displays the effect of gravity on a free-falling object. Your results are to be listed in a table that shows the height of an object dropped from a tower for every second it is falling.

Assuming *t* is the time of free fall, we can make the following observations about the height of an object dropped from a tower:

1. At *t* = 0.0, the object height is the same as the tower height.
2. While the object is falling, its height is the tower height minus the distance it has traveled.
3. Free fall ends when the object height is less than or equal to 0.0.

These requirements determine the design of the `while` loop shown in Fig. 5.7. The object height, `Height`, is initialized to the tower height, `Tower` (from requirement 1). The `while` condition

`Height > 0.0`

ensures that loop exit occurs when the object hits the ground (from requirement 3). Within the loop body, the assignment statement

`Height := Tower - 0.5 * G * Sqr(T)`

Figure 5.7
Dropping an Object
from a Tower

Directory: CHAP5
File: FREEFALL.PAS

```
program FreeFall (Input, Output);
{
  Displays the height of an object dropped
  from a tower until it hits the ground
}
  const
    G = 9.80665;      {gravitational constant for metric units}

  var
    Tower,            {input - height of tower}
    DeltaT,           {input - time interval}
    T,                {output - elapsed time}
    Height : Real;    {output - height of object}
```

▷ ▷ ▷ ▷ ▷

```
begin {FreeFall}
  {Enter tower height and time interval.}
  Write ('Tower height in meters> ');
  ReadLn (Tower);
  Write ('Time in seconds between table lines> ');
  ReadLn (DeltaT);

  {Display object height until it hits the ground.}
  WriteLn;
  WriteLn ('Time' :10, 'Height' :10);
  T := 0.0;
  Height := Tower;
  while Height > 0.0 do
    begin
      WriteLn (T :10:2, Height :10:2);
      T := T + DeltaT;
      Height := Tower - 0.5 * G * Sqr(T)
    end; {while}

  {Object hits the ground.}
  WriteLn;
  WriteLn ('SPLATT!!!')
end. {FreeFall}
```

Sample Run

```
Tower height in meters> 100.0
Time in seconds between table lines> 1.0

      Time    Height
      0.00    100.00
      1.00     95.10
      2.00     80.39
      3.00     55.87
      4.00     21.55

SPLATT!!!
```

computes the object height (from requirement 2), where distance traveled is represented by the formula

$$distance = \tfrac{1}{2} g t^2$$

and g is the gravitational constant.

The number of loop iterations depends on the time interval between iterations (DeltaT) and the tower height (Tower), both of which are input data. During each iteration, the current elapsed time, T, and the current object height, Height, are displayed on a new table line, and new values are assigned to these variables. The message following the table is displayed when the object hits the ground. ▲

Program Style

Displaying a Table

The program in Fig. 5.7 displays a table of output values. Before the loop is reached, the statement

```
WriteLn ('Time' :10, 'Height' :10);
```

displays the two strings that appear in the table headings. Since a string is printed right-justified in its field (see Table 2.13), the rightmost character of the first string appears in column 10 and that of the second string in column 20 (10 + 10).

Within the loop body, the statement

```
WriteLn (T :10:2, Height :10:2);
```

displays a pair of output values each time it is executed. The rightmost digit of the first number appears in column 10 and that of the second number in column 20. Therefore a table consisting of two columns of numbers is displayed, each right-aligned with its respective heading. Make sure that the field width (10, in this case) is big enough to accommodate the largest value to be printed.

Another technique for using loop requirements to design a loop is to work backward from the results to determine which initial values will produce those results. In the next example, we use this technique to determine the initialization steps for a loop.

EXAMPLE 5.4: Working Backward to Determine Loop Initialization ▼

Your 10-year-old cousin is learning the binary number system and has asked you to write a program that displays all powers of 2 that are less than a certain value (say, 10,000). Assuming that each power of 2 is stored in the variable Power, we can make two observations about the loop:

1. Power during the next iteration is 2 times Power during the current iteration.
2. Power must be $\geq$ 10,000 just after loop exit.

Requirement 1 derives from the fact that the powers of 2 are all multiples of 2, and requirement 2 from the fact that only powers less than 10,000 are to be displayed. From requirement 1, we know that Power must be multiplied by 2 in the loop body. From requirement 2, we know that loop exit should occur if Power >= 10000 is true, so the loop repetition condition is Power < 10000.

These considerations lead us to the following outline:

1. Initialize `Power` to _____
2. `while Power < 10000 do`
    `begin`
        3. Display `Power`
        4. Multiply `Power` by 2
    `end`

One way to complete step 1 is to ask what value should be displayed during the first loop iteration. Since the value of any number raised to the power 0 is 1, initializing `Power` to 1,

1. Initialize `Power` to 1

will cause step 3 to display the correct value for `Power` during the first iteration. The second iteration will display 1×2 or 2 (2^1); the third iteration will display 2×2 or 4 (2^2); the fourth iteration will display 4×2 or 8 (2^3); and so on. ▲

Using Templates to Design Loops

Because many loops have similar structures, we can create general frameworks, or templates, to use in designing these common loops.

Counter-Controlled Loops

We used counters to control the loops in Figs. 5.1 and 5.4. Although they can serve many different purposes, we can standardize the steps of a counter-controlled loop in the following template:

Template for Counter-Controlled Loop

1. Set *counter variable* to 0
2. `while` *counter variable* < *final value* `do`
    `begin`
        . . .
        3. Increase *counter variable* by 1
    `end`

Two more common loops are sentinel loops and loops controlled by Boolean flags. These loops, too, can be standardized into templates to help with their design.

Sentinel-Controlled Loops

Many programs with loops read one or more additional data items each time they repeat the loop body. Often we don't know how many data items the loop should process when it begins execution, and so we must find a way to signal the program to stop reading and processing new data.

One approach is to instruct the user to enter a unique data value, called a **sentinel value,** after the last data item. The loop-repetition condition tests each data item and causes loop exit when the sentinel value is read. Choose the sentinel value carefully; it must be a value that could not normally occur as data.

A program that calculates the sum of a collection of exam scores is a candidate for using a sentinel value. if the class is large, the instructor may not know the exact number of students who took the exam being graded. The program should work regardless of class size. The following loop uses Sum as an accumulator variable and Score as an input variable:

1. Initialize Sum to 0
2. Read the first score into Score
3. while Score is not the sentinel do
       begin
           4. Add Score to Sum
           5. Read the next score into Score
       end

Step 2 reads the first data value into Score before the loop is reached. In the loop body, step 4 adds each score to Sum (initial value is 0) and step 5 reads each data value in turn, including the sentinel value. The loop repeats as long as the previous data value read is not the sentinel, each iteration causing the previous data value to be added to Sum and the next data value to be read into Score. Because the loop exit occurs right after the sentinel value is read, the sentinel is not added to Sum.

Two of these steps read data into Score, steps 2 and 5. The initial read before the loop (step 2) reads only the first score and is called the *priming read*. This step is analogous to priming a pump, which is done by pouring a cup of water into the pump chamber before the pump can draw water out of a well.

Figure 5.8 shows a Pascal program that codes this loop. The sentinel value is -1 because all exam scores should be nonnegative. The constant declaration

```
const
  Sentinel = -1;             {sentinel value}
```

associates the constant Sentinel with the sentinel value.

Although it may seem strange at first to see the statement

```
ReadLn (Score);
```

sentinel value

an end marker that follows the last data item

at two different points in the program, this is a perfectly good programming practice and causes no problems. The sample run in Fig. 5.8 processes the scores 55, 33, and 77. The sentinel value (-1) is the last data value read, but it is not included in the sum.

Figure 5.8
Using a Sentinel-
Controlled Loop

Directory: CHAP5
File: SUMSCORE.PAS

```
program SumScores (Input, Output);
{Accumulates the sum of exam scores}

   const
      Sentinel = -1;               {sentinel value}

   var
      Score,                       {input - each exam score}
      Sum : Integer;               {output - sum of scores}

begin {SumScores}
   {Accumulate the sum.}
   Sum := 0;
   WriteLn ('When done, enter -1 to stop.');
   Write ('Enter the first score> ');
   ReadLn (Score);
   while Score <> Sentinel do
      begin
         Sum := Sum + Score;
         Write ('Enter the next  score> ');
         ReadLn (Score)
      end; {while}

   {Display the sum.}
   WriteLn;
   WriteLn ('Sum of exam scores is ', Sum :1)
end. {SumScores}
```

Sample Run

```
When done, enter -1 to stop.
Enter the first score> 55
Enter the next  score> 33
Enter the next  score> 77
Enter the next  score> -1

Sum of exam scores is 165
```

We should verify that the program is correct when no data items remain to be processed. In that case, enter the sentinel value as the "first score." The loop exit would occur right after the first (and only) test of the loop-repetition condition, so the loop body would not execute (zero-iteration loop). Sum would retain its initial value of 0, which would be correct.

Template for a Sentinel-Controlled Loop

1. Read the first value of *input variable*
2. while *input variable* is not equal to the sentinel do
        begin

        . . .
                3. Read the next value of *input variable*
        end

The sentinel value must be a value that would not be entered as a normal data item and must not be processed in the loop body. To enhance program readability, we usually store the sentinel value in a constant.

Loops Controlled by Boolean Flags

flag
a Boolean variable whose value is changed from False to True when a particular event occurs

Another common event-controlled loop is one whose execution is controlled by a Boolean variable. A **program flag,** or **flag,** is a Boolean variable whose value (True or False) signals whether a particular event occurs. The flag value should be set to False initially and reset to True when the event occurs. A flag-controlled loop executes until the event being monitored occurs.

For example, assume a program reads various data characters typed at the keyboard, but we are only interested in digit characters (0, 1, . . .). Consequently, our program should ignore any blanks, letters, symbols, and so on, and store the first digit character that it reads. A Boolean variable, say, DigitRead, could be used as a flag to monitor whether a digit character has been read:

Program variable
```
DigitRead : Boolean   {program flag - value is False until
                       a digit character is read; after a
                       digit character is read, value is True}
```

Because no characters have been read before the data entry loop executes, we should initialize DigitRead to False. The while loop must continue to execute as long as DigitRead is False, because this means that the event "digit character read as data" has not yet occurred. Therefore the loop repetition condition should be not DigitRead, because this condition is True when DigitRead is False. Within the loop body, we will read each data character and set the value of DigitRead to True if that data character is a digit. The while loop follows:

```
DigitRead := False;        {Assume no digit character was read.}
while not DigitRead do
   begin
     Write ('Enter another data character> ');
     ReadLn (NextChar);
     DigitRead := ('0' <= NextChar) and (NextChar <= '9')
   end {while}
```

Inside the loop body, the assignment statement

```
DigitRead := ('0' <= NextChar) and (NextChar <= '9')
```

assigns a value of True to DigitRead if NextChar is a digit character (within the range '0' through '9'); otherwise, DigitRead remains False. If DigitRead becomes True, loop exit occurs; if DigitRead remains False, the loop continues to execute until a digit character is finally read.

Template for a Flag-Controlled Loop

1. Initialize *flag* to False
2. while not *flag* do
    begin

      . . .

        3. Reset *flag* to True if the event being monitored occurs
    end

The last step in the loop body updates the flag value, setting it to True after the first occurrence of the event being monitored.

Exercises for Section 5.4

Self-Check

1. When generating a table in a loop, why is it necessary to add format specifiers to every output list item including integers (which cannot have decimal places)?
2. Why would it be incorrect to move the assignment statement in the sentinel-controlled loop of Fig. 5.8 to the end of the loop body?
3. Rewrite the sentinel-controlled loop in Fig. 5.8 as a flag-controlled loop. In this case the event being monitored would be "sentinel value was read."
4. When would a flag-controlled loop be a better choice than a sentinel-controlled loop?

Programming

1. Write a program to maintain a checkbook. It should first ask for a balance, then for transactions, and enter deposits as positive values and checks as negative values. After each check or deposit, the new balance should be printed. Use 0 as a sentinel value.

2. Write a program segment that allows the user to enter values and prints out the number of positive values entered and the number of negative values entered. Use 0 as the sentinel value.

3. Write a `while` loop that displays all powers of an integer, *n,* less than a specified value, `MaxPower`. On each line of a table, show the power (0, 1, 2, . . .) and the value of the integer *n* raised to that power.

4. Write a loop that prints a table of angle measures along with their sine and cosine values. Assume that the initial and final angle measures (in degrees) are available in `InitDeg` and `FinalDeg` (type `Real`), respectively, and that the change in angle measure between table entries is given by `StepDeg`. *Hint:* Don't forget to change degrees to radians.

5. Write a flag-controlled loop that continues to read pairs of integers until it reads a pair with the property that the first integer in the pair is evenly divisible by the second.

5.5 The for Statement

In addition to the `while` statement, Pascal provides another statement for writing counter-controlled loops. The `for` statement condenses the code for a counter-controlled loop, as you can see by comparing this pseudocode:

Pseudocode for `for` Loop	**Pseudocode for `while` Loop**

`for` *counter* := *initial* `to` *final* `do`
  `begin`
    . . .
  `end {for}`
	counter := *initial*;
	`while` *counter* <= *final* `do`
	    `begin`
	      . . .
	      counter := *counter* + 1
	    `end {while}`

The `for` loop header (the first line) specifies all manipulation of the counter variable (the color lines in the `while` loop). These three operations are as follows:

▶ Initialize *counter* to *initial.*
▶ Test if *counter* <= *final*
▶ Increment *counter* to its next value before each test.

EXAMPLE 5.5 ▼

The following two loops produce the same results:

for **loop**	while **loop**
| ```
{Print N blank lines.}
for Line := 1 to N do
   WriteLn
``` | ```
{Print N blank lines.}
Line := 1;
while Line <= N do
   begin
      WriteLn;
      Line := Line + 1
   end {while}
``` |

If Line is declared as an integer variable, the for statement causes the WriteLn operation to be performed N times. The for loop implementation is shorter because it does not require the assignment statements

```
Line := 1;
Line := Line + 1
```

which initialize and update the counter Line. ▲

We describe the for statement syntax next and diagram it in Fig. 5.9.

SYNTAX DISPLAY

The for Statement

Form: for *counter* := *initial* to *final* do
                statement

             for *counter* := *initial* downto *final* do
                statement

Example: ```
for I := 1 to 5 do
   begin
      ReadLn (InData, NextNum);
      Sum := Sum + NextNum
   end; {for}
```

```
for CountDown := 10 downto 0 do
   WriteLn (Countdown :2)
```

Interpretation: The *statement* that comprises the loop body is executed once for each value of *counter* between *initial* and *final,* inclusive. *initial* and *final* may be constants, variables, or expressions of the same ordinal type as *counter*. Use downto instead of to if *initial* is greater than *final*. In this case, *initial* is decremented by 1 after each loop repetition.

Note 1: The value of *counter* must not be modified in *statement*.

Note 2: The value of *final* is computed once, just before loop entry. Changing the value of *final* in the loop body will have no effect on the number of iterations performed.

Note 3: After loop exit, the *counter* variable is undefined.

Note 4: *statement* is not executed if *initial* is greater than *final*. (In the downto form, *statement* is not executed if *initial* is less than *final*.)
```

Figure 5.9
Syntax Diagram of the for Statement

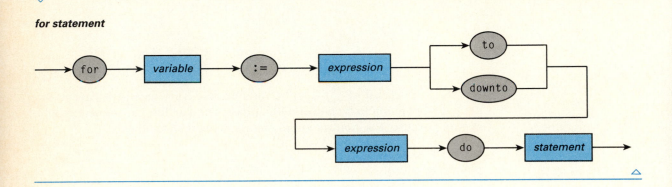

for statement

EXAMPLE 5.6 ▼

The `for` statement in Fig. 5.10 reads payroll data for seven employees and computes and displays each employee's weekly pay. Compare it with the `while` statement shown in Fig. 5.1.

Read the first line of Fig. 5.10 as "`for` each value of `EmpNumber` from `1` to `7 do`." You needn't provide additional Pascal statements to set `EmpNumber` to an initial value or to update the value of `EmpNumber`; these two operations are automatically performed in a `for` loop. ▲

Like a `while` statement, the counter variable in a `for` statement can be used in a computation; unlike a `while` statement, however, its value cannot be changed in the loop body. In the next example, you'll see a `for` statement that uses its counter variable as a function argument.

Figure 5.10
for Loop to Process Seven
Employees

```
for EmpNumber := 1 to 7 do
   begin
      Write ('Hours> ');
      ReadLn (Hours);
      Write ('Rate> $');
      ReadLn (Rate);
      Pay := Hours * Rate;
      WriteLn ('Weekly pay is $', Pay :4:2)
   end; {for}

WriteLn ('All employees processed')
```

EXAMPLE 5.7 ▼

The for loop in Fig. 5.11 prints a list of integer values and their squares and square roots. During each repetition of the loop body, the statements

```
Square := Sqr(I);
Root := Sqrt(I);
```

compute the square and square root of the counter variable I; then the values of I, Square, and Root, are displayed. Table 5.2 traces the execution of the for loop.

Table 5.2
Trace of Program in
Figure 5.11

Statement	I	Square	Root	Effect
	?	?	?	
for I := 1 to MaxI	1			Initialize I to 1.
Square := Sqr(I);		1		Assign 1 to Square.
Root := Sqrt(I);			1.0	Assign 1.0 to Root.
WriteLn ...				Print 1, 1, 1.0.
Increment and test I	2			2 <= 4 is true.
Square := Sqr(I);		4		Assign 4 to Square.
Root := Sqrt(I);			1.4	Assign 1.4 to Root.
WriteLn ...				Print 2, 4, 1.4.
Increment and test I	3			3 <= 4 is true.
Square := Sqr(I);		9		Assign 9 to Square.
Root := Sqrt(I);			1.7	Assign 1.7 to Root.
WriteLn ...				Print 3, 9, 1.7.
Increment and test I	4			4 <= 4 is true.
Square := Sqr(I);		16		Assign 16 to Square.
Root := Sqrt(I);			2.0	Assign 2.0 to Root.
WriteLn ...				Print 4, 16, 2.0.
Increment and test I	5			5 <= 4 is false.
	?			Exit loop.

Figure 5.11
Table of Integers, Squares,
and Square Roots

Directory: CHAP5
File: SQUARES.PAS

▽

```pascal
program Squares (Input, Output);
{Displays a table of integers and their squares and square roots}

  const
    MaxI = 4;                {largest integer in table}

  var
    I,                       {counter variable}
    Square : Integer;        {output - square of I}
    Root : Real;             {output - square root of I}

begin {Squares}
  {Prints a list of integers, their squares, and their square roots}
  WriteLn ('I' :10, 'I * I' :10, 'Square root' :15);
  for I := 1 to MaxI do
    begin
      Square := Sqr(I);
      Root := Sqrt(I);
      WriteLn (I :10, Square :10, Root :15:1)
    end {for}
end. {Squares}
```

Sample Run

```
    I      I * I   Square root
    1        1          1.0
    2        4          1.4
    3        9          1.7
    4       16          2.0
```

△

The trace in Table 5.2 shows that the counter variable I is initialized to 1 when the for loop is reached. After each loop repetition, I is incremented by 1 and tested to see whether its value is still less than or equal to MaxI (4). If the test result is true, the loop body is executed again, and the next values of I, Square, and Root are printed. If the test result is false, the loop is exited.

I is equal to MaxI during the last loop repetition; however, I becomes undefined when the loop is exited. You should not reference the variable I again until it is given a new value. ▲

Type Char Counter Variables

The `for` loop can be used with other ordinal types besides `Integer`. The next example uses a counter variable of type `Char`.

EXAMPLE 5.8 ▼

The next `for` loop displays the uppercase letters on a line. The counter variable, `NextCh`, must be type `Char`.

```
for NextCh := 'A' to 'Z' do
   Write (NextCh);
WriteLn    ▲
```

Counting Down

The examples given so far have used the reserved word `to` and increased the value of the counter variable after each loop repetition. If the reserved word `downto` is used instead, the value of the counter variable decreases after each loop repetition.

EXAMPLE 5.9 ▼

A student wants a table equating Celsius temperatures from 5 degrees to -10 degrees with Fahrenheit temperatures. She could use the following `for` loop:

```
for Celsius := 5 downto -10 do
   begin
      Fahrenheit := 1.8 * Celsius + 32;
      WriteLn (Celsius :10, Fahrenheit :15:1)
   end {for}   ▲
```

Exercises for Section 5.5   *Self-Check*

1. Trace the following program fragments:

   ```
   J := 10;
   for I := 1 to 5 do
      begin
         WriteLn (I, J);
         J := J - 2
      end; {for}
   ```

2. What is the minimum number of times the statement that comprises the `for` loop body can be executed? Give an example program fragment that will execute that minimum number of times.

3. Write `for` loop headers that process all values of `Celsius` (type `Integer`) in the following ranges:
   a. -10 through +10   c. 15 through 50
   b. 100 through 1   d. 50 through -75

4. Variables of which data types can be declared as `for` loop counter variables?

Programming

1. Write a `for` statement that computes the sum of the odd integers in the range 0 to 100, inclusive.
2. Write a program fragment with a `for` statement that accumulates the total number of days for the years 1950 to the year 2000. Remember, any year divisible by 4 is a leap year and has 366 days.

5.6   The repeat Statement

The `repeat` statement specifies a conditional loop that is repeated `until` its condition becomes true. Such a loop is called a *repeat-until* loop. To illustrate, compare two program segments that print the powers of 2 between 1 and 1000:

repeat **statement**	while **statement**
| ```
Power := 1;
repeat
   Write (Power :5);
   Power := Power * 2
until Power >= 1000
``` | ```
Power := 1;
while Power < 1000 do
   begin
      Write (Power :5);
      Power := Power * 2
   end {while}
``` |

logical complements
Boolean expressions with opposite values

The test in the `repeat-until` loop (Power >= 1000) is the **logical complement,** or opposite, of the test in the `while` loop. In the former, the loop body is repeated until the value of Power is greater than or equal to 1000. Since loop repetition *stops* when the condition is true, the test is called a **loop-termination test** rather than a loop-repetition test.

loop-termination test
the condition following `until` that causes loop exit when it becomes `True`

We describe the `repeat` statement syntax and diagram it in Fig. 5.12. Note that there is no need for a `begin-end` bracket around the loop body because the reserved words `repeat` and `until` perform this function.

Figure 5.12
Syntax Diagram of the repeat Statement

SYNTAX DISPLAY

The repeat Statement (repeat-until Loop)

Form: repeat
             loop-body
          until *termination-condition*
Example: repeat
             Write ('Enter a digit> ');
             Read (Ch)
          until ('0' <= Ch) and (Ch <= '9')

Interpretation: After each execution of *loop body, termination-condition* is evaluated. If *termination-condition* is true, loop exit occurs and the next program statement is executed. If *termination-condition* is false, *loop-body* is repeated. The *loop body* always executes at least once.

EXAMPLE 5.10 ▼

The program in Fig. 5.13 uses a repeat-until loop to find the largest value in a sequence of data items. The variable Item holds each data item, and the variable LargestSoFar saves the largest data value encountered. Within the loop, the if statement

```
if Item > LargestSoFar then
   LargestSoFar := Item         {Save the new largest number.}
```

Figure 5.13
Finding the Largest Value

Directory: CHAP5
File: LARGEST.PAS

```
program Largest (Input, Output);
{Finds the largest number in a sequence of integer values}
   const
      MinValue = -MaxInt;       {a very small integer}

   var
      Item,                     {input - each data value}
      LargestSoFar : Integer;   {output - largest value so far}

begin  {Largest}
   {Initialize LargestSoFar to a very small integer.}
   LargestSoFar := MinValue;

   {Save the largest number encountered so far.}
   WriteLn ('Finding the largest value in a sequence:');
   repeat
      Write ('Enter an integer or ', MinValue :1, ' to stop> ');
      ReadLn (Item);
      if Item > LargestSoFar then
         LargestSoFar := Item        {Save the new largest number.}
   until Item = MinValue;

   WriteLn ('The largest value entered was ', LargestSoFar :1)
end. {Largest}
```

▷ ▷ ▷ ▷ ▷ ▷

Sample Run

```
Finding the largest value in a sequence:
Enter an integer or -32767 to stop> -999
Enter an integer or -32767 to stop> 500
Enter an integer or -32767 to stop> 100
Enter an integer or -32767 to stop> -32767
The largest value entered was 500
```

redefines the value of `LargestSoFar` if the current data item is larger than all previous data values.

The constant `MinValue`, which represents a very small integer value, serves two purposes. Initializing `LargestSoFar` to `MinValue` before loop entry makes the condition `Item > LargestSoFar` true during the first iteration, so the first data item is saved as the largest value so far. `MinValue` is also a sentinel value because it is unlikely to be entered as a data item for a program that is finding the largest number in a sequence. ▲

EXAMPLE 5.11 ▼

menu-driven program
a program containing a loop that displays a menu of operations. The user selects the next operation from the menu.

In some applications programs, a menu appears at the top of the screen displaying possible actions. A program that uses a menu to determine its next operation is called a **menu-driven program.** For example, a statistics program might list its possible operations in the following menu form and the program user would enter an integer between 1 and 6 to select the next program operation.

```
1. Compute an average.
2. Compute a standard deviation.
3. Find the median.
4. Find the smallest and largest values.
5. Plot the data.
6. Exit the program.
```

A repeat statement can serve as the main control statement for a menu-driven program, as shown in this pseudocode:

```
repeat
    Display the menu
    Read the user's choice
    Perform the user's choice
until user's choice is exit program
```

The program fragment in Fig. 5.14 implements this loop. For each iteration, procedure `DisplayMenu` displays the menu and then the user's choice is read into `Choice` and passed on to procedure `DoChoice`. The loop repeats until the user's choice is `ExitChoice` (value is 6). ▲

Figure 5.14
Main Control Loop for
Menu-Driven Program

```
repeat
    DisplayMenu;                        {Display the menu choices.}
    WriteLn ('Enter a number between 1 and ', ExitChoice :1);
    ReadLn (Choice);
    DoChoice (Choice)                   {Perform the user's choice.}
until Choice = ExitChoice
```

Complementing a Boolean Expression

To replace a while statement with a repeat statement, you need to know the complement of the while loop repetition condition. To complement a simple comparison, change its operator as shown in the table (e.g., Power >= 1000 and Power < 1000 are complements):

Operator	Operator in Complement
<	>=
<=	>
>	<=
>=	<
=	<>
<>	=

You would form the complement of a Boolean expression by preceding the entire expression with not. For example, the Boolean expression

(Ch >= 'a') and (Ch <= 'z')

is true when Ch is a lowercase letter. The complement of this expression is

not ((Ch >= 'a') and (Ch <= 'z'))

Also, *DeMorgan's theorem*, which is

not (*expression*$_1$ and *expression*$_2$) = (not *expression*$_1$) or (not *expression*$_2$)

not (*expression*$_1$ or *expression*$_2$) = (not *expression*$_1$) and (not *expression*$_2$)

provides another way to complement a Boolean expression containing and and or operators: Write the complement of each individual Boolean expression and change each and to or and each or to and. Using DeMorgan's theorem, the complement of the original expression would be

```
(Ch < 'a') or (Ch > 'z')
```

which is true if `Ch` is not a lowercase letter.

Review of for, while, and repeat Statements

Pascal contains three kinds of loop-control statements: `for`, `while`, and `repeat`. Use the `for` statement to write counting loops, that is, loops for which you know the number of iterations at the beginning of loop execution. The loop-control variable of a `for` statement must belong to an ordinal type (not `Real`).

Use the `while` and `repeat` statements to write event-controlled or conditional loops, loops whose number of iterations depends on the value (`True` or `False`) of a condition. The loop body in a `while` statement is repeated as long as its loop-repetition condition is true; the loop body in a `repeat` statement is repeated until its loop-termination condition becomes true. It is relatively easy to rewrite a `repeat-until` loop as a `while` loop by complementing the condition. However, not all `while` loops can be written as `repeat-until` loops, because the loop body of a `repeat-until` loop will always execute at least once, whereas a `while` loop body may be skipped entirely. For this reason, a `while` loop is preferred over a `repeat-until` loop unless it is certain that at least one loop iteration must always be performed.

To illustrate the three loop forms, Fig. 5.15 presents three versions of a simple counting loop. (The ellipses represent the loop body.) The `for` statement is the best choice in this situation. The `repeat-until` loop must be

Figure 5.15

Comparison of the Three Loop Forms

```
for Count := StartValue to StopValue do        {for loop}
   begin
   ...
   end {for}

Count := StartValue;                           {while loop}
while Count <= StopValue do
   begin
   ...
      Count := Count + 1
   end {while}

Count := StartValue;                           {repeat-until loop}
if StartValue <= StopValue then
   repeat
   ...
      Count := Count + 1
   until Count > StopValue
```

nested in an `if` statement to prevent it from being executed when `Start-Value` is greater than `StopValue`. For this reason, the `repeat-until` version of a counting loop is least desirable.

In Fig. 5.15, `Count`, `StartValue`, and `StopValue` must all be the same ordinal type. The assignment statement

```
Count := Count + 1
```

is used in both the `while` and `repeat` loops to update the loop-control variable `Count`, but is not required in the `for` loop.

Exercises for Section 5.6 **Self-Check**

1. Use DeMorgan's theorem to complement the following conditions:

   a. `(X <= Y) and (X <> 15)` d. `Flag or not (X <> 15.7)`
   b. `(X <= Y) or (Z = 7.5)` e. `not Flag and (X <= 8)`
   c. `(X <> 15) or (Z = 7.5) and (X <= Y)`

2. What would the following `repeat` statement display? What is the difference between `repeat ... until False` and `while False do`?

   ```
   repeat
      WriteLn ('False conditional example.')
   until False
   ```

3. When would you use a `repeat-until` loop rather than a `while` loop?

Programming

1. Write a program fragment that continues to read data values as long as they are not decreasing. The fragment should stop reading whenever a number smaller than the preceding one is entered. Write two versions: one with `repeat` and one with `while`.
2. Write a program fragment for the main control loop in a menu-driven program that updates an account balance (W = withdrawal, D = deposit, Q = quit). Assume that procedures `ProcessWithdrawal` and `ProcessDeposit` already exist and are called with the actual parameter `Balance`. Prompt the user for a transaction code (W, D, or Q) and call the appropriate procedure.

5.7 Nested Loops

Loops can be nested just as `if` statements are. Nested loops consist of an outer loop with one or more inner loops. Each time the outer loop is repeated, the inner loops are reentered, their loop-control expressions are reevaluated, and all required iterations are performed.

EXAMPLE 5.12 ▼

Figure 5.16 shows a sample run of a program with two nested `for` loops. The outer loop is repeated three times (for I equals 1, 2, 3). Each time the outer loop is repeated, the statement

```
WriteLn ('Outer' :5, I :7);
```

displays the string `'Outer'` and the value of I (the outer loop-control variable). Next the inner loop is entered, and its loop-control variable, J, is reset to 1. The number of times the inner loop is repeated depends on the current value of I. Each time the inner loop is repeated, the statement

```
WriteLn ('Inner' :7, I :5, J :5)
```

displays the string `'Inner'` and the value of I and J.

The outer loop-control variable, I, is also the expression whose value determines the number of repetitions of the inner loop. Although this is per-

Figure 5.16
Program with Nested
for Loops

Directory: CHAP5
File: NESTLOOP.PAS

```pascal
program NestLoop (Input, Output);
{Illustrates a pair of nested for loops}

   var
      I, J : Integer;                    {loop-control variables}

begin   {NestLoop}
   WriteLn ('I' :12, 'J' :5);      {Print heading.}
   for I := 1 to 3 do
      begin {outer loop}
         WriteLn ('Outer' :5, I :7);
         for J := 1 to I do
            WriteLn ('Inner' :7, I :5, J :5)
      end {outer loop}
end.    {NestLoop}
```

Sample Run

```
                I    J
Outer           1
   Inner        1    1
Outer           2
   Inner        2    1
   Inner        2    2
Outer           3
   Inner        3    1
   Inner        3    2
   Inner        3    3
```

fectly valid, you cannot use the same variable as the loop-control variable of both an outer and an inner `for` loop in the same nest. ▲

EXAMPLE 5.13 ▼

Program `Triangle` (Fig. 5.17) uses an outer loop (loop-control variable `Row`) and two inner loops to draw an isosceles triangle. Each time the outer loop is repeated, the two inner loops are executed. The first inner loop prints the leading blank spaces; the second inner loop prints one or more asterisks.

The outer loop is repeated five times; the value of `Row` determines the number of repetitions performed by the inner loops. Table 5.3 lists the inner loop-control parameters for each value of `Row`. Four blanks and one asterisk are printed when `Row` is 1, three blanks and three asterisks are printed when `Row` is 2, and so on. When `Row` is 5, the first inner loop is skipped, and nine (2 * 5 - 1) asterisks are printed. ▲

Figure 5.17
Isosceles Triangle Program

Directory: CHAP5
File: TRIANGLE.PAS

▽

```pascal
program Triangle (Input, Output);
{Draws an isosceles triangle}

   const
      NumLines = 5;              {number of rows in triangle}
      Blank = ' ';               {output characters}
      Star = '*';

   var
      Row,                          {loop control for outer loop}
      LeadBlanks,              {loop control for first inner loop}
      CountStars : Integer; {loop control for second inner loop}

begin  {Triangle}
   for Row := 1 to NumLines do
      begin                           {Draw each row.}
         for LeadBlanks := NumLines - Row downto 1 do
            Write (Blank);               {Print leading blanks.}

         for CountStars := 1 to 2 * Row - 1 do
            Write (Star);                   {Print asterisks.}
         WriteLn                            {Terminate line.}
      end  {for Row}
end.  {Triangle}
```

Sample Run

```
    *
   ***
  *****
 *******
*********
```

△

Table 5.3

Inner Loop-Control Parameters

Row	LeadBlanks	CountStars	Effect
1	4 downto 1	1 to 1	Displays 4 blanks and 1 star
2	3 downto 1	1 to 3	Displays 3 blanks and 3 stars
3	2 downto 1	1 to 5	Displays 2 blanks and 5 stars
4	1 downto 1	1 to 7	Displays 1 blank and 7 stars
5	0	1 to 9	Displays 9 stars

Exercises for Section 5.7

Self-Check

1. What is displayed by the following program fragments, assuming M is 3 and N is 5?

    a.
```
for I := 1 to N do
   begin
      for J := 1 to I do
         Write ('*');
      WriteLn
   end {for I}
```
    b.
```
for I := N downto 1 do
   begin
      for J := M downto 1 do
         Write ('*');
      WriteLn
   end {for I}
```

2. Show the output printed by the following nested loops:

```
for I := 1 to 2 do
   begin
      WriteLn ('Outer' :5, I :5);
      for J := 1 to 3 do
         WriteLn ('Inner' :7, I :3, J :3);
      for K := 2 downto 1 do
         WriteLn ('Inner' :7, I :3, K :3)
   end {for I}
```

Programming

1. Write a program fragment that, given an input value *N*, displays *N* rows of the form 1 2 . . . *N*, 2 3 . . . *N* + 1, and so on—a barber pole pattern of numbers. As an example, for an input value of 5, display:

```
1 2 3 4 5
2 3 4 5 6
3 4 5 6 7
4 5 6 7 8
5 6 7 8 9
```

2. Write a program that prints a nicely labeled multiplication table for the digits 0 through 9.

5.8   Debugging and Testing Programs

In Section 2.10, we described the three general categories of errors: syntax errors, run-time errors, and logic errors. Sometimes the cause of a run-time error or the source of a logic error is apparent and the error can be fixed easily. Often, however, the error is not obvious and may require considerable time to locate.

The first step in locating a hidden error is to examine the program output to determine which part of the program is generating incorrect results. Then you can focus on the statements in that section to determine which are at fault. To find problem areas during debugging, insert extra `WriteLn` statements to display intermediate results at different points in your program. For example, if the loop in Fig. 5.8 is not computing the correct sum, the following diagnostic `WriteLn` statement in color will display each value of `Score` and `Sum`. The asterisks highlight the diagnostic output in the debugging runs and the diagnostic `WriteLn` statements in the source program.

```
ReadLn (Score);
while Score <> Sentinel do
   begin
      Sum := Sum + Score;
      WriteLn ('***** score is ', Score, ' sum is ', Sum);
      Write ('Enter the next score> ');
      ReadLn (Score)
   end {while}
```

Be careful when inserting diagnostic `WriteLn` statements. Sometimes you must add a `begin-end` bracket if a single statement inside an `if` or a `while` statement becomes a compound statement when you add a diagnostic `WriteLn`. If you insert a `WriteLn` statement after the last statement in a loop body, don't forget to precede the `WriteLn` with a semicolon.

Once it appears that you have located the error, avoid the temptation to take out the diagnostic `WriteLn` statements. Instead, as a temporary measure, turn the diagnostic statements into comments by enclosing them in braces. In this way, if the same errors crop up again in later testing, removing the braces will be easier than retyping the diagnostic statements.

Off-by-One Loop Errors

A fairly common logic error is a loop that executes one more or one less time than it should. If a sentinel-controlled `while` loop performs an extra repetition, it may erroneously process the sentinel value along with the regular data.

If a `while` loop performs a counting operation, make sure that the initial and final values of the loop-control variable are correct. For example, the following loop body executes $N + 1$ times instead of N times. If you want the loop body to execute exactly N times, change the `while` condition to `Count < N`.

```
Count := 0;
while Count <= N do
  begin
    Sum := Sum + Count;
    Count := Count + 1
  end {while}
```

Checking Loop Boundaries

You can determine whether a loop is correct by checking the *loop boundaries,* that is, the initial and final values of the loop-control variable. For a `for` loop, carefully evaluate the *initial expression* and the *final expression* to see that their values make sense. Then substitute these values everywhere the counter variable appears in the loop body and verify that you get the expected results at the boundaries. As an example, in the `for` loop

```
Sum := 0;
for I := K to N - K do
  Sum := Sum + Sqr(I)
```

check that the first value of the counter variable `I` is supposed to be `K` and that the last value is supposed to be `N - K`. Next check that the assignment statement

```
Sum := Sum + Sqr(I)
```

is correct at these boundaries: When `I` is `K`, `Sum` gets the value of `K` squared, and when `I` is `N - K`, the value of $(N - K)^2$ is added to the previous `Sum`. As a final check, pick some small values of `N` and `K` (say, 3 and 1) and trace the loop execution to see that it computes `Sum` correctly for this case.

Using Debugger Programs

Many computer systems have *debugger programs* to help you debug a Pascal program. A debugger program lets you execute your program one statement at a time (*single-step execution*) so you can see the effect of each statement. You can select several variables whose values will be automatically displayed after each statement executes. This process allows you to trace the program's execution. Besides printing a diagnostic when a run-time error occurs, the debugger indicates the statement that caused the error and displays the values of the variables you selected.

You can also separate your program into segments by setting breakpoints at selected statements. A *breakpoint* is like a fence between two segments of a program. You can request the debugger to execute all statements from the last breakpoint up to the next breakpoint. When the program stops at a breakpoint, you can display selected variables and thus determine whether the program segment executed correctly. If a program segment executes correctly, you will want to execute through to the next breakpoint. If it does not, you may want to set more breakpoints within that segment or perhaps perform single-step execution through that segment.

Testing

After you have corrected all errors and the program appears to execute as expected, test it thoroughly to make sure it works. In Section 4.6, we discussed tracing an algorithm and suggested that you provide enough sets of test data to ensure that all possible paths are traced. The same is true for a completed program. Make enough test runs to verify that the program works properly for representative samples of all possible data combinations.

Exercises for Section 5.8   ***Self-Check***

1. For the `while` loop in the subsection entitled "Off-by-One Loop Errors," add debugging statements to show the value of the loop-control variable at the start of each repetition. Add additional debugging statements to show the value of Sum at the end of each loop repetition.
2. Why does the following code fragment fail? What are the loop boundaries for this code fragment?

```
X := 10;
repeat
  X := X - 1;
  WriteLn (X, Sqrt(X))
until X < 0
```

5.9   Common Programming Errors

Beginners sometimes confuse `if` and `while` statements because both statements contain a condition. Always use an `if` statement to implement a decision step and a `while` statement to implement a conditional loop.

Be careful when you use tests for inequality to control the repetition of a `while` loop. For instance, the following loop is intended to process all transactions for a bank account while the balance is positive:

```
while Balance <> 0.0 do
  Update (Balance)
```

If the bank balance goes from a positive to a negative amount without being exactly `0.0`, the loop will not terminate (an *infinite loop*). This loop would be safer:

```
while Balance > 0.0 do
  Update (Balance)
```

Be sure to verify that the repetition condition for a `while` loop will eventually become false. If you use a sentinel-controlled loop, remember to provide a prompt that tells the program user what value to enter as the sentinel. Make sure that the sentinel value cannot be confused with a normal data item.

If the loop body contains more than one statement, remember to bracket it with `begin` and `end` (unless it is a `repeat-until` loop). Otherwise, only the first statement will be repeated, and the remaining statements will be executed when and if the loop is exited. The following loop will not terminate, because the step that updates the loop-control variable is not considered part of the loop body. The program will continue to print the initial value of `Power` until you instruct the computer to terminate its execution.

```
while Power <= 10000 do
  WriteLn ('Next power of N is ', Power :6);
  Power := Power * N
```

Be sure to initialize to 0 an accumulator variable used for accumulating a sum by repeated addition and to initialize to 1 a variable used for accumulating a product by repeated multiplication. Omitting this step leads to inaccurate results.

The value of the counter variable in a `for` statement either increases by 1 (`to` form) or decreases by 1 (`downto` form) after each repetition. If `Larger` is greater than `Smaller`, the following `WriteLn` statement will not execute because the initial value that would be assigned to `I` is larger than its final value:

```
for I := Larger to Smaller do
  WriteLn (I)
```

Similarly, the next `WriteLn` statement will not execute because the initial value that would be assigned to `I` is smaller than its final value:

```
for I := Smaller downto Larger do
  WriteLn (I)
```

A `repeat-until` loop always executes at least once. Use a `repeat` statement only when certain that there is no possibility of zero loop iterations; otherwise, use a `while` loop.

Be sure to trace each nest of loops carefully, checking the inner and outer loop-control variables. The loop-control variable of an outer `for` statement cannot be changed inside an inner `for` statement. Also, you cannot use the same loop-control variable in two `for` statements within the same nest.

CHAPTER REVIEW

1. To repeat steps in a program, use either of two kinds of loops: counter-controlled (or counting loops) and event-controlled (or conditional loops). For a counter-controlled loop, the number of iterations required can be determined before the loop is entered. For an event-controlled loop, repetition continues until a special event or condition occurs.

   Template for a Counter-Controlled Loop

   Set *counter variable* to 0
   while *counter variable* < *final value* do
       begin
           . . .
           Increase *counter variable* by 1
       end

2. Pascal provides three statements for coding loops: while, for, and repeat. while and repeat can implement both kinds of loops; for can implement only counter-controlled loops.

3. In designing a loop, focus on both loop-control and loop-processing. For loop processing, make sure that the loop body contains steps that perform the operation that must be repeated. For loop control, you must provide steps that initialize, test, and update the loop control variable. Make sure that the initialization step leads to correct program results when the loop body is not executed (zero-iteration loop).

4. There are two common conditional loops: sentinel-controlled and flag-controlled. A sentinel-controlled loop stops repetition right after the sentinel value is read. Choose a value that cannot be a normal data item as the sentinel value. A flag-controlled loop tests a Boolean variable to determine whether a particular event has occurred.

   Template for a Sentinel-Controlled Loop

   Read the first value of *input variable*
   while *input variable* is not equal to the sentinel do
       begin
           . . .
           Read the next value of *input variable*
       end

   Template for a Flag-Controlled Loop

   Initialize *flag* to False
   while not *flag* do
       begin
           . . .
           Reset *flag* to True if the event being monitored occurs
       end

5.   The `while` statement is the most general of the three Pascal loop statements. Unlike a `for` or `while`, the body of a `repeat-until` loop is always executed at least once. In a `for` statement, the counter variable may increase in value (`to` form) or decrease in value (`downto` form) after each loop iteration. Remember that the final value expression for the counter variable is evaluated when the loop is first reached and cannot be changed during loop execution.

6.   Loops can be nested just like `if` statements. Each time an outer loop in a nest is repeated, every inner loop of the nest is reentered and executed to completion.

Summary of New Pascal Constructs

Construct	Effect
while *Statement*	

`Sum := 0;`
`while Sum <= MaxSum do`
  `begin`
    `Write ('Next integer> ');`
    `ReadLn (Next);`
    `Sum := Sum + Next`
  `end {while}`
	A collection of input data items is read, and their sum is accumulated in `Sum`. This process stops when the accumulated sum exceeds `MaxSum`.

for *Statement*	

`for CurMonth := 3 to 9 do`
  `begin`
    `ReadLn (MonthSales);`
    `YearSales := YearSales`
            `+ MonthSales`
  `end {for}`
	The loop body is repeated for each value of `CurMonth` from 3 to 9, inclusive. For each month, the value of `MonthSales` is read and added to `YearSales`.

repeat *Statement*	

`Sum := 0;`
`repeat`
  `ReadLn (NextInt);`
  `WriteLn (NextInt);`
  `Sum := Sum + NextInt`
`until NextInt = 0`
	Integer values are read, and their sum is accumulated in `Sum`. The process terminates after the first zero is read.

Quick-Check Exercises

1.   If the loop condition is a Boolean variable, what type of loop is this?
2.   It is an error if a `while` loop body never executes. True or false?
3.   The priming step for a sentinel-controlled loop is what kind of statement? Where is this statement placed? What is the purpose of a similar statement in the loop body?

4. The sentinel value is always the last value added to a sum being accumulated in a sentinel-controlled loop. True or false?

5. Which loop form (`for`, `repeat`, or `while`)
   a. executes at least once?
   b. is the most general?
   c. condenses the code for a counting loop?
   d. should be used in a menu-driven program?

6. What does the following segment display?

```
Product := 1;
Counter := 2;
while Counter <= 5 do
   begin
      Product := Product * Counter;
      Counter := Counter + 1
   end; {while}
WriteLn (Product)
```

7. A loop that performs an incorrect computation during its last iteration has a problem at the _____.

8. During execution of the following program segment,

```
for I := 1 to 10 do
   begin
      for J := 1 to I do
         Write (I * J);
      WriteLn
   end
```

   a. how many times does the `Write` statement execute?
   b. how many times does the `WriteLn` statement execute?
   c. what is the last value displayed?

9. What will be output by the following fragment?

```
N := 10;
for I := 1 to N do
   begin
      Write (I :3);
      N := N - I
   end; {for}
WriteLn (N :4)
```

Answers to Quick-Check Exercises

1. Flag-controlled loop
2. False
3. An input operation; just before loop entry and as the last statement in the loop body. The input operation in the loop body reads all but the first data item, which is read by the input operation before loop entry.
4. False—the sentinel should not be processed.
5. a. `repeat`   b. `while`   c. `for`   d. `repeat`
6. The value of 1 * 2 * 3 * 4 * 5, or 120.
7. loop boundary

8. a.   1 + 2 + 3 + ... + 9 + 10, or 55   b.   10   c.   100
9.   1 2 3 4 5 6 7 8 9 10 -45

Review Questions

1. How does a sentinel value differ from a program flag as a means of loop control?
2. For correct use of a sentinel value when reading in data, where should the input statements appear?
3. Write a program fragment that allows a user to input several pairs of values for X and Y and, for each pair, computes X raised to the Y power by repeated multiplication. The program should keep obtaining values from the user until a sentinel value of 0 is entered for X.
4. Hand trace the following program given these data:

```
4 2 8 4   1 4 2 1   9 3 3 1   -22 10 8 2   3 3 4 5

program Slopes (Input, Output);
  const
    StopValue = 0.0;
  var
    Slope, Y2, Y1, X2, X1 : Real;

begin {Slopes}
  WriteLn ('Enter four numbers separated by spaces');
  WriteLn ('The last two numbers cannot be the same, but');
  WriteLn ('The program terminates if the first two are.');
  WriteLn ('Enter four numbers> ');
  ReadLn (Y2, Y1, X2, X1);
  Slope := (Y2 - Y1) / (X2 - X1);
  while Slope <> StopValue do
    begin
      WriteLn ('Slope is ', Slope :5:2);
      WriteLn ('Enter four more numbers> ');
      ReadLn (Y2, Y1, X2, X1);
      Slope := (Y2 - Y1) / (X2 - X1)
    end {while}
end. {Slopes}
```

5. Can you always replace a while loop with a for or a repeat loop? Why or why not?
6. Consider the program segment

```
Count := 0;
for I := 1 to N do
  begin
    Read (X);
    if X = I then
      Count := Count + 1
  end {for}
```

a. Write a while loop equivalent to the for loop.
b. Write a repeat-until loop equivalent to the for loop.

Programming Projects

Directory: CHAP5
File: PROJ1.PAS

1. Write a program that will find the smallest, largest, and average values in a collection of N numbers. Read in the value of N before reading each value in the collection of N numbers.

2. Modify Programming Project 1 to compute and display both the range of values in the data collection and the standard deviation of the data collection. To compute the standard deviation, accumulate the sum of the data (Sum) and the sum of the squares of the data values (SumSquares) in the main loop. After loop exit, use the formula

$$Standard\ deviation = \sqrt{\frac{SumSquares - \frac{Sum^2}{N}}{N}}$$

3. Bunyan Lumber Co. needs to create a table of the engineering properties of its lumber. The dimensions of the wood are given as the base and the height in inches. Engineers need to know the following information about lumber:

   cross-sectional area = base × height
   moment of inertia = (base × height³)/12
   section modulus = (base × height²)/6

   The height sizes are 2, 4, 6, 8, and 10 inches. Produce a table with appropriate headings to show these values and the computed engineering properties. Do not duplicate a 2-by-6 board with a 6-by-2 board.

4. Write a program to generate a yearly calendar. The program should accept the year and the day of the week for January 1 of that year (1 = Sunday, 7 = Saturday). Remember, February has 29 days if the year is divisible by 4. The calendar should be printed in the following form (for each month):

```
    January
                      1
 2  3  4  5  6  7  8
 9 10 11 12 13 14 15
16 17 18 19 20 21 22
23 24 25 26 27 28 29
30 31
```

5. a. Write a program to read in a collection of exam scores ranging in value from 1 to 100. Your program should count and print the number of outstanding scores (90–100), the number of satisfactory scores (60–89), and the number of unsatisfactory scores (1–59). It should also display the category of each score. Test your program on the following data:

   63 75 72 72 78 67 80 63 75
   90 89 43 59 99 82 12 100

   b. Modify your program to display the average exam score (a real number) at the end of the run.

6. Write a program to process weekly employee time cards for all employees of an organization. Each employee will have three data items: an identification number, the hourly wage rate, and the number of hours worked during a given

week. Each employee is to be paid time and a half for all hours worked over 40. A tax amount of 3.625% of gross salary will be deducted. The program output should show the employee's number and net pay. Display the total payroll and the average amount paid at the end of the run.

Directory: CHAP5
File: PROJ7.PAS

7. Suppose you own a beer distributorship that sells Piels (ID number 1), Coors (ID number 2), Bud (ID number 3), and Iron City (ID number 4) by the case. Write a program to
    a. read in the case inventory for each brand for the start of the week.
    b. process all weekly sales and purchase records for each brand.
    c. print out the final inventory.
    Each transaction will consist of two data items: the brand identification number (an integer) followed by the amount purchased (a positive integer value) or the amount sold (a negative integer value). The weekly inventory for each brand (for the start of the week) will also consist of two items: the identification number and the initial inventory for that brand. For now, assume that you always have sufficient foresight to prevent depletion of your inventory for any brand. *Hint:* Your data entry should begin with eight values representing the case inventory, followed by the transaction values.

8. Revise Programming Project 7 to make it a menu-driven program. The menu operations supported by the revised program should be (E)nter Inventory, (P)urchase Beer, (S)ell Beer, (D)isplay Inventory, and (Q)uit Program. Negative quantities should no longer be used to represent goods sold.

9. Before high-resolution graphics displays became common, computer terminals were often used to display graphs of equations using only text characters. A typical technique created a vertical graph by spacing over on the screen, then drawing an *. Write a program that displays the graph of an increasing frequency sine wave this way. The program should ask the user for an initial step size in degrees and the number of lines of the graph to display. A sample output begins as:

```
                    *
                         *
                           *
                             *
                               *
                                 *
                                  *
                                   *
                                  *
                                 *
                               *
                             *
                          *
                      *
                  *
             *
         *
     *
  *
 *
```

▼ **What attracted you to the field of computer science?**

▲ I've always enjoyed mathematics and problem solving. Both of my parents work with computers, so I was exposed to them from a very early age. I can remember entering data on keypunch cards at my mother's office at NASA when I was eight or nine years old. In high school, I took a Fortran programming class and a problem-solving class at the local community college. I really enjoyed the logical thinking that was required, and the great feeling you get when you finally debug a complicated program—I even enjoyed pulling all-nighters to get class projects finished! By the time I finished the freshman series of programming courses in college, I was hooked.

▼ **You currently work on intelligent planning systems. When did your interest in artificial intelligence develop? How are intelligent planning systems "intelligent"?**

▲ My interests in artificial intelligence (AI) developed during my junior and senior years in college. I took several psychology classes and an AI class, and decided I really liked the combination of programming and cognitive psychology that AI represents, so I applied to graduate programs in AI, and eventually got my Ph.D. for research in machine learning.

Intelligent planning systems can be used autonomously or as "assistants" for human planners in many domains—such as space shuttle control, manufacturing, emergency response, and project management. These systems take knowledge about causality and problem solving within a specific domain and use general reasoning techniques to formulate plans based on that knowledge. Intelligent planning systems are capable of consolidating information into a plan and then analyzing the plan to determine where there might be bottlenecks, resource overutilization, or conflicts between competing subgoals. Because they can continually synthesize incoming data, intelligent planning systems are a powerful tool with which a human planner can generate and maintain plans for very complex problems.

▼ **Are there problem-solving skills that are invaluable to you in tackling design problems?**

▲ In order to design a new piece of software, you need to be able to specify, very clearly and precisely, what problem it is you're trying to solve. This isn't always easy to do, even if you know what the problem is—and frequently in research, part of the design problem is to identify the problem being solved in the first place. Problem specification requires an ability to take intuitive, abstract, or vague concepts and break them down into manageable pieces; and to take these pieces and describe them "mathematically," in language that is clear enough that you can then start implementing a solution. Implementing a solution requires good programming skills. As I said before, you have to clearly specify, in a programming language, every step of the solution. Equally important are good debugging skills. Debugging requires patience, the application of careful testing methods, and the ability to "step back" from your expectations and observe what's *really* happening. When I helped students in the lab, I would frequently find that they were having trouble debugging their programs because they "knew," or rather

INTERVIEW

Marie desJardins

Marie desJardins graduated from Harvard University with an A.B. in computer science and later obtained a Ph.D. in artificial intelligence from the University of California at Berkeley. While at Berkeley Dr. desJardins was president of WICSE (Women in Computer Science and Engineering). Before entering the computer science industry Dr. desJardins worked as an instructor and lecturer, earning the Danforth Teaching Award for her work with undergraduate students. Since 1991, she has been a member of the Applied Artificial Intelligence Technology Program at SRI International.

thought they knew, what their program was doing, so they weren't testing the parts of the program that were causing the problem.

▼ Through your years as a lecturer and teaching assistant, what topics did you find were most difficult for students learning introductory programming skills?

▲ For beginning students, I think there are two particularly difficult concepts. The first is the idea that computers are actually very simplistic, deterministic devices that do *exactly* what they are told. This means that a computer program has to be correct in every detail: you can't skip any steps, make any assumptions, or have even a tiny error. Because we're so used to giving instructions to other human beings, who are very good at filling in gaps and at asking questions when there's something missing, it's hard at first to get used to the fact that in computer programming you have to specify every single step in order to solve a problem correctly.

The second difficult concept is that of recursion. The idea that a function can call itself with different arguments, and that the new call will eventually return to the spot in the same function where it was called—even if there were many more calls to the function within the recursive call—is not intuitive for most students. I found that different students respond to different explanations of this concept: some can grasp a particular metaphor, some need to "see" recursion happening in hands-on observation, some need to work it through on paper. My favorite part of teaching an introductory programming class is seeing the "Aha!" that many students experience when they finally get an intuitive understanding of recursion.

▼ Looking back at your academic experience, what recommendations do you have for students pursuing computer science studies?

▲ Computer science should be fun most of the time. Different students will enjoy different parts of the programming process—some people really like to design programs; some people like the programming itself; and some people enjoy testing and debugging. Sometimes it can be frustrating, especially when you feel like you've tried everything and just can't get a program to work. I really enjoy working with other people, so that when I get stuck, there's somebody else who knows what I'm working on that I can talk through the problem with. I think that developing the ability to work in a team is really important for computer science classes, and is invaluable in a work environment later on. The other recommendation I'd make is to pursue your other interests—music, history, literature, whatever. Not only will that make you a more well-rounded person (and help you to get away from the terminal every once in a while), but I frequently find that things I've learned in other classes actually come in handy in computer science classes. And you may find that you can combine computers with one or more of those interests, as I did with psychology and CS when I decided to study artificial intelligence.

CHAPTER SIX

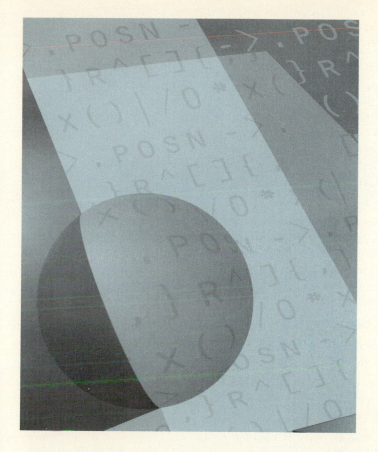

Modular Programming

A carefully designed program constructed using procedures and functions shares some of the properties of a stereo system. Each stereo component is an independent device that performs a specific operation. You might know the purpose of each component, but you certainly have no need to know what electronic parts each contains or how it functions to play or record music.

Electronic audio signals move back and forth over wires linking the stereo components, via plugs on the back of the stereo receiver marked as inputs or outputs. Wires attached to the input plugs carry electronic signals into the receiver, where they are processed. These signals may come from the cassette deck, tuner, or CD player. The receiver sends new electronic signals through the output plugs to the speakers or back to the cassette deck for recording.

The introduction to procedures in Chapter 3 illustrated how to write the separate program components—the procedures—of a program. These procedures (or functions) correspond to the individual steps in a problem solution. In this chapter, you will learn how to connect the modules to create a program system—an arrangement of parts that makes your program function like a stereo system as it passes information from one module to another.

6.1   Introduction to Parameter Lists

Parameter lists provide the communication links between the main program and its modules. Parameters make procedures and functions more versatile because they enable a module to manipulate different data each time it is called. This section describes how programmers use parameters to pass information between a program and its modules, or between two modules.

Actual and Formal Parameters

actual parameter list
parenthesized list of variables (or values) passed to the procedure; follows the procedure name in the procedure call

Each procedure call statement has two parts: a *procedure name* and an **actual parameter list.** To illustrate, consider a procedure Line that draws a line from one point on the screen to another. The procedure call statement

```
Line (X1, Y1, X2, Y2)
```

    ↑   ↑
Procedure **Actual**
name   **parameter**
          list

consists of the procedure name, Line, and the actual parameter list (X1, Y1, X2, Y2). The values of the four *actual parameters* are passed to procedure Line, which draws a line from point (X1, Y1) to point (X2, Y2). To continue drawing from point (X2, Y2) to (X3, Y3), we need the procedure call statement

```
Line (X2, Y2, X3, Y3)
```

In each procedure call, the programmer provides procedure Line with four variables or values that represent the X, Y coordinates of two points on the screen. Because the four coordinates can change each time Line is called, we must represent them somehow in the procedure declaration. To do this, we use dummy names called *formal parameters:*

```
procedure Line (XStart, YStart, XEnd, YEnd : Integer);
```

          ↑   ↑
      Procedure   **Formal parameter list**
        name

formal parameter list
parenthesized list of dummy names (with data types) used in the procedure to represent actual parameters; follows the procedure name in the procedure heading

The **formal parameter list** shows the four formal parameters used inside the procedure to represent the X, Y coordinates of the end points of the line to be drawn. The pair XStart, YStart represents one end point, and the pair XEnd, YEnd represents the other. The formal parameter list also indicates the data type, Integer, of these parameters.

Correspondence Between Actual and Formal Parameters

Procedure Line doesn't know what values it will receive until it is called. The calling program passes the information needed by Line via the actual parameter list, matching each actual parameter with its corresponding formal parameter.

Figure 6.1 shows part of a program containing procedure Line and one call to this procedure. The arrows show the information flow between the four actual and formal parameters. The parameter correspondence is summarized here:

Actual Parameter	corresponds to	Formal Parameter
X1		XStart
Y1		YStart
X2		XEnd
Y2		YEnd

Figure 6.1 shows that the value of main program variable X1 is passed to formal parameter XStart, and so on. Although not shown in the figure, the four actual parameters should have values assigned before the procedure call executes.

Notice that corresponding formal and actual parameters have different names in Fig. 6.1. This presents no problems, because the parameter correspondence is determined by *position* in each parameter list, not by name.

Figure 6.1
Main Program with Call to
Procedure Line

```
program Main (Input, Output);
    var
        X1, X2, Y1, Y2, X3, Y3 : Integer;   Main program variables
                    Formal parameters
    procedure Line (XStart, YStart, XEnd, YEnd : Integer);
    . . .

    end; {Line}

begin {Main}
    . . .
    Line (X1, Y1, X2, Y2);   Actual parameters
    . . .
end. {Main}
```

Information flow between corresponding parameters

EXAMPLE 6.1 ▼

Procedure `ReportSumAve` in Fig. 6.2 computes and displays the sum and the average of two type `Real` values that are passed into the procedure. The comment {input} identifies formal parameters `Num1` and `Num2` as procedure inputs.

local variables

variables declared in a procedure, not in the main program

Two **local variables**, `Sum` and `Average`, are declared in the procedure. Local variables can be accessed only within the procedure. The statements

```
Sum := Num1 + Num2;
Average := Sum / 2.0;
```

assign values to these local variables as follows: The sum of the values passed into parameters `Num1` and `Num2` is stored in `Sum`, and their average is stored in `Average`.

For the procedure call statement

```
ReportSumAve (6.5, 3.5)
```

the value 6.5 is passed to formal parameter `Num1` and the value 3.5 is passed to formal parameter `Num2`. The value assigned to `Sum` is 10.0, and the value assigned to `Average` is 5.0. The procedure displays these two values. The correspondence between the actual and the formal parameters follows:

Actual Parameter	*corresponds to*	*Formal Parameter*
6.5		Num1
3.5		Num2

For the procedure call statement

```
ReportSumAve (X, Y)
```

Figure 6.2
Procedure to Display a
Sum and an Average

Directory: CHAP6
File: REPORTSU.PAS

```
procedure ReportSumAve (Num1, Num2 {input} : Real);
{
   Computes and displays the sum and average of Num1 and Num2.
   Pre : Num1 and Num2 are assigned values.
   Post: The sum and average value of Num1 and Num2 are
         computed and displayed.
}
   var
      Sum,                              {sum of Num1, Num2}
      Average : Real;                   {average of Num1, Num2}

begin {ReportSumAve}
   Sum := Num1 + Num2;
   Average := Sum / 2.0;
   WriteLn ('The sum is ', Sum :4:2);
   WriteLn ('The average is ', Average :4:2)
end; {ReportSumAve}
```

the value of X is passed to formal parameter Num1 and the value of Y is passed to formal parameter Num2:

Actual Parameter	corresponds to	Formal Parameter
X		Num1
Y		Num2

Figure 6.3 shows the main program data area and the data area for procedure ReportSumAve after this procedure call statement executes. The values 8.0 and 10.0 are passed into the formal parameters Num1 and Num2, respectively. The local variables, Sum and Average, are initially undefined; the execution of the procedure body changes the values of these variables to 18.0 and 9.0, respectively. ▲

The Procedure Data Area

Each time a procedure call statement is executed, an area of memory is allocated for storage of that procedure's data. The procedure data area includes storage cells for its formal parameters and any local variables or constants that may be declared in the procedure. Whenever the procedure terminates, the procedure data area is erased; it is re-created empty (all values undefined) when the procedure is called again.

Illegal Parameter Substitution Errors

The data type of each actual parameter must be assignment compatible (see Section 2.5) with the data type of its corresponding formal parameter, or a type mismatch syntax error will occur. How does the Pascal compiler de-

Figure 6.3
Data Areas After Call of
ReportSumAve

termine whether an actual parameter has a correct data type? The Pascal compiler knows the required data type for each actual parameter because a procedure's declaration must precede its first call. The formal parameter list (in the procedure declaration) specifies the data type of each procedure parameter.

Program Style

Choosing Formal Parameter Names

Although you can choose any valid identifiers as formal parameter names, you should continue to follow the convention of picking names that help to document the use of the formal parameter. Remember that the correspondence between an actual and a formal parameter is determined solely by position in the parameter lists, regardless of what names are used.

One purpose of procedures and functions is to facilitate the reuse of previously written and tested modules in future programs. Try to pick meaningful and generic formal parameter names rather than specific names tailored to a particular program application.

Preconditions and Postconditions

The multiple-line comment at the beginning of procedure `ReportSumAve` describes the procedure's operation. For comments that extend over multiple lines, use the commenting style

```
{
    . . . comments . . .
}
```

The comment line

```
Pre : Num1 and Num2 are assigned values.
```

precondition
condition assumed to be true before a procedure or function call

describes the condition that is true before the procedure is called; this condition is known as a **precondition.** The lines

```
Post: The sum and average value of Num1 and Num2 are
      computed and displayed.
```

postcondition
condition assumed to be true after a procedure or function executes

describe the condition that is true after the procedure execution is completed; this condition is called a **postcondition**.

Preconditions and postconditions document the procedure operation for other programmers who may use it. For example, preconditions tell a programmer what must be done before the procedure is called. In this case, two data values must be assigned or read into the actual parameters prior to calling `ReportSumAve`. Postconditions tell a programmer the effect of the procedure's execution on its parameters. In this case, their sum and average are computed and displayed.

Exercises for Section 6.1   ***Self-Check***

1. Consider procedure Down:

```
procedure Down (N : Integer);
begin {Down}
  while N > 0 do
    begin
      Write (N);
      N := N - 1
    end {while}
end;  {Down}
```

a. What is displayed when the procedure call statement Down (3) executes?
b. If M is 5, what happens when the procedure call statement Down (M) executes?
c. What is the value of the actual parameter M after the procedure executes?
d. Where should M be declared, and what should its data type be?
2. Write preconditions and postconditions for procedure Down in Exercise 1.

Programming

1. Write a procedure that computes and displays the square root of a formal parameter X if X is greater than or equal to zero. Otherwise, the procedure should display an error message.

6.2 Returning Information from Procedures

In Section 6.1, we passed information from the main program to the procedure, where the information was processed. Procedures not only process information passed to them, but they also return information to the main program or another procedure for additional processing. This section describes how procedures return information to the calling module.

Variable and Value Parameters

Once again, the communication link between the procedure and the calling module is the parameter list. Formal parameters fall into two categories: value parameters and variable parameters. A **value parameter** receives information passed into a procedure, and a **variable parameter** returns a procedure result by changing its corresponding actual parameter value. So far we have used only value parameters.

Example 6.2 demonstrates the difference between value and variable parameters. As you follow the example, recall that when a procedure call executes, the computer allocates memory space in the procedure data area

value parameter

a type of formal parameter that receives information passed into a procedure

variable parameter

a type of formal parameter that returns a procedure result

for each formal parameter. For input parameters, a copy of the value of each actual input parameter is stored in the memory cell allocated to its corresponding formal parameter. The procedure body can manipulate this value.

EXAMPLE 6.2 ▼

Procedure ComputeSumAve in Fig. 6.4 is similar to ReportSumAve (Fig. 6.2), the main difference being the former has four parameters: two for input (Num1 and Num2) and two for output (Sum and Average). Procedure ComputeSumAve computes the sum and the average of its inputs but does not display them. Instead these values are assigned to formal parameters Sum and Average and returned as procedure results to the calling module.

To see how this procedure works, assume that the main program declares X, Y, Total, and Mean as type Real variables. The procedure call statement

ComputeSumAve (X, Y, Total, Mean)

sets up the correspondence:

Actual Parameter	corresponds to	Formal Parameter
X		Num1
Y		Num2
Total		Sum
Mean		Average

The values of X and Y, associated with formal parameters Num1 and Num2, are passed into the procedure when it is first called. The statement

Sum := Num1 + Num2;

Figure 6.4
Procedure to Compute a
Sum and an Average

Directory: CHAP6
File: COMPUTES.PAS

```
procedure ComputeSumAve (Num1, Num2 {input} : Real;
                         var Sum, Average {output} : Real);
{
  Computes the sum and average of Num1 and Num2.
  Pre : Num1 and Num2 are assigned values.
  Post: The sum and average of Num1 and Num2 are computed
        and returned.
}
begin {ComputeSumAve}
  Sum := Num1 + Num2;
  Average := Sum / 2.0
end; {ComputeSumAve}
```

stores the sum of the procedure inputs in the main program variable `Total` (the third actual parameter). The statement

`Average := Sum / 2.0`

divides the value stored in the main program variable `Total` by `2.0` and stores the quotient in the main program variable `Mean` (the fourth actual parameter). Figure 6.5 shows the main program data area and the procedure data area after the procedure call but before the procedure body begins execution; Fig. 6.6 shows these data areas just after the procedure body executes. The procedure execution sets the values of main program variables `Total` and `Mean` to `18.0` and `9.0`, respectively. ▲

Figure 6.5 points out one important difference between formal parameters used as procedure inputs and those used as procedure outputs. Because formal parameters `Num1` and `Num2` are considered *value parameters,* each receives a copy of its corresponding actual parameter *value,* which the procedure uses in its computations. The *value* passed into formal parameter `Num1` is stored in the procedure data area at the time of the procedure call, and there is no further connection between formal parameter `Num1` and its corresponding actual parameter. The broken arrow in Fig. 6.5 indicates this condition, and its arrowhead shows that data flows in one direction only: from the calling module to the procedure.

Formal parameters `Sum` and `Average`, on the other hand, are *variable parameters.* The compiler stores in the procedure data area the memory *address* of the actual variable that corresponds to each variable parameter.

Figure 6.5
Data Areas After
Procedure Call

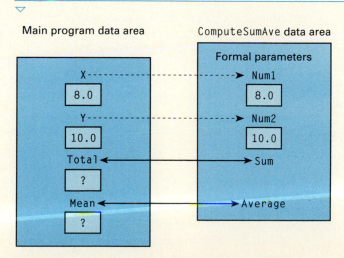

Figure 6.6
Data Areas After
Procedure Execution

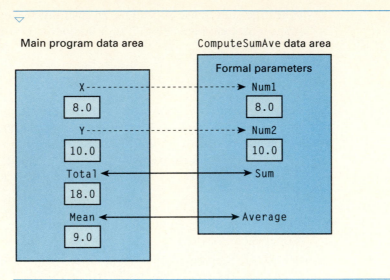

Through this address, the procedure accesses the actual parameter in the calling module, so the procedure can change the actual parameter value or use it in a computation. In Fig. 6.5, this relationship is shown by a double-headed arrow connecting each variable parameter with its corresponding actual parameter. The double-headed arrow indicates that data can flow into the procedure and out of the procedure through a variable parameter.

Because the Pascal compiler must know whether a formal parameter is a value or variable parameter when it translates the procedure declaration, we identify variable parameters by preceding them with the reserved word `var` (see the second line in Fig. 6.4). Notice that `var` appears only in the formal parameter list, not in the actual parameter list.

Variable parameters are more versatile than value parameters because their values can be used in a computation as well as changed by the procedure's execution. Why not make all parameters, even input parameters, variable parameters? The reason is that value parameters offer some protection to data integrity: Because copies of value parameters are stored locally in the procedure data area, Pascal protects the actual parameter's value and prevents it from being erroneously changed by the procedure's execution. For example, if we add the statement

```
Num1 := -5.0
```

at the end of procedure `ComputeSumAve`, the value of formal parameter `Num1` will be changed to `-5.0`, but the value stored in `X` (the corresponding actual parameter) will still be `8.0`.

Should a programmer neglect to declare an output formal parameter as a variable parameter, then its value (not its address) will be stored in the procedure and any change to its value will not be returned to the calling program. This is a very common error in parameter usage.

Program Style

Writing Formal Parameter Lists

In Fig. 6.4 the formal parameter list

```
(Num1, Num2 {input} : Real;
 var Sum, Average {output} : Real);
```

is written on two lines to improve program readability. The value parameters are on the first line with the comment {input} to document their use as procedure inputs. The variable parameters are on the second line with the comment {output}.

Generally we follow the practice shown in Fig. 6.4 in writing formal parameter lists. Input parameters are listed first, and any output parameters are listed last.

When to Use a Variable Parameter or a Value Parameter

How do you decide whether to use a variable parameter or a value parameter? Here are some rules of thumb:

▶ If information is to be passed into a procedure but not returned or passed out of the procedure, then the formal parameter representing that information should be a value parameter (e.g., Num1 and Num2 in Figs. 6.2 and 6.4). A parameter used in this way is called an *input parameter*.

▶ If information is to be returned to the calling program from a procedure, then the formal parameter representing that information must be a variable parameter (e.g., Sum and Average in Fig. 6.4). A parameter used in this way is called an *output parameter*.

▶ If information is to be passed into a procedure, perhaps modified, and a new value returned, then the formal parameter representing that information must be a variable parameter. A parameter used in this way is called an *input/output parameter*.

Although we distinguish output parameters from input/output parameters, Pascal does not. Both kinds of parameters must be declared as variable parameters, so the address of the corresponding actual parameter is stored in the procedure data area when the procedure is called. For an input/output parameter, we assume there are some meaningful data in the actual parameter before the procedure executes; for an output parameter, we make no such assumption.

Passing Expressions to Value Parameters

Assignment-compatible expressions (or variables or constants) can serve as actual parameters corresponding to value parameters. For example, the procedure call statement

```
ComputeSumAve (X + Y, 10.5, MySum, MyAve);
```

calls `ComputeSumAve` to compute the sum (returned in `MySum`) and the average (returned in `MyAve`) of the expression `X + Y` and the real number `10.5`. However, only variables can correspond to variable parameters, so `MySum` and `MyAve` must be declared as type `Real` variables in the calling module. This restriction is imposed because an actual parameter corresponding to a variable parameter may be modified when the procedure executes; it is illogical to allow a procedure to change the value of either a constant or an expression.

Multiple Calls to a Procedure

Recall that parameters enable a procedure to execute one set of instructions on different sets of data each time the procedure is called. In Example 6.3, we demonstrate how a procedure may be called more than once in a given program and process different data in each call.

EXAMPLE 6.3: Sorting Three Numbers ▼

Program `Sort3Numbers` in Fig. 6.7 reads three data values into `Num1`, `Num2`, and `Num3` and rearranges the data so that they are in increasing sequence, with the smallest value in `Num1`. The three calls to procedure `Order` perform this **sorting** operation.

sort
a rearrangement of data such that the data are in increasing sequence

The body of procedure `Order` consists of the `if` statement from Fig. 4.10. The procedure heading contains the formal parameter list

```
(var X, Y {input/output} : Real)
```

which identifies `X` and `Y` as the formal parameters. `X` and `Y` are *input/output parameters* because the procedure uses the current actual parameter values as inputs and may return new values.

After `Order` executes, the smaller of its two parameter values is stored in its first actual parameter and the larger is stored in its second actual parameter. Therefore, the procedure call statement

```
Order (Num1, Num2); {Order the data in Num1 and Num2.}
```

stores the smaller of `Num1` and `Num2` in `Num1` and the larger in `Num2`. In the sample run shown, `Num1` is `8.0` and `Num2` is `10.0`, so these values are not changed by the procedure execution. However, the procedure call statement

```
Order (Num1, Num3); {Order the data in Num1 and Num3.}
```

```pascal
program Sort3Numbers (Input, Output);
{
  Reads three numbers and sorts them
  so that they are in increasing order
}
  var
    Num1, Num2, Num3 : Real;    {three variables being sorted}

  procedure Order (var X, Y {input/output} : Real);
  {
    Orders a pair of numbers represented by X and Y so that
    the smaller number is in X and the larger number is in Y.
    Pre : X and Y are assigned values.
    Post: X is the smaller of the pair and Y is the larger.
  }
    var
      Temp : Real;              {copy of number originally in X}

  begin {Order}
    if X > Y then
      begin {Switch the values of X and Y}
        Temp := X;              {Store old X in Temp.}
        X := Y;                 {Store old Y in X.}
        Y := Temp               {Store old X in Y.}
      end {if}
  end; {Order}

begin {Sort3Numbers}
  WriteLn ('Enter 3 numbers separated by spaces> ');
  ReadLn (Num1, Num2, Num3);

  {Sort the numbers}
  Order (Num1, Num2);    {Order the data in Num1 and Num2.}
  Order (Num1, Num3);    {Order the data in Num1 and Num3.}
  Order (Num2, Num3);    {Order the data in Num2 and Num3.}

  {Print the results.}
  WriteLn ('The three numbers in order are:');
  WriteLn (Num1 :8:2, Num2 :8:2, Num3 :8:2)
end. {Sort3Numbers}
```

Sample Run

```
Enter 3 numbers separated by spaces>
8.0  10.0  6.0
The three numbers in order are:
    6.00    8.00   10.00
```

switches the values of Num1 (initial value is 8.0) and Num3 (initial value is 6.0). Table 6.1 traces the program execution. ▲

Statement	Num1	Num2	Num3	**Effect**
ReadLn (Num1, Num2, Num3);	8.0	10.0	6.0	Enters data
Order (Num1, Num2);				No change
Order (Num1, Num3);	6.0		8.0	Switches Num1 and Num3
Order (Num2, Num3);		8.0	10.0	Switches Num2 and Num3
WriteLn (Num1, Num2, Num3)				Displays 6.0, 8.0, 10.0

Exercises for Section 6.2 **Self-Check**

1. Assume X, Y, and Z are integer variables and X is 5, Y is 7, and Z is 2. Trace the execution of the call Shuffle (X, Y, Z):

```
procedure Shuffle (X, Y : Integer;
                        var Z : Integer);
   var
     Temp : Integer;

begin
  Temp := X;
  X := Y;
  Y := Z;
  Z := Temp
end; {Shuffle}
```

2. a. Show the output displayed by the following program in the form of a table of values for X, Y, Z, and W:

```
program Show (Input, Output);
  var
    W, X, Y, Z : Integer;

  procedure SumDiff (Num1, Num2 : Integer;
                     var Num3, Num4 : Integer);
  begin {SumDiff}
    Num3 := Num1 + Num2;
    Num4 := Num1 - Num2
  end; {SumDiff}

begin {Show}
  X := 5; Y := 3; Z := 7; W := 9;
```

```
          WriteLn ('   X    Y    Z    W');
          SumDiff (X, Y, Z, W);
          WriteLn (X :4, Y :4, Z :4, W :4);
          SumDiff (Y, X, Z, W);
          WriteLn (X :4, Y :4, Z :4, W :4);
          SumDiff (Z, W, Y, X);
          WriteLn (X :4, Y :4, Z :4, W :4);
          SumDiff (Z, Z, X, Y);
          WriteLn (X :4, Y :4, Z :4, W :4);
          SumDiff (Y, Y, Y, W);
          WriteLn (X :4, Y :4, Z :4, W :4)
       end. {Show}
```

    b.   Write the preconditions and postconditions for procedure
         `SumDiff`.

3.   A procedure has four formal parameters: W, X, Y, and Z (all type `Real`).
     During execution, the procedure stores the sum of W and X in Y and the
     product of W and X in Z. Which parameters are inputs and which are
     outputs?

Programming

1.   Write the procedure for Self-Check Exercise 3.
2.   Write a procedure that accepts as input the height *h* and radius *r* of a
     right circular cone and outputs the volume of the cone. The formula for
     the volume of a cone is: *volume* = $\pi r^2 h$.

6.3   Syntax Rules for Procedures with Parameter Lists

This section wraps up our discussion of parameters via syntax displays for
procedure declaration and call, a syntax diagram for formal parameter lists,
and rules for parameter list correspondence.

SYNTAX DISPLAY

Procedure Declaration (Procedure with Parameters)

Form: procedure *pname* (*formal parameters*) ;
           declaration section
           begin
              procedure body
           end;

Example: procedure Highlight (Ch {input} : Char;
                              var NumStars {output} : Integer);
          {
            Displays Ch between two asterisks and returns the
            numbers of asterisks printed.
            Pre : Ch is defined.
            Post: Returns 3 in NumStars if Ch = Border;
                   otherwise, returns 2 in NumStars.
          }

```
            const
               Border = '*';

         begin {Highlight}
            Write (Border);  Write (Ch);  Write (Border);
            if Ch = Border then
               NumStars := 3
            else
               NumStars := 2
         end; {Highlight}
```

Interpretation: The procedure *pname* is declared, followed by the *formal parameters* enclosed in parentheses. The identifiers declared in the *declaration section* are local to the procedure and are defined only during the procedure execution. The *procedure body* describes the data manipulation to be performed by the procedure using the *formal parameters* as dummy names for the actual parameters. Value *formal parameters* receive data passed into the procedure, and variable *formal parameters* (preceded by word var) return procedure results to the calling module.

SYNTAX DISPLAY

Procedure Call Statement (Procedure with Parameters)

Form: *pname* (*actual parameters*)
Example: Highlight ('A', NumAsterisks)
Interpretation: The *actual parameters* are enclosed in parentheses. When procedure *pname* is called into execution, the first *actual parameter* is associated with the first formal parameter, the second *actual parameter* with the second formal parameter, and so on. For a value parameter, the *actual parameter*'s value is stored in the procedure data area and the procedure processes the local value. For a variable parameter, the *actual parameter*'s address is stored in the procedure data area and the procedure processes the *actual parameter*.
Note: The *actual parameters* must satisfy the rules for parameter list correspondence discussed later in this section.

The following syntax diagram shows that a *formal parameter* list is always enclosed in parentheses and consists of one or more lists of identifiers. Each

Formal Parameter List

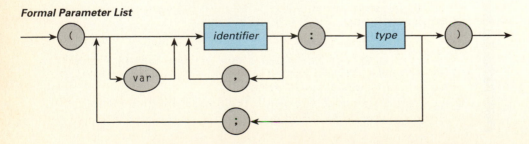

list may be preceded by `var` (optional), and must end with a colon followed by a data type name (e.g., `Real` or `Char`). Identifiers in a list are separated by commas, and lists of identifiers are separated by semicolons.

EXAMPLE 6.4 ▼

The following two formal parameter lists are printed on several lines to improve readability:

```
(Ch3 : Char;              (M, N, O : Integer;
  var X, Y, Z : Real)       var X, Y, Z : Real;
                                A, B, C : Real)
```

In both lists, X, Y, Z are declared as type `Real` variable parameters. `Ch3` is a type `Char` value parameter; A, B, and C are type `Real` value parameters; and M, N, and O are type `Integer` value parameters. ▲

This example points out a common error in formatting formal parameter lists: In the list on the right, the indentation of A, B, and C causes some students to think that the word `var` is implied and that A, B, and C are also variable parameters. Not so! The word `var` must always appear before *each* list of variable parameters.

The formal parameter list also determines the form of any actual parameter list in calls to the procedure. This form is determined during the translation of the program when the compiler processes the procedure declaration.

Later, when it reaches a procedure call statement, the compiler checks the actual parameter list for consistency with the formal parameter list. An actual parameter list may be a list of expressions, variables, or constants separated by commas. An actual parameter list and its corresponding formal parameter list must agree in **N**umber, **O**rder, and **T**ype (**NOT**), as described in the following rules.

Rules for Parameter List Correspondence

1. Correspondence between actual and formal parameters is determined by position in their respective parameter lists. These lists must be the same size, although the names of corresponding actual and formal parameters may differ.
2. For variable parameters, the types of corresponding actual and formal parameters must be identical. For value parameters, the actual parameter must be assignment compatible with its corresponding formal parameter (see Sections 2.5 and 7.6).
3. For variable parameters, an actual parameter must be a variable. For value parameters, an actual parameter may be a variable, a constant, or an expression.

EXAMPLE 6.5 ▼

A main program contains the declarations

```
var
  X, Y : Real;
  M : Integer;
  Next : Char;

procedure Test (A, B : Integer;
                var C, D : Real;
                var E : Char);
```

where only the heading for procedure Test is shown. Procedure Test has two value parameters (A and B) and three variable parameters (C, D, and E). Any of the following procedure call statements would be syntactically correct in the main program:

```
Test (M + 3, 10, X, Y, Next);
Test (M, MaxInt, Y, X, Next);
Test (35, M * 10, Y, X, Next)
```

The first actual parameter list shows that an expression (e.g., M + 3) or a constant (e.g., 10) may be associated with a value formal parameter. The correspondence specified by this parameter list is shown in Table 6.2.

Table 6.2

Parameter Correspondence for Test (M + 3, 10, X, Y, Next)

Actual Parameter	Formal Parameter	Parameter Kind
M + 3	A	Integer, value
10	B	Integer, value
X	C	Real, variable
Y	D	Real, variable
Next	E	Char, variable

All the procedure call statements in Table 6.3 contain syntax errors. The last procedure call statement points out an error often made in using procedures. The last three actual parameters (C, D, E) have the same names as their corresponding formal parameters. However, they are not declared as variables in the main program, so they cannot be used as actual parameters.

Table 6.3
Invalid Procedure Call
Statements

Procedure Call Statement	Error
Test (30, 10, M, X, Next)	Type of M is not Real.
Test (M, 19, X, Y)	Not enough actual parameters.
Test (M, 10, 35, Y, 'E')	Constants 35 and 'E' cannot correspond to variable parameters.
Test (M, 3.0, X, Y, Next)	Type of 3.0 is not Integer.
Test (30, 10, X, X + Y, Next)	Expression X + Y cannot correspond to a variable parameter.
Test (30, 10, C, D, E)	C, D, and E are not declared in the main program.

When writing relatively long parameter lists such as in this example, be careful not to transpose two actual parameters, or a syntax error may result. If no syntax is violated, the procedure execution will probably generate incorrect results.   ▲

Exercises for Section 6.3   **Self-Check**

1. Arrange the other correct parameter lists shown in Example 6.5 in a format similar to Table 6.2.
2. Correct the syntax errors in these formal parameter lists:

    ```
    (var A, B : Integer, C : Real)
    (value M : Integer; var Next : Char)
    (var Account, Real; X + Y , Real)
    ```

3. Assuming the declarations

    ```
    var
      X, Y, Z : Real;
      M, N : Integer;

    procedure Massage (var A, B : Real;
                       X : Integer);
    ```

    which of the following are correct? Which are incorrect and why?

a.	Massage (X, Y, Z)	g.	Massage (A, B, X)
b.	Massage (X, Y, 8)	h.	Massage (Y, Z, M)
c.	Massage (Y, X, N)	i.	Massage (Y+Z, Y-Z, M)
d.	Massage (M, Y, N)	j.	Massage (Z, Y, X)
e.	Massage (25.0, 15, X)	k.	Massage (X, Y, M, 10)
f.	Massage (X, Y, M+N)	l.	Massage (Z, Y, MaxInt)

Programming

1. Write a procedure that displays a table showing all powers of its first argument from zero through the power indicated by its second argument (a positive integer). The procedure also should return the sum of all values displayed. For example, if the first argument is 10 and the second argument is 3, the procedure should display 1, 10, 100, and 1000 and return 1111 as its result.

6.4   Scope of Identifiers

Every identifier in a Pascal program has a domain—the part of the program in which it is defined—called the **scope of the identifier.** An identifier can be referenced only by statements within its scope, which may be local or global as described next.

identifier scope
the part of a program that can reference an identifier declared in the program

Scope Rule 1: Local and Global Scopes

The scope of an identifier is the block (program or procedure) in which it is declared. Therefore, an identifier declared within the main program has **global scope** and can be referenced anywhere in the program. An identifier declared within a module has **local scope** and so can be referenced only within that module and any other modules that it declares.

global scope
the scope of an identifier declared in the main program
local scope
the scope of an identifier declared in a procedure or function

The scope rules apply to all identifiers used in a program, including the names of constants, variables, procedures, and formal parameters. Thus, while a procedure declared in the main program declaration part has global scope, its formal parameter list is part of the procedure block and so has local scope.

Figure 6.8 illustrates scope rule 1 by boxing the program block and each procedure block. We placed each formal parameter list on a separate line to show that it is part of its procedure block. In color type next to each block, we show the identifiers whose scope is that block.

Variables Y and Z are global variables, which means that we can reference these variables anywhere (i.e., in the body of the main program or Proc1 or Proc2). (We will discuss why we cannot make the same statement for global variable X shortly.) Neither the main program nor procedure Proc2 can reference the local identifiers declared in Proc1 (formal parameters M, N, Me and local variables X, You).

Because Proc1 and Proc2 are global identifiers, we would expect that these procedures can be called anywhere. Table 6.4 shows that although procedure Proc2 can call Proc1, procedure Proc1 cannot call Proc2. The reason for this exception is that Proc2 is declared after Proc1, and the declaration of an identifier must precede its first use. If you have one procedure that calls another, be sure to declare the procedure being called before the caller.

Figure 6.8
Scope of Identifiers

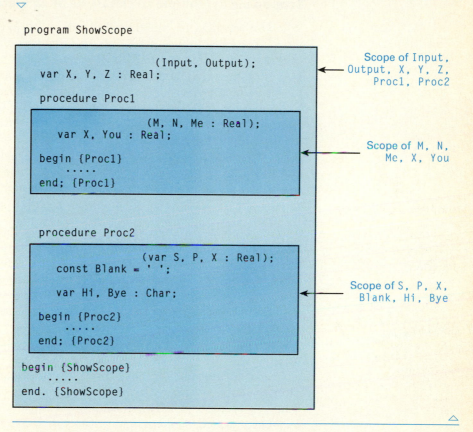

```
program ShowScope
                              (Input, Output);        ──►  Scope of Input,
    var X, Y, Z : Real;                                    Output, X, Y, Z,
                                                           Proc1, Proc2
    procedure Proc1

                      (M, N, Me : Real);
        var X, You : Real;
                                                       ◄── Scope of M, N,
    begin {Proc1}                                          Me, X, You
      .....
    end; {Proc1}


    procedure Proc2

                      (var S, P, X : Real);
        const Blank = ' ';

        var Hi, Bye : Char;                            ◄── Scope of S, P, X,
                                                           Blank, Hi, Bye
    begin {Proc2}
      .....
    end; {Proc2}

begin {ShowScope}
  .....
end. {ShowScope}
```

Table 6.4
Valid Procedure Calls

Program or Procedure Body	Procedures That Can Be Called
ShowScope	Proc1, Proc2
Proc2	Proc1, Proc2
Proc1	Proc1

Table 6.4 shows that a procedure can call itself (a *recursive call*). We discuss recursive calls in Section 6.8.

Notice that identifier X in Fig. 6.8 has three separate declarations (global variable, local variable in Proc1, formal parameter in Proc2) and therefore three different scopes. We know that we cannot declare the same identifier twice in one block, but we can have multiple declarations for an identifier provided they are all in different blocks. Scope rule 2 tells us how Pascal handles multiple declarations of an identifier.

Scope Rule 2: Multiple Declarations of an Identifier

When an identifier has multiple declarations all in different blocks, then the most local declaration is used each time that identifier is referenced.

Scope rule 2 tells us that global identifier X is accessed when we use X in the main program body, that local variable X is accessed when we use X in the body of Proc1, and that formal parameter X is accessed when we use X in the body of Proc2. Because of scope rule 2, we needn't be concerned whether an identifier has been declared elsewhere when we declare and use it in a procedure. If an identifier has been declared elsewhere, Pascal ignores the other declarations when we reference that identifier within the procedure body. This feature simplifies writing procedures for reuse in other programs.

Software Engineering: Avoiding Side Effects

side effect
changing a nonlocal variable that does not correspond to a variable formal parameter through a procedure or function execution

Although global variables can be referenced anywhere in a program, you should avoid referencing them in a procedure body. Changing the value of a global variable in a procedure is called a **side effect** of the procedure execution. Often no documentation exists to indicate that a procedure manipulates a *global* variable; consequently, in a program with many procedures, it may be difficult to locate the statement that assigns an incorrect value to a global variable. If the statement

```
Y := Y + 3.5;      {Example of a side effect}
```

appeared in procedure Proc1, it would cause a side effect (adding 3.5 to global variable Y) whenever that procedure was called. However, a procedure can access a global variable without causing a side effect if the global variable is passed via the parameter list.

The formal parameter list and the local declarations for a procedure explicitly document the data to be manipulated. You should manipulate only local identifiers in a procedure, the only exceptions being global constants and type identifiers (discussed in later chapters). Because Pascal does not allow the value of a constant to be changed, you can reference a global constant in a procedure with no side effects.

Scope for Nested Procedures

Nested procedures occur when we declare one procedure inside another. Scope rule 1 tells us that the scope of an inner procedure is the block in which it is declared. Therefore, an inner procedure can be called by the procedure that declares it and by itself (a recursive call), but an inner procedure cannot be called by the main program or by any procedures outside the nest. This restriction limits the potential reuse of an inner procedure, so we recommend that you do not nest procedures.

Figure 6.9 illustrates the effect of procedure nesting on identifier scope, and Table 6.5 lists the identifiers that can be referenced in each block and

Figure 6.9
Scope for Nested
Procedures

```
program Nested
                        (Input, Output);
    var M, N : Real;

    procedure Outer
                        (var X, Y : Real);
        var P, Q : Real;

        procedure Inner;

            var P, T : Real;
        begin {Inner}
            .....
        end; {Inner}

        begin {Outer}
            .....
        end; {Outer}

    begin {Nested}
        .....
    end. {Nested}
```

Scope of Input,
Output, M,
N, Outer

Scope of
X, Y, P, Q, Inner

Scope of P, T

Table 6.5
Valid Identifier
References for
Fig. 6.9

Program or Procedure Body	Identifiers That Can Be Referenced
Nested	Input, Output (parameters) M, N (global variables) Outer (global procedure)
Outer	Input, Output (parameters of Nested) M, N (global variables) X, Y (parameters) P, Q (local variables) Outer (global procedure) Inner (local procedure)
Inner	Input, Output (parameters of Nested) M, N (global variables) X, Y (parameters for Outer) Q (variable declared in Outer) P, T (local variables) Outer (global procedure) Inner (procedure declared in Outer)

the procedures that can be called. The table shows that procedure Inner can reference its own local variables, all identifiers declared in the main program, and all identifiers declared in procedure Outer except for variable P. The reason for this exclusion is that Inner declares its own local variable P and that declaration takes precedence (scope rule 2).

Illustrating the Scope Rules

Example 6.6 illustrates bad programming practice, where identifier names are not meaningful and are unnecessarily redundant. However, studying this example should help you master the Pascal scope rules.

EXAMPLE 6.6 ▼

Figure 6.10 shows a procedure declared in a main program. W is declared as a variable in both the procedure and the main program; X is declared as a variable in the main program and as a parameter in the procedure; Y is declared as a variable in the main program only.

The main program begins by initializing global variables W, X, and Y to the values shown on the left side of Fig. 6.11. The procedure call statement

```
Change (W);
```

calls procedure Change with main program variable W corresponding to variable parameter X. Figure 6.11 shows the program and procedure data areas just after the procedure call.

In procedure Change, the assignment statement

```
X := 6.0;            {Change parameter X.}
```

stores 6.0 in the main program variable W, and the assignment statement

```
Y := Y + 1.0;        {Side effect - change global Y.}
```

increments the main program variable Y to 4.0 (a side effect). The other two assignment statements in Change affect only its local variables W and Z (W becomes 35.0 and Z becomes 3.0)

The second WriteLn statement in Change displays the values of its local identifiers (W, X, and Z) and the global variable Y just before the procedure return. The WriteLn statement in the main program displays the values of the three main program variables after the return:

```
  W     X     Y
[6.0] [2.0] [4.0]
```

Figure 6.10
Program ScopeRules

Directory: CHAP6
File: SCOPERUL.PAS

```pascal
program ScopeRules (Input, Output);
  var
    W, X, Y : Real;

  procedure Change (var X {input/output} : Real);
    var
      W, Z : Real;

  begin {Change}
    W := 35.0;        {Change local W.}
    X := 6.0;         {Change parameter X.}
    Y := Y + 1.0;     {Side effect - change global Y.}
    Z := 3.0;         {Change local Z.}
    WriteLn ('W' :5, 'X' :5, 'Y' :5, 'Z' :5);
    WriteLn (W :5:1, X :5:1, Y :5:1, Z: 5:1, ' in Change')
  end; {Change}

begin  {ScopeRules}
  W := 5.5;           {Initialize global W.}
  X := 2.0;           {Initialize global X.}
  Y := 3.0;           {Initialize global Y.}
  Change (W);         {Update global W.}
  WriteLn (W :5:1, X :5:1, Y :5:1, ' in ScopeRules' :19)
end. {ScopeRules}
```

Sample Run

```
  W    X    Y    Z
35.0  6.0  4.0  3.0  in Change
 6.0  2.0  4.0         in ScopeRules
```

Figure 6.11
Data Areas After Procedure
Call

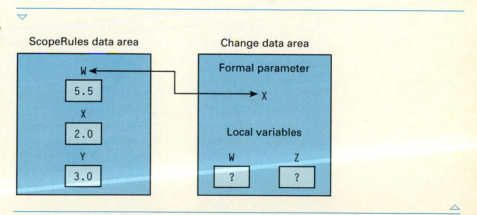

Notice that main program variable X is unchanged and that the value of W is 6.0 (not 35.0).

Consider what happens if X or Y is used as the actual parameter instead of W. That question is left as an exercise at the end of this section.   ▲

Exercises for Section 6.4   **Self-Check**

1. In Fig. 6.8, why can't variable You declared in procedure Proc1 be referenced by the main program or procedure Proc2? Why can't procedure Proc2 be called from within the body of Proc1?
2. In Fig. 6.8, what would be the effect of executing the body of Proc1 as follows?

```
begin {Proc1}
   X := 5.5;
   Y := 6.6;
   M := 2;
   N := 3;
   You := M
end; {Proc1}
```

3. If the statement sequence in Exercise 2 appeared in a different block, some of the assignment statements would be syntactically incorrect. Identify the incorrect statements, and indicate the effect of executing the others if the statement sequence appeared as the body of
    a. Proc2
    b. ShowScope
4. Consider program ScopeRules in Fig. 6.10.
    a. What kind of error would occur if the assignment statement

    ```
    Z := 15.0;
    ```

    were inserted in the main program?
    b. Show the new values of W, X, and Y if X were the actual parameter in the call to procedure Change.
    c. What if Y were the actual parameter in the call to Change?
    d. What would be the effect of making formal parameter X a value parameter?
5. The outline of a program with nested procedures follows. Describe the scope of each identifier, including procedure names.

```
program NestScope (Input, Output);
   const Pi = 3.14159;

   procedure A (var X : Real);
      var B, C : Integer;

      procedure D (var S : Real);
         const Star = '*';
      begin
         . . . . .
```

```
       end; {D}

   begin {A}
       . . . . .
   end; {A}

   procedure F (var X, Y : Real);
      var D : Integer;
   begin
       . . . . .
   end; {F}

begin
    . . . . .
end. {NestScope}
```

6.5 Functions: Modules That Return a Single Result

Functions are independent modules like procedures, except that procedures can return any number of results whereas a function always returns a single result. In Section 3.2, we showed how to call a predefined function by writing a function designator in an expression. For example, the function designator Abs(X + Y) calls the predefined function Abs (absolute value), where the expression X + Y is the actual parameter passed to function Abs. In this section, we study how to write our own functions.

Writing User-Defined Functions

To define your own function, write a function declaration and place it in the declaration part of the calling program. Because a function does not return its result through its parameter list, a function declaration differs in the following ways from a procedure declaration:

▶ A function heading begins with the reserved word function instead of procedure.

```
function Exponent (U, V : Real) : Real;
```

| Function name | Formal parameter list | Type of result |

▶ All function parameters should be value parameters.
▶ The data type of the function result is specified at the end of the function heading, following the formal parameter list.
▶ Within the function body, the function result is defined by assigning a value to the function name. The last value assigned to the function name is returned as the function result.

We illustrate these requirements for user-defined functions in Example 6.7.

EXAMPLE 6.7 ▼

Programmers typically use functions to simplify numeric computations. For instance, since Pascal has no exponentiation operator, a library function for raising a number to a power would be useful. Function Exponent (Fig. 6.12) raises its first argument, U, to the power indicated by its second argument, V (i.e., the function result is U^V). The function heading indicates that Exponent has two type Real value parameters; the type of the result, Real, is placed after the colon.

   The if statement in the function body selects either an assignment statement or a WriteLn statement depending on the value passed into U. If the value of U is 0, the assignment statement

```
Exponent := 0.0
```

executes and defines the function result as 0. If the value of U is positive, the assignment statement

```
Exponent := Exp(V * Ln(U))
```

calls Pascal's built-in functions Exp and Ln to calculate the desired value using the formula derived in Example 3.4. Assigning this value to Exponent defines it as the function result.

   If the value of U is negative, the WriteLn statement displays an error message but no value is assigned to Exponent, so the function result would be undefined. This is consistent with the function precondition, which states

Figure 6.12
Function Exponent

Directory: CHAP6
File: EXPONENT.PAS

```
function Exponent (U, V : Real) : Real;
{
 Returns its first argument raised to the power specified
 by its second argument.
 Pre : U >= 0.0 and V is defined.
 Post: Returns U raised to the power V.
}
begin {Exponent}
   if U = 0.0 then
      Exponent := 0.0          {Result of 0.0 to any power is 0.0}
   else if U > 0.0 then
      Exponent := Exp(V * Ln(U)) {Result is U raised to power V}
   else
      WriteLn ('**** Error in first parameter of Exponent')
end; {Exponent}
```

that function Exponent should be called only when its first parameter is nonnegative.

Notice that the two assignment statements use the function name Exponent without parameters. If you use parameters after the function name, Pascal considers this a recursive call to the function. ▲

Calling a User-Defined Function

If we have a main program with three type Real variables, X, Y, and Z, the main program statement

Z := Exponent(X, Y)

↑   ↑

Function name   Actual parameter list

calls Exponent, passing it the values of actual parameters X and Y. The function body computes the value of X^Y. Upon return from the function, the function result is assigned to Z.

Figure 6.13 shows the main program data area and the function data area right after the function call. For the particular values of X and Y shown (3.0 and 2.5), the function execution defines the function result as 15.59. Figure 6.14 shows the program data area and the function data area after the function body finishes execution but before the function return. Notice that there is no connection between main program variable Z and the memory cell in Exponent's data area that represents the function result. The function result will be assigned to Z after the return to the main program.

Figure 6.13
Data Areas After Function Call

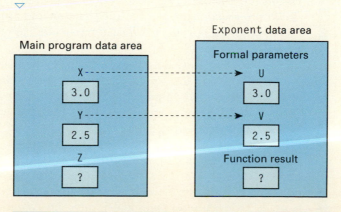

Figure 6.14
Data Areas After Function
Execution But Before
Return

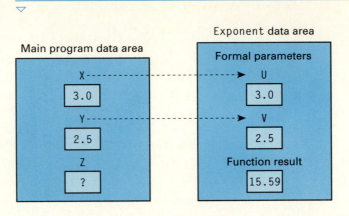

Exponent data area

Main program data area

Formal parameters

Function Declaration

Form:
```
function fname (formal parameters) : ftype;
    local declaration section
begin
    function body
end;
```

Example:
```
function InverseSum (X, Y : Real) : Real;
{Computes 1.0 divided by the sum of X, Y.}
    var
       SumXY : Real; {local storage for the sum of X, Y}

begin {InverseSum}
   SumXY := X + Y;
   InverseSum := 1.0 / SumXY
end; {InverseSum}
```

Interpretation: The function *fname* is declared, followed by the *formal parameters* enclosed in parentheses. The identifiers declared in the *local declaration section* are local to the function and are defined only during the execution of the function. A formal parameter cannot be declared as a local identifier.

The *function body* describes the data manipulation to be performed by the function using the formal parameters as dummy names in the description. When a formal parameter is referenced during function execution, the value of the corresponding actual parameter is manipulated.

The function returns a single result of type *ftype*. The function result is the value assigned to *fname* just prior to the return.

Note 1: The identifier *ftype* must be the name of a standard data type (Integer, Real, Boolean, or Char), a subrange type or enumerated type (described in Chapter 7), or a pointer type (described in Chapter 16).

Note 2: If there are no parameters, omit the *formal parameters* and the parentheses.

SYNTAX DISPLAY

Function Designator (Function Call)

Form: *fname* (*actual parameters*)
Example: InverseSum(3.0, Z)
Interpretation: The *actual parameters* are enclosed in parentheses. When function *fname* is called into execution, the first actual parameter corresponds to the first formal parameter, the second actual parameter corresponds to the second formal parameter, and so on. A function designator must always appear within an expression; after execution, the function result replaces the function designator in that expression.
Note: If there are no parameters, omit the *actual parameters* and the parentheses.

Software Engineering: Avoiding Function Side Effects

Because all function parameters in this book are input parameters, we omit the comment {input} from a function's formal parameter list. This restriction is imposed by programming style considerations, not by Pascal. You could return an additional result from a function by making one of its parameters a variable parameter, but any change to this parameter's value would be an undesirable *side effect* because it would not be expected and would contradict standard programming practice.

Testing Functions

In Example 6.8, we write a function that computes income tax owed and a small program whose sole purpose is to call and test that function. Such a program, used to test the operation of a function or a procedure, is called a **driver program.**

driver program
a small program written to test
a procedure or function

EXAMPLE 6.8 ▼

Figure 4.13 contained an if statement that computed the income tax due for a particular salary based on the tax table shown in Table 4.10. Since this table appears in many different programs, your accountant has decided to place it in function FindTax (Fig. 6.15). The assignment statement

```
MyTax := FindTax(MySalary);
```

calls function FindTax, passing the value of MySalary into input parameter Salary. If the value passed into Salary is within the range of the table, the tax owed is computed and returned as the function result; otherwise, the function returns -1.0 to signal an input salary that is outside the table range.

   Notice how the processing tasks are divided in Fig. 6.15. First, the ReadLn statement enters a salary value in the main program, not in function Find-Tax. The value read is passed into FindTax via its parameter list, as it should be. Never place statements to read a function's input data in the function body.

Figure 6.15
Driver Program with
Function FindTax

```pascal
program Driver (Input, Output);
{Tests function FindTax}

   var
     MySalary,                              {input - salary}
     MyTax      : Real;                     {output - tax}

   function FindTax (Salary : Real) : Real;
   {
    Returns tax amount owed for a salary < $15000.
    Pre : Salary is assigned a value.
    Post: If Salary is within range, returns the tax owed;
          otherwise, returns -1.0.
   }
      const
        MaxSalary = 15000.00; {maximum salary for table}
        OutOfRange = -1.0;     {"tax" for an out-of-range salary}

   begin  {FindTax}
     if Salary < 0.0 then
        FindTax := OutOfRange                {salary too small}
     else if Salary < 1500.00 then        {first range}
        FindTax := 0.15 * Salary
     else if Salary < 3000.00 then          {second range}
        FindTax := (Salary - 1500.00) * 0.16 + 225.00
     else if Salary < 5000.00 then          {third range}
        FindTax := (Salary - 3000.00) * 0.18 + 465.00
     else if Salary < 8000.00 then          {fourth range}
        FindTax := (Salary - 5000.00) * 0.20 + 825.00
     else if Salary <= MaxSalary then     {fifth range}
        FindTax := (Salary - 8000.00) * 0.25 + 1425.00
     else
        FindTax := OutOfRange                {salary too large}
   end; {FindTax}

begin {Driver}
  Write ('Enter a salary less than or equal to $15000.00> $');
  ReadLn (MySalary);
  MyTax := FindTax(MySalary);
  if MyTax >= 0.0 then
     WriteLn ('The tax on $', MySalary :4:2,
              ' is $', MyTax :4:2)
  else
     WriteLn ('Salary $', Salary :4:2, ' is out of table range')
end. {Driver}
```

Sample Run

```
Enter a salary less than or equal to $15000.00> $6000.00
The tax on $6000.00 is $1025.00
```

Second, the function result is computed in the function but is displayed by the `WriteLn` statement in the calling program. Generally, you should use `WriteLn` statements in functions only to display error messages.

Third, notice that the function body defines the function result by assigning a value to the function name, `FindTax`. After the function return, the assignment statement

```
MyTax := FindTax(MySalary);
```

in the main program assigns the function result to `MyTax`. Sometimes beginning programmers incorrectly assign a value to `MyTax`, instead of `FindTax`, in the function body. Because `MyTax` is a global variable, the function would compile without error, but the function result would be undefined so "garbage" would be assigned to `MyTax` after the function return.   ▲

Program Style

Validating Input Parameters

The `if` statement in function `FindTax` tests for an invalid value of the input parameter `Salary` before performing the tax computation. All procedures and functions should validate their input parameters; there are no guarantees that the values passed to an input parameter will be meaningful.

Program Style

Cohesive Modules

Function `FindTax` only computes the payroll tax. It neither reads in a value for `Salary` nor displays the computed result, nor does it display an error message if the value passed to `Salary` is out of range. It simply returns a special value (`-1.0`), and the calling program displays the error message.

Modules that perform a single operation are called *cohesive modules*. Writing cohesive modules is good programming style, for they help to keep functions and procedures relatively compact and easy to read, write, and debug.

Program Style

Writing Driver Programs to Test Modules

The main program body in Fig. 6.15 consists of a statement for data entry, an assignment statement with a function designator in its expression part, and an `if` statement to display the function result. The sole purpose of the program is to test the function `FindTax`. Such a program is called a *driver program*.

Experienced programmers often use driver programs to pretest functions and procedures. Generally the small investment in time and effort required to write a short driver program pays off by reducing the total time spent debugging a large program system that contains several modules.

Self-Check

1. Since both procedures and functions can return a result and procedures are not limited to one output, why do we need functions?
2. For function FindTax in Fig. 6.15, explain why you should not replace each of the assignment statements

    ```
    FindTax := OutOfRange
    ```

    with the WriteLn statement

    ```
    WriteLn (Salary :4:2, ' is out of range')
    ```

3. a. What does the following function do?

    ```
    function Hypot (X, Y : Real) : Real;
    begin {Hypot}
      Hypot := Sqrt(Sqr(X) + Sqr(Y))
    end; {Hypot}
    ```

    b. Write a statement that calls this function with arguments A and B and stores the function result in C.
4. Which of the following tasks would be best implemented as a function and which as a procedure? Justify your answer.
    a. Computing the volume of a cone
    b. Displaying user instructions
    c. Testing whether a data value is in a specified range
    d. Computing the angle and muzzle velocity for a cannon based on the desired range

Programming

1. Write a driver program that tests function FindTax for all values of Salary from -400.00 to 15100.00 in increments of 500.00.
2. Write a function that raises a real number (X) to an integer power (N) by multiplying X by itself N times (use a for loop). Will your function work for negative values of X or N? *Hint:* To make your function work for negative values of N, use Abs(N) as the final expression in the for loop. Then use $X^N = 1 / X^{-N}$ to compute the correct result when N is negative.

6.6 Stepwise Design with Functions and Procedures

Using parameter lists to pass information to and from procedures and functions will improve your problem-solving skills. If the solution to a subproblem cannot be written easily using just a few Pascal statements, code it as a procedure or a function. The following case study demonstrates stepwise design of programs using procedures and functions.

General Sum-and-Average Problem

PROBLEM ▼

Accumulate a sum and average a list of data values using procedure and functions modules. Because these tasks surface in many problems, design a general set of modules you can reuse in other programs.

ANALYSIS ▼

The loop in Fig. 5.4 computed a company's total payroll. We can use a similar loop to compute the sum of a collection of data values. To compute an average, you would divide a sum by the total number of items, being careful not to perform this division if the number of items is 0.

Data Requirements

Problem Inputs

```
NumItems : Integer      {number of data items to be summed}
Item : Real             {each data item}
```

Problem Outputs

```
Sum : Real              {sum of data items}
Average : Real          {average of data}
```

Relevant Formula

average = sum of data / number of data items

DESIGN ▼

Initial Algorithm

1. Read the number of items.
2. Read the data and compute the sum of the data.
3. Compute the average of the data.
4. Print the sum and the average.

The structure chart in Fig. 6.16 documents the data flow between the main problem and its subproblems. We will implement as a separate module each step that has a nontrivial solution; the label under a step denotes the name of the module that implements that step. Each step except the first is implemented in a separate module.

Figure 6.16 clarifies the data flow between the main program and each module. All variables whose values are set by a module are *module outputs*

Figure 6.16
Structure Chart with Data Flow Information

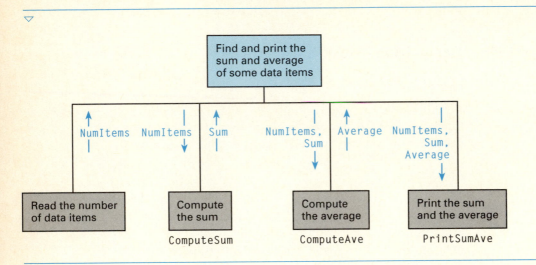

(indicated by an arrow pointing out of the module). All variables whose values are used in a computation but are not changed by the module are *module inputs* (indicated by an arrow pointing into the module). The role of each program variable depends on its usage in a module and changes from step to step in the structure chart.

Because the step *Read the number of data items* defines the value of `NumItems` this variable is an output of this step. Module `ComputeSum` needs the value of `NumItems` to know how many data items to read and sum; consequently, `NumItems` is an input to module `ComputeSum`. The variable `Sum` is an output of module `ComputeSum` but is an input to modules `ComputeAve` and `PrintSumAve`. The variable `Average` is an output of module `ComputeAve` but is an input to module `PrintSumAve`.

IMPLEMENTATION ▼

Using the data flow information in the structure chart, you can write the main program before refining the algorithm. Follow the approach described in Section 3.1 to write the main program. Begin by copying the data requirements into the program declaration part. Declare all the variables that appear in the structure chart in the main program, because they store data passed to a module or results returned from a module. Omit the declaration for variable `Item`, since it does not appear in the structure chart, but be sure to declare it in the module that uses it (`ComputeSum`). Next move the initial algorithm into the program body, writing each algorithm step as a comment (Fig. 6.17).

Figure 6.17
Main Program for General
Sum-and-Average Problem

Directory: CHAP6
File: SUMITEMS.PAS

```pascal
program SumItems (Input, Output);
{Finds and prints the sum and average of a list of data items}

   var
      NumItems : Integer; {input - number of items to be added}
      Sum,                 {output - sum being accumulated}
      Average : Real;      {output - average of the data}
   {
   Insert declarations for procedures ComputeSum and PrintSumAve
   and function ComputeAve here.
   }

begin {SumItems}
   Read the number of items.}
   Write ('How many numbers will be added> ');
   ReadLn (NumItems);

   {Read the data items and compute their sum.}
   ComputeSum (NumItems, Sum);

   {Compute the average of the data.}
   Average := ComputeAve(NumItems, Sum);

   {Print the sum and average.}
   PrintSumAve (NumItems, Sum, Average)
end. {SumItems}
```

To complete the main program, code each algorithm step *in-line* (as part of the main program code) or as a procedure or function call. Code the data entry step in-line, since it consists of a simple Write (for a prompt) and a ReadLn. Modules ComputeSum and ComputeAve return a single result, so you could write them as functions. However, code ComputeSum as a procedure because it reads the data items that are included in the sum. The data entry operations would be a side effect if ComputeSum were a function.

The data flow information in Fig. 6.16 tells you the actual parameters to use in each procedure or function call. In the case of a function, it also tells you the name of the main program variable that will hold the function result. For example, use the assignment statement

```pascal
Average := ComputeAve(NumItems, Sum);
```

to call ComputeAve and set the value of Average. In this call, NumItems and Sum are passed as input parameters to function ComputeAve.

Call ComputeSum using the procedure call statement

```pascal
ComputeSum (NumItems, Sum);
```

where NumItems is an input parameter and Sum is an output parameter.

Call `PrintSumAve` using the procedure call statement

`PrintSumAve (NumItems, Sum, Average)`

where all three parameters are procedure inputs.

Procedure ComputeSum

With the main program complete, you can concentrate on its individual modules, starting with procedure `ComputeSum`. Begin the data requirements for `ComputeSum` with the procedure inputs and outputs. `ComputeSum` also needs two local variables: one for storing each data item (`Item`) and one for loop control (`Count`).

Data Requirements for ComputeSum

Procedure Input

`NumItems : Integer`   `{number of data items to be summed}`

Procedure Output

`Sum : Real`   `{the sum of the data items}`

Local Variables

`Item : Real`   `{each data item}`
`Count : Integer`   `{count of data items summed}`

Before accumulating a sum in a loop, initialize the sum to zero prior to loop entry (see Section 5.2). The loop-control steps must ensure that the correct number of data items are read and included in the sum being accumulated. Since you know the number of items to sum beforehand (`NumItems`), use a counting loop. Use these steps to write the algorithm for `ComputeSum`; Fig. 6.18 shows the code for `ComputeSum`.

Algorithm for ComputeSum

1. Initialize `Sum` to 0
2. for each value of `Count` from 1 to `NumItems` do
 `begin`
      3. Read in the next item.
      4. Add it to `Sum`
 `end`

Figure 6.19 shows the parameter correspondence specified by the procedure call statement

`ComputeSum (NumItems, Sum);`

assuming the value 10 is read into `NumItems` just before the procedure call. The local variables, `Count` and `Item`, are undefined when the procedure is

Figure 6.18
Procedure ComputeSum

Directory: CHAP6
File: SUMITEMS.PAS

```
procedure ComputeSum (NumItems {input} : Integer;
                      var Sum {output} : Real);
{
  Computes the sum of a list of NumItems data items.
  Pre : NumItems is assigned a value.
  Post: NumItems data items are read; their sum is stored in
        Sum.
}

  var
    Count : Integer;          {count of items added so far}
    Item : Real;              {the next data item to be added}

begin  {ComputeSum}
  {Read each data item and add it to Sum.}
  Sum := 0.0;
  for Count := 1 to NumItems do
    begin
      Write ('Next number to be added> ');
      ReadLn (Item);
      Sum := Sum + Item
    end {for}
end; {ComputeSum}
```

Figure 6.19
Parameter Correspondence
for ComputeSum
(NumItems, Sum)

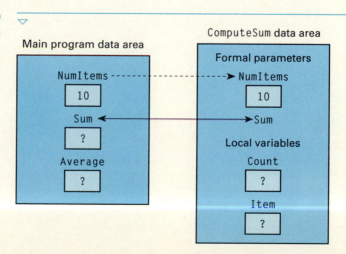

called. The procedure begins by initializing to 0 the main program variable Sum, which corresponds to variable parameter Sum. The for loop reads each data item into local variable Item and adds it to the main program variable Sum. The loop exit and procedure return occur after 10 items have been added.

Function ComputeAve and Procedure PrintSumAve

Both ComputeAve and PrintSumAve are relatively straightforward, as can be seen from their data requirements and algorithms, listed next. Both algorithms test NumItems, because it makes no sense to compute or display the average of the data items if NumItems is not positive. Figure 6.20 shows function ComputeAve, and Fig. 6.21 shows procedure PrintSumAve.

Data Requirements for ComputeAve

Function Inputs

```
NumItems : Integer          {the number of data items}
Sum : Real                  {the sum of all data}
```

Function Output

```
ComputeAve : Real              {the average of the data}
```

Algorithm for ComputeAve

1. if NumItems is positive then
     2.   Set ComputeAve to Sum / NumItems
    else
     3.   Set ComputeAve to 0

Figure 6.20
Function ComputeAve

Directory: CHAP6
File: SUMITEMS.PAS

```
function ComputeAve (NumItems : Integer;
                     Sum : Real) : Real;
{
  Returns the average of NumItems data items with sum of Sum.
  Pre : NumItems and Sum are defined.
  Post: If NumItems is positive, returns Sum / NumItems;
        otherwise, returns zero
}
begin {ComputeAve}
  {Compute the average of the data.}
  if NumItems > 0 then
    ComputeAve := Sum / NumItems
  else
    ComputeAve := 0.0
end; {ComputeAve}
```

Figure 6.21
Procedure PrintSumAve

Directory: CHAP6
File: SUMITEMS.PAS

```
Procedure PrintSumAve  (NumItems {input} : Integer;
                        Sum, Average {input} : Real);
{
  Displays the sum and average of NumItems data items.
  Pre : NumItems, Sum, and Average are defined.
  Post: Displays Sum and also Average if NumItems > 0.
}
begin {PrintSumAve}
  if NumItems > 0 then
    begin
      WriteLn ('The sum is ', Sum :4:2);
      WriteLn ('The average is ', Average :4:2)
    end
  else
    WriteLn ('Sum and average are not defined')
end; {PrintSumAve}
```

Data Requirements for PrintSumAve

Procedure Inputs

```
NumItems : Integer          {the number of data items}
Sum : Real                  {the sum of all data}
Average : Real              {the average of the data}
```

Algorithm for PrintSumAve

1. if NumItems is positive then
> **2.** Display the sum and the average of the data

TESTING ▼

You must insert the function and procedure declarations in the declaration part of program SumItems (after the variable declarations) before you can run the program. In testing SumItems, make sure that the program displays the sum and the average correctly when NumItems is positive and displays an error message when NumItems is zero or negative. Figure 6.22 shows a sample run.

Figure 6.22
Sample Run of SumItems

```
How many numbers will be added> 3
Next number to be added> 5.0
Next number to be added> 6.0
Next number to be added> -7.0
The sum is 4.00
The average is 1.33
```

When to Use a Function or Procedure

In the four steps of the general sum-and-average program (see Fig. 6.16), all but the first step are performed by separate modules. It was obvious that step 1 could be implemented using a `Write` and a `ReadLn`, so that step was written directly in the main program. We used a procedure (`ComputeSum`) for step 2 because its algorithm was relatively complicated. Even though steps 3 and 4 were relatively easy to implement, we used a function (`ComputeAve`) for step 3 and a procedure (`PrintSumAve`) for step 4 because their implementations were rather lengthy. Follow this line of reasoning in determining whether to implement a step as a separate module. From this point on, your main program bodies should consist primarily of a sequence of procedure and function calls.

Multiple Declarations of Identifiers in a Program

The identifiers `Sum` and `NumItems` are declared as global variables in the main program and as formal parameters in the three modules called by the main program. From the discussion of scope of identifiers, you know that each of these declarations has its own scope and that the scope for each formal parameter is the module that declares it. The parameter lists associate global variable `Sum` with each of the other identifiers named `Sum`. The value of global variable `Sum` is initially defined when procedure `ComputeSum` executes because global variable `Sum` corresponds to `ComputeSum`'s output parameter `Sum`. This value is passed into function `ComputeAve` because global variable `Sum` corresponds to `ComputeAve`'s input parameter `Sum`, and so on.

To avoid the confusion of seeing the identifier `Sum` in multiple modules, we could have introduced different names in each module (e.g., `Total`, `My-Sum`). However, the program is easier to read if the name `Sum` is used throughout to refer to the sum of the data values. Make sure that you remember to link these separate uses of identifier `Sum` through parameter lists.

Exercises for Section 6.6   **Self-Check**

1. Procedure `ComputeSum` returns a single value. Why do you think it was not implemented as a function?
2. Draw the main program data area and the function data area for the call to `ComputeAve`, assuming that `Sum` is `100.0` and `NumItems` is `10`.
3. Draw the main program data area and the procedure data area for the call to `PrintSumAve`.

6.7   Debugging and Testing Programs with Modules

As the number of statements in a program or module grows, the possibility of error increases. Keeping each module to a manageable size lowers the likelihood of error and enhances readability and testing of each module.

Just as you can simplify the overall programming process by writing a large program as a set of independent modules, you can simplify testing and debugging a program with multiple modules if you test in stages as the program evolves. Two kinds of testing are used: top-down testing and bottom-up testing. You should use a combination of these methods to test a program and its modules.

Top-Down Testing and Stubs

program system
a main program together with its modules

Whether a single programmer or a programming team is developing a **program system** (a main program and its modules), not all modules will be ready at the same time. It is possible, however, to test the overall flow of control between the main program and its level-1 modules and to test and debug the level-1 modules that are complete. The process of testing the flow of control between a main program and its subordinate modules is called **top-down testing.**

top-down testing
the process of testing flow of control between a main program and its subordinate modules

stub
a module with a heading and minimal body used in testing flow of control

Because the main program calls all level-1 modules, we need a substitute, called a stub, for all modules that are not yet coded. A **stub** consists of a procedure or function heading followed by a minimal body, which should display a message identifying the module being executed and should assign simple values to any outputs. Figure 6.23 shows a stub for procedure ComputeSum that could be used in a test of the main program in Fig. 6.17. The stub arbitrarily assigns a value of 100.0 to output parameter Sum, which is reasonable data for the remaining modules to process. Examining the program output tells us whether the main program calls its level-1 modules in the required sequence and whether data flows correctly between the main program and its level-1 modules.

Bottom-Up Testing and Drivers

A completed module can be substituted for its stub, of course, but always perform a preliminary test of a new module first. Locating and correcting er-

Figure 6.23
Stub for Procedure
ComputeSum

```
procedure ComputeSum (NumItems {input} : Integer;
                         var Sum {output} : Real);
{
   Computes the sum of a list of NumItems data items.
   Pre : NumItems is assigned a value.
   Post: NumItems data items are read; their sum is stored in
         Sum.
}
begin {ComputeSum stub}
   WriteLn ('Procedure ComputeSum entered');
   Sum := 100.0
end; {ComputeSum stub}
```

rors in a single module is easier than in a complete program system. You can test a new module by writing a short driver program similar to the one in Fig. 6.15.

Don't spend a lot of time creating an elegant driver program, because you will discard it as soon as the new module is tested. A driver program should contain only the declarations and executable statements necessary to test a single module. Moreover, it should begin by reading or assigning values to all input parameters and to input/output parameters, then call the module being tested. After calling the module, the driver program should display the module results.

Once you are confident that a module works properly, substitute it for its stub in the program system. The process of separately testing individual modules before inserting them into a program system is called **bottom-up testing**.

bottom-up testing

the process of separately testing individual modules for a program system

Through a combination of top-down and bottom-up testing, you can become fairly confident that the complete program system will be relatively free of errors when it is finally assembled. Consequently, the final debugging sessions should proceed quickly and smoothly.

Debugging Tips for Modular Programs

Here are some suggestions for debugging a program system:

1. As you write the code, carefully place comments to document each module parameter and local identifier. Also use comments to describe the module operation.
2. Leave a trace of execution by placing a `WriteLn` statement that displays the module name at the beginning of the module body.
3. Insert statements that display the values of all input and input/output parameters upon entry to a module. Check that these values make sense.
4. Insert statements that display the values of all module outputs after returning from a module. Hand-compute these values to verify that they are correct. For procedures, make sure that all input/output and output parameters are declared as variable parameters.
5. Make sure that a module stub assigns a value to each of its outputs.

It is a good idea to plan for debugging as you write each module rather than adding debugging steps afterwards. Include the output statements suggested for tips 2 to 4 in the Pascal code for the module. When satisfied that the module works as desired, remove the debugging statements. The simplest way is to change them to comments by enclosing them in braces; if you have a problem later, you can remove the braces, thereby changing the comments back to executable statements.

Another approach to turning debugging statements on and off is to use a global Boolean constant (say, `Debug`), which is declared in the main program. Use the declaration

```
const
  Debug = True;        {Turn debugging on.}
```

during debugging runs, and the declaration

```
const
  Debug = False;       {Turn debugging off.}
```

during normal runs. Within the main program body and its procedures, embed each diagnostic WriteLn statement in an if statement with Debug as its condition. If procedure ComputeSum begins with the following if statement, the WriteLn statements will execute only during debugging runs (Debug is True), as desired:

```
if Debug then
  begin
    WriteLn ('Procedure ComputeSum entered');
    WriteLn ('Input parameter NumItems has value ', NumItems :1)
  end; {if}
```

6.8 Recursive Functions (Optional)

recursive module

a procedure or function that calls itself

factorial of N

the product of all positive integers ≤ N

Pascal allows a function or procedure to call itself. A module that calls itself is a **recursive module.** We describe a recursive function in this section, one that returns an integer value representing the factorial of its argument. The **factorial of N** is the product of all positive integers less than or equal to N and is written in mathematics as $N!$. For example, 4! is the product $4 \times 3 \times 2 \times 1$ or 24.

Figure 6.24 shows a nonrecursive factorial function that uses a loop to accumulate partial products in local variable ProductSoFar. The for statement repeats the multiplication step when N is greater than 1. If N is 0 or 1, the for statement does not execute, so ProductSoFar retains its initial value of 1. After loop exit, the last value of ProductSoFar is assigned to Factorial, thereby defining the function result.

Figure 6.25 shows function Factorial rewritten as a recursive function, in which the if statement implements the following formulas, which form the recursive definition of $N!$:

$$N! = 1 \qquad\qquad \text{for } N = 0 \text{ or } 1$$
$$N! = N \times (N-1)! \qquad \text{for } N > 1$$

When N is greater than 1, instead of executing a loop to repeat the multiplication, as in Fig. 6.24, the statement

```
Factorial := N * Factorial(N-1)
```

executes, which is the Pascal form of the second formula. The expression part of this statement contains a function designator, Factorial(N-1), which calls function Factorial with an argument that is 1 less than the cur-

```
function Factorial (N : Integer) : Integer;
{
  Computes N!
  Pre : N >= 0
  Post: Returns the product 1 * 2 * 3 * . . . * N for N > 1;
        returns 1 when N is 0 or 1.
}
  var
    I,                             {loop-control variable}
    ProductSoFar : Integer;   {accumulated product}

begin {Factorial}
  ProductSoFar := 1;        {Initialize accumulated product.}

  {Perform the repeated multiplication for N > 1.}
  for I := 2 to N do
    ProductSoFar := ProductSoFar * I;

  {Define function result.}
  Factorial := ProductSoFar
end; {Factorial}
```

rent argument. This function call is a *recursive call*. If the argument in the initial call to Factorial is 3, the following chain of recursive calls occurs:

```
Factorial(3) → 3 * Factorial(2) → 3 * (2 * Factorial(1))
```

In the last of these calls, N is equal to 1, so the statement

```
Factorial := 1
```

executes, stopping the chain of recursive calls.

```
function Factorial (N : Integer) : Integer;
{
  Computes N!
  Pre : N >= 0
  Post: Returns the product 1 * 2 * 3 * . . . * N for N > 1;
        returns 1 when N is 0 or 1.
}
begin {Factorial}
  if N <= 1 then
    Factorial := 1
  else
    Factorial := N * Factorial(N-1)
end; {Factorial}
```

When it finishes the last function call, Pascal must return a value from each recursive call, starting with the last one. The last call was `Factorial(1)` and it returns a value of 1. To find the value returned by each call for N greater than 1, multiply N by the value returned from `Factorial(N-1)`. Therefore the value returned from `Factorial(2)` is 2 * the value returned from `Factorial(1)` or 2; the value returned from `Factorial(3)` is 3 * the value returned from `Factorial(2)` or 6 (see Fig. 6.26).

Exercises for Section 6.8   ***Self-Check***

1. Show the chain of recursive calls to function `Mystery` when M is 4 and N is 3. What do you think `Mystery` does?

    ```
    function Mystery (M, N : Integer) : Integer;
    begin {Mystery}
      if N = 1 then
        Mystery:= M
      else
        Mystery:= M * Mystery(M, N-1)
    end; {Mystery}
    ```

Programming

1. Write a recursive function that, given an input value of N, computes N + N-1 + . . . + 2 + 1.
2. Write a function `C(N, R)` that returns the number of different ways *R* items can be selected from a group of *N* items. The mathematical for-

Figure 6.26
Evaluating Factorial(3)

mula for C(N, R) follows. Test C(N, R) using both the recursive and the nonrecursive versions of function Factorial.

$$C(N, R) = \frac{N!}{R!(N-R)!}$$

6.9   Common Programming Errors

Proper use of parameters is difficult for beginning programmers to master, but it is an essential skill. Of the many opportunities for error when you use modules with parameter lists, the obvious pitfall occurs in not ensuring that the actual parameter list has the same number of parameters as the formal parameter list. A syntax error such as number of parameters does not agree with declaration indicates this problem.

Each actual parameter must be assignment compatible with its corresponding formal parameter (for a value parameter) or the same data type (for a variable parameter). An actual parameter that corresponds to a variable formal parameter must be a variable. A violation results in an illegal parameter substitution syntax error.

Return a procedure result to the calling module by assigning a value to a variable parameter. Any such value assigned to a value parameter is stored locally in the procedure and will not be returned. If your procedure seems to execute properly but does not return the expected results, it is possible that you forgot to declare an output or input/output parameter as a variable parameter.

Remember to return all function results by assigning a value to the function name. It is bad programming practice to return a second function result through a variable parameter (function side effect). It is also bad programming practice to directly manipulate a global variable in a procedure or function; all global variables should be passed to a module through its parameter list.

The Pascal scope rules determine where an identifier can be referenced. If an identifier is referenced outside its scope, an identifier not declared syntax error will result.

CHAPTER REVIEW

1. Parameters enable a programmer to pass data to functions and procedures and to return results from procedures. The parameter list provides a highly visible communication path between a module and its calling program. Using parameters enables a module to process different data each time it executes, thereby simplifying reuse of the module in other programs.

2. There are two types of parameters: value parameters and variable parameters. A value parameter is used only for passing data into a module, and a variable

parameter is used to return results from a procedure. The actual parameter that corresponds to a value parameter can be an expression or a constant; the actual parameter that corresponds to a variable parameter must be a variable.

3. The scope of an identifier dictates where it can be referenced. An identifier can be referenced anywhere in the block that declares it. A global variable is one that is declared in the main program, and a local variable is one that is declared in a procedure or function module. A local variable is defined only during the execution of the module, and its value is lost when the module is exited. If there are multiple declarations of an identifier in different blocks, then the compiler uses the most local declaration when translating each block.

4. A function is a module that returns a single result. The function result is defined by assigning a value to the function name inside the function body. Function parameters should be value parameters.

Summary of New Pascal Constructs

Construct	Effect
Function Declaration	
| ```pascal
function Sign (X : Real) : Char;
begin {Sign}
   if X >= 0.0 then
      Sign := '+'
   else
      Sign := '-'
end; {Sign}
``` | Returns a character value that indicates the sign ('+' or '-') of its type Real argument X. |
| ***Procedure Declaration*** | |
| ```pascal
procedure DoIt (X : Real;
                Op : Char;
                var Y: Char;
                var XSign : Char);
begin {DoIt}
   case Op of
      '+' : Y := X + X;
      '*' : Y := X * X
   end; {case}
   XSign := Sign(X)
end; {DoIt}
``` | If Op is '+', returns X + X through Y; if Op is '*', returns X * X through Y. Calls Sign to assign a character value that indicates the sign ('+' or '-') of X to XSign. |
| ***Procedure Call Statement*** | |
| `DoIt (-5.0, '*', Y, MySign)` | Calls DoIt. Passes -5.0 into X, passes '*' into Op, returns 25.0 to Y, returns '-' to MySign. |

Quick-Check Exercises

1. The _____ parameters appear in the procedure call, and the _____ parameters appear in the procedure declaration.
2. Constants and expressions can correspond to formal parameters that are _____ parameters.
3. Formal parameters that are variable parameters must have actual parameters that are _____.
4. Formal parameters that are variable parameters must have actual parameters that are the _____ data type.
5. The data types of corresponding value parameters must be _____.
6. Which is used to test a new module, a driver or a stub?
7. Which is used to test main program flow, a driver or a stub?
8. A(n) _____ occurs when a function assigns a value to a variable parameter or when a procedure changes a global variable.
9. What are the values of main program variables X and Y after the following program executes?

```
program Nonsense (Input, Output);
  var X, Y : Real;

  procedure Silly (X : Real);
    var Y : Real;
  begin
    Y := 25.0;
    X := Y
  end; {Silly}

begin {Nonsense}
  Silly (X)
end. {Nonsense}
```

10. Answer Exercise 9, this time assuming parameter X of Silly is a variable parameter.
11. The parameters of a function should be _____ parameters.
12. The part of a program where an identifier can be referenced is called the _____ of the identifier.
13. True or false: Within a procedure body, any other procedure declared in the program can be called.
14. How does a function return its value?

Answers to Quick-Check Exercises

1. actual, formal
2. value
3. variables
4. same or identical
5. assignment compatible
6. Driver
7. Stub

8. side effect
9. Both are undefined.
10. X is 25.0, Y is undefined.
11. value
12. scope
13. False, a procedure declared later in the main program cannot be called.
14. A function returns its single value by assigning a value to the function name.

Review Questions

1. Write the procedure heading for a procedure called Script that accepts three parameters passed to it. The first parameter is the number of spaces to print at the beginning of a line. The second parameter is the character to print after the spaces, and the third parameter is the number of times to print the second parameter on the same line.

2. Write a function called LetterGrade that has a parameter called Grade and that returns the appropriate letter grade using a straight scale (90–100 is an A, 80–89 is a B, and so on).

3. Why would you choose to make a formal parameter a value parameter rather than a variable parameter?

4. Write a procedure that accepts two real values as input and outputs the sum and difference of the two values.

5. Describe a circumstance where a procedure would give different results if a value parameter in the procedure was changed to a variable parameter.

6. Explain the use of a stub in testing a program.

7. In the chart that follows, write Yes for each procedure on the right that can be referenced (called) by the procedure on the left and No for each procedure that is inaccessible.

```
program ProcScope
     (Input, Output);

  procedure A;

    procedure B;

      procedure C;

      . . .

      end; {C}

    procedure D;

    . . .

    end; {D}

  . . .

  end; {B}
```

Callable Procedures

Calling Procedure	A	B	C	D
A				
B				
C				
D				

```
    .  .  .

    end; {A}

    .  .  .

end. {ProcScope}
```

8. List two reasons for implementing a module as a procedure rather than as a function.

Programming Projects

1. The assessor in your town has estimated the market value of all properties and would like you to write a program that determines the tax owed on each property and the total tax to be collected. The tax rate is 12.5 cents per dollar of assessed value, and the assessed value of each property is 28% of its estimated market value. The market values are as follows:

    $150,000 $148,000 $145,500 $167,000 $137,600 $147,100

    $165,000 $153,350 $128,000 $158,000 $152,250 $148,000

    $156,500 $143,700

    You need to write procedures that correspond to the following procedure headers as part of your solution:

    ```
    procedure PrintInstructions;
    {Displays instructions to the user}

    procedure ProcessProperties (var TotalTax {output} : Real);
    {Reads market values and computes taxes on all properties}

    function ComputeTax (Market : Real) : Real;
    {Computes tax on a property with market value Market}

    procedure PrintSummary (TotalTax {input} : Real);
    {Displays value of TotalTax}
    ```

2. Revise Programming Project 1, assuming a 5% surcharge for all properties with market value over $150,000. Also grant a 10% discount for senior citizens. You will need to enter a second data item for each property to indicate whether its owner is a senior citizen. Write a separate procedure that reads and returns the current property market value and sets a Boolean parameter to True if the owner is a senior citizen.

3. The trustees of a small college are considering a 5.5% pay raise for its faculty members, but first they want to know how much this increase will cost. Write a program that prints the pay raise for each faculty member and the total amount of the raises, then prints the total faculty payroll before and after the raises. Test your program for the following salaries:

$32,500	$24,029.50	$36,000	$43,250
$35,500	$22,800	$30,000.50	$28,900
$43,780	$24,029.50	$44,120.25	$24,100

Refer to Programming Project 1 for a guide as to what procedures and functions will be needed.

4. Revise Programming Project 3, assuming that faculty earning less than $30,000 receive a 7% raise, faculty earning more than $40,000 receive a 4% raise, and all others receive a 5.5% raise. Write a new function that determines the raise percentage. Print the raise percentage as well as the amount for each faculty member.

5. A monthly magazine wants a program that prints out renewal and cancellation notices to its subscribers. Using procedures when advisable, write a program that first reads in the current month number (1 through 12) and year. For each subscription processed, read in four data items: the account number, the month and the year the subscription started, and the number of years paid for the subscription.

    Read in each set of subscription information and print a renewal notice if the current month is either the month prior to expiration or the month of expiration. A cancellation notice should be printed if the current month comes after the expiration month.

    Sample input might be as follows

    ```
    10 94              for a current month of October 1994
    1364  4  94  3     for account 1364, whose 3-year
                       subscription began in April 1994
    ```

6. Write a program that displays a running stopwatch. The user will enter the number of seconds that the stopwatch should run, starting at 0:00:00. Use a counter in your main program to represent the elapsed time and display each value of the counter. Times should be displayed as *hours:minutes:seconds* with leading zeros on the minutes and seconds. Write a procedure that displays a number as two digits with a leading zero. (Just test for less than 10 and output a zero and the number.) Write another procedure that accepts a time and displays it, using the last procedure to display the numbers. Finally, write a procedure that increments a time. Represent an elapsed time with three integer values.

7. The square root of a number N can be approximated by repeated calculation using the formula

    ```
    NG = 0.5(LG + N / LG)
    ```

    where NG stands for next guess and LG stands for last guess. Write a function that implements this process. The first parameter will be a positive real number, the second will be an initial guess of the square root, and the return value will be the computed result.

    The initial guess will be the starting value of LG. The function will compute a value for NG using the formula. The difference between NG and LG is checked to see whether these two guesses are almost identical. If so, the function is exited and NG is returned as the square root; otherwise, the new guess (NG) becomes the last guess (LG), and the process is repeated (i.e., another value is computed for NG, the difference is checked, etc.).

For this program, the loop should be repeated until the magnitude of the difference is less than 0.005 (Delta). Use an initial guess of 1.0 and test the program for the numbers 4, 120.5, 88, 36.01, and 10000.

8. The road stripe painters in your area have allied to form a monopoly. Each painter will paint up to two miles of stripes on the road. For roads longer than two miles, the painter will divide the area to be painted into three equal parts and subcontract each of those parts to three other painters, who will treat their sections the same way. Painters will charge $200.00 for each section they themselves paint and $100.00 to oversee the three they have hired. Write a program that allows a user to enter a road length and computes the cost to paint the entire road. *Hint:* Write a recursive function that returns 200 if the length is less than two miles or adds 100 to three recursive calls to the function with the length divided by 3. Try your program with 2, 54, 55, 100, and 1000 miles.

CHAPTER SEVEN

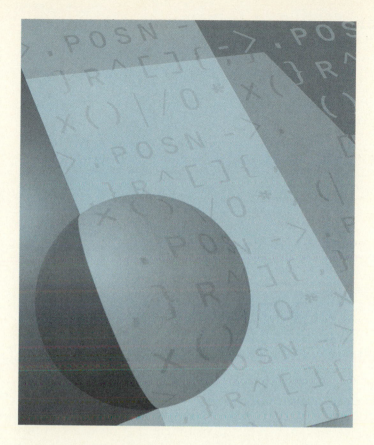

Simple Data Types

simple data type
a data type used to store a single value

We now take a closer look at Pascal's standard data types—`Integer`, `Real`, `Char`, and `Boolean`. We also describe some predefined functions for processing ordinal types.

No programming language can predefine all the data types a programmer may want to use, so Pascal allows a programmer to create new data types. In this chapter, you'll learn how to declare two new kinds of data types: subrange types and enumerated types. All these data types—standard types, subrange types, and enumerated types—are **simple,** or **scalar, data types** because only a single value can be stored in a variable of each type.

7.1   Numeric Data Types: Real and Integer

The data types `Integer` and `Real` represent numeric information. Although most numeric data are real, programmers typically use integers as loop counters and to represent whole-number data, such as exam scores.

Differences Between Numeric Types

We could represent an integer as a real number with a fractional part of 0, so why does Pascal need two numeric data types? On many computers, operations with integers are faster than those with real numbers and integers need less storage space than real numbers. Also, operations with integers are always precise, whereas there may be some loss of accuracy with real numbers.

These differences result from the way numbers are represented in the computer's memory. All data are represented in memory as *binary strings,* strings of 0s and 1s, but the binary string stored for, say, the integer 13 differs from that for the real number 13.0. The actual internal representation is computer dependent, and real numbers often require more bytes of computer memory.

Compare the sample integer and real formats shown in Fig. 7.1. The figure shows that integers are represented by binary numbers. For example, the integer 13 is represented as the binary number 0. . .01101. The leftmost bit represents the sign of the number; positive integers have a sign bit of 0 and negative integers have a sign bit of 1.

Real format (also called *floating-point format*) is analogous to scientific notation. The storage area occupied by a real number is divided into two sections: the *mantissa* and the *exponent.* The *mantissa* is a binary fraction $\geq$ 0.0 and < 1.0, and the *exponent* is a power of 2. The mantissa and the exponent are chosen so that the following formula is correct:

real number = mantissa $\times$ $2^{exponent}$

Because memory cells have a finite size, not all real numbers in the range of reals can be represented precisely.

Real numbers, unlike integers, can have a fractional part, and their range is considerably larger than that of integers. On IBM personal computers, real numbers range in value from 10^{-39} (a very small fraction) to 10^{+38}. The small-

Figure 7.1
Integer and Real Formats

Integer format

Binary number

Real format

Mantissa	Exponent

est positive integer is 1 and the largest integer, MaxInt (a predefined constant), is 32767. On most computers, real numbers require two or three times more storage space (bytes) than integers do.

Numerical Inaccuracies

One of the problems in processing real numbers is the chance of error in representing real data. Just as certain numbers cannot be represented exactly in the decimal number system (e.g., the fraction 1/3 is 0.333333 . . .), so some numbers cannot be represented exactly in real format. The size of this **representational error** depends on the number of binary digits (bits) used in the mantissa: The more bits, the smaller the error.

representational error
an error due to imprecise coding of a decimal number in binary form

For example, the decimal number 0.1 is a real number that cannot be represented exactly in the binary number system, resulting in a small error that would be magnified through repeated computations. Thus, because the result of adding 0.1 ten times is not exactly 1.0, the following loop may fail to terminate on some computers:

```
Trial := 0.0;
while Trial <> 1.0 do
  begin
     . . .

     Trial := Trial + 0.1
  end {while}
```

If the loop repetition test is changed to Trial < 1.0, the loop may execute 10 times on one computer and 11 times on another. To avoid this problem, use integer variables whenever possible in loop-repetition tests.

Other errors occur when manipulating very large and very small real numbers. Adding a large number and a very small number may cause the larger number to "cancel out" the smaller number, resulting in a **cancellation error.** If X is much larger than Y, then X + Y may have the same value as X (e.g., 100000.0 + 0.000001234 is equal to 100000.0 on some computers).

cancellation error
a computational error caused by processing a large number with a much small number

The result of multiplying two very small numbers may be an amount so small it is represented as zero (**arithmetic underflow**). Similarly, if two very large numbers are multiplied, the result may be too large to be represented (**arithmetic overflow**).

arithmetic underflow
an error caused by incorrectly representing a small computational result as zero

arithmetic overflow
an error caused by a computational result that is too large to be represented

Arithmetic overflow can occur even when processing relatively small integer values. For example, if Hours is 24, Min is 60, and Sec is 60, the statement

```
SecInDay := Hours * Min * Sec
```

assigns the number of seconds in a day (86400) to SecInDay. On some computers, this result is too large for type Integer, so you may get a run-time error. To avoid this error, you would be forced to use type Real variables.

Self-Check

1. Assuming a computer exhibits cancellation error such that 1000.0 + 0.0001234 is equal to 1000.0, what would be the result of the following assignment statement. Why?

    X := 1000.0001234;

Programming

1. Since the loop in the section on numerical inaccuracies may not operate correctly, write a loop that outputs the decimal fractions from 0.0 to 1.0 in steps of 0.1 using an integer as the loop counter.

7.2   The Boolean Data Type

Boolean variables have two values, True or False, which Pascal represents as the binary numbers 1 and 0, respectively. We can use the assignment operator with Boolean data and the Boolean operators and, or, not. Boolean expressions are used in if, while, and repeat statements.

Programmers write Boolean expressions that call Boolean functions to enhance program readability. Boolean functions return a value of True or False.

EXAMPLE 7.1: Boolean Functions ▼

We have written an algorithm that contains the following decision step. In this example, we have no interest in the details of the three procedures called in the if statement; we just want to make sure that the correct procedure is called.

```
if Ch is a letter then
   Call procedure ProcessLetter
else if Ch is a digit character then
   Call procedure ProcessDigit
else
   Call procedure ProcessSpecial
```

The if statement that follows implements this algorithm. The first Boolean expression calls function IsLetter (Fig. 7.2) to determine whether Ch is a letter; the second Boolean expression calls function IsDigit to determine whether Ch is a digit. The function designator IsLetter(Ch) returns a value of True if Ch is a letter and a value of False if Ch is not a letter. Similarly, the function designator IsDigit(Ch) returns a value of True if Ch is a digit character and a value of False otherwise.

Figure 7.2
Functions IsLetter
and IsDigit

Directory: CHAP7
File: ISLETTER.PAS

```
function IsLetter (Ch : Char) : Boolean;
{
 Returns True when its argument is a letter; otherwise,
 returns False
}
begin {IsLetter}
   IsLetter := (('A' <= Ch) and (Ch <= 'Z')) or
               (('a' <= Ch) and (Ch <= 'z'))
end; {IsLetter}

function IsDigit (Ch : Char) : Boolean;
{
 Returns True when its argument is a digit character;
 otherwise, returns False
}
begin {IsDigit}
   IsDigit := ('0' <= Ch) and (Ch <= '9')
end; {IsDigit}
```

```
if IsLetter(Ch) then
   ProcessLetter (Ch)
else if IsDigit(Ch) then
   ProcessDigit (Ch)
else
   ProcessSpecial (Ch)
```

Functions IsLetter and IsDigit consist of a statement that assigns a Boolean value to the function name, thereby defining the function result. The value assigned (True or False) depends on the result of the character comparison specified by the Boolean expression. We discuss character comparisons in the next section. ▲

Exercises for Section 7.2

Self-Check

1. Evaluate each of the following when Ch1 is 'a' and Ch2 is '3':
    a. IsLetter(Ch1) and IsDigit(Ch2)
    b. IsLetter(Ch1) or IsDigit(Ch2)
    c. IsLetter(Ch1) and IsDigit(Ch1)
    d. IsLetter(Ch1) or IsDigit(Ch1)

Programming

1. Write a Boolean function that has two integer parameters, M and N, and returns True when the value of M is a divisor of N and False otherwise. Important: Zero is not considered a divisor of any number.

7.3   **The Character Data Type**

The character data type (Char) can store and manipulate individual characters such as those that make up a person's name, address, and other personal data. A type Char literal consists of a single character (a letter, a digit, a punctuation mark, or the like) in apostrophes. If Next is type Char, the assignment statement

```
Next := 'A'
```

stores the letter A in Next.

You can compare character data using relational operators. If Next and First are type Char, the Boolean expressions

```
Next = First
Next <> First
```

determine whether two character variables have the same or different values. The relational operators <, <=, >, and >= allow you to make order comparisons on character data.

To interpret the result of an order comparison, you must know something about the way characters are represented internally in your computer. Each character has its own unique numeric code whose binary form is stored in a memory cell that has a character value. These binary numbers are compared by the relational operators.

Although the actual code is computer dependent, most computers use a character code called ASCII (American Standard Code for Information Interchange). ASCII and two other codes are listed in Appendix C. The digit characters, '0' through '9', are an increasing sequence of consecutive characters in ASCII and have code values of 48 through 57 (decimal). The following order relationship holds for the digit characters regardless of code:

```
'0'<'1'<'2'<'3'<'4'<'5'<'6'<'7'<'8'<'9'
```

The uppercase letters and lowercase letters are also an increasing sequence of consecutive characters. In ASCII, the uppercase letters have the decimal code values 65 through 90 and the lowercase letters have the decimal code values 97 through 122. The following order relationships hold for uppercase and lowercase letters regardless of code:

```
'A'<'B'<'C'< ... <'X'<'Y'<'Z'
'a'<'b'<'c'< ... <'x'<'y'<'z'
```

control character
a character whose "display" causes a special operation

In ASCII the *printable characters* have codes from 32 (the code for a blank or a space) to 126 (the code for the symbol ~). The remaining codes represent normally nonprintable **control characters**. Sending a control character to an output device causes the device to perform a special operation such as returning the cursor to column 1, advancing the cursor to the next line, or ringing a bell.

Exercises for Section 7.3   **Self-Check**

1. Evaluate the following:

    ```
    'A' < 'a'     'A' <> 'a'      'Z' > 'A'       'Z' > 'a'
    '0' <> 0      '0' <= '0'      '3' <= '9'      '9' <= 'A'
    ```

2. What does the following statement do?

    ```
    for Ch := 'A' to 'Z' do
       Write (Ch)
    ```

7.4   Ordinal Functions and Character Functions

Ordinal Data Types

ordinal data type

a data type having a finite set of values that can be listed in order from the first to the last

The data types Integer, Boolean, and Char are classified as **ordinal data types.** The values of an ordinal data type can always be listed in order, with each value having a unique predecessor (except the first) and a unique successor (except the last). For example, the predecessor of 5 is 4 and the successor of 5 is 6.

The order or sequence of an ordinal data type is defined. For example, either -MaxInt or -MaxInt - 1 is the smallest integer, and MaxInt is the largest integer. If -MaxInt - 1 is the smallest, the integers follow the sequence -MaxInt - 1, -MaxInt, . . ., -1, 0, 1, . . ., MaxInt - 1, MaxInt. The order of the Boolean values is False, True.

Ordinal Functions: Ord, Pred, and Succ

The Pascal function Ord determines the *ordinal number,* or relative position, of an ordinal value in its sequence of values. If the parameter of Ord is an integer, the ordinal number returned is the integer itself. For all other ordinal values, the ordinal number of the first value in the sequence is 0, the ordinal number of the second value is 1, and so on. For data type Boolean, Ord(False) is 0 and Ord(True) is 1. If variables A and B belong to the same ordinal type and A < B is true, then Ord(A) < Ord(B) also must be true.

The Pascal function Pred returns the predecessor of its parameter, and the Pascal function Succ returns the successor. These functions, like Ord, can be used only with parameters that are ordinal types.

EXAMPLE 7.2: Ordinal Functions with Integer and Boolean Data ▼

Table 7.1 shows the results of using the Ord, Succ, and Pred functions with an integer or Boolean parameter. The table shows that the largest value in each ordinal type (MaxInt, True) does not have a successor and the smallest does not have a predecessor. ▲

Table 7.1
Results of Some Ord, Succ,
and Pred Functions

Parameter	Ord	Succ	Pred
15	15	16	14
0	0	1	-1
-30	-30	-29	-31
MaxInt	MaxInt	Undefined	MaxInt - 1
-MaxInt	-MaxInt	-MaxInt + 1	Undefined or -MaxInt - 1
False	0	True	Undefined
True	1	Undefined	False

Although you can use the ordinal functions with any of the ordinal types, they are most often used with type Char and the enumerated types, which are discussed in Section 7.7. The ordinal number of a character is based on the character set code used and, therefore, is computer dependent.

EXAMPLE 7.3: Ordinal Functions with Character Data ▼

Table 7.2 shows some results of the Ord, Succ, and Pred functions for ASCII. The table shows that the digit '0' has the ordinal number 48 and the digit '7' has the ordinal number 55 in ASCII. Regardless of the character code used, the value of the expression

Ord('7') - Ord('0')

is 7 because the digit characters must be in consecutive sequence.

Table 7.2
Results of Some Ord, Succ,
and Pred Functions
for ASCII

Parameter	Ord	Succ	Pred
'C'	67	'D'	'B'
'c'	99	'd'	'b'
'0'	48	'1'	'/'
'7'	55	'8'	'6'
'y'	121	'z'	'x'
' '	32	'!'	Unprintable

Table 7.2 also shows that the character 'C' has the ordinal number 67 in ASCII. Since the character 'D' is the successor of the character 'C', it must have an ordinal number of 68. And since the letters are in consecutive sequence in ASCII, the value of the expression

```
Ord('C') - Ord('A')
```

is 2. In ASCII, the lowercase letters have larger code values than the uppercase letters, and the difference in code values for both cases of the same letter is 32 (e.g., `Ord('c') - Ord('C')` is 32). ▲

Character Functions

The function `Chr` returns a character as its result. The character returned is the one whose ordinal number is the function argument. For example, the result of the function reference `Chr(67)` is the character with ordinal number 67 (the letter C in the ASCII code).

If `Ch` is a type `Char` variable, the *nested function reference*

```
Chr(Ord(Ch))
```

has the same value as `Ch`. Therefore, the function `Chr` is the *inverse* of the `Ord` function for the characters.

EXAMPLE 7.4 ▼

Function `UpCase` in Fig. 7.3 returns a type `Char` result—the uppercase form of a lowercase letter passed to its parameter `Ch` (e.g., if `Ch` is 'c', `UpCase` returns 'C'). If `Ch` is 'c', the Boolean expression is true, and the first assignment statement is evaluated as

```
UpCase := Chr(Ord('c') - Ord('a') + Ord('A'))
         Chr(99 - 97 + 65)
         Chr(67) = 'C'
```

Figure 7.3
Function UpCase

Directory: CHAP7
File: UPCASE.PAS

```
function UpCase (Ch : Char) : Char;
{
  Returns the uppercase form of its argument.
  Pre : None.
  Post: Returns the uppercase equivalent of Ch if Ch is
        a lowercase letter; otherwise, returns Ch.
}
begin {UpCase}
  if (Ch >= 'a') and (Ch <= 'z') then
    UpCase := Chr(Ord(Ch) - Ord('a') + Ord('A'))
  else
    UpCase := Ch
end; {UpCase}
```

If Ch does not contain a lowercase letter, function UpCase returns Ch as its result.   ▲

EXAMPLE 7.5: Collating Sequence ▼

A *collating sequence* is a sequence of characters arranged by ordinal number. The program in Fig. 7.4 prints part of Pascal's collating sequence, the characters with ordinal numbers 32 through 90, inclusive. Assuming the ASCII code is used, the first character printed is a blank (ordinal number 32).   ▲

Table 7.3 summarizes the functions introduced in this section, including UpCase, which is not a standard function.

Table 7.3
Ordinal and
Character Functions

Function	Purpose	Argument	Result
Chr(N)	Returns the character whose ordinal number is N	Integer	Char
Ord(N)	Returns the ordinal number of its argument	Any ordinal type	Integer
Pred(N)	Returns the predecessor of its argument	Any ordinal type	Same as argument
Succ(N)	Returns the successor of its argument	Any ordinal type	Same as argument
UpCase(Ch)	Returns uppercase equivalent of argument (not standard)	Char	Char

Figure 7.4
Printing Part of a Collating
Sequence

Directory: CHAP7
File: COLLATE.PAS

```
program Collate (Input, Output);

{Prints part of the collating sequence}
  const
    Min = 32;                          {smallest ordinal number}
    Max = 90;                          {largest ordinal number}

  var
    NextOrd : Integer;                 {each ordinal number}

begin {Collate}
  {Print characters Chr(32) through Chr(90).}
  for NextOrd := Min to Max do
    Write (Chr(NextOrd));              {Print next character.}

  WriteLn
end. {Collate}
```

▷ ▷ ▷ ▷ ▷

Sample Run

```
!="#$%&'()*+,-./0123456789:;<=>@ABCDEFGHIJKLMNOPQRSTUVWXYZ
```

△

Exercises for Section 7.4

Self-Check

1. Evaluate the following:
    a. `Ord(True)`   c. `Succ(False)`
    b. `Pred(True)`   d. `Ord(True) - Ord(False)`
2. Evaluate the following, assuming the letters are consecutive characters.
    a. `Ord('D') - Ord('A')`   f. `Ord('7') - Ord('6')`
    b. `Ord('d') - Ord('a')`   g. `Ord('7') - Ord('6')`
    c. `Succ(Pred('a'))`   h. `Succ(Succ(Succ('d')))`
    d. `Chr(Ord('C'))`   i. `Chr(Ord('A') + 5)`
    e. `Chr(Ord('Z') - Ord('A') + Ord('a'))`
3. Write a `while` loop equivalent to the following `for` loop:

    ```
    for Ch := 'A' to 'Z' do
      WriteLn (Ch, Ord(Ch));
    ```

Programming

1. Write a function `LowCase` that returns as its value the lowercase equivalent of its character argument or, if there is none, returns the value of its argument.

7.5 Subrange Types

subrange type
an ordinal data type whose values are a subset of another ordinal type
host type (base type)
the data type whose range of values is restricted in a subrange type declaration

Pascal allows you to define your own data types. The first user-defined data type we consider is the **subrange type,** where a *subrange* defines a subset of the values associated with a particular ordinal type (the **host type** or **base type**). Subranges indicate the range of values allowed for an ordinal variable, so they enable Pascal to detect when a variable is given a value that is unreasonable in the problem environment.

EXAMPLE 7.6 ▼

To define a subrange, or any new data type, you write a type declaration that begins with the reserved word `type`. This example illustrates the declaration of two subrange types, as well as a variable of each new type:

```
type
  Letter = 'A'..'Z';
  DaysInMonth = 1..31;
```

```
var
   NextChar : Letter;       {NextChar is an uppercase letter.}
   InDay : DaysInMonth;     {InDay is an integer <= 31.}
```

The first subrange, Letter, has the host type Char, so any character value from 'A' to 'Z', inclusive, can be stored in a variable of type Letter. The computer may display an error message and stop program execution if you attempt to read any other character into a variable of type Letter. The assignment statement

```
NextChar := 'a'
```

may cause a compilation error because the character value 'a' is not included in data type Letter. If this error is not detected at compile time, it will cause an out of range run-time error.

DaysInMonth is a subrange with host type Integer. A variable of type DaysInMonth can store the day of the month, a number between 1 and 31 inclusive. The statement

```
ReadLn (InDay)
```

reads a data value into InDay (type DaysInMonth). An out of range run-time error occurs for values < 1 or > 31. ▲

The host type for a subrange is determined by the pair of values that defines the subrange; the ordinal number of the first value must be less than or equal to the ordinal number of the second value. Operations that are valid for the host type can be performed on any of its subrange types. Subrange type identifiers have the same scope rules as other Pascal identifiers.

SYNTAX DISPLAY

Subrange Type Declaration

Form: type *subrange-type* = *minvalue* .. *maxvalue*;
Example: type LowCase = 'a'..'z';
Interpretation: A new data type named *subrange-type* is defined. A variable of type *subrange-type* can be assigned a value from *minvalue* through *maxvalue,* inclusive. The values *minvalue* and *maxvalue* must belong to the same ordinal type (called the host type), and Ord(*minvalue*) must be less than or equal to Ord(*maxvalue*).
Note: *minvalue* and *maxvalue* may be constant identifiers.

Program Style

Motivation for Using Subranges

Most programmers want a program to stop executing as soon as it stores bad data in a variable, and not perform calculations that lead to meaningless results or a run-time error at some later point. Subrange types provide this capability. As soon as a program attempts to store an out-of-range value in a variable whose type is a subrange, the program will stop and indicate an `out of range` error.

Subrange types also enhance program documentation. They clearly indicate to the program reader which variables have a restricted range of values.

The Order of Pascal Declarations

In standard Pascal, the type declarations for a subrange type or any other user-defined data type must come between the constant declarations and the variable declarations in a Pascal block. The form of the declaration part for a standard Pascal block is

constant declarations
type declarations
variable declarations
procedure and function declarations

Although many compilers do not require that this order be followed, you still must declare each identifier before its first use. This means that you must declare a user-defined data type before declaring a variable of that type.

Exercises for Section 7.5

Self-Check

1. Which of the following subranges are illegal and why?
   a. `1..MaxInt`   f. `0..'9'`
   b. `'A'..'Z'`   g. `15..-15`
   c. `-15..15`   h. `'ACE'..'HAT'`
   d. `'A'..'z'`   i. `'a'..'Z'`
   e. `-5.0..5.0`   j. `-MaxInt..-MaxInt + 5`
2. The following type declaration and procedure is supposed to ensure the range of an input number is correct, but it generates `out of range` errors anyway. Why?

```
type
   Year = 1990..2000;          {valid years}

procedure SafeYear (var Y {output} : Year);
begin {SafeYear}
   repeat
     Write ('Input year 1990-2000> ');
     ReadLn (Y)
   until (Y >= 1990) and (Y <= 2000)
end; {SafeYear}
```

Programming

1. Write a type declaration for a type `Month` appropriate to represent the month number and write a procedure `ReadMonth` that has an output parameter M (type `Month`). Your procedure should prompt the user to enter a month as a word and return a valid month number.

7.6 Type Compatibility and Assignment Compatibility

We discussed assignment compatibility in Section 2.5. Now that we can use more data types, we must reexamine our rules for data type compatibility.

Type Identical

type identical data types
data types that are equivalent

Two data types are **type identical** (the same data type) when one of the following conditions holds:

▶ They are declared to be equivalent to each other.
▶ Each data type is declared to be equivalent to a third type identifier.

The type declarations

```
type
   Numbers = Integer;
   PosAndNeg = Numbers;
   IntType = PosAndNeg;
```

have the effect of making Numbers, PosAndNeg, IntType, and Integer identical types. However, Percent and Hundred as declared next are not identical types because each is declared to be identical to the same subrange (1..100), not the same type identifier:

```
type
   Percent = 1..100;
   Hundred = 1..100;
```

Type Compatibility

type compatible data types
data types that can be used
with the same operator

Two data types are **type compatible** if any of the following conditions holds:

▶ They are type identical.
▶ One type is a subrange of the other (for example, Letter and Char in Example 7.6).
▶ Both data types are subranges of the same host type.

Operands that are type compatible can be manipulated together. For example, the expression

```
NextChar <> '3'
```

is syntactically correct as long as NextChar is type Char or Letter. On the other hand, the expression

```
NextChar <> 3
```

causes a syntax error because the integer 3 is not type compatible with NextChar.

Assignment Compatibility

assignment compatible
an expression whose value is
within the range allowed for
the variable receiving it

An expression is **assignment compatible** with a variable if any of the following conditions holds:

▶ Their types are type identical.
▶ They are compatible data types and the value of the expression falls within the range of possible values for the variable.
▶ The variable is type `Real` and the expression is type `Integer`.

If a variable and an expression are assignment compatible, then the expression can be assigned to the variable without error.
  Assuming the declarations

```
type
  Letter = 'A'..'Z';

var
  NextCh : Letter;      {NextCh is an uppercase letter.}
  Ch : Char;
```

the assignment statement

```
NextCh := '3';
```

causes a compile-time error or an `out of range` run-time error because the literal `'3'` is not assignment compatible with the variable `NextCh` (type `Letter`). Because `Ch` is type `Char`, the assignment statement

```
NextCh := Ch;
```

will compile, but it may cause an `out of range` error at run time. This error occurs if the character stored in `Ch` is not an uppercase letter.

Parameter Correspondence and Type Compatibility

What are the requirements for types of corresponding parameters? For variable parameters, each actual parameter must be type identical with its corresponding formal parameter. For value parameters, each actual parameter must be assignment compatible with its corresponding formal parameter.

Exercises for Section 7.6   *Self-Check*

1. Assuming that `I` is type `0..10`, `J` is type `Integer`, and `K` is type `Real`, indicate whether each of the following expressions is assignment compatible with the variable on the left and what constraints are necessary to avoid an out-of-range error:
   a. `K := 3 * I + J`   e. `I := I / J`
   b. `I := 15`   f. `I := J mod 11`
   c. `J := Trunc(K) + 2 * I`   g. `J := 2 * K + 3`
   d. `I := I div J`

2. Explain why a compiler cannot determine whether an `out of range` error may occur at run time for a particular assignment statement.

7.7 Enumerated Types

The solution to many programming problems requires new data types. For example, in a budget program you might want to distinguish among the following categories of expenditures: entertainment, rent, utilities, food, clothing, automobile, insurance, miscellaneous. Although you could create an arbitrary code that associates entertainment with a character value of `'e'`, rent with a character value of `'r'`, and so on, Pascal allows you to create **enumerated types**, each with its own list of meaningful values.

enumerated type
a data type whose list of values is specified by the programmer in a type declaration

For example, the enumerated type `Expenses` has eight possible values enclosed in parentheses:

```
type
   Expenses = (Entertainment, Rent, Utilities, Food,
               Clothing, Automobile, Insurance, Miscellaneous);

var
   ExpenseKind : Expenses;
```

The variable `ExpenseKind` (type `Expenses`) can contain any of the eight values. The following `if` statement tests the value stored in `ExpenseKind`:

```
if ExpenseKind = Entertainment then
   WriteLn ('Postpone until after your payday.')
else if ExpenseKind = Rent then
   WriteLn ('Pay before the fifth of the month!')
. . .
```

EXAMPLE 7.7 ▼

The enumerated type `Day` has the values `Sunday`, `Monday`, and so on:

```
type
   Day = (Sunday, Monday, Tuesday, Wednesday,
          Thursday, Friday, Saturday);       {days of the week}
```

The values associated with an enumerated type must be identifiers; they cannot be numeric, character, or string literals (e.g., `'Sunday'` cannot be a value for an enumerated type). ▲

The scope rules for identifiers apply to enumerated types and their values. Each enumerated type value is treated as a constant identifier in the block containing the type declaration statement. The type declaration must precede any variable declaration that references it.

SYNTAX DISPLAY

Enumerated Type Declaration

Form: `type` *enumerated-type* `=` (*identifier-list*)`;`
Example: `type Class = (Freshman, Sophomore, Junior, Senior);`
Interpretation: A new data type named *enumerated-type* is declared. The values associated with this type are specified in the *identifier-list*. Each value is defined as a constant identifier in the block containing the type declaration statement.
Note: A particular identifier can appear in only one *identifier-list* in a given block.

An identifier cannot appear in more than one enumerated type declaration. The type declaration for `TDay`

```
type
   Day = (Sunday, Monday, Tuesday, Wednesday,
           Thursday, Friday, Saturday);        {days of the week}
   TDay = (Tuesday, Thursday);                  {invalid}
```

is invalid because `Tuesday` and `Thursday` are associated with type `Day`.

Enumerated Type Operators

Like the standard types `Integer`, `Boolean`, and `Char`, each enumerated type is an ordinal type, so the order of its values is fixed when the enumerated type is declared. For type `Day`, the first value in its list (`Sunday`) has ordinal number 0, the next value (`Monday`) has ordinal number 1, and so on. The only operators that can be used with enumerated types are the relational and assignment operators. The following relations are all true:

```
Sunday < Monday
Wednesday = Wednesday
Wednesday >= Tuesday
Entertainment < Rent
```

An assignment statement can define the value of a variable whose type is an enumerated type. In the following example, assume that `Day` has been previously defined as an enumerated type. The variable declaration specifies that `Today` and `Tomorrow` are type `Day`.

```
var
   Today,                       {current day of the week}
   Tomorrow : Day;              {day after Today}
```

The variables can be assigned any of the values listed in the declaration for type `Day`. Consequently, the assignment statements

```
Today := Friday;
Tomorrow := Saturday;
```

assign the value Friday to variable Today and Saturday to variable Tomorrow. After the assignments, the following order relations are all true:

```
Today = Friday
Tomorrow = Saturday
Today < Tomorrow
Today <> Wednesday
Today >= Sunday
```

We can use the ordinal functions Succ, Pred, and Ord with enumerated types. In these examples, assume that Today is Friday and Tomorrow is Saturday:

```
Ord(Today) is 5
Ord(Tomorrow) is 6
Succ(Today) is Saturday
Pred(Today) is Thursday
Pred(Succ(Today)) is Friday
Succ(Tomorrow) is undefined
Pred(Tomorrow) is Friday
```

The next-to-last example is undefined because no value of type Day follows Saturday. Similarly, the value of Pred(Sunday) is undefined. Succ or Pred operations leading to undefined results may cause an out of range error or an overflow error during program execution.

EXAMPLE 7.8 ▼

The following if statement assigns the value of Tomorrow based on the value of Today (both type Day):

```
if Today = Saturday then
  Tomorrow := Sunday
else
  Tomorrow := Succ(Today)
```

Because the days of a week are cyclical, Tomorrow should be set to Sunday when Today is Saturday. The last value (Saturday) in the enumerated type Day is treated separately because Succ(Today) is undefined when Today is Saturday. ▲

Because enumerated types are ordinal types, we can use variables that belong to enumerated types as *counter* variables in for statements and as *case selectors* in case statements. The next two examples illustrate a for statement and a case statement.

EXAMPLE 7.9 ▼

The for loop in Fig. 7.5 reads the hours worked each weekday for an employee and accumulates the sum of the hours worked in WeekHours. If the counter variable Today is declared as the enumerated type Day, the loop ex-

Figure 7.5
Accumulating
Hours Worked

```
WeekHours := 0.0;
for Today := Monday to Friday do
  begin
    Write ('Enter hours for ');
    WriteDay (Today);
    Write ('> ');
    ReadLn (DayHours);
    WeekHours := WeekHours + DayHours
  end; {for}

WriteLn ('Total weekly hours are ', WeekHours :4:2)
```

ecutes for Today equal to Monday through Friday. During each iteration, the calls to Write and WriteDay display a prompt where WriteDay (see Programming Exercise 3 at the end of this section) displays the day name. When Today has the value Monday, the prompt is

```
Enter hours for Monday>
```

Next, each value read into DayHours is added to WeekHours. After loop exit, the final value of WeekHours is displayed. We explain why we need procedure WriteDay next. ▲

Reading and Writing Enumerated Type Values

Because different enumerated types and values can be used in each program, Pascal's input/output procedures were not designed to read or write enumerated type values. However, you can code your own procedures for this purpose.

EXAMPLE 7.10 ▼

Given the declarations

```
type
  Color = (Red, Green, Blue, Yellow);

var
  Eyes : Color;
```

the statement

```
Write (Ord(Eyes) :1)
```

can be used for diagnostic printing during debugging. It does not print the value of Eyes, but it does display the ordinal number of the value that is an integer from 0 (for Red) to 3 (for Yellow).

Procedure `WriteColor` in Fig. 7.6 prints a string that represents a value of type `Color`. If the value of `Eyes` is defined, the statement

```
WriteColor (Eyes)
```

displays the value of `Eyes` as a string. Make sure you understand the difference between the string `'Blue'` and the constant identifier `Blue`. ▲

Programmers often use `case` statements, such as the one in Fig. 7.6, whose case labels are values declared in an enumerated type. Be careful not to use a string such as `'Red'` as a `case` label. This would cause a `constant and case types do not match` syntax error. Remember that only ordinal values or constants (including enumerated constants) can be `case` labels.

It is slightly more difficult to read the value of an enumerated type variable than it is to display it. The next example shows one method.

EXAMPLE 7.11 ▼

Procedure `ReadLnColor` in Fig. 7.7 returns a value of type `Color` through its output parameter `ItemColor`. The loop in Fig. 7.7 repeats until a valid color is assigned to `ItemColor`. The Boolean flag `ValidColor` controls loop repetition and is initialized to `True`. If a valid data character (R, G, B, or Y) is read, the `if` statement assigns its corresponding color value to `ItemColor`. If an invalid data character is read, `ValidColor` is set to `False` and the loop repeats.

If `Black` and `Brown` were added to the list of values for `Color`, it would be necessary to read additional characters when the first letter read was B. We leave this as an exercise (see Programming Exercise 2 at the end of this section). The procedure documentation indicates that `ReadLnColor` calls function `UpCase`. ▲

Figure 7.6
Procedure to Print a Value
of Type Color

Directory: CHAP7
File: WRITECOL.PAS

```
procedure WriteColor (InColor {input} : Color);
{
    Displays the value of InColor.
    Pre : InColor is assigned a value.
    Post: The value of InColor is displayed as a string.
}
begin {WriteColor}
    case InColor of
        Red    : Write ('Red');
        Green  : Write ('Green');
        Blue   : Write ('Blue');
        Yellow : Write ('Yellow')
    end {case}
end; {WriteColor}
```

Figure 7.7
Procedure ReadLnColor

Directory: CHAP7
File: READLNCO.PAS

```pascal
procedure ReadLnColor (var ItemColor {output} : Color);
{
  Assigns a value to ItemColor based on an input character.
  Pre : None
  Post: ItemColor is defined as the color value whose first
        letter is the same as the data character.
  Calls: UpCase (Fig. 7.3)
}
  var
    ColorChar : Char;        {first letter of color name}
    ValidColor : Boolean;    {flag for valid color read}

begin {ReadLnColor}
  repeat
    ValidColor := True; {Assume a valid color will be read.}
    Write ('Enter first letter of color (R, G, B, or Y)> ');
    ReadLn (ColorChar);
    ColorChar := UpCase(ColorChar);  {Convert to uppercase.}

    {Assign the color value or reset ValidColor to False.}
    if ColorChar = 'R' then
      ItemColor := Red
    else if ColorChar = 'G' then
      ItemColor := Green
    else if ColorChar = 'B' then
      ItemColor := Blue
    else if ColorChar = 'Y' then
      ItemColor := Yellow
    else
      ValidColor := False {repeat - valid color was not read.}
  until ValidColor
end; {ReadLnColor}
```

Subranges of Enumerated Types

We can declare subranges of enumerated types. The following declarations
specify that WeekDay (values Monday through Friday) is a subrange of type
Day and that variable SchoolDay is type WeekDay:

```pascal
type
  Day = (Sunday, Monday, Tuesday, Wednesday,
         Thursday, Friday, Saturday);        {days of the week}
  WeekDay = Monday..Friday;                   {weekdays only}

var
  SchoolDay : WeekDay;                        {a weekday}
```

The assignment statement

```pascal
SchoolDay := Monday;
```

is valid, but the assignment statement

```
SchoolDay := Sunday;
```

causes a `Constant out of range` syntax error.

Why Use Enumerated Types?

At this point, you may be wondering whether enumerated types are worth using, considering the effort required to read and write their values. Also, if we need a code to enter the value of an enumerated type variable, why not use that code throughout the program? The reason is that enumerated types make the program considerably easier to read and understand.

EXAMPLE 7.12 ▼

The `if` statement

```
if DayNum = 1 then
   PayFactor := 2.0       {double pay for Sunday}
else if DayNum = 7 then
   PayFactor := 1.5       {time and a half for Saturday}
else
   PayFactor := 1.0       {regular pay}
```

might appear in a payroll program without enumerated types if `Sunday` and `Saturday` are "coded" as the integers 1 and 7, respectively. If we use the enumerated type `Day` and the variable `Today` (type `Day`), we can write this statement as

```
if Today = Sunday then
   PayFactor := 2.0
else if Today = Saturday then
   PayFactor := 1.5
else
   PayFactor := 1.0
```

The second example is obviously more readable because it substitutes values (`Saturday` and `Sunday`) that are meaningful to the problem.   ▲

In a lengthy program, the extra overhead required to implement procedures for reading and writing the values associated with an enumerated type is insignificant. Placing these procedures in your own library of modules will simplify their reuse in future programs.

Another advantage of using enumerated types is the automatic creation of a range of values assignable to a variable. With an integer code, in contrast, any integer value can be assigned unless you take the trouble to declare a subrange type. In the preceding example, any integer value can be assigned to variable `DayNum`, but only one of the seven values listed in the declaration for enumerated type `Day` can be assigned to variable `Today`.

Exercises for Section 7.7   ***Self-Check***

1. Evaluate each of the following expressions, assuming before each operation that `Today` (type `Day`) is `Thursday`:
   a. `Ord(Monday)`
   b. `Ord(Today)`
   c. `Today < Tuesday`
   d. `Succ(Wednesday)`
   e. `Today + 1`
   f. `Ord(Today) + 1`
   g. `Pred(Today)`
   h. `Today >= Thursday`
   i. `Pred(Sunday)`
   j. `Ord(Succ(Succ(Today)))`
2. Indicate whether each of the following type declarations is valid or invalid. Explain what is wrong with each invalid type declaration.
   a. `type Letters = ('A', 'B', 'C');`
   b. `type Letters = (A, B, C);`
      `     TwoLetters = (A, C);`
   c. `type Letters = ('A'..'Z');`
   d. `type Statements = (begin, end, while, for);`
   e. `type`
      `     Day = (Sun, Mon, Tue, Wed, Thu, Fri, Sat);`
      `     WeekDay = Mon..Fri;`
      `     WeekEnd = Sat..Sun;`

Programming

1. Declare an enumerated type `Month` and rewrite the following `if` statement, assuming that `CurMonth` is type `Month` instead of type `Integer`. Also, write the equivalent `case` statement.

   ```
   if CurMonth = 1 then
      WriteLn ('Happy New Year')
   else if CurMonth = 6 then
      WriteLn ('Summer begins')
   else if CurMonth = 9 then
      WriteLn ('Back to school')
   else if CurMonth = 12 then
      WriteLn ('Happy Holidays');
   ```

2. Rewrite procedure `ReadLnColor` (see Fig. 7.7) assuming that `Black` and `Brown` are also values for enumerated type `Color`.
3. Write procedure `WriteDay` for enumerated type `Day`.

7.8 Iterative Approximations (Optional)

Numerical analysis is the branch of mathematics and computer science that develops algorithms for solving computational problems. Problems from numerical analysis include finding solutions to sets of equations, performing operations on matrices, finding roots of equations, and performing mathematical integration. The next case study illustrates methods for iteratively approximating a solution to a computational problem.

CASE STUDY   **Approximating the Value of *e***

....

PROBLEM ▼

Many mathematical quantities can be represented by a series approximation, where a series is represented by a summation of an infinite number of terms. We can use this technique to compute *e* (value is 2.71828 . . .), the base of the natural logarithms.

ANALYSIS ▼

We can approximate the value of *e* by evaluating the series

$$1 + \frac{1}{1!} + \frac{1}{2!} + \frac{1}{3!} + \cdots + \frac{1}{N!}$$

where $N!$ is the factorial of N:

$$N! = N \times (N - 1)! \qquad \text{for } N > 1$$
$$N! = 1 \qquad \text{for } N = 0 \text{ or } 1$$

The previous series can be represented with summation notation as

$$\sum_{i=0}^{N} \frac{1}{i!}$$

where the first term is obtained by substituting 0 for *i* (1/0! is 1/1), the second term is obtained by substituting 1 for *i* (1/1!), and so on. The larger the value of *N*, the more terms will be included in the series, resulting in increased accuracy. The value of *N* is a problem input.

Data Requirements

Problem Input

N : Integer   {number of terms, N, in the sum}

Problem Output

E : Real   {approximate value of e}

Program Variables

IthTerm : Real   {ith term of the series}
I : Integer   {loop-control variable}

DESIGN ▼

Use a counting loop to implement the summation formula.

Initial Algorithm

1. Read in the value of N.
2. Initialize E to 1.0.
3. Initialize the *i*th term to 1.0.
4. for each I from 1 to N do
   begin
        5. Compute the *i*th term in the series.
        6. Add the *i*th term to E.
   end
7. Print the value of E.

IMPLEMENTATION ▼

The program is shown in Fig. 7.8. Inside the for loop, the statement

```
IthTerm := IthTerm / I;
```

computes the value of the *i*th term in the series by dividing the previous term by the loop-control variable I. The formula that follows shows that this division does indeed produce the next term in the series:

$$\frac{\frac{1}{(i-1)!}}{i} = \frac{1}{i \times (i-1)!} = \frac{1}{i!}$$

Because 0! is 1, IthTerm must be initialized to 1.0. The statement

```
E := E + IthTerm;
```

adds the new value of IthTerm to the sum being accumulated in E. Trace the execution of this loop to satisfy yourself that IthTerm takes on the values 1/1!, 1/2!, 1/3!, and so on, during successive loop iterations.

TESTING ▼

To determine whether this algorithm works, run the program for a particular value of N and compare the result with *e*, which is 2.71828183. The sample run shows that the value computed for N (15) is very close to the actual value. How does the value of N affect the accuracy of the final result? Programming Exercise 1 at the end of this section asks you to compute and display a table that demonstrates this.

Exercises for Section 7.8   *Programming*

1. Display a table that shows *e* and *N* for values of *N* from 3 to 15.
2. The value of e^x is represented by the series

Figure 7.8
Series Approximation to *e*

Directory: CHAP7
File: ESERIES.PAS

```
program ESeries (Input, Output);
{Computes the value of e by a series approximation}

   var
      E,                      {output - value being approximated}
      IthTerm : Real;         {ith term in series}
      N,                      {input - number of terms in series}
      I : Integer;            {loop-control variable}

begin {ESeries}
   Write ('Enter the number of terms in the series> ');
   ReadLn (N);

   {Compute each term and add it to the accumulating sum.}
   E := 1.0;                  {initial sum}
   IthTerm := 1.0;            {first term}
   I := 1;
   while I <= N do
      begin
         IthTerm := IthTerm / I;
         E := E + IthTerm;
         I := I + 1
      end; {while}

   {Print the result.}
   WriteLn ('The approximate value of e is ', E :20)
end. {ESeries}
```

Sample Run

```
Enter the number of terms in the series> 15
The approximate value of e is      2.7182818285E+00
```

$$1 + x + x^2/2! + x^3/3! + \cdots + x^n/n! + \cdots$$

Write a program to compute and print the value of this series for any *x* and *n*. Compare the result to `Exp(X)` and print a message `'O.K.'` or `'Not O.K.'`, depending on whether the difference between these results exceeds `0.0001`.

7.9 Common Programming Errors

Be careful when working with complicated expressions, or you may inadvertently omit parentheses or operators. If you omit an operator or a single parenthesis, you will get a syntax error. But if you omit a pair of parentheses, the expression, although syntactically correct, may compute the wrong value.

A useful technique for working with complicated expressions is to break the expression into subexpressions. Assign the subexpressions to temporary variables and manipulate those temporary variables. For example, it is easier to write correctly the three assignment statements

```
Temp1 := Sqrt(X + Y);    {Assign 1st subexpression to Temp1.}
Temp2 := 1.0 + Temp1;    {Assign 2nd subexpression to Temp2.}
Z := Temp1 / Temp2       {Divide the subexpressions.}
```

than the single assignment statement

```
Z := Sqrt(X + Y) / (1.0 + Sqrt(X + Y))
```

which has the same effect. Using three assignment statements is also more efficient because `Sqrt(X + Y)` is evaluated only once; it is evaluated twice in the single assignment statement.

The only operators that you can use with type `Char` data are the relational operators. The Boolean expression

```
3 <> '3'                 {incompatible operands}
```

is invalid because one operand is an integer and the other is a digit character.

Make sure you use parentheses properly in compound Boolean expressions. The Boolean operators `and`, `or`, and `not` have higher precedence than the relational operators, so parentheses are required in expressions such as

```
(-5.0 <= X) and (X <= 5.0)
```

Syntax or run-time errors can occur when you use built-in functions. The argument of the function `Chr` must be type `Integer`; the argument of the functions `Ord`, `Succ`, and `Pred` must be an ordinal type (not type `Real`). The results of the functions `Succ`, `Pred`, and `Chr` will be undefined for certain arguments.

Subranges can help you detect erroneous computations or data. If a value being assigned is outside the subrange, an `out of range` error occurs. The operations that can be performed on a variable with a subrange type are determined by the host type for that subrange. However, a variable whose type is a subrange type cannot correspond to a formal variable parameter whose type is the host type for that subrange.

When you declare enumerated types, remember that only identifiers can appear in the list of values for an enumerated type. Strings, characters, and numbers are not allowed. The same constant identifier cannot appear in more than one enumerated type declaration in a given block. It is permissible, however, for the same constant identifier to appear in more than one subrange type declaration. Remember that no standard procedures are available to read or write the values of an enumerated type.

CHAPTER REVIEW

1. Type `Integer` and `Real` data have different internal representations. `Integer` data are represented as binary numbers with the leftmost bit containing the sign of the number. `Real` data are represented by a binary exponent and mantissa.
2. Arithmetic with `Real` data may not be precise, because not all real numbers can be represented exactly. Other sources of numerical errors include cancellation errors (manipulating a very large number with a very small one) and arithmetic overflow and underflow.
3. The Boolean values, `False` and `True`, are represented as the binary numbers 0 and 1, respectively. Boolean functions can be used to make Boolean expressions more readable.
4. The functions `Pred`, `Succ`, and `Ord` manipulate ordinal data types. The function `Chr`, the inverse of `Ord`, finds the character corresponding to a given ordinal number.
5. Type `Char` data are represented by storing a binary code value for each symbol. The code is computer dependent, but most computers use the ASCII code.
6. You can declare your own data types in Pascal using the reserved word `type`. Subrange type declarations enhance readability by showing which ordinal variables have a restricted range of values. Run-time errors will occur if such variables are assigned out-of-range values.
7. You declare an enumerated type by providing a list of identifiers (values of the data type) enclosed in parentheses. Using enumerated types makes programs more readable because an enumerated type's values are tailored to a particular programming application.
8. Numerical analysis is the branch of mathematics and computer science that develops algorithms for mathematical computation. We demonstrated how to use iterative approximations to evaluate a series that represents the value of *e*.

Summary of New Pascal Constructs

Construct	Effect
Subrange Declaration	
```type Digit = '0'..'9';```	A subrange of the characters is declared. This subrange (named `Digit`) consists of the character values `'0'` through `'9'`.
Enumerated Type Declaration	
```type BColor = (Blue, Black, Brown);```	An enumerated type `BColor` is declared with values `Blue`, `Black`, and `Brown`.

Quick-Check Exercises

1. What value is returned by the following function when its arguments are 5, 7? When its arguments are 7, 5? What does function `ThisDoesWhat` do?

   ```
   function ThisDoesWhat (First, Second : Integer) : Boolean;
   begin
      ThisDoesWhat := (First div Second) = 0
   end; {ThisDoesWhat}
   ```

2. Which of the following can be an enumerated type value: an integer, a real number, an identifier, a Boolean value, a string value?
3. Explain how a subrange type can be used to detect an out-of-range integer value. How about an out-of-range real value?
4. What is the value of each of the following?
   a. `Chr(Ord('a'))`   c. `Ord('7') - Ord('0')`
   b. `Chr(Ord('a') + 3)`   d. `Ord('z') - Ord('a')`
5. Is a subrange type useful for preventing a user from entering an out-of-range value in a `ReadLn` statement? Why or why not?
6. a. Can a variable whose type is a subrange type correspond to a formal variable parameter whose type is the host type?
   b. What if the formal parameter is a value parameter?
7. If two variables are type compatible, can one always be assigned to the other?
8. If the value 1/3 is computed using `Real` variables, why will the result not be exactly 1/3.
9. What is wrong with the following enumerated type declaration?

   ```
   type Prime = (2, 3, 5, 7, 9, 11, 13);
   ```

10. Consider the enumerated type declaration

    ```
    type Class = (Frosh, Soph, Jr, Sr);
    ```

    What is the value of each of the following?

    a. `Ord(Succ(Pred(Soph)))`   b. `Pred(Pred(Jr))`

Answers to Quick-Check Exercises

1. True; false. The function tests $|First| < |Second|$.
2. Only an identifier
3. Pascal generates code that will signal a run-time error when an out-of-range value is stored in a variable whose type is a subrange of the integers. Subranges cannot be defined over the real numbers.
4. a. `'a'`   b. `'d'`   c. 7   d. 25
5. The programmer must ensure that an invalid value is not entered. A subrange type can cause an `out of range` error if an invalid value is entered.
6. a. No   b. Yes
7. Yes, if they are the same type, or if the variable getting a new value is the host type and the other is a subrange of that host. If the variable getting a new value is a subrange type, the new value must be in range.

8. Because of representational error, the fraction $0.333333\ldots$ cannot be represented exactly in either decimal or binary.
9. Integers cannot appear as enumerated type values.
10. a. 1   b. Frosh

Review Questions

1. What are the advantages of the data type Integer over data type Real?
2. List and explain three computational errors that may occur in type Real expressions.
3. Write an enumerated type declaration for Fiscal as the months from July through June. Declare the subrange Winter as December through February.
4. Write procedures for reading and writing values for variables of enumerated type Season:

   ```
   type Season = (Winter, Spring, Summer, Fall);
   ```

5. Write a while loop equivalent to the following for loop. Assume variable Ch is type Char.

   ```
   for Ch := 'A' to 'Z' do
     Write(Ch)
   ```

6. a. Write a case statement that tests whether Today is a working day. Print either of the messages 'Workday' or 'Weekend'. Assume Today is type Day, an enumerated type that has the days of the week as its values.
   b. Is it necessary to guard this case statement?
7. Write a Boolean function that returns True or False based on the following conditions involving its arguments: either Flag is True or Color is Red, or both Money is Plenty and Time is Up. Show any type declarations that may be needed before the function is declared.
8. Write a Boolean function called OvertimeDue that returns a value of True only if a worker's weekly Hours are greater than 40.
9. Write an enumerated type declaration for days of the week and subrange types for weekdays and weekend days. How is the definition of the enumerated type constrained by the subrange requirements?
10. Write the Pascal statements necessary to enter an integer between 0 and 9, inclusive, and convert it to an equivalent character value (e.g., 0 to '0', 1 to '1') to be stored in a character variable Num.
11. Write a Pascal function with Integer argument N and Real argument X that returns as its value the first N terms of the series

$$X + 1/2X^2 + 1/3X^3 + 1/4X^4 + \cdots + 1/NX^N$$

Programming Projects

1. An integer N is divisible by 9 if the sum of its digits is divisible by 9. Develop a program to determine whether the following numbers are divisible by 9 using this technique.

$N = 154368$
$N = 621594$
$N = 123456$

2. Redo Programming Project 1 by reading each digit of the number to be tested into the type `Char` variable `Digit`. Calculate the sum of the numeric values of the digits. *Hint:* The numeric value of `Digit` (type `Char`) is `Ord(Digit) - Ord('0')`.

3. Since communications channels are often noisy, numerous ways have been devised to ensure reliable data transmission. One successful method uses a checksum. A checksum for a message can be computed by summing the ordinal values of the characters in the message and taking the modulo of 64. The ordinal value of a space character is added to this result to obtain the checksum. Since this value is within the range of the displayable characters, it is displayed as a character as well. Write a program that accepts single line messages ending with a period and displays the checksum for each message. Your program should continue displaying checksums until the user enters a line with only a period.

4. Write a program for printing a bar graph that summarizes the rainfall in Bedrock for one year. Include the average monthly rainfall and the maximum monthly rainfall during the year as part of the program output.

    Prompt the user for the amount of rainfall for a particular month and instruct the computer to display an appropriate output line. Assume that no one month will have more than 14 inches of rainfall. Your graph should resemble this one:

```
January  |******************
February |************
             .
             .
             .
         |_____1_____2_____3_____4_____5 ...
                  Inches of Rainfall
```

As part of your solution, write procedures that correspond to the procedure headers shown here:

```
procedure WriteMonth (Month {input} : Integer);
{Writes the string corresponding to the value of Month}

GetMonthlyTotal (Month {input} : Integer;
                 var Inches {output},
                     MaxInches {input/output},
                     TotInches {input/output} : Real);

{
   User is prompted for Inches of rainfall during a Month.
   MaxInches and TotInches are updated so that they contain
   the maximum and total inches of rainfall input so far.
}
```

```
procedure DrawBar (Month {input} : Integer;
                   Inches {input} : Real);
{
  Draws a bar whose length is computed from Inches and whose
  label is determined by the value of Month
}

procedure DrawScaleLine;
{Draws scale and label at bottom of graph}
```

5. The interest paid on a savings account is compounded daily. This means that if you start with StartBal (in dollars) in the bank, at the end of the first day you will have a balance of

$$StartBal \times (1 + Rate/365)$$

where Rate is the annual interest rate (0.10 if the annual rate is 10%). At the end of the second day, you will have

$$StartBal \times (1 + Rate/365) \times (1 + Rate/365)$$

and at the end of N days you will have

$$StartBal \times (1 + Rate/365)^N$$

dollars. Write a program that processes a set of data records, each of which contains values for StartBal, Rate, and N, and computes the final account balance.

6. The bisection method is one way of finding an approximate root for the equation $f(x) = 0$ on the interval XLeft to XRight, inclusive (assuming the function is continuous on this interval). The interval end points (XLeft and XRight) and the tolerance for the approximation (Epsilon) are entered by the user.

    The bisection method calls for the identification of an interval [XLeft, XRight] that is less than Epsilon in length over which $f(x)$ changes sign (from positive to negative or vice versa). The midpoint (XMid = (XLeft + XRight)/2.0) of the interval will be an approximation to the root of the equation when $f(XMid)$ is very close to 0. Of course, if you find a value of XMid so that $f(XMid) = 0$, you have found a very good approximation of the root and the algorithm should stop.

    One way to detect a sign change is to examine the value of the products $f(XLeft) \times f(XMid)$ and $f(XMid) \times f(XRight)$. If one of the products is negative, then a sign change has occurred over that interval (either [XLeft, XMid] or [XMid, XRight]). If neither product is negative, there is no root in the interval XLeft, XRight. If the sign change occurs in the interval [XLeft, XMid], let XRight = XMid and repeat the process. Similarly, if the sign change occurs in the interval [XMid, XRight], let XLeft = XMid and repeat the process. Figure 7.9 shows an example of a root in the interval [XLeft, XMid].

    Write a program that uses the bisection method to determine an approximation to the equation

$$5x^3 - 2x^2 + 3 = 0$$

over the interval [-1, 1] using Epsilon = 0.0001.

Figure 7.9
Root in Interval
[XLeft, XMid]

7. We can approximate the area under the curve described by a function f by dividing the area into a number of rectangles and then accumulating the sum of all the rectangular areas. Figure 7.10 shows an example of the *midpoint method,* so named because the curve intersects each rectangle at its middle (as measured along the x-axis). The area of each rectangle is w (its width) times the function value at its midpoint. The area of the rectangle with left endpoint x_1 is $w \times f(x_1 + w/2)$. If the interval [a, b] is divided into n rectangles, the area under the curve is represented by the sum

$$Area = w \sum_{i=0}^{n-1} f(a + i \times w + w/2)$$

Figure 7.10
Midpoint Method

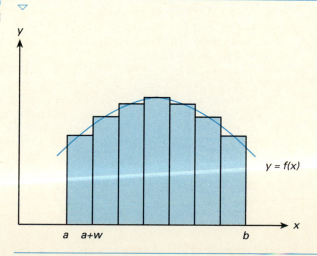

where w is $(b - a)/n$ and the first rectangle begins at $x = a$, the second at $x = a + w$, the third at $x = a + 2w$, and so on.

Write a program that uses the midpoint approximation to find the area under the curve (the value of the definite integral) for the function

$$f(x) = -3x^2 + 2x + 4$$

over the interval $[-2, 3]$. Test your program using several different values of n. The larger n is, the better the approximation should be.

8. A daisy wheel printer uses a print wheel with 95 characters representing the letters with ordinal values of 33 to 127. The printer works by rotating the print wheel left or right a number of steps until the correct letter is under the hammer, then striking. When the printer first starts, the wheel is positioned with the hammer over the letter A. Write a program that can drive a daisy wheel printer. When the user presses a key, output the print wheel move that will most quickly move the correct letter under the hammer for striking and indicate the strike. Pressing return (ordinal value 13) should indicate a carriage advance, and pressing the Escape key (ordinal value 27) will end the program. Always display the shortest move, be it left or right. Remember, the space key does not print anything, repeating a letter does not move the wheel, and keys that don't print should be ignored. Create an enumerated type for the type of rotation (left or right) and a subrange type for the rotation distance.

9. We are used to counting in base 10, but that is not the only possible base. Create a subrange type that can express a base 9 digit using the integers 0 to 8. Write procedures to input, display, increment, and decrement three-digit base 9 numbers, where there is one procedure parameter per digit. Consider only positive numbers.

How did your interest in computer science develop?

During my junior year at Brooklyn College, I took an introductory programming class that I enjoyed immensely—much more than the math classes I was taking towards my major. Since that was the only course offered at my university, I elected to pursue computer science by going on for a master's degree.

Computer science programs were very new at that time—late '60s—and I didn't know much about them. I figured that there had to be more to it than "just" writing programs if master's and Ph.D. degrees were being granted. I also figured that if I hated it, I could always quit. I had a "nothing ventured, nothing gained" attitude.

It turns out that I loved it. For the first time in my life I was really excited about being in school. I've never regretted the decision.

What challenges face students beginning their computer science degrees?

As the field of computer science matures, it also expands. There are now a myriad of architectures, numerous programming languages and programming methodologies, and a host of other issues that did not previously exist. The challenge to educators is to evolve an effective course of study for computer science students. The challenge for students is to understand that there are many different methodologies and architectures and that the first they learned is not necessarily the "best" and only one they should know.

Students must be aware that they are part of a rapidly changing field. They must always be ready for something new and different and view these new concepts as exciting challenges and not as threats to their knowledge base. As exciting as I found the study of computers when I first began, the world to which I was exposed is dull in contrast to what is waiting for students today. Learning to write a program is of critical importance, but never forget that it is simply the means to harnessing the power of the computer and not an end in itself.

When and how did the first supercomputer come to be? How did you become involved in supercomputer research?

Depending on your definition of supercomputer, you might choose any of several different machines as being the first. The CDC 6600, in 1964, and the ILLIAC IV, in 1968, are the first machines that I can think of. One was a production machine and one was a major university research project. I guess it was an inevitable development step that components of a computer would be duplicated as happened with those machines.

I first became involved with supercomputers while on a consulting project. I was hired to develop a Fortran compiler for a new, parallel machine. The experience I gained led me to join the Supercomputing Research Center as a research staff member where I now continue research on using these computers.

What distinguishes a supercomputer from all others?

The term "supercomputer" has been used for some time and has had different meanings over the years. I define a supercomputer as any of a number of different computers that utilize parallelism to achieve greater

INTERVIEW

Judith Schlesinger

Judith Schlesinger is a researcher at the Supercomputing Research Center in Bowie, Maryland, where she is currently involved in creating a system that "predicts" the performance capabilities of a parallel computer for any specified algorithm. Previously Dr. Schlesinger ran her own consulting business—JDS Consulting Services—and worked at the University of Denver, where she designed and implemented the master's program in computer science. Dr. Schlesinger earned her Ph.D. from Johns Hopkins University.

speed of processing. Machines utilizing only pipelining or multiple function units are not generally considered to be supercomputers even though these are considered to be forms of parallelism. A supercomputer would use vector registers, multiple processors (numbering from just a few to thousands), or a combination of both to achieve massive speedups in processing.

These machines process data just as computers have always done: they store data in memory, apply computations to the data, and communicate results with the user or with other computers. However, depending on their configuration, these machines do introduce new programming issues related to how data is stored and accessed, what algorithms are most effective, and, what is the best way to program each machine to exploit all of its capabilities. Currently, a great deal of research is ongoing in these and related areas.

These machines can reduce the time it takes to run a program to completion. Jobs that required days of dedicated computer time can now be run in minutes; jobs that required weeks can now be run in days. These are gross estimates of the kinds of time improvements that have been achieved but I think they make the point. If a researcher in weather prediction, say, can now see results of data processed in minutes rather than days or weeks, we are that much closer to getting accurate weather forecasting. Certainly, everyone should be aware of the improved weather forecasts we now receive over those of just a few years ago.

▼ **In what ways do supercomputers currently affect our lives?**

▲ There are always applications that need more than whatever computer capability is available. These are the applications that are always being run on the biggest and fastest machines. Weather prediction, DNA and drug modeling, fluid dynamics, (financial) market modeling, demographic modeling, and oceanic and atmospheric modeling are just a few of many uses for supercomputers.

Very few of us are going to awaken any time in the near future and know that a supercomputer has directly affected our lives. However, as models of our environment, atmosphere, and oceans are improved, as medical breakthroughs are made, as new solutions to old problems (pollution, waste elimination, ecosystem destruction, etc.) are discovered due to the increased capabilities of supercomputers, we will assuredly be feeling the impact of these machines on our lives.

▼ **How does your research affect the computing industry as a whole?**

▲ The computing industry is very different from the days when everything was a mainframe. From individual desktop computers and more powerful workstations, to loosely coupled networks and workstation "farms," to very large vector and parallel machines, we now have an array of different architectures to meet different needs. Research and technology that are on the cutting edge today will be the production tools of tomorrow. The only current way to achieve significantly greater speeds from computers is to make them parallel. So, while supercomputer research focuses on specific uses, knowledge and skill being acquired will ultimately benefit everyone.

CHAPTER EIGHT

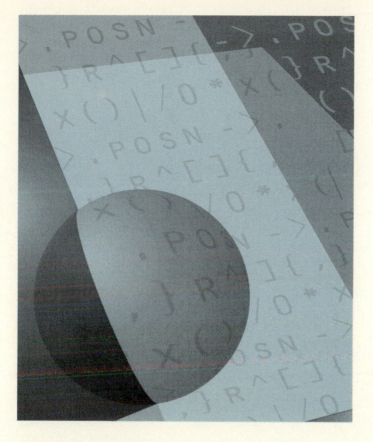

Text Files

interactive program
a program that reads all data from the keyboard and displays all output on the screen

All the example programs presented so far have been interactive. An **interactive program** reads all input data from the keyboard and displays all output on the screen. Interactive input and output is fine for programs that process small amounts of data, but this procedure is less effective for programs that must process large amounts of data. To improve efficiency, we can use data files for storing program input and output. Pascal can process two kinds of data files: text files and binary files. This chapter describes text files.

The input and output procedures we have used for interactive programs work with text files. In this chapter, we will describe one new procedure, Read, that is particularly useful for reading data from text files, in addition to describing several new procedures and functions for text files.

8.1   Text Files, Data Files, and Output Files

A **text file** is a collection of individual characters stored under the same name on a disk. You can save all of the data to be processed by a program in a text file before you run that program. You can then instruct the program to read its data from the text file rather than reading it from the keyboard. A **data file** (or **input file**) is a file that contains the input data for a program. A data file may be a text file or a binary file (Chapter 15).

One advantage of a data file is that you can access it using an editor program (or word processor) and can correct any errors before the data file is processed by a program. Another advantage is that a data file can be read over and over again by a program. This property facilitates debugging because your program can read its data from the same data file each time it is run. In an interactive program, you would have to reenter each individual data item during every run of the program.

You can also instruct a program to write its results to a text file instead of to the screen, giving you a permanent version on disk of the program results. That disk file can be printed or even used as a data file for a second program that will process it further. An **output file** is a file that contains a program's results.

Organization of Information in a Text File

You can create and save a text file by using an editor. Each character that you type resides temporarily in main memory and is displayed on the screen. When you save the file, the information displayed on the screen is stored as a stream of characters on disk (see Fig. 8.1).

The text file in Fig. 8.1 contains a total of 25 characters or bytes, including digit characters, periods, blanks, letters, and two special characters, <eoln> and <eof>. <eoln>, the *end-of-line* character, is stored in a text file each time the Return key on the keyboard is pressed. <eof>, the *end-of-file* character, is automatically inserted after the last character of a text file when the text file is saved. A text file can have many <eoln> characters but only one <eof> character.

Figure 8.1
Text File as a Stream of Characters

| 1 | 5 | 9 | 0 | 0 | . | 0 | 0 | | J | J | <eoln> | 2 | 5 | 0 | 0 | 0 | . | 0 | 0 | | S | P | <eoln> | <eof> |

Although the text file is *physically* stored on disk as one long stream of characters, it is *logically* organized as a sequence of characters separated into lines by <eoln> characters. If you use an editor to access the text file in Fig. 8.1, it will look like the information in Fig. 8.2, except that you will not see the <eoln> and <eof> characters.

You can view a text file using an editor or you can display a text file on the screen using an operating system command such as

>TYPE *filename*

where *filename* is the name of the text file. Each file line will be displayed on a separate line of the screen. You can also get a hard copy of a text file by sending it to a printer.

Reading Data from a Text File

You can use Pascal's ReadLn procedure to read data from a text file. Let's consider a program that contains the variable declarations

```
var
    Salary : Real;         {input - a salary}
    First, Last : Char;    {input - initials}
    Separator : Char;      {input - blank between Salary and First}
    MyData : Text;         {a text file used as a data file}
```

The last line declares MyData as a variable of type Text, which is the predefined data type for a text file. The statement

```
ReadLn (MyData, Salary, Separator, First, Last)
```

has five parameters: a Text file variable, a Real variable, and three Char variables. It reads four data items from file MyData, storing the first in Salary, the second in Separator, the third in First, and the fourth in Last. If MyData represented the text file in Fig. 8.2 and the first line were being read, this statement would store 15900.00 in Salary, the blank character in Separator, and the letter J in First and Last.

How does Pascal know to read the data from the text file instead of the keyboard? This is determined by the first parameter in the call to ReadLn. If the first parameter is a variable of type Text, Pascal reads data from the file indicated by that variable; otherwise, Pascal reads data from the keyboard.

Figure 8.2
Logical Organization of
Text File in Fig. 8.1

```
15900.00 JJ<eoln>
25000.00 SP<eoln><eof>
```

ReadLn processes each line of a text file just like a data line entered at the keyboard. The first line of the file identified by variable MyData begins with a sequence of digit characters containing a decimal point. When ReadLn is reading data into a type Real variable, it skips any leading blanks and reads all numeric characters up to the next blank or <eoln> character; consequently, it stores the real number 15900.00 in Salary. The next character to be read is the blank character between the digit 0 and the first letter J; this blank is stored in Separator. The two letter J's are stored in First and Last.

Some of the characters on a data line may be processed by ReadLn but not stored. The statement

```
ReadLn (MyData, Salary)
```

reads and stores in Salary the next number in a line of file MyData; it then skips the remaining characters on the data line (through the next <eoln>). This is not considered an error. The next ReadLn operation would begin reading data from the next data line of file MyData.

Procedure Read

A second input procedure, Read, also reads data from the keyboard or from a file. Unlike ReadLn, however, procedure Read processes only as many data characters as are needed to satisfy its input list.

EXAMPLE 8.1 ▼

The statements

```
Read (MyData, Salary);        {Read Salary from MyData.}
Read (MyData, Separator);     {Read the blank character.}
Read (MyData, First, Last);   {Read initials from MyData.}
ReadLn (MyData)        {Skip past <eoln> character in MyData.}
```

have the same effect as

```
ReadLn (MyData, Salary, Separator, First, Last)
```

The first Read statement reads into Salary the characters that comprise a real number, stopping at the blank character; the second Read statement reads the blank character into Separator; the third Read statement reads the next two characters into First and Last; the ReadLn statement skips past the <eoln> character to the start of the next data line. Figure 8.3 shows the effect of executing these statements when the first line of file MyData is being read. The blank character is shown as the symbol □ in Separator. ▲

Review of Read and ReadLn

The number of characters read by Read or ReadLn depends on the type of variable receiving the data. When reading data into a type Char variable, a single character is read. When reading data into a numeric variable, the program skips over any leading blanks, control characters, or <eoln> characters

Figure 8.3
Effect of Read on First Line
of File MyData

until it encounters a character that is not a blank, a control character, or
`<eoln>`. That first character must be a sign or a digit; if it is not, an execution
error such as `Non-digit found while reading number` occurs, and the
program stops. If the first character is a sign or a digit, the program continues
reading numeric characters (including a decimal point for type `Real`) until it
encounters a blank, a control character, or an `<eoln>`. For `ReadLn` only, the
`<eoln>` character is also read but not stored.

SYNTAX DISPLAY

Read, ReadLn Procedures

Form: Read (*infile*, *input list*)
             ReadLn (*infile*, *input list*)

Example: Read (InData, X, Y, Z)
             ReadLn (InData, Ch1, Ch2)

Interpretation: A sequence of characters is read from the file identified by
infile (type `Text`) into the variables specified in *input list*. The type of each
variable in *input list* must be `Boolean`, `Char`, `Integer`, `Real`, or a subrange of
`Char` or `Integer`. If the data type of a variable is `Char`, only a single character
is read into that variable. If the data type of a variable is `Integer` or `Real`, any
leading blanks or `<eoln>` characters are skipped and a sequence of numeric
characters (including a decimal point for `Real`) is read and stored in that variable. After the *input list* for `Read` is satisfied, the next character to be read is
the one that follows the last character that was read. If `ReadLn` is called, the
next character to be read is the one that follows the next `<eoln>` character. If
infile is omitted or is `Input`, the data items are read from the keyboard.

Table 8.1 lists several examples of Read and ReadLn statements and their effects. Assume that X is type Real, N is type Integer, C is type Char, and the first character processed is the first character in the file shown on the right. The next character to be read after each Read or ReadLn operation is shown in color.

Table 8.1
Effects of Read and ReadLn

Statement and Effect	Next Character to Be Read
Read (InData, X, N, C) X is 1234.56, N is 789, C is ' '	1234.56□789□A345.67<eoln> W<eoln><eof>
ReadLn (InData, X, N, C) X is 1234.56, N is 789, C is ' '	1234.56□789□A345.67<eoln> W<eoln><eof>
Read (InData, X, C, N) X is 1234.56, C is ' ', N is 789	1234.56□789□A345.67<eoln> W<eoln><eof>
ReadLn (InData, X, C, N) X is 1234.56, C is ' ', N is 789	1234.56□789□A345.67<eoln> W<eoln><eof>
Read (InData, C, X, N) C is '1', X is 234.56, N is 789	1234.56□789□A345.67<eoln> W<eoln><eof>
ReadLn (InData, C, X, N) C is '1', X is 234.56, N is 789	1234.56□789□A345.67<eoln> W<eoln><eof>
ReadLn (InData, X, N); Read (InData, C) X is 1234.56, N is 789, C is 'W'	1234.56□789□A345.67<eoln> W<eoln><eof>
ReadLn (InData, X); ReadLn (InData, C) X is 1234.56, C is 'W'	1234.56□789□A345.67<eoln> W<eoln><eof>

Notice in Table 8.1 that C contains the blank character after the first four operations. In all these cases, C follows X or N in the input list. Therefore, a sequence of numeric characters up to (but not including) the blank character is read into X or N and the blank character is read into C.

Writing Results to a Text File

Use procedures Write and WriteLn to write results to a text file in the same way that you write to the screen. If the first parameter in a call to Write or WriteLn is a variable of type Text, the output characters are sent to the file identified by that variable rather than to the screen. Whenever WriteLn is used, an <eoln> character is placed in the file after the last output character.

A program writes a numeric value to a file as a sequence of digit characters. The minus character (−) precedes a negative number. The decimal point character (.) is inserted in a type Real value. You can use format specifications when writing to a text file (see Section 2.8).

SYNTAX DISPLAY

Write, WriteLn Procedures

Form: Write (*outfile, output list*)
            WriteLn (*outfile, output list*)
Example: Write (MyResult, Salary)
            WriteLn (MyResult, Hours :3:1, ' $', Salary :4:2)
Interpretation: The characters specified by *output list* are written to the end of file *outfile*. Each item in *output list* must be a string literal or an expression of type Boolean, Char, Integer, or Real or a subrange of Char or Integer. If an expression is type Char, a single character is written to file *outfile;* otherwise, multiple characters may be written. Format specifications may be included in the *output list*. When WriteLn is called, an <eoln> character is written to *outfile* after the last character specified by the *output list*. If *outfile* is omitted or is Output, the output results are written to the screen.

The Keyboard and Screen as Text Files

In interactive programming, Pascal treats data entered at the keyboard as if they were read from the system file Input. On most systems, these data are stored temporarily in an **input buffer** (a storage area) until you press the Return key. Up to that point, you can edit the data in the input buffer using the backarrow key to erase characters and retyping them. Pressing the Return key inserts the <eoln> character in the input buffer and enables your program to begin processing the data line.

input buffer
a temporary storage area for input data

Although the <eof> character could be placed in system file Input, we normally use a sentinel value in interactive programming to indicate the end of data. To enter the <eof> character in file Input, you press the Control key and a letter simultaneously (for example, Ctrl-Z on IBM personal computers).

Displaying characters on the screen is equivalent to writing characters to system file Output. The WriteLn procedure places the <eoln> character in this file, thereby moving the cursor to the start of the next line of the screen. Both Input and Output are text files because their individual components are characters.

EXAMPLE 8.2 ▼

The statements

```
Write (Output, 'Enter a salary value> ');
ReadLn (Input, Salary)
```

display a prompting message on the screen (file Output) and read a value typed at the keyboard (file Input) into Salary. They are equivalent to the more familiar statements

```
Write ('Enter a salary value> ');
ReadLn (Salary)  ▲
```

Exercises for Section 8.1   ***Self-Check***

1. a. For a computer program that handles the booking of airline reservations, would it be preferable to use a data file or to enter the data interactively? Explain your answer.
   b. What about a program for printing student transcripts at a university?
2. Explain when `Read` might be preferred to `ReadLn` as a means of obtaining numeric data from the user of an interactive program.
3. Let X be type `Real`, N type `Integer`, and C type `Char`. Indicate the contents of each variable after each `Read` or `ReadLn` operation, assuming that the file consists of the following lines:

   ```
   123 3.145 XYZ<eoln>
   35 Z<eoln>
   ```

   a. `ReadLn (InData, N, X); Read (InData, C)`
   b. `Read (InData, N, X, C)`
   c. `Read (InData, N, X, C, C)`
   d. `ReadLn (InData, N); Read (InData, C)`
   e. `ReadLn (InData, X); Read (InData, C, N)`
   f. `ReadLn (InData, C, C, C, X); Read (InData, N)`
   g. `Read (InData, N, X, C, C, C, C, N)`
   h. `Read (InData, N, X, C, C, C, C)`

4. Repeat Exercise 3, substituting `WriteLn` for `ReadLn`, `Write` for `Read`, and `OutData` for `InData`. Show file `OutData` after each part. Assume that N is 512, X is 0.123, and C is '*'.
5. If text files are physically stored on disk as one long stream of characters, how can they appear as multiple lines on the screen of a text editor program?

8.2 Procedures and Functions for Text Files

So far we have shown how to declare a text file, how to read from a text file used as a data file, and how to write output results to a text file used as an output file. In this section, we describe the additional procedures and functions needed to use a text file in a Pascal program.

To use a text file, you must carry out the following operations:

1. Declare variables used to identify text files as type `Text`.
2. List the file variables in the program heading.
3. Provide the directory name of the actual disk file that corresponds to each file variable.

4. For a text file that is being used as a data file, open the file and reset its file location marker to the first character in the file.
5. For a text file that is being used as an output file, open the file by creating an initially empty file on disk.
6. Use the file variable as the first parameter in all read or write operations involving the text file.

We have already discussed operations 1 and 6; the remaining operations are described next.

External and Internal Names for Files

disk directory
a list of descriptive information about the files stored on a disk, including each file's directory name

To enable Pascal to access a file saved on disk, you must provide its directory name, which is the name used to identify it in a disk's directory. A **disk directory** contains the directory names of all files stored on a disk together with other relevant information such as when a file was last modified, its size in bytes, and its disk address.

A file's directory name must follow whatever conventions apply on your particular computer system. For example, some systems limit a file name to eight characters, a period, and a three-letter extension. Many programmers use the extension .DAT or .TXT to designate a text file.

You need to communicate to the operating system the directory names of any files you are using so that the system knows the correspondence between file variables (internal names) and directory names (external names). This process is system dependent. Your instructor will give you the details for your particular system; we will show you some examples later in this section.

Opening a Text File

opening a file
preparing a file for input or for output

Before a program can use a text file, the file must be prepared for input or output, or **opened.** A text file cannot be opened for both input and output at the same time. That is, if you are in the process of reading data from a text file, you cannot begin to write output results to the same file.

Reset Procedure

The procedure call statement

```
Reset (InData)
```

file location marker
a marker in each file that points to the next character to be processed in the file

prepares file `InData` for input to the program by moving its file location marker to the beginning of the file. The **file location marker** points to the next character to be processed in the file. After the `Reset` operation has been performed, the next character to be read is always the first character in the file. The `Reset` operation must be done before any characters are read from file `InData`, but, of course, the operation will fail if file `InData` was not previously saved on disk. To read and process a file a second time in the same program run, perform the Reset operation again.

Figure 8.4 shows file MyData after the Reset operation. The file location marker points to the first character.

Reset Procedure

Form: Reset (*infile*)
Example: Reset (MyData)
Interpretation: File *infile* is prepared for input, and the file location marker for *infile* is moved to the first character in the file. The Reset operation is automatically performed on system file Input, so Reset (Input) is not required.

Rewrite Procedure

The procedure call statement

Rewrite (OutData)

prepares file OutData for receiving output. If the disk has no file corresponding to file OutData, a new, initially empty file is created. If a file corresponding to OutData is already saved on disk, its file location marker moves to the beginning of the file, effectively erasing the old file data.

Rewrite Procedure

Form: Rewrite (*outfile*)
Example: Rewrite (MyData)
Interpretation: File *outfile* is prepared for output, and *outfile* is initialized to an empty file. Any data previously stored in file *outfile* are lost. The Rewrite operation is automatically performed on system file Output, so Rewrite (Output) is not required.

Techniques for Specifying Directory Names

Some Pascal systems use an extended form of the Reset and Rewrite procedures to associate a file name used in a Pascal program with the file's directory name. For example, the procedure call statements

Figure 8.4
File MyData After
Reset (MyData)

15900.00 JJ<eoln>25000.00 SP<eoln><eof>

File location marker

```
Reset (InData, 'INDATA.DAT');
Rewrite (OutData, 'OUTFILE.DAT');
```

specify that file variable `InData` corresponds to disk file `INDATA.DAT` and that file variable `OutData` corresponds to disk file `OUTFILE.DAT`. Note that this use of `Reset` and `Rewrite` is non-standard and may not be supported on your system.

In Turbo Pascal, the `Assign` statement is used to associate a file variable with a disk file. The statements

```
Assign (InData, 'INDATA.DAT');
Assign (OutData, 'OUTFILE.DAT');
```

must precede the `Reset` or `Rewrite` statement.

In VAX Pascal, the `Open` statement is used for this purpose.

```
Open (InData, 'INDATA.DAT', Old);
Open (OutData, 'OUTFILE.DAT');
```

The parameter `Old` indicates that file `'INDATA.DAT'` was previously created.

Testing for the End of a File: Function EOF

When reading a data file, you need to know when you have reached the end of the file. One way is to count the number of characters processed and compare this count to the number of characters in the file. Another way is to add a sentinel character at the end of each file. Both methods are unnecessary.

Each file automatically ends with an `<eof>` character, and Pascal's built-in function `EOF` (for End Of File) tests whether the next character to be read in a file is the `<eof>` character. The function designator

```
EOF(InFile)
```

returns `True` if all data characters in file `InFile` have been processed (i.e., the next character to be read is the `<eof>` character). It returns `False` if there are more characters remaining to be read.

SYNTAX DISPLAY

EOF Function

Form: EOF(*filename*)
Example: EOF(InFile)
Interpretation: EOF returns True if the next character in file *filename* is `<eof>`; otherwise, EOF returns False.
Note: If *filename* is omitted, the input file is assumed to be the system file `Input` (the keyboard). If a read operation is attempted when EOF(*filename*) is True, an `Attempt to read past the end of the input file` error occurs and the program stops.

Putting it All Together

Examples 8.3 and 8.4 use all the file operators discussed so far.

EXAMPLE 8.3: Writing a Table to an Output File ▼

The program in Fig. 8.5 reads a file containing a list of numbers (one per line) and writes each number followed by its square root and square to an output file. The program heading lists the three text files that are processed, including file Output (the screen).

After opening the files, the program writes the table heading to the output file. Inside the while loop, the ReadLn statement reads each number from the input file, and the WriteLn statement writes three output results to the next line of the output file. Although the number of characters in a data line may vary, the program always writes 37 characters per output line, including

Figure 8.5
Program SquareAndRoot

Directory: CHAP8
File: SQUAREAN.PAS

```
program SquareAndRoot (Output, InFile, OutFile);
{Writes a table of squares and square roots to a file.}
   var
      InFile,                    {input file}
      OutFile : Text;            {output file}
      NextNum : Real;            {next number}

begin {SquareAndRoot}
   {Prepare files for input and output.}
   Reset (InFile);                  {Open InFile for input.}
   Rewrite (OutFile);               {Open OutFile for output.}

   {Write table heading to output file.}
   WriteLn (OutFile, 'N' :10:2,
            'Square root' :15:2, 'Square' :12:2);

   {Read each number and write each line of the output file.}
   while not EOF(InFile) do
      begin
         ReadLn (InFile, NextNum);          {Read next number.}
         WriteLn (OutFile, NextNum :10:2,
                  Sqrt(NextNum) :15:2, Sqr(NextNum) :12:2)
      end; {while}

   WriteLn ('Table of roots and squares is in file SQUARES.TXT')
end. {SquareAndRoot}
```

Sample Run

```
Table of roots and squares is in file SQUARES.TXT
```

the `<eoln>` character. The numbers that are read from the data file and written to the output file do not appear on the screen. Notice that there is no need for a prompt inside the loop because the data items are not entered interactively.

Notice also that no priming read is needed when using function `EOF` to control loop repetition. Instead, the `ReadLn` statement inside the loop reads all data lines including the first. If the data file is empty, the `while` loop body does not execute. In this case, the output file would contain only the table heading, which was already written. We show a sample data file (left) and corresponding output file (right) next.

File InFile	File OutFile (SQUARES.TXT)

```
                               N   Square root      Square<eoln>
100<eoln>                  100.00        10.00   10000.00<eoln>
4.00<eoln><eof>              4.00         2.00      16.00<eoln><eof>
```

After the loop exit, the directory name of the output file (SQUARES.TXT) is written to the screen, so the program user knows where to look for the file. ▲

Testing for the End of a Line: Function EOLN

Pascal also provides a function `EOLN` (for End Of LiNe) that enables a program to detect the `<eoln>` characters that separate a text file into lines. Function `EOLN` returns `True` when the next data character is `<eoln>`; otherwise, `EOLN` returns `False`.

SYNTAX DISPLAY

EOLN Function

Form: EOLN(*filename*)
Example: EOLN(InFile)
Interpretation: The function result is `True` if the next character in file *filename* is `<eoln>`; otherwise, the function result is `False`.
Note: If *filename* is omitted, the input file is assumed to be the system file `Input` (the keyboard). In standard Pascal, it is an error to call the `EOLN` function if `EOF`(*filename*) is `True`.

EXAMPLE 8.4: Copying a Line of a File ▼

Procedure `CopyLine` in Fig. 8.6 copies one line of its first file parameter to its second file parameter. The `while` loop copies each character up to the `<eoln>` from file `InFile` to `OutFile`. After loop exit, the statements

```
ReadLn (InFile);                    {Skip the <eoln>.}
WriteLn (OutFile)                   {Write it to OutFile.}
```

skip over the `<eoln>` character in `InFile` and write the `<eoln>` character to `OutFile`. ▲

Figure 8.6
Procedure CopyLine

**Directory: CHAP8
File: COPYLINE.PAS**

```
procedure CopyLine (var InFile {input file},
                        OutFile {output file} : Text);
{
 Copies one line of file InFile to file OutFile.
 Pre  : InFile is opened for input and OutFile for output.
 Post : Each character on the current line of file InFile is
        copied to OutFile. The <eoln> character is the last
        character written to OutFile and the file location
        marker for InFile is at the start of the next line.
}
 var
   Next : Char;        {each file character}

begin {CopyLine}
  {Copy all characters up to the <eoln>.}
  while not EOLN(InFile) do
    begin
      Read (InFile, Next);
      Write (OutFile, Next)
    end; {while}

  {Process the <eoln> character.}
  ReadLn (InFile);                {Skip the <eoln>.}
  WriteLn (OutFile)               {Write it to OutFile.}
end; {CopyLine}
```

Although procedure CopyLine does not actually read the <eoln> character into Next, a Pascal program can read the <eoln> character. When this
happens, standard Pascal stores the blank character in the variable receiving
<eoln> as its data item.

EXAMPLE 8.5: Copying a File ▼

The file copy program in Fig. 8.7 copies one line at a time from its input file
(InFile) to its output file (OutFile). Before each repetition of the while
loop, function EOF tests whether the end of file InFile has been reached. If
the <eof> character is next, EOF(InFile) is True and not EOF(InFile) is
False, so loop exit occurs. If the file does contain more data characters,
EOF(InFile) is False and not EOF(InFile) is True, so CopyLine executes and copies the next line. ▲

Program Style

Using ReadLn After a Loop

After the loop in Fig. 8.6 is exited, the statement

```
ReadLn (InFile);                       {Skip the <eoln>.}
```

Figure 8.7
Program CopyFile

Directory: CHAP8
File: COPYFILE.PAS

```pascal
program CopyFile (Output, InFile, OutFile);
{Copies a data file by writing each line to an output file.}
  var
     InFile,                     {input file}
     OutFile : Text;             {output file}

{Insert procedure CopyLine (Fig. 8.6) here.}

begin {CopyFile}
  {Prepare files for input and output.}
  Reset (InFile);                       {Open InFile for input.}
  Rewrite (OutFile);                     {Open OutFile for output.}

  {Copy the data file line by line.}
  while not EOF(InFile) do
     CopyLine (InFile, OutFile);    {Copy the next line.}
  WriteLn ('Data file is copied to COPYFILE.TXT')
end. {CopyFile}
```

Sample Run

```
Data file is copied to COPYFILE.TXT
```

executes, skipping over the <eoln> character. Placing ReadLn (InFile) right after a loop that uses not EOLN(InFile) as its loop-repetition test causes ReadLn to process the <eoln> character that caused loop repetition to terminate. If the <eoln> character were not processed, the next Read or ReadLn would read it instead of the first character in the next data line; possibly causing unexpected program results and a run-time error. In fact, if this statement were omitted from CopyLine, the loop in CopyFile (Fig. 8.7)

```pascal
while not EOF(InFile) do
  CopyLine (InFile, OutFile);    {Copy the next line.}
```

would execute forever. The next character to process after a return from CopyLine would always be the <eoln> character. Consequently, in the next call to CopyLine, its while loop would be skipped and the statement

```pascal
WriteLn (OutFile)                 {Write it to OutFile.}
```

would write another <eoln> character to OutFile instead of writing the next data line. This process would continue until the program user terminated the program.

File Parameters in User-Defined Procedures

File parameter InFile is listed as a variable parameter in the parameter list for procedure CopyLine. Because InFile represents an input file, it may seem strange to declare it as a variable parameter. However, Pascal requires all file parameters to be variable parameters because a local copy of a large file would require too much memory.

Using EOLN with Keyboard Data

You can use the EOLN function with parameter Input to test for the <eoln> character when reading data from the keyboard. Recall that the <eoln> character is placed in system file Input when the Return key is pressed. The statement

```
CopyLine (Input, OutFile)
```

passes Input as the first file parameter to procedure CopyLine (see Fig. 8.6), so the next data line typed at the keyboard would be written to file OutFile.

It is easy to misuse EOLN or EOF to test for the <eoln> or <eof> character in the keyboard data. If you forget to specify the file parameter and write the function designator as just EOLN (as in while not EOLN do), Pascal will use system file Input as the default file parameter. Similarly, if you forget to use a file parameter with Read or ReadLn, Pascal will use Input by default, so your program will pause until you type in a data line.

Exercises for Section 8.2   ***Self-Check***

1. Find the errors in the following fragment assuming InFile is type Text and Next is type Char. Which file is the input file, which file is the output file, and which file is tested by function EOLN?

   ```
   Rewrite (InFile);
   Reset (Input);
   while not EOLN do
     begin
       Read (InFile, Next);
       Write (Next)
     end; {while}
   ```

2. Assume you are given an input file with integers, one per line, in it. Assuming variable NumData is type Text, what statements would be required to prepare for reading the file?

Programming

1. Write a procedure that reads a file that has integers, one per line, and computes the sum of the integers. The input to the procedure is a file variable. The procedure output is the sum. If the file is empty, the sum should be zero.

2. Write a program that compresses a file by writing every other character in the file to an output file. The new file will contain approximately half as many characters as the original.
3. Write a procedure that returns a count of the number of occurrences of a particular character on the current line of a data file. The internal file name and the character being counted should be procedure inputs; the count of characters should be a procedure output.

8.3 Using Text Files

If one program writes its output to a disk file rather than to the screen, a second program may use that output file as its data file. In effect, the two programs communicate with each other through the disk file. The following case study develops a program whose output file is another program's data file.

CASE STUDY **Preparing a Payroll File**

PROBLEM

Your company's accountant has asked you to write two payroll programs. The first program will read a data file containing employee salary data, with data for each employee stored on two consecutive lines. The first line will house the employee's name. The second line will start with an indicator of employee status, with an H for an hourly employee or an S for a salaried employee. Either the employee's hourly rate (for an hourly employee) or the employee's annual salary (for a salaried employee) will follow. For hourly employees only the second line will end with an additional data value—the number of hours worked that week. A sample data file with one salaried and one hourly employee follows:

Data File

```
Peter Liacouras<eoln>
S 260000.00<eoln>
Caryn Koffman<eoln>
H 10.00 40.0<eoln><eof>
```

The first program should write each employee's name to an output file, followed by a line containing the employee's computed gross salary for the week. It should also compute and write to the screen the total payroll amount for the week. As shown in the following output file, the second line of the output file should list a salaried employee's annual salary (e.g., $260,000) divided by 52. The fourth line of the output file should list the product of an hourly employee's rate ($10.00) and hours (40.0).

Output File

```
Peter Liacouras<eoln>
5000.00<eoln>
Caryn Koffman<eoln>
400.00<eoln><eof>
```

The second program will read the output file and write payroll checks based on the contents of that file. For example, the first check issued should be for $5000.00 made out to Peter Liacouras.

ANALYSIS ▼

We will write the first program now and leave the second one as an exercise (see Programming Project 1 at the end of this chapter). The program must copy each employee's name to the output file. It must also compute each employee's weekly salary, write it to the output file, and add it to the payroll total.

Data Requirements

Problem Inputs (from Input File InEmp)

```
each employee's name
the category (hourly or salaried) of each employee
the pay rate for each employee
the hours worked for an hourly employee
```

Problem Outputs (to Output File OutEmp)

```
each employee's name
each employee's weekly salary
```

Problem Output (to screen)

```
Payroll : Real     {the payroll total}
```

DESIGN ▼

The main program prepares the files for input and output and calls procedure `ProcessEmp` to process all employees and accumulate the total payroll (step 2 in the following algorithm). After `ProcessEmp` is finished, the main program displays the final payroll total.

Algorithm for Main Program

1. Prepare files `InEmp` and `OutEmp`.
2. Process all employees and compute payroll total.
3. Display the payroll total.

Analysis and Design of ProcessEmp

`ProcessEmp` allocates storage for the variables that store an employee's salary data and final salary. The data requirements for `ProcessEmp` follow.

Data Requirements for ProcessEmp

Input Parameter

`InEmp : Text`   {file of employee data}

Output Parameter

`OutEmp : Text`   {payroll file}

Input/Output Parameter

`Payroll : Real`   {the payroll amount so far}

Local Variables

```
HourOrSal : Char   {input - hourly or salaried indicator}
Hours : Real       {input - hours worked}
Rate : Real        {input - hourly rate}
Salary : Real      {output - gross salary}
```

The algorithm for `ProcessEmp` follows. Step 3 of `ProcessEmp` is performed by procedure `CopyLine` (see Fig. 8.6). Step 4 is performed by procedure `ReadData` and step 5 is performed by function `ComputeSal`. Figure 8.8 shows the structure chart.

Algorithm for ProcessEmp

1. Initialize payroll total to 0.0.
2. `while` there are more employees `do`
   `begin`
      3. Read next employee's name from `InEmp` and write it to `OutEmp`.
      4. Read next employee's salary data.
      5. Compute next employee's weekly salary.
      6. Write next employee's salary to `OutEmp` and add it to payroll total.
   `end`

IMPLEMENTATION ▼

Coding the Main Program

Figure 8.9 shows the main program. Besides text files `InEmp` and `OutEmp`, the only variable declared in the main program is `Payroll`. We declare the variables needed to store and process an individual employee's data in `ProcessEmp`. This step is consistent with the policy of declaring a variable in the highest-level module that accesses it.

Figure 8.8

Structure Chart for Writing the Payroll File

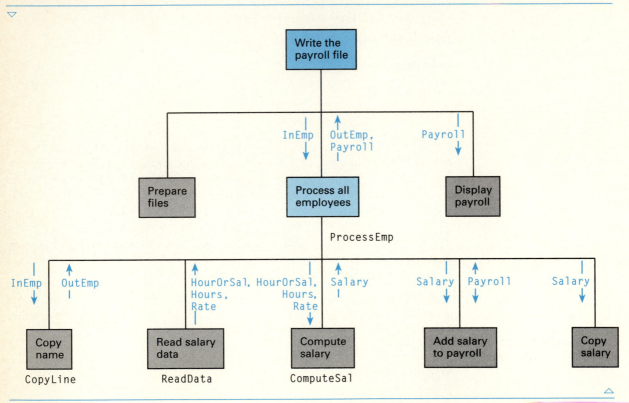

Figure 8.9

Writing a Payroll File

Directory: CHAP8
File: WRITEPAY.PAS

```
program WritePayroll (Output, InEmp, OutEmp);
{
  Writes each employee's name and weekly salary to an
  output file and computes total payroll amount.
}
  var
    InEmp,                  {data file}
    OutEmp : Text;          {output file}
    Payroll : Real;         {output - total payroll}

{Insert CopyLine, ReadData, ComputeSal, & ProcessEmp here.}

begin {WritePayroll}
  {Prepare InEmp and OutEmp.}
  Reset (InEmp);
  Rewrite (OutEmp);

  {Process all employees and compute payroll total.}
  ProcessEmp (InEmp, OutEmp, Payroll);
```

▷ ▷ ▷ ▷ ▷ ▷

```
{Display result.}
   WriteLn ('Total payroll is $', Payroll :4:2)
end. {WritePayroll}
```

Sample Run

```
Total payroll is $5400.00
```

△

Coding the Modules

Figure 8.10 shows procedure ProcessEmp and its subordinate modules. Procedure ReadData reads the first data character and then reads either one or two numeric values, depending on whether the first character is S or H. Function ComputeSal computes the gross weekly salary for an employee, and that amount is assigned to Salary after the function return.

The while loop in ProcessEmp tests whether the next character is <eof>. If it is not, ProcessEmp calls CopyLine to copy the next employee's name from the input file (InEmp) to the output file (OutEmp). CopyLine processes every other line of file InEmp, starting with the first line.

Figure 8.10
ReadData, ComputeSal, and ProcessEmp

Directory: CHAP8
File: WRITEPAY.PAS

▽

```
procedure ReadData (var InEmp {input file} : Text;
                    var HourOrSal {output} : Char;
                    var Rate {output},
                        Hours {output} : Real);
{
 Reads the employee salary data.
 Pre  : File InEmp is opened for input.
 Post : HourOrSal contains the first data character on
        the data line.
        If HourOrSal is H, Rate contains the hourly rate
        and Hours contains the hours worked. If HourOrSal
        is S, Rate contains the annual salary and Rate is
        undefined. Otherwise, Hours and Rate are undefined.
}
begin {ReadData}
  Read (InEmp, HourOrSal);
  if HourOrSal = 'H' then
    ReadLn (InEmp, Rate, Hours)   {Read hourly rate and hours.}
  else if HourOrSal = 'S' then
    ReadLn (InEmp, Rate)          {Read annual salary.}
  else
    begin
      ReadLn (InEmp);                  {Skip past <eoln>.}
      WriteLn ('Invalid character ', HourOrSal)
    end {if}
end; {ReadData}
```

▷ ▷ ▷ ▷ ▷ ▷

```
function ComputeSal (HourOrSal : Char;
                     Rate,
                     Hours : Real) : Real;
{
 Computes the weekly gross salary.
 Pre : HourOrSal and Rate are defined.
 Post: If HourOrSal is H, returns Rate * Hours;
       if HourOrSal is S, returns Rate / 52;
       otherwise, result is undefined.
}
begin
   if HourOrSal = 'H' then
     ComputeSal := Rate * Hours
   else if HourOrSal = 'S' then
     ComputeSal := Rate / 52.0
end; {ComputeSal}

procedure ProcessEmp (var InEmp {input file},
                          OutEmp {output file} : Text;
                      var Payroll {output} : Real);
{
 Processes all employees and computes payroll total.
 Pre : InEmp is prepared for input and OutEmp for output.
 Post: All employee names and weekly salaries are written
       to OutEmp and the sum of their salaries is returned
       through Payroll.
}
   var
     HourOrSal : Char;{input - hourly or salaried indicator}
     Hours,            {input - hours worked}
     Rate,             {input - hourly rate}
     Salary : Real;    {output - gross salary}

begin  {ProcessEmp}
   Payroll := 0.0;
   while not EOF(InEmp) do
     begin
       CopyLine (InEmp, OutEmp);      {Copy employee name.}
       {Read salary data.}
       ReadData (InEmp, HourOrSal, Rate, Hours);
       Salary := ComputeSal(HourOrSal, Rate, Hours);
       if (HourOrSal = 'H') or (HourOrSal = 'S') then
         begin {good data}
           Payroll := Payroll + Salary;
           WriteLn (OutEmp, Salary :4:2)
         end {good data}
       else
         WriteLn (OutEmp, 'Salary is undefined')
     end {while}
end; {ProcessEmp}
```

Next, the statement

```
ReadData (InEmp, HourOrSal, Rate, Hours);
```

in `ProcessEmp` calls `ReadData` to read an employee's salary data from `InEmp` and to advance the file location marker to the first letter of the next employee's name. If the character read into `HourOrSal` is not H or S, `ReadData` writes an error message to the screen and skips to the start of the next data line. The next statement in `ProcessEmp`

```
Salary := ComputeSal(HourOrSal, Rate, Hours);
```

calls `ComputeSal` to compute the weekly gross salary and to assign it to `Salary`. Finally, the statements

```
Payroll := Payroll + Salary;
WriteLn (OutEmp, Salary :4:2)
```

add the current employee's gross salary to `Payroll` and write it to file `Out-Emp` provided `Salary` is defined.

TESTING ▼

Run the payroll program with sample payroll data to determine whether it computes weekly salaries and payroll correctly for both hourly and salaried employees. Also see what happens when the first character of an employee's salary data is not H or S. In this case, the program should display an error message and continue on to process the next employee's data. Check whether the program correctly processes later employees or whether errors propagate, causing an error in one employee's data to invalidate all other results.

The Importance of Advancing Past the <eoln> Character

It is easy to make an error when reading character data mixed with numeric data. Many problems are caused by not advancing past the <eoln> character. For example, consider what would happen if `ReadData` used the statement

```
Read (InEmp, Rate);
```

to read a salaried employee's data instead of calling procedure `ReadLn`. The difficulty is that the `Read` procedure advances the file location marker for file `InEmp` up to the <eoln> character but not past it:

```
S 260000.00<eoln>
           ↑
    File location marker
```

When CopyLine is called to copy the second employee's name, the while loop exit occurs immediately, without reading the name, because the next character is the <eoln> character. The <eoln> character is processed just before CopyLine returns to procedure ProcessEmp, and the next character is now the first letter of an employee's name. When ReadData is called again, the statement

```
Read (InEmp, HourOrSal);
```

reads the first letter, C, of the second employee's name, so an error message will be displayed on the screen.

Exercises for Section 8.3   **Self-Check**

1. a. What would be the effect, if any, of trailing blanks at the end of data lines in the data file for the program in Fig. 8.9?
   b. What would be the effect of blank lines?
2. Why does placing employee names and salary amounts on separate lines of file OutEmp simplify writing the program to print the payroll checks?

Programming

1. Write a program that reads file OutEmp produced by program WritePayroll (Fig. 8.9) and displays a count of the number of employees processed by WritePayroll and their average salary.

8.4   Debugging with Files

Preparing a data file that contains a representative set of test data for a new program makes it easier to debug a program. Each time it is run, the program can read the test data from this file, eliminating the need to retype the data items.

8.5   Common Programming Errors

The file name used in your program may differ from the directory name of the associated disk file. All file names must be declared as file variables (type Text) except for system files Input and Output. Don't forget to list all file variables in the program heading.

Always use the Reset or Rewrite procedure to prepare a file for input or output (except for system files Input and Output). If you rewrite an existing file, the data on that file may be lost. Make sure that you do not inadvertently place the Reset or Rewrite statement in a loop. If you do, a Read operation in the loop will repeatedly read the first file component; a Write operation in the loop will repeatedly write the first file component.

The `Read` or `ReadLn` procedure can be used only after a file has been prepared for input. Similarly, the `Write` or `WriteLn` procedure can be used only after a file has been prepared for output. When performing file input or output, be sure to specify the file name as the first procedure parameter; otherwise, the system file `Input` or `Output` will be assumed. The following loop will execute forever because data are read from system file `Input` (the default file) instead of file `MyData`, which is being tested for the `<eoln>` character:

```
while not EOLN(MyData) do
  begin
    Read (Next);        {incorrect read from keyboard}
    Write (Next)
  end; {while}
```

When you use function `EOLN` or `EOF` to control data entry, don't forget to include the data file name as the function argument. Remember to skip over the `<eoln>` character, using `ReadLn`, after you have reached the end of a data line. Be careful not to try to read data when the file location marker is at `<eof>`.

If you press the Return key an extra time when you have finished creating a data file, you may place an extra empty line at the end of the data file. The following file contains one number per line and an empty line at the end:

```
500<eoln>
37<eoln>
<eoln><eof>
```

Although the empty line may seem harmless, if we use the `while` header

```
while not EOF(InData) do
```

to control a loop that reads and processes one number per line, the empty line will cause the loop to execute one extra time.

CHAPTER REVIEW

1. You can read a program's data from a text file and write its results to a text file by specifying a file variable (type `Text`) as the first parameter in a `Read(Ln)` or `Write(Ln)`.
2. The `<eoln>` character separates a text file into lines. The `EOLN` function can test for an `<eoln>` character, and the `WriteLn` statement places an `<eoln>` character in a text file. An `<eoln>` character that is read into a type `Char` variable is stored as a blank in standard Pascal.
3. When text files are processed, sequences of characters are transferred between main memory and disk storage. The data type of a variable used in an input list must be `Char`, `Integer`, `Real`, or a subrange of `Char` or `Integer`. Besides the above, you can use Boolean variables and string literals in an output list.

4. The Reset procedure moves the file location marker for an input file to the first character in the file. The Rewrite procedure creates an empty output file. The EOF function tests whether the end of the file has been reached and returns True if the next character is the <eof> character.

Summary of New Pascal Constructs

Construct	Effect
File Declaration	
```var MoreChars, MoreDigits : Text; I : Integer; NextCh : Char;```	MoreChars and MoreDigits are text files.
Reset and Rewrite Procedures	
```Reset (MoreDigits); Rewrite (MoreChars);```	MoreDigits is prepared for input, and MoreChars is prepared for output.
Read and Write Procedures	
```Read (MoreDigits, I); WriteLn (MoreChars, 'number: ', I);```	The next integer is read from file MoreDigits into variable I (type Integer). The string 'number: ' is written to MoreChars followed by the value of I.
EOF Function	
```Reset (MoreDigits); Rewrite (MoreChars); while not EOF(MoreDigits) do begin ReadLn (MoreDigits, I); WriteLn (MoreChars, I) end; {while}```	File MoreDigits is prepared for input to the program and file MoreChars for output from the program. The first integer value on each line of file MoreDigits is written to a separate line of file MoreChars.
EOLN Function	
```Reset (MoreDigits); while not EOLN(MoreDigits) do begin Read (MoreDigits, NextCh); Write (Output, NextCh) end; {while} ReadLn (MoreDigits)```	File MoreDigits is prepared for input. Each character on the first line is read to NextCh and displayed on the screen. ReadLn advances the file location marker for MoreDigits to the first character of the second line.

Quick-Check Exercises

1. Either _____ or _____ must be performed before a file can be read or written.
2. The _____ character separates a _____ file into lines, and the _____ character appears at the end of a file.
3. What data types can be read from or written to a text file?
4. Is it ever permissible to pass a file as a value parameter to a procedure?
5. True or false: The name of a variable of type Text must be the same as the directory name of the corresponding file.
6. Can a text file be used for both input and output by the same program?
7. Correct the following segment:

```
Reset (Number);
while not EOF do
    Read (InFile, Number);
```

Answers to Quick-Check Exercises

1. Reset, Rewrite
2. <eoln>, text, <eof>
3. Any of the standard data types (or a subrange thereof) except Boolean can be read; any of the standard types (or a subrange thereof) or a string literal can be written.
4. No.
5. False, the file's directory name need not be the same as the file variable name.
6. Yes, but it may not be open for both input and output at the same time.
7. ```
   Reset (InFile);
   while not EOF(InFile) do
       Read (InFile, Number);
   ```

Review Questions

1. List three advantages to using files for input and output instead of interactive input and output.
2. a. Explain the difference between a file's internal and external names.
   b. What conventions are followed for choosing each name?
   c. Which name appears in the file variable declaration?
   d. Which name appears in an operating system command?
3. Explain how Read and ReadLn differ in reading data items from a text file.
4. Let X be type Real, N type Integer, and Ch type Char. Indicate the contents of each variable after each input operation is performed, assuming the file consists of the following lines and that the Reset (InData) operation occurs before each sequence of statements:

```
23 53.2 ABC<eoln>
145 Z<eoln><eof>
```
```

a. Read (InData, N, X);
    ReadLn (InData, Ch)
b. ReadLn (InData, Ch, N)
c. ReadLn (InData);
    Read (InData, X, Ch)

5. Write a loop that reads up to 10 integer values from a data file and displays them on the screen. If there are not 10 integers in the file, the message That's all folks should be displayed after the last number.

6. Write a procedure that copies several data lines typed at the keyboard to a text file. The copy process should be terminated when the user enters an empty line.

7. Write a procedure that will open a data file, read the first character from the file, and write that to a new file. The procedure should not write the second file if the first file is empty.

Programming Projects

Directory: CHAP8
File: PROJ1.PAS

1. Write a procedure that reads the data for one employee from file OutEmp produced by program WritePayroll (see Section 8.3) and writes a payroll check to an output file. The format of the check should be similar to this one:

```
Temple University        Check No.      12372
Philadelphia, PA         Date:       03-17-94

Pay to the
Order of:  Peter Liacouras    $ 5000.00

                         Jane Smith
                         Bursar
```

2. Write a program that reads the initial check number and the data from the keyboard and then writes checks using the procedure from Programming Project 1 and a data file generated by running program WritePayroll. Write a separator line consisting of 80 underscore characters between checks.

3. Each year the state legislature rates the activity of the faculty of each state-supported college and university. The rating is based on reports submitted by the faculty members indicating the average number of hours worked per week during the school year. Each faculty member is rated, and the university receives an overall rating.

   The faculty activity ratings are computed as follows:
   a. "Highly productive" means over 55 hours per week reported.
   b. "Satisfactory" means reported hours per week are between 35 and 55.
   c. "Overpaid" means reported hours per week are less than 35.
   Read the following data from a file (assuming all names are padded with blanks in the data file to 10 characters):

Name	Hours
Herm	63
Flo	37
Jake	20

Name	Hours
Maureen	55
Saul	72
Tony	40
Al	12

As part of your solution, your program should include procedures that correspond to the procedure headers shown next:

```
procedure PrintHeader;
{Displays table heading}

procedure DisplayProductivity (Hours {input} : Real);
{Displays productivity ranking based on value of Hours}

procedure ProcessName (var FacHours {input} : Text);
{Reads and displays one faculty name from file FacHours}

procedure ProcessData (var FacHours {input} : Text;
                            var Count {input/output} : Integer;
                            var Sum {input/output} : Real);
{
  Reads all data lines from file FacHours and displays body
  of table and returns number of faculty (Count) and the sum
  of their hours worked (Sum). Calls: ProcessName and
  DisplayProductivity.
}
```

Directory: CHAP8
File: PROJ4.PAS

4. Compute the monthly payment and the total payment for a bank loan, given the following:
   a. The amount of the loan
   b. The duration of the loan in months
   c. The interest rate for the loan
   Your program should read in one loan at a time, perform the required computation, and print the values of the monthly payment and the total payment.
      Test your program with at least the following data (and more if you want):

Loan	Months	Rate
16000	300	12.50
24000	360	13.50
30000	300	15.50
42000	360	14.50
22000	300	15.50
300000	240	15.25

Hints:
a. The formula for computing a monthly payment is

$$monthpay = \frac{ratem \times expm^{months} \times loan}{expm^{months} - 1.0}$$

where

$ratem = rate/1200.00$

$expm = (1.0 + ratem)$

You will need a loop to multiply *expm* by itself *months* times.
b.   The formula for computing the total payment is

$$total = monthpay \times months$$

5.   Use the solution to Programming Project 4 as the basis for writing a program that will write a data file containing a table of the following form:

```
            Loan Amount: $1000
Interest  Duration  Monthly  Total
Rate      (years)   Payment  Payment
6.00      20        ——       ——
6.00      25        ——       ——
6.00      30        ——       ——
6.25      20        ——       ——
```

The output file produced by your program should contain payment information on a $1000 loan for interest rates from 6% to 10% with increments of 0.25%. The loan durations should be 20, 25, and 30 years.

6.   Because text files can grow very large, some computer systems supply a handy utility program that displays the head and tail of a file, where the head is the first four lines and the tail is the last four lines. Write a program that displays the head of the file, a line of dots, and the tail of the file. If the file is eight or less lines long, just display the entire file.

7.   Whatsamata U offers a service to its faculty in computing grades at the end of each semester. A program processes three weighted test scores and calculates a student's average and letter grade (based on an A as 90–100, a B as 80–89, etc.). Read the student data from a file and write each student's name, test score, average, and grade to an output file.

Write a program to provide this valuable service. The data will consist of the three test weights followed by three test scores and a student ID number (four digits) for each student. Calculate the weighted average for each student and the corresponding letter grade. This information should be printed along with the initial three test scores. The weighted average for each student is equal to

$$(weight_1 \times score_1) + (weight_2 \times score_2) + (weight_3 \times score_3)$$

For summary statistics print the highest average, the lowest average, the average of the averages, and the total number of students processed.
Sample data:

```
0.35  0.25  0.4     test weights
00  76    88  1014      test scores and ID
```

8. Write a program that reads in a string of characters that represent a Roman numeral and then converts it to Arabic form (an integer). The character values for Roman numerals are as follows:

M	1000
D	500
C	100
L	50
X	10
V	5
I	1

    Test your program with the following data: IX (9), LXXXVII (87), CCXIX (219), MCCCLIV (1354), MMDCLXXIII (2673), MCDLXXVI (1476).

INTERVIEW

Donna Auguste

Donna Auguste is a technical director in the Multimedia Services Engineering and Development group at U S WEST Technologies. Previously, Ms. Auguste managed the Apple software engineering team that developed the industry's first Personal Digital Assistant, the Apple Newton. Her tireless commitment to projects and dynamic leadership skills have become her trademarks in the software development industry. Ms. Auguste began her studies at the University of California—Berkeley, where she earned a bachelor of science degree in electrical engineering and computer science. She then studied three years in the Carnegie-Mellon computer science Ph.D. program researching intelligent computer-aided instruction and user modeling.

▼ **What areas of computer science first attracted your interest? What was your first job in the industry?**

▲ I chose to study electrical engineering and computer science because I was very interested in how computers are designed, built, and used. During college, my strongest technical interest became artificial intelligence. I enjoyed exploring how to develop computers that could adapt to the needs of the people using them as tools. My first job in the industry was at Lawrence Livermore Lab in California. I was a systems programmer, implementing magnetic fusion energy physics programs on LLL's new Cray computer. This was during the summer between my freshman and sophomore years in college. Later, I did summer internships at Bell Labs in Murray Hill, New Jersey, and at Xerox Palo Alto Research Center in California. When I got out of school I worked on expert system technology at Intellicorp for six years.

▼ **You have worked on a wide range of specialized projects—knowledge-based expert systems for 3M and other artificial intelligence software for Intellicorp, and Apple's Newton MessagePad. How difficult is it to adapt your management and engineering skills to the needs of these projects?**

▲ From my point of view, everything I do uses everything I've ever learned. For example, skills I learned during childhood about valuing different perspectives of diverse people are the same skills that I used in blending a diverse engineering team for developing Newton software. I've been a relatively introverted "nerd" all my life, but my mother and sisters made sure that I developed strong verbal communication skills in addition to academic skills; now I use those communication skills every day in the workplace. My involvement in BESSA, the Black Engineering and Science Students' Association at UC Berkeley, was also very beneficial to me. Through BESSA, I met others with technology interests similar to my own; we worked on projects together to explore electrical engineering, computer science, and mechanical engineering ideas. As I took on leadership roles in BESSA, eventually serving as president, I began to develop my management and leadership skills. Technically, I draw daily from theory and practice in my engineering, science, and math background. Hands-on technical apprenticeships during college, as a complement to the theory I was learning, were invaluable in preparing me to use and re-use fundamental technical skills.

▼ **Your current position involves developing multimedia software for interactive television. How do you set expectations for the team? Do you foresee any constant obstacles to achieving the goals you establish?**

▲ We're designing and implementing our broadband multimedia technology with maximum flexibility to support a variety of applications. Our customers will tell us what they're interested in when we begin field testing the early technology. The product goals develop as we receive feedback from the marketplace. We plan to listen to our customers and respond rapidly to their interests.

   Major obstacles? Nothing out of the ordinary for developing new technology products. Network latencies are a foreseeable challenge. This is primarily because we are implementing the technology with computers and other network components that each require nanosecond and millisecond response times. Cumulatively, that adds up to a delay. Our customers expect response time close to an "instantaneous TV experience." We have to be creative with the technology in order to meet that expectation.

▼ **As a team manager, what are the key concepts you apply in directing your team?**

▲ LISTEN—All of us are experts at something related to our product development, so we ask each other a lot of questions and we listen to each other.
LEARN—Everyone on the team needs to constantly be in learning mode. For products based on (our!) brand-new technology, we have to realize that we're making this up as we go along.
HAVE FUN!

▼ **What next? Where do you see your career in the next few years?**

▲ There are lots of exciting options in this field. I have thoroughly enjoyed working in technology start-up environments—like my work at Intellicorp. I've also learned a tremendous amount and enjoyed working in larger corporate environments such as Apple and U S WEST. Outside of work, I devote a lot of time to learning and writing music—using a computer to help with composing and arranging—and enjoy this tremendously. My external interests, such as writing and music, may contribute to my choices in the future.

▼ **What recommendations do you have for students currently learning the introductory concepts of problem solving with computers?**

▲ I have one primary recommendation: Learn to give yourself honest feedback about progress toward your goals. Whether your goal is to master certain problem-solving techniques or to solve a very specific problem, you need to factor in input from others and give yourself your own feedback about whether or not your solution(s) will move you toward that goal. Re-examine solutions that do not move you toward your goals, and adjust them. The computer is one of many tools that you can apply to discover solutions. Understand what it can and cannot do as a problem-solving tool in your hands. Learn to trust your own intuition about how and when to use it.

CHAPTER NINE

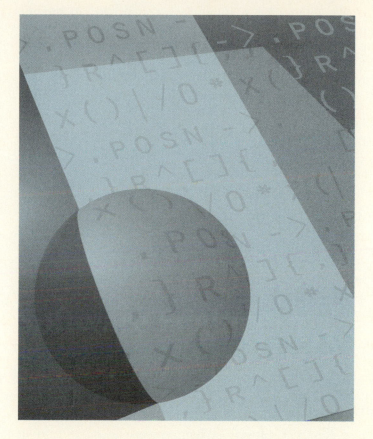

Software Engineering

The programs you've written and studied so far have been relatively short and designed to solve specific problems. Many problems, particularly those in industry, require larger, more complex programs. This type of large system programming, called *programming in the large,* is the focus of this chapter.

To implement large programs, professional programmers use a collection of tools and techniques for program design, coding, testing, and maintenance. The study and use of these tools and techniques is called **software engineering.** One technique to simplify the writing of large programs reuses code that accomplishes a particular task. In several earlier

software engineering
the study and use of tools and techniques for designing, coding, testing, and maintaining large software systems

programs, you've extended problem solutions from one problem to another, but for the most part your programs were not general enough to solve more than one problem. To program a large system efficiently, the problem solution must be modularized so that many different programmers can write and test different sections of the program. Quite often a module used in one program can be part of another program. This chapter illustrates the benefits of libraries of modules in writing efficient, modular programs.

In addition to discussing how large programs are designed and written, this chapter also introduces testing techniques. Because this chapter describes concepts used by software professionals, it concludes with a discussion of professional behavior, ethics, and responsibilities.

9.1 Programming in the Large

To solve large-scale programming problems, programmers must have some way of attacking the problem systematically and managing its complexity. The techniques professional programmers use for this purpose are not very different from those you have been practicing so far. Programmers use the software development method to structure their solution, and they implement their solution by writing a collection of small, well-defined modules. Wherever possible, they reuse modules written to solve earlier problems. This section discusses how professional programmers use the software development method to develop a computer application or software system.

The System/Software Life Cycle

system/software life cycle
the steps in the development
of a software system

Because the development of a software system proceeds in stages from its initial inception to its ultimate obsolescence, programmers refer to these different stages as the **system/software life cycle** (SLC). The system/software life cycle, like the software development method, consists of the following six steps:

1. Requirements specification
   a. Prepare a complete and unambiguous problem statement.
   b. Submit the requirements document to the users and analysts for review and obtain their written approval.
2. Analysis
   a. Understand the problem; determine problem outputs and required inputs.
   b. Evaluate alternative solutions.
   c. Choose the preferred solution.
3. Design
   a. Perform a top-down design of the system.
   b. For each module, identify key data elements and subordinate procedures using structure charts.

4. Implementation
    a. Write algorithms and pseudocode descriptions of individual procedures.
    b. Code the solution.
    c. Debug the code.
5. Testing and verification
    a. Test the code, verifying that it is correct.
    b. Include users and special testing teams in all system tests.
6. Operation, follow-up, and maintenance
    a. Run the completed system.
    b. Evaluate its performance.
    c. Remove new bugs as they are detected.
    d. Make required changes to keep the system up to date.
    e. Verify that changes are correct and do not adversely affect the system's operation.

Problem analysis should always precede problem solution (synthesis). Steps 1 and 2 of the SLC (requirements specification and analysis) are the analysis part, and steps 3 and 4 (design and implementation) are the synthesis part. System users take the lead in developing the initial requirements specification for a proposed software system. System analysts work closely with users to understand more thoroughly the problem requirements and to evaluate possible alternative solutions.

The SLC is iterative. During the design phase (step 3), problems may arise that necessitate modifying the requirements specification. Similarly, during implementation (step 4) it may become necessary to reconsider decisions made in the design phase. Systems analysts and system users must approve all changes.

Once implemented, the system must be thoroughly tested before entering its final stage (operation and maintenance). System changes identified in these stages may require repetition of earlier stages of the SLC to correct errors found during testing or to accommodate changes required by external sources (for example, a change in federal or state tax regulations).

Estimates vary as to the time necessary for each stage. For example, a typical system may require a year to proceed through the first four stages, three months of testing, then four or more years of operation and maintenance. Because the programmers who maintain the system may not have participated in its original design or implementation, software must be designed and documented so that it can be easily maintained.

Requirements Specification

Although we have illustrated most phases of the SLC (our software development method) in solving case studies, we have not studied in detail the requirements specification process. Programming problems used as examples for learning a programming language tend to be stated simply so that students can focus on the rudiments of the language and on programming techniques. For these reasons, each case study was preceded by a brief statement of the problem, and we began our solutions with the analysis phase.

To illustrate the requirements specification process, assume you have been given the following problem specification for a telephone directory program.

PROBLEM ▼

Write an interactive telephone directory program that contains a collection of names and telephone numbers. The directory user should be able to insert a new entry in the directory, retrieve an entry from the directory, change a directory entry, and delete a directory entry.

To plan the program, you need to know the format of the input data, the desired form of any output screens or printed forms, and the need for data validation. You might ask the user the following questions, among others:

▶ Is an initial list of names and numbers to be stored in the directory beforehand, or are all entries to be inserted at the same time? If there is an initial list, is it stored in a data file or will it be entered interactively?

▶ If the file is a text file, what are the formatting conventions (e.g., will the name start in position 1 and the phone number in position 20)? Are the name and number on the same data line or on separate lines?

▶ Is the final directory printed or stored as a file on disk?

▶ Can more than one number be associated with a particular name? If so, should the first number, the last number, or all numbers be retrieved?

▶ Is there a limit on the length of a name? How are the names stored (e.g., *lastname, firstname,* or *firstname lastname*)?

▶ Are phone numbers stored as numbers or as strings of characters? Do they contain area codes? Are there any special characters, such as hyphens and parentheses, in a phone number? Should you check for illegal characters in a number or for numbers that are too short or too long?

As you can see, the initial problem statement leaves plenty of questions unanswered. To complete the requirements specification, you should get answers to these questions and more.

Prototyping

prototyping
developing a system by adding successive refinements to an initial system model

An alternative to traditional system development is prototyping. In **prototyping**, systems analysts work closely with system users to develop a prototype, or model, of the actual system and refine that prototype in stages. Initially the prototype has few working features and just mimics the input/output interaction of the users with the system. At each stage, the users and the analysts decide what changes should be made and what new features should be added; these changes are then incorporated into the prototype. The process continues until a complete prototype is available that performs all the functions of the final system. The analysts and the users can then decide whether to use the prototype as the final system or as the basis of the design for a new system, which will perform the same operations as the prototype but which will be more efficient.

Programming Teams

One major difference between programming in college and in industry is that in industry it is rare for a large software project to be implemented by a single programmer. Most often, a large project is assigned to a team of programmers after the problem specification and analysis phases are complete. The team members then coordinate the overall organization of the project and meet regularly to exchange information and report progress.

Each team member is responsible for a set of modules, some of which may be accessed by other team members. After the initial organizational meeting, each team member should provide the other members with a specification for each procedure that he or she is implementing. Such a specification is similar to the documentation provided for each procedure in this text. It consists of a brief statement of the purpose of the procedure, its pre- and postconditions, and its formal parameter list. This information is all that a potential user of the procedure needs to know to call the procedure correctly.

Normally one team member acts as "librarian" by assuming responsibility for determining the status of each module in the system. Initially, the library of modules consists of a stub for each new module. As a module is completed and tested, its updated version replaces the version currently in the library. The librarian keeps track of the date that each version of a module is inserted into the library and makes sure that all programmers use the latest version of any module.

Exercises for Section 9.1   **Self-Check**

1. Which phase or phases of the software life cycle are of most concern to the systems analyst? To the librarian?
2. List the six phases of the software life cycle. Which phase is usually the longest?

9.2 Module Libraries

Whether programming as an individual or as a member of a team, we must be able to divide a program into a set of self-contained modules. In Pascal, these modules can be procedures or functions. The philosophy behind modular programming is one we've used in small programs: procedural abstraction.

Procedural Abstraction Revisited

Procedural abstraction is the philosophy that procedure development should separate the concern of *what* is to be achieved by a procedure from the details of *how* it is to be achieved. In other words, you can specify what you expect a procedure to do, then use that procedure in the design of a problem solution before you know how to implement the procedure.

To visualize the process, consider the implementation of two steps of an algorithm coded as procedure calls in the main program:

The main program calls two procedures, Proc1 and Proc2, to accomplish its first two tasks. The details of how these tasks are to be accomplished will be provided in the procedure declarations for Proc1 and Proc2 when they are written.

The practice of procedural abstraction in programming is analogous to following a recipe in cooking. An inexperienced cook working alone might follow without deviation each step in the recipe in the sequence in which it is listed. An experienced chef, on the other hand, would do much of the preparatory work (such as chopping ingredients, preparing the sauce) ahead of time or distribute these assignments to helpers. The chef would not care how, or in what sequence, these tasks were completed, as long as they were ready before needed in the final assembly and cooking. The experienced chef is using procedural abstraction, while the inexperienced cook is not.

Sample Library Modules

As you progress through this course, you will write many procedures and functions. You should try to keep each new module as general as possible so that you can reuse it in other applications. You will eventually build up a sizable personal library. Reusing tried and tested modules is always much more efficient than starting from scratch. Each new module that you write will have to be thoroughly tested and debugged whereas the modules in your personal library should be error free.

Efficient programmers write library modules to perform useful operations that are not included in standard Pascal. You wrote one such module, function UpCase (Fig. 7.3), which converts a lowercase letter to uppercase. Because Pascal's ReadLn procedure cannot read a Boolean value, you might want to write your own input procedure for this purpose.

EXAMPLE 9.1 ▼

Procedure ReadLnBool (Fig. 9.1) returns True if the data line begins with t or T and False if it begins with f or F. The statement

```
NextChar := UpCase(NextChar);
```

converts the first data character to uppercase.   ▲

EXAMPLE 9.2 ▼

Procedure EnterInt (Fig. 9.2) is another useful input module that should be part of your personal library. It reads and returns an integer value within a specified range (e.g., an integer from -5 to +5).   ▲

Program Style

Validating a Library Procedure's Parameters

Procedure EnterInt begins by checking whether its user correctly entered its input parameters, MinN and MaxN. If the parameters define an empty range, an error message is displayed and the while loop is skipped. Make sure that you

---

Figure 9.1
Procedure ReadLnBool

Directory: CHAP9
File: READLNBO.PAS

```pascal
procedure ReadLnBool (var BoolVal {output} : Boolean);
{
  Reads a Boolean value (represented by a T or F) into
  BoolVal.
  Pre :  None.
  Post:  BoolVal is set to True if T or t is read;
         BoolVal is set to False if F or f is read.
  Calls: function UpCase (Fig. 7.3)
}
  var
    NextChar : Char;               {data character}

begin {ReadLnBool}
  repeat
    Write ('Type T or F> ');
    ReadLn (NextChar);
    NextChar := UpCase(NextChar);
    BoolVal := (NextChar = 'T')          {Is NextChar 'T'?}
  until (NextChar = 'T') or (NextChar = 'F')
end; {ReadLnBool}
```

Figure 9.2
Procedure EnterInt

Directory: CHAP9
File: ENTERINT.PAS

```
procedure EnterInt (MinN, MaxN {input} : Integer;
                         var N {output} : Integer);
{
 Reads an integer between MinN and MaxN into N.
 Pre : MinN and MaxN are assigned values.
 Post: Returns in N the first data value
       between MinN and MaxN if MinN <= MaxN is true;
       otherwise, N is not defined.
}
  var
    Done : Boolean;    {program flag - loop control}

begin {EnterInt}
  if MinN <= MaxN then
    Done := False         {no valid value in N as yet}
  else
    begin
      WriteLn ('Error - empty range for EnterInt');
      Done := True              {N is undefined.}
    end; {if}

  {Keep reading until valid number is read.}
  while not Done do
    begin
      Write ('Enter an integer from ');
      Write (MinN :1, ' to ', MaxN :1, '> ');
      ReadLn (N);
      Done := (MinN <= N) and (N <= MaxN)  {Is N valid?}
    end {while}
end; {EnterInt}
```

carefully validate input parameters for procedures that are candidates for inclusion in a library. Since library procedures can be reused many times and by many different programmers, this extra effort can pay valuable dividends.

Exercises for Section 9.2

Self-Check

1. Why is it important that, when library procedures change, the procedure parameters remain the same?

Programming

1. Write procedure `EnterChar` that returns a data character that lies within a specified range of characters. Your procedure should display an error message if the specified range is invalid.
2. Write a program that tests the procedure written in Programming Exercise 1. Describe how you can effectively test the procedure using this test program, and list all input you will use for testing.

9.3 Abstract Data Types

In many programming problems, you need to process information relating to the day of the week. To facilitate this processing, you can declare an enumerated type Day that has as its values the days of the week. You would have to write your own procedures for reading and writing the days of the week, because Pascal cannot read and write enumerated type values directly. This combination of a data type and procedures for processing that type is called an **abstract data type (ADT)**.

abstract data type (ADT)
a combination of a data type and procedures and functions for manipulating the data type
specification
a comment describing an ADT
implementation
the code for the ADT

Figure 9.3 shows one possible form for the abstract data type, called DayADT, just described. An ADT is separated into two sections: specification and implementation. The ADT **specification** is one long comment which contains all the information a programmer needs to know to use the ADT. The ADT **implementation** contains the actual code including the data type declaration.

Figure 9.3
Abstract Data Type DayADT

Directory: CHAP9
File: DAYADT.PAS

```
{
    SPECIFICATION for abstract data type DayADT

    Structure: Day is an enumerated data type whose values
        represent the days of the week.

    Operators:

    ReadLnDay (var ADay : Day) : Reads a value into ADay.

    WriteDay (ADay : Day) : Displays the value of ADay.

    IMPLEMENTATION
}
    type
        Day = (Sunday, Monday, Tuesday, Wednesday,
                Thursday, Friday, Saturday);

    {Insert function UpCase here (see Fig. 7.3)}

    procedure ReadLnDay (var ADay {output} : Day);
    {
     Reads a value into ADay.
     Pre : None.
     Post: ADay is assigned a value when the two characters
            read are SU, MO, TU, WE, TH, FR, or SA;
            Value of ADay corresponds to data characters.
     Calls:UpCase
    }
```

▷ ▷ ▷ ▷ ▷ ▷

```
    var
      DayCh1,                   {input - first letter in day}
      DayCh2  : Char;           {input - second letter in day}
      ValidDay : Boolean; {flag - indicates whether data are
                                  valid}

    begin {ReadLnDay}
      repeat
        Write ('Enter the first two letters of the day name> ');
        ReadLn (DayCh1, DayCh2);
        DayCh1 := UpCase(DayCh1);
        DayCh2 := UpCase(DayCh2);

        {Convert to day of week}
        ValidDay := True;                     {Assume valid day.}
        if (DayCh1 = 'S') and (DayCh2 = 'U') then
          ADay := Sunday
        else if (DayCh1 = 'M') and (DayCh2 = 'O') then
          ADay := Monday
        else if (DayCh1 = 'T') and (DayCh2 = 'U') then
          ADay := Tuesday
        else if (DayCh1 = 'W') and (DayCh2 = 'E') then
          ADay := Wednesday
        else if (DayCh1 = 'T') and (DayCh2 = 'H') then
          ADay := Thursday
        else if (DayCh1 = 'F') and (DayCh2 = 'R') then
          ADay := Friday
        else if (DayCh1 = 'S') and (DayCh2 = 'A') then
          ADay := Saturday
        else
          ValidDay := False     {Day is not valid - repeat loop}
      until ValidDay
    end; {ReadLnDay}

    procedure WriteDay (ADay {input} : Day);
    {
     Displays the value of ADay.
     Pre : ADay is defined.
     Post: Displays a string corresponding to the value of ADay.
    }
    begin {WriteDay}
      case ADay of
        Sunday    : Write ('Sunday');
        Monday    : Write ('Monday');
        Tuesday   : Write ('Tuesday');
        Wednesday : Write ('Wednesday');
        Thursday  : Write ('Thursday');
        Friday    : Write ('Friday');
        Saturday  : Write ('Saturday')
      end {case}
    end; {WriteDay}
```

Using Abstract Type Day

You should insert function `UpCase` where indicated and save `DayADT` as a separate disk file, `DAYADT.PAS`. When you use `DayADT` in a new program, this file can be read from disk and inserted in the declaration part of the new program following the variable declarations. Move the declaration for type `Day` so that it appears with the other type declarations in the new program and precedes the declaration of any variable of type `Day`. If your compiler allows procedures to be declared before variables, you can insert the entire ADT right after the last type declaration in the new program. This is nonstandard and would not be possible on all Pascal compilers.

Some Pascal compilers have **compiler directives**, which are special lines inserted in the program file that provide instructions to the compiler. Often, a compiler directive instructs the compiler to include a previously saved file into another file that is being compiled. For example, in VAX Pascal (implemented on Digital Equipment Corporation VAX computers), the line

compiler directive
program lines that provide
instructions to the compiler

```
%Include 'DAYADT.PAS'
```

instructs the compiler to include file `DAYADT.PAS` at the point where this comment appears in the program being compiled. The lines in file `DAYADT.PAS` would be inserted and translated. Any syntax errors would be displayed.

Alternatively, some compilers allow you to compile source files that are not complete Pascal programs as separate program modules (for example, VAX Pascal modules or Turbo Pascal units). In this case, a file containing Pascal code similar to `DayADT` could be compiled as a separate program module, resulting in an object file that would be saved on disk. You could then write a new program that uses `DayADT` without including this code in your new program (called a **client** of `DayADT`).

client
the user (a program) of an
abstract data type

After compiling the client program, you could instruct the linker to link its object code with that of module `DayADT`. You could then load the resulting object code file for the client program into memory and run it. Appendix D discusses how to create and use separate module files in VAX Pascal and Appendix E discusses how to do this in Turbo Pascal.

For our purposes, we will assume that the disk file for `DayADT` must be inserted directly in the source file of any new program that uses it. We will use comments such as

```
{Insert data type Day from DayADT.}
{Insert procedures ReadLnDay and WriteDay from DayADT.}
```

to remind you to do this; you should perform the insertion manually or by using a compiler directive if one is available on your system.

EXAMPLE 9.3 ▼

The program shown in Fig. 9.4 is a driver program that tests DayADT. It reads and displays the "day of the week" stored in variable Today (type Day). Notice that WriteDay does not advance the cursor to the next line, so we used the statement pair

```
WriteDay (Today);
WriteLn;
```

to display the value of Today and to advance the cursor.   ▲

Exercises for Section 9.3   *Self-Check*

1. Draw a structure chart for program TestDay that shows the data flow between program procedures.

Programming

1. Write an ADT MonthADT that contains the declaration for an enumerated type Month, procedures ReadMonth and WriteMonth, and function

Figure 9.4
Testing DayADT

Directory: CHAP9
File: TESTDAY.PAS

```
program TestDay (Input, Output);
{Test abstract data type DayADT (Fig. 9.3).}

   {Insert data type Day from DayADT.}

   var
      Today : Day;                {input - day being read}

   {Insert procedures ReadLnDay and WriteDay from DayADT.}

begin {TestDay}
   WriteLn ('What day is Today?');
   ReadLnDay (Today);
   Write ('Today is ');
   WriteDay (Today);
   WriteLn;
   if Today = Sunday then
      WriteLn ('Today is the first day of the week')
end. {TestDay}
```

Sample Run

```
What day is today?
Enter the first two letters of the day name> SU
Today is Sunday
Today is the first day of the week
```

> MonthEquivalent. Function MonthEquivalent has an integer argument of 1 through 12 and returns a value of type Month.
>
> 2. Write a client program that tests your MonthADT.

9.4 Testing Large Programs

It doesn't matter how carefully designed and efficient a program is if it doesn't do what it is supposed to do. One way to show that a program is correct is by testing it. But how much testing should be done? Often errors appear in a software product after it is delivered, some of the more notable errors having caused power brownouts, telephone network saturation, and space flight delays.

Preparing a Test Plan Early

A test plan specifies how the software will be tested, when the tests will take place, and who will do the testing. Normally, testing is done by the programmer, by other members of the programming team who did not code the module being tested, and by users of the software product. Some companies have special testing groups that are expert at finding bugs in other programmers' code.

Even though testing and verification appear at the end of the system life cycle, software development will proceed more smoothly if you consider the tests that each module will go through as it is being designed. If the test plan is developed early in the design stage, testing can take place concurrently with design and coding. The earlier an error is detected, the easier and less expensive it is to correct.

By thinking about testing early, you can write each module so that it will be able to handle correctly many situations that would otherwise cause problems or execution errors. A good programmer will practice **defensive programming** and include code that detects unexpected or invalid data values. For example, if a procedure has the precondition

defensive programming
guarding against program
failure due to invalid
data entry

```
{Pre : N greater than zero}
```

it would be a good idea to place the if statement

```
if N <= 0 then
    WriteLn ('Invalid value for parameter N - ', N :1);
```

at the beginning of the procedure. This if statement will provide a diagnostic message in the event that the parameter passed to the procedure is invalid.

Similarly, if a data value read from the keyboard is supposed to be between 0 and 40, a defensive programmer would use procedure EnterInt (see Fig. 9.2), as shown next:

```
WriteLn ('Enter number of hours worked:');
EnterInt (0, 40, Hours)
```

The first two parameters of `EnterInt` define the range of acceptable values for its third parameter.

Structured Walkthroughs

structured walkthrough
a detailed, step-by-step presentation of the algorithm to other members of the programming team whose purpose is to find design errors overlooked by the programmer

In one important testing technique, called a **structured walkthrough,** the programmer describes, or "walks through," the logic of a new module as part of a presentation to other members of the programming team. During the walkthrough, team members attempt to identify design errors or bugs that the programmer may have overlooked before they become part of the code.

Black Box Versus White Box Testing

black box testing
a testing process that assumes that the tester has no knowledge of the code; tester must compare a system's performance with its specification

There are two ways to test a module or a complete system: black box, or specification-based, testing and white box testing. **Black box testing** assumes that the program tester has no idea of the code inside the module or system. The tester's job is to verify that the module does what its specification says it will. For a procedure, this means ensuring that its postconditions are satisfied whenever its preconditions have been met. For a system, this means ensuring that it does indeed satisfy its original requirements specification. Because the tester cannot look inside the module or system, he or she must prepare sufficient sets of test data to determine that the system outputs are correct for all valid system inputs. The tester especially should check the **system boundaries**, that is, particular values for the program variables where the system performance changes. A boundary for a payroll program would be the value of hours worked that triggers overtime pay. Moreover, the module or system should not crash when presented with invalid inputs. Black box testing most often is done by a special testing team or by program users.

system boundaries
values that cause a change in system performance

white box testing
a testing process that assumes the tester knows how the system is coded and requires checking all possible execution paths

In **white box testing,** the tester has full knowledge of the code for the module or system and must verify that each and every section of code has been thoroughly tested. For a selection statement (`if` or `case`), this means checking all possible paths through the selection statement. The tester must determine that the correct path is chosen for all possible values of the selection variable, taking special care at the boundary values where the path changes.

For a loop, the tester must check that it always performs the correct number of iterations and that the number of iterations is not off by 1. The tester must also verify that the computations inside the loop are correct at the boundaries, that is, for the initial and final values of the loop-control variable. Finally, the tester must make sure that the module or system still meets its specification when a loop executes zero times and that there are no circumstances under which the loop could execute forever.

Integration Testing

Section 6.7 discussed the differences between top-down and bottom-up testing. Another type of testing is called *integration testing*. In integration testing, the program tester must determine whether the individual components of a system that have been tested separately (using top-down or bottom-up testing or some combination) can be integrated with other like components. Each phase of integration testing deals with larger units, progressing from individual modules, through subsystems, and ending with the entire system. For example, after two subsystems have been completed, integration testing must determine whether the two subsystems can work together. Once the entire system has been completed, integration testing must determine whether that system is compatible with other systems in the computing environment in which it will be used.

Exercises for Section 9.4   *Self-Check*

1.   Explain why a procedure interface error would not be discovered through white box testing.
2.   Devise a set of data to test procedure `EnterInt` (Fig. 9.2) using each of the following:
     a.   White box testing
     b.   Black box testing

9.5   Formal Methods of Program Verification

In Section 9.4, we asked, How much testing is enough? Although we described testing procedures and recommended that testing go hand-in-hand with program design and implementation, we really did not answer the question directly. How would a systems analyst know for sure that the testing team has tried enough different sets of test data or that all possible paths through the program have been executed?

formal verification

using formal techniques to prove that a program is correct

To address this issue, computer scientists have developed an alternative method of demonstrating the correctness of a program called **formal verification**. In this method, the verifier uses formal rules to prove that a program meets its specification in the same way that a mathematician proves a theorem using definitions, axioms, and previously proved theorems.

A thorough discussion of formal verification is beyond the scope of this book. However, we introduce two key concepts, assertions and loop invariants, and use them to help document and clarify some modules.

Assertions

assertion

a logical statement that is always true

Part of formal verification concerns documenting a program through **assertions**—logical statements about the program that are "asserted" to be true.

An assertion is written as a comment and describes what is supposed to be true about the program variables at that point.

EXAMPLE 9.4 ▼

The following program fragment contains a sequence of assignment statements, each followed by an assertion written as a comment:

```
A := 5;             {assert: A is 5}
X := A;             {assert: X is 5}
Y := X + A;         {assert: Y is 10}
```

The truth of the first assertion, {A is 5}, follows from executing the first statement with the knowledge that 5 is a constant. The truth of the second assertion, {X is 5}, follows from executing X := A with the knowledge that A is 5. The truth of the third assertion, {Y is 10}, follows from executing Y := X + A with the knowledge that X is 5 and A is 5. The assertions document the change in a program variable after each assignment statement executes.   ▲

The goal of formal verification is to prove that a program fragment meets its specification. For the preceding fragment, this means proving that the final assertion, or *postcondition* (in this case, {Y is 10}), follows from the initial presumption, or *precondition* (in this case, {5 is a constant}), after the program fragment executes. The assignment rule (described next) is critical to this process. If we know that {A is 5} is true, the assignment rule allows us to make the assertion {X is 5} after executing the statement X := A.

The Assignment Rule

```
{P(A)}
X := A;
{P(X)}
```

Explanation: If P(A) is a logical statement (assertion) about A, the same statement will be true of X after the assignment statement X := A executes.

For our purposes, we use assertions as a documentation tool to improve our understanding of programs rather than as a method of formally proving them correct. Our assertions will be written in informal English, not in a formal language for logical statements. We have already used assertions to document the effect of executing a procedure.

Preconditions and Postconditions

A procedure's precondition is a logical statement about its input parameters. A procedure's postcondition may be a logical statement about its output parameters, or it may be a logical statement describing the change in program state caused by the procedure's execution. Any of the following activities changes the program state: changing the value of a variable, writing additional program output, reading new input data.

EXAMPLE 9.5 ▼

The precondition and the postcondition for procedure EnterInt (see Fig. 9.2) are repeated next:

```
procedure EnterInt (MinN, MaxN {input} : Integer;
                         var N {output} : Integer);
{
  Reads an integer between MinN and MaxN into N.
  Pre : MinN and MaxN are assigned values.
  Post: Returns in N the first data value between MinN and
        MaxN if MinN <= MaxN is true; otherwise, N is not
        defined.
}
```

The precondition tells us that input parameters MinN and MaxN are defined before the procedure begins execution. The postcondition tells us that the procedure's execution assigns the first data value between MinN and MaxN to the output parameter N whenever MinN <= MaxN is true. ▲

Loop Invariants

loop invariant
a logical statement about variables processed in the loop that is true just before the first loop repetition and remains true after each loop repetition

Errors frequently occur in loops because it is difficult to determine that a loop body executes exactly the right number of times or that loop execution causes the desired change in program variables. A special type of assertion, a loop invariant, helps prove that a loop meets its specification. A **loop invariant** is a logical statement about variables processed by a loop that is true before the loop is entered and after each execution of the loop body. It must therefore be true just after the loop is exited. An invariant is so-called because it is a relationship that remains true as loop execution progresses.

As an example of a loop invariant, let's examine the following loop, which accumulates the sum of the integers 1, 2, . . . , N, where N is a positive integer, and Sum, I, and N are type Integer:

```
{
  Accumulate the sum of integers 1 through N in Sum.
  assert: N >= 1
}
Sum := 0;
I := 1;
while I <= N do
   begin
      Sum := Sum + I;
      I := I + 1
   end; {while}

{assert: Sum is 1 + 2 + 3 + . . . + N-1 + N}
```

The first assertion, {N >= 1}, is the precondition for the loop, and the last assertion is its postcondition.

We stated previously that the loop invariant must be true before the loop begins execution and after each loop repetition. Since it traces the loop's progress, the loop invariant should be a logical statement about the loop-control variable I and the accumulating sum.

Figure 9.5 sketches the loop's progress for the first three iterations of the loop. At the end of the third iteration, I is 4 and Sum is 6—the sum of all integers less than 4 (1 + 2 + 3). When loop repetition finishes, I will be N+1 and Sum will contain the desired result (1 + 2 + 3 + . . . + N). Therefore we propose the invariant

```
{invariant: I <= N+1 and Sum is 1 + 2 + . . . + I-1}
```

In English, this means that, after each loop repetition, I must be less than or equal to N+1 and Sum is equal to the sum of all positive integers less than I.

You may be wondering why the first part of the invariant is I <= N+1 instead of I <= N. The reason is that the loop invariant must be true after the last iteration of the loop. Since the last step taken in the loop body is to increment I, the last value assigned to I just prior to loop exit is N+1.

The loop invariant also must be true before loop execution begins. At that point, I is 1 and 1 <= N+1 is true for N >= 1 (the precondition). Also, the invariant requires that the value of Sum be equal to the summation of all positive integers less than 1. Because Sum is initialized to 0, this is also the case.

In program verification, the loop invariant proves that the loop meets its specification. For our purposes, we will use the loop invariant to document what we know about the loop's behavior, and we will place it just before the loop body, as shown next.

Figure 9.5

Sketch of Summation Loop

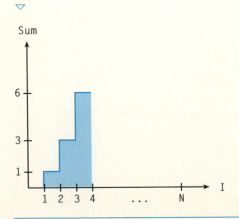

```
{
 Accumulate the sum of integers 1 through N in Sum.
 assert: N >= 1
}
Sum := 0;
I := 1;
while I <= N do
   {invariant: I <= N+1 and Sum is 1 + 2 + . . . + I-1}
   begin
      Sum := Sum + I;
      I := I + 1
   end; {while}

{assert: Sum is 1 + 2 + 3 + . . . + N-1 + N}
```

Loop Invariants as a Design Tool

Some computer scientists recommend writing the loop invariant as a preliminary step before coding the loop. The invariant serves as a specification for the loop and as a guide to determining the loop initialization, the loop repetition condition, and the loop body. For example, the following loop invariant describes a summation loop that adds N data items:

```
{invariant:
   Count <= N and
   Sum is the sum of all data read so far
}
```

From the loop invariant we can infer the following:

▶ The loop initialization is

```
Sum := 0.0;
Count := 0;
```

▶ The loop repetition test is

```
Count < N
```

▶ The loop body is

```
Read (Next);
Sum := Sum + Next;
Count := Count + 1
```

Given all this information, it becomes a simple task to write the summation loop (see Programming Exercise 2 at the end of this section).

Invariants and the for Statement

Since the loop invariant states what we know to be true about a loop after each iteration, we should be able to write an invariant for a for statement as well as a while statement. So that the loop invariant will remain true, we will assume that the loop-control variable in a `for` statement is incremented just before loop exit and retains its final value. This assumption allows us to use a loop invariant to document the following `for` loop:

```
{assert: N >= 1}

Sum := 0;
for I := 1 to N do
   {invariant: I <= N+1 and Sum is 1 + 2 + . . . + I-1}
   Sum := Sum + I;

{assert: Sum is 1 + 2 + 3 + . . . + N-1 + N}
```

More Loop Invariants

This subsection provides another example of the use of a loop invariant and assertions to document a loop.

EXAMPLE 9.6 ▼

Figure 9.6 shows a sentinel-controlled `while` loop that computes the product of a collection of data values. Loop exit occurs after the sentinel value (value of `Sentinel`) is read. The loop invariant indicates that `Product` is the product of all values read before the current one and that none of these values

Figure 9.6
Sentinel-Controlled Loop
with Invariant

```
{
 Compute the product of a sequence of data values.
 assert: Sentinel is a constant.
}
Product := 1;
WriteLn ('When done, enter ', Sentinel :1, ' to stop.');
WriteLn ('Enter the first number> ');
ReadLn (Num);
while Num <> Sentinel do
   {invariant:
      Product is the product of all prior values read into Num
      and no prior value of Num was the sentinel
   }
   begin
      Product := Product * Num;
      WriteLn ('Enter the next number> ');
      ReadLn (Num)
   end; {while}

{assert:
   Product is the product of all numbers
   read into Num before the sentinel.
}
```

was the sentinel. The preconditions and postconditions for the loop are written as assertions. ▲

Self-Check

1. a. Write the loop invariant and the assertion following the loop for the `while` loop in procedure `EnterInt` (Fig. 9.2).
   b. What other assertions should be added to procedure `EnterInt` to facilitate its verification?
2. If the sentinel-controlled loop in Fig. 9.6 were rewritten as a flag-controlled loop, what would the new loop invariant look like? The flag `NoZero` should remain true until a zero value is read.
3. In Programming Exercise 1, why is `Number >= 0` used instead of `Number > 0`?

Programming

1. Write a function that returns the count (`Count`) of the number of nonzero digits in an arbitrary integer (`Number`). Your solution should include a `while` loop for which the following loop invariant is valid:

   ```
   {invariant:
       Count >= 0 and Number >= 0 and the original
       Number has been divided by 10 Count times.
   }
   ```

   and this assertion would be valid following the loop:

   ```
   {assert: Number is 0 and Count is the number of digits in N.}
   ```

2. Write a program fragment that implements the loop whose invariant is described in the subsection "Loop Invariants as a Design Tool."

9.6 Ethics and Responsibilities

Software engineers and computer programmers should act like the professionals they are. As part of their jobs, computer programmers may access large data banks that contain sensitive personnel information, information that is classified "secret" or "top secret," or financial transaction data. Programmers should behave in a socially responsible manner and not retrieve information they are not entitled to see. They should not use any information that they access for their own personal gain or do anything that would be considered illegal, unethical, or harmful to others.

The media often report stories of "computer hackers" who have broken into secure data banks. Some hackers sell classified information to intelligence agencies of other countries. Others retrieve similar information for their own amusement, as a prank, or just to demonstrate that they can. Regardless of the intent, such activity is illegal and subject to government prosecution.

Another illegal activity sometimes practiced by hackers is the insertion of special code, called a *virus,* into a computer's disk memory. A virus may cause sporadic activities to occur that disrupt the operation of the host computer. For example, unusual messages may appear on the screen at certain times. Viruses can also cause the host computer to erase portions of its own disk memory, thereby destroying valuable information and programs. Viruses are spread from one computer to another when data are copied from the infected disk and processed by a different computer. Certainly, these kinds of activities should not be considered harmless pranks; they are illegal and often cause irreparable damage.

A programmer who changes information in a database containing financial records is guilty of *computer theft* or *computer fraud*. Such acts are a felony and can lead to fines and imprisonment.

Another example of unprofessional behavior is using someone else's program or code without permission. While it is certainly permissible to use procedures in libraries that have been developed for reuse by your own company's programmers, you should not use another programmer's personal code or code from another company without permission. Failure to obtain such permission could lead to an expensive lawsuit against you or your company.

Many commercial software packages are protected by copyright laws and cannot be copied or duplicated. It is illegal to make additional copies of copyrighted software that you may be using at work for use on your home computer. In addition to being illegal, using software copied from another computer increases the possibility that your computer will receive a virus. You should act ethically and honor any copyright agreements that pertain to a particular software package.

Exercises for Section 9.6   **Self-Check**

1. Why might it be easier for a computer programmer to commit computer theft than for other users of a computer system?
2. What might be some ethical responsibilities of the program tester?

9.7 Common Programming Errors

To use a library procedure, you must know the name of the library file in which the procedure is found and have a description of the procedure interface. Specifically, you must know the Number, Order, and Type (NOT) of the procedure's parameters. Make sure that all variable formal parameters correspond to actual parameters that are variables of the same or identical type. Also make sure that all preconditions for a procedure's parameters (as listed in the procedure interface) are satisfied before each call to the procedure. Finally, the library containing the procedure you are using must be linked to your program before you attempt to run it.

The rules for using an abstract data type (ADT) are different in each Pascal system. In Turbo Pascal, you can encapsulate an ADT in a unit; in VAX Pascal, you can encapsulate an ADT in a module. The client program must communicate the names of any ADTs used to the Pascal compiler. You must also compile the ADT before you compile the Pascal program. In Turbo Pascal, the ADT is automatically linked to the object code; in VAX Pascal, you must do this during the link step.

If your system does not support separate compilation of ADTs, you must insert the data type and procedure declarations directly in the main program or the client of the ADT. Make sure that each declaration from the ADT is inserted before its first reference.

CHAPTER REVIEW

1. A large program or system has a life cycle consisting of the following phases:

   ▶ Requirements specification
   ▶ Analysis
   ▶ Design
   ▶ Implementation
   ▶ Testing and verification
   ▶ Operation, follow-up, and maintenance

2. During the requirements specification phase, programmers and analysts in the programming team work together with users to ensure that everyone understands the planned capabilities of the new program system.

3. Use of a library of procedures and functions facilitates the implementation phase. Program development proceeds more quickly and smoothly if you reuse previously tested modules in a new program instead of writing new modules.

4. Using module libraries simplifies apportioning pieces of a large project to members of a programming team. A library's procedures and functions can be imported and reused.

5. You can create an abstract data type by placing a data type declaration together with procedures and functions that operate on data of that type in a separate file.

6. The test plan for a large program should be developed during the design phase. The test plan discusses the kind of testing to be done, the amount of testing, and who will do the testing. Programmers should keep the test plan in mind as they implement the program's modules.

7. Different techniques for testing include structured walkthroughs, black box testing, white box testing, and integration testing. A programming team should use all of these techniques.

8. Formal verification is an alternative to testing. Assertions and loop invariants are logical statements. An assertion is always true. A loop invariant is a logical statement that is true before the first loop repetition and after each repetition of the loop.

Quick-Check Exercises

1. Place the following six phases of the software life cycle (SLC) in their correct order:

testing and verification	design	requirements specification
operation and maintenance	implementation	analysis

2. In which phases are users of a software product likely to participate?
3. In which phases of the SLC are programmers and analysts likely to participate?
4. What is the name given to a collection of reusable functions and procedures?
5. Name the two sections of an abstract data type. Where is the data type declaration found? Where are the procedure declarations found?
6. _____ testing requires the use of test data that exercise each statement in a module.
7. _____ testing focuses on testing the functional characteristics of a module.
8. Why is a loop invariant not equivalent to placing an assertion at the beginning of the loop body?
9. The use of loop invariants is useful for which of the following: loop control, loop design, loop verification?
10. Write a loop invariant for the following code segment:

```
Product := 1;
Counter := 2;
while Counter <= 5 do
   begin
      Product := Product * Counter;
      Counter := Counter + 1
   end;
```

Answers to Quick-Check Exercises

1. Requirements specification, analysis, design, implementation, testing and verification, operation and maintenance
2. Requirements specification, testing and verification, operation and maintenance
3. All phases
4. Library
5. Specification and implementation sections; implementation; implementation
6. White box
7. Black box
8. The assertion must be true before each iteration of the loop; the loop invariant must be true before and after each iteration.
9. Loop design, loop verification
10. ```
    {invariant:
        Counter <= 6 and
        Product contains product of all integers < Counter
    }
    ```
    ```

Review Questions

1. Define the terms *procedural abstraction* and *loop invariant*.
2. Which of the following are likely to occur in a programmer's library of procedures? Explain your answers.
   a. A procedure that raises a number to a specified power
   b. A procedure that writes the user instructions for a particular program
   c. A procedure that displays the name of an application program in block letters
   d. A procedure that displays the block letter M
3. Define an abstract data type for the positions on a baseball team (pitcher, catcher, infield, outfield) with procedures to read and write those positions and code the ADT as a unit.
4. Write the specification for an abstract data type Money that allows you to do basic arithmetic operations (addition, subtraction, multiplication, and division) on real numbers having exactly two digits to the right of the decimal point.
5. Which of the following statements is incorrect?
   a. Loop invariants are used in loop verification.
   b. Loop invariants are used in loop design.
   c. A loop invariant is always an assertion.
   d. An assertion is always a loop invariant.
6. Briefly describe a test plan for the telephone directory program described in Section 9.1. Assume that integration testing is used.
7. Write a procedure that computes the average number of characters found on the lines of a text file. Include loop invariants and any other assertions necessary to verify that the procedure is correct.

Programming Projects

1. Write an abstract data type that consists of data type ColorType and operators for reading and writing the colors (red, yellow, green, blue, black, brown, orange, purple, and white).
2. Create a library of procedures (or functions) that can be used to determine the following information for an integer input parameter:
   a. Is it a multiple of 7, 11, or 13?
   b. Is the sum of the digits odd or even?
   c. What is the square root value?
   d. Is it a prime number?

   Write a client program that tests your library procedures using the following input values: 104, 3773, 13, 121, 77, and 3075.

Directory: CHAP9
File: PROJ3.PAS

3. Each month a bank customer deposits $50 into a savings account. Assume that the interest rate is fixed and is a problem input. The interest is calculated on a quarterly basis. For example, if the account earns 6.5% annually, it earns one-fourth of 6.5% every three months. Write a program to compute the total investment, the total amount in the account, and the interest accrued for each of the 120 months of a 10-year period. Assume that the rate is applied to all funds in the account at the end of a quarter, regardless of when the deposits were made.

Print all values accurate to two decimal places. The table printed by your program when the annual interest rate is 6.5% should begin as follows:

MONTH	INVESTMENT	NEW AMOUNT	INTEREST	TOTAL SAVINGS
1	50.00	50.00	0.00	50.00
2	100.00	100.00	0.00	100.00
3	150.00	150.00	2.44	152.44
4	200.00	202.44	0.00	202.44
5	250.00	252.44	0.00	252.44
6	300.00	302.44	4.91	307.35
7	350.00	357.35	0.00	357.35

4. Redo Programming Project 3, adding columns to allow comparison of interest compounded monthly (one-twelfth of annual rate every month) with continuously compounded interest. The formula for continuously compounded interest is

$$amount = principal \times e^{\,rate \times time}$$

where *rate* is the annual interest rate and *time* is expressed in years.

5. Many computer program user interfaces place windows on the screen that consist of a user area enclosed in a border. In the top edge of the border, the title of the window is displayed centered. Write a library module to create such windows on the screen. Your module should include a procedure that accepts the window's coordinates, the character displayed in the border, and the title (5 characters). Supply a program that adequately tests the library module.

6. You have been assigned the task of writing a library module to compute factorials and Fibonacci numbers. Since this library module will be a component of the flight software of a satellite, it is of utmost importance that it be absolutely correct. Therefore you are to supply loop invariants for all loops and sufficient assertions to show program correctness. You must also supply a test program and a written test procedure that will support your claims of correctness.

   Factorials are described in detail in Section 6.8. For a given number N, the Nth Fibonacci number is computed as follows: If N is 0 or 1, the Fibonacci number is 1. Otherwise, the Fibonacci number is the sum of the last two Fibonacci numbers. As an example, the first eight Fibonacci numbers are 1, 1, 2, 3, 5, 8, 13, 21. Each number is the sum of the previous two. Do not use a recursive solution for either of these problems.

▼ **What was the major influence on your choosing computer science as a profession?**

▲ I like to program. I think that's a primary reason why most people are in the profession. In ancient times (the early 1960s), quite a bit of effort was required to get near a computer, and you would be crazy to even try to do it if you didn't like it. Getting a hundred-line program to work was something that might require a week's work, since one-day turnaround was common. You turned in your card deck one day and got your printout the next day. Under those circumstances, you were strongly motivated to outsmart the system, and it was quite satisfying to be able to actually do so.

▼ **Why are algorithms and data structures fundamental to computer science?**

▲ Algorithms and data structures represent an abstraction of the notion of a particular program running on a particular machine. This abstraction has served us well, because algorithms and data structures have been remarkably robust across generations of machines. The best available sorting method today is the same as the best available sorting method 30 years ago, and the same goes for data structures and algorithms for searching and many other problems. Thus, though one might think that new technology would make old methods obsolete, it has turned out that algorithms and data structures can be thought of as representative of the knowledge built up over the years in all the programs that have been written. When you develop a program for sorting or searching or some other classical problem, then either you are inventing something that has eluded others over the years, or you are reinventing some classical algorithm. The former happens sufficiently often to make the field still exciting, even for newcomers, and the latter happens sufficiently often that it is worthwhile to study the best classical methods and take advantage of others' experience.

▼ **Is there a connection between famous classical problems like Towers of Hanoi, dining philosophers, or traveling salesman and the study of areas like software engineering or computer graphics?**

▲ Most of the "classical problems" in computer science are not too old and not too far removed from practical problems. Anyone involved in a serious endeavor solving a practical problem with a computer is very likely to encounter recursion (as typified by Towers of Hanoi), synchronization (as typified by dining philosophers), and NP-completeness (as typified by the traveling salesman problem). An educated computer scientist will have a better chance to cope, having studied the classical problems.

▼ **Universal models of computation, Turing machines and the like, seem like games theoreticians play that aren't that important for computing professionals making a living in the real world. What is the link between computational models and applications?**

▲ Sometimes there are direct links. Often the very best way to solve a problem is to invent an abstract machine (computational model) suited to the problem, then write a simple simulator for the machine. Other times the links are indirect but also very important. For example, inten-

INTERVIEW
▼

Robert Sedgewick

Robert Sedgewick is a professor of computer science at Princeton University. He has held visiting research positions at Xerox PARC, Institute for Defense Analyses, and INRIA. Sedgewick is a widely published author whose research interests include mathematical analysis of algorithms, structures and algorithms, and program visualization.

sive study of computational models related to problems like the traveling salesman problem has led to the development of the theory of "NP-completeness," which tells the practicing programmer not to expect to easily find a tricky way to solve the traveling salesman problem efficiently, and that there are a vast number of similar "NP-complete" problems. By studying the theory, one can perhaps learn to more easily recognize (and perhaps avoid) the onset of NP-completeness in practice. This is a very significant advance over the situation faced by practicing programmers even in 1975.

▼ **What major events do you foresee in research in algorithms and data structures in the 1990s?**

▲ Serendipity is one of the most attractive aspects of working in research. No one can know where the real breakthroughs will come, so I'll pass on this question.

▼ **Among the goals of studying algorithms is the design of more efficient programs. Efficiency of a similar kind is also a goal for those who build computers—the architects. In what ways do hardware and software designers share information to achieve common goals?**

▲ Given a specific program, a good hardware designer can build a machine that will do an outstanding job executing that program, but a great hardware designer will come up with a machine that is fast for a large class of similar programs. Conversely, given a specific machine, a good software designer can write a program that will run fast on a large class of similar machines. The best way to generalize in both cases is through abstraction: Settle on a specific set of operations that the hardware should be built to perform and that should be used to build the software. Common goals are best served when both sides agree on the same set of operations. Actually, this is frequently the case in successful machine designs. Note that this goes back to your earlier question on the value of models of computation.

CHAPTER TEN

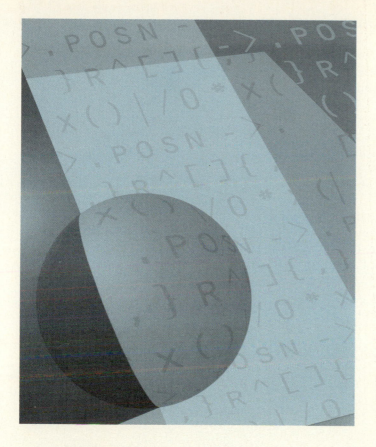

Arrays

data structure
a composite of related data items stored under the same name

Simple data types, whether built-in (Integer, Real, Boolean, Char) or user-defined (e.g., enumerated type Day), use a single memory cell to store a variable. To solve many programming problems, it is more efficient to store related data items together than to store each data item in a different variable. A program that processes exam scores for a class, for example, would be easier to write if all the scores were stored together and could be accessed as a group. Pascal allows a programmer to group such related data items together into a single composite **data structure.** In this chapter, we look at one such data structure: the array.

10.1   The Array Data Structure

array
a collection of data items of the same type

The **array** is a data structure in which we store a collection of data items of the same type (e.g., all the exam scores for a class). By using an array, we can associate a single variable name (e.g., Scores) with the entire collection of data (see Fig. 10.1). We can also reference individual items in the array. The naming process is like the one used to describe families and their members. The Koffman household refers to all five members of my immediate family, and individual names—Deborah Koffman, for example—designate individuals in my family.

Pascal stores an array in consecutive storage locations in main memory, one item per memory cell. We can perform some operations, such as passing the array as a parameter to a procedure, on the whole array. We also can access individual items stored in the array (called **array elements**) and process them like other simple variables. In this section, we describe how to declare arrays in Pascal programs and how to reference individual array elements.

array element
a data item that is part of an array

Declaring Arrays

Normally, we first describe the structure of an array in an *array type declaration*. Then we can allocate storage for one or more arrays of that type.

                        8 elements   Element type
```
type
  RealArray = array [1..8] of Real;   {array type declaration}
var
  X : RealArray;                       {Allocate storage for array X.}
```

In this example, the array type, RealArray, is declared in the type declaration. The symbols [1..8] tell Pascal to allocate 8 memory cells for any variable with type RealArray. Because variable X is declared with type RealArray, X is an array of 8 elements, and each element contains a single Real value.

Keep in mind that an array type declaration does not cause the Pascal compiler to allocate storage space in memory. The array type merely describes the structure of an array. Only variables actually store information

Figure 10.1
Array Scores with Five
Array Elements

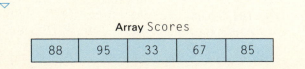

Array Scores

| 88 | 95 | 33 | 67 | 85 |

and require storage. Pascal does not allocate storage space until a variable of this type is declared.

SYNTAX DISPLAY

Array Type Declaration

Form: `type`
           array type = `array` [*subscript type*] `of` *element type*;
Example: `type`
           `SmallArray = array [1..5] of Char;`
Interpretation: The identifier *array type* describes a collection of array elements; each element can store an item of type *element type*. The *subscript type* can be either of the standard ordinal types `Boolean` or `Char`, an enumerated type, or a subrange type. There is one array element for each value in the *subscript type*.

The *element type* describes the type of each element in the array. All elements of an array are the same type.

Note 1: The standard types `Real` and `Integer` cannot be used as a *subscript type*; however, a subrange of the integers can be a *subscript type*.
Note 2: The *element type* can be any standard or user-defined type.

Note 1 in the syntax display states that the standard types `Integer` and `Real` cannot be used as subscript types. Type `Integer` is not allowed because an array with subscript type `Integer` would have one element for each integer in the range `-MaxInt` to `MaxInt` (a very large array!). Type `Real` is not allowed because it is not an ordinal type.

Array Subscripts

To process the data stored in an array, we must be able to access its individual elements. We use the array name (a variable) followed by the array subscript (sometimes called an **index**) to do so. The **array subscript,** enclosed in brackets, selects a particular array element for processing and must be assignment compatible with the subscript type specified in the array type declaration.

If X is a variable of type `RealArray`,

```
type
  RealArray = array [1..8] of Real;   {array type declaration}
var
  X : RealArray;                {Allocate storage for array X.}
```

the subscript type is the `Integer` subrange `1..8`, so the allowable subscripts are integers in this subrange. We therefore use `X[1]` (read as "X sub 1") to reference the first element of array X, `X[2]` for the second element, and `X[8]` for the eighth element (see Fig. 10.2). We cannot use `X[0]` or `X[9]` to reference elements in array X. (Why not?)

We call a variable followed by a subscript in brackets (e.g., `X[1]`) a **subscripted variable**. A subscripted variable has the same data type as the ar-

array subscript (index)
a value or expression enclosed in brackets after the array name, specifying which array element to access

subscripted variable
a variable followed by a subscript in brackets

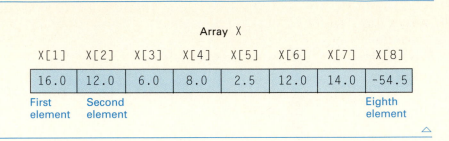

Figure 10.2
The Eight Elements of
Array X

Array X

X[1]   X[2]   X[3]   X[4]   X[5]   X[6]   X[7]   X[8]

| 16.0 | 12.0 | 6.0 | 8.0 | 2.5 | 12.0 | 14.0 | -54.5 |

First   Second   Eighth
element   element   element

ray element it references. Because the elements of array X are type Real, we can manipulate X[1] like any other Real variable. Specifically, we can use X[1] with the arithmetic operators, the relational operators, and the assignment operator. We also can pass X[1] as a parameter to procedures Read(Ln) and Write(Ln) and to any of Pascal's built-in functions that accept type Real parameters.

To store a value in an array element, we write an assignment statement of the form

subscripted variable := *expression*

To retrieve or access a value stored in an array element, just write the corresponding subscripted variable in an expression.

EXAMPLE 10.1: Storing and Retrieving Values in an Array ▼

Let X be the array first shown in Fig. 10.2. Some statements that manipulate elements of this array are shown in Table 10.1. The contents of array X after execution of these statements are shown in Fig. 10.3. Notice that only array elements X[3] and X[4] have changed, because they are the only ones that are assigned new values.

Table 10.1
Storing and Retrieving
Values in Array X

Statement	Explanation
WriteLn (X[1])	Displays the value of X[1], or 16.0.
X[4] := 25.0	Stores the value 25.0 in X[4].
Sum := X[1] + X[2]	Stores the sum of X[1] and X[2], or 28.0, in the variable Sum.
Sum := Sum + X[3]	Adds X[3] to Sum. The new Sum is 34.0.
X[4] := X[4] + 1.0	Adds 1.0 to X[4]. The new X[4] is 26.0.
X[3] := X[1] + X[2]	Stores the sum of X[1] and X[2] in X[3]. The new X[3] is 28.0

Figure 10.3
Array X After Execution of
Statements in Table 10.1

Figure 10.3
Array X After Execution of
Statements in Table 10.1

Each subscript in Table 10.1 is a literal enclosed in square brackets (e.g., [4]). In Example 10.2, we show that an array subscript may be an expression that is assignment compatible with the subscript type. ▲

EXAMPLE 10.2: Manipulating Array Elements ▼

The statements in Table 10.2 manipulate elements in array X (Fig. 10.3). I is a type Integer variable with value 6. When I is 6, the subscripted variable X[I + I] references element X[12], which is not in the array. To indicate this, Pascal would display an Index expression out of bounds run-time error.

Table 10.2
Using Subscript
Expressions with Array X

Statement	Effect
Write (8, X[8])	Displays 8 and -54.5 (value of X[8])
Write (I, X[I])	Displays 6 and 12.0 (value of X[6])
Write (X[I] + 1)	Displays 13.0 (value of X[6] + 1)
Write (X[I] + I)	Displays 18.0 (value of X[6] + 6)
Write (X[I + 1])	Displays 14.0 (value of X[7])
Write (X[I + I])	Illegal attempt to display X[12]
Write (X[2 * I - 4])	Displays -54.5 (value of X[8])
Write (X[Trunc(X[5])])	Displays 12.0 (value of X[2])
X[I] := X[I + 1]	Assigns 14.0 (value of X[7]) to X[6]
X[I - 1] := X[I]	Assigns 14.0 (new value of X[6]) to X[5]
X[I] - 1 := X [I - 1]	Illegal assignment statement

The last Write statement in Table 10.2 uses X[5] as an argument for function Trunc and Trunc(X[5]) as a subscript expression. X[5] has the value 2.5 and Trunc(X[5]) is 2, so the value of X[2] (not X[5]) is printed. An error would occur if the value of Trunc(X[5]) were outside the allowable range (1 through 8).

Two different subscripts are used in the last three assignment statements in the table. The first assignment statement copies the value of X[7] to X[6] (subscripts I + 1 and I); the second assignment statement copies the value of X[6] to X[5] (subscripts I and I - 1). The last assignment statement causes a syntax error because X[I] - 1 is an expression, not a variable. ▲

SYNTAX DISPLAY

Array Element Reference

Form: *array name* [*subscript*]

Example: X[3 * I - 2]

Interpretation: The *subscript* must be an expression that is assignment compatible with the subscript type specified in the declaration for *array name*. If the expression is the wrong data type, the syntax error Index type is not compatible with declaration is detected. If the expression value is not in range, an index expression out of bounds error occurs during run time.

More Array and Subscript Types

The arrays declared so far had subscript types that were subranges of the integers and were used to store numeric values. This, of course, is not required in Pascal, because subscript types can be any ordinal type (except Integer) and array elements can be any standard or previously declared type. A number of different array types are described in Table 10.3.

As the table shows, the array Name has 10 elements and can store the letters of a person's name. The array Fahrenheit, with 21 elements, stores the Fahrenheit temperature equivalent to each Celsius temperature in the range -10 through +10 degrees Celsius. For example, Fahrenheit[0] would be the Fahrenheit temperature, 32.0, corresponding to 0 degrees Celsius. Arrays LetterCount and LetterFound have the same subscript type (i.e., the uppercase letters) but different element types. The array Answers has only two elements, with subscript values True and False.

EXAMPLE 10.3 ▼

The declaration section for a plant operations program is shown next. The type declaration declares two simple data types, EmpRange and Day, and two array types, EmpArray and DayArray. Two arrays, Vacation and Plant-Hours, are declared in the variable declarations.

```
const
  NumEmp = 8;                          {number of employees}

type
  EmpRange = 1..NumEmp;                {subscript range}
  EmpArray = array [EmpRange] of Boolean;
  Day = (Sunday, Monday, Tuesday, Wednesday,
         Thursday, Friday, Saturday);
  DayArray = array [Day] of Real;
```

Table 10.3
Some Array Types and
Applications

Array Type	Subscript Type	Application

`type NameArray =`
`  array [1..10] of Char;`
`var Name : NameArray;`
	integer subrange	`Name[1] := 'A';` stores a person's name using 10 characters.

`type Temps =`
`  array [-10..10] of Real;`
`var Fahrenheit : Temps;`
	integer subrange	`Fahrenheit[0] := 32.0;` stores Fahrenheit temperatures equivalent to -10 through 10 degrees Celsius.

`type Counters =`
`  array ['A'..'Z'] of Integer;`
`var LetterCount : Counters;`
	character subrange	`LetterCount['A'] := 0;` stores the number of times each uppercase letter occurs.

`type Flags =`
`  array ['A'..'Z'] of Boolean;`
`var LetterFound : Flags;`
	character subrange	`LetterFound['X'] := False;` stores a set of Boolean values indicating which letters occur and which do not.

`type BoolCounts =`
`  array [Boolean] of Integer;`
`var Answers : BoolCounts;`
	Boolean	`Answers[True] := 15;` stores the number of true answers and false answers to a quiz.

```
var
   Vacation : EmpArray;
   PlantHours : DayArray;
```

Consider the declaration for array type `EmpArray` first. The subscript type is `EmpRange` (the subrange `1..NumEmp`), so the subscript type for an array of type `EmpArray` (e.g., `Vacation`) is `1..8`. Each element of array `Vacation` can store a Boolean value (see Fig. 10.4). The contents of this array could indicate which employees are on vacation (`Vacation[1]` is `True` if employee 1 is on vacation). If employees 1, 3, 5, and 7 are on vacation and the rest are not, array `Vacation` would have the values shown in Fig. 10.4.

Next consider the declaration for array type `DayArray`. Because the subscript type is the enumerated type `Day`, the subscripts for an array of type `DayArray` are the enumerated type values `Sunday`, `Monday`, and so on. Because `PlantHours` is type `DayArray`, each element of array `PlantHours` can store a type `Real` value. The array element `PlantHours[Sunday]` could indicate how many hours the plant was operating on `Sunday` of the past week.

Figure 10.4
Arrays Vacation and PlantHours

The array in Fig. 10.4 indicates that the plant was closed on the weekend and operated a single shift on `Monday` and `Thursday` (open `8.0` hours), double shifts on `Tuesday` and `Friday`, and triple shifts on `Wednesday`.

We could eliminate the declarations for the constant `NumEmp` and data type `EmpRange` and just declare the array type `EmpArray`:

```
type
   EmpArray = array [1..8] of Boolean;
```

There are three advantages to the original declarations, however. First, it is easy to change the declared size of array `Vacation`: By simply redefining the constant `NumEmp`, we change the array size. Second, the constant `NumEmp` can be referenced in the program body. Finally, the data type `EmpRange` can be used as a type identifier elsewhere in the program. ▲

Anonymous Array Types

Although we will not do so in this text, it is possible to declare an array without first declaring its type. The variable declaration

```
var
   X : array [1..20] of Integer;   {anonymous type array}
```

anonymous type
an unnamed type used in a variable declaration

allocates storage for an array `X` of 20 integers. Because there is no array type declaration, the type of array `X` is an **anonymous type**. It is bad programming practice to declare arrays with anonymous types.

Exercises for Section 10.1 *Self-Check*

1. Given the statements `Y := X3` and `Y := X[3]`, supply type and variable declaration such that these statements are valid. Assume `Y` is of type `Real`.
2. If an array is declared to have 10 elements, can you always reference the array elements using subscripts 1 through 10?
3. For the following declarations, how many memory cells are reserved for data and what type of data can be stored there? Is the memory allocated after the type declaration or after the variable declaration?

```
type
   IndexRange = 1..5;
   AnArray = array [IndexRange] of Char;

var
   Grades : AnArray;
```

4. Describe the following array types and indicate how many elements can be stored in arrays of each type:
   a. `array [1..20] of Char`
   b. `array ['0'..'9'] of Boolean`
   c. `array [-5..5] of Real`
   d. `array [Boolean] of Char`

5. Write the variable and type declarations for only the valid array descriptions:
   a. subscript type `Boolean`, element type `Real`
   b. subscript type `'A'..'F'`, element type `Integer`
   c. subscript type `Char`, element type `Boolean`
   d. subscript type `Integer`, element type `Real`
   e. subscript type `Char`, element type `Real`
   f. subscript type `Real`, element type `Char`
   g. subscript type `Day` (enumerated type), element type `Real`
6. Provide array type declarations for representing the following:
   a. A group of rooms (living room, dining room, kitchen, etc.) that have a given area
   b. Elementary school grade levels (1 through 6) with a given number of students per grade
   c. A group of colors with letter values assigned according to the first letter of their name (e.g., `'B'` for blue)

10.2 Sequential Access to Array Elements

Many programs require that all the elements of an array be processed in sequence, starting with the first element. To enter data into an array, print its contents, or perform other sequential processing tasks, we would use a `for` loop whose loop-control variable (I) is also the array subscript (X[I]). Increasing the value of the loop-control variable by 1 would cause the next array element to be processed.

EXAMPLE 10.4: Storing Data in an Array ▼

The array `Cube`, declared as follows, stores the cubes of the first 10 integers (for example, `Cube[1]` is 1, `Cube[10]` is 1000):

```
type
   IndexRange = 1..10;
   IntArray = array [IndexRange] of Integer;

var
   Cube : IntArray;        {array of cubes}
   I : Integer;            {loop-control variable}
```

The `for` statement

```
for I := 1 to 10 do
   Cube[I] := I * I * I
```

stores values into this array as follows:

Array Cube

[1]	[2]	[3]	[4]	[5]	[6]	[7]	[8]	[9]	[10]
1	8	27	64	125	216	343	512	729	1000

▲

EXAMPLE 10.5: Reading and Displaying an Array ▼

Data must always be read into an array one element at a time, and displayed one array element at a time. In Fig. 10.5, the declarations

```
const
   MaxItems = 8;                          {number of data items}

type
   IndexRange = 1..MaxItems;
   RealArray = array [IndexRange] of Real;

var
   X : RealArray;                         {array of data}
   I : IndexRange;                        {loop-control variable}
```

allocate storage for an array X of `Real` elements with subscripts in the range 1..8. Three `for` loops process the array X, and the loop-control variable I ($1 \le I \le 8$) is the array subscript in each loop. The first `for` loop

```
for I := 1 to MaxItems do
  Read (X[I]);
```

reads one data value into each array element (the first item is stored in X[1],
the second item in X[2], etc.). The Read statement is repeated for each value
of I from 1 to 8; each repetition causes a new data value to be read and
stored in X[I]. The subscript I determines which array element will receive
the next data value.

Figure 10.5
Table of Differences

**Directory: CHAP10
File: SHOWDIFF.PAS**

```
program ShowDiff (Input, Output);
{
  Computes the average value of an array of data and
  prints the difference between each value and the average
}
  const
    MaxItems = 8;                      {number of data items}

  type
    IndexRange = 1..MaxItems;
    RealArray = array [IndexRange] of Real;

  var
    X : RealArray;                     {array of data}
    I : IndexRange;                    {loop-control variable}
    Average,                           {average value of data}
    Sum    : Real;                     {sum of the data}

begin {ShowDiff}
  {Enter the data.}
  Write ('Enter ', MaxItems :1, ' numbers> ');
  for I := 1 to MaxItems do
    Read (X[I]);

  {Compute the average value.}
  Sum := 0.0;                          {Initialize Sum.}
  for I := 1 to MaxItems do
    Sum := Sum + X[I];                 {Add each element to Sum.}
  Average := Sum / MaxItems;           {Get average value.}
  WriteLn ('The average value is ', Average :3:1); WriteLn;

  {Display the difference between each item and the average.}
  WriteLn ('Table of differences between X[I] and average');
  WriteLn ('I' :4, 'X[I]' :8, 'Difference' : 14);
  for I := 1 to MaxItems do
    WriteLn (I :4, X[I] :8:1, X[I] - Average :14:1)
end. {ShowDiff}
```

▷ ▷ ▷ ▷ ▷ ▷

Sample Run

```
Enter 8 numbers> 16.0  12.0  6.0  8.0  2.5  12.0  14.0  -54.5
The average value is 2.0

Table of differences between X[I] and average
   I     X[I]      Difference
   1     16.0          14.0
   2     12.0          10.0
   3      6.0           4.0
   4      8.0           6.0
   5      2.5           0.5
   6     12.0          10.0
   7     14.0          12.0
   8    -54.5         -56.5
```

The last `for` loop,

```
for I := 1 to MaxItems do
  WriteLn (I :4, X[I] :8:2, X[I] - Average :14:2)
```

displays a table that shows each array element, `X[I]`, and the difference between that element and the average value, `X[I] - Average`.

The second `for` loop,

```
Sum := 0.0;                     {Initialize Sum to zero.}
for I := 1 to MaxItems do
  Sum := Sum + X[I];            {Add each element to Sum.}
```

accumulates the sum of all eight elements of array `X` in the variable `Sum`. Each time the `for` loop is repeated, `I` increases by 1, so the statement

```
Sum := Sum + X[I];              {Add each element to Sum.}
```

adds the next element of array `X` to `Sum`. The execution of this program fragment is traced in Table 10.4 for the first three repetitions of the loop.   ▲

Table 10.4
Partial Trace of for Loop

Statement Part	I	X[I]	Sum	Effect
`Sum := 0.0;`			0.0	Initializes `Sum`.
`for I := 1 to MaxItems do` `  Sum := Sum + X[I]`	1	16.0	 16.0	Initializes `I` to 1; adds `X[1]` to `Sum`.
increment and test `I` `  Sum := Sum + X[I]`	2	12.0	 28.0	2 <= 8 is True; adds `X[2]` to `Sum`.
increment and test `I` `  Sum := Sum + X[I]`	3	6.0	 34.0	3 <= 8 is True; adds `X[3]` to `Sum`.

Exercises for Section 10.2 *Self-Check*

1. The following sequence of statements changes the contents of array X displayed in Fig. 10.5. Describe what each statement does to the array, and show the final contents of array X after all statements execute.

```
I := 3;
X[I] := X[I] + 10.0;
X[I - 1] := X[2 * I - 1];
X[I + 1] := X[2 * I] + X[2 * I + 1];
for I := 5 to 7 do
   X[I] := X[I + 1];
for I := 3 downto 1 do
   X[I + 1] := X[I]
```

2. Write program statements that do the following to array X shown in Fig. 10.5:
   a. Replace the third element with 7.0
   b. Copy the element in the fifth location into the first one
   c. Subtract the first element from the fourth and store the result in the fifth element
   d. Increase the sixth element by 2
   e. Find the sum of the first five elements
   f. Multiply each of the first six elements by 2 and place each product in an element of the array AnswerArray
   g. Display all even-numbered elements on one line

Programming

1. Write a loop to compute the product of all elements of an array of real numbers. Write a suitable type for this array.

10.3 Arrays as Parameters and Operands

In this section, we show how to pass individual array elements and entire arrays as parameters. We also discuss another operation that can be performed on whole arrays: copying an array.

Array Elements as Parameters

In Fig. 10.5 the subscripted variable X[I] is an actual parameter for the Pascal Read and WriteLn procedures. We can pass individual array elements as actual parameters to procedures or functions that we write. In this case, the formal parameters must have the same data type as the array elements.

EXAMPLE 10.6 ▼

Procedure Switch in Fig. 10.6 exchanges the values of its two type Real parameters. The procedure call statement

```
procedure Switch (var P, Q {input/output} : Real);
{
  Exchanges the values of P and Q.
  Pre : P and Q are assigned values.
  Post: P has the value passed into Q and vice versa.
}
  var
    Temp : Real;         {temporary variable for the exchange}

begin {Switch}
  Temp := P;
  P := Q;
  Q := Temp
end; {Switch}
```

```
Switch (X[2], X[1])
```

uses this procedure to exchange the contents of the first two elements (type Real) of array X from Fig. 10.5. The actual parameter X[2] corresponds to formal parameter P, and the actual parameter X[1] to formal parameter Q. This correspondence is shown in Fig. 10.7.

   Although we can pass array elements as actual parameters, we cannot use them as formal parameters. The procedure declaration

```
procedure Switch (var X[I], X[J] {input/output} : Real);
```

would cause a syntax error because the formal parameter names must be Pascal identifiers.   ▲

Copying an Array

In all array operations so far, we processed one array element at a time. Pascal allows us, however, to copy an entire array of values by using the assignment operator. To illustrate, given the declarations

Figure 10.7
Parameter Correspondence
for Switch (X[2], X[1])

```
const
  MaxSize = 100;

type
  IndexRange = 1..MaxSize;
  TestArray = array [IndexRange] of Real;

var
  X, Y : TestArray;
```

the assignment statement

```
X := Y                        {copy array Y to array X}
```

copies each value in array Y to the corresponding element of array X (i.e., Y[1] is copied to X[1], Y[2] to X[2], and so forth). Array copies can be performed only when the arrays involved are the same array type.

Array Parameters

We can write modules that have array parameters. The module can manipulate some or all of the elements corresponding to its actual array parameter.

EXAMPLE 10.7: Initializing an Array ▼

Figure 10.8 shows a procedure that sets the initial values of all elements of an array of type TestArray to InValue. We can use the procedure call statements

```
FillArray (X, 0.0);
FillArray (Y, 1.0)
```

to fill arrays X and Y declared earlier. After these statements execute, array X will contain all zeros and array Y will contain all ones.

In procedure FillArray, the formal array parameter is declared as a variable parameter of type TestArray. The following procedure heading

Figure 10.8
Procedure FillArray

Directory: CHAP10
File: FILLARRA.PAS

```
procedure FillArray (var W {output} : TestArray;
                     InValue {input} : Integer);
{
  Sets all elements of its array parameter to InValue.
  Pre : InValue is defined.
  Post: W[I] = InValue, for 1 <= I <= MaxSize.
}
  var
    I : IndexRange;          {array subscript and loop control}

begin {FillArray}
  for I := 1 to MaxSize do
    W[I] := InValue
end; {FillArray}
```

```
procedure FillArray (var W : array [IndexRange] of Real;
                          InValue {input} : Integer);
```

is invalid because each parameter type must be an identifier. ▲

Variable and Value Array Parameters

When an array is passed as a variable parameter, Pascal passes the address of the first actual array element into the procedure data area. Because the array elements are stored in adjacent memory cells, the entire array of data can be accessed. The procedure directly manipulates the actual array.

When an array is passed as a value parameter, a local copy of the array is made when the procedure is called. The local array is initialized so that it contains the same values as the corresponding actual array. The procedure manipulates the local array, and any changes made to the local array do not alter the contents of the actual array.

Example 10.8 illustrates these differences, assuming the following declarations:

```
const
  MaxSize = 5;

type
  IndexRange = 1..MaxSize;
  TestArray = array [IndexRange] of Real;

var
  X, Y, Z : TestArray;
```

EXAMPLE 10.8 ▼

Although it is possible to use a single assignment statement to copy one array to another, the assignment statement

```
Z := X + Y        {illegal addition of arrays}
```

is invalid because the operator + cannot have an array as an operand. You might use procedure AddArray (Fig. 10.9) to add two arrays of type Test-Array.

The parameter correspondence for arrays established by the procedure call statement

```
AddArray (X, Y, Z)
```

is shown in Fig. 10.10. Arrays A and B in the procedure data area are local copies of arrays X and Y. As indicated by the solid arrow, the address of the first element of array Z is stored in parameter C. The procedure results are stored directly in array Z. After execution of the procedure, Z[1] will contain the sum of X[1] and Y[1], or 3.5; Z[2] will contain 6.7; and so on. Arrays X and Y will be unchanged. ▲

Figure 10.9
Procedure AddArray

Directory: CHAP10
File: ADDARRAY.PAS

```pascal
procedure AddArray (A, B {input} : TestArray;
                    var C {output} : TestArray);
{
  Stores the sum of A[I] and B[I] in C[I]. Array elements
  with subscripts 1..MaxSize are summed, element by element.
  Pre : A[I] and B[I] (1 <= I <= MaxSize) are defined.
  Post: C[I] := A[I] + B[I] (1 <= I <= MaxSize).
}
  var
    I : IndexRange;            {loop control and array subscript}

begin {AddArray}
  {Add corresponding elements of each array.}
  for I := 1 to MaxSize do
    C[I] := A[I] + B[I]
end; {AddArray}
```

Program Style

Efficiency of Variable Parameters Versus Protection of Value Parameters

Parameters A and B in Fig. 10.9 are declared as value parameters because they only store data passed into procedure AddArray and their values should not be changed by AddArray. Pascal must create a local copy of

▶▶▶▶▶▶

Figure 10.10
Parameter Correspondence for AddArray (X, Y, Z)

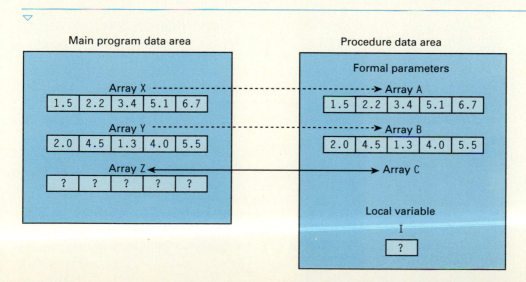

these two arrays each time procedure `AddArray` is called. This copying uses valuable computer time and memory space. If the arrays being copied are very large, the program may terminate with an error because all its memory space has been used.

To conserve time and memory space, experienced programmers sometimes declare arrays that are used only for module inputs as variable parameters rather than as value parameters. This means, however, that the corresponding actual array is directly manipulated by the module and is no longer protected from accidental modification by the module. Any changes made to the actual array are an undesirable side effect of the module's execution. If an array corresponds to a value parameter, the changes are made to a local copy, and the actual array is unaffected. To avoid side effects, declare array parameters used only for module inputs as value parameters unless the arrays are quite large (say, more than 500 elements).

EXAMPLE 10.9: Comparing Two Arrays ▼

Function `SameArray` in Fig. 10.11 determines whether two arrays (of type `TestArray`) are identical. We consider two arrays to be identical if the first element of one is the same as the first element of the other, the second element of one is the same as the second element of the other, and so forth.

We can determine that the arrays are not identical by finding a single pair of unequal elements. Consequently, the `while` loop may be executed anywhere from one time (first elements unequal) to `MaxSize` - 1 times. Loop exit occurs when a pair of unequal elements is found or just before the last pair is tested.

After loop exit, the Boolean assignment statement

```
SameArray := (A[I] = B[I])              {Define result.}
```

defines the function result. If loop exit occurs because the pair of elements with subscript `I` are not equal, the function result is `False`. If loop exit occurs because the last pair of elements is reached (`I` = `MaxSize`), the function result is `True` if the elements at `I` are equal and `False` if they are not.

As an example of how you might use function `SameArray`, the `if` statement

```
if SameArray(X, Y) then
  Z := X
else
  AddArray (X, Y, Z)
```

either copies array X to array Z (when X and Y are identical) or stores the sum of arrays X and Y in array Z (when X and Y are not identical).

Because the arrays have `MaxSize` elements, a common error is to use the condition

```
(I <= MaxSize) and (A[I] = B[I])
```

```
function SameArray (A, B : TestArray) : Boolean;
{
  Returns a value of True if the arrays A, B are identical;
  otherwise, returns a value of False.
  Pre : A[I] and B[I] (1 <= I <= MaxSize) are defined.
  Post: Returns True if A[I] = B[I] for all I in range
        1..MaxSize; otherwise, returns False.
}
  var
    I : Integer;                    {array subscript}

begin
  I := 1;                          {Start with first pair.}
  {Test corresponding elements of arrays A and B.}
  while (I < MaxSize) and (A[I] = B[I]) do
    {invariant:
        1 <= I <= MaxSize and
        A[I] = B[I] for all prior values of I
    }
    I := I + 1;                    {Advance to next pair.}

  {assert:
      An unequal pair was found or all but the
      last pair were compared.
  }
  SameArray := (A[I] = B[I])                {Define result.}
end;  {SameArray}
```

as the `while` condition in Fig. 10.11, causing all element pairs to be tested by the `while` condition if the arrays are equal. When `I` is `MaxSize + 1`, the first part of this condition evaluates to `False` but the second part still must be evaluated. This can lead to an `index expression out of bounds` error because array element `A[MaxSize + 1]` does not exist. ▲

The next case study demonstrates two different methods for array access: sequential access and random access. We discuss their differences after the case study.

CASE STUDY   Home Budget Problem

PROBLEM ▼

Write a program that keeps track of monthly expenses by category. The program should read each expense amount, add it to the appropriate category total, and print the total expenditure by category. The input data consist of the category and the amount of each purchase made during the past month.

ANALYSIS ▼

The budget categories are entertainment, food, clothing, rent, tuition, insurance, and miscellaneous. The program must accumulate seven separate totals, each of which can be associated with a different element of a seven-element array. The program must read each expenditure, determine to which category it belongs, and then add that expenditure to the appropriate array element. After processing all expenditures, the program should print a table that shows each category and its accumulated total. As in all programs that accumulate a sum, each total must be initialized to zero.

You could simply use an array with subscripts 1 through 7 to store your budget entries, but the program would be more readable if you declared a data type `BudgetCat` and used this data type as the array subscript type. To enhance modularity and ease of development, you can treat the `BudgetCat` data type as an abstract data type and declare it, together with its operators `ReadBudgetCat` and `WriteBudgetCat`, in ADT `BudgetCatADT` (see Programming Exercise 4 at the end of this section). Data type `BudgetCat`, shown next, has an extra "category," `Done`, which is used to indicate that all expenditures have been processed.

Data Requirements

Data Type

```
BudgetCat = (Entertainment, Food, Clothing, Rent,
             Tuition, Insurance, Miscellaneous, Done);
```

Problem Inputs

Each expenditure and its category

Problem Output

```
Budget : BudgetArray    {array of expense totals}
```

DESIGN ▼

Initial Algorithm

1. Initialize all category totals to zero.
2. Display the possible budget categories.
3. Read each expenditure and add it to the appropriate total.
4. Print the accumulated total for each category.

Structure Chart and Refinements

The structure chart in Fig. 10.12 shows the relationships among steps 1, 3, and 4, which manipulate the array `Budget`. Procedures `Initialize` and

Figure 10.12
Structure Chart for Home
Budget Problem

PostIt store information in this array, and procedure *Report* displays this information. Step 2 is implemented by procedure *DisplayMenu* (not shown), which simply lists the budget categories for the benefit of the program user.

IMPLEMENTATION ▼

Coding the Main Program

Figure 10.13 shows the program. The main program contains declarations for the data type *BudgetArray* and the array *Budget* (type *BudgetArray*). Array *Budget* appears in each parameter list and is passed between each procedure and the main program.

The loop-control variable *NextCat* (type *BudgetCat*) is declared as a local variable in each procedure. In procedure *Initialize*, the assignment statement

```
Budget[NextCat] := 0.0
```

is repeated once for each value of *NextCat* and sets each element of *Budget* to *0*. In procedure *Report* the statements

```
WriteBudgetCat (NextCat);  {Display budget category.}
WriteLn (Budget[NextCat] :15:2)
```

call procedure *WriteBudgetCat* (from ADT *BudgetCatADT*) to display a budget category name and *WriteLn* to display the category total.

Procedure *PostIt* must read each expenditure and add it to the appropriate array element. The total of all entertainment expenditures is accumulated in *Budget[Entertainment]*, all food expenditures are accumulated in *Budget[Food]*, and so forth.

Figure 10.13
Home Budget Program

Directory: CHAP10
File: HOMEBUDG.PAS

```pascal
program HomeBudget (Input, Output);
{Prints a summary of all expenses by budget category}

  type
    {Insert data type BudgetCat from BudgetCatADT.}

    BudgetArray = array [BudgetCat] of Real;    {array type}

  var
    Budget : BudgetArray;           {output - array of totals}

  {
    Insert procedures ReadBudgetCat and WriteBudgetCat
    from BudgetCatADT.
  }

  procedure Initialize (var Budget {output} : BudgetArray);
  {
    Initializes array Budget to all zeros.
    Pre : None.
    Post: Each element of Budget is 0.0.
  }
    var
      NextCat : BudgetCat;              {loop-control variable}
                                    {       array subscript}
  begin {Initialize}
    for NextCat := Entertainment to Miscellaneous do
      Budget[NextCat] := 0.0
  end; {Initialize}


  procedure DisplayMenu;
  {Displays the budget categories}
    var
      NextCat : BudgetCat;

  begin
    WriteLn ('LIST OF BUDGET CATEGORIES:');
    for NextCat := Entertainment to Done do
      begin
        WriteBudgetCat (NextCat);
        WriteLn
      end {for}
  end; {DisplayMenu}
```

▷ ▷ ▷ ▷ ▷ ▷

```pascal
procedure PostIt (var Budget {input/output} : BudgetArray);
{
   Reads each expenditure amount and adds it to the
   appropriate element of array Budget.
   Pre : Each array element Budget[NextCat] is 0.0.
   Post: Each array element Budget[NextCat] is the sum of
         expense amounts for category NextCat.
}
begin {PostIt stub}
   WriteLn ('Procedure PostIt entered')
end; {PostIt stub}

procedure Report (Budget {input} : BudgetArray);
{
   Prints the expenditures in each budget category.
   Pre  : Array Budget is defined.
   Post : Displays each budget category name and amount.
   Calls: WriteBudgetCat
}
   var
      NextCat : BudgetCat;           {loop-control variable,}
                                     {array subscript}
begin {Report}
   WriteLn;                            {Display table heading.}
   WriteLn ('  Category     ' :15, 'Expenses' :15);
   {Print each category name and the total.}
   for NextCat := Entertainment to Miscellaneous do
      begin
         WriteBudgetCat (NextCat);   {Display category.}
         WriteLn (Budget[NextCat] :15:2)
      end {for}
end; {Report}

begin  {HomeBudget}
   {Initialize array Budget to all zeros.}
   Initialize (Budget);

   {Display list of budget categories.}
   DisplayMenu;

   {Read and process each expenditure.}
   PostIt (Budget);

   {Print the expenditures in each category.}
   Report (Budget)
end. {HomeBudget}
```

Coding Procedure PostIt

Procedure PostIt, shown in Fig. 10.14, uses procedure ReadBudgetCat (from ADT BudgetCatADT) to read the budget category. Procedure PostIt calls ReadBudgetCat to read the next category into NextCat. The while

Figure 10.14
Procedure PostIt

Directory: CHAP10
File: HOMEBUDG.PAS

```pascal
procedure PostIt (var Budget {input/output} : BudgetArray);
{
   Reads each expenditure amount and adds it to the
   appropriate element of array Budget.
   Pre  : Each array element Budget[NextCat] is 0.0.
   Post : Each array element Budget[NextCat] is the sum of
          expense amounts for category NextCat.
   Calls: ReadBudgetCat
}
   var
      NextCat : BudgetCat;     {next budget category}
      Expense : Real;          {expenditure amount}

begin  {PostIt}
   {Read each budget category and expense and add to Budget.}
   ReadBudgetCat (NextCat);
   while NextCat <> Done do
      {invariant:
          no prior value of NextCat is Done
          and Budget[NextCat] is the sum of all budget entries
          so far for each category NextCat.
      }
      begin
         Write ('Enter the expenditure amount $');
         ReadLn (Expense);
         Budget[NextCat] := Budget[NextCat] + Expense;
         WriteLn;
         ReadBudgetCat (NextCat)
      end {while}
end; {PostIt}
```

loop body is executed for each value of NextCat that is not Done (the sentinel). The assignment statement

```pascal
Budget[NextCat] := Budget[NextCat] + Expense;
```

adds the expense amount to whatever element of array Budget is selected by NextCat.

TESTING ▼

Before running the program, you must create and save the disk file that contains ADT BudgetCatADT (see Programming Exercise 4 at the end of this section). A sample run of the home budget program in Fig. 10.15 indicates that the input data do not have to be in order by category. You should verify that all budget categories without expenses remain zero and that invalid category values do not cause the program to terminate prematurely. Notice that

Figure 10.15

Sample Run of Home
Budget Program

```
LIST OF BUDGET CATEGORIES:
Entertainment
Food
Clothing
Rent
Tuition
Insurance
Miscellaneous
Done

Enter the first letter of the category> C
Enter the expenditure amount $25.00

Enter the first letter of the category> M
Enter the expenditure amount $25.00

Enter the first letter of the category> C
Enter the expenditure amount $15.00

Enter the first letter of the category> E
Enter the expenditure amount $675.00

Enter the first letter of the category> D

    Category        Expenses
    Entertainment    675.00
    Food               0.00
    Clothing          40.00
    Rent               0.00
    Tuition            0.00
    Insurance          0.00
    Miscellaneous     25.00
```

it is sufficient to enter only the first letter of each budget category because all
are unique.

Sequential Versus Random Access to Arrays

The home budget program illustrates two common ways of selecting array
elements for processing. Often we need to manipulate all elements of an array in some uniform manner (for instance, we might want to initialize them
all to zero). In such situations, it makes sense to process the array elements
in sequence (*sequential access*), starting with the first and ending with the
last. In procedures `Initialize` and `Report`, we accomplish sequential access by using a `for` loop whose loop-control variable is also the array subscript.

In procedure PostIt, the order in which the array elements are accessed depends completely on the order of the data. The value read into NextCat determines the element to be incremented. This approach is called *random access* because the order is not predictable.

Self-Check

1. When is it better to pass an entire array of data, rather than individual elements, to a procedure?
2. When is a copy of an entire array made for an array that is a procedure parameter? What happens to the copy after the procedure executes?
3. In function SameArray (Fig. 10.11), what will be the value of I when the statement

    ```
    SameArray := (A[I] = B[I])
    ```

    executes if array A is equal to array B? If the third elements do not match? If only the last elements do not match?

Programming

1. Write a procedure that assigns a value of True to element I of the output array if element I of one input array has the same value as element I of the other input array; otherwise, assign a value of False. If the input arrays have subscript type IndexType, the output array should have the following type:

    ```
    type
       BoolArray = array [IndexType] of Boolean;
    ```

2. Write a procedure that copies each value stored in one array to the corresponding element of another array. For example, if the arrays are InArray and OutArray, copy InArray[1] to OutArray[1], then copy InArray[2] to OutArray[2], and so on.
3. Write an array equivalent of the Switch procedure of Fig. 10.6 that does not allocate a local, temporary array. Hence SwitchArray, given input arrays Aarray and Barray, would switch Aarray[1] with Barray[1], Aarray[2] with Barray[2], and so on.
4. Write ADT BudgetCatADT. *Hint:* See DayADT in Fig. 9.3.

10.4 Subarray Processing

Usually, it isn't known prior to program execution exactly how many elements will be stored in an array. As an example, a professor processing exam scores might have 150 students in one class, 200 in the next, and so on. Because you must declare the array size before program execution begins (at *compile time*), you must allocate enough storage space so that the program can process the largest expected array without error.

When you read the array data into memory, you should begin filling the array starting with the first element and be sure to keep track of how many data items are actually stored in the array. The part of the array that contains data is called the **filled subarray.** The **length** of the filled subarray is the number of data items that are actually stored in the array.

filled subarray
the portion of an array that contains actual data
length of a subarray
the number of elements in a subarray

EXAMPLE 10.10 ▼

The array Scores, declared as follows, can accommodate a class size of up to 250 students. Each array element can contain an integer value.

```
const
   ClassSize = 250;          {maximum class size}

type
   ClassIndex = 1..ClassSize;  {subscript type for ScoreArray}
   ScoreArray = array [ClassIndex] of Integer;

var
   Scores : ScoreArray;        {array of exam scores}
   ClassLength : Integer;       {length of filled subarray}
```

Procedure ReadScores in Fig. 10.16 reads up to 250 exam scores and prints a warning message when the array is filled. The output parameter ClassLength represents the length of the filled subarray and is initialized to zero. Within the while loop, the statements

Figure 10.16
Reading Part of an Array

Directory: CHAP10
File: READSCOR.PAS

```
procedure ReadScores (var Scores {output} : ScoreArray;
                      var ClassLength {output} : Integer);
{
  Reads an array of exam scores (Scores)
  for a class of up to ClassSize students.
  Pre : None.
  Post: The filled subarray is Scores[1..ClassLength]
        and ClassLength is the number of values read
        (0 <= ClassLength <= ClassSize).
}
  const
    Sentinel = -1;             {sentinel score}

  var
    TempScore : Integer;     {temporary storage for a score}

begin
  Write ('Enter next score after the prompt or enter ');
  WriteLn (Sentinel :1, ' to stop:');

  {Read each array element until done.}
  ClassLength := 0;                {initial class length}
  Write ('Score> ');
```

▷ ▷ ▷ ▷ ▷ ▷

```
    ReadLn (TempScore);
    while (TempScore <> Sentinel) and (ClassLength < ClassSize) do
       {invariant:
          No prior value of TempScore is Sentinel,
          ClassLength <= ClassSize,
          and Scores[1..ClassLength] is the filled subarray
       }
       begin
          ClassLength := ClassLength + 1; {Increment ClassLength.}
          Scores[ClassLength] := TempScore;     {Save the score.}
          Write ('Score> ');
          ReadLn (TempScore)
       end; {while}

    {assert: Sentinel was read or array is filled.}
    if TempScore <> Sentinel then
       WriteLn ('Cannot store ', TempScore, '- array is full.')
end;   {ReadScores}
```

△

```
ClassLength := ClassLength + 1; {Increment ClassLength.}
Scores[ClassLength] := TempScore;     {Save the score.}
```

increment `ClassLength` and store the score just read (value of `TempScore`) in the next array element. After loop exit, the value of `ClassLength` is the length of the filled subarray.

In any subsequent processing of array `Scores`, use the variable `ClassLength` to limit the number of array elements processed. Because only the subarray with subscripts 1 through `ClassLength` (i.e., `Scores[1..ClassLength]`) contains meaningful data, array elements with subscripts larger than `ClassLength` should not be manipulated. `ClassLength` should be passed as a parameter to any procedure that processes the filled subarray.   ▲

Exercises for Section 10.4   **Self-Check**

1. In procedure `ReadScores`, what prevents the user from entering more than `ClassSize` scores?
2. Given the ability to do subarray processing, what are the consequences of always declaring a larger array bounds than is needed?
3. Why do we read the next data value into `TempScore` instead of reading it directly into the next array element?

Programming

1. Rewrite the `while` loop in `ReadScores` as a `repeat-until` loop. Why is the `while` loop better? Why can't we use a `for` loop?

10.5   Searching and Sorting an Array

This section discusses two common problems in processing arrays: *searching* an array to determine the location of a particular value and *sorting* an array to rearrange the array elements in numerical order. As an example of an array search, we might want to search the array to determine which student, if any, got a particular score. An example of an array sort would be rearranging the array elements so that they are in increasing order by score. Such a sort would be helpful if we wanted to display the list in order by score or if we needed to locate several different scores in the array.

Finding the Smallest Value in an Array

We begin by solving a simpler search problem: finding the smallest value in an array.

Algorithm for Finding the Smallest Value in an Array

1. Assume that the first element is the smallest so far and save its subscript as the subscript of the smallest so far.
2. for each array element do
    3. if the current element < the smallest so far then
        4. Save the subscript of the current element as the subscript of the smallest so far.

Function FindMin in Fig. 10.17 implements this algorithm for an array of type ScoreArray (see Example 10.10). During each iteration of the loop, MinIndex is the subscript of the smallest element so far and W[MinIndex] is its value. The function returns the last value assigned to MinIndex, which is the subscript of the smallest value in the array. Parameters StartIndex and EndIndex define the boundaries of the subarray W[StartIndex..EndIndex] whose smallest value is being found. Passing these subscripts as arguments results in a more general function.

Note that function FindMin returns the subscript (or index) of the smallest value, not the smallest value itself. Assuming Next is type Integer, and ClassLength is the number of array elements containing data, the following statements display the smallest value in array Scores (type ScoreArray):

```
IndexOfMin := FindMin(Scores, 1, ClassLength);
WriteLn ('The smallest exam score is ', Scores[IndexOfMin] :1)
```

Although not as easy to read, the single statement that follows is equivalent; it uses the function designator as the subscript expression.

```
WriteLn ('The smallest exam score is ',
        Scores[FindMin(Scores, 1, ClassLength)] :1)
```

Figure 10.17
Function FindMin

Directory: CHAP10
File: FINDMIN.PAS

```
function FindMin (W {input} : ScoreArray;
                  StartIndex, EndIndex {input} : ClassIndex) :
                                                 Integer;
{
  Returns the subscript of the smallest element in the
  subarray W[StartIndex..EndIndex].
  Pre : StartIndex and EndIndex are defined and
        W[StartIndex..EndIndex] is part of the filled subarray.
  Post: Returns K if W[K] <= W[I] for all I in subrange
        StartIndex..EndIndex. If the smallest value appears in
        two or more elements, K is the subscript of the first.
}
  var
    MinIndex,               {index of smallest so far}
    NextIndex : Integer;    {index of current element}

begin {FindMin}
  MinIndex := StartIndex;   {Assume first entry is smallest.}
  for NextIndex := StartIndex + 1 to EndIndex do
    if W[NextIndex] < W[MinIndex] then
      MinIndex := NextIndex; {Value at NextIndex is smallest.}

  {assert:
    All elements are examined and
    MinIndex is the index of the smallest element.
  }
  FindMin := MinIndex                 {Define result.}
end; {FindMin}
```

Searching an Array

We can search an array for a particular score by comparing each array element, starting with the first, to the *target score,* the value we are seeking. If a match occurs, we have found the target score in the array and can return its subscript as the search result. Otherwise, we continue searching until we either get a match or test all array elements without success.

Data Requirements for Search Function

Input Parameters

```
Scores: ScoreArray         {array to be searched}
ClassLength : ClassIndex   {number of elements in Scores}
Target : Integer           {score being searched for}
```

Function Output

The subscript of the first element containing `Target` or zero if `Target` was not found

Program Variables

```
Next : Integer      {subscript of next score to test}
NoTarget: Boolean   {program flag - true if target
                      has not been found in elements
                      tested so far}
```

Algorithm for Search Function

1. Start with the first array element.
2. Set `NoTarget` to `True`.
3. `while` the target is not found and there are more elements `do`
   4. `if` the current element contains the target score `then`
         Set `NoTarget` to `False`.
      `else`
         Try the next element.
5. `if` the target was not found `then`
      Return 0.
   `else`
      Return the target's subscript.

The `while` loop in step 3 executes until it finds an array element that contains the target score or it has tested all array elements without success. Step 4 compares the current array element (selected by subscript `Next`) to the target score and sets `NoTarget` to `False` if they match. If they do not match, the subscript `Next` is increased by 1. After loop exit, the `if` statement (step 5) defines the function result as 0 (target was not found) or as the value of `Next` when the match occurred. Figure 10.18 shows function `Search`.

The program flag `NoTarget` controls loop repetition and communicates the results of the search loop to the `if` statement that follows the loop. `No-Target` is set to `True` before entering the search loop and reset to `False` as soon as a tested element matches the target. The only way `NoTarget` can remain true throughout the entire array search is if no array element matches the target. The `if` statement returns 0 when `NoTarget` remains true; otherwise, it returns the value of subscript `Next` that caused `NoTarget` to be changed to `False`.

The loop invariant is

```
{invariant:
   Target was not found in subarray Scores[1..Next - 1]
   and Next is <= ClassLength + 1.
}
```

Figure 10.18
Function Search

**Directory: CHAP10
File: SEARCH.PAS**

```
function Search (Scores : ScoreArray;
                 ClassLength : ClassIndex;
                 Target : Integer)      : Integer;
{
  Searches for Target in array Scores.
  Pre : 1 <= ClassLength <= ClassSize and
        Scores[1..ClassLength] is the filled subarray.
  Post: Returns the subscript of Target if found;
        otherwise, returns zero.
}
  var
    Next : Integer;          {index of the current score}
    NoTarget : Boolean;      {program flag - true if target
                             has not been found in elements
                             tested so far}

begin  {Search}
  {Compare each element of Scores to Target until done.}
  Next := 1;                 {Start with the first score.]
  NoTarget := True;          {Target is not found.}
  while NoTarget and (Next <= ClassLength) do
    {invariant:
        Target was not found in subarray Scores[1..Next - 1]
        and Next is <= ClassLength + 1.
    }
    if Scores[Next] = Target then
      NoTarget := False       {Target is found.}
    else
      Next := Next + 1;       {Advance to next score.}

  {assert:
    Target was found or all elements tested without success.
  }
  if NoTarget then
    Search := 0                        {Target was not found.}
  else
    Search := Next         {Target found at Scores[Next].}
end; {Search}
```

This means that for each value of Next (starting with 1), the target was not found in an array element with a smaller subscript than Next. Because Next <= ClassLength + 1 must also be true after loop exit, Scores[ClassLength] is the last array element that can be compared to the target.

In the following sketch of array Scores,

Array Scores

[1] [2]   . . .   [Next-1] [Next] . . . [ClassLength]

Elements tested without success	Elements not yet tested

the elements in the color part of the array are the ones that have already been tested, and the element with subscript `Next` will be tested in the current loop iteration. If `Scores[Next]` does not match the target, the portion of the array in color will grow by one element, and the value of `Next` will increase by 1.

The invariant is true before the first iteration (`Next` is 1) because there are no array elements that precede the element with subscript 1. If the current element matches the target, loop exit will occur without changing `Next`, so the invariant will still be true. If `Next` becomes `ClassLength + 1`, all array elements will have been tested without success (the entire array will be in color), and loop exit will occur.

Sorting an Array

Many programs execute more efficiently if the data they process are sorted before processing begins. For example, a check processing program executes more quickly if all checks are in order by checking account number. Other programs produce more understandable output if the information is sorted before it is displayed. For example, your university might want your instructor's grade report sorted by student ID number. In this section, we describe one simple sorting algorithm from among the many that have been studied by computer scientists.

The *selection sort* is a fairly intuitive sorting algorithm. To perform a selection sort of an array with N elements (subscripts `1..N`), we locate the smallest element in the array and then switch the smallest element with the element at subscript 1, thereby placing the smallest element at position 1. Then we locate the smallest element remaining in the subarray with subscripts `2..N` and switch it with the element at subscript 2, thereby placing the second smallest element at position 2. Then we locate the smallest element remaining in the subarray with subscripts `3..N` and switch it with the element at subscript 3, and so on.

Figure 10.19 traces the operation of the selection sort algorithm on a subarray of length 4. The first array shown is the original array. Then we show each step as the next smallest element is moved to its correct position. The subarray in color represents the portion of each array that is sorted. Note that, at most, N-1 exchanges will be required to sort an array with N elements.

Algorithm for Selection Sort

1. `for Fill := 1 to N-1 do`
      2. Find the position of the smallest element
           in subarray `Scores[Fill..N]`.
      3. `if Fill` is not the position of the smallest element `then`
           4. Exchange the smallest element with the one at position
                `Fill`.

Figure 10.19
Trace of Selection Sort

`Fill` is `1`. Find the smallest element in subarray `Scores [1..4]` and swap it with `Scores[1]`.

`Fill` is `2`. Find the smallest element in subarray `Scores [2..4]` — no swap needed.

`Fill` is `3`. Find the smallest element in subarray `Scores [3..4]` and swap it with `Scores[3]`.

We can use function `FindMin` (see Fig. 10.17) to perform step 2. Procedure `SelectSort` in Fig. 10.20 implements the selection sort algorithm for the array `Scores` with `ClassLength` elements. Local variable `IndexOfMin` holds the index of the smallest exam score found so far in the current subarray. At the end of each pass, we call procedure `Switch` (see Fig. 10.6) to exchange the elements with subscripts `IndexOfMin` and `Fill` when `IndexOfMin` and `Fill` differ. After execution of procedure `SelectSort`, the exam scores will be in increasing order by exam score. We must modify procedure `Switch` to accept type `Integer` parameters.

The loop invariant for the outer loop

```
{invariant:
    The elements in Scores[1..Fill-1] are in
    their proper place and Fill <= ClassLength.
}
```

summarizes the progress of the selection sort. The subarray whose elements are in their proper place is shown in the color part of array `Scores` in the

Figure 10.20
Selection Sort Procedure

Directory: CHAP10
File: SELECTSO.PAS

```
procedure SelectSort (var Scores {input/output} : ScoreArray;
                          ClassLength {input} : Integer);
{
 Sorts the data in array Scores.
 Pre : 1 <= ClassLength <= ClassSize and the
        filled subarray is Scores[1..ClassLength].
 Post: The values in Scores[1..ClassLength] are in
        increasing order.
 Calls:Procedures Switch and FindMin
}
   var
     Fill, {index of element to contain next smallest score}
     IndexOfMin : Integer;       {index of next smallest element}

begin {SelectSort}
   for Fill := 1 to ClassLength - 1 do
     begin
       {invariant:
          The elements in Scores[1..Fill-1] are in
          their proper place and Fill <= ClassLength.
       }
       {Find smallest score in Scores[Fill..ClassLength].}
       IndexOfMin := FindMin(Scores, Fill, ClassLength);

       {Exchange elements at Fill and IndexOfMin.}
       if IndexOfMin <> Fill then
          Switch (Scores[IndexOfMin], Scores[Fill])
     end {for Fill}
end; {SelectSort}
```

following sketch. The remaining elements are not yet in place and are all larger than Scores[Fill-1].

Array Scores

[1] [2]	. . .	[Fill-1]	[Fill]	. . .	[ClassLength]
Elements in their proper place			**Elements larger than** Scores[Fill-1]		

During each pass, the portion of the array in color grows by one element and Fill is incremented to reflect this. When Fill is equal to ClassLength, the first ClassLength-1 elements will be in their proper place, so Scores[ClassLength] must also be in its proper place.

Program Style

Creating and Using General Purpose Modules

Function `FindMin` is a general purpose module that finds the smallest element in any subarray of its array parameter. Writing `FindMin` in this way enables us to use it in procedure `SelectSort`, simplifying the coding of `SelectSort`.

Exercises for Section 10.5   **Self-Check**

1. For the `Search` function in Fig. 10.18, what happens if
   a. the last student score matches the target?
   b. several scores match the target?
2. Trace the execution of the selection sort on the following two lists:

   10   55   34   56   76   5   5   15   25   35   45   45

   Show the arrays after each exchange occurs. How many exchanges are required to sort each list? How many comparisons?
3. How could you modify the selection sort algorithm to get the scores in descending order (largest score first)?

Programming

1. Write a procedure to find the next to the smallest element of an array. Assume that there are no duplicate entries in the array. Return `StartIndex` if the array only has one item.
2. Another method of performing the selection sort is to place the largest value in position `N`, the next largest in position `N-1`, and so on. Write this version.
3. A technique for implementing an array search without introducing a program flag is to use a `while` loop that increments `Next` as long as both of the following statements are true: The target does not match the current element, and `Next` is less than `ClassLength`. After loop exit, the element at position `Next` can be retested to determine the function result. If the element matches the target, the result is `Next`; otherwise, the result is `0`. Write the function body.

10.6   Analysis of Algorithms: Big-O Notation (Optional)

Many algorithms for searching and sorting arrays are available. Because arrays can have many elements, executing these algorithms can be very time consuming. Therefore, it is important to have some idea of the relative efficiency of different algorithms. Given the difficulty of measuring precisely the performance of an algorithm or program, programmers normally try to approximate the effect on an algorithm of a change in the number of items, N, that the algorithm processes. Programmers can compare two algorithms by seeing how each algorithm's execution time increases with N.

For example, if

$$2N^2 + N - 5$$

expresses the relationship between processing time and N, the algorithm is an $O(N^2)$ algorithm, where O is an abbreviation for order of magnitude. This notation is known as *Big-O notation*. The reason that this is an $O(N^2)$ algorithm instead of an $O(2N^2)$ algorithm or an $O(2N^2 + N - 5)$ algorithm is that the fastest-growing term (the one with the largest exponent) is dominant for large N and we ignore constants.

To search an array of N elements for a target using function `Search`, we have to examine all N elements if the target is not present in the array. If the target is in the array, then we have to search only until we find it. However, the target could be anywhere in the array—it is equally likely to be at the beginning of the array as at the end. So on average we have to examine $N/2$ array elements to locate a target value in an array. This means that an array search is an $O(N)$ process, so the growth rate is linear.

To determine the efficiency of a sorting algorithm, we focus on the number of array element comparisons and exchanges that it requires. Performing a selection sort on an array with N elements requires $N - 1$ comparisons during the first pass through the array, $N - 2$ comparisons during the second pass, and so on. Therefore the total number of comparisons is represented by the series

$$1 + 2 + 3 + \cdots + (N - 2) + (N - 1)$$

The value of this series is expressed in the closed form

$$N \times (N - 1)/2 = N^2/2 - N/2$$

so the number of comparisons performed in sorting an array of N elements is $O(N^2)$.

The number of array element exchanges varies, depending on the initial ordering of the array elements. If an element is already in its correct position, it is not exchanged. If the array happens to be sorted before procedure `SelectSort` is called, all its elements will be in their proper place, so there will be zero exchanges (*best-case situation*). If no elements are in their correct positions, there will be one exchange at the end of each pass through the array, or a total of $N - 1$ exchanges (*worst-case situation*). Therefore, the number of array element exchanges for an arbitrary initial ordering is between zero and $N - 1$, which is $O(N)$.

Because the number of comparisons is $O(N^2)$, selection sort is a *quadratic sort* (i.e., its growth rate is proportional to the square of the number of elements). What difference does it make whether an algorithm is an $O(N)$ process or an $O(N^2)$ process? Table 10.5 evaluates N and N^2 for different values of N. A doubling of N causes N^2 to increase by a factor of 4. Since N^2 increases much more quickly than *N*, the performance of an $O(N)$ algorithm is not as adversely affected by an increase in array size as is an $O(N^2)$ algorithm. For large values of *N* (say, 100 or more), the differences in performance for an $O(N)$ and an $O(N^2)$ algorithm are significant (see the last three lines of Table 10.5).

N	N^2
2	4
4	16
8	64
16	256
32	1024
64	4096
128	16384
256	65536
512	262144

Other factors besides the number of comparisons and exchanges affect an algorithm's performance. For example, one algorithm may take more time preparing for each exchange or comparison than another. Or one algorithm might exchange subscripts, whereas another might exchange the array elements themselves, which can be more time-consuming. Another measure of efficiency is the amount of memory required by an algorithm.

Exercises for Section 10.6 **Self-Check**

1. Determine how many times the `WriteLn` statement is displayed in each of the following fragments. Indicate whether the program fragment is $O(N)$ or $O(N^2)$.

    a. ```
for I := 1 to N do
    for J := 1 to N do
        WriteLn (I, J)
```

    b. ```
for I := 1 to N do
    for J := 1 to 2 do
        WriteLn (I, J)
```

    c. ```
for I := 1 to N do
    for J := N downto I do
        WriteLn (I, J)
```
```

Programming

1. Write a program fragment that displays the values of $Y1$ and $Y2$, defined as follows, for values of N from 10 to 100 in increments of 10. Does the result surprise you?

    $Y1 = 100N + 10$

    $Y2 = 5N^2 + 2$

10.7 Arrays with Type Char Elements and Subscripts

Many arrays contain numerical values, such as exam scores or hours worked. The arrays we introduce in this section store character data. In addition to storing character data in arrays, we can use characters as array subscripts.

Arrays of Characters

You can store a character string such as a person's name in memory using an array of characters. The following declarations allocate storage for array Name.

```
const
  StringSize = 20;

type
  IndexRange = 1..StringSize;
  CharArray = array [IndexRange] of Char;

var
  I : IndexRange;          {array subscript and loop control}
  Name : CharArray;        {array of 20 characters}
```

You can process array Name just like you process any other array in Pascal. A loop is necessary to read data into array Name or to display its contents. The loop below

```
for I := 1 to StringSize do
  Read (Name[I]);
ReadLn
```

reads 20 characters into array Name. We show the array Name next for a data line consisting of the characters George Washington followed by three spaces.

Array Name

The fragment

```
Write ('The first president is ');
for I := 1 to StringSize do
  Write (Name[I]);
WriteLn
```

displays the line

```
The first president is George Washington
```

Arrays with Type Char Subscripts

Often you can use an array with subscript type Char (or a subrange of Char) to simplify a program that processes characters. Example 10.11 and the case study that follows use arrays whose subscripts are the uppercase letters.

EXAMPLE 10.11 ▼

The program in Fig. 10.21 displays the number of occurrences of each letter in a line of text. It uses array LetterCount (subscript type 'A'..'Z') to store the number of occurrences of each letter (e.g., LetterCount['A'] is the number of occurrences of the letter A). Procedure CountLetters reads each data character into Ch and increments the element of array LetterCount selected by data character Ch. Function UpCase (see Figure 7.3) converts the case of each letter read to uppercase so that both t and T cause the count for

Figure 10.21
Counting Letters in a Line

Directory: CHAP10
File: CONCORDA.PAS

```
program Concordance (Input, Output);
{
  Finds and prints the number of occurrences of each letter.
  The case of each letter is immaterial. Letters with counts
  of zero are not displayed.
}
  type
    Letter = 'A'..'Z';
    CountArray = array [Letter] of Integer;

  var
    LetterCount : CountArray; {output - array of counts}

  {Insert procedure FillCountArray and function UpCase
   (Fig. 7.3) here.}

  procedure CountLetters (var LetterCount {output} : CountArray);
  {
   Counts the number of occurrences of each letter.
   Pre  : LetterCount is initialized to all zeros.
   Post : Reads next data line and LetterCount[Ch] is the
          number of occurrences of letter Ch in the line.
  }
```

▷ ▷ ▷ ▷ ▷

```
    var
      Ch : Char;                         {each data character}

   begin {CountLetters}
     WriteLn ('Type in a data line:');
     while not EOLN do
       begin
         Read (Ch);                      {Get next character.}
         Ch := UpCase(Ch);               {Convert to uppercase.}
         if (Ch >= 'A') and (Ch <= 'Z') then
           LetterCount[Ch] := LetterCount[Ch] + 1
       end; {while}
     ReadLn                              {Skip the <eoln>.}
   end; {CountLetters}

   procedure PrintCount (LetterCount {input} : CountArray);
   {
    Prints counts of letters.
    Pre  : LetterCount is initialized.
    Post : Displays each letter and its count if non-zero.
   }
     var
       NextChar : Letter;               {loop control and subscript}

   begin {PrintCount}
     WriteLn;
     WriteLn ('Letter', 'Occurrences' :16);
     for NextChar := 'A' to 'Z' do
       if LetterCount[NextChar] > 0 then
         WriteLn (NextChar :6, LetterCount[NextChar] :16)
   end; {PrintCount}

begin  {Concordance}
  {Initialize LetterCount.}
  FillCountArray (LetterCount, 0);

  {Count the letters in a line.}
  CountLetters (LetterCount);

  {Print counts of letters that are in the line.}
  PrintCount (LetterCount)
end. {Concordance}
```

Sample Run

```
Type in a data line:
This is it!

Letter   Occurrences
     H            1
     I            3
     S            2
     T            2
```

letter T to be incremented. Procedure `FillCountArray` is similar to `FillArray` (see Fig. 10.8). Procedure `PrintCount` displays a table showing each letter and the number of occurrences of each letter.   ▲

CASE STUDY ## Cryptogram Generator Problem

A cryptogram is a coded message formed by substituting a code character for each letter of the original message. Computers can be programmed to generate these coded messages.

PROBLEM ▼

Create a cryptogram program in which the substitution is performed uniformly throughout the original message—for instance, every A is replaced by an S, every B is replaced by a P, and so forth. All punctuation (including spaces between words) remains unchanged.

ANALYSIS ▼

The program must examine each character in the message and replace each character that is a letter by its code symbol. We can store the code symbols in an array `Code` with subscript type `'A'..'Z'` and element type `Char`. The character stored in `Code['A']` will be the code symbol for the letter `'A'`. This will enable us to look up the code symbol for a letter simply by using that letter as an index to the array `Code`. In the sample array `Code` shown next, every letter is replaced by the next letter in the alphabet and letter Z is replaced by A.

Array `Code`

['A']	['B']	['C']		['Y']	['Z']
B	C	D	. . .	Z	A

Data Requirements

Problem Inputs

`Code : array [Letter] of Char    {array of code symbols}`

Each message character

Problem Outputs

Each character of the cryptogram

DESIGN ▼

Initial Algorithm

1. Read in the code symbol for each letter.
2. Read each message character and display the cryptogram.

Algorithm Refinements and Structure Chart

As shown in the structure chart (Fig. 10.22), procedure `ReadCode` performs step 1 and procedure `Encrypt` performs step 2. The data requirements and algorithms for these procedures follow.

Local Variable for ReadCode

```
NextLetter : 'A'..'Z'    {Loop-control variable and
                          array subscript}
```

Algorithm for ReadCode

1. Display the alphabet.
2. `for` each letter `do`
    3. Read in the code symbol and store it in array `Code`.

Local Variable for Encrypt

```
Ch : Char    {each message character}
```

Algorithm for Encrypt

1. `while` there are more message characters `do`
    `begin`
       2. Read the next message character.
       3. Display the message character or its code symbol.
    `end`

IMPLEMENTATION ▼

The program in Fig. 10.23 assumes that the uppercase letters are consecutive characters, as they are in the ASCII character set.

Figure 10.22
Structure Chart for
Cryptogram Generator

```pascal
program Cryptogram (Input, Output);

{Generates cryptograms corresponding to input messages}

  type
    Letter = 'A'..'Z';
    CodeArray = array [Letter] of Char;

  var
    Code : CodeArray;          {input - array of code symbols}

  {Insert function UpCase (Fig. 7.3) here.}

  procedure ReadCode (var Code {output} : CodeArray);
  {
    Reads in the code symbol for each letter.
    Pre : None.
    Post: 26 data values are read into array Code.
  }
    var
      NextLetter : Letter;              {each letter}

  begin {ReadCode}
    WriteLn ('First specify the code.');
    WriteLn ('Enter a code symbol under each letter.');
    WriteLn ('ABCDEFGHIJKLMNOPQRSTUVWXYZ');
    {Read each code symbol into array Code.}
    for NextLetter := 'A' to 'Z' do
      Read (Code[NextLetter]);
    ReadLn;                           {Skip the <eoln>.}
    WriteLn                           {Skip a line.}
  end;   {ReadCode}

  procedure Encrypt (Code {input} : CodeArray);
  {
    Reads each character and prints it or its code symbol.
    Pre : Array Code is defined.
    Post: Reads a data line. A code symbol was printed for
          each letter; each nonletter was printed
  }
    var
      Ch : Char;        {input - each message character}

  begin  {Encrypt}
    WriteLn ('Enter each character of your message:');
    while not EOLN do
      begin
        Read (Ch);
        Ch := UpCase(Ch);                {Convert to uppercase.}
        if (Ch >= 'A') and (Ch <= 'Z') then
          Write (Code[Ch])              {Print code symbol.}
        else
          Write (Ch)                    {Print nonletter.}
      end; {while}
```

▷ ▷ ▷ ▷ ▷ ▷

```
      ReadLn                              {Skip the <eoln>.}
    end; {Encrypt}

begin  {Cryptogram}
  {Read in the code symbol for each letter.}
  ReadCode (Code);

  {Read each character and print it or its code symbol.}
  Encrypt (Code)
end. {Cryptogram}
```

Sample Run

```
First specify the code.
Enter a code symbol under each letter.
ABCDEFGHIJKLMNOPQRSTUVWXYZ
BCDEFGHIJKLMNOPQRSTUVWXYZA

Enter each character of your message:
A tiny one!#
B UJOZ POF!#
```

TESTING ▼

In the preceding sample run, the code symbol for each letter is entered directly beneath that letter and read by procedure ReadCode. The sample run ends with two lines of output: the first contains the message; the second contains its cryptogram. For a simple test, try using each letter as its own code symbol. In that case, both lines should be the same. Make sure the program encodes lowercase as well as uppercase letters. The program should not change characters that are not letters.

Exercises for Section 10.7 **Self-Check**

1. What changes would have to be made to the cryptogram generator so that, given the same code, it would decode rather than encrypt?

Programming

1. Make changes to the cryptogram program to encode the blank character and the punctuation symbols , ; : ? ! . . *Hint:* Use subscript type Char.
2. The cryptogram generator program does not work correctly if the user inputs the same code symbol more than once. Modify ReadCode so that such an error forces the user to reenter an unambiguous code.

10.8 Debugging Programs with Arrays

When debugging programs (or modules) that process arrays, it is best to test them on arrays having a small number of elements. If constants are used in array size declarations, then these constants should be small values. After your program is error free, you can change the constants to their normal values.

When debugging a module with an array parameter, be sure that the module works for special cases. Some special cases are:

▶ Sorting an array whose elements are already ordered
▶ Searching for a target that matches the first or last value in an array
▶ Reading a list of array data with more data items than array elements

10.9 Common Programming Errors

The most common error in the use of arrays is a subscript expression whose value goes outside the allowable range during program execution, causing an `index expression out of bounds` run-time error.

Subscript range errors most often are caused by an incorrect subscript expression. If the subscript is also the loop-control variable and is incremented before each loop iteration, subscript range errors can result from nonterminating loops or from loops that execute one more time than required.

Subscript range errors are most likely for subscript values at the loop boundaries. If these values are in range, it is likely that all other subscript references in the loop are in range as well.

As with all Pascal data types, make sure there are no type inconsistencies. The subscript type and element type used in all array references must correspond to those specified in the array type declaration.

Similarly, two arrays used in an array copy statement or as corresponding parameters must be type identical. Remember to use only identifiers without subscripts as formal array parameters and to specify the types of all array parameters using identifiers.

CHAPTER REVIEW

1. Arrays are data structures that store collections of data items of the same type. An array is characterized by its subscript type and element type. You declare an array type before you declare a variable (the array) with that type. Pascal allocates storage at compile time for each array listed in the variable declarations.

2. You can reference the entire collection of data using the array name; you can reference individual items using the array name followed by a subscript (a subscripted variable). The subscript must be a constant or expression that is com-

patible with the subscript type for that array. Array subscripts can be integers, characters, enumerated type values, and Boolean values.

3. You can use a `for` statement to reference the individual elements of an array in sequence. Some common array operations written using `for` loops are initializing arrays, reading arrays, and printing arrays. You can also reference array elements in arbitrary or random order (called *random access*).

4. You can write modules that have array parameters. When you call a procedure that has an array as a value parameter, a copy of the array is stored in the procedure data area and manipulated. The actual array is a module input and cannot be changed. When you call a procedure that has an array as a variable parameter, the address of the first actual array element is passed to the procedure and the actual array is manipulated. This enables you to change the contents of the actual array which is a module output.

5. You can write modules that search an array for a specific target value and sort the array so that its contents are ordered in an increasing, or decreasing, sequence. You can use Big-O notation to compare the efficiency of two searching or sorting algorithms.

Summary of New Pascal Constructs

Construct	Effect
Array Declaration	
```type IndexRange = 1..10; IntArray = array [IndexRange] of Integer; var Cube, Count : IntArray;```	The data type `IntArray` describes an array with 10 type `Integer` elements. `Cube` and `Count` are arrays with this structure.
Array References	
```for I := 1 to 10 do Cube[I] := I * I * I;```	Saves I cubed in the `Ith` element of array `Cube`.
```if Cube[5] > 100 then Write (Cube[1], Cube[2])```	Displays the first two cubes, if `Cube[5]` is greater than 100.
Array Copy	
```Count := Cube```	Copies contents of array `Cube` to array `Count`.

Quick-Check Exercises

1. What is a data structure?
2. Which standard types cannot be array subscript types? Array element types?
3. Can values of different types be stored in an array?

4. If an array is declared to have 10 elements, must the program use all 10?
5. When can the assignment operator be used with array operands? Answer the same question for the equality operator.
6. The two methods of array access are ＿＿＿＿＿＿＿ and ＿＿＿＿＿＿＿.
7. The ＿＿＿＿＿＿＿ loop allows us to access the elements of an array in ＿＿＿＿＿＿＿ order.
8. What is a filled subarray? What is its length? What is the relationship between the last element in a filled subarray and its length?
9. Explain why variable parameters are a more efficient use of memory when passing arrays to a procedure.
10. Declare variables `Name` and `Hours` that can be used to store a person's name (up to 20 letters) and the hours worked each day of the week in separate arrays.

Answers to Quick-Check Exercises

1. A data structure is a grouping of related values in memory.
2. `Real` and `Integer`; all can be element types.
3. No.
4. No.
5. If the arrays are the same type; if the arrays are strings.
6. Random, sequential
7. `for`, sequential
8. A filled subarray is the portion of an array that has meaningful data. Its length is the number of elements in the filled subarray. The last element's subscript is the same as the length.
9. A local copy of each array used as a value parameter is made when a procedure is called.
10.
```
type
    IndexRange = 1..20;
    NameArray = array [IndexRange] of Char;
    Day = (Sunday, Monday, Tuesday, Wednesday,
           Thursday, Friday, Saturday);
    HourArray = array [Day] of Real;

var
    Hours : HourArray;
    Name : NameArray;
```

Review Questions

1. Identify the error in the following code segment. When will the error be detected?

```
program Test (Input, Output);
    type
      AnArray = array [1..8] of Integer;

    var
      X : AnArray;
      I : Integer;
```

```
begin {Test}
  for I := 1 to 9 do
    X[I] := I
end. {Test}
```

2. Declare an array of reals called `Week` that can be referenced by using any day of the week as a subscript, where `Sunday` is the first subscript.

3. Indicate which of the assignment statements in the following code segment are incorrect. For each incorrect statement, describe what the error is and when it will be detected.

```
program Errors (Input, Output);
  type
    AnArray = array [1..8] of Real;

  var
    X, Y : AnArray;
    I : Integer;

begin
  I := 1;
  X[I] := 7.329;
  X[1..8] := 9.25;
  X(I) := -23.5;
  X := Y;
  X[1..5] := Y[1..5]
end;
```

4. What are two common ways of selecting array elements for processing?

5. How would the parameters differ for two procedures that manipulate arrays if one does subarray processing and the other does not?

6. The parameters for a procedure are two arrays (type `RealArray`) and an integer that represents the length of the arrays. The procedure copies the first array in the parameter list to the other array in reverse order. Write the procedure.

7. What would be a valid reason for not passing an array that provides input to a procedure as a value parameter?

8. How many exchanges are required to sort the following list of integers using selection sort? How many comparisons?
   20 30 40 25 60 80

9. What is the efficiency of selection sort in Big-O notation? Why?

Programming Projects

Directory: CHAP10
File: PROJ1.PAS

1. Write a program for the following problem. You are given a file that contains a collection of scores (type `Integer`) for the last exam in your computer course. You are to compute the average of these scores and assign grades to each student according to the following rule:

   If a student's score is within 10 points (above or below) of the average, assign a grade of `Satisfactory`. If a student's score is more than 10 points higher than the average, assign a grade of `Outstanding`. If a student's score is more than 10 points below the average, assign a grade of `Unsatisfactory`.

The output from your program should consist of a labeled two-column list that shows each score and its corresponding grade. As part of the solution, your program should include functions and procedures that correspond to the function and procedure headers that follow:

```
procedure ReadStuData (var RawScores {input} : Text;
                       var Score {output} : ArrayType;
                       var Count {output} : Integer;
                       var TooMany {output} : Boolean);
{
  Reads exam scores from file RawScores into array Scores.
  Count contains number of students read. TooMany is set
  to True if RawScores contains more than ClassSize scores.
}

procedure PrintGrade (OneScore {input} : Integer;
                      Average {input} : Real);
{Prints student grade after comparing OneScore to Average}

function Mean (Score : ArrayType; Count : Integer) : Real;
{Computes average of Count student scores}

procedure PrintTable (Score {input} : ArrayType;
                      Count {input} : Integer);
{
  Prints a table showing each student's score and grade
  on a separate line.
  Calls: PrintGrade.
}
```

2. Redo Programming Project 1, assuming that each line of file RawScores contains a student's ID number (an integer) and an exam score. Allocate three arrays for storing ID numbers, exam scores, and grades. Modify procedure ReadStuData to read the ID number and the score from the Ith data line into array elements ID[I] and Score[I], respectively. Write a new procedure AssignGrades that assigns values to the array Grades based on the exam scores. Modify procedure PrintTable to display a three-column table with the following headings:

```
ID      Score       Grade
```

3. Write a program to read N data items into two arrays, X and Y, of size 20. Store the product of corresponding elements of X and Y in a third array, Z, also of size 20. Print a three-column table displaying the arrays X, Y, and Z. Then compute and print the square root of the sum of the items in Z. Make up your own data, with N less than 20.

4. If an array is sorted, we can search for an item in the array much faster by dividing the array and searching decreasing halves. This is called a binary search. Given a beginning and an end in an array, the binary search determines a middle index and compares the middle value to the search value. If they are equal, the procedure can return a found condition. If the middle is less than the search value, we search to the right of the middle, repeating the same process. Write a binary search procedure for an array of integers and a test program that

searches for each value in an ordered array of 1000 numbers (1 to 1000). Have the program count the total number of comparisons required. Compare this number to the 5,005,500 comparisons required by the simple search function.

5. The results of a true–false exam given to a computer science class have been coded for input to a program. The information available for each student consists of a student identification number and the student's answers to 10 true–false questions. The available data are as follows:

Student Identification	Answer String
0080	FTTFTFTTFT
0340	FTFTFTTTFF
0341	FTTFTTTTTT
0401	TTFFTFFTTT
0462	TTFTTTFFTF
0463	TTTTTTTTTT
0464	FTFFTFFTFT
0512	TFTFTFTFTF
0618	TTTFFTTFTF
0619	FFFFFFFFFF
0687	TFTTFTTFTF
0700	FTFFTTFFFT
0712	FTFTFTFTFT
0837	TFTFTTFTFT

Write a program that first reads in the answer string representing the 10 correct answers (use FTFFTFFTFT as data). Next read each student's data into two arrays. Then compute and store the number of correct answers for each student in the corresponding element of another array. Determine the best score, Best. Then print a three-column table that displays the ID number, the score, and the grade for each student. The grade should be determined as follows: If the score is equal to Best or Best-1, give an A; if it is Best-2 or Best-3, give a C. Otherwise, give an F.

6. An array can be used to represent a polynomial. If we consider a polynomial such as $a + bx + cx^2 + dx^3$, we could put *a, b, c,* and *d* in array locations indexed by 1, 2, 3, and 4, respectively. The maximum index of the array would determine the maximum degree of the polynomial we could compute. Write a program that will input a polynomial of degree up to 10 and output a table of the computed values of the polynomial for *x* values from -1.0 to 1.0 in steps of 0.1.

7. The results of a survey of the households in your township are available for public scrutiny. Each record contains data for one household, including a four-digit integer identification number, the annual income for the household, and

the number of household members. Write a program to read the survey results into three arrays and perform the following analyses:

a. Count the number of households included in the survey and print a three-column table displaying the data. (Assume that no more than 25 households were surveyed.)

b. Calculate the average household income and list the identification number and income of each household that exceeds the average.

c. Determine the percentage of households that have incomes below the poverty level. Compute the poverty level income using the formula

$$p = \$6500.00 + \$750.00 \times (m - 2)$$

where m is the number of members of each household. This formula shows that the poverty level depends on the number of family members, m, and that the poverty level income increases as m gets larger.

Test your program on the following data.

Identification Number	Annual Income	Household Members
1041	12,180	4
1062	13,240	3
1327	19,800	2
1483	22,458	8
1900	17,000	2
2112	18,125	7
2345	15,623	2
3210	3,200	6
3600	6,500	5
3601	11,970	2
4725	8,900	3
6217	10,000	2
9280	6,200	1

8. Assume that your computer has the very limited capability of reading and writing only single-integer digits and adding together two integers consisting of one decimal digit each. Write a program that can read in two integers of up to 30 digits each, add these digits together, and display the result. Test your program using pairs of numbers of varying lengths.

Hints: Store the two numbers in two integer arrays of size 30, one digit per array element. If the number is less than 30 digits in length, enter enough leading zeros (to the left of the number) to make the number 30 digits long.

You will need a loop to add the digits in corresponding array elements starting with subscript 30. Don't forget to handle the carry digit if there is one! Use a

Boolean variable to indicate whether the sum of the last pair of digits is greater than 9.

9. A prime number is any number divisible only by one and itself. Write a program to compute all the prime numbers less than 2000. One way to generate prime numbers is to create an array of Boolean values that are true for all prime numbers, false otherwise. Initially set all the array entries to true. Then, for every number from 2 to 1000, set the array locations indexed by multiples of the number (but not the number itself) to false. When done, output all numbers whose array location is true. These will be the prime numbers.

10. Write an interactive program that plays the game of Hangman. Read the word to be guessed into `Word`. The player must guess the letters belonging to `Word`. The program should terminate when either all letters have been guessed correctly (player wins) or a specified number of incorrect guesses have been made (computer wins).

   Hint: Use `Solution` to keep track of the solution so far. Initialize `Solution` to a string of symbols `'*'`. Each time a letter in `Word` is guessed, replace the corresponding `'*'` in `Solution` with that letter.

CHAPTER ELEVEN

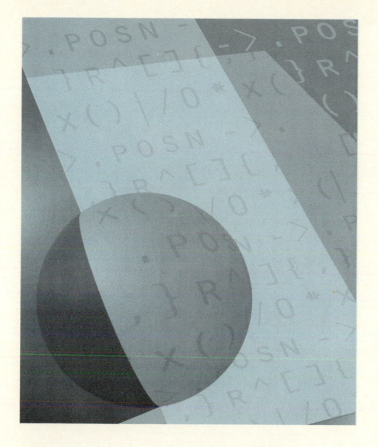

Packed Arrays and Multidimensional Arrays

multidimensional array
an array with two or more dimensions

We can store strings in packed arrays of characters using Pascal's assignment operator. We can use relational operators to compare strings and procedures Write and WriteLn to display them.

The array data structure also allows a programmer to organize information in arrangements that are more complex than the linear or one-dimensional arrays you've seen so far. We can declare and use arrays with several dimensions, each with a different subscript type. Although **multidimensional arrays** allow more flexibility in arranging data than one-dimensional arrays, the rules for element types are the same: The array elements may be simple or structured, but they must all be the same type.

11.1   Strings and Packed Arrays of Characters

In Section 10.7, we showed how to store a character string in an array of characters. You can also store a character string in a packed array. Using a **packed array** for string storage enables Pascal to store more than one character in each computer memory cell. Besides using packed arrays for more efficient storage, Pascal permits operations on packed arrays that simplify string processing.

packed array of characters
an array that can house multiple characters in a single memory cell

Declaring Packed Arrays

We declare two packed arrays, `FirstName` and `LastName`, next.

```
const
   StringLength = 10;

type
   String10 = packed array [1..StringSize] of Char;

var
   FirstName, LastName : String10;
```

string variable (string)
a variable that stores a packed array of characters

Variables `FirstName` and `LastName` are called **string variables**, or **strings**, of length 10 (value of `StringLength`) because they can each store a character string consisting of exactly ten characters.

You can assign a string literal to a string variable. The statement

```
FirstName := 'A.C. Jones';    {Assign a string to FirstName}
```

stores the string value `'A.C. Jones'` in the string variable `FirstName`:

Array `FirstName`

[1]	[2]	[3]	[4]	[5]	[6]	[7]	[8]	[9]	[10]
A	.	C	.		J	o	n	e	s

Because `FirstName` and `LastName` are both the same type, the assignment statement

```
LastName := FirstName          {copy FirstName to LastName}
```

copies the string value stored in `FirstName` to `LastName`.

Each string value stored in a string variable must have the same length as the string variable receiving it. The string assignments

```
FirstName := 'Jones';          {invalid - string too short}
FirstName := 'A.C. Johnson'    {invalid - string too long}
```

would cause a `type conflict of operands` syntax error because they violate this rule.

SYNTAX DISPLAY

String Variable Declaration

Form: type *string type* = packed array [1..*size*] of Char;
Example: type String10 = packed array [1..10] of Char;
Interpretation: The identifier *string type* denotes an array type that can store a string value consisting of *size* characters.
Note: The subscript type for *string type* must begin with 1.

String Comparison

Function SameArray in Fig. 10.11 determines whether two arrays of real numbers are identical. You don't need to write a function to compare strings because Pascal allows them to be operands of the relational operators. Assuming that AlphaStr and BetaStr are string variables of length 3, the statement

```
Same := (AlphaStr = BetaStr)        {Are strings identical?}
```

assigns the value True to Same when AlphaStr and BetaStr contain the same string. The assignment statement

```
Differ := (AlphaStr <> BetaStr)     {Are strings different?}
```

assigns the value True to Differ when AlphaStr and BetaStr contain different strings. Finally, the assignment statement

```
Same := (AlphaStr = 'Rob')
```

assigns the value True to Same when AlphaStr contains the string 'Rob'.

Using the relational operators <,<=, >, and >=, it is also possible to compare equal length strings for *lexicographic*, or alphabetical, order. Pascal bases the result on the collating sequence (order of characters) for your computer.

For example, the condition

```
AlphaStr < BetaStr
```

is true if the string stored in AlphaStr is considered less than the string stored in BetaStr. Pascal determines this by comparing corresponding characters in both strings, starting with the first pair. If the characters are the same, then the next pair is checked. If the characters in position I are the first different pair, then AlphaStr is less than BetaStr if AlphaStr[I] is less than BetaStr[I].

The conditions shown in Table 11.1 are true for the character codes shown in Appendix C. The last column shows why each condition is true.

Table 11.1
Some True String
Comparisons

AlphaStr	Operator	BetaStr	Reason Condition Is True
'AAA'	<	'ZZZ'	'A' < 'Z'
'AZZ'	<	'ZZZ'	'A' < 'Z'
'ZAZ'	<	'ZZA'	'A' < 'Z'
'AZZ'	<	'BAA'	'A' < 'B'
'B11'	>	'A99'	'B' > 'A'
'B11'	<	'B12'	'1' < '2'
'ACE'	<	'AID'	'C' < 'I'
'123'	>	'103'	'2' > '0'
'123'	>=	'123'	all characters equal
'30 '	>=	'123'	'3' > '1'

The last line of Table 11.1 shows the curious result that '30 ' >= '123' is true. This result is based solely on the relationship between the first pair of different characters, '3' and '1'. To avoid these funny results, you should replace any blanks in numeric strings with zeros.

Displaying String Variables

We discussed how to assign string values and how to compare strings. You can also display strings using Write or WriteLn. The statements

```
Write ('Hello ', FirstName);
WriteLn ('. Good to see you.')
```

display the line

```
Hello A.C. Jones. Good to see you.
```

when FirstName contains the string 'A.C. Jones'. As shown, a string variable can appear without a subscript as a parameter in a Write or WriteLn statement. When this is done, the variable's contents are printed as a single string.

You can use a format specification when displaying a string variable. The statements

```
Write ('Hello ', FirstName :4);
WriteLn ('! Good to see you.')
```

display the line

```
Hello A.C.! Good to see you.
```

Since the field width 4 is less than the length (10) of string FirstName, only the first 4 characters of FirstName are displayed. If the field width is larger than the string length, leading blanks are displayed before the string. Table 11.2 provides some examples.

Table 11.2
Displaying a
Formatted String

Statement	Effect
`Write (FirstName : 10)`	`A.C. Jones`
`Write (FirstName : 6)`	`A.C. J`
`Write (FirstName : 12)`	`   A.C. Jones`

In summary, the following statements are true for string variables.

▶ You can assign a string literal to a string variable of the same length.
▶ You can display a string variable by passing it as a parameter to `Write` or `WriteLn`.
▶ You can compare a string variable to another string variable or a string literal of the same length.

Notice that we said nothing about reading a string in the list above. Unfortunately standard Pascal does not allow the use of string variables as parameters for `Read` or `ReadLn`. We will discuss how to read a string shortly.

Referencing Individual Characters in a String

For the most part, we can manipulate individual characters of a string just like any type `Char` variable. For example, if `FirstName` contains the string `'A.C. Jones'`, the statements

```
FirstName[1] := 'D';
FirstName[6] := 'B'
```

change the contents of `FirstName` to `'D.C. Bones'`. If `NextChar` is type `Char`, the statement

```
NextChar := FirstName[2]
```

stores a period in `NextChar`. The condition

```
FirstName[I] = '.'
```

compares the `I`th character in `FirstName` to the period character (value is `True` when `I` is 2 or 4).

You cannot pass a string element to a type `Char` variable parameter. However, you can read individual characters directly into a string variable. The statement

```
Read (FirstName[1])
```

replaces the first character in string `FirstName` with the next data character read.

Abstract Data Type StringADT

Because operations with strings are common, you should include in your library an abstract data type `StringADT` that contains a declaration for data type `StringType` and procedure `ReadLnString` for reading a string from either the keyboard or a data file. Table 11.3 shows the specification for `StringADT`.

Table 11.3
Specification for String
Abstract Data Type

Structure
A string is a sequence of exactly `StringLength` characters stored in a variable of type `StringType`.

Operator
The description of the operator uses the following parameters:

    `InFile` (type `Text`)
    `InString` (type `StringType`)
    `CurLength` (type `Integer`)

`ReadLnString (var InFile, var InString, var CurLength)`: Reads
    a data string of up to `StringLength` characters from file `InFile` into
    `InString` and returns the number of characters read through `CurLength`.

Let's consider the specification for `ReadLnString` in Table 11.3. Assume that each data string appears at the end of a line, followed by `<eoln>`. The number of characters actually read and stored in a string variable is limited by its declared length (`StringLength`). If `ReadLnString` encounters the `<eoln>` before reading `StringLength` characters, it should store the blank character in all array elements that did not receive data (called **padding a string**). If there are more than `StringLength` characters before the `<eoln>`, `ReadLnString` should store only the first `StringLength` characters, and ignore the remaining characters.

padding a string
storing blank characters after
the last character read into a
string

Figure 11.1 shows the implementation for `StringADT`. A variable of type `StringType` can store a string with 20 characters.

The `while` loop in `ReadLnString` reads each data character and stores it in the element of `InString` selected by counter `CurLength`. The loop invariant

```
{invariant:
    InString[1..CurLength] contains characters read so far
    and CurLength <= StringLength
    and <eoln> was not reached.
}
```

Figure 11.1
Implementation of
StringADT

Directory: CHAP11
File: STRINGADT.PAS

▽

```
{Implementation of StringADT}

  const
    StringLength = 20;          {the string length}

  type
    StringIndex = 1..StringLength;
    StringType = packed array [StringIndex] of Char;



  procedure ReadLnString (var InFile {input} : Text;
                          var InString {output} : StringType;
                          var CurLength {output} : Integer);
  {
   Reads a data string from file InFile into InString and
   returns the number of characters read through CurLength.
   Pre : StringLength is the length of a string
         variable of type StringType and file InFile
         is opened for input.
   Post: Reads up to StringLength characters from file InFile
         into InString and advances to the next data line. If
         <eoln> is reached before InString is filled, stops
         reading characters and pads the rest of the string
         with blanks. Stores the count of characters read
         in CurLength (0 <= CurLength <= StringLength).
  }
    const
      Pad = ' ';                    {character used for padding}

    var
      I : Integer;          {loop control and index to string}

  begin  {ReadLnString}
    {Read each character and store it in InString.}
    CurLength := 0;                  {no characters read}
    while (not EOLN(InFile)) and (CurLength < StringLength) do
      {invariant:
          InString[1..CurLength] contains characters read so far
          and CurLength <= StringLength
          and <eoln> was not reached.
      }
      begin
        CurLength := CurLength + 1; {Increment character count.}
        Read (InFile, InString[CurLength])   {Read a character.}
      end;   {while}
```

▷ ▷ ▷ ▷ ▷ ▷

```
  {assert: at end of line or string is filled}
  ReadLn (InFile);                     {Advance to next line}

  {Pad rest of string with blanks}
  for I := CurLength + 1 to StringLength do
    InString[I] := Pad
end;   {ReadLnString}
```

indicates that, at the end of each loop iteration, the subarray In-String[1..CurLength] contains the data characters read so far. In the following sketch of array InString, the array elements containing data characters are in color. During each iteration of the loop, the value of CurLength increases by one and the portion of the array in color grows by one element.

Array InString

[1] [2] ... [CurLength]	...	[StringLength]
Elements containing data		

Loop exit occurs when the <eoln> is reached or after StringLength characters are read. After loop exit, the statement

```
ReadLn (InFile);                     {Advance to next line}
```

advances to the next line of file InFile, skipping over any extra characters at the end of the current data line.

Next, the for statement stores a blank character in all array elements that did not receive data. If CurLength is equal to StringLength (all array elements are filled), the for loop body is skipped.

Table 11.4 shows the values returned through InString and CurLength for three calls to procedure ReadLnString when StringLength is 5, not 20. For the last call, only the uppercase letters are read and stored; the lowercase letters are skipped.

Table 11.4
Results of Calls to
ReadLnString

StringLength	Data String	InString	CurLength
5	ABC<eoln>	'ABC '	3
5	ABCDE<eoln>	'ABCDE'	5
5	ABCDEfg<eoln>	'ABCDE'	5

If you use Input as the first parameter in a call to ReadLnString, the data string will be read from the keyboard. Because of differences in the way Pascal systems perform interactive input, `ReadLnString` may not always perform as expected.

Returning the count of characters actually read through `CurLength` enables a client program to display the data string without showing the blank padding. If `AString` is type `StringType` and `ALength` is type `Integer`, the statements

```
ReadLnString (Input, AString, ALength);
WriteLn ('*', AString :ALength, '*')
```

read a data string into `AString` and display only the first `ALength` characters between asterisks. So if `StringLength` is 20 and the data line is

```
a short one<eoln>
```

the following line would be displayed:

```
*a short one*
```

Exercises for Section 11.1   *Self-Check*

1. What would be returned by `ReadLnString` through `InString` and `CurLength` for the data string

    ```
    The quick fox jumped<eoln>
    ```

    when `StringLength` is 10, 20, and 25?
2. If an assignment statement is used to store a string in a packed array, what must be true about the length of the string? What can be done if this is not the case?
3. What is the difference between determining if two arrays of real numbers are the same and determining if two packed arrays of characters are the same? What, if any, are the restrictions on the subscript types of the two packed arrays being compared?

Programming

1. Write a procedure that finds the actual length of a string that is padded with blanks. Do not include the blank padding in the actual length.
2. Write a procedure that stores the reverse of an input string parameter in its output parameter (for example, if the input string is `'happy '`, the output string should be `'yppah '`). The actual length of the string being reversed (excluding blank padding) should also be an input parameter.
3. Write a program that uses the procedure in the preceding exercise to determine whether a string is a palindrome. (A palindrome is a string that reads the same left to right as it does right to left; for example, `'level'`.)

11.2 Using Strings

Now that you can store character strings in memory, you can improve your capability to manipulate textual data. Suppose that you would like to find a summer job. You need a program that creates form letters to help you inquire about possible job opportunities.

Printing a Form Letter

PROBLEM ▼

You would like a program that can help in writing job application letters. Each letter will be written to a separate output file for printing.

ANALYSIS ▼

A letter consists of a heading, a salutation, the body, and a closing. The heading, salutation, and the first line of the body will be different for each letter, but the body and the closing will be the same. First, you'll use an editor to create the letter body and the closing and save it as a text file (`BodyFile`). To individualize each letter, you want to enter data for the first part of the letter at the keyboard and then write the first part of the letter to the output file (`Letter`). Next, you can write the rest of the letter from file `BodyFile` to the output file.

An example of the data entry process for the first part of the letter follows. The information you'll enter is in color.

```
Today's date          > July 27, 1995
Employer name         > Peter Liacouras
Company name          > Temple University
Address               > Broad and Montgomery Streets
City, state, and zip> Philadelphia, PA  19122
```

This data would be inserted in the first several lines written to the output file, as shown in Fig. 11.2.

Data Requirements

Problem Inputs

```
BodyFile : Text            {the body of the letter}
Date : StringType          {today's date}
Employer : StringType      {employer's name}
Company : StringType       {company name}
Address : StringType       {company address}
CityStZip : StringType     {city, state, and zip}
```

Problem Outputs

```
Letter : Text              {the complete letter}
```

Figure 11.2
First Lines of File Letter

```
                                              July 27, 1995

       Peter Liacouras
       Temple University
       Broad and Montgomery Streets
       Philadelphia, PA  19122

       Dear Peter Liacouras:

       I am interested in applying for a job at Temple University.
```

DESIGN ▼

Initial Algorithm

1. Read the preamble data from the keyboard and write it to `Letter`.
2. Copy the letter body to `Letter`.

The structure chart (Fig. 11.3) shows that procedures `Preamble` and `WriteBody` perform steps 1 and 2, respectively.

IMPLEMENTATION ▼

Coding the Main Program

The main program body shown in Fig. 11.4 prepares both text files and calls procedures `Preamble` and `WriteBody`. They, in turn, call procedure

Figure 11.3
Structure Chart for
Form Letter Program

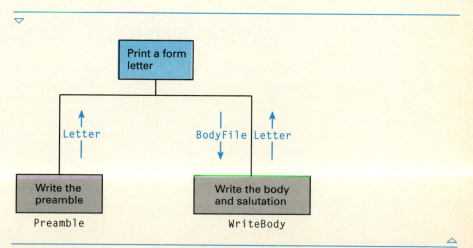

Figure 11.4
Form Letter
Writing Program

Directory: CHAP11
File: FORMLETT.PAS

```pascal
program FormLetter (Input, Output, BodyFile, Letter);
{
  Writes a job application letter to an output file. The data
  for the letter preamble is read from the keyboard; the letter
  body is copied from a data file to the output file.
}
  const
    StringLength = 40;

  type
    StringType = packed array [1..StringLength] of Char;

  var
    BodyFile,                      {input - body of letter}
    Letter    : Text;              {output - completed letter file}

  {Insert procedure ReadLnString (see Fig. 11.1) here.}
  {Insert procedures Preamble and WriteBody here.}

begin {FormLetter}
  Reset (BodyFile);
  Rewrite (Letter);
  WriteLn (Output, 'Writing job application letter.');
  Preamble (Letter);
  WriteBody (BodyFile, Letter);
  WriteLn (Output, 'Letter copied to output file.')
end. {FormLetter}
```

ReadLnString declared in StringADT (Fig. 11.1). The main program displays a message before data entry begins and a message after the letter is completed.

Coding the Procedures

Procedure Preamble (see Fig. 11.5) reads from the keyboard the strings needed for the letter heading and salutation. After data entry, the strings read into DateString, Employer, Company, Address, CityStZip are written to file Letter.

   Procedure WriteBody (Fig. 11.6) copies the body of the letter (not shown) from the input file to the output file. The while loop copies each line of the data file to the output file.

TESTING ▼

Test procedure ReadLnString using a driver program first. Try to read strings from the keyboard as well as a data file. See what happens when the

Figure 11.5
Procedure Preamble

Directory: CHAP11
File: FORMLETT.PAS

```
procedure Preamble (var Letter {output} : Text);
{
   Writes a preamble for a job application letter to a file.
   Pre : The output file is opened.
   Post: Writes the heading, salutation, and first sentence of
         a job application letter using data entered at the
         keyboard.
   Calls: ReadLnString
}
  const
    PageWidth = 50;                              {start of date}

  var
    DateString,                          {input - data strings}
    Employer, Company,                   {         "          }
    Address, CityStZip : StringType;     {         "          }
    DateLen,  EmpLen, CompLen,
    AddLen, CityLen    : Integer;        {length of each string}

begin  {Preamble}
  {Enter all data}
  Write ('Today''s date        > ');
  ReadLnString (Input, DateString, DateLen);
  Write ('Employer name       > ');
  ReadLnString (Input, Employer, EmpLen);
  Write ('Company name        > ');
  ReadLnString (Input, Company, CompLen);
  Write ('Address             > ');
  ReadLnString (Input, Address, AddLen);
  Write ('City, state, and zip> ');
  ReadLnString (Input, CityStZip, CityLen);

  {Write letter preamble.}
  WriteLn (Letter, ' ' :PageWidth, DateString :DateLen);
  WriteLn (Letter);
  WriteLn (Letter, Employer);
  WriteLn (Letter, Company);
  WriteLn (Letter, CityStZip);
  WriteLn (Letter);
  WriteLn (Letter, 'Dear ', Employer :EmpLen, ':');
  WriteLn (Letter);
  Write (Letter, 'I am interested in applying for a job at ');
  WriteLn (Letter, Company :CompLen, '.');
  WriteLn (Letter)
end; {Preamble}
```

data lines are longer than the length of the receiving string variable and when the data line is exactly the same length as the string variable. When you run the form letter program, try using an empty file BodyFile.

Figure 11.6
Procedure WriteBody

Directory: CHAP11
File: FORMLETT.PAS

```
procedure WriteBody (var BodyFile {input},
                         Letter   {output} : Text);
{
  Copies the body of a job application letter from a data
  file to an output file.
  Pre : The input file and output file are opened.
  Post: Writes the letter body to the output file.
  Calls: ReadLnString
}
  var
    OneLine : StringType;          {next data line}
    LineLength : Integer;          {length of line read}

begin {WriteBody}
  {Copy each line until done}
  while not EOF(BodyFile) do
    begin
      ReadLnString (BodyFile, OneLine, LineLength);
      WriteLn (Letter, OneLine :LineLength)
    end {while}
end; {WriteBody}
```

Exercises for Section 11.2   ***Self-Check***

1. Procedure `Preamble` displays several character strings. What method is
    used so that the blank padding is not displayed?

Programming

1. Assume that the technique used in procedure `Preamble` to keep the
    blank padding from being displayed does not work on your computer.
    Write a procedure `WriteString` that displays characters 1 through
    `CurLength` of a string where the string and `CurLength` are passed as
    parameters.

11.3 Two-Dimensional Arrays: Arrays of Arrays

Two-dimensional arrays, the most common of the multidimensional arrays,
store information normally represented in tabular form. An example would
be a classroom seating plan that lists each student's name in the location
(row and seat) of that student's desk (see Fig. 11.7).

Figure 11.7
Classroom Seating Plan (11
Rows and 9 Seats per Row)

Declaring Two-Dimensional Arrays

Examples 11.1 to 11.3 demonstrate how to declare two-dimensional arrays.

EXAMPLE 11.1 ▼

A familiar two-dimensional object is a tic-tac-toe board. The declarations

```
type
   MoveRange = 1..3;
   BoardArray = array [MoveRange, MoveRange] of Char;
                             ↗                ↗
                        First          Second
                        dimension      dimension
var
   TicTacToe : BoardArray;
```

allocate storage for array `TicTacToe` (see Fig. 11.8), which is type `BoardArray`. An array of type `BoardArray` has two dimensions, each with subscript type `MoveRange`. Therefore `TicTacToe` is a two-dimensional array with three rows and three columns. This array has nine elements, each of which must be referenced by specifying a row subscript (1, 2, or 3) and a column subscript (1, 2, or 3).

To reference an element of a two-dimensional array, you must specify the array name and provide two subscript expressions. The first subscript is the row subscript, and the second subscript is the column subscript. The subscripted variables

Figure 11.8
A Tic-Tac-Toe Board Stored
as Array TicTacToe

```
TicTacToe[2, 3]              TicTacToe[2][3]

↑        ↗     ↖             ↑       ↗      ↖
Array   Row    Column        Array   Row     Column
name    subscript subscript  name    subscript subscript
```

select the array element in row 2, column 3 of the array in Fig. 11.8; it contains the character O. The form `TicTacToe[2, 3]` is more commonly used. ▲

EXAMPLE 11.2 ▼

Your instructor wants to store the seating plan (Fig. 11.7) for a class on a computer. The declarations

```
const
   RowMax = 11;               {number of rows in the room}
   SeatsPerRow = 9;           {number of seats in a row}
   StringSize = 10;           {characters in a string}

type
   RowRange = 1..RowMax;
   SeatRange = 1..SeatsPerRow;
   StringIndex = 1..StringSize;
   StringType = packed array [StringIndex] of Char;
   SeatPlan = array [RowRange, SeatRange] of StringType;

var
   MyClass : SeatPlan;        {seating plan for MyClass}
```

allocate storage for a two-dimensional array of strings called `MyClass`. Array `MyClass` could be used to hold the first names of the students seated in a classroom with 11 rows and 9 seats in each row. Because each string contains 10 characters, the array requires 990 bytes of storage ($11 \times 9 \times 10$). The statement

```
MyClass[6, 5] := 'Marilyn'
```

places a student named `Marilyn` in row 6, seat 5, the center of the classroom. ▲

EXAMPLE 11.3 ▼

The declarations

```
const
   NumberSalesPeople = 5;          {number of salespeople}

type
   People = 1..NumberSalesPeople;
   Quarter = (Fall, Winter, Spring, Summer);
   SalesArray = array [People, Quarter] of Real;

var
   Sales : SalesArray;
```

Figure 11.9
Array Sales

	[Fall]	[Winter]	[Spring]	[Summer]
[1]	1200.00	1250.00	1700.00	1200.00
[2]	3500.00	2400.00	1500.00	1000.00
[3]	4500.00	3000.00	2500.00	1500.00
[4]	2500.00	2000.00	3000.00	1200.00
[5]	1250.00	2500.95	2700.00	1500.00

allocate storage space for a two-dimensional array of real numbers called Sales. The first dimension is type People and the second type Quarter. The array contains 20 (5 × 4) elements (see Fig. 11.9). Sales[1, Winter] stores the amount of sales (1250.00) for salesperson 1 during the Winter quarter. ▲

Arrays of Arrays

Arrays can have elements that are structured types rather than simple types. You can think of a multidimensional array as an array of arrays. The declarations

```
type
   MoveRange = 1..3;
   BoardRow = array [MoveRange] of Char;
   BoardArray = array [MoveRange] of BoardRow;

var
   TicTacToe : BoardArray;
```

allocate storage for the array TicTacToe shown in Fig. 11.8. These statements declare BoardRow as an array type with three elements of type Char and BoardArray as an array type with three elements of array type Board-Row. Consequently, the variable TicTacToe (type BoardArray) is an array of arrays, or a two-dimensional array.

SYNTAX DISPLAY

Array Type Declaration (Multidimensional)

Form:
```
type
   multidim = array [subscript₁, subscript₂, ... , subscriptₙ]
              of element type;
```

or

```
type
   multidim = array [subscript₁] of array [subscript₂] ...
              of array [subscriptₙ] of element type;
```

Example: `type`

```
        Month = (Jan, Feb, Mar, Apr, May, Jun,
                 Jul, Aug, Sep, Oct, Nov, Dec);
        Candidate = 'A'..'E';
        Precinct = 1..10;
        YearRange = 1900..1999;
        YearByMonth = array [YearRange, Month] of Real;
        Election = array [Candidate] of array
                     [Precinct] of Integer;
```

Interpretation: *subscript$_i$* represents the subscript type of dimension i of array type *multidim*. Each subscript type can be either of the standard ordinal types `Boolean` or `Char`, an enumerated type, or a subrange type. The *element type* can be any standard data type or a previously defined simple or structured data type.

Storage of Two-Dimensional Arrays

Pascal compilers store two-dimensional arrays in adjacent memory cells to simplify accessing the individual elements. The elements of a two-dimensional array normally are stored in order by row (i.e., first row 1, then row 2, etc.), a process called *row-major order.* To access a particular array element, the compiler computes the *offset* of that element from the first element stored. To perform this computation, the compiler must know the size of each element in bytes and the number of elements per row. Both values are available from the array type declaration.

For example, the array `TicTacToe` would be stored as shown in Fig. 11.10. In this array, each row has three elements, each occupying one byte of storage. The offset for element `TicTacToe[`*row, col*`]` is computed from the formula

Figure 11.10
Array TicTacToe
in Memory

$$offset = rowsize \times (row - 1) + (col - 1)$$

Because *rowsize* is 3 (i.e., 3 columns per row), this formula gives a value of 0 as the offset for element `TicTacToe[1,1]` and a value of 5 as the offset for element `TicTacToe[2,3]`.

Exercise for Section 11.3   **Self-Check**

1. Assuming the following declarations,

    ```
    type
      RowRange = 1..5;
      ColRange = 1..4;
      MatrixType = array [RowRange, ColRange] of Real;

    var
      Matrix : MatrixType;
    ```

    answer these questions:

    a. How many elements are in array `Matrix`?
    b. Write a statement to display the element in row 3, column 4.
    c. What is the offset for this element?
    d. What formula computes the offset for `Matrix[I,J]`?

11.4 Processing Two-Dimensional Arrays

We have two methods for accessing elements of a one-dimensional array: random access and sequential access. For a two-dimensional array or table, we have three methods of access:

1. *Random access.* The order is arbitrary, depending on data entered by the program user.
2. *Row-by-row access.* All elements in the first row are processed, then all elements in the second row, and so on.
3. *Column-by-column access.* All elements in the first column are processed, then all elements in the second column, and so on.

Nested loops are used to access a two-dimensional array, either row-by-row or column-by-column. In row-by-row access, the outer loop-control variable is the row subscript and the inner loop-control variable is the column subscript. These roles are reversed in column-by-column access, as shown in the following templates summarizing the loop forms.

Template for Row-by-Row Access of Array Table

```
for row-subscript ... do          {Specify the row.}
  for column-subscript ... do      {Access each column of row.}
    Process Table[row-subscript, column-subscript]
```

Template for Column-by-Column Access of Array Table

```
for column-subscript ... do        {Specify the column}
  for row-subscript ... do          {Access each row of column.}
    Process Table[row-subscript, column-subscript]
```

Here are some of the more common operations that we perform on two-dimensional arrays and their recommended method of access:

▶ Initialize all array elements to a specified value—either row-by-row or column-by-column access.
▶ Find the sum of all the elements in a table—either row-by-row or column-by-column access.
▶ Display the elements in a table—row-by-row access.
▶ Find the sum for each row—row-by-row access.
▶ Find the sum for each column—column-by-column access.
▶ Update array elements as determined by input data—random access.

We show how to perform some of these operations next.

Initializing an Array

Procedure `Initialize` (Fig. 11.11) initializes each element of its array parameter `Sales` (Fig. 11.9) to `InValue`. The procedure accesses the array elements row-by-row. The outer `for` loop cycles through the rows and the inner `for` loop cycles through the columns. During the first iteration of the outer loop `NextPerson` is 1, so the inner loop sets the four array elements in

Figure 11.11
Initializing a Two-Dimensional Array

Directory: CHAP11
File: SALESANA.PAS

```
procedure Initialize (var Sales {output} : SalesArray;
                          InValue {input} : Real);
{
  Initializes all elements of its array parameter to InValue.
  Pre  : InValue is defined.
  Post : Sets each element of its array parameter to InValue.
}
  var
    NextPerson : People;           {Row subscript}
    NextQuarter : Quarter;         {Column subscript}

begin {Initialize}
  for NextPerson := 1 to NumberSalesPeople do
    for NextQuarter := Fall to Summer do
      Sales[NextPerson, NextQuarter] := InValue
end; {Initialize}
```

row 1 to InValue. Next, it sets the four array elements in row 2 to InValue, and so on.

Computing Row Sums

For the array shown in Fig. 11.9, computing the sum for one row will give the annual sales total for one person (e.g., 1200.00 + 1250.00 + 1700.00 + 1200.00 is the annual sales total for the first salesperson). The program fragment

```
Sum := 0.0;
for NextQuarter := Fall to Summer do
  Sum := Sum + Sales[1, NextQuarter];
WriteLn ('Sales for person 1 are $', Sum :3:2)
```

computes this sum by adding the four array elements in row 1 to Sum. Notice that only the column subscript changes with each loop iteration. The fragment initializes Sum to 0 before the loop and displays its final value after loop exit.

You must use nested loops to find the sum for every row. Procedure SumRows (Fig. 11.12) performs this operation. Instead of displaying each sum,

Figure 11.12

Procedure SumRows and Type RowArray

Directory: CHAP11
File: SALESANA.PAS

```
type
  RowArray = array [People] of Real;

procedure SumRows (Sales {input} : SalesArray;
                       var RowSum {output} : RowArray);
{
 Sums the rows of array Sales, returning the sums in RowSum.
 Pre  : Array Sales is defined.
 Post : RowSum[I] is the sum of elements in row I.
}
  var
    NextPerson : People;        {Row subscript}
    NextQuarter : Quarter;      {Column subscript}
    Sum : Real;                 {Each row sum}

begin {SumRows}
  for NextPerson := 1 to NumberSalesPeople do
    begin
      Sum := 0.0;
      for NextQuarter := Fall to Summer do
        Sum := Sum + Sales[NextPerson, NextQuarter];
      RowSum[NextPerson] := Sum      {Return next row sum}
    end {outer for}
end; {SumRows}
```

the procedure returns the sum for row I in array element RowSum[I](type RowArray). We declare type RowArray before the procedure.

Procedure SumRows accesses the array elements row-by-row. Its outer for loop cycles through the rows and its inner for loop cycles through the columns. The outer loop initializes Sum to 0 before each pass through the columns and assigns its final value after each pass to the element of array RowSum selected by the row subscript.

Computing Column Sums

Computing the sum for each column would give us the annual sales for each quarter (e.g., 1200.00 + 3500.00 + 4500.00 + 2500.00 + 1250.00 gives us the total sales during the Fall quarter). To compute the sum for a given column, we must add the five elements in each row of that column. Procedure SumColumns (Fig. 11.13) accesses the array elements column-by-column and returns the four column sums through array ColSum. Fig. 11.14 shows the relationship among arrays Sales, RowSum, and ColSum.

Figure 11.13
Procedure SumColumns
and Type ColArray

Directory: CHAP11
File: SALESANA.PAS

```
type
   ColArray = array [Quarter] of Real;

procedure SumColumns (Sales {input} : SalesArray;
                          var ColSum {output} : ColArray);
{
  Sums the columns of array Sales, returning the sums in ColSum
  Pre  : Array Sales is defined.
  Post : ColSum[I] is the sum of elements in column I.
}
   var
      NextPerson : People;              {Row subscript}
      NextQuarter : Quarter;            {Column subscript}
      Sum : Real;                       {Each column sum}

begin {SumColumns}
   for NextQuarter := Fall to Summer do
      begin
         Sum := 0.0;
         for NextPerson := 1 to NumberSalesPeople do
            Sum := Sum + Sales[NextPerson, NextQuarter];
         ColSum[NextQuarter] := Sum      {Return next column sum}
      end {outer for}
end; {SumColumns}
```

CASE STUDY   **Analysis of Sales Data**

PROBLEM ▼

The sales manager of your company needs a sales analysis program to track sales performance by salesperson and by quarter. The program will read all sales transactions from a text file. The data for each transaction will be the salesperson's number, the quarter in which the sale took place, and the sales amount. The sales transactions should be in no particular order. After reading all sales transactions, the program should display a table in the form shown in Fig. 11.14, which includes the totals by person and by quarter.

ANALYSIS ▼

You will need separate arrays to hold the sales table, the row sums, and the column sums.

Data Requirements

Problem Inputs

Sales transactions file

```
Sales : SalesArray;    {array of sales amounts}
```

Problem Outputs

```
RowSum : RowArray;     {array of row sums}
ColSum : ColArray;     {array of column sums}
```

Figure 11.14
Array Sales, RowSum, and ColSum

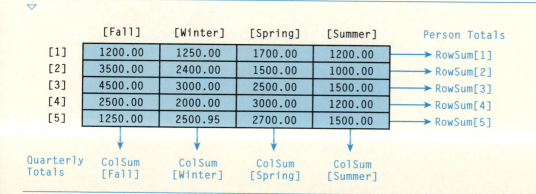

	[Fall]	[Winter]	[Spring]	[Summer]	Person Totals
[1]	1200.00	1250.00	1700.00	1200.00	→ RowSum[1]
[2]	3500.00	2400.00	1500.00	1000.00	→ RowSum[2]
[3]	4500.00	3000.00	2500.00	1500.00	→ RowSum[3]
[4]	2500.00	2000.00	3000.00	1200.00	→ RowSum[4]
[5]	1250.00	2500.95	2700.00	1500.00	→ RowSum[5]

Quarterly Totals   ColSum [Fall]   ColSum [Winter]   ColSum [Spring]   ColSum [Summer]

DESIGN

Initial Algorithm

1. Initialize all elements of the sales array to zero.
2. Read in the sales data.
3. Compute the row sums.
4. Compute the column sums.
5. Display the sales table showing the row and column sums.

IMPLEMENTATION ▼

Coding the Main Program

We have already written procedures for steps 1, 3, and 4 (Figs. 11.11–11.13). We will write the main program next (Fig. 11.15) and then write the procedures for steps 2 and 5.

Figure 11.15

Sales Analysis
Main Program

Directory: CHAP11
File: SALESANA.PAS

```pascal
program SalesAnalysis (Input, Output, SalesFile);
{Reads in sales figures for one year and stores them in a table
 organized by salesperson and quarter. Displays the table and
 the annual totals for each person and the sales totals for
 each quarter.
}
  const
    NumberSalesPeople = 5;        {number of salespeople}

  type
    People = 1..NumberSalesPeople;
    Quarter = (Fall, Winter, Spring, Summer);
    SalesArray = array [People, Quarter] of Real;
    RowArray = array [People] of Real;
    ColArray = array [Quarter] of Real;

  var
    SalesFile : Text;            {file of sales data}
    Sales : SalesArray;          {2-D sales table}
    RowSum : RowArray;           {row totals}
    ColSum : ColArray;           {column totals}

{Insert procedures Initialize, SumRows, and SumColumns.}
{Insert procedures ReadQuarter, ReadTable and DisplayTable.}

begin {SalesAnalysis}
  Initialize (Sales, 0.0);
  ReadTable (SalesFile, Sales);
  SumRows (Sales, RowSum);
  SumColumns (Sales, ColSum);
  DisplayTable (Sales, RowSum, ColSum)
end. {SalesAnalysis}
```

Coding Procedure ReadTable

Procedure ReadTable (Fig. 11.16) reads in the sales table data from the sales transaction file after preparing the data file for input. Each transaction specifies the salesperson, the quarter in which the sale took place, and the sales amount. Procedure ReadQuarter (see Programming Exercise 1 at the end of this section) returns the sales quarter value read through its second parameter and a Boolean value through its third parameter, indicating whether a valid quarter was read.

Figure 11.16
Procedure ReadTable

Directory: CHAP11
File: SALESANA.PAS

```
procedure ReadTable (var SalesFile {input} : Text;
                     var Sales {output} : SalesArray);
{
 Reads the sales table data from a data file and saves the
 sales results in a sales table.
 Pre  : Sales is initialized to all zeros.
 Post : Each entry of Sales represents the sum of sales
        for a particular salesperson and quarter.
 Calls: ReadQuarter to read the sales quarter.
}
  var
    TranAmount : Real;              {transaction amount}
    TranPerson : Integer;           {salesperson number}
    TranQuarter : Quarter;          {sales quarter}
    ValidQuarter : Boolean;         {flag indicating whether
                                      a valid quarter was read}

begin {ReadTable}
  {Prepare data file for input.}
  Reset (SalesFile);

  {Read and store all valid sales data.}
  while not EOF(SalesFile) do
    begin
      Read (SalesFile, TranPerson);
      ReadQuarter (SalesFile, TranQuarter, ValidQuarter);
      ReadLn (SalesFile, TranAmount);
      if ValidQuarter and (TranPerson >= 1) and
                          (TranPerson <= 5) then
        Sales[TranPerson, TranQuarter] :=
              Sales[TranPerson, TranQuarter] + TranAmount
      else
        WriteLn ('Invalid person or quarter - ',
                 'person is ', TranPerson :1,
                 '; amount is ', TranAmount :3:2)
    end {while}
end; {ReadTable}
```

The `if` statement tests whether the salesperson and quarter are valid. If so, the statement

```
Sales[TranPerson, TranQuarter] :=
      Sales[TranPerson, TranQuarter] + TranAmount
```

adds the current sales amount to the total being accumulated for the salesperson selected by `TranPerson` (row subscript) and `TranQuarter` (column subscript). Because the data are in no particular order, the array elements are randomly accessed.

Coding Procedure DisplayTable

You should display the information in a two-dimensional array in the same way that humans visualize it: as a table whose rows correspond to the array's first dimension and whose columns correspond to the array's second dimension. To accomplish this, access and display the array elements row-by-row.

Procedure `DisplayTable` (Fig. 11.17) displays the data in the sales table array in the form shown in Fig. 11.14. Besides the array data (first parameter), the procedure also displays the row sums (second parameter) and column sums (third parameter). To enhance readability, `DisplayTable` also displays the row and column labels shown in Fig. 11.14.

Figure 11.17
Procedure DisplayTable

Directory: CHAP11
File: SALESANA.PAS

```
procedure DisplayTable (Sales {input} : SalesArray;
                        RowSum {input} : RowArray;
                        ColSum {input} : ColArray);
{
 Displays the sales table data in table form and the row
 and column sums.
 Pre  : Sales, RowSum, and ColSum are defined.
 Post : The values stored in the three arrays are displayed.
}
  var
    NextPerson : People;              {Each salesperson}
    NextQuarter : Quarter;            {Each quarter}

begin
  {Display the heading.}
  WriteLn;
  WriteLn ('SALES TABLE' :40);
  WriteLn ('[Fall]' :20, '[Winter]' :10, '[Spring]' :10,
                          '[Summer]' :10, ' Person Totals');

  {Display one table row for each salesperson.}
  for NextPerson := 1 to NumberSalesPeople do
    begin
      Write ('[' :8, NextPerson :1, ']');
```

▷ ▷ ▷ ▷ ▷ ▷

```
      for NextQuarter := Fall to Summer do
        Write (Sales[NextPerson, NextQuarter] :10:2);
      WriteLn (RowSum[NextPerson] : 14:2)
    end; {for NextPerson}

  {Display the column totals.}
  WriteLn;
  Write ('Quarterly' :10);
  for NextQuarter := Fall to Summer do
    Write (ColSum[NextQuarter] :10:2);
  WriteLn;
  WriteLn ('Totals')
end; {DisplayTable}
```

TESTING ▼

To test the sales analysis program, create a sample data file. Verify that incorrect data for salesperson or quarter do not cause an index expression out of bounds error during run time. Figure 11.18 shows a sample run. The person totals column and quarterly totals row should both sum to the same amount (4200.00 for the sample run).

Exercises for Section 11.4 **Self-Check**

1. For each fragment, which array locations are displayed and in which order?
   a. for NextQuarter := Fall to Summer do
         Write (Sales[1, NextQuarter])
   b. for NextPerson := 1 to 5 do
         Write (Sales[NextPerson, Spring]);

Figure 11.18
Sample Run of Sales
Analysis Program

```
Invalid person or quarter - person is 6; amount is 1200.00
Invalid person or quarter - person is 3; amount is 850.00

                         SALES TABLE
              [Fall]   [Winter]  [Spring]  [Summer] Person Totals
        [1]  1000.00      0.00      0.00   1500.00       2500.00
        [2]     0.00      0.00    100.00    500.00        600.00
        [3]   100.00      0.00   1000.00      0.00       1100.00
        [4]     0.00      0.00      0.00      0.00          0.00
        [5]     0.00      0.00      0.00      0.00          0.00

Quarterly 1100.00      0.00   1100.00   2000.00
Totals
```

```
    c.  for NextQuarter := Fall to Summer do
          begin
            for NextPerson := 1 to 5 do
              Write (Sales[NextPerson, NextQuarter]);
            WriteLn
          end; {for}
```

Programming

1. Procedure `ReadQuarter` reads two characters representing the quarter (`FA`, `WI`, `SP`, `SU`) from a data file and returns the corresponding quarter value (`Fall`, `Winter`, `Spring`, `Summer`) if the data characters are correct. Write procedure `ReadQuarter`.
2. Write an array type declaration for 10 × 10 square matrices that contain real numbers.
3. For the array type declared in Programming Exercise 2, do the following:
    a. Write a loop that computes the sum of the elements in row 5.
    b. Write a loop that computes the sum of the elements in column 6.
    c. Write nested loops that compute the sum of all the array elements.
4. Write a function that determines who has won a game of tic-tac-toe. The function should first check all rows to see whether one player occupies all the cells in that row, next check all columns, and then check the two diagonals. The function should return a value from the enumerated type (`NoWinner`, `XWins`, `OWins`).

11.5 Three-Dimensional Arrays

Pascal does not limit the number of dimensions an array may have, though arrays with only two and three dimensions are most common. Be aware that large amounts of memory space can be allocated for storage of a multidimensional array. For that reason, avoid passing multidimensional arrays as value parameters. In this section, we study some examples of three-dimensional arrays.

EXAMPLE 11.4 ▼

The array `RoomHeat` (Fig. 11.19) declared as

```
type
   Length = 1..12;      {12 feet long}
   Width = 1..10;       {10 feet wide}
   Height = 1..8;       {8 feet high}
   TempArray = array [Length, Width, Height] of Real;

var
   RoomHeat : TempArray;
```

Figure 11.19
Array RoomHeat

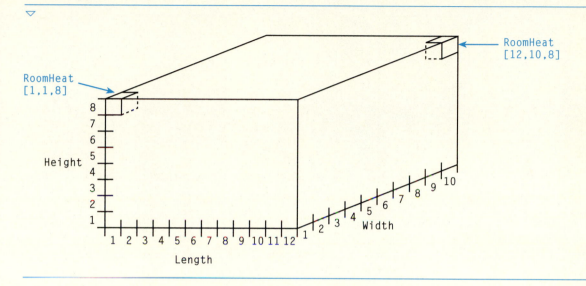

has three dimensions and requires three subscripts. The first subscript can have values from 1 to 12; the second, from 1 to 10; and the third, from 1 to 8. A total of 12 × 10 × 8, or 960, real numbers can be stored in the array RoomHeat. We can use this array to store the room temperature measured at discrete points in a 12-by-10-foot room with an 8-foot ceiling. ▲

EXAMPLE 11.5 ▼

Your job is to computerize a small office. The first step is to store the information in your boss's two file cabinets, labeled "Business" and "Personal" (Fig. 11.20). Each file cabinet contains two drawers, and each drawer has 26 folders labeled A through Z. Each folder contains a memo of up to 255 characters. The following declarations allocate storage for an array Office that will hold all the information in the two filing cabinets:

```
const
   MemoLength = 255;

type
   CabinetType = (Business, Personal);
   DrawerType = (Top, Bottom);
   FolderType = 'A'..'Z';
   Memo = packed array [1..MemoLength] of Char;
   FileCabinet = array [CabinetType, DrawerType, FolderType]
                                      of Memo;
```

Figure 11.20
Office Files to Be
Computerized

```
var
  Office : FileCabinet;
```

You need three subscripts to access an element of this array. The subscripted variable `Office[Business, Top, 'A']` accesses the folder with label `A` in the open drawer shown in Fig. 11.20. The statement

```
Write (MemoFile, Office[Business, Top, 'A'])
```

copies the memo in this folder to output file `MemoFile` (type `Text`).

The array `Office` occupies a large amount of storage space. Using 1K bytes to mean 1024 bytes, the array would require 26K bytes of storage ($2 \times 2 \times 26 \times 256$).   ▲

EXAMPLE 11.6 ▼

A university offers 50 courses at each of five campuses. The registrar's office wants to break down enrollment information according to student rank. To do this, they need to store the enrollment information in a three-dimensional array with 1000 elements ($50 \times 5 \times 4$). This array is declared next and is shown in Fig. 11.21.

```
const
  MaxCourse = 50;                    {maximum number of courses}

type
  Campus = (Main, Ambler, Center, Delaware, Montco);
  Rank = (Freshman, Sophomore, Junior, Senior);
  CourseRange = 1..MaxCourse;
  ClassArray = array [CourseRange, Campus, Rank] of Integer;
```

Figure 11.21
Three-Dimensional Array ClassEnroll

```
var
   ClassEnroll : ClassArray;              {class enrollment}
   CurCampus : Campus;                    {current campus}
   ClassRank : Rank;                      {current rank}
   Total : Integer;                       {student totals}
```

The subscripted variable `ClassEnroll[1, Center, Senior]` represents the number of seniors taking course 1 at Center campus.

The program fragment

```
Total := 0;
for ClassRank := Freshman to Senior do
   Total := Total + ClassEnroll[1, Center, ClassRank]
```

computes the total number of students of all ranks in course 1 at Center campus.

The program fragment

```
Total := 0;
for CurCampus := Main to Montco do
   for ClassRank := Freshman to Senior do
      Total := Total + ClassEnroll[1, CurCampus, ClassRank]
```

computes the total number of students in course 1 (regardless of rank or campus). ▲

Exercises for Section 11.5 *Self-Check*

1. Declare a three-dimensional array type in which the first subscript consists of letters from 'A' to 'F', the second subscript consists of integers from 1 to 10, and the third consists of the user-defined type Day (days of the week). Real numbers will be stored in the array. How many elements can be stored in an array of this type?

2. Declare a three-dimensional array that can keep track of the number of students in the math classes (Math1, Algebra, Geometry, Algebra2, Trigonometry, Calculus) at your old high school according to the grade level and the gender of the students. How many elements are in this array?

3. Extend row-major order to three dimensions and show how the array ClassEnroll might be stored. What would be the offset for the array element ClassEnroll[1, Center, Senior] and the general formula for ClassEnroll[*i, j, k*]?

Programming

1. Redefine MaxCourse (Example 11.6) as 5, and write code fragments that perform the following operations:
   a. Enter the enrollment data.
   b. Find the number of juniors in all classes at all campuses. Count students once for each course in which they are enrolled.
   c. Find the number of sophomores on all campuses who are enrolled in course 2.
   d. Compute and print the number of students at Main campus enrolled in each course and the total number of students at Main campus in all courses. Count students once for each course in which they are enrolled.
   e. Compute and print the number of upper-class students in all courses at each campus, as well as the total number of upper-class students enrolled. (Upper-class students are juniors and seniors.) Again, count students once for each course in which they are enrolled.

11.6   Common Programming Errors

A variable of type packed array [1..N] of Char is a string variable of length N (a constant) and can store a string value consisting of exactly N characters. Pascal detects an incompatible type syntax error if you assign a string value that is too short or too long to a string variable. If you assign one string variable to another, they must both be the same length.

When you use multidimensional arrays, make sure the subscript for each dimension is consistent with its declared type. If any subscript value is out of range, you may get an `index expression out of bounds` error during run time.

If you use nested `for` loops to process the array elements, make sure that loop-control variables used as array subscripts are in the correct order. The order of these variables determines the sequence in which the array elements are processed.

CHAPTER REVIEW

1. Allocate a string variable whose type is a packed array of characters for storing a string literal or data item. You can perform assignment, comparison, and display operations more easily on a string variable because the entire string can be processed as a unit rather than element by element.
2. Use two-dimensional arrays, or arrays of arrays, to represent tables of information and game boards. You can use arrays of higher dimension to represent more complicated organizations of information.
3. Access the elements of a multidimensional array in a systematic way using nested loops. The correspondence between the loop-control variables and the array subscripts determines the order in which the array elements are processed. To access a two-dimensional array row-by-row, use the row subscript as the outer loop-control variable and the column subscript as the inner loop-control variable. Reverse this order to access the elements column-by-column.

Summary of New Pascal Constructs

Construct	Effect
Declaring String Variables	

`type`
`  String10 = packed array [1..10] of Char;`
`var`
`  Name : String10;`
	The data type `String10` describes a packed array of 10 characters. `Name` is a string variable of length 10.

Operations on Strings	
`Name := 'R. Koffman'`	Saves `'R. Koffman'` in `Name`.
`WriteLn (Name)`	Displays `'R. Koffman'`.
`if Name > 'Daffy Duck' then`	Compares `Name` to `'Daffy Duck'`.

Construct	Effect
Declaring Multidimensional Arrays	
```type Day = (Sunday,Monday,Tuesday,Wednesday, Thursday,Friday,Saturday); Matrix = array [1..52, Day] of Real; var Sales : Matrix;```	`Matrix` describes a two-dimensional array with 52 rows and 7 columns (days of the week). `Sales` is an array of this type and can store 364 real numbers.
Multidimensional Array References	
`Write (Sales[3, Monday])`	Displays the element of `Sales` for day `Monday` of week 3.
```for Week := 1 to 52 do for Today := Sunday to Saturday do Sales[Week, Today] := 0.0```	Initializes each element of `Sales` to 0.
`ReadLn (Sales[1, Sunday])`	Reads the value for the first `Sunday` into `Sales`.

Quick-Check Exercises

1. When can the assignment and relational operators be used with array operands?
2. Can you store a string of length five in the variable declared below using an assignment statement? If not, why not?

   ```
   var
      AString : packed array [6..10] of Char;
   ```

3. Declare variables `First` and `Last` that may be used to store a person's first name and last name (maximum of 20 characters each) into separate strings. How would you read a data string into `First` or `Last`?
4. What are the three modes of access for a two-dimensional array?
5. What is the difference between row-major and column-major order? Which does Pascal use?
6. Write the type declaration for an array that stores the current worm population in a stack of worm boxes. The boxes are arranged in a rectangular pallet of 10 boxes × 7 boxes and there are 5 pallets in a stack.
7. Write a program segment to display the sum of the values (type `Real`) in each column of a two-dimensional array `Table` with data type `array [1..5, 1..3] of Real`. How many column sums will be displayed? How many elements are included in each sum?
8. Write the type declaration for an array that stores the batting averages by position (`Catcher`, `Pitcher`, `FirstBase`, etc.) for each of 10 baseball teams in two leagues (`American` and `National`).

Answers to Quick-Check Exercises

1. The assignment operator can be used with two arrays of the same type. Relational operators can be used with two packed arrays of characters with a subscript type of the form `1..N`.
2. No, subscript type must be the subrange type `1..5`.
3.  ```
    type
        AString = packed array [1..20] of Char;

    var
        First, Last : AString;
    ```
    Use procedure `ReadLnString` or a loop with a `Read` operation to read data into `First` or `Last`.
4. Random access, row-by-row access, column-by-column access
5. In row-major order, the first row of the array is placed at the beginning of the memory area allocated to the array. It is followed by the second row, and so on. In column-major order, the first column is placed at the beginning of the array memory area. Pascal uses row-major order.
6.  ```
    type
        LengthRange = 1..10;
        WidthRange = 1..7;
        StackRange = 1..5;
        WormStack = array [LengthRange, WidthRange, StackRange]
                              of Integer;
    ```
7.  ```
    for Column := 1 to 3 do
        begin
            ColumnSum := 0.0;
            for Row := 1 to 5 do
                ColumnSum := ColumnSum + Table[Row, Column];
            WriteLn ('Sum for column ', Column :1, ' is ',
                        ColumnSum :3:2)
        end {for Column}
    ```
    Three column sums; five elements added per column
8.  ```
    type
        League = (American, National);
        Team = 1..10;
        Position = (Pitcher, Catcher, FirstBase,
                    SecondBase, ThirdBase, ShortStop,
                    LeftField, CenterField, RightField);
        BAArray = array [League, Team, Position] of Real;
    ```

Review Questions

1. List three advantages of using packed arrays of characters.
2. Declare an array that can be used to store each title of the `Top40` hits for each week of the year given that the `TitleLength` will be 20 characters.
3. Write the declaration of the array `YearlyHours` to store the hours each of five employees works each day of the week, each week of the year.
4. Write a procedure to compute and display the total number of hours worked by each employee on a specified day (an input parameter).

5. Write a procedure to compute and display the total number of hours worked by a given employee (an input parameter).

6. Write the declarations for the array `CPUArray` that will hold 20 elements of type `CPU` where `CPU` is an array type that contains storage for five real items.

Programming Projects

Directory: CHAP11
File: PROJ2.PAS

1. Write a set of procedures to manipulate a pair of matrices. Provide procedures for addition, subtraction, and multiplication. Each procedure should validate its input parameters (i.e., check all matrix dimensions) before performing the required data manipulation.

2. Write a program that uses a two-dimensional array to store election results. The program should call the following procedures. Parameter `Tally` stores the election results.

Procedure `Initialize (var Tally)`: Reads in the number of precincts (up to 10) and the letter (up to J) corresponding to the last candidate; initializes all vote totals to zero.

Procedure `ReadTally (var Tally)`: Reads in the votes by precinct for each candidate.

Procedure `WriteTable (Tally)`: Displays the election results in the form shown.

Procedure `CountBallot (var Tally)`: Determines the count of votes received by each candidate and the corresponding percentage of the total votes cast.

Procedure `FindWinner (Tally, var Cand1, var Cand2, var Over50)`: Determines the letters of the highest-scoring candidate (`Cand1`) and the second-highest-scoring candidate (`Cand2`) and sets `Over50` to `True` if the highest scoring candidate receives more than 50% of the vote.

Procedure `DisplayWinner (Cand1, Cand2, Over50)`: Displays the name of `Cand1` and the message `Won the election` if `Over50` is true; otherwise, displays the message `Runoff election between 2 highest-scoring candidates` and `Cand1` and `Cand2`.

Write a main program that calls these procedures, and run the program for the data in the following table and also when candidate C receives only 108 votes in precinct 4.

Precinct	Candidate A	Candidate B	Candidate C	Candidate D
1	192	48	206	37
2	147	90	312	21
3	186	12	121	38
4	114	21	408	39
5	267	13	382	29

3. Modify Programming Project 2 to make it an interactive menu-driven program. Menu options should include initializing the vote table (prompt the user for the

number of candidates, their names, and the number of precincts), displaying the vote table with row and column totals, displaying the precinct totals, displaying the candidates' names and votes received (raw count and percentage of votes cast), displaying winner's name (or names in the event of a tie), and exiting the program.

4. For the sales analysis problem (see Section 11.4) provide these procedures:

   `EditData (var Sales)`: Prompts the user to determine the person, quarter, and new amount for a sales entry to be changed and then changes that entry.

   `SaveTable (Sales)`: Stores the table values in an output file. Writes each table entry in the same format as sales transactions in the data file.

   Add these options to the program and test them. Change the main program so that it is a menu-driven program.

5. The Queen in the game of chess can move horizontally, vertically, or diagonally on an 8 × 8 board. Write a program that displays a chess board as characters. The squares of the chess board are displayed as one of the following letters: E for an empty and available square, Q if the square now contains a queen and X if the location is protected by a queen already on the board. The board starts with all locations empty. The user can place Queens by supplying a row and column location that contains an E. The program ends when there are no E squares left. Try to see how many Queens you can place on the board. It is possible to place 8.

INTERVIEW

▼

Patrick H. Winston

Patrick H. Winston is a professor of computer science at the Massachusetts Institute of Technology and director of the interdepartmental Artificial Intelligence Laboratory there. He is also author of Artificial Intelligence *and co-author of* Lisp, *two of the most widely used texts on these subjects. He is currently involved in the study of learning, precedent-based reasoning, common-sense problem solving, problem solving via abstraction, and applications of artificial intelligence (AI) to database mining, scheduling, and dynamic resource allocation.*

▼ **People often seem confused about what artificial intelligence is and is not. In your text, *Artificial Intelligence*, you define the goals of AI as "[attempting] to make computers more useful [and] to understand the principles that make intelligence possible." Has your thinking about the goals of AI changed since that was written nine years or so ago?**

▲ I would say my sense of the goals of AI is more precise perhaps, but not fundamentally changed. Now I tend to say that the engineering goal of artificial intelligence is to solve real-world problems using artificial intelligence as an armamentarium of ideas about representing knowledge, using knowledge, and assembling systems. The scientific goal, on the other hand, is to determine which ideas about representing knowledge, using knowledge, and assembling systems account for various sorts of intelligence.

▼ **Of all the choices you could have made, why did you choose AI? What influenced you most in that decision?**

▲ Well, I have always wanted to understand what thinking is all about. When I was a graduate student, I looked for answers, as many do, by taking subjects offered in psychology and neuroanatomy. But even though I learned a lot, I felt that something was missing. Luckily, that was about the time I heard that the students of Marvin Minsky and Seymour Papert were not only trying to understand intelligence, they were trying to *produce* it. I resolved instantly to be one of those students. And when I did, I learned that what was missing was the idea that you can study the computations that make intelligence possible without concerning yourself too much with the particular computer that happens to be performing those computations, be it natural or made of silicon.

▼ **What comes to mind when you think of the major achievements in AI over the past decade? Who do you think has benefited the most from the accomplishments of AI?**

▲ Lots. Especially in the last half of the decade, which has been especially exciting because so much conventional wisdom has been overturned. For example, we now know that the memory required to do visual recognition need not involve any explicit three-dimensional models—an idea that used to seem ridiculous 10 years ago. But this is just one example; similar stories can be told for just about every subfield of AI. I've taken to telling my students that the exams stay the same from year to year, but all the answers change.

▼ **One sometimes hears of the MIT or Carnegie-Mellon or some other institutional view of artificial intelligence, suggesting that several views of AI are extant. Do you think such diversity of viewpoints exists in the field, and if so do you think it's healthy?**

▲ Certainly there are lots of approaches, and many are championed by advocates with almost religious zeal. And on the whole, this is a good thing because AI, like most fields, benefits from diverse ideas and excited people. And besides, any adequate account of intelligence, from a computational point of view, is unlikely to rest on just a few elegant laws like electromagnetism rests on Maxwell's equations. There is room for lots of approaches to be right with respect to some part of the total picture.

▼ What significant achievements can we look forward to in AI in the 1990s?

▲ Making predictions in AI is always dangerous because there are critics who take failure to meet some claimed objective at a predicted time to mean *never* instead of *not yet*. Also, we still need breakthroughs in AI, and it is hard to predict when someone will have a breakthrough idea. But if you force me, nevertheless, to hazard something, I would claim that the results of the past few years suggest that the next decade will be the decade of learning. Ten years from now, we will know a great deal about how to learn using a combination of already known facts and a little observation, and conversely, we will know a great deal about how to dig regularities out of lots of data with no background knowledge. Some of this is bound to change the world, at least in a minor way, and maybe in a major way, especially if the technolgy can be harnessed, for example, to individually tailored product marketing or to, say, pharmaceutical development.

CHAPTER TWELVE

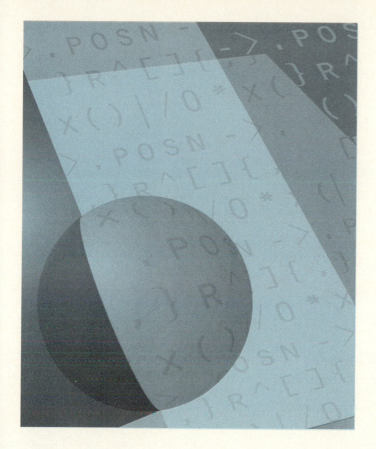

Records

We introduce a new structured data type in this chapter: records. Like arrays, records are composed of related data items, but, unlike arrays, record components can contain data of different types. We could use a record to store various items of information about a person: name, address, year of birth, and gender, for example. We could not save this information in an array because name and address would be strings, year of birth would be an integer, and gender would be a character.

Finally, we can use arrays whose elements are records and records whose components are other records to represent more complex organizations of information.

12.1   **The Record Data Type**

Although arrays are useful as data structures that can collect related data, they are limited because all the data they store must be of the same type. Many programming problems can be easily solved if we are able to organize related data having different data types. With the **record** data structure, we can store related data of different types in a single data structure. In this section, we show how to declare and process records.

Declaring Record Types

To keep organized, accessible information about her staff members, the manager of a software firm wants to save the information like the following about each employee:

```
ID: 1234
Name: Caryn Jackson
Gender: F
Number of Dependents: 2
Hourly Rate: 6.00
Total Wages: 240.00
```

We can store this information in a record with six data elements. The **record data type** is a template that describes the format of each record including the name and type of each data element, or record **field.** To store the preceding information, we can use the record type `Employee` shown next with two integer fields, a string field, a character field (for gender), and two real fields:

```
const
   StringLength = 13;

type
   StringIndex = 1..StringLength;
   IDRange = 1111..9999;
   StringType = packed array [StringIndex] of Char;

   Employee = record
               ID : IDRange;
               Name : StringType;
               Gender : Char;
               NumDepend : Integer;
               Rate, TotWages : Real
             end; {Employee}
```

The type declaration for record `Employee` is bracketed by the words `record` and `end`. Each field description consists of the field name (a Pascal identifier) followed by the field data type. A colon separates the field name from the data type. The field data type can be a standard data type (`Char`, `Integer`, `Real`), a user-defined simple type (`IDRange`), or a structured data type (`StringType`).

A variable declaration is required to allocate storage space for a record. The record variable `Clerk` (see Fig. 12.1) is declared:

```
var
  Clerk : Employee;
```

The record variable `Clerk` has the structure specified in the declaration for record type `Employee`. Thus the memory allocated consists of storage space for six distinct values.

As with other identifiers in Pascal programs, field names should describe the information to be stored and the data type should be appropriate for that kind of information. For example, record type `Employee` uses a string field for storage of an employee's name.

SYNTAX DISPLAY

Record Type Declaration

Form:
```
type
    rec type = record
                      id list₁  :  type₁;
                      id list₂  :  type₂;
                          . . .
                      id listₙ  :  typeₙ
                end;
```
Example:
```
type
      Complex = record
                      RealPart, ImaginaryPart : Real
                end;
```

Interpretation: The identifier *rec type* is the name of the record structure being described. Each *id list$_i$* is a list of one or more field names separated by commas; the data type of each field in *id list$_i$* is specified by *type$_i$*.

Notes: Field names must be unique within a record type. Each *type$_i$* can be any standard or user-defined data type, including a structured type. If *type$_i$* is a user-defined data type, it can be defined either before the record or as part of the record description.

Figure 12.1
Record Variable Clerk

Accessing Record Fields

We can access a field in a record by using a *field selector,* which consists of
the record variable name followed by the field name. A period separates the
record name from the field name:

record-variable . field-name

EXAMPLE 12.1 ▼

The following statements store data in the record variable Clerk. Figure 12.1
shows the contents of Clerk after these statements execute.

```
Clerk.ID := 1234;                    {Store 1234 in ID field.}
Clerk.Name := 'Caryn Jackson';  {Store string in Name field.}
Clerk.Gender := 'F';                 {Store F in Gender field.}
Clerk.NumDepend := 2;                {Store 2 in NumDepend field.}
Clerk.Rate := 6.00;                  {Store 6.00 in Rate field.}
Clerk.TotWages := 0.0;               {Initialize TotWages field.}
Clerk.TotWages := Clerk.TotWages + 40.0 * Clerk.Rate
```

Once data are stored in a record, they can be manipulated in the same
way as other data in memory. For example, the last assignment in our example computes the clerk's new total wages by adding this week's wages to her
previous total wages (0.0 in this case). The computed result is saved in the
record field Clerk.TotWages.

The statements

```
Write ('The clerk is ');
case Clerk.Gender of
  'F', 'f' : Write ('Ms. ');
  'M', 'm' : Write ('Mr. ')
end; {case}
Write (Clerk.Name)
```

display the clerk's name after an appropriate title ('Ms. ' or 'Mr. '); the
output line follows:

```
The clerk is Ms. Caryn Jackson
```
▲

Arrays as Record Fields

The Name field of record Clerk is a string, which is really a packed array of
characters:

Clerk.Name `Caryn Jackson`

We can reference individual characters in an array field by writing the field
selector followed by a subscript enclosed in brackets:

```
Record
variable    Field
   ↓
Clerk.Name[I]
   ↗        ↑
 String   Subscript
 variable
```

The `for` loop that follows accesses each character, from the first (C) to the last (n):

```
Write ('The clerk''s initials are: ');
for I := 1 to StringLength do
  if (Clerk.Name[I] >= 'A') and (Clerk.Name[I] <= 'Z') then
    Write (Clerk.Name[I]);
WriteLn
```

The `if` statement condition is true if `Clerk.Name[I]` is an uppercase letter, so the program fragment displays the output line

```
The clerk's initials are: CJ
```

Exercises for Section 12.1   **Self-Check**

1. Each part in an inventory is represented by its part number, a descriptive name, the quantity on hand, and the price. Define a record type `Part`.
2. A computer graphics program computes the intensity of *pixels* (picture elements) on the screen. Define a record type `Pixel` for this program that will represent a pixel, where each pixel has an integer *X* and *Y* location, and real valued intensities for colors red, green, and blue.

12.2   Records as Operands and Parameters

In addition to accessing individual record fields to perform arithmetic operations, logical operations, or input or output operations, programmers often need to write procedures that process entire records. Usually it is more convenient to pass the record itself as a procedure parameter rather than to pass the individual fields. Programmers also need to copy the contents of one record variable to another. This section describes operations on entire records.

Record Copy or Assignment

We can copy all the fields of one record variable to another record variable of the same type with a record copy (assignment) statement. To illustrate, if `Clerk` and `Janitor` are both record variables of type `Employee`, the statement

```
Clerk := Janitor       {copy Janitor to Clerk}
```

copies each field of `Janitor` into the corresponding field of `Clerk`.

Records as Parameters

A record can be passed as a parameter to a function or a procedure, provided the actual parameter is the same type as its corresponding formal parameter. The use of records as parameters can shorten parameter lists considerably, because one parameter (the record variable) can be passed instead of several related parameters.

You can't use Pascal's input procedures to read data from the keyboard or a text file into an entire record. Similarly, you can't use Pascal's output procedures to write the contents of an entire record to the screen or a text file. You will need to code your own procedures to perform these common operations, as we show in Examples 12.2 and 12.3. Each procedure has a single parameter: the record to be read or written.

EXAMPLE 12.2: Reading a Record ▼

Procedure `ReadEmployee` in Fig. 12.2 reads data into all fields of a record variable of type `Employee`. The procedure call statement

```
ReadEmployee (Clerk)
```

causes the data read to be stored in record variable `Clerk`.   ▲

Figure 12.2
Procedure ReadEmployee

Directory: CHAP12
File: READEMPL.PAS

```
procedure ReadEmployee (var AnEmp {output} : Employee);
{
  Reads one employee record into AnEmp.
  Pre  : None.
  Post : Data are read into record AnEmp.
  Calls: procedure ReadLnString (Fig. 11.1)
}
  var
    NameLen: Integer;       {length of Name read}
begin {ReadEmployee}
  Write ('ID> ');
  ReadLn (AnEmp.ID);
  Write ('Name> ');
  ReadLnString (Input, AnEmp.Name, NameLen);
  Write ('Gender (F or M)> ');
  ReadLn (AnEmp.Gender);
  Write ('Number of dependents> ');
  ReadLn (AnEmp.NumDepend);
  Write ('Hourly rate> ');
  ReadLn (AnEmp.Rate);
  Write ('Total wages to date> ');
  ReadLn (AnEmp.TotWages)
end; {ReadEmployee}
```

EXAMPLE 12.3: Writing a Record ▼

In a grading program, the summary statistics for an exam are the average score, the highest and lowest scores, and the standard deviation. Previously we would have stored these data in separate variables, but now we are able to group them together as a record:

```
type
   ScoreRange = 0..100;
   ExamStats = record
                  Low, High : ScoreRange;
                  Average, StandardDev : Real
               end; {ExamStats}
```

Procedure `PrintStat` (Fig. 12.3) displays the value stored in each field of its record parameter (type `ExamStats`). ▲

Exercises for Section 12.2   **Self-Check**

1. What does the following fragment do? Provide the declarations for variables `Exam1` and `Exam2`.

    ```
    PrintStat (Exam1);
    Exam2 := Exam1;
    Exam2.High := Exam2.High - 5.0;
    PrintStat (Exam2)
    ```

2. Which of the following are incorrect and why for `Exam1` and `Exam2` from Exercise 1? Correct each invalid statement.
    a. `var Exam1, Exam 2 : Exam;`
    b. `Exam1 := Exam2`
    c. `ReadLn (Exam1.Average)`
    d. `Exam1.High := Exam2`

Figure 12.3
Procedure PrintStat

Directory: CHAP12
File: PRINTSTA.PAS

```
procedure PrintStat (Exam {input} : ExamStats);
{
   Prints the exam statistics.
   Pre : The fields of record parameter Exam are assigned
         values.
   Post: Each field of Exam is displayed.
}
begin {PrintStat}
   WriteLn ('High score: ', Exam.High :1);
   WriteLn ('Low score: ', Exam.Low :1);
   WriteLn ('Average: ', Exam.Average :3:1);
   WriteLn ('Standard deviation: ', Exam.StandardDev :3:1)
end; {PrintStat}
```

    e.   `Exam2.Low := Exam1.High`
    f.   `Exam2.Low := Exam1.Average`
    g.   `WriteLn (Exam1)`

Programming

1.   Write a procedure that reads in the data for a pixel and returns the data through its parameter. See Self-Check Exercise 2 for Section 12.1.

12.3 The with Statement

Writing the complete field selector each time you reference a field of a record is tedious business. Instead, you can use the `with` statement to shorten the field selector. This `with` statement processes the record variable `Clerk` shown in Fig. 12.1:

```
with Clerk do
  begin
    Write ('The clerk is ');
    case Gender of
      'F', 'f' : Write ('Ms. ');
      'M', 'm' : Write ('Mr. ')
    end; {case}
    WriteLn (Name);

    TotWages := TotWages + 40.0 * Rate;
    WriteLn ('The clerk''s total wages are $', TotWages :4:2)
  end; {with}
```

As you can see, you needn't specify both the record variable and the field names inside a `with` statement. Because the record variable `Clerk` is identified in the `with` statement header, only the field name is needed, not the complete field selector (e.g., `Rate` instead of `Clerk.Rate`). The `with` statement is particularly useful when you are manipulating several fields of the same record variable.

SYNTAX DISPLAY

with Statement

Form: `with` *record var* `do`
          statement
Example: `with Clerk do`
          `if NumDepend > 3 then`
             `Rate := 1.5 * Rate`
Interpretation: *statement* can be a single statement or a compound statement. *record var* is the name of a *record* variable. Anywhere within *statement*, you can reference a field of *record var* by specifying only its field name.

EXAMPLE 12.4 ▼

Many programs need to keep track of the time of day, and normally do so by updating the time of day after a certain period has elapsed. The record type Time is declared as follows, assuming a 24-hour clock:

```
type
   Time = record
            Hour : 0..23;
            Minute, Second : 0..59
          end; {Time}
```

Procedure ChangeTime in Fig. 12.4 updates the time of day, TimeOfDay (type Time), after a time interval, ElapsedTime, which is expressed in seconds. Each statement that uses the mod operator updates a particular field of the record represented by TimeOfDay. The mod operator ensures that each updated value is within the required range; the div operator converts multiples of 60 seconds to minutes and multiples of 60 minutes to hours.

Using the with statement simplifies writing procedure ChangeTime. Without it, the first assignment statement would be coded as

```
NewSec := TimeOfDay.Second + ElapsedTime;   {total seconds}   ▲
```

Figure 12.4
Procedure ChangeTime

Directory: CHAP12
File: CHANGETI.PAS

```
procedure ChangeTime (ElapsedTime {input} : Integer;
                      var TimeOfDay {input/output} : Time);
{
  Updates the time of day, TimeOfDay, assuming a 24-hour clock
  and an elapsed time of ElapsedTime in seconds.
  Pre : ElapsedTime and record TimeOfDay are assigned
        values.
  Post: TimeOfDay is incremented by ElapsedTime.
}

  var
     NewHour, NewMin, NewSec : Integer; {temporary variables}

begin {ChangeTime}
   with TimeOfDay do
      begin
         NewSec := Second + ElapsedTime;       {total seconds}
         Second := NewSec mod 60;              {seconds over 60}
         NewMin := Minute + (NewSec div 60);   {total minutes}
         Minute := NewMin mod 60;              {minutes over 60}
         NewHour := Hour + (NewMin div 60);    {total hours}
         Hour := NewHour mod 24                {hours over 24}
      end {with}
end;   {ChangeTime}
```

Program Style

A Word of Caution About the with Statement

Although the `with` statement is helpful in reducing the length of program statements that manipulate record components, it also can reduce the clarity of those statements. For example, in the preceding assignment statement, the field selector `TimeOfDay.Second` shows clearly that `Second` is a field of record parameter `TimeOfDay`. This role is not documented as clearly in the statement

```
NewSec := Second + ElapsedTime;    {total seconds}
```

used in procedure `ChangeTime`.

Exercises for Section 12.3 **Self-Check**

1. If a procedure declared a local variable with name `Second`, how would the use of `with` be restricted if a variable of type `Time` were also declared?
2. If all fields of variable `Now` (type `Time`) are initially 0, how is `Now` changed by the execution of the following fragment?

```
ChangeTime (3600, Now);
ChangeTime (7125, Now)
```

Programming

1. Write a procedure that initializes all fields of a variable of type `Time` to 0.
2. Write a function that accepts a parameter of type `Time` and computes the equivalent time in seconds. Return the result as a real number. (Why?)

12.4 Arrays of Records

Arrays and records are two basic data structures in Pascal. Just as we use the basic program modules, procedures and functions, as building blocks of larger programs, we can use these basic data structures to model more complicated organizations of data.

Storing a Database as an Array of Records

database

a collection of facts or information about related items usually organized as a file or table of records

One common method of organizing data in real life is to build a **database**, a collection of facts or information about related items. A hospital, for example, might maintain a database of employees, a database of patients, and a database of prescription drugs. We could use a record to represent each item in a database, and we could use an array of records to store each database in memory. Often we read a database from a disk file before we access it and we write a database out to disk when we are finished updating it.

A simple example of a database is a collection of student records for a class. For each student, we might want to store the student's name, three exam scores, the average score, and the student's grade. We can store the information for each student in a record of type `Student`. The data structure declared next stores the class data in an array of student records. Array `Class` is shown in Fig. 12.5.

```
const
    MaxClass = 200;
    StringLength = 20;
    NumberExams = 3;

type
    ClassIndex = 1..MaxClass;
    StringIndex = 1..StringLength;
    ExamIndex = 1..NumberExams;
    StringType = packed array [StringIndex] of Char;
    ScoreArray = array [ExamIndex] of Integer;
    Student = record
                    Name : StringType;
```

Figure 12.5
Array of Records

```
                   Scores : ScoreArray;
                   Average : Real;
                   Grade : Char
                 end; {Student}

    StudentArray = array [ClassIndex] of Student;

var
  Class : StudentArray;
```

In Fig. 12.5, the data for the first student are stored in record `Class[1]`. The individual data items are `Class[1].Name`, `Class[1].Scores[1]`, `Class[1].Scores[2]`, `Class[1].Scores[3]`, `Class[1].Average` and `Class[1].Grade`. Notice that two subscripts are needed to access an exam score. The first subscript selects an element of array `Class`; the second subscript selects an element of the `Scores` array. As shown, `Class[1].Scores[1]` is 90.

EXAMPLE 12.5 ▼

Procedure `ReadClass` (Fig. 12.6) reads data into the array of student records. The procedure returns two results: the array of student data and the number of student records stored. The `for` statement

```
for I := 1 to ClassSize do
  ReadStudent (Class[I])
```

Figure 12.6
Procedure ReadClass

Directory: CHAP12
File: READCLAS.PAS

```
procedure ReadClass (var Class {output} : StudentArray;
                     var ClassSize {output} : Integer);
{Returns the number of students in the class through
 ClassSize. Fills the subarray Class[1..ClassSize] with
 student data.
 Pre  : None
 Post : 1 <= ClassSize <= MaxClass and Class[I] contains
        the input data for the Ith student.
 Calls: EnterInt (Fig. 9.2) and ReadStudent
}
  var
    I : Integer;           {loop control and array subscript}

begin {ReadClass}
  WriteLn ('Enter number of students:');
  EnterInt (1, MaxClass, ClassSize);

  {Read the student data.}
  WriteLn ('Enter each student''s data:');
  for I := 1 to ClassSize do
    ReadStudent (Class[I])
end; {ReadClass}
```

fills the array `Class`. Each time `ReadStudent` (see Programming Exercise 1 at the end of this section) is called, the record returned (type `Student`) will be stored as the Ith element (1 ≤ I ≤ `ClassSize`) of array `Class`. The details of reading each record are left to procedure `ReadStudent`.   ▲

Using the with Statement with an Array of Records

Be careful when you use a `with` statement to process an array of records. For example, the `with` statement that begins

```
with Class[I] do
```

uses the subscripted variable `Class[I]` as its record variable. The particular array element referenced depends on the value of I. If I is undefined or is out of range, a run-time error will result.

If I is updated inside the `with` statement, the array element referenced will not change. For example, the following statements display the first student's name `MaxClass` times. Because I is 1 when the `with` statement is reached, `Class[1]` is the record referenced in the `with` statement body. Even though the `for` loop changes the value of I, `Class[1]` is still the record referenced, so `Class[1].Name` will be displayed repeatedly.

```
I := 1;
{incorrect attempt to display all student names}
with Class[I] do
  for I := 1 to ClassSize do
    WriteLn (Name)
```

The correct way to sequence these statements is

```
{Display all student names.}
for I := 1 to ClassSize do
  with Class[I] do
    WriteLn (Name)
```

Now all student names will be printed, because I is changed by the `for` statement external to the `with` statement. Each time the `with` statement is reached, it references a new record. Whenever a `for` statement accesses an array of records in sequential order, the `with` statement should be nested inside the `for` statement, not vice versa.

Effect of Data Structures on Program Design

The data structure chosen for a problem can have a significant effect on program design. When you code procedures that process the class data, take advantage of the fact that each student's data are stored in a separate record and use procedures associated with that record type. For example, procedure `ReadClass` calls procedure `ReadStudent` to read each student record. Often you will find that procedures like `ReadStudent` will already be coded. This choice of data structure simplifies coding `ReadClass`.

An alternative for storing the student data would be to use four separate arrays: one array with MaxClass elements could store all the student names, a two-dimensional array (MaxClass × 3) could store the exam scores, and two more arrays with MaxClass elements could store the average score and semester grade for each student. The Ith student's data would be stored in row I of all four arrays (see Fig. 12.7).

Although we will not go into detail on how to process these arrays, it should be clear that procedure ReadClass would be much more complicated. Instead of filling one array of records, it would need to read data into four separate arrays, one with two dimensions.

Another possibility for storing the class data would be to combine the student information with information about the class as a whole in a single record. Record type GradeBook declared next has three fields: ClassID for storing the class identification (a string), ClassSize for storing the class size, and Class for storing the student data. Figure 12.8 sketches record variable MyClass (type GradeBook).

```
type
    {Insert declarations for StringType and StudentArray.}
    GradeBook = record
                ClassID : StringType;
                ClassSize : Integer;
                Class : StudentArray
            end; {GradeBook}

var
    MyClass : GradeBook;        {a grade book page}
```

You can store all the information for a class in one record variable (e.g., MyClass) of type GradeBook. Use MyClass.ClassID to access the class

Figure 12.7
Four Arrays for
Student Data

Figure 12.8
Record Variable MyClass

identification, `MyClass.ClassSize` to access the number of students, `MyClass.Class[I]` to access the Ith student record, `MyClass.Class [I].Name` to access that student's `Name`, and `MyClass.Class[I].Score[1]` to access that student's first exam score.

You can rewrite procedure `ReadClass` to read the class identification, class size, and student data into a record of this type (see Programming Exercise 2 at the end of this section). The new procedure would have just one parameter because all information about the class would be read into different fields of the same record. Example 12.6 shows how to sort the array field `Class` so its records are in alphabetical order by student name.

EXAMPLE 12.6 ▼

Procedure `SortStudents` (Fig. 12.9) sorts the class array so that all student data are in sequence by student name. Compare it to procedure `SelectSort` shown in Fig. 10.20.

Procedure `SwitchStu` exchanges the student records at positions `Fill` and `IndexOfMin` of array field `Class`. Notice that `SwitchStu` uses three record copy statements to exchange all student data, not just the student names.

Function `FindMinName` (see Programming Exercise 3 at the end of this section) returns the position of the student record with the alphabetically smallest name in the subarray `Class[Fill..ClassSize]`. The array field `Class` is the first function argument and it should correspond to a formal parameter of type `StudentArray`. ▲

Figure 12.9
Procedures SwitchStu and
SortStudents

Directory: CHAP12
File: SORTSTUD.PAS

```
procedure SwitchStu (var Stu1, Stu2 {input/output} : Student);
{Switches the values stored in Stu1 and Stu2.}
   var
      TempStu : Student;              {temporary student record}

begin {SwitchStu}
   TempStu := Stu1;       Stu1 := Stu2;       Stu2 := TempStu
end; {SwitchStu}

procedure SortStudents (var MyClass {input/output} :
                                          GradeBook);

{
 Sorts the data in array field Class of record MyClass.
 Pre : The record MyClass is defined and the filled
        subarray is MyClass.Class[1..MyClass.ClassSize].
 Post: The records in MyClass.Class[1..MyClass.ClassSize] are
        in alphabetical order by student name.
 Calls: Procedures SwitchStu and FindMinName.
}
   var
      Fill,                     {index of element to be filled next}
      IndexOfMin : Integer;     {index of next smallest element}

begin {SortStudents}
   with MyClass do
      for Fill := 1 to ClassSize - 1 do
         begin
            {invariant:
                The records in MyClass.Class[1..Fill-1] are in
                their proper place and Fill <= MyClass.ClassSize.
            }
            {Find position of student with smallest name.}
            IndexOfMin := FindMinName(Class, Fill, ClassSize);

            {Exchange students at positions Fill and IndexOfMin.}
            if IndexOfMin <> Fill then
               SwitchStu (Class[IndexOfMin], Class[Fill])
         end {for and with}
end; {SortStudents}
```

Exercises for Section 12.4   *Self-Check*

1.   For the array of records Class (see Fig. 12.5), what value is displayed by each valid statement? Correct the invalid statements.
   a.   WriteLn (Class[1].Name[4])
   b.   WriteLn (Class[1].Score[4])
   c.   WriteLn (Class.Grade[3])
   d.   WriteLn (Class[1].Name)
   e.   WriteLn (Class[1].Name[4].Grade)

```
f.  WriteLn (Class[1].Grade)
g.  WriteLn (Class[1])
h.  WriteLn (Class.Name[4])
```

Programming

1. Write procedure ReadStudent. Read each student's name and score; leave the grade field undefined.
2. Write a modified procedure ReadClass to read all class data into a record of type GradeBook. Assume that the number of records and class identification are data items and are returned as procedure results along with the student array.
3. Write function FindMinName (see Fig. 10.17).

12.5 **Hierarchical Records**

hierarchical record

a record with one or more record fields

In addition to constructing arrays with record components, it is possible to declare a record type with fields that are other record types. A record with one or more fields that are record types is a **hierarchical record.**

In this section, we modify record type Employee by adding new fields for storage of the employee's address, starting date, and date of birth. The record type NewEmployee is declared in Fig. 12.10, along with two additional record types, Date and Address. Programmer is a record variable of type NewEmployee. The hierarchical structure of this record variable is shown in Fig. 12.11. This diagram provides a graphic display of the record form.

Figure 12.10
Declaration of a
Hierarchical Record

Directory: CHAP12
File: READNEWE.PAS

```
const
    StringLength = 14; {length of all strings except zipcode}
    ZipStringSize = 5; {length of zipcode string}

type
    IDRange = 1111..9999;
    StringIndex = 1..StringLength;
    ZipIndex = 1..ZipStringSize;
    StringType = packed array [StringIndex] of Char;
    ZipString = packed array [ZipIndex] of Char;
    Month = (January, February, March, April, May, June, July,
             August, September, October, November, December);

    Employee = record
                  ID : IDRange;
                  Name : StringType;
                  Gender : Char;
                  NumDepend : Integer;
                  Rate, TotWages : Real
               end; {Employee}
```

▷ ▷ ▷ ▷ ▷

```
Address = record
            Street, City, State : StringType;
            ZipCode : ZipString
          end; {Address}

Date = record
         ThisMonth : Month;
         Day : 1..31;
         Year : 1900..1999
       end; {Date}

NewEmployee = record
                PayData : Employee;
                Home : Address;
                StartDate, BirthDate : Date
              end; {NewEmployee}
```

```
var
  Programmer : NewEmployee;
```

△

Record `Programmer` has fields `PayData`, `Home`, `StartDate`, and `Birth-Date`. Each of these fields is itself a record (called a *subrecord* of `Programmer`). The fields of each subrecord are indicated under that subrecord.

To reference a field in this diagram, we must trace a complete path to it starting from the top of the diagram. For example, the field selector

`Programmer.StartDate`

references the subrecord `StartDate` (type `Date`) of the variable `Programmer`. The field selector

`Programmer.StartDate.Year`

references the `Year` field of the subrecord `Programmer.StartDate`. The field selector

`Programmer.Year`

is incomplete (which `Year` field?) and would cause a syntax error. The record copy statement

`Programmer.StartDate := DayOfYear`

is valid if `DayOfYear` is a record variable of type `Date`. This statement copies each field of `DayOfYear` into the corresponding field of the subrecord

`Programmer.StartDate`

In many situations we can use the `with` statement to shorten the field selector. The statement

```
with Programmer.StartDate do
  WriteLn ('Year started: ', Year:4, ', day started: ', Day:1)
```

Figure 12.11
Record Variable Programmer (Type NewEmployee)

displays two fields of the subrecord `Programmer.StartDate`. The computation for updating total wages could be written as

```
with Programmer.PayData do
   TotWages := TotWages + Rate * 40.0
```

The `with` statement

```
with Programmer do
   WriteLn (PayData.Name, ' started work in ',StartDate.Year:4)
```

displays an output line of the form

```
Caryn Jackson  started work in 1986
```

It is also possible to nest `with` statements. The following nested `with` statement also displays the preceding output line.

```
with Programmer do
   with PayData do
      with StartDate do
         WriteLn (Name, ' started work in ', Year :4)
```

The record variable name (`Programmer`) must precede the field names, as shown. The order of the field names `PayData` and `StartDate` is not important.

We can also use a list of record variable names and field names in a `with` statement. The statement

```
with Programmer, PayData, StartDate do
  WriteLn (Name, ' started work in ', Year :4)
```

is equivalent to the one just discussed.

Procedure `ReadNewEmp` in Fig. 12.12 could be used to read in a record of type `NewEmployee`. It calls procedures `ReadEmployee` (see Fig. 12.2), `ReadAddress`, and `ReadDate` (see the programming exercise at the end of this section).

Exercises for Section 12.5   **Self-Check**

1. What must be the type of `NewAddress` if the following statement is correct?

    ```
    Programmer.Home := NewAddress
    ```

2. Write Pascal statements to perform the following actions:
    a. Increase the programmer's salary by 10%.
    b. Display the city, state, and zip code of the programmer.
    c. Display the programmer's month of birth.
    d. Display the month the programmer started working.

    Programming

1. Write procedures `ReadAddress` and `ReadDate`.

Figure 12.12
Procedure ReadNewEmp

Directory: CHAP12
File: READNEWE.PAS

```
procedure ReadNewEmp (var NewEmp {output} : NewEmployee);
{
    Reads a record into record variable NewEmp.
    Pre  : None.
    Post : Reads data into all fields of record NewEmp.
    Calls: Procedures ReadEmployee (see Fig. 12.2),
           ReadAddress, and ReadDate (see programming exer-
           cise)
}
begin {ReadNewEmp}
  with NewEmp do
    begin
      ReadEmployee (PayData);
      ReadAddress (Home);
      ReadDate (StartDate);
      ReadDate (BirthDate)
    end {with}
end; {ReadNewEmp}
```

12.6   Data Abstaction and Object-Oriented Programming

Procedural abstraction is the philosophy that procedure development should separate the concern of *what* is to be achieved by a procedure from the details of *how* it is to be achieved. Using procedural abstraction, you can specify what you expect a procedure to do, then use that procedure in the design of a problem solution before you know how to implement the procedure. Applying procedural abstraction in combination with top-down design results in modular programs that are easier to read and maintain than nonmodular programs.

Data Abstraction

data abstraction
program design technique that focuses on the data objects needed by a program and the operations on those objects

In this section, we introduce another type of abstraction, data abstraction. The idea of **data abstraction** is to specify *what* data objects are needed for a problem and *what* operations must be performed on these objects without being overly concerned with *how* the data objects will be represented and stored in memory. This approach allows us to use the data objects in our programs before pinning down the details of their actual organization in memory and before implementing them. Applying data abstraction and procedural abstraction results in a set of reusable program units that serve as building blocks for future software development.

You have already practiced data abstraction—you have used the data type `Real` to represent real numbers, without knowing much about the internal representation of this data type on a computer. In fact, `Real` representations vary considerably from one computer to another. Some computers use a floating-point processor to perform real arithmetic; others use software to perform real arithmetic. The point is that you have been using real literals, variables, and operations with confidence, without knowing or even caring how they are represented.

Data abstraction enables you to make implementation decisions in stages. At the top levels of the design, you focus on how to use a data object and on what *operators* (procedures and functions) are needed; at the lower levels of design, you work out the implementation details.

instance of a data object
a variable with the same type as the data object

To use a data object in a client program, you must declare a variable of that type. A variable with the same type as a data object is called an **instance** of the object.

Information Hiding

information hiding
concealing the details of a low-level module's implementation form a higher-level module

When writing a client program that uses a data object, you are still at the top level and may not know the details of the data object's implementation. Therefore, when the client module accesses the data object, it can do so only through its operators. Concealing the details of a data object's implementation is called **information hiding.**

To see how information hiding works, let's consider how we might organize and process information to be stored in a personal telephone directory. At the very least, we would want to store each person's name and telephone number in the directory. If we assume that we have operator functions named `GetName` and `GetNumber`, we can write programs that manipulate the information in a particular entry without knowing how the person's name and number are actually stored. If `AnEntry` is an entry in our telephone directory, the function designator `GetName(AnEntry)` returns the name stored in `AnEntry` and the function designator `GetNumber(AnEntry)` returns the number stored in `AnEntry`. To the user of these functions, it makes no difference whether `AnEntry` is a record with two string fields or an array containing two string elements. The implementor, however, must know the internal organization of data type `AnEntry` before coding these functions. Both `GetName` and `GetNumber` are called **accessor operators** because they access a data object and return a value stored in that object.

accessor operator
a function or procedure that retrieves a value stored in a data object

From a software engineering viewpoint, not knowing the details of a data object's implementation is an advantage rather than a limitation. It allows the designer to modify the data object at a later date and possibly choose a more efficient method of internal representation or implementation. Because the client module accesses a data object only through its operators, the client will not have to be rewritten and may not even need to be recompiled after the data object is modified.

Encapsulation

A goal of software engineering is to write *reusable code,* which can be reused in many different applications, preferably without having to be recompiled. One method *encapsulates,* or combines, a data type together with its operators in a separate program module. In Section 9.3, we stated that the combination of a data type together with its operators is called an *abstract data type* (ADT).

Figure 12.13 illustrates an abstract data type. The data values stored in the ADT are hidden inside the oval wall. The purpose of this wall is to indicate that these data values can be accessed only by going through the ADT's operators.

specification
description of the data type and operators of an ADT

Before coding an ADT, you should write its **specification**, which provides a complete description of the data type and its operators and, therefore, contains all the information needed by a programmer who uses the ADT. In some versions of Pascal (but not in standard Pascal), you can implement each ADT as a separate program unit, saved in its own file. You can compile the ADT, creating an object file, and the linker can link the object file with other programs that use it. If you were careful to include a fairly complete set of operator procedures in the ADT, you will not need to modify or recompile the ADT before reusing it in a new application.

Figure 12.13
Diagram of an ADT

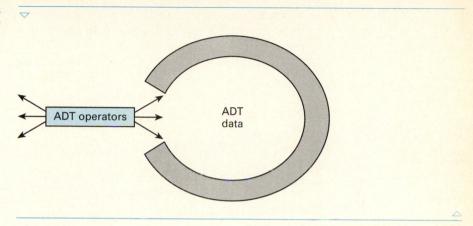

Object-Oriented Programming

Object-oriented programming (OOP) has become very popular in the past few years. One important reason for this popularity is that object-oriented programming facilitates writing reusable program modules. A second reason is the availability of objects in languages like Turbo Pascal and C++.

object
the encapsulation of data fields together with operators in a single entity

Turbo Pascal (but not standard Pascal) allows the programmer to encapsulate data fields along with operators in a single entity known as an **object**. Object types can be defined so that their data fields can only be manipulated by their operators. For this reason, objects are a natural means of implementing abstract data types.

Objects may be defined in a hierarchical manner with descendant types inheriting attributes from their ancestor types. This enables the programmer to create new objects from existing objects rather than starting from scratch.

ADT for a Telephone Directory Entry

We mentioned earlier that a telephone directory entry should contain a person's name and telephone number. We will assume that both of these data items are character strings and that each entry has a unique name whose value we use to distinguish between entries. A data object component used in this way is called a **key**. Table 12.1 provides a specification for ADT `Entry`.

key
a data object component that has a unique value for each instance of the data object

Before we write the specification (Table 12.1), we list the operators that might be required to process a directory entry.

Operators for a Directory Entry

▶ Create and define an entry.
▶ Read and store data for an entry.
▶ Display an entry.
▶ Test whether two entries have the same key value.

▶ Retrieve the name of an entry.
▶ Retrieve the phone number of an entry.

Table 12.1
Specification for ADT Entry

Structure
A telephone directory entry contains two strings representing the person's name and telephone number.

Operators
The descriptions of the operators use the following parameters:

```
AnEntry,Entry2 are type Entry
AName is a name string
ANumber is a phone number string
InFile is type Text
```

`Init (var AnEntry, AName, ANumber)` Stores `AName` and `ANumber` in an entry.

`ReadEntry (var AnEntry, var InFile)` Reads a name and phone number from file `InFile` into an entry.

`EqualTo(AnEntry, Entry2)` (function) Tests whether `AnEntry` and `Entry2` have the same key value.

`GetName(AnEntry, AName)` Returns through `AName` the name associated with an entry.

`GetNumber(AnEntry, ANumber)` Returns through `ANumber` the number associated with an entry.

`DisplayEntry (AnEntry)` Displays a name and phone number.

As shown in Table 12.1, operators `Init` and `ReadEntry` store data in a directory entry. Operator `DisplayEntry` displays an entry, and operators `GetName` and `GetNumber` retrieve the data values stored in an entry. Operator `EqualTo` determines whether two entries have the same key value.

Figure 12.14 shows the Pascal code for `EntryADT`. Data type `Entry` is a record type with two fields: `Name` and `Number`. Procedure `ReadEntry` calls

Figure 12.14
Abstract Data Type
EntryADT

Directory: CHAP12
File: ENTRYADT.PAS

```
{
 Implementation of EntryADT.
 Uses module StringADT (Fig. 11.1).

 Insert declarations for StringLength (value is 12),
 StringIndex, and StringType from StringADT.
}

  type
    Entry = record
              Name,                    {Name is key field.}
```

▷ ▷ ▷ ▷ ▷ ▷

```
            Number : StringType
          end; {Entry}

{Insert procedure ReadLnString from StringADT.}

procedure Init (var AnEntry {output} : Entry;
                    AName,
                    ANumber : StringType);
{
 Creates a directory entry with contents AName and
 ANumber.
 Pre : AName and ANumber are defined.
 Post: AName and ANumber are stored in a directory entry.
}
begin {Init}
  AnEntry.Name := AName;
  AnEntry.Number := ANumber
end; {Init}

procedure ReadEntry (var AnEntry {output} : Entry;
                         var InFile {input} : Text);
{
 Reads a name and phone number from file InFile
 into an entry. If Input is the second actual parameter,
 reads from the keyboard.
 Pre : InFile is opened.
 Post: Name and number are read into a directory entry.
 Calls: ReadLnString from StringADT
}
  var
    CurLength : Integer;  {length of string read}

begin {ReadEntry}
  ReadLnString (InFile, AnEntry.Name, CurLength);
  ReadLnString (InFile, AnEntry.Number, CurLength)
end; {ReadEntry}

procedure GetNumber (AnEntry : Entry;
                         var ANumber : StringType);
{
 Returns the phone number stored in a directory entry.
 Pre : AnEntry is defined.
 Post: Returns phone number through ANumber.
}
begin {GetNumber}
  ANumber := AnEntry.Number
end; {GetNumber}

procedure GetName (AnEntry : Entry;
                       var AName : StringType);
{
 Returns the name stored in a directory entry.
 Pre : AnEntry is defined.
```

▷ ▷ ▷ ▷ ▷ ▷

```
   Post: Returns name through AName.
}
begin {GetName}
  AName := AnEntry.Name
end; {GetName}

function EqualTo (AnEntry, Entry2 : Entry) : Boolean;
{
 Determines whether AnEntry and Entry2 have the same key.
 Pre : AnEntry and Entry2 are defined.
 Post: Returns True if keys are equal;
       otherwise, returns False.
}
begin {EqualTo}
  EqualTo := (AnEntry.Name = Entry2.Name)
end; {EqualTo}

procedure DisplayEntry (AnEntry {input} : Entry);
{
 Displays the contents of a directory entry.
 Pre : AnEntry is defined.
 Post: Name and number are displayed.
}
begin {DisplayEntry}
  WriteLn (AnEntry.Name);
  WriteLn (AnEntry.Number)
end; {DisplayEntry}
```

△

ReadLnString (from StringADT) to read two data strings from a text file (parameter InFile). If InFile corresponds to Input, ReadEntry reads data from the keyboard.

Figure 12.15 diagrams EntryADT. As with any ADT, a client module should access the data fields only through the operators listed on the left.

Using EntryADT

Figure 12.16 shows a small driver program that tests EntryADT. First, the program creates an empty directory entry (MyEntry) and then it reads and stores data into that entry. Next, it reads a name (NewName) and displays the telephone number (MyNumber) if that name was stored; otherwise, it displays a Not listed message. Finally, it displays the directory entry.

Program Style

Use of Init

We call procedure Init to create an empty directory entry before calling ReadEntry to read data into that entry. Although we needn't call Init first, we usually follow the convention of creating an instance of a data object before referencing that instance.

Figure 12.15
Sketch of EntryADT

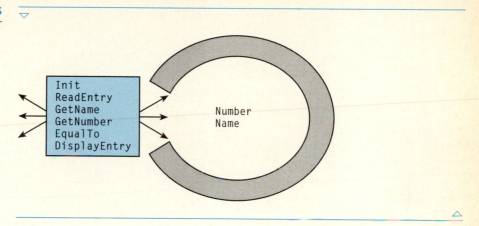

```
Init
ReadEntry
GetName
GetNumber
EqualTo
DisplayEntry
```

Number
Name

Figure 12.16
Driver Program for
EntryADT

Directory: CHAP12
File: CLIENTRY.PAS

```
program ClientEntry (Input, Output);
{
  Driver program to test EntryADT.
  Uses StringADT (Fig. 11.1) and EntryADT (Fig. 12.14).
}

  const
    NullString = '            ';    {string of 12 blanks.}


  {
    Insert declarations for StringLength (value is 12),
    StringIndex,and StringType from StringADT. Insert
    declaration for Entry from EntryADT.
  }

  var
    MyEntry, NewEntry : Entry;      {input - directory entries}
    NewName,                     {input - name being searched for}
    MyNumber : StringType; {output - number of directory entry}
    CurLength : Integer;              {length of string read}

  {Insert ReadLnString from StringADT and operators from
   EntryADT.}

begin {ClientEntry}
  {Create your personal entry.}
  Init (MyEntry, NullString, NullString);  {Create empty entry.}
  WriteLn ('Enter your personal directory entry:');
  ReadEntry (MyEntry, Input);                {Read your entry.}
```

▷ ▷ ▷ ▷ ▷ ▷

```
{Check for match and display result.}
WriteLn;
Write ('Enter a name to match> ');
ReadLnString (Input, NewName, CurLength);  {Read search key.}
Init (NewEntry, NewName, NullString);          {Store key in
                                                    NewEntry.}

if EqualTo(MyEntry, NewEntry) then
   begin
     GetNumber (MyEntry, MyNumber);
     WriteLn ('Number is ', MyNumber)
   end
else
   WriteLn ('Not listed');

{Display your directory entry.}
WriteLn;
WriteLn ('Your directory entry follows:');
DisplayEntry (MyEntry)
end. {ClientEntry}
```

Sample Run

```
Enter your personal directory entry:
Judy Wilson
215-555-9876

Enter a name to match> Judy Wilson
Number is 215-555-9876

Your directory entry follows:
Judy Wilson
215-555-9876
```

Program Style

Hiding a Record's Internal Representation

In Fig. 12.16, the if statement

```
if EqualTo(MyEntry, NewEntry) then
   begin
     GetNumber(MyEntry, MyNumber);
     WriteLn ('Number is ', MyNumber)
   end
else
   WriteLn ('Not listed');
```

uses operators EqualTo and GetNumber to process records AnEntry and Entry2 (type Entry). Since Entry is a record type with fields ID and Name, we could use the following if statement instead:

▶▶▶▶▶▶

```
if MyEntry.Name = NewEntry.Name then
   WriteLn ('Number is ', MyEntry.Number)
else
   WriteLn ('Not listed');
```

Although shorter, this if statement is less desirable because it is dependent on the internal organization of data type Entry and would have to be rewritten if data type Entry were modified.

Exercises for Section 12.6 **Self-Check**

1. List the Pascal operators and standard functions that should be considered part of the complete specifications for the following built-in data types:
   a. Real   b. Char   c. Boolean

2. What is information hiding? Why is it important to a software designer?

3. What does the following program segment do? What does it display for the two records shown? What data types are required for MyEmp, YourEmp, Name1, and Name2?

```
Init (MyEmp, 'Jennie Moss ', '215-555-1233');
Init (YourEmp, 'Jackie Moss ', '215-555-1234');
if EqualTo(MyEmp, YourEmp) then
   WriteLn ('Duplicate entry!')
else
   begin
      Name1 := GetName(MyEmp);
      Name2 := GetName(YourEmp);
      WriteLn (Name1, '***** ', Name2)
   end; {if}
```

4. Suppose you were asked to provide an ADT that would allow up to 10 type Entry items to be placed in a phone book. What would be the structure for the phone book? Describe, but don't write, operators for adding a new phone book entry and finding an entry by name in the phone book.

Programming

1. Code the operators in Self-Check Exercise 4.

12.7 Variant Records (Optional)

variant record
a record that has a fixed and a varying component
fixed part
the part of a record that is always the same
variant part
the part of a record that is changeable

All record variables of type NewEmployee have the same form and structure. It is possible, however, to use **variant records** to store data collections in which some fields are always the same (the **fixed part**) and some fields may be different (the **variant part**).

For example, we might want to include additional information about an employee based on marital status. For all married employees, we might want to know the spouse's name and the number of children. For all divorced employees, we might want to know the date of the divorce. For all single employees, we might want to know whether the employee lives alone.

This new employee type, Executive, is declared in Fig. 12.17 and uses several data types declared earlier in Fig. 12.10.

Figure 12.17
Record Type Executive and
Record Variable Boss

Directory: CHAP12
File: EXECUTIVE.PAS

```
const
  StringLength = 14;   {length of all strings except zipcode}
  ZipStringSize = 5;   {length of zipcode string}

type
  IDRange = 1111..9999;
  StringIndex = 1..StringLength;
  ZipIndex = 1..ZipStringSize;
  StringType = packed array [StringIndex] of Char;
  ZipString = packed array [ZipIndex] of Char;
  Month = (January, February, March, April, May, June, July,
           August, September, October, November, December);

  Employee = record
               ID : IDRange;
               Name : StringType;
               Gender : Char;
               NumDepend : Integer;
               Rate, TotWages : Real
             end; {Employee}

  Address = record
              Street, City, State : StringType;
              ZipCode : ZipString
            end; {Address}

  Date = record
           ThisMonth : Month;
           Day : 1..31;
           Year : 1900..1999
         end; {Date}

  MaritalStatus = (Married, Divorced, Single);
  Executive = record
                PayData : Employee;
                Home : Address;
                StartDate, BirthDate : Date;
                case MS : MaritalStatus of
                  Married  : (SpouseName : StringType;
                              NumberKids : Integer);
                  Divorced : (DivorceDate : Date);
                  Single   : (LivesAlone : Boolean)
              end; {Executive}

var
  Boss : Executive;
```

The fixed part of a record always precedes the variant part. The fixed part of record type `Executive` has the form of record type `NewEmployee`. The variant part follows the line

```
case MS : MaritalStatus of
```

which defines a special field `MS`, of type `MaritalStatus`. The value of the **tag field** `MS` (`Married`, `Divorced`, or `Single`) indicates the form of the remainder of the record. If the value of the tag field is `Married`, there are two additional fields, `SpouseName` (type `StringType`) and `NumberKids` (type `Integer`); otherwise, there is only one additional field, `DivorceDate` (type `Date`) or `LivesAlone` (type `Boolean`).

tag field
the record field whose value determines the form of that record's variant part

Figure 12.18 shows three variants of record variable `Boss`, starting with the tag field. The fixed parts of all these records (not shown) have the same form.

For each variable of type `Executive`, the compiler allocates sufficient storage space to accommodate the largest of the record variants. However, only one variant is defined at any given time, and that particular variant is determined by the tag field value.

The amount of storage required for each variant depends on how many bytes are used to store integer values and enumerated type values on a particular computer. The first variant in Fig. 12.18 requires 14 bytes of storage (one byte per character of the spouse's name) and should be the largest.

EXAMPLE 12.7 ▼

If the value of the tag field `Boss.MS` is `Married`, then only the variant fields `SpouseName` and `NumberKids` can be referenced correctly; all other variant fields are undefined. Assuming the first variant shown in Fig. 12.18 is stored in record `Boss`, the program fragment

Figure 12.18
Three Variants of Record Variable Boss

Boss.MS	Married
Boss.SpouseName	Elliot Koffman
Boss.NumberKids	3

Boss.MS	Divorced
Boss.DivorceDate.ThisMonth	May
Boss.DivorceDate.Day	20
Boss.DivorceDate.Year	1989

Boss.MS	Single
Boss.LivesAlone	True

```
with Boss do
   begin
      WriteLn ('The spouse''s name is ', SpouseName, '.');
      WriteLn ('They have ', NumberKids :1, ' children.')
   end {with}
```

displays the lines

```
The spouse's name is Elliot Koffman.
They have 3 children.
```

We must ensure that the variant fields that are referenced are consistent with the current tag field value. The compiler and the run-time system do not normally check this. If the value of Boss.MS is not Married when the preceding fragment is executed, the information displayed will be meaningless. For that reason, a case statement is often used to process the variant part of a record. Using the tag field as the case selector, we can ensure that only the currently defined variant is manipulated.   ▲

EXAMPLE 12.8 ▼

The fragment in Fig. 12.19 displays the data stored in the variant part of record Boss. The value of Boss.MS determines what information is displayed.   ▲

Figure 12.19
Displaying a Variant
Record

```
{Display the variant part.}
with Boss do
   case MS of
      Married :
         begin
            WriteLn ('The spouse''s name is ', SpouseName, '.');
            WriteLn ('They have ', NumberKids :1, ' children.')
         end; {Married}
      Divorced :
         with DivorceDate do
            WriteLn ('Divorced on ', Ord(ThisMonth) + 1 :2,
                     '/', Day :2, '/', Year :4);
      Single :
         if LivesAlone then
            WriteLn ('Lives alone')
         else
            WriteLn ('Does not live alone')
   end {case}
```

SYNTAX DISPLAY

Record Type with Variant Part

Form:
```
type
  rec type = record
               id list₁ : type₁;
               id list₂ : type₂;
               . . .
               id listₙ : typeₙ;
```
Fixed part

```
             case tag : tag type of
               label₁ : (field list₁);
               label₂ : (field list₂);
               . . .
               labelₖ : (field listₖ)
             end;
```
Variant part

Example:
```
type
  Face = record
           Eyes : Color;
         case Bald : Boolean of
           True : (WearsWig : Boolean);
           False : (HairColor : Color)
         end;
```

Interpretation: The fixed part is declared before the word `case`. The variant part starts with the reserved word `case`. The identifier *tag* is the name of the *tag* field of the record; the tag field name is separated by a colon from its type (*tag type*), which must be type `Boolean`, an enumerated type, or a subrange of an ordinal type.

The case labels (*label₁*, *label₂*, . . . , *labelₖ*) are lists of values of the tag field as defined by *tag type*. *Field list₁* describes the record fields associated with *label₁*. Each element of *field list₁* specifies a field name and its type; the elements in *field list₁* are separated by semicolons. *Field list₁* is enclosed in parentheses.

Note 1: All field names must be unique. The same field name may not appear in the fixed and variant parts or in two field lists of the variant part.

Note 2: An empty field list (no variant part for that case label) is indicated by an empty pair of parentheses, ().

Note 3: A field list may have a variant part, and that part must follow the fixed part of that field list.

Note 4: There is only one `end` for the record type declaration; there is no separate `end` for the `case`.

When you initially store data in a record with a variant part, the tag field value should be read first. Once the value of the tag field is defined, data can be read into the variant fields associated with that value.

Self-Check

1. How many bytes do you need to store each variant for a record of type `Executive`, assuming two bytes for an integer or an enumerated type value and one byte for a character or a Boolean value? Don't include the tag field in your calculations.

2. Write a statement that displays `Boss.SpouseName` if defined or the message `Not married`.

Programming

1. Write a procedure to display a record of type `Face` as declared in the syntax display in this section.

12.8 Common Programming Errors

The most common error when using records is incorrectly specifying the record field to be manipulated. The full field selector (record variable and field name) must be used, unless the record reference is nested inside a `with` statement or the entire record is to be manipulated. So far we have discussed the latter option only for record copy statements and for records passed as parameters.

If a record variable name is listed in a `with` statement header, only the field name is required to reference fields of that record inside the `with` statement. You still must use the full field selector to reference fields of any other record variable.

Errors in Arrays of Records

When an array of records is processed, the array name and the subscript must be included as part of the field selector (e.g., `X[I].Key` references field `Key` of the `I`th record). If you use a `for` statement to process all array elements in sequence, then you must nest any `with` statement that references the array records inside the `for` statement, as shown here:

```
for I := 1 to N do
  with X[I] do
```

As the loop-control variable `I` changes, the next array record is processed by the `with` statement. If the nesting order is reversed, as in

```
with X[I] do
  for I := 1 to N do
```

then the same array record is processed `N` times. The record that is processed is determined by the value of `I` when the `with` statement is first reached. Changing the value of `I` inside the `with` statement has no effect.

Errors in Variant Records

For variant records, remember that the value of the tag field determines the form of the variant part that is currently defined. Manipulating any other variant causes unpredictable results. You must ensure that the correct variant is being processed—the computer does not check this. So always reference a variant record in a `case` statement with the tag field as the `case` selector to ensure that the proper variant part is being manipulated.

CHAPTER REVIEW

1. Use records to store a collection of related data items of different types. Reference individual record fields using a field selector consisting of the record variable name and a period followed by the field name.
2. You can assign one record variable to another record variable of the same type (record copy statement) or pass a record as a parameter to a procedure or function.
3. You can shorten a field selector using a `with` statement. If you specify the record variable name in a `with` statement header, then you only need to write the field name inside the `with` statement.
4. Using arrays of records to organize data collections can simplify programming. A procedure that processes the entire array of records can call other procedures to process each individual record.
5. Represent more complicated data organizations using hierarchical records (records with record components). Use variant records to store data with both a fixed and varying component.
6. Through data abstraction, you can focus on data objects and their required operations. You can write clients that manipulate these objects without knowledge of the objects' internal structure or organization. Information hiding enables you to process data objects and access the information they store through their operators. If a data object's implementation should change, you will not need to rewrite its client programs.

Summary of New Pascal Constructs

Construct	Effect
Record Declaration	
```type Part = record ID : 1111..9999; Quantity : Integer; Price : Real end; {Part} var Nuts, Bolts : Part;```	A record type `Part` is declared with fields that can store two integers and a real number. `Nuts` and `Bolts` are record variables of type `Part`.

Construct	Effect

Record Variant Declaration

```
type
  ChildKind = (Girl, Boy);
  Child = record
              First, Last : Char;
              Age : Integer;
          case Sex : ChildKind of
              Girl : (Sugar, Spice :
                               Real);
              Boy : (Snakes, Snails,
                      Tails : Integer)
          end; {Child}
var
  Kid : Child;
```

A record type with a variant part is declared. Each record variable can store two characters and an integer. One variant part can store two real numbers, and the other can store three integers. The record variable `Kid` is type `Child`.

Record Reference

```
TotalCost := Nuts.Quantity
               * Nuts.Price;
WriteLn (Bolts.ID :4)
```

Multiplies two fields of `Nuts`.
Prints `ID` field of `Bolts`.

Record Copy

```
Bolts := Nuts
```

Copies record `Nuts` to `Bolts`.

with Statement

```
with Bolts do
  Write (ID :4, Price :8:2)
```

Prints two fields of `Bolts`.

Declaring Arrays of Records

```
type
  AElement = record
                Data : Real;
                Key : Integer
             end; {AElement}
  DataArray = array [1..10] of
                AElement;
var
  MyData : DataArray;
```

`DataArray` is an array type with 10 elements of type `AElement` (a record). Each element has fields named `Data` and `Key`.

`MyData` is a variable of type `DataArray`.

Referencing an Array of Records

```
MyData[1].Data := 3.14159;
MyData[10].Key := 9999;
```

The real value 3.14159 is stored in the first `Data` field of array `MyData`; the value 9999 is stored in the last `Key` field.

Construct	Effect
Referencing a Record Variant	

<pre>with Kid do
  case Sex of
    Girl :
      begin
        Write (Pounds of sugar>');
        ReadLn (Sugar)
      end; {Girl}
    Boy :
      begin
        Write ('Count of snakes>');
        ReadLn (Snakes)
      end {Boy}
  end {case and with}</pre>
	Uses a `case` statement to read data into the variant part of record variable `Kid`. If tag field `Sex` is `Girl`, reads a value into the field `Sugar`. If tag field `Sex` is `Boy`, reads a value into the field `Snakes`.

Quick-Check Exercises

1. What is the primary difference between a record and an array? Which would you use to store the catalog description of a course? To store the names of the students in the course?
2. Write a type declaration that describes a computer display that is 640 columns by 480 rows of pixels, where each pixel has a red, green, and blue intensity value (of integer type).
3. When can you use the assignment operator with record operands? When can you use the equality operator?
4. For `AStudent` declared as follows, provide a statement that displays the initials of `AStudent`:

```
type
   StringIndex = 1..StringLength;
   StringType = packed array [StringIndex] of Char;
   Student = record
                First, Last : StringType;
                Age, Score : Integer;
                Grade : Char
             end; {Student}

var
   AStudent : Student;
```

5. If an integer uses two bytes of storage and a character one, and `StringLength` is 20, how many bytes of storage are occupied by `AStudent`?
6. Write a procedure that displays a variable of type `Student`.
7. Why do we use a `with` statement? What is a disadvantage of using the `with` statement?

8. Write the type declaration for a data structure that stores a player's name, salary, fielding position, batting average, fielding percentage, and number of hits, runs, runs batted in, and errors.

9. Write the type declaration for a data structure that stores the information in Quick-Check Exercise 8 for a team of 25 players.

10. _____ is hiding low-level details of implementation from a higher-level module.

11. When should you use a record variant?

Answers to Quick-Check Exercises

1. The values stored in an array must all be the same type, whereas the values stored in a record do not have to be the same type; record for catalog item; array for list of names.

2.
```
type
   Pixel = record
                 Red, Blue, Green : Integer
             end; {Pixel}
   Screen = array [1..640, 1..480] of Pixel;
```

3. When the records are the same type; never

4. `WriteLn (AStudent.First[1], AStudent.Last[1])`

5. 45

6.
```
procedure WriteStudent (OneStu {input} : Student);
   begin
      WriteLn ('Student is ', OneStu.FirstName,
                ' ', OneStu.LastName);
      WriteLn ('Age is ', OneStu.Age :1);
      WriteLn ('Score is ', OneStu.Score :1);
      WriteLn ('Grade is ', OneStu.Grade)
   end;
```

7. A `with` statement allows us to shorten field selectors. It is helpful when we must reference several fields of the same record. Its disadvantage is that it makes the program less readable because it separates the record variable name from the field name. It is particularly confusing when there are multiple records of the same type or when a record has nested subrecords.

8.
```
type
   Position = (Pitcher, Catcher, FirstBase,
                SecondBase, ThirdBase, ShortStop,
                LeftField, CenterField, RightField);
   StringIndex = 1..StringLength;
   StringType = packed array [StringIndex] of Char;
   Player = record
                 Name : StringType;
                 Salary : Real;
                 FieldPos : Position;
                 BatAve, FieldPct : Real;
                 Hits, Runs, RBIs, Errors : Integer
             end; {Player}
```

```
 9. type
       Position = ...
       StringIndex = ...
       StringType = ...
       Player = ...
       TeamArray = array [1..25] of Player;
```
10. Information hiding
11. When an object has some fields that are always the same and some fields that may be different

Review Questions

1. Declare a record called `Subscriber` that contains the fields `Name`, `Street-Address`, `MonthlyBill` (how much the subscriber owes), and which paper the subscriber receives (`Morning`, `Evening`, or `Both`).

2. Write a Pascal program to enter and then print out the data in record `Competition` declared as follows:

```
const
   StringLength = 20;

type
   StringIndex = 1..StringLength;
   StringType = packed array [StringIndex] of Char;
   OlympicEvent = record
                     Event,
                     Entrant,
                     Country : StringType;
                     Place : Integer
                  end; {OlympicEvent}
var
   Competition : OlympicEvent;
```

3. Identify and correct the errors in the following program.

```
program Report (Input, Output);
   type
      String12 = packed array [1..12] of Char;
      SummerHelp = record
                      Name : String12;
                      StartDate : String12;
                      HoursWorked : Real
                   end; {SummerHelp}

   var
      Operator : SummerHelp;

begin {Report}
   with SummerHelp do
      begin
         Name := 'Stan Viceroy';
         StartDate := 'June 1, 1995';
         HoursWorked := 29.3
```

```
      end; {with}
   WriteLn (Operator)
 end. {Report}
```

Use the following declarations for Review Questions 4 through 9.

```
const
   TotalEmployees = 20;

type
   EmpRange = 1..TotalEmployees;
   Employee = record
                 ID : Integer;
                 Rate, Hours : Real
              end; {Employee}
   EmpArray = array [EmpRange] of Employee;

var
   Employees : EmpArray;
```

4. Write the function `TotalGross` that will return the total gross pay given the data stored in array `Employees`.

5. Explain what is wrong with the following fragment and fix it:

```
I := 1;
with Employees[I] do
   while I <= TotalEmployees do
      begin
         WriteLn (Hours :12:2);
         I := I + 1
      end {while}
```

6. Explain what is wrong with the following fragment and fix it:

```
I := 1;
while (Employees[I].ID <> 999) and (I<=TotalEmployees) do
   I := I + 1;
```

7. Write a fragment that displays the ID number of each employee who works between 10 and 20 hours per week.

8. Write a fragment that displays the ID number of the employee who works the most hours.

9. Write a procedure that, given an employee ID, displays the wages of that employee.

10. Write the declarations for the record `Quotations` that contains an integer count of the number of quotations stored and an array of up to 100 records of type `Quote`. Each record of type `Quote` should have the following fields: `The-Quote` (80 characters in length), `Author` (30 characters), and `Year` (integer).

11. Explain why the principle of information hiding is important to the software designer.

12. Write an abstract data type specification for describing a radio station. A station has a four-letter call sign, can be AM or FM, and has a real number frequency.

13. Write the variant declaration for `Supplies`, which consists of `Paper`, `Ribbon`, or `Labels`. For `Paper`, the information needed is the number of sheets per

box and the size of the paper. For `Ribbon`, the size, color, and kind (`Carbon` or `Cloth`) are needed. For `Labels`, the size and number per box are needed. For each supply, the cost, the number on hand, and the reorder point also must be stored. Use whatever data types are appropriate for each field.

Programming Projects

Directory: CHAP12
File: PROJ1.PAS

1. Represent an article of clothing using a record that consists of the article's description (a string), color (enumerated type `ColorType`), and price. Write a new abstract data type `ClothingADT` with operators that read and display a single article of clothing. `ClothingADT` should use the ADT developed for Programming Project 1 in Chapter 9. Use `ClothingADT` in a client program that reads and displays the data for each clothing item from a text file in which each item's data takes up three lines: description, color, price. Read each item's data into the same program variable.

2. Modify Programming Project 1 to display a summary table that indicates the count of items read in each color. Also, display the total value of all items. You should use an array of integers with subscript type `ColorType` to keep track of the count of items in each color.

3. A number expressed in scientific notation is represented by its mantissa (a decimal fraction) and its exponent. Write a procedure that reads separately the mantissa and exponent of a number and stores them in a record with two `Real` fields. Write a procedure that prints the contents of each record as a real value. Also write a procedure that computes the sum, the product, the difference, and the quotient of the two numbers. Test your procedures.

4. We all have demands on our time and must determine the best use of that time. Write a program that allows a user to enter up to 40 activities and then computes a maximum number of nonoverlapping activities that can be performed. Each activity has a description (40 character string), a start time (of type `Time`), and an end time (also of type `Time`).

   There is an easy way to generate such a list. Sort the list of activities by increasing end time. Then select the first item in this list, which takes up time until its end time. Thereafter, select the next item in the sorted list with a start time after the previously selected item's end time (so that it is not overlapped by that item). Continue this process until the list is exhausted. The selected items are surely in order and do not overlap. This is the maximum number of activities that can be performed.

5. Write a student grading program that uses the data structure `GradeBook` declared in Section 12.4. Provide the following procedures. Assume that parameter `MyClass` is type `GradeBook`.

   `ReadExamFile (var InFile, var MyClass)`: Reads in the student exam data from data file `InFile`. Reads each student's name and stores three exam scores per student.

   `AddStudent (var MyClass)`: Reads a student record from the keyboard and adds it to the collection of student records.

   `GetStudent (MyClass, StudentName, var StuData)`: Returns through `StuData` the record for the student specified by `StudentName`.

`PutStudent (var MyClass, StudentName, StuData)`: Stores new exam data (passed through `StuData`) in the record for the student specified by `StudentName`.

`AssignGrade (var MyClass)`: Computes the average exam score for each student. Assigns letter grades using a predetermined exam scale (e.g., 90–100, A; 80–89, B; and so on).

`EditStudent (var MyClass)`: Prompts the user for the name of a student whose grade may be changed; reads in the new grade and calls `PutStudent` to make the change.

`DisplayGrade (MyClass)`: Displays the information stored in array `MyClass` in a legible format.

Write a menu-driven program which tests these procedures.

6. Use a three-dimensional array to represent a building (floors 1 to 3, wings A and B, and rooms 1 to 5). Each entry in the array will be a record containing a person's name and phone number. Provide operators to create an initially empty building (all names are blank), read data into the building, display the entire building, display a particular floor of the building, retrieve the entry for a particular room, and store a new entry in a particular room. To designate a particular room, the program user must enter the floor number, wing letter, and room number as data. You will also need an abstract data type to represent, read, and display a single entry.

7. Write a program that simulates the movement of radioactive particles in a 20-by-20-foot two-dimensional shield around a reactor. Particles enter the shield at some random position in the shield coordinate space. Once a particle enters the shield, it moves 1 foot/second in one of four directions. The direction for the next second of travel is determined by a random number between 1 and 4 (forward, backward, left, right). A change in direction is interpreted as a collision with another particle, which results in a dissipation of energy. Each particle can have only a limited number of collisions before it dies. A particle exits the shield if its position places it outside the shield coordinate space before K collisions occur. Determine the percentage of particles that exit the shield, where K and the number of particles are input as data items. Also compute the average number of times a particle's path crosses itself during travel time within the shield. *Hint:* Mark each array position occupied by a particle before it dies or exits the shield.

8. Many supermarkets use computerized scanning equipment that allows the checkout clerk to drag an item across a sensor that reads the bar code on the product container. After the computer reads the bar code, the store inventory database is examined, the item's price and product description are located, counts are reduced, and a receipt is printed. Your task is to write a program that simulates this process.

    Your program will need to read the inventory information from the data file on disk into an array of records. The data in the inventory file is written one item per line, beginning with a 2-digit product code, followed by a 30-character product description, its price, and the quantity of that item in stock. Your program will need to copy the revised version of the inventory to a new data file after all purchases have been processed.

Processing customers' orders involves reading a series of product codes representing each person's purchases from a second data file. A zero product code is used to mark the end of each customer order. As each product code is read, the inventory list is searched to find a matching product code. Once located, the product price and description are printed on the receipt, and the quantity on hand is reduced by 1. At the bottom of the receipt, you are to print the total for the goods purchased by the customer.

INTERVIEW
▼

Adele Goldberg

Adele Goldberg is the chairman and founder of ParcPlace Systems. ParcPlace Systems provides a broad range of products and services based on object-oriented technologies, including development tools for Smalltalk and for C ++, that serve the applications development needs of corporate programmers. Previously, Dr. Goldberg was a research laboratory manager at Xerox PARC, where she wrote several books on the Smalltalk-80 system (Smalltalk-80: The Language, *with David Robson, and* Smalltalk-80: The Interactive Programming Environment) *and led the effort to design, implement, and distribute the Smalltalk-80 development system on standard microprocessors.*

▼ **What influenced you to become a computer scientist?**

▲ I received a bachelor's degree in mathematics from the University of Michigan, where my degree work had been mostly theoretical. However, I worked as a programmer at the Center for Research on Learning and Teaching at the university and I also worked in an IBM business office in Chicago. After seeing what kind of work was available and seeing opportunities in the application of computing to education, I decided to obtain more advanced training. I attended graduate school in information sciences at the University of Chicago and arranged to do my doctoral research at Stanford University at the Institute for Mathematical Studies in the Social Sciences (IMSSS). My particular long-term interests were, and still are, in the use of computers to augment both formal and informal learning.

▼ **How did your interests in learning lead you to the Smalltalk development team?**

▲ My interests in the use of computer technology for learning naturally led me to consider accessibility issues; that is, to be truly beneficial, tools taught in the classroom should be accessible wherever and whenever the person thinks of using them. When I met Alan Kay, I immediately resonated with his ideas for the Dynabook, a personal computer that would have the same portability and ease of use as a printed book. The vision of the Dynabook incorporated the vision of a system structure in which people would find immediately usable applications but would also be able to easily learn how to specify applications and uses of their own invention. I joined Xerox Palo Alto Research Center in 1973, shortly after the start of the Smalltalk project. All the people involved in the Smalltalk project were, at one time or another, invited into the Dynabook project by Alan, who was looking for people to tackle the software and hardware issues associated with creating a truly personalizable and accessible system. Creating a language that would be easy enough to be accessible by almost anyone, yet powerful enough to allow the user to customize the system, was part of the challenge.

▼ **Smalltalk, the first uniformly object-oriented language, revolutionized programming for the personal computer in the 1980s. How was the language developed?**

▲ Smalltalk is based on ideas gleaned from the Simula language and from early work on visual programming, such as Sutherland's Sketchpad. The earliest versions of Smalltalk were highly influenced by the tales of success from MIT with the Logo Project. We started out with the notion of a single language that would be learnable by children as well as adults, although I found that this spectrum was better understood as a series of tightly related languages. The Smalltalk system evolved gradually over the years, with an interesting research cycle: We would design and implement the language along with the user interface and development tools, reimplement any known applications, invent and implement new applications, then determine what was hard and what was easy to implement and why. We would then modify the language system design and repeat the cycle. The vision of the language remained the same, but its embodiment changed because of new ideas about usage and how to learn and also because of new technologies.

▼ **What is object-oriented programming, and to what do you attribute its popularity?**

▲ Software engineering technology encompasses all aspects of engineering, from programming languages to analysis and design methods to measures. By object-oriented technology, we mean technology that embodies the use of objects. An object is a software description of a set of behaviors that occur in the real world. Programming using object-oriented languages involves an analysis of the required system behaviors, and then the design of which parts of a system will take responsibility for providing these behaviors. These system parts are called objects. The behaviors are often referred to as the services provided by the objects. Objects are describable as compositions or refinements of other objects. An important aspect of object-oriented programming is designing the relationships among the objects.

My early work with the Smalltalk project focused on determining design factors that contributed to learnability. This included devising pedagogical techniques, setting up special resource centers, and teaching. I typically taught students ages 10–13 years old. I observed that they were able to learn to program when they extended and customized example programs. This is one of the basic concepts behind object programming. An object is the basic system component, or building block, and lends itself to customization or extension, making it unnecessary for a programmer to start from scratch with every application. An object consists of some private memory and a set of operations. It responds to a set of messages that specify which of its operations should be carried out. Messages may request an operation, but do not specify how it should be carried out. This not only minimizes interdependence between system components, but makes it possible for a user to employ an object without knowing the details of its internal implementation. This model of communicating objects applies to the most primitive objects as well as the high-level interaction between the computer and user in the Smalltalk system, and was important to us as we worked toward a powerful but very accessible system.

The modularity of object-oriented systems is a key reason for their popularity today. The value of modularity becomes apparent when designing and implementing large applications. As long as the message interface on which other objects depend is not destroyed, components may be redesigned, tested, and implemented without disrupting the rest of the program's operation. The other reason is the somewhat inaccurate belief that you cannot have a graphical, interactive application unless you use an object-oriented style of implementation.

▼ **What advice would you give a student majoring in computer science today?**

▲ I would like students to understand that studies in computer science cannot be treated in isolation from a vision of how technology can be put to work to improve some aspect of work, education, or recreational life. We study programming languages, we invent new technologies for hardware and software, we study mathematics and psychology, and we study the introduction of technology into large and small organizations. And all these studies are directed at applying our knowledge of the foundations of computing science to improve our ability to employ the computer as a tool.

CHAPTER THIRTEEN

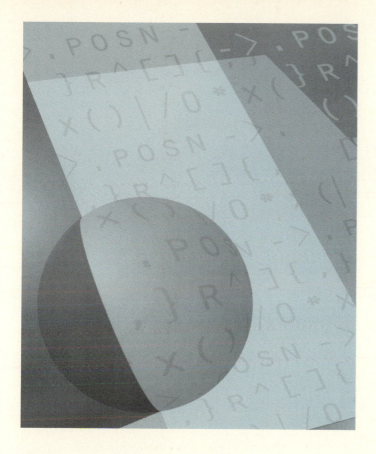

Recursion

recursive module
a procedure or function that calls itself

A recursive procedure or function is one that calls itself. Each time it is called, the **recursive module** can operate on different parameters. Recursion can be an alternative to iteration (looping), although a recursive solution is usually less efficient, in terms of computer time, than an iterative one because of the overhead for the extra procedure calls. In many instances, however, recursion enables us to specify a natural, simple solution to a problem that otherwise would be difficult to solve. For this reason, recursion is an important and powerful tool in problem solving and programming.

13.1 Recursive Modules

In this section, we demonstrate recursion by using a simple function and we develop rules for writing recursive modules from this example. Consider the computer solution to the problem of multiplying 6 by 3, assuming you can add but not multiply. The problem of multiplying 6 by 3 can be split into two problems:

Problem 1: Multiply 6 by 2.

Problem 2: Add 6 to the result of problem 1.

Because your computer can add, it can solve problem 2 but not problem 1. Problem 1, however, is simpler than the original problem. We can split problem 1 into two problems, 1.1 and 1.2, leaving three problems to solve, two of which are additions.

Problem 1.1: Multiply 6 by 1.

Problem 1.2: Add 6 to the result of problem 1.1.

Problem 2: Add 6 to the result of problem 1.

Even though your computer cannot multiply, you can program it to recognize that the result of multiplying any number by 1 is that number. Therefore solving problem 1.1 (the answer is 6) and problem 1.2 gives the solution to problem 1 (the answer is 12). Solving problem 2 gives the final answer, 18.

Figure 13.1 implements this approach to multiplication as the recursive Pascal function `Multiply`, which returns the product, M × N, of its two arguments. If N is greater than 1, the statement

```
Multiply := M + Multiply(M, N-1)      {recursive step}
```

executes, splitting the original problem into the two simpler problems:

Figure 13.1
Recursive Function
Multiply

Directory: CHAP13
File: MULTIPLY.PAS

```
function Multiply (M, N : Integer) : Integer;
{
   Performs multiplication using + operator.
   Pre : M and N are defined and N > 0.
   Post: Returns M * N.
}
begin {Multiply}
   if N = 1 then
      Multiply := M                        {stopping case}
   else
      Multiply := M + Multiply(M, N-1)    {recursive step}
end; {Multiply}
```

Problem 1: Multiply M by N-1.

Problem 2: Add M to the result.

The first of these problems is solved by calling `Multiply` again with N-1 as its second argument. If the new second argument is greater than 1, there will be additional calls to function `Multiply`. We call this case (N > 1) the **recursive step** because it contains a call to function `Multiply`.

recursive step
the step in a program or algorithm that contains a recursive call

Note the two different uses of the identifier `Multiply` in the recursive step in Fig. 13.1. The one without parameters defines the function result; the other calls the function recursively.

When the condition N = 1 is finally true, the statement

```
Multiply := M                          {stopping case}
```

stopping case
the statement that causes recursion to terminate

executes, so the answer is M. We call this case (N = 1) the **stopping case** because it is always the last case reached.

Tracing a Recursive Function

Hand-tracing an algorithm's execution demonstrates how that algorithm works. We can trace the execution of the function designator `Multiply(6, 3)` by drawing an activation frame that corresponds to each call of the function. An **activation frame** is a device that shows the parameter values for each call and summarizes its execution.

activation frame
a device showing the parameter values for each recursive call and its execution

Figure 13.2 shows the three activation frames generated to solve the problem of multiplying 6 by 3. The part of each activation frame that executes before the next recursive call is in color; the part that executes after the return from the next call is in gray. The darker the color of an activation frame, the greater the depth of recursion.

The value returned from each call appears alongside each black arrow. The return arrow from each function call points to the operator +, because the addition is performed just after the return.

Figure 13.2 shows that there are three calls to function `Multiply`. Parameter M has the value 6 for all three calls; parameter N has the values 3, 2, and finally 1. Because N is 1 in the third call, the value of M (6) is returned as the result of the third and last call. After the return to the second activation frame, the value of M is added to this result, and the sum (12) is returned as the result of the second call. After the return to the first activation frame, the value of M is added to this result, and the sum (18) is returned as the result of the original call to function `Multiply`.

Properties of Recursive Problems and Solutions

Problems that can be solved by recursion have the following characteristics:

▶ One or more stopping cases have a simple, nonrecursive solution.

Figure 13.2
Trace of Function Multiply

▶ The other cases of the problem can be reduced (using recursion) to problems that are closer to stopping cases.
▶ Eventually the problem can be reduced to stopping cases only, which are relatively easy to solve.

Follow these steps to solve a recursive problem:

1. Understand the problem.
2. Determine the stopping cases.
3. Determine the recursive steps.

The recursive algorithms that we write generally consist of an `if` statement with the form:

```
if the stopping case is reached then
    Solve it.
else
    Split the problem into simpler cases using recursion.
```

Figure 13.3 illustrates these steps. Assume that for a particular problem of size *N*, we can split the problem into one of size 1 that we can solve (a stopping case) and one of size *N* - 1. We can split the problem of size *N* - 1 into another problem of size 1 and a problem of size *N* - 2, which we can split further. If we split the problem *N* times, we end up with *N* problems of size 1, all of which we can solve.

A Recursive Procedure

In Fig. 13.4, `Reverse` is a recursive procedure that reads in a string of length N and prints it out backward. If the procedure call statement

`Reverse (5)`

is executed, the five characters entered are displayed in reverse order. If the characters `abcde` are entered when this procedure is called, the lines

`abcde`
`edcba`

appear on the screen. The color letters are entered as data and the black letters are printed. If the procedure call statement

`Reverse (3)`

is executed instead, only three characters are read, and the lines

`abc`
`cba`

terminating condition
a condition that is true when a recursive module reaches a stopping case

appear on the screen.

Like most recursive procedures, the body of procedure `Reverse` consists of an `if` statement that evaluates a **terminating condition**, N = 1. When

Figure 13.3
Splitting a Problem into Smaller Problems

Figure 13.4
Procedure Reverse

Directory: CHAP13
File: REVERSE.PAS

```
procedure Reverse (N : Integer);
{
  Displays a string of length N in
  the reverse order from which it is entered.
  Pre : N is greater than or equal to one.
  Post: Displays N characters.
}
  var
    Next : Char; {next data character}

begin {Reverse}
  if N = 1 then
    begin {stopping case}
      Read (Next);
      Write (Next)
    end {stopping case}
  else
    begin {recursion}
      Read (Next);
      Reverse (N-1);
      Write (Next)
    end {recursion}
end; {Reverse}
```

the terminating condition is true, the problem has reached a stopping case—a data string of length 1—and the `Read` and `Write` statements are executed.

When the terminating condition is false (N > 1), the recursive step (following `else`) is executed and the `Read` statement enters the next data character. The procedure call statement

```
Reverse (N-1);
```

calls the procedure recursively, with the parameter value decreased by 1. The character just read is not displayed until later, because the `Write` statement follows the recursive procedure call. Consequently, the `Write` statement cannot be performed until after the procedure execution is completed and control is returned to the `Write` statement. For example, the character that is read when N is 3 is not displayed until after the procedure execution for N equal to 2 is done. Hence, this character is displayed after the characters that are read when N is 2 and N is 1.

To see why this is so, trace the execution of the procedure call statement

```
Reverse (3)
```

The trace shown in Fig. 13.5 assumes the letters `abc` were entered as data. The trace shows three activation frames for procedure `Reverse`, each beginning with a list of the initial values of N and Next for that frame. The value of

Figure 13.5
Trace of Reverse (3)

N is passed into the procedure when it is called, because N is a value parameter; the value of Next is initially undefined, because Next is a local variable.

The statements in color in Fig. 13.5 are recursive procedure calls and result in a new activation frame, as indicated by the colored arrows. A procedure return occurs when the procedure end is reached, as indicated by the word Return and a black arrow pointing to the statement in the calling frame to which the procedure returns. Tracing the colored arrows and then the black arrows in Fig. 13.5 gives us the list of statements in Fig. 13.6. To help you understand this list, all the statements for a particular activation frame are indented to the same column.

Figure 13.6
Sequence of Statements
for Reverse (3)

Call Reverse with N equal to 3.
    Read the first character (a) into Next.
    Call Reverse with N equal to 2.
        Read the second character (b) into Next.
        Call Reverse with N equal to 1.
            Read the third character (c) into Next.
            Display the third character (c).
            Return from third call.
        Display the second character (b).
        Return from second call.
    Display the first character (a).
    Return from original call.

Note the three calls to procedure Reverse, each with a different parameter value. The procedure returns always occur in the reverse order of the procedure calls; that is, we return from the last call first, then we return from the next to last call, and so on. After we return from a particular execution of the procedure, the procedure displays the character that was read into Next just prior to that procedure call. The expression **unwinding the recursion** describes the return from a series of recursive calls.

unwinding the recursion
the process of returning from a series of recursive calls

Exercises for Section 13.1   **Self-Check**

1. Show how the problem generated by the function designator Multiply(5, 4) can be split into smaller problems as in Fig. 13.3.
2. Trace the execution of Multiply(5, 4).
3. Given the following procedure and the call WhatDo (4), what would be the output?

```
procedure WhatDo (I : Integer);
begin {WhatDo}
  if I > 1 then
    begin
      Write (I :2);
      WhatDo (I - 1);
      Write (I :2)
    end {if}
end; {WhatDo}
```

Programming

1. Write a recursive function Divide(A, B) to compute A div B using only integer subtraction and no multiplication or division.

13.2   Parameter and Local Variable Stacks

stack
a data structure in which the last component stored is the first one removed

Pascal uses a special data structure called a **stack** to keep track of the values of the parameters of a recursive module as they change from call to call. A stack is analogous to a stack of dishes or trays. In a buffet, clean dishes are always placed on top of the stack of dishes. When a dish is needed, the last one placed on the stack, the one on top, is removed. This causes the next to last dish placed on the stack to move to the top of the stack.

Whenever a new procedure call occurs, the parameter value associated with that call is placed on the top of the parameter stack. Also, a new memory cell whose value is initially undefined is placed on top of the stack that is maintained for each local variable. In procedure Reverse, whenever N or Next is referenced, the value at the top of the corresponding stack is always used. When a procedure return occurs, the value currently at the top of each stack is removed, and the value just below it moves to the top.

Stacks for Procedure Reverse

As an example, let's look at the two stacks right after the first call to Reverse. There is one cell on each stack, as follows:

After first call to Reverse

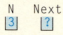

The letter a is read into Next just before the second call to Reverse.

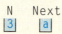

After the second call to Reverse, the number 2 is placed on top of the stack for N, and the top of the stack for Next becomes undefined again. The value in color is at the top of each stack.

After second call to Reverse

The letter b is read into Next just before the third call to Reverse:

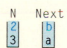

However, Next becomes undefined again right after the third call:

After third call to Reverse

During this execution of the procedure, the letter c is read into Next, and c is echo printed immediately because N is 1 (the stopping case):

The procedure return causes the values at the top of the stack to be removed:

After first return

Because control is returned to a `Write` statement, the value of `Next (b)` at the top of the stack is then displayed. Another return occurs, causing the values currently at the top of the stack to be removed:

After second return

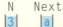

Again, control is returned to a `Write` statement, and the value of `Next (a)` at the top of the stack is displayed. The third and last return removes the last pair of values from the stack, and `N` and `Next` both become undefined:

After third return

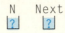

Chapter 17 shows you how to declare and manipulate stacks yourself. Because these steps are all done automatically by Pascal, we can write recursive procedures without worrying about the stacks.

Implementation of Parameter Stacks in Pascal

For illustrative purposes, we have used separate stacks for `N` and `Next` in our discussion; the compiler, however, actually maintains a single stack. Each time a call to a procedure or a function occurs, all its parameters and local variables are pushed onto the stack along with the memory address of the calling statement. The latter gives the computer the return point after execution of the procedure or function. Although multiple copies of a procedure's parameters may be saved on the stack, only one copy of the procedure body is in memory.

Exercises for Section 13.2   ***Self-Check***

1. Why is `N` a value parameter in Fig. 13.4?
2. Assume the characters `*+-/` are entered for the procedure call statement

   `Reverse (4)`

   Show the contents of the stacks immediately after each procedure call and return.
3. For the function designator `Multiply(5, 4)`, show the stacks after each recursive call.

13.3   Recursive Mathematical Functions

Many mathematical functions are defined recursively. An example is the factorial of a number n (represented as $n!$):

▶   0! is 1

▶   *n*! is $n \times (n - 1)!$,   for $n > 0$ Definition of *n*!

Thus $4! = 4 \times 3! = 4 \times 3 \times 2!$, and so on. It is easy to implement this recursive mathematics definition as a recursive function in Pascal.

EXAMPLE 13.1 ▼

Function `Factor` in Fig. 13.7 computes the factorial of its argument N. The recursive step

```
Factor := N * Factor(N-1)
```

implements the second line of the factorial definition. This statement means that the result of the current call (argument N) is determined by multiplying the result of the next call (argument N-1) by N.

    A trace of

```
Fact := Factor(3)
```

is shown in Fig. 13.8. The value returned from the first call, `Factor(3)`, is 6, and this value is assigned to `Fact`. Be careful when you use the factorial function; its value increases rapidly and could lead to an integer-overflow error (for example, 10! is 24320). ▲

Although the recursive implementation of function `Factor` follows naturally from its definition, this function can be implemented easily using iteration. The iterative version (`FactorIt`) is shown in Fig. 13.9. Notice that `FactorIt` contains a loop as its major control structure, whereas the recursive version contains an `if` statement. Also, a local variable, `Factorial`, is needed in `FactorIt` to hold the accumulating product.

Figure 13.7
Recursive Function Factor

Directory: CHAP13
File: FACTOR.PAS

```
function Factor (N : Integer) : Integer;
{
  Computes the factorial of N (N!).
  Pre : N is defined and N >= 0.
  Post: Returns N!
}
begin {Factor}
  if N = 0 then
    Factor := 1
  else
    Factor := N * Factor(N-1)
end; {Factor}
```

Figure 13.8
Trace of Fact := Factor(3)

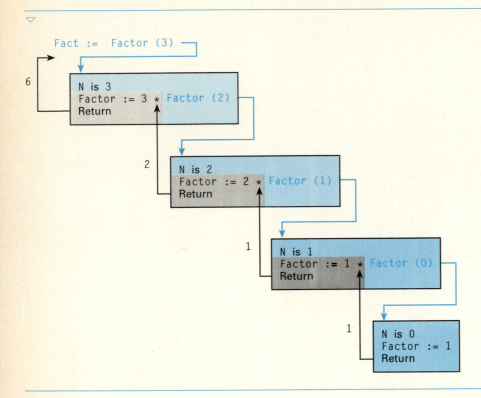

Figure 13.9
Iterative Function FactorIt

Directory: CHAP13
File: FACTORIT.PAS

```
function FactorIt (N : Integer) : Integer;
{
  Computes the factorial of N (N!).
  Pre : N is defined and N >= 0.
  Post: Returns N!
}
  var
    I,                        {loop-control variable}
    Factorial : Integer;   {the accumulating product}

begin {FactorIt}
  Factorial := 1;
  for I := 2 to N do
    Factorial := Factorial * I;

  FactorIt := Factorial        {Define result.}
end; {FactorIt}
```

EXAMPLE 13.2 ▼

The Fibonacci series is a sequence of numbers that have varied uses. They were originally intended to model the growth of a rabbit colony. We will not describe that model here, but you can see that the Fibonacci sequence 1, 1, 2, 3, 5, 8, 13, 21, 34, . . . increases rapidly. The fifteenth number in the sequence is 610 (that's a lot of rabbits!). The Fibonacci sequence is defined as follows:

▶ Fib_1 is 1.
▶ Fib_2 is 1.
▶ Fib_n is $Fib_{n-2} + Fib_{n-1}$, for $n > 2$.

   Verify for yourself that the sequence of numbers in the preceding paragraph is correct.
   A recursive function that computes the `Nth` Fibonacci number is shown in Fig. 13.10. Although easy to write, the Fibonacci function is not very efficient, because each recursive step generates two calls to function `Fibonacci`. ▲

EXAMPLE 13.3 ▼

Euclid's algorithm for finding the greatest common divisor of two positive integers, M and N, is defined recursively as follows. The *greatest common divisor* (GCD) of two integers is the largest integer that divides them both.

▶   `GCD(M, N)` is N if N `<=` M and N divides M.
▶   `GCD(M, N)` is `GCD(N, M)` if M `<` N.
▶   `GCD(M, N)` is `GCD (N`, remainder of M divided by N).

Figure 13.10
Recursive Function
Fibonacci

Directory: CHAP13
File: FIBONACC.PAS

```
function Fibonacci (N : Integer) : Integer;
{
  Computes the Nth Fibonacci number.
  Pre : N is defined and N > 0.
  Post: Returns the Nth Fibonacci number.
}
begin  {Fibonacci}
  if N <= 2 then
     Fibonacci := 1
  else
     Fibonacci := Fibonacci(N-2) + Fibonacci(N-1)
end; {Fibonacci}
```

Figure 13.11
Function GCD

Directory: CHAP13
File: FINDGCD.PAS

```
program FindGCD (Input, Output);

{Prints the greatest common divisor of two integers}
   var
      M, N : Integer;                {two input items}

   function GCD (M, N : Integer) : Integer;
   {
      Finds the greatest common divisor of M and N.
      Pre : M and N are defined and both are > 0.
      Post: Returns the greatest common divisor of M and N.
   }
   begin {GCD}
      if (N <= M) and (M mod N = 0) then
         GCD := N
      else if M < N then
         GCD := GCD(N, M)
      else
         GCD := GCD(N, M mod N)
   end; {GCD}

begin {FindGCD}
   Write ('Enter two positive integers> ');
   ReadLn (M, N);
   WriteLn ('Their greatest common divisor is ',
            GCD (M, N) :1)
end. {FindGCD}
```

Sample Run

```
Enter two positive integers> 24 84
Their greatest common divisor is 12
```

This algorithm states that the GCD is N if N is the smaller number and if N divides M. If M is the smaller number, then the GCD determination should be performed with the arguments transposed. If N does not divide M, the answer is obtained by finding the GCD of N and the remainder of M divided by N. The declaration and use of function GCD are shown in Fig. 13.11. ▲

Exercises for Section 13.3 **Self-Check**

1. What is the output of the following program? What does function Puzzle compute?

```
program TestPuzzle (Input, Output);

   function Puzzle (N : Integer) : Integer;
   begin  {Puzzle}
```

```
      if N = 1 then
         Puzzle := 0
      else
         Puzzle := 1 + Puzzle(N div 2)
    end;  {Puzzle}

  begin {TestPuzzle}
    WriteLn (Puzzle(8))
  end. {TestPuzzle}
```

2.   Complete the following recursive function, which calculates the value of a number (Base) raised to a power (Power). Assume that Power is positive.

```
     function PowerRaiser (Base, Power : Integer) : Integer;
     begin
        if Power = _____ then
           PowerRaiser := _____
        else
           PowerRaiser := _____
     end;
```

3.   What would happen if the terminating condition for function Fibonacci is N <= 1?

4.   If a program had the statement F := Fibonacci(5), how many calls to Fibonacci would be performed?

Programming

1.   Write a recursive function, FindSum, that calculates the sum of successive integers starting at 1 and ending at N (e.g., FindSum(N) = 1 + 2 + . . . + (N-1) + N).

2.   Write an iterative version of the Fibonacci function.

3.   Write an iterative function for the greatest common divisor.

13.4 Recursive Modules with Array Parameters

So far our recursive examples have used parameters that are simple types. Recursive modules also can process parameters that are structured types. This section shows recursive modules with array parameters.

CASE STUDY **Summing the Values in an Array**

PROBLEM ▼

Write a recursive function that finds the sum of the values in an array X with subscripts 1..N.

ANALYSIS ▼

The stopping case occurs when N is 1, that is, the sum is X[1] for a single-element array. If N is not 1, then we must add X[N] to the sum we get when we add the values in the subarray with subscripts 1..N-1.

Data Requirements

Problem Inputs

```
X : IntArray       {array of integer values}
N : Integer        {number of elements in the array}
```

Problem Output

The sum of the array values

DESIGN ▼

Initial Algorithm

1. if N is 1 then
   2. The sum is X[1].
   else
   3. Add X[N] to the sum of values in the subarray with subscripts 1..N-1.

IMPLEMENTATION ▼

Function FindSum in Fig. 13.12 implements this algorithm. The result of calling FindSum for a small array (N is 3) is also shown.

TESTING ▼

Figure 13.13 traces the function call FindSum(X, 3). As before, the colored part of each activation frame executes before the next recursive function call,

---

Figure 13.12
Using Recursive Function
FindSum

Directory: CHAP13
File: TESTFIND.PAS

```
program TestFindSum (Input, Output);

{Tests function FindSum}

  type
    IndexRange = 1..20;
    IntArray = array [IndexRange] of Integer;

  var
    N : Integer;
    X : IntArray;
```

▷ ▷ ▷ ▷ ▷

```
function FindSum (var X : IntArray;
                      N : Integer) : Integer;

{
   Finds the sum of the values in elements 1..N of array X.
   Pre : Array X and N are defined and N > 0.
   Post: Returns sum of first N elements of X.
}
begin {FindSum}
   if N = 1 then
      FindSum := X[1]
   else
      FindSum := X[N] + FindSum(X, N-1)
end; {FindSum}

begin {TestFindSum}
   N := 3;
   X[1] := 5;  X[2] := 10;  X[3] := -7;
   WriteLn ('The array sum is ', FindSum(X, 3) :3)
end. {TestFindSum}
```

Sample Run

```
The array sum is 8
```

Figure 13.13
Trace of FindSum(X, 3)

and each colored arrow points to a new activation frame. The gray part of each activation frame executes after the return from a recursive call, and each black arrow indicates the return point (the operator +) after a function execution. The value returned is indicated alongside the black arrow. The value returned for the original call, `FindSum(X, 3)`, is 8, which is printed.

Recursive Boolean Functions

Functions that return Boolean values (`True` or `False`) also can be written recursively. These functions do not perform a computation, yet their result is still determined by evaluating an expression (type `Boolean`) containing a recursive call. The function in Example 13.4 searches an array and the one in Example 13.5 compares two arrays.

EXAMPLE 13.4: Recursive Array Search ▼

The Boolean function `Member` in Fig. 13.14 returns the value `True` if the argument `Target` is in the subarray `X[1..N]`; otherwise, it returns the value `False`. For a single-element array (a stopping case), the result is determined by comparing `X[1]` and `Target`. For larger arrays, the result is `True` if the last element, `X[N]`, equals `Target` (another stopping case). Otherwise, the result depends on whether `Target` occurs in the subarray `X[1..N-1]`, as indicated by the recursive step:

```
Member := Member(X, Target, N-1) {Search rest of array.}
```

Figure 13.14
Recursive Function
Member

Directory: CHAP13
File: MEMBER.PAS

```
function Member (var X : IntArray;
                     Target,
                     N : Integer) : Boolean;

{
  Searches for Target in array X with subscripts 1..N.
  Pre : Target, N, and array X are defined and N > 0.
  Post: Returns True if Target is located in array X;
        otherwise, returns False.
}
begin {Member}
  if N = 1 then
    Member := (X[1] = Target)          {Check single element.}
  else if X[N] = Target then
    Member := True                     {Found - return True.}
  else
    Member := Member(X, Target, N-1) {Search rest of array.}
end; {Member}
```

Figure 13.15
Trace of Function Member

The function result is the value assigned to Member when a stopping case is reached.

The function designator Member(X, 10, 3) is traced in Fig. 13.15 for the array X defined in Fig. 13.12. The value returned is True, because the expression X[N] = Target is True when N is 2 (the second activation frame). ▲

EXAMPLE 13.5: Comparing Two Arrays ▼

The Boolean function Equal returns the value True if two arrays, say X and Y, of N elements are the same (e.g., X[1] = Y[1], X[2] = Y[2], . . ., X[N] = Y[N]). This function (see Fig. 13.16) looks similar to function Member. For single-element arrays, the function result depends on whether X[1] = Y[1]. For larger arrays, the result is False if X[N] <> Y[N]. Otherwise, the result depends on whether the subarrays with subscripts 1..N-1 are equal. ▲

Program Style

Variable Array Parameters in Recursive Modules

Earlier we stated that programmers often declare large arrays as variable parameters to conserve memory even if the arrays are input parameters. We recommend that you do this for recursive modules; otherwise, a separate copy of an array parameter would be made for each recursive call.

Figure 13.16
Recursive Function Equal

Directory: CHAP13
File: EQUAL.PAS

```
function Equal (var X, Y : IntArray;
                    N : Integer) : Boolean;
{
   Compares arrays X and Y with elements 1..N.
   Pre : Arrays X and Y are defined and N > 0.
   Post: Returns True if arrays X and Y are equal; otherwise,
         returns False.
}
begin {Equal}
   if N = 1 then
      Equal := (X[1] = Y[1])          {Compare 1-element arrays.}
   else if X[N] <> Y[N] then
      Equal := False                  {Found an unequal pair.}
   else
      Equal := Equal(X, Y, N-1)       {Compare rest of arrays.}
end; {Equal}
```

Comparison of Iterative and Recursive Functions

In function MemberIt (Fig. 13.17), the iterative version of Member, a loop is needed to examine each array element. Without recursion it is not possible to use the function name in an expression, so a local variable, Found, is needed to represent the result so far. Before the return from the function, the final value of Found is assigned as the function result.

The iterative function would execute faster than the recursive version. However, many programmers would argue that the recursive version is esthetically more pleasing. It is certainly more compact (a single if statement) and requires no local variables. Once you are accustomed to thinking recursively, the recursive form is somewhat easier to read and understand than the iterative form.

Some programmers like to use recursion as a conceptual tool. Once they have written the recursive form of a function or procedure, they can always translate it into an iterative version if run-time efficiency is a constraint. In the next section, we will describe a much more efficient searching algorithm.

Exercises for Section 13.4   ***Self-Check***

1. Trace the execution of recursive function Equal for the three-element arrays X (element values 1, 15, 10) and Y (element values 1, 5, 7).
2. Answer Exercise 1 for the recursive function Member and array X when searching for 15 and for 3.
3. What does the following recursive function do? Trace its execution on array X in Exercise 1.

Figure 13.17
Iterative Function
MemberIt

Directory: CHAP13
File: MEMBERIT.PAS

```
function MemberIt (var X : IntArray;
                       Target,
                       N : Integer) : Boolean;
{
  Searches for Target in array X with subscripts 1..N.
  Pre : Target, N, and array X are defined and N > 0.
  Post: Returns True if Target is located in array X;
        otherwise, returns False.
}
  var
    Found : Boolean;                    {local flag}
    I : Integer;                        {loop-control variable}

begin {MemberIt}
  Found := False;                       {Assume Target not found.}
  {Search array X for Target.}
  I := 1;                               {Start at beginning.}
  while not Found and (I <= N) do
    if X[I] = Target then
      Found := True                     {Found Target.}
    else
      I := I + 1;                       {Try next element.}

  {assert: Target is found or all elements are tested.}
  MemberIt := Found                     {Define result.}
end; {MemberIt}
```

```
function Mystery (X : IntArray;
                      N : Integer) : Integer;

  var
    Temp : Integer;
begin {Mystery}
  if N = 1 then
    Mystery := X[1]
  else
    begin
      Temp := Mystery(X, N-1);
      if X[N] > Temp then
        Mystery := X[N]
      else
        Mystery := Temp
    end {if}
end; {Mystery}
```

Programming

1. Write a recursive procedure that returns the smallest value in an array
    and its location.

13.5 Binary Search

This section describes a recursive search algorithm called binary search. Binary search is an example of an $O(\log_2 N)$ algorithm—a significant improvement over the sequential search algorithm, $O(N)$ (see Section 10.6).

Recursive Binary Search

Section 10.5 demonstrated one technique for searching for a target key in an array. Function Search (Fig. 10.18) performs a sequential search of its array argument and returns the index of the target key or the value 0 if the target is not present. Because the function requires N comparisons to determine that a target key is not in an array of N elements, sequential search is not very efficient for large arrays ($N > 100$). If the elements of the array being searched have been sorted and are in sequence by key value, we can make use of a more efficient search algorithm known as binary search.

Function Search returns 0 for a failed search. However, if 0 is allowed as a valid subscript for the array being searched, then returning 0 as the function value is inconclusive. To eliminate this ambiguity, we can implement an array-search algorithm as a procedure that has two output parameters: the index of the target value if found and a program flag indicating whether the target was found.

PROBLEM ▼

Write an improved search algorithm that takes advantage of the sorted array elements and allows the use of 0 as a subscript in the array being searched.

ANALYSIS ▼

The *binary-search algorithm* uses the ordering of array elements to eliminate half the array elements with each probe into the array. Consequently, if the array has 1000 elements, it either locates the target value or eliminates 500 elements with its first probe, 250 elements with its second probe, 125 elements with its third probe, and so on. For this reason, a binary search of an ordered array is an $O(\log_2 N)$ process. This means that you could use the binary-search algorithm to find a name in a large metropolitan telephone directory using 30 or fewer probes.

Because the array is ordered, all we have to do is compare the target value with the middle element of the subarray we are searching. If their values are the same, we are done. If the middle element value is larger than the target value, we should search the left half of the subarray; otherwise, we should search the right half of the subarray.

The subarray being searched has subscripts First..Last. The variable Middle is the subscript of the middle element in this range. Figure 13.18 shows an example in which the target is 35, First is 1, Last is 9, and Middle is 5. The right half of the array (subscripts Middle..Last) is eliminated by the first probe.

Last must be reset to Middle - 1 to define the new subarray to be searched, and Middle should be redefined as shown in Fig. 13.19. The target value, 35, would be found on this probe.

The binary-search algorithm can be defined clearly using recursion. The stopping cases are as follows:

▶ The array bounds are improper (First > Last).
▶ The middle value is the target value.

In the first case, the procedure returns False as the value of the program flag and the index of the target value is not defined. In the second case, True is returned as the value of the program flag and Middle is returned as the index of the target value. The recursive step is to search the appropriate subarray.

Data Requirements

Problem Inputs

```
Table  : IntArray    {array of integers to be searched}
Target : Integer     {target being searched for}
First  : Integer     {first subscript in the subarray}
Last   : Integer     {last subscript in the subarray}
```

Problem Outputs

```
Index : Integer     {location of Target in Table}
Found : Boolean     {flag - set to True if Target found}
```

Figure 13.18
First Probe of Binary
Search

Figure 13.19
Second Probe of Binary
Search

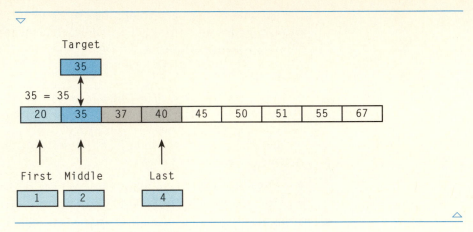

DESIGN ▼

Binary-Search Algorithm

1.   Compute the subscript of the middle element.
2.   `if` the array bounds are improper `then`
      3.   Return with failure.
    `else if` the target is the middle value `then`
      `begin`
        4.   Middle value is target location.
        5.   Return with success.
      `end`
    `else if` the target is less than the middle value `then`
      6.   Search subarray with subscripts `First..Middle - 1`.
    `else`
      7.   Search subarray with subscripts `Middle + 1..Last`.

For each of the recursive steps (steps 6 and 7), the bounds of the new subarray must be listed as actual parameters in the recursive call. The actual parameters define the search limits for the next probe into the array.

IMPLEMENTATION ▼

In the initial call to the recursive procedure, `First` and `Last` should be defined as the first and last elements of the entire array, respectively. For example, you could use the procedure call

```
BinSearch (X, 35, 1, 9, Location, Success);
```

to search an array X with subscripts `1..9` for the target value 35 (assuming X has type `IntArray`). The position of the target element in array X will be returned as the value of the actual parameter `Location` if 35 is found. The actual parameter `Success` will be set to `True` if 35 is found and will be `False` otherwise. Procedure `BinSearch` is shown in Fig. 13.20.

The assignment statement

```
Middle := (First + Last) div 2;
```

computes the subscript of the middle element by finding the average of `First` and `Last`. The value has no meaning when `First` is greater than `Last`, but it does no harm to compute it.

TESTING ▼

Check for targets in the first and last elements of the array. Check for targets that are not present. Check the algorithm for even- and odd-length arrays and for arrays with lower subscripts that are negative. Also check arrays with

Figure 13.20
Recursive Binary Search Procedure

Directory: CHAP13
File: BINSEARC.PAS

```
procedure BinSearch (var Table {input} : IntArray;
                         Target {input} : Integer;
                         First, Last {input} : Integer;
                         var Index {output} : Integer;
                         var Found {output} : Boolean);
{
  Pre : The elements of Table are in increasing order and
        First and Last are defined.
  Post: If Target is in the array, return its position
        in Index and set Found to True; otherwise, set
        Found to False and leave Index undefined.
}
  var
    Middle : Integer;

begin {BinSearch}
  Middle := (First + Last) div 2;   {Compute middle
                                              subscript.}
  if First > Last then              {Test array bounds.}
    Found := False
  else if Target = Table[Middle] then
    begin
      Found := True;                    {successful search}
      Index := Middle
    end
  else if Target < Table[Middle] then
    BinSearch (Table, Target, First, Middle - 1,
            Index, Found)
  else
    BinSearch (Table, Target, Middle + 1, Last,
            Index, Found)
end; {BinSearch}
```

multiple target values. See what happens when the array size gets very large, say, 1000.

Exercises for Section 13.5 **Self-Check**

1. Trace the execution of `BinSearch` for the array shown in Fig. 13.19 and a `Target` value of 40.
2. What would happen if `BinSearch` were called with the precondition of elements in increasing order violated? Would `BinSearch` still find the item?

Programming

1. Sorting algorithms need to know where in a sorted array a new item should be inserted. Write a recursive function `InsertLocation` that returns a location where `Target` could be inserted into an array and still maintain correct ordering.

13.6 Problem Solving with Recursion

To solve the Towers of Hanoi problem, you must move a specified number of disks that gradually increase in size from one tower (or one peg) to another. Legend has it that the world will come to an end when the problem is solved for 64 disks. You may be familiar with a children's game that is a 3-disk version of this puzzle.

The version of the problem shown in Fig. 13.21 has five disks (numbered 1 through 5) and three towers or pegs (lettered A, B, and C). The goal is to move the five disks from peg A to peg C subject to the following rules:

1. Only one disk may be moved at a time, and this disk must be the top disk on a peg.
2. A larger disk can never be placed on top of a smaller disk.

Figure 13.21
Towers of Hanoi

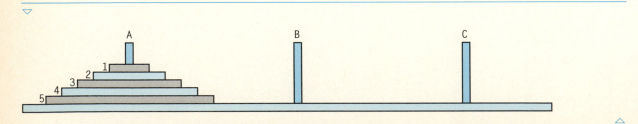

A stopping case of the problem is the movement of only one disk (e.g., "move disk 2 from peg A to peg C"). Simpler problems than the original would be to move four disks subject to conditions 1 and 2, to move three disks, and so on. We therefore want to split the original five-disk problem into one or more problems involving fewer disks. Let's consider splitting the original problem into three problems:

1. Move four disks from peg A to peg B.
2. Move disk 5 from peg A to peg C.
3. Move four disks from peg B to peg C.

Step 1 moves all disks but the largest to tower B, an auxiliary tower. Step 2 moves the largest disk to the goal tower, tower C. Step 3 then moves the remaining disks from B to the goal tower, where they will be placed on top of the largest disk. Let's assume that we can perform step 1 and step 2 (a stopping case); Fig. 13.22 shows the status of the three towers after completion of these steps. At this point it should be clear that we can solve the original five-disk problem if we can complete step 3 (move four disks from peg B to peg C). In step 3, peg C is the goal tower and peg A becomes the auxiliary tower.

Unfortunately, we still don't know how to perform step 1 or step 3. Both steps, however, involve four disks instead of five, so they are easier than the original problem. We should be able to split them into even simpler problems. In step 3, we must move four disks from peg B to peg C, so we can split it into two 3-disk problems and a single 1-disk problem:

3.1 Move three disks from peg B to peg A.
3.2 Move disk 4 from peg B to peg C.
3.3 Move three disks from peg A to peg C.

Figure 13.23 shows the towers after completion of steps 3.1 and 3.2. The two largest disks are now on peg C. Once we complete step 3.3, all five disks will be on peg C. Although we still do not know how to solve steps 3.1

Figure 13.22
Towers of Hanoi After Steps 1 and 2

Figure 13.23

Towers of Hanoi After Steps 1, 2, 3.1, and 3.2

and 3.3, they are at least simpler problems than the four-disk problem from which they are derived.

By splitting each *N*-disk problem into two problems involving (*N* - 1) disks and a one-disk problem, we eventually reach the point where all the cases manipulate only one disk, cases that we know how to solve. Next, we use this process to write a Pascal program that solves the Towers of Hanoi problem.

CASE STUDY   **Towers of Hanoi Problem**

PROBLEM ▼

Solve the Towers of Hanoi problem for N disks, where N is a parameter.

ANALYSIS ▼

The solution to the Towers of Hanoi problem consists of a printed list of individual disk moves. We need a recursive procedure that moves any number of disks from one peg to another, using the third peg as an auxiliary. The role of each peg (source, destination, auxiliary) changes with each call.

Data Requirements

Problem Inputs

```
FromPeg : 'A'..'C'      {the from peg}
ToPeg : 'A'..'C'        {the to peg}
AuxPeg : 'A'..'C'       {the auxiliary peg}
N : Integer             {number of disks to be moved}
```

Problem Output

A list of individual disk moves

DESIGN ▼

Initial Algorithm

1. `if N is 1 then`
      2. Move disk 1 from the *from* peg to the *to* peg.
  `else`
    `begin`
        3. Move `N-1` disks from the *from* peg to the *auxiliary* peg using
             the *to* peg as an intermediary.
        4. Move disk `N` from the *from* peg to the *to* peg.
        5. Move `N-1` disks from the *auxiliary* peg to the *to* peg using the
             from peg as an intermediary.
    `end`

If `N` is 1, a stopping case is reached. If `N` is greater than 1, the recursive step (following `else`) splits the original problem into three smaller subproblems, one of which (step 4) is a stopping case. Each stopping case displays a move instruction. Verify that the recursive step generates the three original sub-problems, repeated next, when `N` is 5, the *from* peg is `A`, and the *to* peg is `C`.

1. Move four disks from peg A to peg B.
2. Move disk 5 from peg A to peg C.
3. Move four disks from peg B to peg C.

IMPLEMENTATION ▼

The implementation of this algorithm is shown as procedure `Tower` in Fig. 13.24. Procedure `Tower` has four parameters. The procedure call statement

`Tower ('A', 'C', 'B', 5)`

solves the problem posed earlier of moving five disks from tower `A` to tower `C` using `B` as an auxiliary peg.

In Fig. 13.24, the stopping case (move disk 1) is implemented as a call to procedure `WriteLn`. Each recursive step consists of two recursive calls to `Tower`, with a call to `WriteLn` sandwiched between them. The first recursive call solves the problem of moving `N-1` disks to the *auxiliary* peg. The call to `WriteLn` displays a message to move disk `N` to the *to* peg. The second recursive call solves the problem of moving the `N-1` disks back from the *auxiliary* peg to the *to* peg.

TESTING ▼

The procedure call statement

`Tower ('A', 'C', 'B', 3)`

Figure 13.24
Recursive Procedure Tower

Directory: CHAP13
File: TOWER.PAS

```
procedure Tower (FromPeg,
                 ToPeg,
                 AuxPeg {input} : Char;
                 N       {input} : Integer);
{
  Moves N disks from FromPeg to ToPeg
  using AuxPeg as an intermediary.
  Pre : FromPeg, ToPeg, AuxPeg, and N are defined.
  Post: Displays a list of move instructions that transfer
        the disks.
}
begin {Tower}
  if N = 1 then
    WriteLn ('Move disk 1 from peg ', FromPeg,
             ' to peg ', ToPeg)
  else
    begin {recursive step}
      Tower (FromPeg, AuxPeg, ToPeg, N-1);
      WriteLn ('Move disk ', N :1, ' from peg ', FromPeg,
               ' to peg ', ToPeg);
      Tower (AuxPeg, ToPeg, FromPeg, N-1)
    end {recursive step}
end; {Tower}
```

solves a simpler three-disk problem: to move three disks from peg A to peg C. Its execution is traced in Fig. 13.25; the output generated is shown in Fig. 13.26. Verify for yourself that this list of steps does solve the three-disk problem.

Comparison of Iterative and Recursive Procedures

It is interesting to consider that procedure Tower in Fig. 13.24 will solve the Towers of Hanoi problem for any number of disks. The three-disk problem results in a total of 7 calls to procedure Tower and is solved by 7 disk moves. The five-disk problem would result in a total of 31 calls to procedure Tower and is solved in 31 moves. In general, the number of moves required to solve the N-disk problem is $2^N - 1$. Because each procedure call requires the allocation and initialization of a local data area in memory, computer time increases exponentially with problem size. For this reason, be careful about running the program with a value of N larger than 10.

The dramatic increase in processing time for larger towers is a function of the problem, not of recursion. In general, however, if there are recursive and iterative solutions to the same problem, the recursive solution requires more time and space because of the extra procedure calls.

Figure 13.25
Trace of Tower ('A', 'C', 'B', 3)

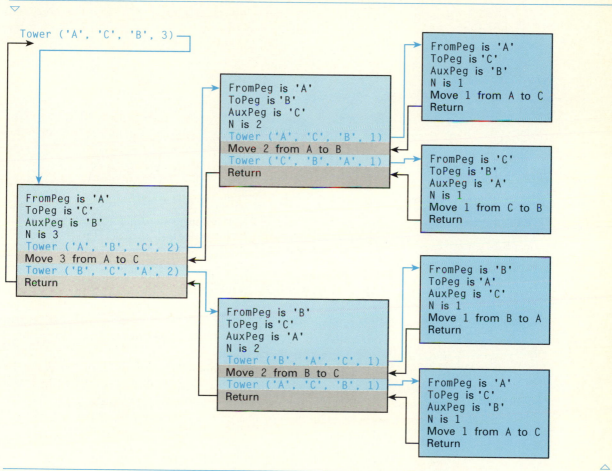

Figure 13.26
Output Generated by
Tower ('A', 'C', 'B', 3)

Although recursion was not really needed to solve the simpler problems in this chapter, it was extremely useful in formulating an algorithm for the Towers of Hanoi. For certain problems, recursion leads naturally to solutions that are much easier to read and understand than their iterative counterparts. In those cases, the benefits gained from increased clarity far outweigh the extra cost in time and memory of running a recursive program.

Exercises for Section 13.6 **Self-Check**

1. What problems are generated when you attempt to solve the problem "Move three disks from peg B to peg A"? When you attempt to solve the problem "Move three disks from peg A to peg C"?
2. How many moves are needed to solve the six-disk problem?

Programming

1. Write a main program that reads in a data value for N (the number of disks) and calls procedure Tower to move N disks from A to B.

13.7 Debugging Recursive Algorithms

You may find it difficult to observe the output displayed by a recursive procedure as it executes. If each recursive call generates several output lines and there are many recursive calls, the output will scroll down the screen faster than you can read. On most systems, you can stop the screen temporarily by pressing a control-character sequence (for example, Ctrl-S). You press another control sequence (for example, Ctrl-Q) to resume the display. You can also declare NextChar as a type Char variable in the recursive procedure and insert the lines

```
Write ('Press any key to continue> ');
Read (NextChar)
```

just before a recursive call. These lines cause your program to pause and to resume execution when you press a key.

13.8 Common Programming Errors

The most common problem with a recursive function or procedure is that it may not terminate properly. For example, if the terminating condition is not correct or is incomplete, the procedure may call itself indefinitely or until all available memory is used up. Normally, a stack overflow run-time error indicates that a recursive procedure is not terminating. Make sure you identify all stopping cases and provide a terminating condition for each one. Also be sure that each recursive step leads to a situation that is closer to a stopping case and that repeated recursive calls eventually lead to stopping cases only.

Large arrays or other data structures used as value parameters can quickly consume all available memory. Unless absolutely essential for data protection, arrays should be passed as variable parameters. Any expression such as N-1 must be passed as a value parameter.

CHAPTER REVIEW

1. A recursive module or function is one that calls itself. You can use recursion to solve problems by splitting them into smaller versions of themselves.
2. Each recursive module has one or more stopping cases and recursive steps. The stopping cases can be solved directly; the recursive steps lead to recursive calls of the module.
3. Recursive modules can be used with parameters that are simple types or structured types. Recursive functions can implement mathematical operations that are defined by recursive definitions.
4. Binary search is a recursive search procedure that can search a large array in $O(\log N)$ time.

Quick-Check Exercises

1. How are stacks used in recursion?
2. Can the stopping case also have a recursive call in it?
3. Which control statement is always in a recursive procedure or function?
4. What are the two uses of the function name in a recursive function?
5. What is the relation between a terminating condition and a stopping case?
6. Returning from a series of recursive calls is called _____ the recursion.
7. What is the problem with value array parameters in recursion?
8. In a recursive problem involving N items, why must N be a value parameter?
9. What causes a stack overflow error?
10. What can you say about a recursive algorithm that has the following form?

    ```
    if condition then
       Perform recursive step.
    ```

Answers to Quick-Check Exercises

1. The stack is used to hold all parameter and local variable values and the return point for each execution of a recursive module.
2. No, if it did, recursion would continue.
3. The if statement

4. To assign a value to the function and to call it recursively
5. A recursive module reaches a stopping case when a terminating condition is true.
6. Unwinding
7. A copy of the array must be pushed onto the stack each time a call occurs. All available stack memory could be exhausted.
8. If N was a variable parameter, it would not be possible to use the expression N-1 as an actual parameter in a recursive call.
9. Too many recursive calls—all stack memory is allocated.
10. Nothing is done when the stopping case is reached.

Review Questions

1. Differentiate between a recursive step and a stopping case in a recursive algorithm.
2. Discuss the time and space efficiency of recursive procedures versus iterative procedures.
3. What basic characteristics must a problem have for a recursive solution to be applicable?
4. Write a recursive procedure that prints the accumulating sum of ordinal values corresponding to each character in a string. For example, if the string value is 'a boy', the first value printed would be the ordinal number of a, then the sum of ordinals for a and the space character, then the sum of ordinals for a, space, b, and so on.
5. Differentiate between the use of value and variable parameters in a recursive procedure. When would each be applicable?
6. Convert the following program from an iterative process to a recursive function that calculates an approximate value for e, the base of the natural logarithms, by summing the series

   $1 + 1/1! + 1/2! + \ldots + 1/N!$

   until additional terms do not affect the approximation:

```
program ELog (Input, Output);

   var
      ENL, Delta, Fact : Real;
      N : Integer;

begin {ELog}
   ENL := 1.0;
   N := 1;
   Fact := 1.0;
   Delta := 1.0;
   repeat
      ENL := ENL + Delta;
      N := N + 1;
      Fact := Fact * N;
      Delta := 1.0 / Fact
   until ENL = (ENL + Delta);
   Write ('The value of e is ', E :18:15)
end. {ELog}
```

Programming Projects

1.   The expression for computing $c(n, r)$, the number of combinations of n items taken r at a time, is

$$c(n, r) = n!/r!(n - r)!$$

Write and test a function for computing $c(n, r)$, given that $n!$ is the factorial of n.

2.   A palindrome is a word that is spelled exactly the same when the letters are reversed, for example, level, deed, and mom. Write a recursive function that returns the Boolean value `True` if a word passed as a parameter is a palindrome.

3.   Write a recursive procedure that lists all subsets of pairs of letters for a given set of letters, for example,

```
['A','C','E','G'] →['A','C'], ['A','E'], ['A','G'],
                    ['C','E'], ['C','G'], ['E','G']
```

4.   Write a procedure that accepts an 8 × 8 array of characters that represents a maze. Each position can contain either an `'X'` or a blank. Starting at position `[1,1]`, list any path through the maze to get to location `[8,8]`. Only horizontal and vertical moves are allowed (no diagonal moves). Make sure your algorithm avoids retracing previously tried paths. If no path exists, write a message indicating this condition.

Moves can be made only to locations that contain a blank. If an `'X'` is encountered, that path is blocked and another must be chosen. Use recursion.

5.   Programming Project 6 in Chapter 7 described the bisection method, which finds an approximate root for the equation $f(X) = 0$ on the interval `XLeft` to `XRight`, inclusive (assuming the function is continuous on this interval). The interval end points (`XLeft` and `XRight`) and the tolerance for the approximation (`Epsilon`) are input by the user.

One stopping criterion for the bisection method is the identification of an interval `[XLeft,XRight]` that is less than `Epsilon` in length over which $f(X)$ changes sign (from positive to negative or vice versa). The midpoint `[XMid = (XLeft + XRight)/2.0]` of the interval will be an approximation to the root of the equation when `f(XMid)` is very close to zero. Of course, if you find a value of `XMid` such that `f(XMid) = 0`, you have found a very good approximation of the root, and the algorithm should also stop.

To perform the recursive step, replace either `XLeft` or `XRight` with `XMid`, depending on which one has the same sign as `XMid`. Write a program that uses the bisection method to determine an approximation to the equation

$$5x^3 - 2x^3 + 3 = 0$$

over the interval `[-1,1]` using `Epsilon = 0.0001`.

6.   Write a program that finds the size of a blob in a rectangular grid where a blob is a connected group of filled cells. Represent the grid as an 8 × 8 array. Read the data for the array, designating each cell as filled or empty. Also enter the starting cell for the blob you are investigating. If the starting cell is not in the grid or the starting cell is empty, the blob has a size of 0. Otherwise, the size of a blob is determined by moving out from the start cell to its eight neighbors (assuming the cell is not on a grid boundary) and determining the size of the blob

each neighbor is part of. Add 1 to this sum to account for the start cell. Make sure you reset a cell to empty when it is counted as part of a blob.

7.   Write a program that, given a list of up to 10 integer numbers and a sum, will find a subset of the numbers whose total is that sum if one exists or indicate that none exists otherwise. For example, for the list 5, 13, 23, 9, 3, 3 and sum = 28, your program should find 13, 9, 3, 3.

8.   MergeSort is an $O(N \times \log N)$ sorting technique with the following recursive algorithm:

`if` the array to sort has more than 1-element `then`
   `begin`
      MergeSort the left-half of the array.
      MergeSort the right-half of the array.
      Merge the two sorted subarrays to form the sorted array.
   `end`

For example: to MergeSort the array 10, 20, 15, 6, 5, 40, follow these steps:

MergeSort the subarray 10, 20, 15 giving 10, 15, 20.

MergeSort the subarray 6, 5, 40 giving 5, 6, 40.

Merge the two sorted subarrays giving 5, 6, 10, 15, 20, 40.

Each call to MergeSort above will generate two more recursive calls (one for a 1-element array and one for a 2-element array). MergeSort for a 1-element array is a stopping case. See Section 15.3 for a discussion of merging.

CHAPTER FOURTEEN

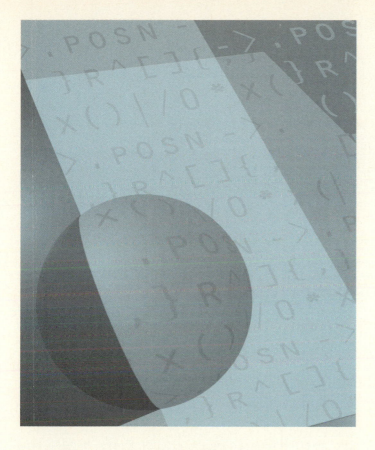

Sets

This chapter introduces a new user-defined, structured data type: sets. Sets are useful for determining whether a variable has a value that is included in a list of values. In this chapter, you will learn what sets are, which operators are used with sets, and how to use them in programs.

14.1   Set Data Type

set
an unordered list of elements
that are values of the same
ordinal type

set element (set member)
a value in a set

Sets are structured variables that contain lists of integers, characters, or enumerated type values. A set is like an array in that it can house a collection of simple elements. Unlike an array, however, the elements of a set are not ordered.

You probably have studied sets in a mathematics course. In mathematics, a set is represented by a list of **set elements,** or **set members,** enclosed in curly braces. For example, the set {1, 3, 5, 7, 9} is the set of odd integers from 1 through 9. In Pascal, set elements are enclosed in square brackets so the preceding set is written as [1, 3, 5, 7, 9]. Because the elements of a set are not ordered, the set [9, 5, 7, 1, 3] is equivalent to [1, 3, 5, 7, 9].

Declaring Sets

You declare a set or set variable just as you declare other structured types. First declare a set data type and then declare a variable of that type.

EXAMPLE 14.1   ▼

The declarations

```
type
  DigitSet = set of 0..9;   {set type of integer elements}

var
  Odds, Evens, Middle, Mixed : DigitSet;          {4 sets}
```

declare a set type DigitSet and four set variables: Odds, Evens, Middle, and Mixed. Each set variable of type DigitSet can contain between zero and 10 elements chosen from the integers in the subrange 0..9. Although memory space is allocated for four sets, their contents are undefined. To work with a set, you must define it using a set assignment, as shown shortly.   ▲

SYNTAX DISPLAY

Set Type Declaration

Form: type
         set type = set of *base type*;
Example: type
         LetterSet = set of 'A'..'Z';
Interpretation: The identifier *set type* is defined over the values specified in *base type*. A variable declared to be of type *set type* is a set whose elements are chosen from the values in *base type*. The *base type* must be an ordinal type.
Notes: Most implementations limit the number of values in the *base type* of a set. Usually this limit is the same as the number of values in the data type Char (128 or 256), allowing you to declare set of Char as a set type. Given this limitation, you cannot use the data type Integer as a *base type,* but you can use a subrange of type Integer with up to 128 or 256 values.

Set Assignment and Set Literals

The set assignment statement places values in a set. The statements

```
Odds := [1, 3, 5, 7, 9];
Evens := [0, 2, 4, 6, 8]
```

set literal
a list of values enclosed in brackets

assign values to two of the set variables declared in Example 14.1. Each assignment statement assigns a set literal to a set variable, where a **set literal** is a list of values from the set base type enclosed in brackets. After these assignments, the set `Odds` contains the set of odd digits in the subrange 0 through 9, and the set `Evens` contains the set of even digits in the same range. We could use these two sets to determine whether a variable contained an odd or an even number.

The set literal `['0'..'9','+','-','E','.']` is the set of characters that can appear in a real number. This set contains 14 elements. It is more convenient to use the *subrange notation* `'0'..'9'` to denote the 10 digit characters rather than list each digit character separately.

SYNTAX DISPLAY

Set Literal

Form: [*list-of-elements*]
Example: `['+', '-', '*', '/', '<', '>', '=']`
Interpretation: A set is defined whose elements are the *list-of-elements* enclosed in brackets. The elements of a set must belong to the same ordinal type or to compatible ordinal types (defined in Section 7.6). Commas separate elements in the *list-of-elements*. A group of consecutive elements may be specified with subrange notation (i.e., *minvalue .. maxvalue,* where *minvalue* and *maxvalue* are type-compatible expressions and *minvalue* is considered less than or equal to *maxvalue*).

SYNTAX DISPLAY

Set Assignment

Form: *set var* := *set expression*
Example: `Uppercase := ['A'..'Z']` {set of uppercase letters}
Interpretation: The variable, *set var,* is defined as the set whose elements are determined by *set expression*. The *set expression* may be a set literal or another set variable. Alternatively, a *set expression* may specify the manipulation of two or more sets using the set operators. The base type of *set var* and *set expression* must be type compatible, and all the elements in *set expression* must be included in the base type of *set var*.

Empty Set and Universal Set

empty set
a set having zero elements denoted by [ ]

Two special set literals are associated with each set type: the empty set and the universal set. The **empty set** has zero elements and is denoted by a pair of brackets, `[ ]`. To create an empty set, you must use an assignment such as

```
Middle := []
```

undefined set
a set variable that is declared
but is not assigned any values
universal set
a set containing all possible
values for a set

An empty set can be distinguished from an **undefined set,** where the set is declared but its elements are unknown.

A **universal set** contains all the values in the base type for a particular set type. For a set of type `DigitSet` (Example 14.1), the base type is the subrange `0..9` so a universal set would be denoted as `[0..9]`. The assignment

```
Mixed := [0..9]
```

defines set variable `Mixed` as a universal set. We often initialize a set variable to the empty set or universal set before using it.

Sets with Enumerated Type Values

You also can define sets with values chosen from your own enumerated data type.

EXAMPLE 14.2 ▼

In the following declarations, we declare and use an enumerated type (`Cars`) as the base type for a set type (`CarSet`). Next, we declare three set variables of type `CarSet`:

```
type
  Cars = (Dodge, Ford, Lincoln, Cadillac, Fiesta, Pontiac,
          Corvette, Buick, Chevrolet, Mercury, Mustang);
  CarSet = set of Cars;

var
  Avis, Hertz, Merger : CarSet;
```

The assignments

```
Avis := [Dodge, Lincoln, Fiesta];
Hertz := [Dodge..Cadillac, Mercury];
Merger := [Dodge..Mustang]
```

define the set `Avis` consisting of the three elements listed, the set `Hertz` consists of five elements (what are they?), and the set `Merger`, which is the universal set for type `CarSet`.

You may place a set variable on the right of the assignment statement, provided both set variables have compatible base types. The next assignment changes the value of set `Merger`:

```
Merger := Hertz   ▲
```

Exercises for Section 14.1 *Self-Check*

1. Which of the following sets are valid? Which are invalid? What are the elements of the valid sets?
    a. `[1, 3, 1..5]`   d. `['1', '3', 'A'..'C']`
    b. `['1', '3', '1'..'5']`   e. `[1, 10, 500..501]`
    c. `[1, 3, '1'..'5']`

The *difference* of set A and set B (set operator -) is the set of elements that are in set A but not in set B:

```
[1,3,4] - [1,2,4] is [3]
[1,3] - [2,4] is [1,3]
['A','C','F'] - ['B','C','D','F'] is ['A']
['A','C','F'] - ['A','C','D','F'] is []
['A','C','D','F'] - ['A','C','F'] is ['D']
```

commutative operator
an operator that produces the same result regardless of the order of its operands

The set operator - is not **commutative.** This means that A - B and B - A can have different values. The set operators + and *, however, are commutative.

In Pascal expressions, the operators +, *, and - specify arithmetic operations when their operands are type Real or Integer, and they specify set operations when their operands are sets. When an operator has more than one meaning, this condition is called **operator overloading.** The precedence rules for the operators +, *, and - are the same regardless of their use (see Table 4.5). When in doubt, use parentheses to specify the intended order of evaluation.

operator overloading
giving an operator more than one meaning

Often a new element must be inserted into an existing set. Such an insertion is achieved by forming the union of the existing set and a **unit set,** which contains only the new element. The set [2], which follows, is a unit set:

unit set
a set containing a single element enclosed in brackets

```
[1,3,4,5] + [2] is [1,2,3,4,5]
```

Avoid the common error of omitting the brackets around a unit set. For example, the expressions

```
[1,3,4,5] + 2        {2nd operand is not a set}
Avis + Cadillac      {2nd operand is not a set}
```

are invalid because one operand is a set and the other is a constant (see Example 14.2). Likewise, the expression

```
[Avis] + [Cadillac]  {1st operand is not a set}
```

is invalid; the brackets around Avis are not needed because Avis is a set.

Set Relational Operators

The relational operators =, <>, <=, and >= compare two sets. The two sets being compared must have the same base type. The result of a comparison is a Boolean value.

The operators = and <> test whether two sets contain the same elements:

```
[1,3] = [1,3] is True     [1,3] <> [1,3] is False
[1,3] = [2,4] is False    [1,3] <> [2,4] is True
[1,3] = [3,1] is True     [1,3] <> [3,1] is False
  [] = [1] is False         [] <> [1] is True
```

As indicated by the next-to-last line, the order in which the elements of a set are listed is not important ([1,3] and [3,1] denote the same set). However, we normally list the elements of a set in increasing ordinal sequence.

The relational operators `<=` and `>=` determine subset and superset relationships:

▶ Set A is a *subset* of set B (A `<=` B) if every element of A is also an element of B:

```
[1,3] <= [1,2,3,4] is True
[1,3] <= [1,3] is True
[1,2,3,4] <= [1,3] is False
[1,3] <= [] is False
[] <= [1,3] is True
```

The empty set, [ ], is a subset of every set.

▶ Set A is a *superset* of set B (A `>=` B) if every element of B is also an element of A:

```
[1,3] >= [1,2,3,4] is False
[1,3] >= [1,3] is True
[1,2,3,4] >= [1,3] is True
[1,3] >= [] is True
[] >= [1,3] is False
```

The set operators are summarized in Table 14.1.

Table 14.1
Set Operators

Operator	Meaning	Example
+	Set union	`['A'] + ['B'] is ['A', 'B']`
–	Set difference	`['A', 'B'] - ['A'] is ['B']`
*	Set intersection	`['A', 'B'] * ['A'] is ['A']`
=	Set equality	`['A', 'B'] = ['B', 'A'] is True`
<>	Set inequality	`['A', 'B'] <> ['A'] is True`
<=	Subset	`['A', 'B'] <= ['A'] is False`
>=	Superset	`['A', 'B'] >= ['B'] is True`

Reading and Writing Sets

Like most other data structures, a set cannot be a parameter of the standard Read or Write procedures. Data items to be stored in a set must be read individually and inserted in an initially empty set using the set union operator.

EXAMPLE 14.4: Reading Sets ▼

Procedure ReadSet in Fig. 14.1 reads a sentence terminated by . and inserts the uppercase form of each letter in the set represented by parameter Letters (set type CharSet). The statement

Figure 14.1
Procedure ReadSet

Directory: CHAP14
File: READSET.PAS

```
procedure ReadSet (var Letters {output} : CharSet);
{
  Reads a sentence terminated by a period and
  stores the uppercase form of each letter in Letters.
  Pre  : None.
  Post : Returns through Letters all the letters read
         before the period.
  Calls: function UpCase (Fig. 7.3)
}
  const
    Sentinel = '.';                     {sentinel character}

  var
    NextChar : Char;                    {next input character}

begin  {ReadSet}
  Letters := [];                        {Initialize Letters.}
  WriteLn ('Enter a sentence ending with symbol ', Sentinel);
  Read (NextChar);                      {Read first character.}
  while NextChar <> Sentinel do
    {invariant:
        No prior value of NextChar is the sentinel and
        Letters contains each uppercase letter read so far.
    }
    begin
      NextChar := UpCase(NextChar);     {Convert to uppercase.}
      if NextChar in ['A'..'Z'] then
        Letters := Letters + [NextChar];   {Insert a letter.}
      Read (NextChar)                   {Read next character.}
    end  {while}

  {assert: Last character read was the sentinel.}
end; {ReadSet}
```

```
Letters := [];                        {Initialize Letters.}
```

initializes set Letters to the empty set, and the if statement

```
if NextChar in ['A'..'Z'] then
  Letters := Letters + [NextChar];   {Insert a letter.}
```

inserts each new uppercase letter in set Letters.   ▲

EXAMPLE 14.5: Writing Sets ▼

To print a set, you must test whether every value in the base type is a set element. Only values that are set elements should be printed. Procedure PrintSet in Fig. 14.2 prints the uppercase letters in the set represented by its parameter Letters. If you call PrintSet with ['A', 'C', 'Z'] as its parameter, PrintSet displays {A, C, Z, }.   ▲

Figure 14.2
Procedure PrintSet

**Directory: CHAP14
File: PRINTSET.PAS**

```
procedure PrintSet (Letters {input} : CharSet);
{
   Prints the uppercase letters in set Letters.
   Pre : Letters is defined.
   Post: Each uppercase letter in Letters is displayed.
}
   var
      NextLetter : Char;            {loop-control variable}

begin {PrintSet}
   Write ('{');
   for NextLetter := 'A' to 'Z' do
      if NextLetter in Letters then
         Write (NextLetter, ', ');            {Print a set member.}
   WriteLn ('}')
end; {PrintSet}
```

Exercises for Section 14.2   ***Self-Check***

1. Given that A is the set [1,3,5,7], B is the set [2,4,6], and C is the set [1,2,3], evaluate the following set expressions.

    a.   A + (B - C)   g.   C + (A - C)
    b.   A + (B * C)   h.   C - (A - B)
    c.   A + B + C   i.   (C - A) - B
    d.   (C - A) <= B   j.   A - C - [5,7] = []
    e.   [] <= A * B * C   k.   2 in A
    f.   A + B <> [1..7]   l.   2 in A + B

2. Given two sets A and B, write a Boolean expression to determine whether A is a proper subset of B. A is a proper subset of B if every element of A is in B and one element in B is not in A.

Programming

1. Modify PrintSet to print a set of type DigitSet.

14.3 Common Programming Errors

Remember that a set variable, like any variable, must be initialized before it can be manipulated. It is tempting to assume that a set is empty and then to begin processing it without initializing it to the empty set, [ ], through an explicit assignment.

Many Pascal operators can be used with sets. The meaning of the operator changes when its operands are sets instead of numbers. Remember to use a unit set (a set of one element) when you insert or delete a set element. The set union operation in the expression

```
['A','E','O','U'] + 'I'        {incorrect set union}
```

is incorrect and should be rewritten as

```
['A','E','O','U'] + ['I']      {correct set union}
```

Because a set cannot be an operand of the standard Read or Write procedure, you must read in the elements of a set individually and insert them into an initially empty set using the set union operator. To print a set, you must test each value in the base type of a set for set membership. Only those values in the set should be printed.

CHAPTER REVIEW

1. The set data type stores a collection of elements of the same type (called the base type). Each value in the base type of a set either is a member of the set or is not. Unlike an array, a value can be saved only once in a set, and the set elements are unordered (e.g., [1,5,2,4] is the same set as [1,2,4,5]).
2. Use the set membership operator in to determine whether a particular value is a set element. The operators +, *, and - perform set union, set intersection, and set difference, respectively, when used with set operands. The relational operators = and <> test for set equality and inequality; the relational operators <= and >= test for subset and superset relationships.

Summary of New Pascal Constructs

Construct	Effect
Set Type Declaration	
`type` `   DigitSet = set of 0..9;`	Declares a set type DigitSet whose base type is the set of digits from 0 through 9.
`var` `   Digits, Primes : DigitSet;`	Digits and Primes are set variables of type DigitSet.
Set Assignment	

`Digits := [];`
`Primes := [2,3,5] + [7];`
`Digits := Digits + [1..3];`
`Digits := [0..9] - [1,3,5,7,9];`
 	
`Digits := [1,3,5,7,9] * Primes`
	Digits is the empty set.
	Primes is the set [2,3,5,7].
	Digits is the set [1,2,3].
	Digits is the set [0,2,4,6,8].
	Digits is the set [3,5,7].

Set Relations	

`Primes <= Digits`
 	
`Primes >= []`
	True if Primes is a subset of Digits.
	Always True.

Construct	Effect
`Primes <> []`	`True` if `Primes` contains any element.
`[1,2,3] = [3,2,1]`	`True` because sets are unordered.

Quick-Check Exercises

1. What is the universal set?
2. Which can have the most elements: a set union, an intersection, or a difference? Which of these operators is not commutative?
3. Can you have a set whose base type is `Integer` or `Char`? How about a subrange type with host type `Integer` or `Char`?
4. Does it make any difference in which order the elements of a set are inserted? Does it make any difference if an element is inserted more than once into the same set?
5. Given that `Set1` is `[1..3]`, what are the contents of the following sets?
   a. `Set2 := Set1 + [4,5,6];`
   b. `Set3 := Set1 - Set2;`
   c. `Set4 := Set3 + [4,7];`
   d. `Set5 := Set4 + [4,6];`
   e. `Set6 := Set5 * Set2;`

Answers to Quick-Check Exercises

1. The set containing all the values in the base type
2. The union of two sets. The set difference (operator `-`) is not commutative.
3. You cannot use `Integer` as a base type, but you can use `Char`. A subrange of `Integer` or `Char` can be the base type.
4. No; no
5. a. `[1..6]`   b. `[]`   c. `[4,7]`   d. `[4,6,7]`   e. `[4,6]`

Review Questions

1. Why may we be unable to declare a set whose base type is `Char` (in some versions of Pascal)?
2. Which of the following could be declared as a set? Provide a set declaration for those that can and explain why not for those that cannot.
   a. All integers
   b. All integers from 50 to 80
   c. All integers from 1900 to 2000
   d. All real numbers from 0 to 1
   e. All characters from A to Z
   f. All Boolean values
   g. The first 10 multiples of 9

3. Write the declarations for a set, `Oysters`, whose values are the months of the year (enumerated type `Month`). Initialize `Oysters` to the set of all months whose names contain the letter r. Write an assignment statement that inserts the month `May` in this set and deletes the month `September`.

4. The following `for` loop prints each member of a set whose elements are values of enumerated type `Day`. Write the declaration for set `TestSet`. Rewrite the loop as a `while` loop whose repetition condition is `TestSet <> []`. Use the set operator `–` to delete each set element after it is displayed.

```
for Today := Sunday to Saturday do
  if Today in TestSet then
    WriteDay (Today)
```

5. Provide the declarations for the following two sets. What are the intersection and the union of sets `Vowel` and `Letter`? What are the two set differences?

```
Vowel := ['Y', 'U', 'O', 'I'];
Letter := ['A' .. 'P'];
```

Programming Projects

1. We have a group of ten people: Crissa, Neil, Patricia, Noel, Mary, Martin, Donald, John, Ruth, and Bill. Each person has a set of people to whom they tell secrets. Your task is to write a program that inputs the names of the people each person tells secrets to and determines everyone who will find out the secret, assuming Crissa knows it first. You will create two sets: people who know the secret and have told everyone to whom they tell secrets and people who know the secret but haven't told anyone yet. Initially the first set is empty and Crissa is in the second set. Your program will have a loop that selects a member of the second set, moves all the people that member tells secrets to into the second set only if they are not already in the first or second set, and moves the selected member to the first set. When the second set is empty, your program is complete.

2. Write a Pascal program to play the game TaxMan. In this game, a user plays against the computer with the object of accumulating the most points. The user selects a number from 1 to 40. If the number is still available, the user is credited with points equal to the number chosen and the computer is credited with points equivalent to the sum of the unclaimed factors of the number chosen. The user may not choose a number that has no factors. After a number is chosen, it and its factors are removed from the set of available numbers. The computer gets all unclaimed numbers added to its score when the game ends.

    To illustrate, consider the game played with the set of numbers 1 to 6. If the user selects 6, the computer gets all factors of 6, namely, 3, 2, 1, and the score is tied. Now only 4 and 5 are left to choose from; since the factors of 4 (2 and 1) have been removed from the set of available numbers and 5 has no factors other than itself and 1, the computer wins, 15 to 6. The user should have chosen 5 first, then 4, and then 6. Then the user would have won, 15 to 7.

3. Write a procedure that reads in an array of cards and stores it in an array of sets, one set for each suit. Use an enumerated type for the suits and one for the card face values. The data for each card will be presented in the form of a character

representing the suit and a character representing the card face value
(`'2'..'9'`, `'T'`, `'J'`, `'Q'`, `'K'`, `'A'`).

4. Consider a hand of cards read in Programming Project 3 as a bridge hand and evaluate it. Award points for each card according to the following method:

Card Face Value	Points
`2..10`	0
`jack`	1
`queen`	2
`king`	3
`ace`	4

Also add one point for each suit that has only two cards, two points for each suit that has only one card, and three points for each suit that is missing.

Directory: CHAP14
File: PROJ5.PAS

5. Write a program to scan a line of characters containing an equation and calculate the result. Assume all operands are integers. Conduct tests to determine whether the equation is valid.

   Valid operations are +, -, /, *, and ^, where +, -, /, and * have their typical functions and ^ indicates the value to its left is raised to the power of the operand to its right (which must be positive).

   Numbers may be negative. All operations are done in left-to-right order (no operator precedence). For example,

   `2 + 3 ^ 2 + 36 * 1`

   would be

   `5 ^ 2 + 36 * 1 = 25 + 36 * 1 = 61 * 1 = 61`

   Use sets to verify the equations' operations, and ignore all blanks. Output should consist of an equal sign (=) and then the answer. If an equation is invalid, display the message ** `INVALID` **.

6. Rewrite Programming Project 5 to allow operands (including exponents) that are either integers or real numbers. You should read the characters of the operands one at a time and convert them to their equivalent numeric value.

CHAPTER FIFTEEN

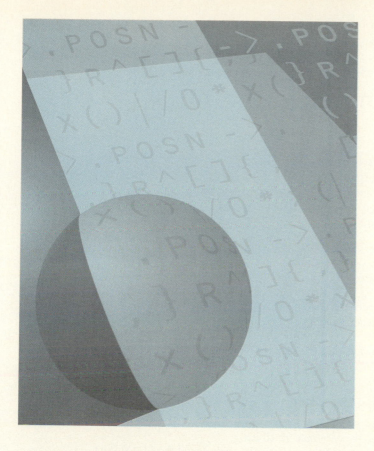

External Data Structures: Files

access in random order
processing the elements of
a data structure in arbitrary
order

access in sequential order
processing all elements of a
data structure starting with the
first element and ending with
the last element

This chapter covers the file data structure. Like arrays, files are ordered collections of elements of the same type. Because files are located in secondary memory (disk) rather than in main memory, they can be much larger than arrays. Moreover, the elements of an array can be accessed in arbitrary, or **random**, **order**; files in standard Pascal, in contrast, can be accessed only in **sequential order**. This means that file component 1, component 2, . . . , component $(N - 1)$ must be accessed before file component N.

Files should be familiar to you from your work on Chapter 8, where the files were *text files,* or files of characters. In this chapter, we will work with files whose components can be any simple or structured type. For example, we may have a file of integers or a file of records. These nontext files are called *binary files*.

15.1 Text File ADT and Binary File ADT

Text File ADT

In Chapter 8, you learned about the structure of text files and the operations that can be performed on them. In this section, we will summarize this information as a formal specification for a text file abstract data type (see Table 15.1). This formal description will help us extend the text file data type to files that have other components besides characters.

Table 15.1

Specification for Text File ADT

Structure

A text file is an ordered collection of characters from the Pascal character set stored on disk. The character <eoln> denotes the end of a line, and the character <eof> denotes the end of the file. The characters in the file are processed sequentially, starting with the first. A file location marker keeps track of the next character to be processed.

Operators

The descriptions of the operators use the following parameters:

> F is a file variable
> *input list* is a list of simple variables
> *output list* is a list of simple variables, simple values, and strings

Reset (F)   Opens file F for input (reading), placing the file location marker at the first character.

Rewrite (F)   Opens file F for output (writing), placing the file location marker at the beginning of an empty file.

Read (F, *input list*)   Reads data from file F into the variables specified in *input list*. If F is missing, it reads data from system file Input.

ReadLn (F, *input list*)   Same as Read except that it advances the file location marker for file F to the start of the next line after performing the data entry.

Write (F, *output list*)   Writes values in *output list* to file F. If F is missing, it writes to system file Output.

WriteLn (F, *output list*)   Same as Write except that it writes an <eoln> to file F after all values.

EOF(F)   (function) Returns True if the <eof> is the next character in file F; otherwise, it returns False.

EOLN(F)   (function) Returns True if an <eoln> is the next character in file F; otherwise, it returns False.

Next we show how to use these operators with other file types. Three of these operators—ReadLn, WriteLn, and EOLN—can be used only with Text files because they process the <eoln> character, which cannot appear in other file types.

Declaring Binary Files

binary file
a file whose components are stored on disk in the same form as in main memory

In addition to text files, we can declare new file types whose components are any type, simple or structured, except for another file type. Files with nontext components are binary files. A component of a **binary file** is stored on disk using the same binary form as it has in main memory.

The declarations

```
type
   NumberFile = file of Integer;

   StringType = packed array [1..20] of Char;
   Book = record
            StockNum : Integer;
            Author,
            Title : StringType;
            Price : Real;
            Quantity : Integer
         end; {Book}

   BookFile = file of Book;

var
   Numbers : NumberFile;      {file with integer components}
   Books : BookFile;          {file with book components}
```

define a record type (Book), two file types (NumberFile and BookFile), and two file variables (Numbers and Books). File Numbers is a file with simple components (type Integer) and file Books is a file with structured components (record type Book).

Files Numbers and Books are binary files. File Numbers can contain a collection of integers. File Books can contain a collection of records of type Book.

SYNTAX DISPLAY

File Type Declaration

Form: type
                file type = file of *component type*;
Example: type
             Item = record
                      ID : Integer;
                      Salary : Real
                   end; {Item}

             ItemFile = file of Item;

Interpretation: A new type *file type* is declared whose components must be type *component type*. Any standard or previously declared data type, except for another file type, or a structured type with a file type as one of its constituents, can be the component type.

Writing Information to a Binary File

How do we store information in a binary file? We must use procedure Write to store a variable or value of the same type as the file components. The statement

```
Write (Numbers, 1234)
```

writes the integer 1234 to binary file Numbers declared earlier. When we use Write with a binary file, the first parameter must be the file variable name and the second parameter must be a variable or value of the same type as the file components. We can write only one file component at a time. The statement

```
Write (Numbers, 1234, -999)    {invalid Write of 2 values}
```

is invalid because it attempts to write two integer values to file Numbers.

When writing an integer to binary file Numbers, Pascal copies its value from memory (internal storage) directly to disk (external storage). The same amount of memory is needed in both places. When Pascal writes an integer to a text file, the internal binary value is converted to a string of ASCII digit characters and the number of external bytes required depends on the length of this string. For example, the integer 1 requires a single byte of storage in a text file whereas the integer 16954 requires 5 bytes of storage in a text file (digit character 1, digit character 6, and so on). Both integers require the same number of bytes when stored in a binary file of integers.

We can write the internal binary form of a record variable directly to a binary file. If MyBook is a record variable (type Book) and Books is type file of Book, the statement

```
Write (Books, MyBook);
```

writes a new component to binary file Books. Recall that the statement

```
Write (Output, MyBook)      {invalid parameters for Write}
```

is invalid because Output is a text file (the screen) and Pascal does not allow us to write a record variable directly to a text file.

Reading Information from a Binary File

We retrieve file components in a similar manner. The statements

```
Read (Books, MyBook);
Read (Numbers, NextNum)
```

read the next component of a binary file (the first parameter) to the variable indicated by the second parameter. The binary image stored in the next file component is copied directly to the variable. The file location marker selects the file component to be read and is advanced to the next component after each Read operation.

Binary File ADT

We summarize all these points in the following specification for a binary file ADT (Table 15.2).

Table 15.2
Specification for Binary File ADT

Structure
A binary file is an ordered collection of simple or structured components that are all the same type. A binary file is terminated by an <eof> character. The components in a binary file are processed sequentially, starting with the first. A file location marker keeps track of the next component to be processed.

Operators
The descriptions of the operators use the following parameters:

> F is a file variable
> *recvar* is a variable of the same type as the components of file F

Reset (F)   Opens file F for input (reading), placing the file location marker at the first character.
Rewrite (F)   Opens file F for output (writing), placing the file location marker at the beginning of an empty file.
Read (F, *recvar*)   Reads the next component from file F into *recvar* and advances the file location marker.
Write (F, *recvar*)   Writes the binary image of *recvar* as the next component of file F. If file F has simple components, a literal can be used in place of *recvar*.
EOF(F)   (function) Returns True if the <eof> is the next character in file F; otherwise, it returns False.

Exercises for Section 15.1 **Self-Check**

1. If your computer stores a type Real value in memory in six bytes, how many bytes are required to store six real numbers in a binary file? Answer the same question for a text file in which each number is written using WriteLn, format specifier :4:2, and <eoln>, which requires two bytes. Are there any circumstances under which either of your answers might change?

2. Could both the binary file and the text file in Exercise 1 store all the same numbers? If not, provide some number that could be stored by one but not the other.
3. How many bytes are used to store each component of file Books? Assume two bytes for an integer and six bytes for a real number.

15.2 Creating and Using Binary Files

Unlike a text file, a binary file cannot be created by using an editor program. The only way to create a binary file is by writing its components using a program. In this section, we show how to create a file with simple components and a file with structured components.

Creating and Using a File of Integers

Program EchoFile in Fig. 15.1 first creates and then echo prints file Numbers whose components are the integers from 1 to 1000. You can envision file Numbers as:

File Numbers

1	2	3	4	5	6	. . .	998	999	1000	\<eof\>

EchoFile begins by preparing file Numbers for output (the Rewrite statement). The for loop then creates a file of integer values, and the statement

```
Write (Numbers, I);          {Write each integer to Numbers.}
```

copies each value of I (1 to 1000) to file Numbers.

Next, file Numbers is prepared for input (the Reset statement). The while loop echo prints each value stored in Numbers until the end of file Numbers is reached (EOF(Numbers) is True). Within the loop, the statement

```
Read (Numbers, NextInt);   {Read next integer into NextInt.}
```

reads the next file component (an integer value) into variable NextInt. The statement

```
WriteLn (Output, NextInt :4)              {Display it.}
```

displays this value on a separate line of the screen (system file Output).

Creating a File of Records

Figure 15.2 creates a binary file, Inventory, that represents the inventory of a bookstore. Each file component is a record of type Book, because Inventory is declared as type BookFile (file of Book). The information saved

Figure 15.1
Program EchoFile

Directory: CHAP15
File: ECHOFILE.PAS

```
program EchoFile (Output, Numbers);

{Creates a file of integer values and echo prints it}

   const
     NumInt = 1000;              {number of integers in the file}

   type
     NumberFile = file of Integer;

   var
     Numbers : NumberFile; {file of integers}
     I,                         {loop-control variable}
     NextInt : Integer; {each integer read from file Numbers}

begin {EchoFile}
   Rewrite (Numbers);  {Initialize Numbers to an empty file.}

   {Create a file of integers.}
   for I := 1 to NumInt do
     Write (Numbers, I);    {Write each integer to Numbers.}

   {Echo print file Numbers.}
   Reset (Numbers);                 {Prepare Numbers for input.}
   while not EOF(Numbers) do
     begin
       Read (Numbers, NextInt);  {Read next integer into
                                              NextInt.}

       WriteLn (Output, NextInt :4)    {Display it.}
     end {while}

end. {EchoFile}
```

in each component consists of a four-digit stock number, the book's author and title (strings), the price, and the quantity on hand.

The main program calls procedure `ReadBook` to enter the data for each book from the terminal into record variable `OneBook`. `ReadBook` first reads the book's stock number. If the stock number is not the sentinel, `ReadBook` calls procedure `ReadLnString` (Fig. 11.1) to read the author and title strings. After `OneBook` is defined, the statement

```
Write (Inventory, OneBook);   {Copy the book to Inventory.}
```

copies it to file `Inventory`.

The binary file created when the program in Fig. 15.2 is run is shown on page 568. The last record serves as a sentinel. The `StockNum` field (value is 9999) is the only field of the sentinel record that has its value defined.

```
program BookInventory (Input, Output, Inventory);
{
 Creates a book file from keyboard data.
 Uses module StringADT (Fig. 11.1).
}
  const
    Sentinel = 9999;                  {sentinel stock number}

{
 Insert declarations for StringLength (value is 20),
 StringIndex, and StringType from StringADT.
}

  type
    StockRange = 1111..9999;         {range of stock numbers}
    Book = record
             StockNum : StockRange;
             Author,
             Title   : StringType;
             Price : Real;
             Quantity : Integer
           end;   {Book}
    BookFile = file of Book;

  var
    Inventory : BookFile;            {the book file}
    OneBook : Book;                  {each book}

{Insert procedure ReadLnString from StringADT.}

  procedure ReadBook (var OneBook {output} : Book);
  {
   Reads a book from the keyboard into OneBook.
   Pre  : None.
   Post : Data are read from the keyboard into each field of
          the record represented by parameter OneBook.
   Calls: ReadLnString
  }
    var
      CurLen : Integer;      {length of a data string}

  begin {ReadBook}
    with OneBook do
      begin
        Write ('Stock number> ');
        ReadLn (StockNum);
```

▷ ▷ ▷ ▷ ▷ ▷

```
            if StockNum <> Sentinel then
               begin
                  Write ('Author> ');
                  ReadLnString (Input, Author, CurLen);
                  Write ('Title> ');
                  ReadLnString (Input, Title, CurLen);
                  Write ('Price $');
                  ReadLn (Price);
                  Write ('Quantity> ');
                  ReadLn (Quantity)
               end {if}
         end; {with}
      WriteLn
   end; {ReadBook}

begin  {BookInventory}
   Rewrite (Inventory);          {Prepare Inventory for output.}

   {Read and copy each book until done.}
   WriteLn ('Enter the data requested for each book.');
   WriteLn ('Enter a stock number of 9999 when done.');
   ReadBook (OneBook);                      {Read first book.}
   while OneBook.StockNum <> Sentinel do
      begin
         Write (Inventory, OneBook); {Copy the book to Inventory.}
         ReadBook (OneBook)                   {Read next book.}
      end; {while}

   Write (Inventory, OneBook);  {Write sentinel record to file.}

   WriteLn ('File Inventory completed.')
end. {BookInventory}
```

Sample Run

```
Enter the data requested for each book.
Enter a stock number of 9999 when done.
Stock Number> 1234
Author> Robert Ludlum
Title> The Parsifal Mosaic
Price $17.95
Quantity> 10

Stock Number> 7654
Author> Blaise Pascal
Title> Pascal Made Easy
Price $50.00
Quantity> 1

Stock Number> 9999
File Inventory completed.
```

File Inventory

1234	7654	9999	∧
Robert Ludlum	Blaise Pascal	?	e
The Parsifal Mosaic	Pascal Made Easy	?	o
17.95	50.00	⋮	f
10	1	?	∨

Array of Records and Files of Records

Program BookInventory stores a binary file of book records on disk. If you need to change the file contents, you first must read each record to be modified into main memory. For a file not overly large, you could store all its records in an array of records, update the array, and then write the modified array back to the file.

Reading the array data from a binary file is easier and more efficient than reading it from a text file. You can copy the binary image of each file record directly into its corresponding array element. If InvenArray is an array of records of type Book (up to MaxBook records), the following while loop reads the records of file Inventory into InvenArray:

```
Reset (Inventory);                  {Open the file for input.}
Next := 0;                          {InvenArray is empty.}
while not EOF(Inventory) and (Next < MaxBook) do
   begin
      Next := Next + 1;             {Access next element.}
      Read (Inventory, InvenArray[Next]) {Store book in array.}
   end; {while}

if not EOF(Inventory) then
   WriteLn ('Warning - file too large for array.');
BookCount := Next;                  {Save count of books.}
```

After modifying InvenArray, you should write its new contents to file Inventory, one record at a time. The next for loop accomplishes this:

```
Rewrite (Inventory);                {Open the file for output.}
for Next := 1 to BookCount do
   Write (Inventory, InvenArray[Next])   {Write book to file.}
```

Exercises for Section 15.2 *Self-Check*

1. Complete the following program. What does it do?

```
program Mystery (Data, OutData);
   type
      NumberType = file of _____;
```

```
var
   Data   :_____;
   OutData :_____;
   Next : Integer;

begin
   _____(Data);
   _____(OutData);
   while not EOF(_____) do
      begin
         Read (_____, Next);
         if Next < 50 then
            begin
               Write (_____ , Next);
               WriteLn (_____, Next :2, ' failed exam')
            end {if}
      end {while}
end. {Mystery}
```

2. Why doesn't it matter that some of the fields of the sentinel record are not defined? Under what circumstances might this present a problem?

3. Write all the declarations necessary for a file whose components are student records, where each record consists of a student ID number and an array of five scores. Write a loop that reads each student's record from the file and displays the student's ID number and first score.

Programming

1. Write a procedure that resets file `Inventory` and displays each inventory record on the screen. Call procedure `WriteBook` to display each record.

2. Write procedure `WriteBook`.

15.3   File Merge

Like most data structures, a file frequently needs modification or updating after it has been created. You may want to modify one or more fields of an existing record, delete a record, insert a new record, or simply display the current field values for a record.

In the last section, we discussed reading the entire file into an array and then updating the array. This approach is not feasible if the file is very large or if we want to insert or delete some records. In these cases, the best approach is to create a new file whose records are based on the original file. To do this, we must read each record of the current file, perhaps modify it, and then write it to the new file.

One common update operation is a file merge. In a **file merge**, two files of the same type are combined into a third file. If the records in the two original files are ordered according to a key field, the records in the new file

file merge
a combination of two or more compatible files to form a new file that preserves the ordering of the records by key field

must also be in order by key field. Recall that a record's *key field* contains a unique value that identifies the record.

Merging Two Files

PROBLEM ▼

Whenever it receives a new shipment of books, the bookstore prepares a file (Update) that describes the new shipment. To keep our inventory file (Inventory) up to date, we need a program to combine, or merge, the update file with the inventory file.

ANALYSIS ▼

We will assume that the records on both files are in order by stock number. We also reserve the largest stock number (9999) as a special sentinel value always found at the end of each file.

Our task is to create a third file (NewInven) from the data in the two existing files. If a stock number appears in only one of the files, then its corresponding record will be copied directly to NewInven. If a stock number appears in both files, then the data from file Update will be copied to NewInven, because that is the most recent information; however, the Quantity field of the record written to NewInven must be the sum of both Quantity fields (the quantity shipped plus the quantity on hand). The records in the new file must be in order by stock number.

Figure 15.3 illustrates the new file that results from merging two small sample files. For simplicity, only the Stock and Quantity fields of all three files are shown. The only stock numbers appearing on all three files are 4234 and the sentinel stock number (9999). The original inventory file (Inventory) and the update file (Update) each contain four records (including the sentinel); the

Figure 15.3
Sample File Merge ▽

File NewInventory

new inventory file (NewInven) contains six records (including the sentinel), in order by stock number. Records 1111 and 8955 are copied directly from file Inventory, records 6345 and 7789 are copied directly from file Update, and record 4234 is a combination of the data on files Inventory and Update.

The data requirements and the algorithm for a Merge procedure are described next. Because we are writing a procedure, the type declarations, which should appear in the main program, would be similar to those in Fig. 15.2.

Data Requirements

Procedure Inputs

```
Inventory : BookFile    {current inventory file}
Update : BookFile       {file of new books received}
```

Procedure Outputs

```
NewInven: BookFile      {new inventory file}
```

Local Variables

```
InvenBook : Book        {current record from Inventory}
UpdateBook : Book       {current record from Update}
```

DESIGN ▼

Algorithm for File Merge

1. Prepare files Inventory and Update for input and file NewInven for output.
2. Read the first record from Inventory into InvenBook and from Update into UpdateBook.
3. Copy all records that appear in only one input file to NewInven. If a record appears in both input files, sum both Quantity values before copying record UpdateBook to NewInven.

Refinements and Program Structure

Step 3 compares each pair of records stored in InvenBook and UpdateBook. Because the records in file NewInven must be in order by stock number, the record with the smaller stock number is written to NewInven. Another record is then read from the file containing the record just written, and the comparison process is repeated. If the stock numbers of UpdateBook and InvenBook are the same (a record appears in both files), the new value of UpdateBook.Quantity is computed, the modified record is written to NewInven, and the next records are read from both input files.

Step 3 Refinement

3.1 while there are more records to read do
       3.2 if InvenBook.StockNum < UpdateBook.StockNum then

    3.3 Write `InvenBook` to `NewInven` and read the next record
         of `Inventory` into `InvenBook`.
  `else if InvenBook.StockNum > UpdateBook.StockNum then`
    3.4 Write `UpdateBook` to `NewInven` and read the next record
         of `Update` into `UpdateBook`.
  `else`
    3.5 Modify the `Quantity` field of `UpdateBook`, write
         `UpdateBook` to `NewInven`, and read the next record
         from `Inventory` and `Update`.
3.6 Write the sentinel record to `NewInven`.

    Let's trace this refinement, assuming `InvenBook` and `UpdateBook` initially contain the first file records:

InvenBook   UpdateBook   NewInven

1111
30

4234
55

→

1111
30

Because 1111 is less than 4234, record `InvenBook` is copied to file `NewInven` (Step 3.3), and the next record is read into `InvenBook`:

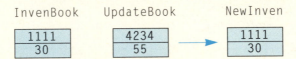

InvenBook   UpdateBook   NewInven

4234
15

4234
55

→

1111	4234
30	70

    Now the stock numbers are equal, so the quantity fields are summed (Step 3.5), the new record with stock number 4234 is written to file `NewInven`, and the next records are read into `InvenBook` and `UpdateBook`:

InvenBook   UpdateBook   NewInven

8955
90

6345
10

→

1111	4234	6345
30	70	10

This time the record in `UpdateBook` is copied to `NewInven` (Step 3.4), the next record is read into `UpdateBook`, and the merge continues.

    What happens when the end of one input file is reached? The stock number for the current record of that file will be 9999 (the maximum), so each record read from the other input file will be copied directly to file `NewInven`. When the ends of both input files are reached, the `while` loop is exited and the sentinel record is written to file `NewInven` (Step 3.6).

    Procedure `CopySmaller` implements Steps 3.2 through 3.5. The structure chart for the `Merge` procedure is shown in Fig. 15.4.

IMPLEMENTATION ▼

Procedure `Merge` is shown in Fig. 15.5. The only output displayed on the screen as a result of executing this procedure is the message `File merge`

Figure 15.4
Structure Chart for
Procedure Merge

completed. After the procedure's execution, you may want to echo print file NewInven. To do so, reset file NewInven and then write individual fields of each record to the screen. When certain that file NewInven is correct, you can use an operating system command to rename it Inventory. You could then use the new file Inventory as the input inventory file and merge it with another Update file at a later time.

You can adapt the merge procedure to perform other update operations. For example, you could merge a file that represents the daily sales of all books (file Sales) with file Inventory to generate an updated inventory file at the end of each day. If the quantity field of each record in file Sales is subtracted from the quantity field of the corresponding record in file Inventory, the difference would represent the quantity remaining in stock. You could even delete records whose quantity fields became negative or zero by simply not copying such records to NewInven.

Program Style

Analysis of the Merge Procedure

Several questions arise about the merge procedure in Fig. 15.5. For example, what happens if an input file is empty or contains only the sentinel record? Because procedure Merge always reads at least one record, an execution error will occur if either input file is empty. If a file contains only the sentinel record, then only the sentinel record will be read from that file, and all the records in the other file will be copied directly to file NewInven. If both input files contain only the sentinel record, the while loop will be exited immediately, and only the sentinel record will be copied to file NewInven after loop exit.

```pascal
procedure CopySmaller (var InvenBook,
                           UpdateBook {input/output} : Book;
                       var Inventory {input}, Update {input},
                           NewInven {output} : BookFile);
begin {CopySmaller}
  if InvenBook.StockNum < UpdateBook.StockNum then
    begin {<}
      Write (NewInven, InvenBook);          {Copy InvenBook.}
      Read (Inventory, InvenBook)
    end {<}
  else if InvenBook.StockNum > UpdateBook.StockNum then
    begin {>}
      Write (NewInven, UpdateBook);         {Copy UpdateBook.}
      Read (Update, UpdateBook)
    end {>}
  else
    begin {=}
      UpdateBook.Quantity := UpdateBook.Quantity +
                             InvenBook.Quantity;
      Write (NewInven, UpdateBook);   {Copy new UpdateBook.}
      Read (Inventory, InvenBook);    {Read both records.}
      Read (Update, UpdateBook)
    end {=}
end;   {CopySmaller}


procedure Merge (var Inventory, Update {input},
                     NewInven {output}        : BookFile);
{
 Merges data on files Inventory and Update to file NewInven.
 Pre  : Files Inventory and Update are existing files ordered
        by stock number, ending with a sentinel stock number.
 Post : Each record appearing in only Inventory or Update is
        copied to NewInven. If a stock number appears in
        both files, the Quantity fields are summed and the
        remaining fields are copied from Update. File NewInven
        is ordered by stock number and ends with the sentinel.
 Calls: CopySmaller
}
  var
    Inventory,              {old inventory file}
    Update,                 {update file}
    NewInven : BookFile;    {new inventory file}
    InvenBook,              {current record of file Inventory}
    UpdateBook : Book;      {current record of file Update}

begin {Merge}
  {
   Prepare Inventory and Update for input,
   NewInven for output.
  }
```

```
Reset (Inventory);
Reset (Update);
Rewrite (NewInven);

{Read the first record from Inventory and Update.}
Read (Inventory, InvenBook);
Read (Update, UpdateBook);
{
 Copy all records from file Inventory and Update
 to NewInven.
}
while (InvenBook.StockNum <> Sentinel) or
      (UpdateBook.StockNum <> Sentinel) do
  CopySmaller (InvenBook, UpdateBook, Inventory,
               Update, NewInven);

{Write the sentinel record to NewInven.}
Write (NewInven, InvenBook);

WriteLn ('File merge completed.')
end; {Merge}
```

Finally, how efficient is the merge procedure if the end of one file is reached much sooner than the other? This imbalance would result in the stock number 9999 being repeatedly compared to the stock numbers on the file that is not yet finished. It would be more efficient to exit the `while` loop when the end of one file is reached, then copy all remaining records on the other file directly to file `NewInven`. This modification is left as an exercise at the end of this section.

TESTING ▼

To test the merge procedure, provide files that contain only the sentinel record as well as files with one or more actual records. Make sure that the merge procedure works properly regardless of which of the two input files has all its records processed first. Also make sure that there is exactly one sentinel record on the merged file.

Exercises for Section 15.3 *Self-Check*

1. In procedure `Merge`, what three assumptions are made about the two files that are merged? Must the two input files have the same number of records?
2. What happens if a record from one input file has the same stock number as a record from the other input file? What happens if one input file has two consecutive records with the same stock number?

3. What would happen if the or in the while condition in procedure Merge were changed to and?

Programming

1. Modify procedure Merge, assuming that its input files do not contain a sentinel record. In this case, there should not be a sentinel record on the merged file. Exit from the merge loop when the end of either file is reached and then copy the remaining records from the unfinished file.

15.4   File Buffer Variable

Unlike other Pascal data structures, a file is located in secondary storage rather than main memory. Therefore, you must first transfer data from a file into main memory (by a Read operation) before you can manipulate the data.

file buffer variable
a data area in main memory that contains a copy of the file component currently selected by the file location marker

To simplify file access, Pascal allocates within main memory a **file buffer variable** for each file declared in a program. The buffer variable acts as a "window" through which file data can be accessed. The buffer variable for a data file contains a copy of the file component currently selected by the file location marker. During a file read, as the file location marker moves, the file buffer variable is automatically updated.

Accessing a file's data through its buffer variable is more efficient because it eliminates the need to allocate memory space for a variable that stores the current file component (for example, record OneBook in Fig. 15.2). It also saves the processing time required to copy the current file component into that variable.

We denote the file buffer variable by writing the file name followed by a caret (^). Therefore, we use Inventory^ to represent the file buffer variable for file Inventory, and we use the field selector Inventory^.Author to access its Author field. The with statement

```
with Inventory^ do
  begin
    WriteLn ('Stock number of book sold is ', StockNum :4);
    Quantity := Quantity - 1;
    SalesTotal := SalesTotal + Price
  end {with}
```

manipulates the StockNum, Price, and Quantity fields of the record currently in the file buffer variable of file Inventory.

Get and Reset

The Reset operator moves the file location marker to the beginning of a file and stores the file's first component in its file buffer variable. The effect of the statement

```
Reset (Inventory)
```

follows:

Inventory^   **File** Inventory

| 1111
Ashenhurst
·
·
· | | 1111
Ashenhurst
·
·
· | 1234
Baker
·
·
· | 1345
Carnegie
·
·
· |

↑
File location marker

The statement

```
Get (Inventory)
```

advances the file location marker to the next file component, and automatically updates the file buffer variable:

Inventory^   **File** Inventory

| 1234
Baker
·
·
· | | 1111
Ashenhurst
·
·
· | 1234
Baker
·
·
· | 1345
Carnegie
·
·
· |

↑
File location marker

When the file location marker is at the last file component, the next `Get` operation causes the file buffer variable to become undefined, and `EOF(Inventory)` becomes `True`.

SYNTAX DISPLAY

Reset Procedure (Effect on File Buffer Variable)

Form: `Reset (infile)`
Example: `Reset (Inventory)`
Interpretation: Moves the file location marker for file *infile* to the beginning of file *infile*, and stores the first file component in file buffer variable *infile^*.
Note: Pascal performs the `Reset` operation automatically on system file `Input`, so `Reset (Input)` is not needed and may cause an error.

SYNTAX DISPLAY

Get Operator

Form: `Get (infile)`
Example: `Get (Inventory)`
Interpretation: Advances the file location marker for file *infile*, and stores the next file component in file buffer variable *infile^*.

Note: The effect of the Get operation is undefined if EOF(*infile*) is True before or after the Get is executed. The Reset operation for a file must precede the first Get for that file (except for system file Input).

Put and Rewrite

We write to a file in Pascal by appending data to the end of the file. You can write data stored in a file buffer variable to a file using the Put operator. The statement

Put (*outfile*)

appends the current contents of file buffer variable *outfile*^ to the end of file *outfile*. The data to be transferred must be stored in file buffer variable *outfile*^ before the Put is executed. The statement

Rewrite (*outfile*)

must execute before the first Put operation.

EXAMPLE 15.1 ▼

Procedure BuildSmall in Fig. 15.6 creates an abbreviated inventory file, SmallInv, that consists only of the stock number and quantity of every record in file Inventory. You must declare file types BookFile and Small-BookFile in the calling program. You need not declare record variables for storing the current record of each of these files.

Figure 15.6
Procedure BuildSmall

Directory: CHAP15
File: BUILDSMA.PAS

```
procedure BuildSmall (var Inventory {input} : BookFile;
                      var SmallInv {output} : SmallBookFile);
{
  Creates a new inventory file (SmallInv) containing only
  stock numbers and quantities of the records in Inventory.
  Pre : Inventory is defined.
  Post: SmallInv contains a smaller version of each record in
        Inventory.
}
begin  {BuildSmall}
  {Initialize buffer variable for Inventory & open SmallInv.}
  Reset (Inventory);
  Rewrite (SmallInv);

  {Copy stock number & quantity from Inventory to SmallInv.}
  while not EOF(Inventory) do
    begin
      {Define buffer variable SmallInv^.}
```

▷ ▷ ▷ ▷ ▷ ▷

```
        SmallInv^.StockNum := Inventory^.StockNum;
        SmallInv^.Quantity := Inventory^.Quantity;
        Put (SmallInv);                    {Append data to SmallInv.}
        Get (Inventory)                    {Access next record.}
      end {while}
  end; {BuildSmall}
```

Each assignment statement

```
SmallInv^.StockNum := Inventory^.StockNum;
SmallInv^.Quantity := Inventory^.Quantity;
```

copies one field from the file buffer variable for `Inventory` to the file buffer variable for `SmallInv`. The statement

```
Put (SmallInv);                    {Append data to SmallInv.}
```

appends the data just copied to file `SmallInv`; the statement

```
Get (Inventory);                    {Access next record}
```

updates the file buffer variable for `Inventory` so that it contains the next record. ▲

SYNTAX DISPLAY

Rewrite Procedure (Effect on File Buffer Variable)

Form:　　Rewrite (*outfile*)
Example:　Rewrite (SmallInv)
Interpretation: Returns the file location marker for file *outfile* to the beginning of file *outfile*, thereby erasing any data that might be stored on the file. The file buffer variable *outfile*^ becomes undefined. Pascal performs the `Rewrite` operation automatically on system file `Output`, so `Rewrite (Output)` is not needed and may cause an error.

SYNTAX DISPLAY

Put Operator

Form:　　Put (*outfile*)
Example:　Put (SmallInv)
Interpretation: Appends the contents of file buffer variable *outfile*^ to the end of file *outfile*. The file buffer variable must be defined before the `Put` operation; it becomes undefined after the `Put` operation.
Note: A `Rewrite` operation must precede the first `Put` operation (except for system file `Output`).

Get and Put versus Read and Write

`Get` and `Read` may both access data stored in a file. The `Read` procedure reads the current file component into a local variable of the same type. The statement

```
Read (Inventory, NextBook)
```

stores the next component of file `Inventory` in the variable `NextBook` and advances the file location marker for `Inventory`.

A local variable is not needed with `Get` because the data in the file buffer variable may be accessed directly. However, you can still use `Get` to store data in a local variable if you desire. The statements

```
NextBook := Inventory^;
Get (Inventory)
```

have the same effect as the preceding `Read` statement. They copy the current file component (contents of `Inventory^`) into `NextBook`, and advance the file location marker to the next file component.

The statement

```
Write (NewInven, NextBook)
```

writes the data stored in variable `NextBook` to file `NewInven`. You can also do this using the statements

```
NewInven^ := NextBook;
Put (NewInven)
```

The assignment statement defines the file buffer variable `NewInven^`; the `Put` operation appends this data to the end of file `NewInven`.

Exercises for Section 15.4   ***Self-Check***

1. Complete the program segment below so that each number in the input file is doubled in the output file.

    ```
    program Mystery (_____, _____);
       type
          NumberFile = file of Integer;

       var
          InFile, OutFile : _____;

    begin
       Reset (_____);
       Rewrite (_____);
       while not EOF(_____) do
          begin
             _____^ := 2 * _____^;
             Put (_____);
             Get (_____)
          end {while}
    end. {Mystery}
    ```

2. Indicate how you would modify procedures `Merge` and `CopySmaller` (see Fig. 15.5) to use `Get` and `Put` instead of `Read` and `Write`. Also,

manipulate the file buffer variables directly instead of using local variables `UpdateBook` and `InvenBook`.

Programming

1. Rewrite procedure `BuildSmall` to copy every other record of file `Inventory` to file `SmallInv`.

15.5 Common Programming Errors

Always declare each binary file type and a file variable of that type, and be sure to prepare a binary file before attempting to read its records or write to it. Open the file using `Reset` (for an input file) or `Rewrite` (for an output file). Don't forget to pass the file variable as the first of two parameters for each `Read` or `Write` operation; the second parameter must be a variable of the same type as the file components.

You can perform a number of operations with text files that you cannot perform with binary files. Because binary files are not segmented into lines, you cannot use the `EOLN` function or `ReadLn` and `WriteLn` procedures. Also, you cannot create or modify a binary file using an editor program. A binary file must be created by running a program before it can be used.

You can access the current file component through the file buffer variable. Avoid the common error of writing the operators that manipulate the file buffer variable as `Get` (*infile^*) or `Put` (*outfile^*). The caret should be deleted and the operators written as `Get` (*infile*) or `Put` (*outfile*).

CHAPTER REVIEW

1. The file type `Text` is predefined. Its components are the Pascal characters and a special character, `<eoln>`. The `EOLN` function can test for an `<eoln>`, and the `WriteLn` statement places one in a text file.
2. You can declare and manipulate binary files whose components may be any simple or structured type (except for a structured type with a file type component).
3. Binary files have an advantage over `Text` files in that the binary image of a file component can be transferred directly between a variable in main memory and a binary file. The variable involved in the data transfer must be the same type (simple or structured) as the components of the binary file.
4. You can access a file's data through its file buffer variable. You do not need to allocate a separate variable in main memory for storing a file component. Use the operators `Reset` and `Rewrite` to initialize the file buffer variable. Use `Get` to retrieve the next file component and `Put` to append the contents of the file buffer variable to the end of its file.

Summary of New Pascal Constructs

Construct	Effect
File-Type Declaration	
```type DigitFile = file of Integer; var MoreDigits : DigitFile;```	Declares a file type `DigitFile` whose components are integers. `MoreDigits` is a file of type `DigitFile`.
Get Operator	
```Reset (MoreDigits); I := MoreDigits^; Get (MoreDigits); Write (MoreDigits^)```	Stores the first integer in file `MoreDigits` in the file buffer variable and copies it to `I`. Displays the second integer.
Put Operator	
```Rewrite (MoreDigits); MoreDigits^ := 99; Put (MoreDigits)```	Opens a new file `MoreDigits` whose first component is `99`.

Quick-Check Exercises

1. What data types can be read from or written to a text file?
2. What data types can be read from or written to a binary file?
3. Binary and text files can be created using any standard text editor. True or false?
4. If we have a file of integers and each integer requires 2 bytes, how many bytes would be required to store 20 integers using a binary file? Would a text file require the same number, more, or less?
5. Comment on the correctness of this statement: It is more efficient to use a text file because the computer knows that each component is a single character that can be copied into a single byte of main memory; with a binary file, however, the size of the components may vary.
6. What limits the number of records that can be written to a file?
7. What limits the number of records that can be read from a file? How do you know when you have read them all?
8. What happens if the `Reset` operation is performed on a file that has just been created in a program? If the `Rewrite` operation is performed on the same file?
9. How does the Pascal compiler know how big to make the file buffer variable for a file?
10. The _____ operator stores the first file record in the file _____ _____. The _____ operator stores the record pointed to by the file _____ _____ in the file _____ _____ and advances the file _____ _____. The _____ operator copies the record in the file _____ _____ to the file and advances the file _____ _____.

Answers to Quick-Check Exercises

1. Any of the standard data types (or a subrange thereof) except type Boolean can be read; any of the standard data types (or a subrange thereof) plus strings can be written.
2. The file's component type, which is any simple or structured type (except for an object) that does not have a file type as one of its constituents.
3. True for text files, False for binary files
4. 40 bytes. Unless each integer can be written in two characters or less, the text file would require more bytes.
5. The statement is not correct. It is true that two binary files may have components of different sizes, but all the components of a particular file must be the same data type and the same size. This size can be determined from the type declarations. Because no data conversions are necessary when you use binary files, binary files are more efficient than text files.
6. The only limit is the available space on disk.
7. The number of records that were written to the file when it was created. Use the `EOF` function to test for the end-of-file mark.
8. `Reset` prepares the file for input so we can echo print it if we want to check the records that were written. `Rewrite` causes the data in the file to be lost.
9. The file buffer variable is the same size as the file components, which can be determined from the type declarations.
10. The `Reset` operator stores the first file record in the file *buffer variable*. The `Get` operator stores the record pointed to by the file *location marker* in the file *buffer variable* and advances the file *location marker*. The `Put` operator copies the record in the file *buffer variable* to the file and advances the file *location marker*.

Review Questions

1. Given the following program fragment, why would the two numbers be readable in the future if a binary file is used and not if a text file is used?

```
Write (OutFile, 1234);
Write (OutFile, 5678)
```

2. What can always be said about the length of a binary file? Can the same be said about a text file?
3. Explain the difference between writing the integer `12345` to a binary file and to a text file. How many bytes of external storage would be needed for each file? Which operation would be faster?
4. Consider file `EmpStat` (type `EmpFile`) that contains records for up to 15 employees. The data for each employee consist of the employee's name (20 characters), social security number (11 characters), gross pay for the week (real), taxes deducted (real), and the net pay (real) for the week. Write a program called `PayReport` that will create a text file `ReportFile` with the heading line

```
NAME      SOC-SEC-NUM      GROSS      TAXES      NET
```

followed by two blank lines, then the pertinent information under each column heading. `ReportFile` should contain up to 18 lines of information after `PayReport` is executed.

5. What are the characteristics of a binary file?

6. Imagine for a moment that you are a college professor who uses a computerized system to maintain student records. Write the type and variable declarations for a file that will consist of multiple records of type `StudentStats`. The statistics kept on each student are `GPA`, `Major`, `Address` (consisting of `Name`, `StreetAddress`, `City`, `State`, and `ZipCode`), and `ClassSchedule` (consisting of up to six records of `Class`, each containing `Description`, `Time`, and `Days` fields). Use whatever data types are appropriate for each field.

7. Explain the use and manipulation of a file buffer variable.

8. Write a procedure that will read a file of names and `Put` every other name in a file. Use file buffer variables.

Programming Projects

1. Write a program to create a file of records, each containing a person's last name, first name, birth date, and sex. Create a new file of records containing only first names and sex. Also print out the complete name of every person whose last name begins with the letter A, C, F, or P through Z and who was born in a month beginning with the letter J.

2. Create separate text files for the salesmen and for the saleswomen in your furniture store. For each employee, include an employee number (four digits), a name, and a salary. Each file should be in order by employee number. Merge these two files into a third file (binary) that also has a gender field containing one of the values in the type (`Female`, `Male`). After the file merge operation, find the average salary for all employees. Then search the new file and print a list of all female employees earning more than the average salary and a separate list of all male employees earning more than the average salary. *Hint:* You will have to search the new file once for each list. Your program should include procedures corresponding to the following procedure headers:

```
procedure ReadOneRec (var DataFile {input} : Text;
                          Sex {input} : Gender;
                          var EmpRec {output} : EmployeeRec);
{
 Reads one employee record from text file DataFile and
 assigns Sex value to appropriate EmpRec field.
}

procedure MergeFile (var MaleFile, FemaleFile {input} :
                                                 Text;
                         var OutFile {output} : EmployeeFile);
{
 Merges the records from the two input files, adds gender
 field to the output record.
 Calls: ReadOneRec.
}
```

```
procedure FindAveSalary (var EmpFile {input} :
                                        EmployeeFile;
                        var Average {output} : Real);
{Computes average salary using all employee records}

procedure PrintHigh (Sex {input} : Gender;
                     var EmpFile {input} : EmployeeFile;
                     Average {input} : Real);
{
  Print gender-specific list of persons earning more than
  Average salary.
}
```

3. Write a procedure that will merge the contents of three sorted files by ID number and write the merged data to an output file. The parameters to the procedure will be the three input files and the one output file. The file records will be of the form

```
Data = record
         ID : Integer;
         Name : StringType;
         Salary : Real
       end; {Data}
```

Assume there is no sentinel record. Test your procedure with some sample data.

4. Cooking recipes can be stored on a computer and, with the use of files, quickly referenced.
    a. Write a procedure that will create a text file of recipes from information entered at the terminal. The format of the data to be stored is
       (1) recipe type (Dessert, Meat, etc.)
       (2) subtype (for Dessert, use Cake, Pie, or Brownies)
       (3) name (for cake, German Chocolate)
       (4) number of lines in the recipe to follow
       (5) the actual recipe
       Items 1–4 should be on separate lines.
    b. Write a procedure that will accept as parameters a file and a record of search parameters that will cause all recipes of a type, all recipes of a subtype, or a specific recipe to be written.

5. College football teams need a service to keep track of records and vital statistics. Write a program that will maintain this information in a file. An update file will be "posted" weekly against the master file of all team statistics to date, and all the records will be updated. All the information in both files will be stored in order by ID number. Each master record will contain the team's ID number; team name; number of games won, lost, and tied; total yards gained by the team's offense; total yards gained by the other teams against this one; total points scored by this team; and total points scored by the other teams against this one.

    For this program, use the master file Teams and update Teams from file Weekly. Write the updated information to a file called NewTeams. In addition, each record of the weekly file should be echo printed. At the completion of processing the files, write a message indicating the number of weekly scores processed, the team that scored the most points, and the team with the most offensive yardage for this week.

6. Write a program that takes a master file of college football information and prints out teams that match a specified set of search parameters. Some information you might want to print: all teams with a won/lost percentage in a certain range; all teams within a certain range of points scored or scored upon; all teams with a certain range of yardage gained or given up; all teams with a certain number of games won, tied, or lost. (*Note:* The won/lost percentage is calculated by dividing number of games won by total games played; ties count as half a game won.)

Directory: CHAP15
File: PROJ7.PAS

7. Write a program that updates a file of type `Inventory` (see Section 15.3). Your program should be able to modify an existing record, insert a new record, and delete an existing record. Assume that the update requests are in order by stock number and that they have the form

```
type
   ChangeKind = (Delete, Insert, Modify);
   UpdateReq = record
                 case Change : ChangeKind of
                    Delete : (StockNumber : StockRange);
                    Insert : (NewBook : Book);
                    Modify : (ModBook : Book)
               end; {UpdateReq}
```

Each update request should be read from a binary file. Only the stock number appears in an update request for a deletion. The new book record is supplied for a request to insert a record or to modify an existing record. Your program should also print an error message for invalid requests, such as an attempt to delete a record that does not exist, an attempt to insert a new record with the same stock number as an existing record, or an attempt to modify a record that does not exist.

8. Redo Programming Project 7 as a menu-driven program.

9. It is relatively easy to sort in memory, as we have seen. Sorting a disk file is called *external sorting*. One way to perform an external sort is to store each record's key and record number in an array, sort the array by key field using selection sort, read the file records in sorted order using `Seek` and the sorted record numbers, and then write them to a new sorted file. Write a procedure that performs an external sort on the following records, sorting on the integer value `EmpNum`, creating a new sorted file. Write a suitable test program for your procedure. Compare the number of bytes sorted in memory to the number of bytes in the entire file.

```
Employee = record
             EmpNum : Integer;
             Name, Street, City, State,
             Zip, Department : StringType
           end;
```

CHAPTER SIXTEEN

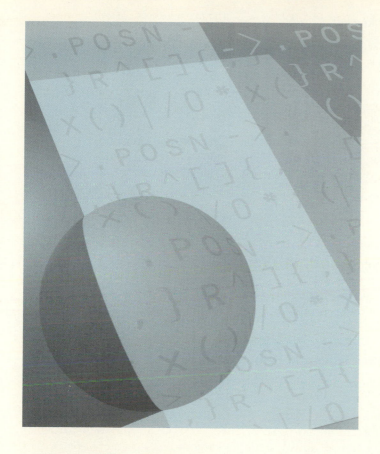

Pointers and Linked Lists

In this chapter, we shift our attention from static structures, such as arrays and records, to dynamic data structures. Unlike static structures, in which the size of the data structure is established during compilation and remains unchanged throughout program execution, dynamic data structures expand and contract as a program executes. The particular dynamic data structure we will study is called a linked list. A *linked list* is a collection of elements (called *nodes*) that are records. Each node has a special field, called a pointer, that connects it to the next node in the list.

Linked list

Linked lists are extremely flexible. It is easy to add new information by creating a new node and inserting it between two existing nodes. It is also relatively easy to delete a node.

In this chapter, you will learn how to store information in linked lists and how to process this information. In Chapter 17, we will examine other examples of dynamic data structures, including stacks, queues, and binary trees.

16.1 Pointer Types and Pointers

The nodes in a linked list are joined by pointers. This section discusses what pointers are and how to use them.

Declaring Pointer Types and Pointer Variables

pointer variable (pointer)
a variable whose contents are a memory cell address

We can declare pointer types in Pascal and then pointer variables that are pointer types. However, unlike other variables that may contain a particular value (or a collection of related values), **pointer variables** contain addresses or locations in memory. That is, we store the address of a particular data object (i.e., a record, array, or simple variable) in a pointer variable. For example, the declarations

```
type
  RealPointer = ^Real;

var
  P : RealPointer;
```

identify `RealPointer` as the name of a pointer type. We read `^Real` as "pointer to `Real`." The variable declaration specifies that P is a pointer variable of type `RealPointer` and allows us to store the *memory address* of a type `Real` variable in P.

SYNTAX DISPLAY

Pointer Type Declaration

Form: type *pointertype* = ^ *datatype*;
Example: type RealPointer = ^Real;
Interpretation: Type *pointertype* is a data type whose values are memory cell addresses. A data element whose address is stored in a variable of type *pointertype* must be type *datatype*.

Allocating and Accessing New Storage Cells

The statement

```
New (P)
```

calls the Pascal procedure `New`, which allocates storage for a type `Real` value and places the address of this memory cell in pointer variable P. Once storage is allocated for the type `Real` value pointed to by P, we can store a value in that memory cell and manipulate it. **Dynamic allocation** is the process of allocating new storage during program execution.

The actual memory address stored in pointer variable P is a number that has no meaning to us. Consequently, we represent the value of P by drawing an arrow to a memory cell:

The `?` in the memory cell with label P^ indicates that its contents are undefined just after `New (P)` is executed. In Pascal, the symbol P^ indicates the contents of the data area (memory cells) pointed to by P. The ^ (caret), called the *dereferencing operator*, follows the pointer name.

Pascal allocates storage at different times for the memory cells shown in the preceding diagram. Storage is allocated for pointer variable P during compilation when its variable declaration is reached. Storage is allocated for the cell with label P^ when the `New` statement is executed.

The data type of P determines the size and structure of the data area pointed to by P. Because P was declared as type `RealPointer` (i.e., `type RealPointer = ^Real`), P points to a memory area large enough to hold a `Real` value.

The contents of a memory cell pointed to by P are processed just like any other type `Real` variable. The statement

```
P^ := 15.0
```

assigns `15.0` as the contents of the memory cell pointed to by P.

If `Val1` is a type `Real` variable, the statement

```
Val1 := P^ + 10.0
```

adds `10.0` and the contents of the cell pointed to by P and stores the sum (`25.0`) in `Val1`. The Boolean expression `Val1 <= P^` compares `Val1` to the contents of the cell pointed to by P, so its value is `False`. The statement

```
WriteLn ('The contents of cell pointed to by P are ', P^ :2:1)
```

displays the value of P^ as `15.0`.

SYNTAX DISPLAY

New Procedure

Form: New (*pointervar*)

Example: New (P)

Interpretation: Storage for a new data area is allocated, and the address of this data area is stored in pointer variable *pointervar*. If *pointervar* is type *pointertype*, the internal representation and size of the new data area are determined from the declaration for *pointertype*. Use *pointervar*^ to reference this data area.

Pointer Operations

Pointer variables do differ from variables of other types. A pointer variable can contain *only* a memory address. For the pointer variable P declared earlier (type ^Real), the following statements would be invalid because a type Integer or type Real value cannot be assigned to a pointer variable:

```
P := 1000;        {invalid assignment}
P := 15.5;        {invalid assignment}
```

The value (an address) of a pointer variable cannot be displayed, so the statement

```
WriteLn (P);      {invalid attempt to display an address}
```

would also be invalid.

If P and Q are both pointer variables of the same type, they can be manipulated with the assignment operator and the relational operators = and <>. For example, the *pointer assignment statement*

```
Q := P
```

copies the address stored in pointer variable P to pointer variable Q. As a result, both P and Q point to the same memory area, and we can reference the following cell using either P^ or Q^:

In this instance, the Boolean expression P = Q is True and P <> Q is False.

To summarize, the operators that can be used with pointer variables are :=, =, and <> and both operands must be pointer variables of the same type.

Pointers to Records

We can declare pointers to structured data types as well as to simple data types. Most commonly, we declare pointers to records. The declarations

```
type
  String2 = packed array [1..2] of Char;
  Electric = record
                Current : String2;
                Volts : Integer
             end; {Node}

  EPointer = ^Electric;

var
  P, Q : EPointer;   {pointers to records of type Electric}
```

identify `EPointer` as a pointer type. A pointer variable of type `EPointer` points to a record of type `Electric` with two fields: `Current` and `Volts`.

Variables P and Q are pointer variables that can be used to point to records of type `Electric` (denoted by P^ and Q^). The statement

```
New (P)
```

allocates storage for a record of type `Electric` and stores its memory address in pointer P. The data fields of record P^ are initially undefined.

Recall that we used the field selector `Student.Name` to reference the `Name` field of record variable `Student`. We can also use a field selector to reference a field of a record pointed to by a pointer variable. For example, the field selector `P^.Current` references the `Current` field of the record pointed to by P (record P^). The assignment statements

```
P^.Current := 'AC';
P^.Volts := 115
```

define the fields of the record pointed to by P as shown here:

The statement

```
WriteLn (P^.Current, P^.Volts :4)
```

displays the data fields of the record pointed to by P. For the record in the preceding diagram, the statement displays the line

```
AC 115
```

The statement

```
New (Q)
```

stores the address of a new record of type `Electric` in pointer Q. The next statements copy the contents of the record pointed to by P (record P^) to the record pointed to by Q (record Q^), and change the `Volts` field of record Q^:

```
Q^ := P^;
```

```
Q^.Volts := 220
```

Finally the pointer assignment statement

```
Q := P
```

resets pointer Q to point to the same record as pointer P. The old record pointed to by Q still exists in memory but can no longer be accessed. Such a record is called an **orphan**.

orphan
a data area in memory that can't be accessed because its address is no longer stored in a pointer variable

Exercises for Section 16.1   *Self-Check*

1. If P and Q are type `EPointer`, explain the effect of each valid assignment statement. Which are invalid?
    a. `P^.Current := 'CA'`   e. `P^.Volts := Q^ Volts`
    b. `P^ := Q^`   f. `P := Q`
    c. `P.Current := 'HT'`   g. `P^.Current := Q^.Volts`
    d. `P := 54`   h. `Q^ := P`
2. If A, B, and C are type `EPointer`, draw a diagram of pointers and memory cells after the following operations. Indicate any orphaned data areas.
    a. `New(A)`   d. `A := B`
    b. `New(B)`   e. `B := C`
    c. `New(C)`   f. `C := A`

Programming

1. For the following record type, write a program fragment that creates a collection of seven pointers, allocates memory for each pointer, and places the musical notes do, re, mi, fa, so, la, and ti in the data areas:

```
type
   String2 = packed array [1..2] of Char;
   MusicNote = record
                  Note : String2
               end; {MusicNote}

   MusicNoteP = ^MusicNote;
```

16.2   Manipulating the Heap

heap

the area in main memory used
for the dynamic allocation of
storage

When New executes, where in memory is the new record stored? Pascal maintains a storage pool of available memory cells called a **heap** and allocates memory cells from this pool whenever procedure New is executed.

Effect of the New Statement on the Heap

If P is a pointer variable of type EPointer (declared in the last section), the statement

```
New (P);
```

allocates memory space for a record that stores two characters and an integer variable. The memory cells in this record are originally undefined (they retain whatever data were last stored in them), and the memory address of the first cell allocated is stored in P. Allocated cells are no longer considered part of the heap. The only way to reference allocated cells is through pointer variable P (for example, P^.Current or P^.Volts).

Figure 16.1 shows the pointer variable P and the heap before and after the execution of New (P). The *before* diagram shows pointer variable P as undefined before the execution of New (P). The *after* diagram shows P pointing to the first of four memory cells allocated for the new record (assuming that four memory cells can accommodate a record of type Electric). The cells still considered part of the heap are in gray.

For example, if the memory cells with addresses 1000 through 2000 were originally in the heap, after the execution of New (P) the memory cells with addresses 1000 through 1003 would no longer be part of the heap. The address 1000 would instead be stored in pointer variable P, and that cell would contain the first byte of P^.Current; memory cell 1002 would contain the first byte of P^.Volts.

Returning Cells to the Heap: The Dispose Procedure

The procedure call statement

```
Dispose (P);
```

returns the memory cells pointed to by P to the heap, restoring the heap to the state shown on the left of Fig. 16.1. At this point, the value of pointer variable P becomes undefined and the data formerly associated with P^ are

Figure 16.1
Heap Before and After
New (P)

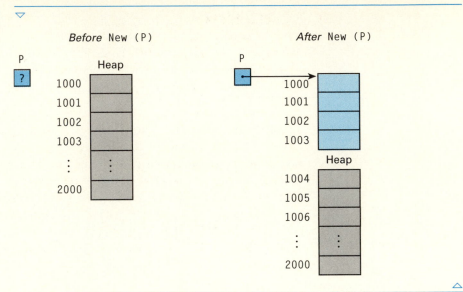

no longer accessible. The four cells that are returned to the heap can be reused later when another New statement is executed.

Often more than one pointer points to the same record. For that reason, be careful when you return the storage occupied by a record to the heap. If cells are reallocated after they are returned, errors may result if they are later referenced by another pointer that still points to them. Make sure you have no need for a particular record before you return the storage occupied by it.

SYNTAX DISPLAY

The Dispose Procedure

Form: Dispose (*pointervar*)
Example: Dispose (P)
Interpretation: The memory cells in the data area whose address is stored in pointer *pointervar* are returned to the heap. These cells can be reallocated when procedure New is called.

Exercise for Section 16.2   *Self-Check*

1. In a program that is allocating memory space for temporary data items, what would be the consequences of failing to use Dispose when the data items are no longer needed?

16.3   Linked Lists

We can arrange groups of dynamically allocated records into a flexible data structure called a **linked list.** Linked lists are like chains of children's "pop beads," where each bead has a hole at one end and a plug at the other (see Fig. 16.2). We can connect the beads in the obvious way to form a chain and easily modify it. We can remove the color bead by disconnecting the two beads at both its ends and reattaching this pair of beads, add a new bead by connecting it to the bead at either end of the chain, or break the chain somewhere in the middle (between beads A and B) and insert a new bead by connecting one end to bead A and the other end to bead B. We show how to perform these operations to rearrange the records in a linked list next.

In this section, we use pointers to create linked lists. We can add a pointer field to a record and then build a linked list by connecting records with pointer fields. We call a record in a linked list a **node.**

Declaring Nodes

To declare a record type with a pointer field, we first declare a pointer type (`NodePointer`) and then a record type. To illustrate:

```
type
   String3 = packed array [1..3] of Char;
   NodePointer = ^Node;
   Node = record
            AWord : String3;
            Count : Integer;
            Link : NodePointer
          end; {Node}

var
   P, Q, R : NodePointer;   {pointers to records of type Node}
```

A pointer variable of type `NodePointer` points to a record of type `Node` with three fields: `AWord`, `Count`, and `Link`. The first two fields store a string and an integer value; the third field, `Link` (type `NodePointer`), stores an address, as shown in the following diagram:

Figure 16.2
Children's Pop Beads in a Chain

Pop bead   Chain of pop beads

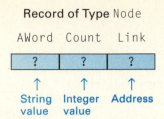

Record of Type Node

Notice that the type declaration for NodePointer refers to the identifier Node, which is not yet declared. The declaration of a pointer type is the *only* situation in which Pascal allows us to reference an undeclared identifier. The pointer type must be declared before any node that has a field of this type.

Connecting Nodes

The statements

```
New (P);
New (Q);
```

allocate storage for two records of type Node.

The assignment statements

```
P^.AWord := 'hat';   P^.Count := 2;
Q^.AWord := 'top';   Q^.Count := 3
```

define two fields of each node, as shown in Fig. 16.3. The Link fields are still undefined.

The statement

```
P^.Link := Q
```

stores the address of record Q^ in the Link field of record P^, thereby connecting node P^ to node Q^ (see Fig. 16.4).

The Link field of the first node, P^.Link, points to the second node in the list and contains the same address as pointer Q. We can therefore use either field selector Q^.AWord or P^.Link^.AWord to access the AWord field of the second node in the list.

Figure 16.3
Nodes P^ and Q^

Figure 16.4
List with Two Elements

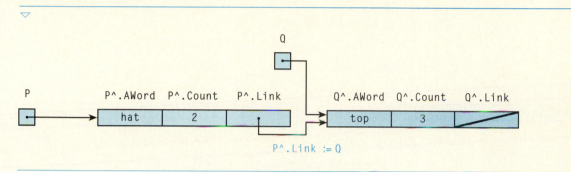

$$P^{\wedge}.Link := Q$$

We normally store a special pointer value, nil, in the pointer field of the last element in a list. We can use either of the following statements to accomplish this result. We usually represent the value nil by drawing a diagonal line in a pointer field:

```
Q^.Link := nil   |   P^.Link^.Link := nil
```

Inserting a Node in a List

To insert a new node between nodes P^ and Q^, we start with the statements

```
New (R);
R^.AWord := 'the';  R^.Count := 5;
```

They allocate and initialize a new node (R^), which is pointed to by pointer R. The statements

```
{1}     P^.Link := R;    {Connect node P^ to node R^.}
{2}     R^.Link := Q     {Connect node R^ to node Q^.}
```

assign new values to the Link fields of node P^ (statement {1}) and node R^ (statement {2}). Statement {1} connects node P^ to node R^; statement {2} connects node R^ to node Q^. Figure 16.5 shows the effect of these statements. The color arrows show the new values of the pointer fields; the gray arrow shows the old values.

Notice in Fig. 16.5 that we no longer need pointer variables Q and R to access the list nodes because we can reach each node by following a trail of pointers from pointer variable P. The first node (node P^) is called the **list head.** Table 16.1 shows some valid references to the list data, starting from the list head.

list head

the first node in a list

Figure 16.5
Inserting Node R^ in a List

Table 16.1
References to List Nodes in
Fig. 16.5

Field Selector	Data Referenced
P^.AWord	hat
P^.Link	Link field of first node
P^.Link^.AWord	the
P^.Link^.Link	Link field of second node
P^.Link^.Link^.Count	3

Insertion at the Head of a List

Although we usually insert new data items at the end of a data structure, it is easier and more efficient to insert a new item at the head of a list. The following program fragment allocates a new node and inserts it at the head of the list pointed to by P. Pointer OldHead points to the original list head. After the insertion, P points to the new list head which is linked to the old list head, as shown in Fig. 16.6. The color arrows show the new values of the pointer fields; the gray arrow shows the old values.

```
OldHead := P;              {Save pointer to old list head.}
New (P);                   {Point P to a new node.}
P^.Link := OldHead         {Connect new list head to old list head.}
```

Insertion at the End of a List

Inserting an item at the end of a list is less efficient because we usually do not have a pointer to the last list element and so must follow the pointer trail

Figure 16.6
Insertion at the List Head

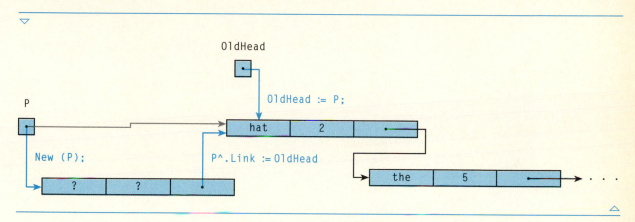

from the list head to the last list node and then perform the insertion. When `Last` is pointing to the last list node (Fig. 16.7), the statements

```
New (Last^.Link);       {Attach a new node to list end.}
Last^.Link^.Link := nil            {Mark new list end.}
```

connect a new node to the end of the list and set its `Link` field to `nil`.

Deleting a Node

To delete a node from a linked list, we simply change the `Link` field of the node that points to it (its *predecessor*). We want the predecessor to point to the node that follows the one being deleted (its *successor*). For example, to delete node `R^` from the three-element list in Fig. 16.8, we change the `Link` field of node `P^` to point to the successor of node `R^`. The statement

Figure 16.7
Insertion at the End of a List

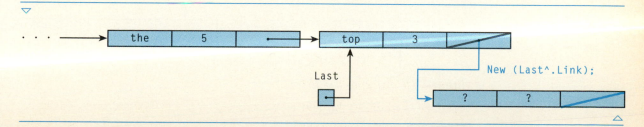

```
P^.Link := R^.Link;   {Bypass node R^.}
```

copies the address in the `Link` field of node `R^` to the `Link` field of node `P^`, thereby deleting node `R^` from the list. Then, we use the statements

```
R^.Link := nil;        {Disconnect R^ from its successor.}
Dispose (R)            {Return storage to the heap.}
```

to disconnect node `R^` from the list and return its storage to the heap.

Traversing a List

traversing a list

processing the nodes in a list
starting with the list head and
ending with the last node

In many list processing operations, we must process each node in the list in sequence, a procedure called **traversing a list.** We start at the list head and follow the trail of pointers.

One typical operation performed on most data structures is to display the data structure's contents. To display the contents of a list, we must display only the values of the information fields, not the link fields. Procedure `PrintList` in Fig. 16.9 displays the information fields of each node in the list shown in Fig. 16.8 (after the deletion). The procedure call statement

```
PrintList (P);
```

displays the output lines

```
hat 2
top 3
```

The `while` condition

```
Head <> nil
```

Figure 16.8
Deleting a List Node

Figure 16.9
Procedure PrintList

Directory: CHAP16
File: PRINTLIS.PAS

```
procedure PrintList (Head {input} : ListPointer);
{
  Displays the list pointed to by Head.
  Pre : Head points to a list whose last node has a pointer
        field of nil.
  Post: The data fields of each list node are displayed and
        the last value of Head is nil.
}
begin {PrintList}
  {Traverse the list until the end is reached.}
  while Head <> nil do
    {invariant: No prior value of Head was nil.}
    begin
      Write (Head^.AWord);
      WriteLn (Head^.Count :2);
      Head := Head^.Link                  {Advance to next node.}
    end {while}
end; {PrintList}
```

is common in loops that process lists. If the list to be displayed is empty, this condition is true initially and the loop body is skipped. If the list is not empty, the loop body executes and the last statement in the loop,

```
Head := Head^.Link        {Advance to next node.}
```

advances the pointer `Head` to the next list element, which is pointed to by the `Link` field of the current list element. After the last data value in the list is printed, this statement assigns the address `nil` to `Head` and loop exit occurs.

Because `Head` is a value parameter, a local copy of the pointer to the first list element is established when the procedure is entered. This local pointer is advanced, but the corresponding pointer in the calling program remains unchanged. What would happen to our list if `Head` was a variable parameter?

Program Style

Warning About Variable Parameters for Pointers

Consider the effect of parameter `Head` being a variable parameter instead of a value parameter. This would allow the procedure to change the corresponding actual parameter, regardless of our intentions. In `PrintList` and in many similar procedures, the last value assigned to the pointer parameter is `nil`. If `Head` is a variable parameter, the corresponding actual parameter

▶▶▶▶▶▶

would be set to `nil`, thereby disconnecting it from the list to which it pointed before the procedure call.

Passing a pointer as a value parameter protects that pointer from being changed by the procedure. However, you should realize that any changes made to other pointers in the list during the procedure's execution will remain.

Circular Lists and Two-Way Lists (Optional)

You can traverse a list in only one direction, and you can't move past the last element. To circumvent these restrictions, programmers use either circular or two-way lists.

Circular Lists

circular list
a list in which the last list node contains a pointer to the first list node

A **circular list** is one in which the last list node points back to the list head. In the following circular list, you can start anywhere in the list and still access all list elements:

Two-Way Lists

two-way (doubly linked) list
a list in which each node has a pointer to its predecessor and successor

In a **two-way,** or **doubly linked, list,** each node has two pointers: one to the node's successor (`Right`) and one to the node's predecessor (`Left`). For the node `Next^` shown here,

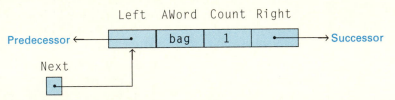

the statement

`Next := Next^.Right`

moves pointer `Next` to the successor node, and the statement

`Next := Next^.Left`

moves pointer `Next` to the predecessor node.

Exercises for Section 16.3 **Self-Check**

1. For the three-element list in Fig. 16.5, explain the effect of each fragment. Assume the list is restored to its initial state before each fragment executes.

```
a.  R^.Link := P              f.  P^.Link := nil
b.  P^.Link := R              g.  P^.Link := Q^.Link
c.  P := P^.Link              h.  P^.Aword := R^.AWord
d.  P^.Count :=               i.  P^.Link^.Link := nil
        P^.Link^.Link^.Count  j.  while P <> nil do
e.  New (Q^.Link);                  begin
    Q^.Link^.AWord := 'zzz';            P^.Count :=
    Q^.Link^.Count := 0;                    P^.Count + 1;
    Q^.Link^.Link := nil              P := P^.Link
                                    end
```

2. How would you delete the node at the head of a list? How would you delete a node if you were given only a pointer to the node to be deleted and a pointer to the list head?

Programming

1. Write a function that finds the length of a list.
2. Write a fragment to advance pointer `Last` to the last node of a list whose head is `P^`. Then insert a new list node at the end of the list. Make sure you consider the special case of an initially empty list (`P` is `nil`).

16.4 Linked List ADT

A linked list can store any collection of records (e.g., student records for a class, or a telephone directory) and its flexibility makes it an ideal data structure when there are frequent insertions and deletions. Table 16.2 provides the specification for a linked list abstract data type.

Table 16.2
Specification for Linked List Abstract Data Type

Structure

A linked list is a collection of elements of the same type (`Entry`). Each element has a key field which uniquely identifies it. Elements can be inserted, deleted, or replaced.

Operators

The descriptions of the operators use the following parameters:

AList	(type LinkList)
AnEntry	(type Entry)
InFile	(type Text)
Success	(type Boolean)

Several operators use the `Boolean` parameter `Success` to indicate whether the operation succeeds (returns `True`) or fails (returns `False`).

Table 16.2 Specification for Linked List Abstract Data Type *(continued)*	`Init (var AList)` Creates a linked list that is initially empty. `ReadList (var AList, var InFile)` Reads the entries from a text file and stores them in the linked list. `Insert (var AList, AnEntry, var Success)` Inserts a new entry at the beginning of the list. `Search (AList, AnEntry, var Success)` Returns through `Success` an indication of whether a record with the same key as `AnEntry` appears in the linked list. `Replace (var AList, AnEntry, var Success)` Replaces the entry having the same key as `AnEntry` with `AnEntry`. `Delete (var AList, AnEntry, var Success)` Deletes the entry having the same key as `AnEntry`. `Retrieve (AList, var AnEntry, var Success)` Retrieves the entry having the same key as `AnEntry`. `GetCount (AList)` (function) Returns the count of entries in the list. `DisplayList (AList)` Displays all list entries.

Implementation of LinkListADT

A linked list starts off with zero nodes, expanding as new nodes are inserted and shrinking when existing nodes are deleted. We can represent a linked list using a record with two fields: a pointer field, `Head`, which points to the first list node, and an `Integer` field, `Count`, which keeps track of the number of nodes. When we declare a variable of type `LinkList`, storage is allocated at compile time for this record only. Storage is allocated for the linked list nodes at run time as needed.

Figure 16.10 shows the type declarations for `LinkListADT`. To enhance reusability, we will assume that the elements housed in our linked list are declared in a separate abstract data type (`EntryADT`) that provides operators for reading a record (`ReadEntry`), displaying a record (`DisplayEntry`), and testing whether two records have the same key (`EqualTo`). We will import this module into `LinkListADT`.

Figure 16.10
Type Declarations for
LinkListADT

Directory: CHAP16
File: LINKLIST.PAS

```
{
  Implementation of LinkListADT.
  Uses module EntryADT (Fig. 12.14).

  Insert declarations for type Entry from EntryADT.
}

  type
    ListPointer = ^ListNode;
```

▷ ▷ ▷ ▷ ▷ ▷

```
ListNode = record
               Info : Entry;          {information part}
               Link : ListPointer     {connector to next node}
           end; {ListNode}

LinkList = record
               Head : ListPointer;    {pointer to first node}
               Count : Integer        {number of nodes}
           end; {LinkList}
{
   Insert operators ReadEntry, DisplayEntry, and EqualTo
   from EntryADT.
}
```

Init, Insert, and ReadList

Figure 16.11 shows three linked list operators: Init, Insert, and ReadList. Procedure Init initializes its parameter (AList) to an empty list by setting the count of entries to 0 and the pointer Head to nil.

Procedure Insert places a new entry at the beginning of the list rather than the end because insertion at the beginning is easier. In Insert, the statements

Figure 16.11
Init, Insert, and ReadList

Directory: CHAP16
File: LINKLIST.PAS

```
procedure Init (var AList {output} : LinkList);
{
 Creates an initially empty list.
 pre : none
 post: Defines AList as a linked list with 0 elements.
}
begin {Init}
  AList.Count := 0;
  AList.Head := nil
end; {Init}


procedure Insert (var AList {input/output} : LinkList;
                      AnEntry {input} : Entry;
                      var Success {output} : Boolean);
{
 Inserts entry AnEntry into a list.
 pre : AnEntry is defined.
 post: Inserts AnEntry as the first list element of
       list AList and sets Success to True.
}
```

▷ ▷ ▷ ▷ ▷

```
    var
       OldHead : ListPointer;       {pointer to old list head}

begin {Insert}
   OldHead := AList.Head;              {Save pointer to old head.}
   New (AList.Head);                   {Point Head to a new node.}
   AList.Head^.Info := AnEntry; {Store new entry in new head.}
   AList.Head^.Link := OldHead;    {Link new head to old head.}
   AList.Count := AList.Count + 1; {Increase count of nodes.}
   Success := True
end;   {Insert}


procedure ReadList (var AList {output} : LinkList;
                       var InFile {input} : Text);
{
 Reads data records from a data file into a list.
 pre : InFile has been saved as a text file.
 post: Entries in InFile are stored in the list AList.
}
    var
       AnEntry : Entry;               {a new entry}
       Success : Boolean;             {flag}

begin {ReadList}
   Reset (InFile);                    {Open the data file.}

   {Read each record and insert it in the list.}
   while not EOF(InFile) do
      begin
         ReadEntry (AnEntry, InFile);       {Read next entry.}
         Insert (AList, AnEntry, Success)  {Insert AnEntry.}
      end {while}
end; {ReadList}
```

△

```
OldHead := AList.Head;        {Save pointer to old head.}
New (AList.Head);             {Point Head to a new node.}
AList.Head^.Info := AnEntry;  {Store new entry in new head.}
AList.Head^.Link := OldHead;  {Link new head to old head.}
```

store AnEntry's data at the head of the list. The first statement stores the address of the current list head in OldHead, and the next two allocate a new head node and store AnEntry in it. The last statement connects the new list head to the rest of the list.

The while loop in ReadList reads each entry's data (using procedure ReadEntry) and calls Insert to store the data in a new node at the head of the linked list. Each entry is stored in the list in the reverse order from which it is read (i.e., the last entry read is stored in the list head).

Figure 16.12 traces the insertion of the first two data records, assuming each data record contains a person's name and number. In each diagram, the color arrows show pointers that are changed by procedure `Insert`.

Search

We often use recursive algorithms to process linked data structures. A recursive search algorithm follows.

Algorithm for List Search

1. `if` the list is empty `then`
Return with `Success` set to `False`.
`else if` the first list node contains `AnEntry`'s key `then`
Return with `Success` set to `True`.
`else`
Search the rest of the list.

Figure 16.12
Inserting the First Two
Data Records

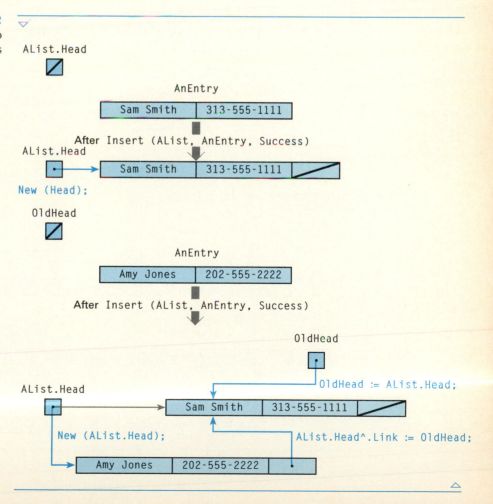

If the list is empty, the value of Success must be False. If the head of the list matches AnEntry, the value of Success must be True. Otherwise, the recursive step "Search the rest of the list" searches the list whose head is the second element of the previous list. This step causes the first element of successively smaller lists to be compared to AnEntry until the list being searched is empty (first stopping case—return False through Success) or its head matches AnEntry (second stopping case—return True through Success). Figure 16.13 traces the algorithm during an unsuccessful search, showing the list head (pointed to by First) for each recursive call.

Operator Search (Fig. 16.14) calls procedure DoSearch to start the search, passing the list head as the first parameter to DoSearch. Procedure DoSearch implements the recursive search algorithm. In DoSearch, the condition EqualTo(AnEntry, First^.Info) compares the key field of AnEntry to the key field of the current list head. The statement

```
DoSearch (First^.Link, AnEntry, Success)
```

advances First to the second element of the current list, causing the rest of the list to be searched. The recursion stops as soon as a value is assigned to

Figure 16.13
Search for AnEntry's Key

Figure 16.14
DoSearch
and Search

Directory: CHAP16
File: LINKLIST.PAS

```
procedure DoSearch (First {input} : ListPointer;
                    AnEntry {input} : Entry;
                    var Success {output} : Boolean);
{
 Performs recursive search.
 pre : First points to the head of the list being searched.
 post: If AnEntry's key is found, Success is set to True;
       otherwise, Success is set to False.
}
begin {DoSearch}
  if First = nil then
    Success := False
  else if EqualTo(AnEntry, First^.Info) then
    Success := True
  else
    DoSearch (First^.Link, AnEntry, Success)
end; {DoSearch}

procedure Search (AList {input} : LinkList;
                  AnEntry {input} : Entry;
                  var Success {output} : Boolean);
{
 Calls DoSearch to search for AnEntry's key in AList.
 pre : AnEntry is defined.
 post: If AnEntry's key is found, Success is set to True;
       otherwise, Success is set to False.
}
begin {Search}
  DoSearch (AList.Head, AnEntry, Success)
end; {Search}
```

`Success` and, after unwinding from the recursion, that value is returned to the program that called `Search`.

Replace and Delete

Operators `Replace` (Fig. 16.15) and `Delete` (Fig. 16.16) are modeled after `Search`. Both call recursive procedures (`DoReplace` or `DoDelete`) to compare the key of `AnEntry` to the first element of successively smaller lists. Because both recursive procedures can modify the list, `First` is a variable parameter.

What happens when the current list head matches `AnEntry`'s key? In `DoReplace`, the statement

```
First^.Info := AnEntry;    {Replace item with AnEntry.}
```

Figure 16.15
DoReplace
and Replace

Directory: CHAP16
File: LINKLIST.PAS

```
procedure DoReplace (var First {input/output} : ListPointer;
                         AnEntry {input} : Entry;
                         var Success {output} : Boolean);
{
 Performs recursive replacement.
 pre : First points to the head of the list being searched.
 post: Entry with same key as AnEntry is replaced and
       Success is True; otherwise, Success is False.
}
begin {DoReplace}
   if First = nil then
      Success := False
   else if EqualTo(AnEntry, First^.Info) then
      begin {found key}
         First^.Info := AnEntry;   {Replace item with AnEntry.}
         Success := True
      end {found key}
   else
      DoReplace (First^.Link, AnEntry, Success)
end; {DoReplace}

procedure Replace (var AList {input/output} : LinkList;
                       AnEntry {input} : Entry;
                       var Success {output} : Boolean);
{
 Substitutes AnEntry for entry in AList with matching key.
 pre : AnEntry is defined.
 post: Entry with same key as AnEntry is replaced and
       Success is True; otherwise, Success is False.
}
begin {Replace}
   DoReplace (AList.Head, AnEntry, Success)
end; {Replace}
```

replaces the data stored in the current list head with `AnEntry`. In `DoDelete`, the statement

```
First := First^.Link;                {Bypass old head.}
```

deletes the current list head, which is then returned to the heap (by `Dispose`). Both procedures set `Success` to `True`, and procedure `Delete` decrements the data field `AList.Count`.

Using LinkListADT

Figure 16.17 shows a client program for `LinkListADT`. The program reads in an initial list of three items and displays it using `DisplayList`

Figure 16.16
DoDelete
and Delete

Directory: CHAP16
File: LINKLIST.PAS

```
procedure DoDelete (var First {input/output} : ListPointer;
                        AnEntry {input} : Entry;
                        var Success {output} : Boolean);
{
 Performs recursive deletion.
 pre : First points to the head of the list being searched.
 post: If AnEntry is found, it is deleted and
       Success is True; otherwise, Success is False.
}
   var
     ToDelete : ListPointer; {pointer to node to delete.}

begin {DoDelete}
   if First = nil then
     Success := False
   else if EqualTo(AnEntry, First^.Info) then
     begin {found key}
       ToDelete := First;              {Delete list head.}
       First := First^.Link;           {Bypass old head.}
       ToDelete^.Link := nil;      {Disconnect old head.}
       Dispose (ToDelete);         {Return node to heap.}
       Success := True
     end {found key}
   else
     DoDelete (First^.Link, AnEntry, Success)
end; {DoDelete}

procedure Delete (var AList {input/output} : LinkList;
                      AnEntry {input} : Entry;
                      var Success {output} : Boolean);
{
 Deletes the entry in AList with the same key as AnEntry.
 pre : AnEntry is defined.
 post: If AnEntry is found, it is deleted and
       Success is True; otherwise, Success is False.
}

begin {Delete}
   DoDelete (AList.Head, AnEntry, Success);
   if Success then                {Decrement Count after deletion.}
     AList.Count := AList.Count - 1
end; {Delete}
```

(see Programming Exercise 1 for Section 16.4). Next it reads and inserts a new item at the head of the list and displays the four-element list. Finally, it deletes the item just inserted and displays the original list again.

```
program ListClient (Input, Output, InFile);
{
  Imports EntryADT and LinkListADT.

  Insert type declaration for Entry from EntryADT and
  ListPointer, ListNode, and LinkList from LinkListADT.
}
  var
    MyList : LinkList;        {Linked list to be tested}
    InFile : Text;           {Data file with list data}
    NewEntry : Entry;        {New entry for linked list}
    Success : Boolean;       {Program flag}


  {
  Insert procedure ReadEntry from EntryADT and Init, Insert,
  ReadList, Search, Replace, and Delete from LinkListADT.
  }

begin
  Init (MyList);                  {Create initial linked list.}
  ReadList (MyList, InFile);      {Read data into linked list.}
  WriteLn ('Initial list:');
  WriteList (MyList);  WriteLn;      {Display initial list.}

  {Insert a new entry or change an entry in the list.}
  Write ('Type in a new entry> ');
  ReadEntry (NewEntry, Input);          {Read new entry.}
  Search (MyList, NewEntry, Success);   {Is it in the list?}
  if Success then
    begin
      WriteLn ('Found key - replace entry');
      Replace (MyList, NewEntry, Success)    {Yes, replace it.}
    end
  else
    Insert (MyList, NewEntry, Success);     {No, insert it.}
  WriteLn ('List after insertion or replacement:');
  WriteList (MyList);  WriteLn;

  {Delete the entry just inserted.}
  Delete (MyList, NewEntry, Success);

  WriteLn ('List after deletion of new entry:');
  WriteList (MyList)
end.
```

Sample Run

```
Initial list:
Bill
555-123-4567
```

▷ ▷ ▷ ▷ ▷

```
Sam
555-111-2222
Carol
555-123-6789

Type in a new entry> Robin
555-222-3333
List after insertion or replacement:
Robin
555-222-3333
Bill
555-123-4567
Sam
555-111-2222
Carol
555-123-6789

List after deletion of new entry:
Bill
555-123-4567
Sam
555-111-2222
Carol
555-123-6789
```

Exercises for Section 16.4 **Self-Check**

1. Verify that operator `Insert` works properly when the list being inserted into is an empty one. How does the `nil` pointer get stored in the `Link` field of the list element being inserted?

2. Assume a linked list contains the three strings `'Hat'`, `'Boy'`, `'Cat'`. What successive lists are searched when operator `Search` is called and the target key is `'Boy'`? When the target key is `'Cup'`?

3. Why is it easier to insert a new list element at the head of a list rather than the end? How would you perform an insertion at the end of a list for the linked list declared in Fig. 16.10? Why is this an *O(N)* operation? How could you change the linked list declaration so that insertion at the end of a list would be an *O*(1) operation?

4. How could a linked list be implemented using an array of records rather than pointers? How would you represent the links? How would you add new items? What are the disadvantages of this approach? How could you handle deletions to recover the array locations for future use?

Programming

1. Write operators `Retrieve`, `GetCount`, and `DisplayList`.

2. Write an iterative version of `Search`.
3. Write a recursive procedure to display the list in reverse order.

16.5 Common Programming Errors

Syntax Errors

Be sure to use the dereferencing operator ^ where it is needed. If `P` is a pointer variable, `P^.X` should be used to reference field `X` of the record pointed to by `P`.

The `New` and `Dispose` procedures allocate and deallocate storage, respectively. Both procedures require a parameter that is a pointer variable. `New (P)` is correct, while `New (P^)` is incorrect.

Run-Time Errors

Several run-time errors can occur when traversing linked data structures. For example, if pointer `Next` is supposed to point to each node in the linked list, make sure `Next` is initialized to point to the list head.

Watch out for infinite loops caused by failure to advance a pointer down a list. The `while` statement

```
while Next <> nil do
   Write (Next^.Data);
   Next := Next^.Link;
```

executes forever because the pointer assignment statement is not included in the loop body, so `Next` is not advanced down the list.

A run-time error can occur when the pointer `Next` is advanced too far down the list and `Next` takes on the value `nil`, indicating the end of the list. If pointer `Next` has the value `nil`, the `while` condition

```
while (Next <> nil) and (Next^.ID <> 9999) do
```

causes a run-time error on some systems because `Next^.ID` is undefined when `Next` is `nil`. The `while` condition should be rewritten as

```
while (Next^.Link <> nil) and (Next^.ID <> 9999) do
```

Problems with heap management can also cause run-time errors. If your program gets stuck in an infinite loop while you are creating a dynamic data structure, it could consume all memory cells on the storage heap. This situation leads to a `heap overflow` run-time error.

Similar problems can occur with recursive procedures. If a recursive procedure does not terminate, you can get a `stack overflow` error.

Make sure your program does not attempt to reference a list node after the node is returned to the heap. All pointers to a node being returned should be assigned new values so that the node can never be accessed unless it is reallocated.

Debugging Tips

It is difficult to debug programs that manipulate pointers, because the value of a pointer variable cannot be printed. Consequently, you often will find it more informative to trace the execution of such a program by printing an information field that uniquely identifies the list element being processed instead of the pointer itself.

When writing driver programs to test and debug list operators, you can create a small linked list by using the New statement to allocate several nodes and linking them into a list by using assignment statements (see Section 16.3). You also can use assignment statements to put information into the nodes, prior to linking them.

CHAPTER REVIEW

1. A pointer is a variable whose contents are a memory cell address. You can perform assignment and comparison operations on pointers, but you can't read or write pointer values.

2. The procedure call New (P) dynamically allocates storage for a memory area whose address is stored in pointer variable P. The data type of pointer P determines the structure of this data area, which is referenced as P^. The memory cells for this data area are taken from Pascal's heap. When the data area P^ is no longer needed, use the procedure call Dispose (P) to return it to the storage heap.

3. If data area P^ itself contains a pointer field, you can connect it to another like data area, thereby building a linked list. Linked lists are flexible data structures that shrink and expand as a program executes. It is relatively easy to insert and delete nodes of a linked list.

4. You can use a record of type LinkList declared in the linked list ADT in Section 16.4 to point to a linked list. The operators of LinkListADT perform search, insert, replace, and delete operations on a linked list, as well as reading records from a data file into a linked list and displaying the contents of a linked list.

Summary of New Pascal Constructs

Construct	Effect
Pointer Type Declaration	

`type`
`  Pointer = ^Node;`
`  Node = record`
`    Info : Integer;`
	The type identifier Pointer is declared as a pointer to a record of type Node, where Node is a record type containing a field (Link) of type Pointer.

Construct	Effect
`    Link : Pointer` `end; {Node}`	
`var` `  Head : Pointer;`	`Head` is a pointer variable of type `Pointer`.
New Procedure	
`New (Head)`	A new record of type `Node` is allocated. This record is pointed to by `Head` and is referenced by `Head^`.
Dispose Procedure	
`Dispose (Head)`	The memory space occupied by the record `Head^` is returned to the storage pool.
Pointer Assignment	
`Head := Head^.Link`	The pointer `Head` is advanced to the next node in the dynamic data structure pointed to by `Head`.

Quick-Check Exercises

1. Procedure _____ allocates storage space for a data object that is referenced through a _____; procedure _____ returns the storage space to the _____.
2. What is the major advantage of using pointer representations of lists instead of using arrays to store list-like structures?
3. Assume a linked list contains a pointer, `Rear`, to the last list element. Write the statements necessary to insert an element `NewItem` at the rear of the list instead of at the list head.
4. When an element is deleted from a linked list represented using pointers, it is automatically returned to the heap. True or false?
5. All pointers to a node that is returned to the heap are automatically reset to `nil` so they cannot reference the node returned to the heap. True or false?
6. Why would the following code fragment cause a run-time error? Assume `Link` is a pointer and `Data` is an integer. How could it be fixed?

```
while Head <> nil do
   Head := Head^.Link;
WriteLn ('Last data item in list is: ', Head^.Data);
```

7. If a linked list contains three elements with values `'Him'`, `'Her'`, and `'Its'` and `H` is a pointer to the list head, what is the effect of the following statements? Assume the data field is `Pronoun`, the link field is `Next`, and `N` and `P` are pointer variables.

```
N := H^.Next;
N^.Pronoun := 'She'
```

8. Answer Exercise 7 for the following segment:

```
P := H^.Next;
N := P^.Next;
P^.Next := N^.Next;
Dispose (N)
```

9. Answer Exercise 7 for the following segment:

```
N := H;
New (H);
H^.Pronoun := 'His';
H^.Next := N
```

10. When is it advantageous to use a linked-list data structure? When would an array be a better choice?

Answers to Quick-Check Exercises

1. New; pointer; `Dispose`; heap
2. Storage space is allocated as needed and not all at once.
3.
```
New (Rear^.Link);
Rear := Rear^.Link;
Rear^.Info := NewItem;
Rear^.Link := nil;
Count := Count + 1
```
4. False (`Dispose` must be called).
5. False
6. At loop exit, `Head` will be `nil`, so `Head^.Data` is invalid.

```
Last := nil;                          {Assume list is empty.}
while Head <> nil do
   begin
      Last := Head;                   {Set Last to old Head.}
      Head := Head^.Link              {Advance Head.}
   end; {while}

if Last <> nil then
   WriteLn ('Last data item in list is: ', Last^.Data);
```

7. `'Her'` is replaced by `'She'`.
8. The third list element is deleted.
9. A new list node with value `'His'` is inserted at the front of the list.
10. When the number of elements is variable or insertions and deletions are frequent. When elements must be accessed randomly.

Review Questions

1. Define the term *linked list*. How are the list nodes connected? How many pointer variables would you need to access all nodes of a linked list with five nodes?
2. Why are recursive procedures often used for processing linked data structures?

3.   Why is it more efficient to insert at the front of a list than at the end? What is the time in Big-O notation for insertion at the front of a list? At the end of a list? How can insertion at the end of a list be made more efficient?

4.   If a linked list of data elements is in sorted order, could we perform a binary search on that list in $O(\log_2 N)$ time? Why or why not.

5.   Give the missing type declarations and show the effect of each of the following statements. What does the fragment do?

```
New (P);
P^.Data := 'ABC';
New (P^.Next);
Q := P^.Next;
Q^.Data := 'abc';
Q^.Next := nil
```

Assume the following type declarations for Questions 6 through 9:

```
type
   StringIndex = 1..10;
   StringType = packed array [StringIndex] of Char;
   ListPointer = ^Node;
   Node = record
                Name : StringType;
                Link : ListPointer
             end; {Node}

   HeadNode = record
                   Head : ListPointer;
                   NumItems : Integer
                end; {HeadNode}

   var
      List : HeadNode;
```

6.   Write a program segment that places the names Washington, Roosevelt, and Kennedy in successive elements of the linked list referenced by record `List`. Define `List.NumItems` accordingly.

7.   Write an operator called `DeleteLast` that removes the last element from any list referenced by record `List`.

8.   Write a procedure called `CopyList` that creates a linked list with new nodes that contain the same data as the linked list referenced by `List`.

9.   Write a procedure to delete all nodes with `Name` field equal to `Target` (a parameter) from a linked list referenced by record `List`.

Programming Projects

1.   Write a procedure that uses the selection sort strategy to create a sorted copy of a linked list, assuming `EntryADT` contains an operator `LessThan` for comparing entries.

2.   Write a linked-list merge procedure similar to the file merge procedure from Chapter 15 that creates a new sorted linked list by merging two linked lists that have been sorted using the procedure from Programming Project 1.

3. Modify Programming Project 1 at the end of Chapter 10 so that student grades are stored in a linked list rather than in an array of scores.

4. The singly-linked list presented in this chapter makes it easy to process the list elements in order, but processing in reverse order is very difficult and time consuming. One solution is to use a two-way list (see Section 16.3). Create a new two-way list ADT based on the linked list ADT, and include a new procedure to display the list in reverse. Write a suitable test program for your ADT.

5. A polynomial can be represented as a linked list, where each node contains the coefficient and the exponent of a term of the polynomial. The polynomial $4x^3 + 3x^2 - 5$ would be represented as the following linked list:

Write an abstract data type `Polynomial` that has operators for creating a polynomial, reading a polynomial, and adding and subtracting a pair of polynomials. Store the terms for each polynomial in decreasing order by exponent. *Hint:* To add or subtract two polynomials, traverse both lists. If a particular exponent value is present in either one, it also should be present in the result polynomial unless its coefficient is zero.

6. Each student in the university takes a different number of courses, so the registrar has decided to use a linked list to store each student's class schedule and an array of records to represent the whole student body. A portion of this data structure follows.

The records show that the first student (`ID` is 1111) is taking section 1 of `CIS120` for 3 credits and section 2 of `HIS001` for 4 credits; the second student (`ID` is 1234) is not enrolled, and so on. Write declarations for this data structure. Provide operators for creating the original array of student ID numbers, inserting a student's initial class schedule, adding a course, and dropping a course. Write a menu-driven program that uses these operators.

7. Many programs create multiple, overlapping windows on the screen. With overlapping windows comes the concept of a window being on top and a front-to-back ordering of windows. If windows are drawn from back to front, their appearance matches the expected results. Write a program that maintains a linked list of colored rectangles representing windows in front-to-back order. Your program should have a menu that allows the user to enter a letter for a rectangle, the color of the rectangle, and its screen location. Other menu options should allow the screen to be redrawn and any window to be moved to the top.

CHAPTER SEVENTEEN

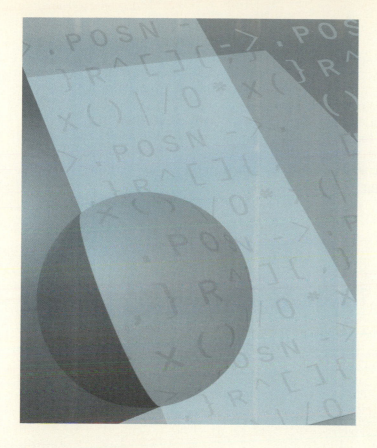

Dynamic Data Structures

Linked lists are just one type of dynamic data structure. In this chapter, we introduce three others: stacks, queues, and binary search trees. We provide only a brief overview of these structures; you will cover them in more detail in advanced courses in computer science.

17.1 Stacks

stack

a data structure in which only the top element can be accessed

A **stack** is a data structure in which only the top element can be accessed. To illustrate, the plates stored in the spring-loaded device in a buffet line perform like a stack. A customer always takes the top plate; when a plate is removed, the plate beneath it moves to the top.

The following diagram shows a stack of three characters. The letter C, the character at the top of the stack, is the only one we can access. We must remove C from the stack in order to access the symbol +. Removing a value from a stack is called **popping the stack,** and storing a data item in a stack is called **pushing** it onto the stack.

pop

removing the top element of a stack

push

placing a new top element on the stack

Stacks as Linked Lists

We can think of a stack as a linked list in which all insertions and deletions are performed at the list head. A list representation of the stack containing C, +, and 2 is

Top

Pointer variable Top points to the list head. We can access only the character in node Top^, the letter C. Next we draw the stack after we push the symbol * onto it:

Top

last-in, first-out (LIFO) structure

a data structure in which the last element stored is the first to be removed

If we pop this stack, we retrieve the symbol * and restore the stack to its earlier state. A stack is called a **last-in, first-out (LIFO) structure** because the last element stored in a stack is always the first one removed.

Stack ADT

Table 17.1 provides a specification for a stack ADT. Besides operators Init, Push, and Pop, we include operators Retrieve and IsEmpty. Operator Retrieve accesses the top element on a stack without removing it. Operator IsEmpty determines whether a stack has any elements.

Structure
A stack consists of a collection of elements all of the same data type (type `StackData`) and ordered by their placement on the stack. New elements are pushed onto the top of the stack. Only the element that was last pushed onto the stack can be popped or retrieved.

Operators
The following descriptions assume these parameters:

`S` (type `Stack`)
`X` (type `StackData`)
`Success` (type `Boolean`)

`Init (var S)` Creates an empty stack.
`Push (var S, X)` The value in `X` is placed on the top of the stack.
`Pop (var S, var X, var Success)` If the stack is not empty, the value at the top of the stack is removed, its value is placed in `X`, and `Success` is set to `True`. If the stack is empty, `X` is not defined and `Success` is set to `False`.
`Retrieve (S, var X, var Success)` If the stack is not empty, the value at the top of the stack is copied into `X`, and `Success` is set to `True`. If the stack is empty, `X` is not defined and `Success` is set to `False`. In either case, the stack is not changed.
`IsEmpty(S)` (function) Returns `True` if the stack is empty; otherwise, returns `False`.

Implementing a Stack ADT

The stack ADT is relatively easy to implement. Like a list, a stack node contains a data field, `Info`, that is type `StackData` (imported from `StackDataADT`) and a pointer field, `Link`. Record type `Stack` has a single data field, `Top`. Figure 17.1 shows the type declarations for a stack ADT.

Figure 17.1
Type Declarations for
StackADT

Directory: CHAP17
File: STACKADT.PAS

```
{
  Implementation of StackADT.
  Imports module StackDataADT.

  Insert declarations for type StackData from StackDataADT.
}

  type
    StackPointer = ^StackNode;
    StackNode = record
                  Info : StackData;      {information part}
                  Link : StackPointer    {link to successor}
                end; {StackNode}

    Stack = record
              Top : StackPointer    {top of stack pointer}
            end; {Stack}
```

Figure 17.2 shows the stack operators. `Init` and `Push` work just like linked list operators `Init` and `Insert`. In `Pop`, the statements

```
X := S.Top^.Info;          {Copy value at top of stack into X.}
S.Top := S.Top^.Link;      {Reset pointer to top of stack.}
```

retrieve the data at the top of the stack (`S.Top^.Info`) and change pointer `Top` to point to the successor of the node at the top of the stack. Operator `Retrieve` is left as an exercise.

Exercises for Section 17.1 **Self-Check**

1. Explain the difference between operators `Pop` and `Retrieve`.
2. Assume stack S is a stack of characters. Perform the following sequence of operations, then indicate the result of each operation and the new stack if it is changed. Rather than draw the stack each time, use the notation |2+C/ to represent a stack of four characters, where the last symbol on the right (/) is at the top of the stack.

Figure 17.2
Operators for
StackADT

Directory: CHAP17
File: STACKADT.PAS

```
procedure Init (var S {output} : Stack);
{
  Creates an empty stack.
  Pre : None.
  Post: An empty stack is created.
}
begin {Init}
  S.Top := nil            {Set top-of-stack pointer to nil.}
end; {Init}


procedure Push (var S {input/output} : Stack;
                    X {input} : StackData);
{
  Pushes X onto a stack.
  Pre : X is defined.
  Post: S.Top^.Info contains X.
}
  var
    OldTop : StackPointer;  {pointer to old top of stack}

begin {Push}
  OldTop := S.Top;         {Save old top of stack.}
  New (S.Top);             {Allocate new node at top of stack.}
  S.Top^.Info := X;        {Store X in new node.}
  S.Top^.Link := OldTop    {Link new node to old stack.}
end; {Push}
```

▷ ▷ ▷ ▷ ▷ ▷

```
procedure Pop (var S {input/output} : Stack;
               var X {output} : StackData;
               var Success {output} : Boolean);
{
  Pops the top of stack S into X.
  Pre : S is a stack.
  Post: Content of X is data at top of stack S, which
        is then removed from S. Sets Success to indicate
        success (True) or failure (False) of pop operation.
}
  var
    OldTop : StackPointer;      {pointer to old top of stack}

begin {Pop}
  if S.Top = nil then
    Success := False
  else
    begin
      OldTop := S.Top;        {Save old top of stack.}
      X := S.Top^.Info;       {Copy value at top of stack into X.}
      S.Top := S.Top^.Link;   {Reset pointer to top of stack.}
      Dispose (OldTop);       {Return top node to the heap.}
      Success := True
    end {if}
end; {Pop}

function IsEmpty (S : Stack): Boolean;
{
  Pre : Stack is defined.
  Post: Returns True if stack is empty; otherwise, False.
}
begin {IsEmpty}
  IsEmpty := (S.Top = nil)
end; {IsEmpty}

{Insert Retrieve here.}
```

```
    Init (S);
    Push (S, '$');
    Push (S, '-');
    Pop (S, NextCh, Success);
    Retrieve (S, NextCh, Success);
    Success := IsEmpty(S)
```

3. It is helpful to include a field, NumItems, in record type Stack containing a count of the number of elements on the stack. What changes would be required to the type declaration and the stack operators if field NumItems were included?

4. How could a stack ADT be implemented using an array instead of a linked list? What are two disadvantages to this approach?

Programming

1. Implement operator `Retrieve`.
2. Write an operator `EmptyStack` that will empty a stack of all elements, freeing all memory used by the stack elements.
3. Write an operator `CopyStack` that uses the stack operators to make a copy of an existing stack. The new stack will contain a duplicate of each node in the original stack. *Hint:* You will need to pop each node and store its data in a temporary stack.
4. Provide a declaration for a stack data object assuming the stack data will be housed in an array instead of a linked list. Write operators `Push` and `Pop`.

17.2 Stack Applications

In Section 13.2, we showed how compilers use stacks to store procedure and function parameters. Compilers also use stacks for data storage while translating expressions. In general, we use stacks in a program to remember a sequence of data objects or actions in the reverse order from that in which they were encountered.

We examine two cases that use stacks. In the first, we use a stack to remember characters read in from a data line so they can be displayed in reverse order. In the second, we use a stack to store open parentheses read from an arithmetic expression so we can determine whether they are matched by corresponding closed parentheses.

CASE STUDY   **Reversing a Data Line**

Write a program that reads a data line and displays the characters in reverse order.

ANALYSIS ▼

We use a stack of characters as the primary data structure for this program. Push each data character onto the stack and then pop each character and display it. If the data line contains the word `house`, the character `e` will be stored at the top of the stack (see Fig. 17.3). The letter `e` is the first letter popped and displayed, `s` is the next letter popped, and so on.

Data Requirements

Problem Input

each data character

Figure 17.3
Pushing house onto a Stack

Problem Output

each character on the stack

Program Variable

```
S : Stack
```

DESIGN ▼

Initial Algorithm

1. Create an empty stack.
2. Push each data character onto the stack.
3. Pop each character from the stack and display it.

IMPLEMENTATION ▼

The program is shown in Fig. 17.4. Because S is a stack of characters, unit StackDataADT should contain the declaration

```
type
   StackData = Char;   {stack of characters}
```

The program calls operator Init to create an empty stack S. The loop in procedure FillStack reads each character in the data line and pushes it onto the stack. The loop in procedure DisplayStack repeats until stack S is empty. During each repetition, it pops the top character and displays it.

Figure 17.4
Program PrintReverse

Directory: CHAP17
File: PRINTREV.PAS

```
program PrintReverse (Input, Output);
{
   Reads a line of characters and displays it in reverse.

   Imports StackDataADT and StackADT.

   Insert type declarations for StackData
   from StackDataADT and Stack from StackADT.
}
```

▷ ▷ ▷ ▷ ▷ ▷

```
var
   S : Stack;        {stack of characters read}

{Insert Init, Push, Pop, and IsEmpty from StackADT.}

procedure FillStack (var S {output} : Stack);
{
   Reads data characters and pushes them onto stack S.
   Pre : S is an empty stack.
   Post: S contains the data characters in reverse order.
}
   var
      NextCh : Char;         {next character}

begin {FillStack}
   Write ('Type a data line and press Enter> ');
   while not EOLN do
      begin
         Read (NextCh);
         Push (S, NextCh)    {Push next character on stack S.}
      end {while}
end; {FillStack}

procedure DisplayStack (var S {input/output} : Stack);
{
   Pops each character from stack S and displays it.
   Pre : Stack S is defined.
   Post: Stack S is empty and all characters are displayed.
}
   var
      Success : Boolean;
      NextCh : Char;         {each character from the stack}

begin {DisplayStack}
   while not IsEmpty(S) do
      begin
         Pop (S, NextCh, Success);   {Pop next character off.}
         Write (NextCh)
      end; {while}
   WriteLn
end; {DisplayStack}

begin {PrintReverse}
   Init (S) ;
   FillStack (S);
   DisplayStack (S)
end. {PrintReverse}
```

Sample Run

```
Type a data line and press Enter> house
esuoh
```

Checking for Balanced Parentheses

Another application of a stack is to determine whether the parentheses in an expression are balanced. For example, the expression

```
(a + b * (c / (d - e))) + (d / e)
1          2   3    321 1     1
```

has balanced parentheses. We can solve this problem without using a stack by ignoring all characters except the symbols (and). We start a counter at 1 and add 1 for each open parenthesis that follows another open parenthesis and subtract 1 for each closed parenthesis that follows another closed parenthesis. Because we are ignoring all other symbols, the parentheses being considered do not have to be consecutive characters. If the expression is balanced, the final count will be 1, and it will always be positive.

This task becomes more difficult if we expand our notion of parentheses to include braces and brackets. For example, the expression

```
(a + b * {c / [d - e]}) + (d / e)
```

is balanced, but the expression

```
(a + b * {c / [d - e}) + (d / e)
```

is not because the subexpression [d - e} is incorrect.

PROBLEM ▼

The set of open parenthesis symbols is {, [, and (. An expression is balanced if each subexpression that starts with the symbol { ends with the symbol }; the same is true for the symbol pairs [,] and (,). In other words, the unmatched open parenthesis nearest to each closed parenthesis must have the correct shape (e.g., if } is the closed parenthesis in question, the symbol { must be the nearest unmatched open parenthesis).

ANALYSIS ▼

Solving this problem without stacks would be fairly difficult, but with stacks it becomes easy. First, scan the expression from left to right, ignoring all characters except for parenthesis symbols (including braces and brackets). Push each open parenthesis symbol onto a stack of characters. For a closed parenthesis symbol, pop an open parenthesis from the stack and see whether it matches the closed parenthesis. If the symbols don't match or the stack is empty, there is an error in the expression. If they do match, continue the scan.

Data Requirements

Problem Input

```
Expression : StringType     {expression to be checked for
                                        balanced parentheses}
```

Problem Output

The function result indicating whether the parentheses in `Expression` are balanced

Program Variables

```
ParenStack : Stack {stack of open parentheses}
Balanced : Boolean {flag indicating whether
                     parentheses are balanced}
NextCh : Char       {next character in Expression}
Index : Integer     {index of the next character}
OpenParen : Char    {open parenthesis at the top of the
                     stack}
CloseParen : Char   {closed parenthesis being matched}
```

DESIGN ▼

Initial Algorithm

1. Create an empty stack of characters.
2. Assume that the expression is balanced (`Balanced` is `True`).
3. `while` the expression is balanced and still in the expression do
   `begin`
      4. Get the next character in the expression.
      5. `if` the next character is an open parenthesis `then`
         6. Push it onto the stack.
         `else if` the next character is a closed parenthesis `then`
            `begin`
               7. Pop the top of the stack.
               8. `if` stack was empty or its top was incorrect `then`
                     Set `Balanced` to `False`.
            `end {if}`
   `end {while}`
9. The expression is balanced if `Balanced` is `True` and the stack is empty.

The `if` statement in Step 5 tests each character in the expression, ignoring all characters except for open and closed parenthesis symbols. If the next character is an open parenthesis symbol, it is pushed onto the stack. If the next character is a closed parenthesis symbol, the nearest unmatched open parenthesis is retrieved (by popping the stack) and compared to the closed parenthesis (Steps 7 and 8). If the next character is not an open or closed parenthesis symbol, it is ignored.

IMPLEMENTATION ▼

Figure 17.5 shows a function that determines whether its input parameter (an expression) is balanced. The `if` statement in the `while` loop tests for open and closed parenthesis symbols. Each open parenthesis is pushed onto stack `ParenStack`. For each closed parenthesis, procedure `Pop` retrieves the nearest unmatched open parenthesis from the stack. If the stack is empty, `Pop` sets `Balanced` to `False`, causing the `while` loop exit. Otherwise, the `case` statement sets `Balanced` to indicate whether the character popped matches the current closed parenthesis symbol. After loop exit occurs, the function result is defined. It is true only when the expression is balanced and the stack is empty.

Figure 17.5
Function IsBalanced

```
function IsBalanced (Expression : StringType) : Boolean;
{
  Determines whether Expression is balanced with respect
  to parentheses.
  Pre  : Expression is defined.
  Post : Returns True if Expression is balanced;
           otherwise, returns False.
  Imports: Stack, Push, Pop and IsEmpty from StackADT.
}
  var
    ParenStack : Stack;      {stack of open parentheses}
    NextCh,                  {next character in Expression}
    CloseParen,              {parenthesis to be matched}
    OpenParen : Char;        {open parenthesis at top of stack}
    Index : Integer;         {index to Expression}
    Balanced : Boolean;      {program flag}

begin {IsBalanced}
  Init (ParenStack);              {Create an empty stack.}
  Balanced := True;
  Index := 1;
  while Balanced and (Index <= Length(Expression)) do
    {invariant:
        All closed parentheses so far were matched and
        Index <= Length(Expression) + 1.
    }
    begin
      NextCh := Expression[Index];    {Access next character.}
      if NextCh in [ '(', '[', '{' ] then
        Push (ParenStack, NextCh)       {Push open parenthesis.}
      else if NextCh in [ ')', ']', '}' ] then
        begin {Matches open paren?}
          CloseParen := NextCh;
```

▷ ▷ ▷ ▷ ▷ ▷

```
                  {Get nearest unmatched open parenthesis.}
                  Pop (ParenStack, OpenParen, Balanced); {Pop stack.}
                  if Balanced then
                    {Check for match.}
                    case CloseParen of
                      ')' : Balanced := (OpenParen = '(' );
                      ']' : Balanced := (OpenParen = '[' );
                      '}' : Balanced := (OpenParen = '{' )
                    end {case}
                end; {Matches open paren?}
              Index := Index + 1      {Access next character.}
            end; {while}

       {Define function result.}
       IsBalanced := Balanced and IsEmpty(ParenStack)
     end; {IsBalanced}
```

TESTING ▼

Write a driver program to test function IsBalanced. This program must import the type declaration for StackData (type is Char) from StackDataADT, record type Stack (from StackADT), and StringType from StringADT. Be sure to use several balanced and unbalanced expressions to test IsBalanced, as well as an expression without parentheses.

Exercises for Section 17.2 **Self-Check**

1. Trace the execution of function IsBalanced for each of the following expressions. Your trace should show the stack after each Push or Pop operation. Also show the values of Balanced, OpenParen, and CloseParen after each parenthesis is processed.

    ```
    (a + b * {c / [d - e]}) + (d / e)
    (a + b * {c / [d - e}}) + (d / e)
    ```

Programming

1. Write a main program to test function IsBalanced.

17.3 **Queues**

queue
a data structure in which elements are inserted at one end and removed from the other end

A **queue** (pronounced "Q") is a listlike structure in which items are inserted at one end and removed from the other end. In contrast, stack elements are inserted and removed from the same end (the top of the stack).

In a queue, the element that has been stored the longest is removed first, so a queue is called a **first-in, first-out (FIFO) structure.** A queue can be used to model a line of customers waiting at a checkout counter or a stream of jobs waiting to be printed by a printer.

Figure 17.6(a) shows a queue of three customers waiting for service at a bank. The name of the customer who has been waiting the longest is Mc-Mann (pointed to by Front); the name of the most recent arrival is Carson (pointed to by Rear). Customer Front^ will be the first one removed from the queue when a teller becomes available, and pointer Front will be reset to point to Wilson. Any new customers will be inserted after Carson in the queue, and pointer Rear will be adjusted accordingly. Figure 17.6(b) shows the queue after removing customer McMann, and Figure 17.6(c) shows the queue after inserting customer Perez.

Figure 17.6
Queue of Customers

Queue ADT

Table 17.2 provides the specification for a queue ADT. We implement the queue ADT next.

Table 17.2
Specification of Queue Abstract Data Type

Structure
A queue consists of a collection of elements all of the same data type and ordered according to time of arrival. The element that was inserted first is the only one that may be removed or examined. Elements are removed from the front of the queue and inserted at the rear of the queue.

Operators
The following descriptions assume these parameters:

> Q (type `Queue`)
> El (type `QueueData`)
> Success (type `Boolean`)

`Init (Q)`   Creates an empty queue.
`Insert (var Q, El)`   The item in `El` is inserted at the rear of the queue.
`Remove (var Q, var El, var Success)`   If the queue is not empty, the element at the front of the queue is removed and copied to `El`, and `Success` is set to `True`. If the queue is empty, `El` is not changed, and `Success` is set to `False`.
`IsEmpty(Q)`   (function) Returns `True` if the queue is empty; otherwise, returns `False`.
`GetSize(Q)`   (function) Returns the number of elements in the queue.

Implementing QueueADT

If we implement a queue as a linked list, removing elements from a queue is no different from removing them from a stack—the element at the front of the queue is removed next. Because new elements are inserted at the rear of the queue, however, we need a pointer to the last list element as well as the first. We can implement a queue as a record with two pointer fields, `Front` and `Rear`. Pointer `Front` points to the node at the front of the queue, and pointer `Rear` points to the node at the rear of the queue. Because we might also want to know how many elements are in a queue, we will add a third field, `Size`. Each queue node is a record with an information part and a link to the next queue node. Figure 17.7 shows the declarations for `QueueADT`.

Next we implement the queue operators. `Init` (Fig. 17.8) sets pointer fields `Front` and `Rear` to `nil`. If the queue is not empty, `Remove` uses the statements

```
El := Q.Front^.Info;            {Retrieve its data.}
Q.Front := Q.Front^.Link;       {Delete old first node.}
```

Figure 17.7
Type Declarations
for QueueADT

Directory: CHAP17
File: QUEUEADT.PAS

```
▽
{
 Implementation of QueueADT.
 Imports module QueueDataADT.

 Insert declarations for type QueueData from QueueDataADT.
}

 type
   QueuePointer = ^QueueNode;
   QueueNode = record
                 Info : QueueData;      {information part}
                 Link : QueuePointer    {link to successor}
               end; {QueueNode}

   Queue = record
             Front,                     {pointer to queue front}
             Rear :  QueuePointer;      {pointer to queue rear}
             Size : Integer             {size of queue}
           end; {Queue}
                                                                △
```

to retrieve the data stored in Q.Front^.Info and reset Q.Front to point to
the successor of the node whose data is retrieved.

If the queue is empty, Insert allocates a new node and points Q.Front
and Q.Rear to this node. Otherwise, the statements

```
New (Q.Rear^.Link);  {Attach a node at end of queue.}
Q.Rear := Q.Rear^.Link      {Point Rear to new node.}
```

Figure 17.8
Operators for
QueueADT

Directory: CHAP17
File: QUEUEADT.PAS

```
▽
procedure Init (var Q {output} : Queue);
{
  Creates an empty queue.
  Pre : None.
  Post: Initializes a queue of zero elements.
}
begin {Init}
  Q.Front := nil;
  Q.Rear  := nil;
  Q.Size  := 0
end; {Init}

procedure Remove (var Q {input/output} : Queue;
                  var El {output} : QueueData;
                  var Success {output} : Boolean);
```

◁ ◁ ◁ ◁ ◁ ◁

```
{
  Removes the element at the front of the queue
  and copies it into El.
  Pre : The queue has been created.
  Post: If the queue is not empty, El contains its
        first element, Front points to new first element,
        and Success indicates success or failure.
}
  var
    OldFront : QueuePointer;        {temporary pointer}

begin {Remove}
  if Q.Front = nil then
    Success := False                {Queue is empty.}
  else
    begin
      {Remove the element at the front of the queue.}
      OldFront := Q.Front; {Point OldFront to first node.}
      El := Q.Front^.Info;              {Retrieve its data.}
      Q.Front := Q.Front^.Link;    {Delete old first node.}
      OldFront^.Link := nil;            {Disconnect it.}
      Dispose (OldFront);               {Deallocate storage.}
      Q.Size := Q.Size - 1;         {Decrement size of Q.}
      Success := True
    end {if}
end; {Remove}

procedure Insert (var Q {input/output} : Queue;
                      El {input} : QueueData);
{
  Inserts El in a queue.
  Pre : The queue has been created.
  Post: Inserts El in a new node and resets Rear to point
        to the new node. Also points Front to the new node
        if the queue has 1 element.
}
begin {Insert}
  if Q.Rear = nil then
    begin {empty queue}
      New (Q.Rear);                 {Point Rear to first node.}
      Q.Front := Q.Rear            {Point Front to first node.}
    end {empty queue}
  else
    begin {extend queue}
      New (Q.Rear^.Link); {Attach a node at end of queue.}
      Q.Rear := Q.Rear^.Link       {Point Rear to new node.}
    end; {extend queue}

  Q.Rear^.Info := El;                 {Define new node's data.}
  Q.Rear^.Link := nil;
  Q.Size := Q.Size + 1                {Increment size of Q.}
end; {Insert}
```

▷ ▷ ▷ ▷ ▷ ▷

```
function IsEmpty (Q : Queue) : Boolean;
{
    Tests for an empty queue.
    Pre : Queue has been created.
    Post: Returns True if queue is empty; otherwise,
          returns False.
}
begin {IsEmpty}
  IsEmpty := (Q.Front = nil)
end; {IsEmpty}

{Insert operator GetSize here.}
```

attach a new node to node Q.Rear^ and reset Q.Rear to point to the new node (Fig. 17.6c). Next, the statements

```
Q.Rear^.Info := El;          {Define new node's data.}
Q.Rear^.Link := nil;
```

store the data passed through parameter El in the new node and set its Link field to nil.

Exercises for Section 17.3 *Self-Check*

1. Redraw the queue in Fig. 17.6 after the insertion of customer Harris and the removal of one customer from the queue. Which customer is removed? How many customers are left? Show pointers First and Rear after each operation.
2. Trace the operation of procedures Insert and Remove as the operations in Question 1 are performed. Show before and after values for all pointers.
3. What changes would be made to Insert to create a new operator, RudeInsert, that inserts at the front of the queue rather than at the end?
4. In a circular queue, the node at the rear points to the node at the front of the queue (see circular lists in Section 16.3). Draw the queue in Fig. 17.6 as a circular queue with just one pointer field named Rear. Explain how you would access the queue element at the front of a circular queue.

Programming

1. Write operator GetSize.
2. Add a new operator, Display, that displays the data stored in a queue. Use QueueDataDisplay to display each node's data.
3. Is it possible to simulate the operation of a queue using two stacks? Write an ADT for the queue data object, assuming two stacks are used

for storing the queue. What performance penalty do we pay for this implementation?

17.4 Binary Trees

We can extend the concept of linked data structures to structures containing nodes with more than one pointer field. One such structure is a *binary tree* (or *tree*) whose nodes contain two pointer fields. Because one or both pointers can have the value `nil`, each node in a binary tree can have 0, 1, or 2 successor nodes.

Figure 17.9 shows two binary trees. For tree (a), each node stores a three-letter string. The nodes on the bottom of this tree have zero successors and are called **leaf nodes**; all other nodes have two successors. For tree (b), each node stores an integer. The nodes containing 40 and 45 have a single successor; all other nodes have no or two successors. A recursive definition of a binary tree is: A **binary tree** is either empty (no nodes) or it consists of a node, called the **root**, and two disjoint binary trees called its **left subtree** and **right subtree**, respectively.

In the definition for binary tree, the phrase *disjoint subtrees* means that a node cannot be in both a left and a right subtree of the same root node. For the trees shown in Fig. 17.9, the nodes containing FOX and 35 are the root nodes for each tree. The node containing DOG is the root of the left subtree

leaf node
a binary tree node with no successors
root node
the first node in a binary tree
left subtree
the part of a tree pointed to by the left pointer of the root node
right subtree
the part of a tree pointed to by the right pointer of the root node

Figure 17.9
Binary Trees

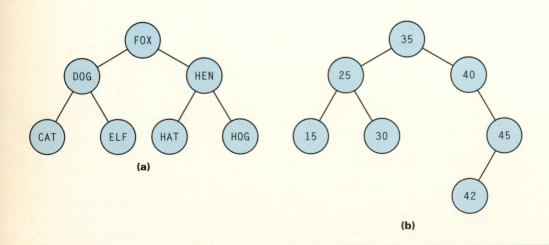

(a)

(b)

of the tree whose root is FOX; the node containing CAT is the root of the left subtree of the tree whose root is DOG; the node containing CAT is a leaf node because both its subtrees are empty trees.

A binary tree resembles a family tree and the relationships among its members are described using the same terminology as for a family tree. In Fig. 17.9(a) the node containing HEN is the *parent* of the nodes containing HAT and HOG. Similarly, the nodes containing HAT and HOG are *siblings,* because they are both *children* of the same parent node. The root of a tree is an *ancestor* of all other nodes in the tree, and they in turn are *descendants* of the root node.

For simplicity, we did not show the pointer fields in Fig. 17.9. Be aware that each node has two pointer fields and that the nodes in (b) containing integers 45 and 42 are stored as follows.

Binary Search Tree

In the rest of this chapter, we focus our attention on a particular kind of binary tree called a binary search tree. A binary search tree is a tree structure that stores data in such a way that they can be retrieved very efficiently. Every item stored in a binary search tree has a unique key.

A **binary search tree** is either empty or has the property that the item in its root has a larger key than each item in its left subtree and a smaller key than each item in its right subtree. Also, its left and right subtrees must be binary search trees.

The trees in Fig. 17.9 are examples of binary search trees; each node has a single data field that is its key. For tree (a), the string stored in every node is alphabetically larger than all strings in its left subtree and alphabetically smaller than all strings in its right subtree. For tree (b), the number stored in every node is larger than all numbers in its left subtree and smaller than all numbers in its right subtree. Notice that this must be true for every node in a binary search tree, not just the root node. For example, the number 40 must be smaller than both numbers stored in its right subtree (45, 42).

Searching a Binary Search Tree

Next we explain how to search for an item in a binary search tree. To find a particular item, say El, we compare El's key to the root item's key. If El's key is smaller, we know that El can only be in the left subtree so we search it. If El's key is larger, we search the root's right subtree. We now write this recursive algorithm in pseudocode; the first two cases are stopping cases.

Algorithm for Searching a Binary Search Tree

1. `if` the tree is empty then
    The target key is not in the tree.
`else if` the target key is in the root item `then`
    The target key is found in the root item.
`else if` the target key is smaller than the root's key `then`
    Search the left subtree.
`else`
    Search the right subtree.

Figure 17.10 traces the search for 42 in a binary search tree containing integer keys. The pointer `Root` indicates the root node whose key is being compared to 42 at each step. The colored arrows show the search path. The search proceeds from the top (node 35) down to the node containing 42.

Building a Binary Search Tree

Before we can retrieve an item from a binary search tree, we must, of course, build the tree. This process requires that we read a collection of data items that is in no particular order and insert each one individually, making sure that the expanded tree is a binary search tree. A binary search tree builds from the root node down, so we must store the first data item in the root node. To store each subsequent data item, we must find its parent node in the tree, attach a new node to the parent, and then store that data item in the new node.

When inserting an item, we must search the existing tree to find that item's key or to locate its parent node. If our search is successful, the item's key is already in the tree, so we will not insert the item. (Duplicate keys are not allowed.) If unsuccessful, the search will terminate at the parent of the item. If the item's key is smaller than its parent's key, we attach a new node as the parent's left subtree and insert the item in this node. If the item's key is larger than its parent's key, we attach a new node as the parent's right subtree and insert the item in this node. The following recursive algorithm maintains the binary search tree property; the first two cases are stopping cases.

Algorithm for Insertion in a Binary Search Tree

1. `if` the tree is empty then
    Insert the new item in the tree's root node.
`else if` the root's key matches the new item's key `then`
    Skip insertion—duplicate key.
`else if` the new item's key is smaller than the root's key `then`
    Insert the new item in the root's left subtree.
`else`
    Insert the new item in the root's right subtree.

Figure 17.10
Searching for key 42

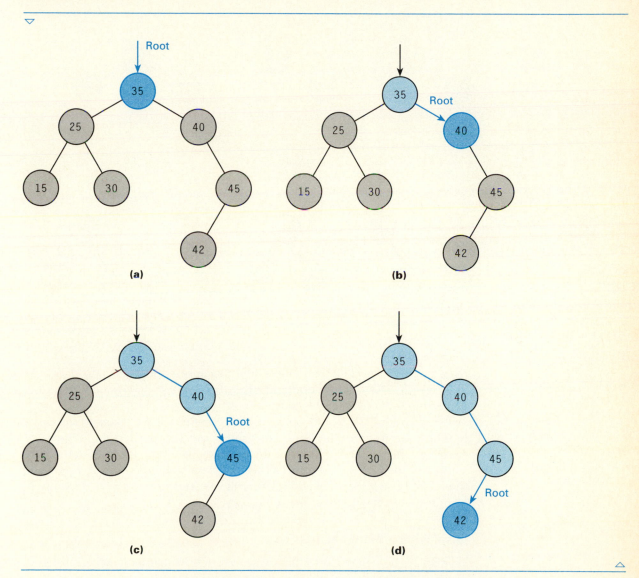

(a)

(b)

(c)

(d)

Figure 17.11 builds a tree from the list of keys: 40, 20, 10, 50, 65, 45, 30. The search path followed when inserting each key is shown in color.

The last node inserted (bottom right diagram) contains the key 30 and is inserted in the right subtree of node 20. Let's trace how this happens. Target key 30 is smaller than 40, so we insert 30 in the left subtree of node 40; this tree has 20 in its root. Target key 30 is greater than 20, so we insert 30 in the

Figure 17.11
Building a Binary Search Tree

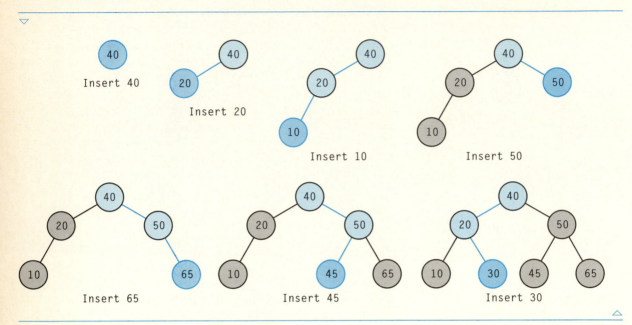

right subtree of node 20, an empty tree. Because node 20 has no right sub-tree, we allocate a new node and insert target 30 in it; the new node becomes the root of 20's right subtree.

Be aware that we would get a very different tree if we changed the order in which we inserted the keys. For example, if we inserted the keys in increasing order (10, 20, 30, . . .), each new key would be inserted in the right subtree of the previous key and all left pointers would be nil. The resulting tree would resemble a linked list. We will see later (Section 17.6) that the insertion order also affects search efficiency.

Displaying a Binary Search Tree

To display the contents of a binary search tree so that its items are listed in order by key value, use the next recursive algorithm.

Algorithm for Displaying a Binary Search Tree

1. if the tree is not empty then
    begin
       2. Display left subtree.
       3. Display root item.

4. Display right subtree.
```
end
```

For each node, the keys in its left subtree are displayed before the key in its root; the keys in its right subtree are displayed after the key in its root. Because the root key value lies between the key values in its left and right subtrees, the algorithm displays the items in order by key value as desired. Because the nodes' data components are displayed in order, this algorithm is also called an **inorder traversal.**

Table 17.3 traces the sequence of calls generated by the display algorithm for the last tree in Fig. 17.11. Completing the sequence of calls for the last step shown, "Display right subtree of node 40.", is left as an exercise at the end of this section. The trace so far displays the item keys in the sequence: 10, 20, 30, 40.

inorder traversal
displaying the items in a binary search tree in order by key value

Table 17.3
Trace of Tree Display Algorithm

Display left subtree of node 40.

  Display left subtree of node 20.

    Display left subtree of node 10.

      Tree is empty—return from displaying left subtree of node 10.

    Display item with key 10.

    Display right subtree of node 10.

      Tree is empty—return from displaying right subtree of node 10.

    Return from displaying left subtree of node 20.

  Display item with key 20.

  Display right subtree of node 20.

    Display left subtree of node 30.

      Tree is empty—return from displaying left subtree of node 30.

    Display item with key 30.

    Display right subtree of node 30.

      Tree is empty—return from displaying right subtree of node 30.

    Return from displaying right subtree of node 20.

  Return from displaying left subtree of node 40.

Display item with key 40.

Display right subtree of node 40.

1. Are the following trees binary search trees? Show the list of keys as they would be displayed by an inorder traversal of each tree. If these trees were binary search trees, what key values could be stored in the left subtree of the node containing key 50?

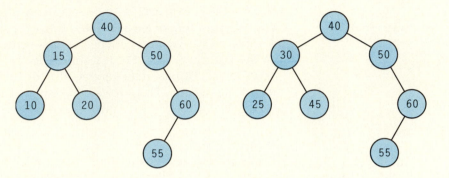

2. Complete the trace started in Table 17.3.
3. Show the binary search trees that would be created from the following lists of keys. Which tree do you think would be the most efficient to search? What can you say about the binary search tree formed in parts (b) and (c)? What can you say about the binary search tree formed in part (d)? How do you think searching it would compare to searching a linked list with the same keys?
    a. 25, 45, 15, 10, 60, 55, 12

    b. 25, 12, 55, 10, 15, 45, 60

    c. 25, 12, 10, 15, 55, 60, 45

    d. 10, 12, 15, 25, 45, 55, 60
4. What would be displayed by an inorder traversal of each tree in Question 3?

17.5 Binary Search Tree ADT

We now write the specification for a binary search tree abstract data type (Table 17.4). Besides the operators discussed so far (`Search`, `Insert`, and `Display`), we include an operator, `Retrieve`, to return the tree item whose key matches a target key.

Table 17.4
Specification for a Binary
Search Tree ADT

Structure
A binary search tree is a collection of elements (nodes) such that each has a unique key value and 0, 1, or 2 subtrees connected to it. The key value in each

Table 17.4
Specification for a Binary
Search Tree ADT
(continued)

node of a binary search tree is larger than all key values in its left subtree and smaller than all key values in its right subtree.

Operators

The following descriptions assume these parameters:

```
Tree (type SearchTree)
El (type TreeData)
Success (type Boolean)
```

`Init (var Tree)`   Creates an empty binary search tree; must be called before any other operators.

`Search (Tree, El, var Success)`   Searches a tree to find a node with the same key as `El`. If found, sets `Success` to `True`; otherwise, sets `Success` to `False`.

`Insert (var Tree, El, var Success)`   Inserts item `El` into the binary search tree and sets `Success` to `True`. If there is already an element with the same key as `El`, `Success` is set to `False`, and no insertion is performed.

`Retrieve (Tree, var El, var Success)`   Retrieves through `El` the tree element with the same key as item `El` and sets `Success` to `True`. If there is no tree element with the same key as `El`, sets `Success` to `False`.

`Display (Tree)`   Displays the tree elements in order by key value.

Implementing the Binary Search Tree ADT

The declarations for `SearchTreeADT` are shown in Fig. 17.12. Each binary search tree node contains a data field, `Info`, of type `TreeData` (imported

Figure 17.12
Type Declarations for
SearchTreeADT

Directory: CHAP17
File: SEARCHTR.PAS

```
{
  Implementation of SearchTreeADT.
  Imports module TreeDataADT.

  Insert declarations for type TreeData from TreeDataADT.
}

  type
    Branch = ^TreeNode;
    TreeNode = record
                 Info : TreeData;    {information part}
                 Left,               {pointer to left subtree}
                 Right : Branch      {pointer to right subtree}
               end; {TreeNode}

    SearchTree = record
                   Root : Branch     {pointer to root node}
                 end; {SearchTree}
```

from `TreeDataADT`) and two pointers, `Left` and `Right`, that connect it to its children:

Binary search tree node

Record type `SearchTree` contains a single pointer field, `Root`, that points to the root node of a tree.

Init, Search, and Retrieve

We will start with operators `Init` and `Search` (Fig. 17.13). `Init` sets the `Root` pointer of its tree parameter to `nil`. Procedure `Search` initiates a search for the tree node with the same key as item `El`, the target item, by

Figure 17.13
Init, Search, and
DoSearch

Directory: CHAP17
File: SEARCHTR.PAS

```
{
    Insert functions EqualTo and LessThan and procedure
    DisplayItem from TreeDataADT.
}
procedure Init (var Tree {output} : SearchTree;
{
    Creates an empty tree. Must be called first.
    Pre : None.
    Post: Root pointer is set to nil.
}
begin {Init}
    Tree.Root := nil
end; {Init}

procedure DoSearch (ARoot {input} : Branch;
                    El {input} : TreeData;
                    var Success {output} : Boolean);
{
    Searches for the item with same key as El in the
    subtree pointed to by ARoot.
    Pre : El and ARoot are defined.
    Post: If El's key is not found, Success is False;
          otherwise, Success is True.
}
begin {DoSearch}
    if ARoot = nil then
        Success := False                      {Tree is empty.}
    else if EqualTo(El, ARoot^.Info) then
        Success := True                       {Target is found.}
    else if LessThan(El, ARoot^.Info) then
        DoSearch (ARoot^.Left, El, Success)   {Search left.}
```

▷ ▷ ▷ ▷ ▷ ▷

```
      else
        DoSearch (ARoot^.Right, El, Success)      {Search right.}
    end; {DoSearch}

    procedure Search (Tree {input} : SearchTree;
                      El {input} : TreeData;
                      var Success {output} : Boolean);
    {
      Searches for the item with same key as El in a binary
      search tree.
      Pre : The tree is defined.
      Post: If El's key is located, Success is True;
            otherwise, Success is False.
    }
    begin {Search}
      DoSearch (Tree.Root, El, Success) {Start at tree root.}
    end; {Search}
```

calling `DoSearch`. Procedure `DoSearch` implements the recursive search algorithm illustrated in Fig. 17.10, beginning at the root of the tree to be searched. Functions `EqualTo` and `LessThan` compare the keys of item `El` and the root node in the obvious way (`EqualTo` tests for equality, `LessThan` tests if `El`'s key is less than the root's key). Both functions are operators for `TreeDataADT`.

Operator `Retrieve` (see Programming Exercise 1 at the end of this section) returns the tree element with the same key as `El`. Its implementation would be similar to that of `Search`. When `DoRetrieve` (like `DoSearch`) locates `El`'s key, use the statements

```
El := ARoot^.Info;        {Return tree element with same key.}
Success := True           {Target is found and retrieved.}
```

to return the tree data through `El` (a variable parameter) and to indicate the result of the retrieval operation.

Insert

Operator `Insert` is shown in Fig. 17.14. It calls recursive procedure `DoInsert` to perform the actual insertion, beginning at the root of the tree. `DoInsert` implements the insertion algorithm illustrated in Fig. 17.11.

In `DoInsert` if parameter `ARoot` is `nil`, the statements

```
New (ARoot);              {Connect ARoot to new node.}
ARoot^.Left := nil;         {Make new node a leaf.}
ARoot^.Right := nil;
ARoot^.Info := El;        {Insert El in node ARoot^.}
```

Figure 17.14
DoInsert and Insert

```
procedure DoInsert (var ARoot {input/output} : Branch;
                        El {input} : TreeData;
                        var Success {output} : Boolean);
{
   Inserts item El in the tree pointed to by ARoot.
   Pre : ARoot and El are defined.
   Post: If a node with same key as El is found, Success
         is set to False. If an empty tree is reached,
         points ARoot to a new node containing El and
         sets Success to True.
}
begin {DoInsert}
   {Check for empty tree.}
   if ARoot = nil then
      begin {Attach new node}
         New (ARoot);              {Connect ARoot to new node.}
         ARoot^.Left := nil;        {Make new node a leaf.}
         ARoot^.Right := nil;
         ARoot^.Info := El;       {Insert El in node ARoot^.}
         Success := True
      end {Attach new node}
   else if EqualTo(El, ARoot^.Info) then
      Success := False                   {Duplicate key.}
   else if LessThan(El, ARoot^.Info) then
      DoInsert (ARoot^.Left, El, Success)    {Insert left.}
   else
      DoInsert (ARoot^.Right, El, Success)   {Insert right.}
end; {DoInsert}

procedure Insert (var Tree {input/output} : SearchTree;
                      El {input} : TreeData;
                      var Success {output} : Boolean);
{
   Inserts item El into a binary search tree.
   Pre : El is defined and the tree is defined.
   Post: Success is True if the insertion is performed.
         If there is a node with the same key value as El,
         Success is False.
}
begin {Insert}
   DoInsert (Tree.Root, El, Success)
end; {Insert}
```

allocate a new tree node that is pointed to by ARoot and store El's data in it. The new node is a leaf node because its pointers are nil. The node that has ARoot as its left or right pointer is the parent of the new node. Figure 17.15 illustrates this for the insertion of 30 in a binary search tree. The right pointer of node 20 is nil before the insertion takes place.

Figure 17.15
Inserting a Node in a Tree

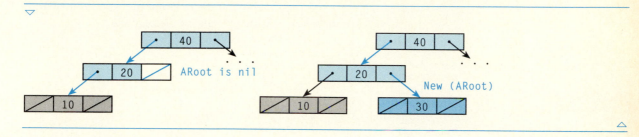

Display

Operator `Display` (Fig. 17.16) calls recursive procedure `DoDisplay` to display the tree items in order by key. `DoDisplay` calls operator `DisplayItem` (part of `TreeDataADT`) to display each item.

Figure 17.16
Display and DoDisplay

```
procedure DoDisplay (ARoot {input} : Branch);
{
  Displays a binary search tree in key order.
  Pre : ARoot points to a binary search tree or is nil.
  Post: Displays each node in key order.
}
begin {DoDisplay}
  if ARoot <> nil then
    begin {recursive step}
      DoDisplay (ARoot^.Left);        {Display left subtree.}
      DisplayItem (ARoot^.Info);      {Display root item.}
      DoDisplay (ARoot^.Right)        {Display right subtree.}
    end {recursive step}
end; {DoDisplay}

procedure Display (Tree {input} : SearchTree);
{
  Displays the elements of a binary search tree.
  Pre : Tree is the header node of a binary search tree.
  Post: Each element of the tree is displayed. The elements
        are displayed in ascending order by key value.
}
begin  {Display}
  DoDisplay (Tree.Root)
end; {Display}

{Insert procedures Retrieve and DoRetrieve here.}
```

Self-Check

1. Explain the effect of the following program segment if `MyTree` is type `SearchTree` and `TreeData` is type `Integer`. Draw the tree built by the sequence of insertions. What values would be displayed?

```
begin
    Init (MyTree);
    Insert (MyTree, 3000, Success);
    Insert (MyTree, 2000, Success);
    Insert (MyTree, 4000, Success);
    Insert (MyTree, 5000, Success);
    Insert (MyTree, 2500, Success);
    Insert (MyTree, 6000, Success);
    Search (MyTree, 2500, Success);
    Search (MyTree, 1500, Success);
    TreeData := 6000;
    Retrieve (MyTree, TreeData, Success);
    Display (MyTree)
end.
```

2. Deleting an entry in a binary tree is more difficult than inserting one. Given any node that is to be deleted in a tree, what are the three cases for deletion and what must be done in each case? Be sure your approach preserves the binary search tree order.

Programming

1. Write `Retrieve` and `DoRetrieve`.
2. Write an operator that reads a list of data items from a binary file into a binary search tree. Use `Insert` to place each item where it belongs.

17.6   Efficiency of a Binary Search Tree

Searching a linked list for a target data value is an $O(N)$ process. In other words, the time required to search a list increases linearly with the size of the list. Searching a binary search tree can be a much more efficient process. If the left and right subtrees of every node are the exact same size, each move to the left or the right during a search eliminates the elements of the other subtree from the search process. Since they need not be searched, the number of nodes we do have to search is cut in half in each step. This is a *best-case analysis,* since, in reality, it is unlikely that a binary search tree will have exactly the same number of nodes in the left and right subtrees of each node. However, this best-case analysis is useful for showing the power of the binary search tree.

As an example, if N is 1023 it will require searching 10 trees ($N = 1023$, 511, 255, 127, 63, 31, 15, 7, 3, 1) to determine that a target is missing. It should require fewer than 10 probes to find a target that is in the tree. The number 1024 is a power of 2 (1024 is 2 raised to the power 10), so searching such a tree is an $O(\log_2 N)$ process ($\log_2 1024$ is 10). Keep in mind that not all binary search trees will have equal size left and right subtrees!

What difference does it make whether an algorithm is an $O(N)$ process or an $O(\log_2 N)$ process? Table 17.5 evaluates $\log_2 N$ for different values of N. A doubling of N causes $\log_2 N$ to increase by only 1. Since $\log_2 N$ increases much more slowly with N, the performance of an $O(\log_2 N)$ algorithm is not as adversely affected by an increase in N.

Table 17.5
Values of N Versus $\log_2 N$

N	$\log_2 N$
32	5
64	6
128	7
256	8
512	9
1,024	10

Exercises for Section 17.6 **Self-Check**

1. Given the binary tree that follows, how many comparisons are needed to find each of the following keys or to determine that the key is not present? List the keys compared to the target for each search.
   a. 50 b. 55 c. 10 d. 65 e. 52 f. 48

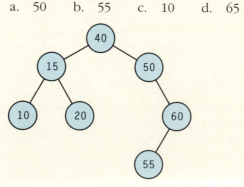

2. Why is it unlikely that a given binary tree will have exactly the name number of elements in the left and right subtrees of every node? For what numbers of nodes is this possible?

3. If the elements of a binary tree are inserted in order, what will the resulting tree look like? What is the Big-O notation for searching in this tree?
4. The binary search introduced in Chapter 13 also performed searches in $O(\log_2 N)$ time. Name two advantages of a binary tree over the binary search. Name one disadvantage.

17.7 Common Programming Errors

Because the procedures in this chapter manipulate pointer fields, you should review the errors described in Chapter 16. Make sure that recursive procedures do, in fact, terminate. Be careful when passing pointers to dynamic data structures as procedure parameters. If a pointer is passed as a variable parameter and is moved down the data structure, you might disconnect some nodes from the data structure.

CHAPTER REVIEW

1. A stack is a LIFO (last-in, first-out) structure in which all insertions (push operations) and deletions (pop operations) are done at the list head. Stacks have many varied uses in computer science including saving parameter lists for recursive modules and translating arithmetic expressions.
2. A queue is a FIFO (first-in, first-out) structure in which insertions are done at one end and deletions (removals) at the other. Queues are used to save lists of items waiting for the same resource (e.g., a printer).
3. A binary tree is a linked data structure in which each node has two pointer fields leading to the node's left and right subtrees. Each node in the tree belongs to either the left or right subtree of an ancestor node, but it cannot be in both subtrees of an ancestor node.
4. A binary search tree is a binary tree in which each node's key is greater than all keys in its left subtree and smaller than all keys in its right subtree. Searching for a key in a binary search tree is an $O(\log_2 N)$ process.

Quick-Check Exercises

1. If A, B, and C are inserted into a stack and a queue, what would be the order of removal for the stack? For the queue?
2. Often computers allow you to type characters ahead of the program's use of them. Should a stack or a queue be used to store these characters?
3. Write a program segment that removes the element just below the top of the stack. Use the stack operators.
4. Assume the left pointer of each node in the following tree is `nil`. Is it a binary search tree? What would be displayed by its inorder traversal? Write a sequence for inserting these keys that would create a binary search tree whose `nil` pointers were all at the lowest level. Is there more than one such sequence?

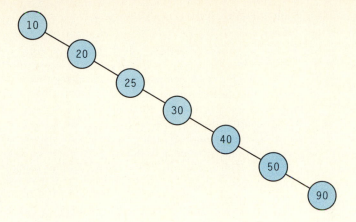

5. If a binary search tree has an inorder traversal of 1, 2, 3, 4, 5, 6, and the root node contains 3 and has 5 as the root of its right subtree, what do we know about the order that numbers were inserted in this tree?

6. A node in a binary search tree can have a maximum of two children. True or false?

7. What is the relationship between the left child, the right child, and their parent in a binary search tree? Between the right child and the parent? Between a parent and all descendants in its left subtree?

8. When is searching a binary search tree more efficient than searching an ordered linked list?

Answers to Quick-Check Exercises

1. For stack: C, B, A; for queue: A, B, C
2. Queue
3. ```
   Pop (S, X, Success);
   Pop (S, Y, Success);
   Push (S, X);
   ```
4. Yes; 10, 20, 25, 30, 40, 50, 90; 30, 20, 10, 25, 50, 40, 90; yes
5. 3 was inserted first and 5 was inserted before 4 and 6.
6. True
7. Left child < parent < right child
   Parent > all its descendants
8. When the left and right subtrees of each node are similar in size

Review Questions

1. Show the effects of each of the following operations on stack S and the parameters for Pop:

```
Init (S);
Push (S, '+');
Pop (S, X1, Success1);
Pop (S, X2, Success2);
```
```

```
Push (S, '(');
Push (S, ')');
Pop (S, X3, Success3);
Pop (S, X4, Success4);
```

2. Write a stack operator that reverses the order of the top two stack elements if the stack has more than one element. Use `Push` and `Pop`.

3. Answer Question 1 for a queue Q of characters. Replace `Push` with `Insert` and `Pop` with `Remove`.

4. Write a queue operator `MoveToRear` that moves the element currently at the front of the queue to the rear of the queue. The element that was second in line will be at the front of the queue. Do this using operators `Insert` and `Remove`.

5. Write a queue operator `MoveToFront` that moves the element at the rear of the queue to the front of the queue. Do this using `Insert` and `Remove`.

6. Discuss the differences between a simple linked list and a binary tree. Consider such things as the number of pointer fields per node, search technique, and insertion algorithm.

7. How can you determine whether a binary tree node is a leaf?

8. Trace an inorder traversal of the following tree as it would be performed by operator `Display` of `SearchTreeADT`.

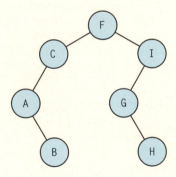

9. What happens when all the elements for a binary search tree are read and inserted in key order? In reverse key order? How does this affect the performance of programs that use the tree?

Programming Projects

1. Write a client program that uses the queue ADT to simulate a typical session for a bank teller. Change `QueueData` to represent a customer at a bank. Store the customer's name, the transaction type, and the amount in the customer record. After every five customers are processed, display the size of the queue and the names of the customers who are waiting.

   Your program should include procedures corresponding to the following procedure headers as part of your solution:

```
procedure WriteCust (OneCust {input} : Customer);
{Displays a single customer record}
```

```
procedure ReadCust (var OneCust {output} : Customer);
{Reads a single customer record from the keyboard}

procedure Arrive (var WaitingLine {input/output} : Queue;
                      var Success {output} : Boolean);
{
  Simulates the arrival of a single customer.
  Calls: ReadCust
}

procedure Depart (var WaitingLine {input/output} : Queue;
                      var Success {output} : Boolean);
{
  Simulates the departure of a single customer.
  Calls: WriteCust
}

procedure Show (WaitingLine {input} : Queue);
{
  Displays size and contents of the customer queue.
  Calls: WriteCust
}
```

2. Carry out Programming Project 1 using a stack instead of a queue.

Directory: CHAP17
File: PROJ3.PAS

3. Write a program to monitor the flow of an item into and out of a warehouse. The warehouse will have numerous deliveries and shipments for this item (a widget) during the time period covered. A shipment out is billed at 50% over the cost of a widget. Unfortunately, each shipment received may have a different cost associated with it. The firm's accountants have instituted a last-in, first-out system for filling orders. This means that the newest widgets are the first ones sent out to fill an order. This inventory system can be represented using a stack, with the Push procedure inserting a shipment received and the Pop procedure deleting a shipment out. Each data record will consist of the following items:

S or O: shipment received or order to be sent
Quantity: quantity received or shipped out
Cost: cost per widget (for a shipment received only)
Vendor: character string that names company sent to or received from

Write the necessary procedures to store shipments received and to process orders. The output for an order will consist of the quantity and the total cost for all widgets in the order. *Hint:* Each widget price is 50% higher than its cost. The widgets used to fill an order may come from multiple shipments with different costs.

4. Redo Programming Project 3, this time assuming widgets are shipped using a first-in, first-out strategy. Use a queue to store the widget orders.

5. A *dequeue* might be described as a double-ended queue, that is, a structure in which elements can be inserted or removed from either end. Write an ADT that contains the declarations and operators for a dequeue.

6. The radix sorting algorithm uses an array of 10 queues (numbered 0 through 9) to simulate the operation of the old card-sorting machines. The algorithm re-

quires one pass to be made for every digit of the numbers being sorted. For example, a list of three-digit numbers would require three passes through the list. During the first pass, the least significant digit (the ones digit) of each number is examined and the number is inserted at the rear of the queue whose subscript matches the digit. After all numbers have been processed, the elements of each queue, beginning with `Queue[0]`, are copied one at a time to the end of an eleventh queue prior to beginning the next pass. The process is repeated for the next most significant digit (the tens digit) using the order of the numbers in the eleventh queue. The process is repeated for the next most significant digit (the hundreds digit). After the final pass, the eleventh queue will contain the numbers in sorted order. Write a program that implements radix sort using our `QueueADT`.

7. Use a binary search tree to maintain an airline passenger list. Each passenger record should contain the passenger name (record key), class (`Economy`, `Business`, `FirstClass`), and number of seats. The main program should be menu driven and allow the user to display the data for a particular passenger, display the entire list, create a list, insert a node, delete a node, and replace the data for a particular passenger. When deleting a node, simply change the number of assigned seats to zero and leave the passenger's node in the tree.

8. Save each word appearing in a block of text in a binary search tree. Also save the number of occurrences of each word and the line number for each occurrence. Use a stack for the line numbers. After all words have been processed, display each word in alphabetical order. Along with each word, display the number of occurrences and the line number for each occurrence.

9. The fastest binary tree is one which is as close to balanced as possible. However, there is no guarantee that elements will be inserted in the right order. It is possible to build a balanced binary tree if the elements to be inserted are in order in an array. Write a procedure and test program that, given a sorted array of elements, builds a balanced binary tree. Augment the binary search tree ADT to count the number of nodes that are searched to find an element and display the number of nodes that are searched to find each item in the tree. *Hint:* The root of the tree should be the middle (median) of the array; this project is easier to do if you use recursion.

10. Write a procedure that performs an inorder traversal of a binary tree without using recursion. It will be necessary to use a stack. Write a suitable test program for your procedure.

APPENDIX A

Reserved Words, Standard Identifiers, Operators, Functions, and Procedures

Reserved Words

and	end	nil	set
array	file	not	then
begin	for	of	to
case	function	or	type
const	goto	packed	until
div	if	procedure	var
do	in	program	while
downto	label	record	with
else	mod	repeat	

Standard Identifiers

Constants:

False, True, MaxInt

Types:

Integer, Boolean, Real, Char, Text

Program parameters:

Input, Output

Functions:

Abs, ArcTan, Chr, Cos, EOF, EOLN, Exp, Ln, Odd, Ord, Pred, Round, Sin, Sqr, Sqrt, Succ, Trunc

Procedures:

Get, New, Pack, Page, Put, Read, ReadLn, Reset, Rewrite, Unpack, Write, WriteLn

Operator	Operation	Type of Operand(s)	Result Type
:=	Assignment	Any type except file types	—
Arithmetic			
+ (unary)	Identity	Integer or real	Same as operand
- (unary)	Sign Inversion		
+	Addition	Integer or real	Integer or real
-	Subtraction		
*	Multiplication		
div	Integer division	Integer	Integer
/	Real division	Integer or real	Real
mod	Modulus	Integer	Integer
Relational			
=	Equality	Ordinal, real, string, set or pointer	Boolean
<>	Inequality		
<	Less than	Ordinal, real, or string	Boolean
>	Greater than		
<=	Less than or equal *or* Subset	Ordinal, real, or string / Set	Boolean
>=	Greater than or equal *or* Superset	Ordinal, real, or string / Set	Boolean
in	Set membership	First operand is any ordinal, second is its set type	Boolean
Logical			
not	Negation		
or	Disjunction	Boolean	Boolean
and	Conjunction		
Set			
+	Union		
-	Set difference	Any set type	Same as operand
*	Intersection		

Table A.2
Standard Functions

Name	Description of Computation	Argument	Result
Abs	The absolute value of the argument	Real/integer	Same as argument
Exp	The value of *e* (2.71828) raised to the power of the argument	Real/integer	Real
Ln	The logarithm (to the base *e*) of the argument	Real/integer (positive)	Real
Sqr	The square of the argument	Real/integer	Same as argument
Sqrt	The positive square root of the argument	Real/integer (positive)	
Round	The closest integer value to the argument	Real	Integer
Trunc	The integral part of the argument	Real	Integer
ArcTan	The arc tangent of the argument	Real/integer	Real
Cos	The cosine of the argument	Real/integer (radians)	Real
Sin	The sine of the argument	Real/integer (radians)	Real
Chr	Returns the character whose ordinal number is its argument	Integer	Char
Odd	Returns True if its argument is an odd number; otherwise, returns False	Integer	Boolean
Ord	Returns the ordinal number of its argument	Ordinal	Integer
Pred	Returns the predecessor of its argument	Ordinal	Ordinal
Succ	Returns the successor of its argument	Ordinal	Ordinal

Procedure Call	Description
Dispose (P)	Returns the record pointed to by pointer variable P to free storage.
Get (F)	Advances the file-position pointer for file F to its next component and assigns the value of the component to F^.
New (P)	Creates a record of the type pointed to by pointer P and saves its address in P.
Pack (U, I, P)	Copies the elements in unpacked array U, starting with U[I], to packed array P, starting with the first element.
Page (F)	Advances the printer to a new page before printing the next line of the file F.
Put (F)	Appends the current contents of F^ to file F.
Read (F, *variables*)	Reads data from file F to satisfy the list of *variables*. If F is not specified, file Input is read.
ReadLn (F, *variables*)	Reads data from text file F to satisfy the list of *variables*. Skips any characters at the end of the last line read.
Reset (F)	Resets the file-position pointer for file F to the beginning. File F can then be read.
Rewrite (F)	Resets the file-position pointer for file F to the beginning; any prior contents are lost. File F can then be written.
Unpack (P, U, I)	Copies the elements in packed array P, starting with first element, to unpacked array U, starting with the U[I].
Write (F, *outputs*)	Writes the data in the order specified by *outputs* to file F. If F is not specified, the data are written to file Output.
WriteLn (F, *outputs*)	Writes the data in the order specified by *outputs* to text file F. Writes an end-of-line mark after the data.

Pascal Syntax Diagrams

program

program parameters

body

declaration part

label declaration

constant definition

type definition

variable declaration

statement label

constant

unsigned constant

identifier

function declaration

procedure declaration

formal parameter list

type

enumerated type

subrange type

pointer type

array type

record type

field list

variant

file type

set type

compound statement

statement

assignment statement

procedure call statement

if statement

while statement

for statement

case statement

case label

repeat statement

with statement

goto statement

actual parameter

expression

simple expression

term

factor

function designator

set value

variable

unsigned number

signed number

integer

real

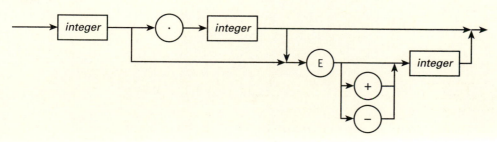

A P P E N D I X   C

Character Sets

The charts in this appendix show the following character sets: ASCII (American Standard Code for Information Interchange), EBCDIC (Extended Binary Coded Decimal Interchange Code), and CDC* Scientific. Only printable characters are shown. The ordinal number for each character is shown in decimal. For example, in ASCII, the ordinal number for A is 65 and the ordinal number for z is 122. The blank character is denoted by a □.

ASCII

Left Digit(s):	Right Digit:									
	0	**1**	**2**	**3**	**4**	**5**	**6**	**7**	**8**	**9**
3			□	!	"	#	$	%	&	'
4	(	)	*	+	,	-	.	/	0	1
5	2	3	4	5	6	7	8	9	:	;
6	<	=	>	?	@	A	B	C	D	E
7	F	G	H	I	J	K	L	M	N	O
8	P	Q	R	S	T	U	V	W	X	Y
9	Z	[	\	]	^	_	`	a	b	c
10	d	e	f	g	h	i	j	k	l	m
11	n	o	p	q	r	s	t	u	v	w
12	x	y	z	{			}	~			

Codes 00–31 and 127 are nonprintable control characters.

EBCDIC

Left Digit(s):	Right Digit: 0	1	2	3	4	5	6	7	8	9
6					□					
7					¢	.	<	(	+	|
8	&									
9	!	$	*	)	;	¬	-	/		
10							^	,	%	—
11	>	?								
12			:	#	@	'	=	"		a
13	b	c	d	e	f	g	h	i		
14						j	k	l	m	n
15	o	p	q	r						
16			s	t	u	v	w	x	y	z
17								\	{	}
18	[	]								
19				A	B	C	D	E	F	G
20	H	I								J
21	K	L	M	N	O	P	Q	R		
22							S	T	U	V
23	W	X	Y	Z						
24	0	1	2	3	4	5	6	7	8	9

Codes 00–63 and 250–255 are nonprintable control characters.

CDC

Left Digit:	Right Digit: 0	1	2	3	4	5	6	7	8	9
0	:	A	B	C	D	E	F	G	H	I
1	J	K	L	M	N	O	P	Q	R	S
2	T	U	V	W	X	Y	Z	0	1	2
3	3	4	5	6	7	8	9	+	-	*
4	/	(	)	$	=	□	,	.	≡	[
5	]	%	≠	↱	∨	∧	↑	↓	<	>
6	≤	≥	¬	;						

A P P E N D I X   D

VAX Pascal Modules

In VAX Pascal, a *module* is a separately compilable program structure. A module heading line contains the reserved word `module` instead of `program`. A module does not require a `begin` line, but its last line is always `end`.

    Figure D.1 shows abstract data type DayADT (see Fig. 9.3) written as a VAX Pascal module. The module begins with the lines

```
[Inherit ('Utility.PEN'), Environment ('DayADT.PEN')]
module DayADT (Input, Output);
```

The VAX Pascal reserved word `Inherit` precedes the list of files (`Utility.PEN`) that are needed to compile the current module. If multiple files are needed, a list of their names should appear within the parentheses; each name should be enclosed in apostrophes with a comma between names. The VAX Pascal reserved word `Environment` precedes the name of the environment file (`DayADT.PEN`) that will be created by compiling the current module. The module name (`DayADT`) and its parameters (`Input` and `Output`) appear after the VAX Pascal reserved word `module`.

Figure D.1
Module DayADT

```
[Inherit ('Utility.PEN'), Environment ('DayADT.PEN')]
module DayADT (Input, Output);
{
   Specification of DayADT

   Structure:  Day is an enumerated data type whose values
               represent the days of the week.

   Operators:  ReadLnDay and WriteDay read and display a value
               of type Day.

   Implementation of DayADT
}
   type
     Day = (Sunday, Monday, Tuesday, Wednesday,
            Thursday, Friday, Saturday);
```

▷ ▷ ▷ ▷ ▷ ▷

```
     procedure ReadLnDay (var ADay : Day;
                          var ValidDay : Boolean);
     {
      Reads two data characters and stores the value represented
      by the data in ADay. Sets ValidDay to indicate whether
      the data are valid.
      Pre  : None
      Post : ADay is assigned a value if the two characters
             read are SU, MO, TU, WE, TH, FR, or SA;
             otherwise, ADay is undefined.
             ValidDay is set to True if ADay is defined;
             otherwise, ValidDay is set to False.
      Uses : UpCase from module Utility.
     }

        var
          DayCh1,                          {input-first letter in day}
          DayCh2 : Char;                   {input-second letter in day}

     begin {ReadLnDay}
       .
       .
       .
     end; {ReadLnDay}

     procedure WriteDay (ADay {input} : Day);
     {
      Displays the value of ADay.
      Pre : ADay is defined.
      Post: Displays a string corresponding to the value of ADay.
     }
     begin
       .
       .
       .
     end; {WriteDay}
end.    {DayADT}
```

△

Module DayADT contains declarations for data type Day and its operator procedures, ReadLnDay and WriteDay. (To conserve space, we did not write out the actual procedure bodies.)

Using Module DayADT

The heading for module DayADT indicates that DayADT is a client of another module named Utility, which contains function UpCase (see Fig. 7.3). The lines

```
[Inherit ('Utility.PEN', 'DayADT.PEN')]
program TestDayUtility (Input, Output);
```

indicate that program `TestDayUtility` is a client program of both modules `DayADT` and `Utility`. Notice that the reserved word `Environment` is not used in a program heading.

Compiling Modules and Client Programs

Module `DayADT` must be saved in a separate file named `DayADT.PAS`. This file must be compiled before any of its clients. Because `DayADT` uses module `Utility`, you must remember to compile module `Utility` first. Once `DayADT` has been compiled, you can compile any client program (or any other module) that uses it.

When you compile module `DayADT`, VAX Pascal creates its environment file (`DayADT.PEN`) and saves its object code in file `DayADT.OBJ`. After compiling a client program but prior to running it, you must link the client's object code file to the object code files for all the modules that it uses.

APPENDIX E

Turbo Pascal Units

In Turbo Pascal, a *unit* is a separately compilable program structure. The first line of a unit begins with the reserved word `unit` instead of `program`. A unit does not require a `begin` line, but its last line is always `end`.

Figure E.1 shows abstract data type `DayADT` (see Fig. 9.3) written as a Turbo Pascal unit. Each unit begins with an interface section, which is followed by an implementation section. The Turbo Pascal reserved words `interface` and `implementation` denote these separate sections. The *interface* section contains declarations for new data types declared in the unit and the procedure or function header for each operator declared in the unit. Each procedure or function header is followed by a comment that describes the operation the module performs and its preconditions and postconditions. The complete procedure and function declarations appear in the implementation section. (To conserve space, we do not write out the actual procedure bodies.)

Figure E.1
Unit DayADT

```
unit DayADT;
{
   Specification of DayADT
   Structure:  Day is an enumerated data type whose values
               represent the days of the week.
}

interface
  type
    Day = (Sunday, Monday, Tuesday, Wednesday,
           Thursday, Friday, Saturday);

  procedure ReadLnDay (var ADay {output} : Day;
                       var ValidDay {output} : Boolean);
  {
   Reads two data characters and stores the value represented
   by the data in ADay. Sets ValidDay to indicate whether the
   data are valid.
   Pre : None
   Post: ADay is assigned a value if the two characters
         read are SU, MO, TU, WE, TH, FR, or SA;
         otherwise, ADay is undefined.
```

▷ ▷ ▷ ▷ ▷

```
                    ValidDay is set to True if ADay is defined;
                    otherwise, ValidDay is set to False.
            Uses: UpCase from unit Utility
          }

      procedure WriteDay (ADay {input} : Day);
      {
      Displays the value of ADay.
      Pre : ADay is defined.
      Post: Displays a string corresponding to the value of ADay.
      }

implementation
    uses Utility;    {contains function UpCase}

    procedure ReadLnDay (var ADay {output} : Day;
                             var ValidDay {output} : Boolean);
        var
          DayCh1,                       {input - first letter in day}
          DayCh2 : Char;                {input - second letter in day}

        begin {ReadLnDay}
         .
         .
         .
        end; {ReadLnDay}

        procedure WriteDay (ADay {input} : Day);
        begin {WriteDay}
         .
         .
         .
        end; {WriteDay}
end. {DayADT}
```

The interface section for unit DayADT contains all the information Turbo Pascal needs to compile a client program that references data type Day or calls operator ReadLnDay or WriteDay. It also contains information a programmer would need to use the unit. The actual implementation of the operators is "hidden" in the implementation section, because the compiler does not need to know those details when it compiles a client program. Similarly, a programmer needs to know only how to call an operator, not how that operator is implemented.

The uses Statement

The uses statement

```
uses Utility;       {contains function UpCase}
```

indicates that unit `DayADT` is a client of another unit named `Utility`, which declares function `UpCase` (see Fig. 7.3). Similarly, any client of unit `DayADT` must contain the statement

`uses DayADT`

A client of both `DayADT` and `Utility` needs the statement

`uses DayADT, Utility;`

If the client is a program, the `uses` statement should follow the `program` statement. If the client is another unit, the `uses` statement should come after the `interface` line or the `implementation` line of the client. If the client references data type `Day` in its own interface section, the `uses` statement must come after the `interface` line. If the only references to data type `Day` and operators `WriteDay` and `ReadLnDay` appear in the client's implementation section, the `uses` statement can come after the `implementation` line.

Compiling Client Programs

Unit `DayADT` must be saved in a separate file named `DayADT.PAS`. This file must be compiled before any of its clients and should be compiled to disk. You can accomplish this by changing the destination from memory to disk in the Compile submenu before compiling unit `DayADT`. Because `DayADT` uses unit `Utility`, you must remember to compile unit `Utility` to disk first. Once `DayADT` has been compiled, you can compile any client program (or any other unit) that uses it.

When you compile unit `DayADT`, Turbo Pascal saves its object code in file `DayADT.TPU`. Prior to running a client program, Turbo Pascal links the client's object code file to the object code files for all the units that the client program uses.

Using PcPix/MacPix and Dr. Pascal

Two Pascal systems are being made available in conjunction with this text. Both were developed by the Visible Software company and both implement all of standard Pascal. This means that the programs you develop on your home IBM-PC or Macintosh will work as described in this text, and will also run properly on your school's computers (which is not true of many microcomputer Pascal systems). This appendix describes these systems and tells you how to obtain them.

The first Pascal system, PcPix™ (or MacPix™ for Macintosh) is a command-line interpreter that runs programs and reports syntax or execution errors. It does not have debugging or editing capabilities, so it must be used in conjunction with a text editor. PcPix/MacPix is available free to purchasers of this book via the Internet, through a file transfer process called FTP.

The second system, Dr. Pascal®, runs programs and reports errors, and also provides a complete programming environment in the manner of Turbo Pascal (described in Appendix G). Dr. Pascal has built-in editing, so moving from editing to running to debugging requires only a single keystroke (or mouse-click on the Macintosh). Also, Dr. Pascal is unique in its ability to run programs visibly. Statements, procedures, and variables—even structured variables—are automatically shown as the program runs. Unlike primitive debuggers in which you must request one variable at a time, Dr. Pascal makes your entire Pascal program visible with one keystroke. Purchasers of this book can order Dr. Pascal at a substantial discount using the coupon at the back of the book.

Obtaining PcPix or MacPix via FTP

To obtain PcPix or MacPix, you must access the Internet and transfer a file from an Internet computer to your own computer (PC or Mac). PcPix and MacPix are available via anonymous FTP from the publisher of this book, at the address aw.com, in the koff.cs1.pascal subdirectory.

Using FTP and then de-archiving files can be complicated. We will give a brief description here, but if you are new to using FTP it is best to consult an experienced Internet user or your instructor.

These instructions describe how to retrieve PcPix or MacPix with a UNIX FTP program; your Internet connection may use different commands. Begin by using FTP to connect to aw.com:

```
ftp aw.com
```

Once connected to aw.com, log in as "anonymous" using your own e-mail address as the password. Then, change to the directory for this book by typing

```
cd aw.computer.science
cd koff.cs1.pascal
```

Upper and lower case must match the names as shown. You can get a list of available files with the `ls` command (`ls -l` and `dir` also work). Before retrieving the files available in this directory, it is a good idea to look at the README file to see if changes have been made since this book went to press. Retrieve the file to your local computer:

```
get README
```

On your local computer, read the file with an editor or a utility such as MORE.

The PcPix files are grouped together as a "zip" archive, called PCPIX.ZIP. The FTP program must be set to "binary" or "type 1", or the received file will not be usable. Once PCPIX.ZIP is on your own PC, use a program like the shareware program PKUNZIP to extract the individual files.

For MacPix, the file is called MacPix.sit.hqx and it will be stored as a Bin-Hex, StuffIt archive. Once the file is on your Macintosh, you will need a program like the shareware program StuffIt Lite to unstuff the files in it.

Using PcPix and MacPix

First use a text editor or word processor to write your Pascal programs. If you use a word processor, you must be sure to save the file using an option your word processor will call ASCII or "plain text" or "text export." On the Macintosh, use TeachText or SimpleText to create plain text files.

You start PcPix with a command line that includes the name of the program to be run. (From Microsoft Windows, use a DOS window to run PcPix.) For example, if the program is in a file called HELLO.PAS, the MS-DOS command to run it would be

```
PCPIX HELLO.PAS
```

You start MacPix by double-clicking on the MacPix icon. A file dialog box opens and you select the file containing the Pascal program you want to run.

PcPix or MacPix first displays the message `Translation begins . . .` and processes the Pascal code. If there are syntax errors, it will show them with a brief explanation. Otherwise it will display `Execution begins . . .` and then run your program.

Further information on using PcPix and MacPix is provided on the documentation file included with each interpreter.

Dr. Pascal

Dr. Pascal is an integrated system for writing, running, and debugging Pascal programs. Its "visible" capability lets users look inside their programs as they run—a capability that facilitates discovering errors and understanding how programs work. Dr. Pascal has many features that make it easier to write, test, and modify Pascal programs. Dr. Pascal offers these advantages:

▶ *Dr. Pascal will help you to do well in this course.* An integrated environment like Dr. Pascal makes it easier to do the course's programming problems. Dr. Pascal's visible capability highlights each line as it executes and continuously updates the values of variables. This makes it easier for you to understand new concepts and to learn Pascal.

▶ *Dr. Pascal will save you time and frustration.* Dr. Pascal is much faster to use than PcPix/MacPix and other command-line oriented systems. You can instantly move from editing to compiling to debugging, back to editing, each with a single keystroke. Error checking is extensive. Even for errors other systems do not detect, requiring you to spend time finding them—such as "uninitialized variable" and "pointer already disposed"—Dr. Pascal immediately detects them and points out their location. The combination of visibility and error checking means that you find errors quickly, get programs finished faster, and are more confident that they are working correctly.

▶ *Dr. Pascal is compatible with this book and with other Pascal systems.* Dr. Pascal fully implements American (IEEE, ANSI) and international (ISO, BSI) Pascal standards. This means it will work correctly with the examples in this book, and programs you write with it will run correctly on the greatest number of other computers and other Pascal systems. Dr. Pascal also implements some features of the new standard for Extended Pascal.

How to Order Dr. Pascal

A coupon in the back of this book can be used to order Dr. Pascal at a substantial discount. It can also be used to order other Pascal software packages: an extended Pascal compiler for MS-DOS or two disks of public-domain Pascal software.

The Extended Pascal Compiler is a professional optimizing compiler, which produces executable programs (.EXE) for MS-DOS. It provides four levels of Pascal standards: ISO/ANSI Standard Pascal, the new Extended Pascal standard, or either of these with DOS-specific extensions. The Extended Pascal Compiler is a professional product that can support major commercial software development projects.

One public-domain disk includes software tools for programming projects. The other, Pascal-S, is a working compiler for a subset of Pascal, with documentation, useful for understanding how a language compiler works. The public-domain disks are not commercial products but source-code Pascal programs for use as tools or simply as examples of moderately large, real-world programs.

Dr. Pascal comes complete with a user's manual and a single-user license. To order, fill in the coupon and mail it with your payment. Or call the number listed and give the information on the form—name, address, phone, and whether disk should be Macintosh, PC 3.5" or PC 5.25"—with your credit card number. Be sure to mention "order code AW-1," meaning you have purchased this book so you qualify for the $39 price for Dr. Pascal (plus $4 shipping) rather than the normal price of $89. Dr. Pascal will be shipped by priority mail (domestic) or air mail (foreign) within 2–7 days of receipt of your order.

Instructors: Dr. Pascal can be adopted for student use and ordered through your college bookstore—this is easier than having each student order by mail. Also, schools can purchase Dr. Pascal site licenses for PC, Macintosh, and some minicomputers. For purchase orders, the FEIN/SSN is 227–64–0041. Contact Visible Software for more information:

Visible Software, Box 949, Newark, DE 19715–0949, phone (302) 455–9400

Using Turbo Pascal

When you switch on, or *boot up*, a personal computer, the operating system is loaded into memory from the hard disk (designated as disk drive C) and begins execution. If you are using MS-DOS, the operating system issues the prompt

```
C>
```

to inform you that it is ready for you to type in the next operation. Enter the following commands in color:

```
C>CD \BP\BIN
C>Turbo
```

to enter the Turbo Pascal integrated environment. The first command (CD, for Change Directory) makes the subdirectory \BP\BIN, which contains Turbo Pascal, the active disk directory. This command is installation dependent, so you may need to enter a different subdirectory (for example, \TP\BIN). Typing in Turbo puts you in the Turbo Pascal integrated environment.

If you are using Windows, type in

```
C>Win
```

You will see a screen display that shows icons (pictures) for several applications programs. To enter the Turbo Pascal integrated environment, move the mouse cursor to the Turbo Pascal icon and click the left mouse button twice in rapid succession.

Turbo Pascal Menus

Once in the Turbo Pascal integrated environment, you can create new programs, modify old ones, and compile and run those programs. You can interact with the environment through the *menu screens*. The top line in Fig. G.1 is Turbo Pascal's Main menu (File, Edit, Search, and so on). If your computer has a mouse, you can select a Main menu item by positioning the mouse cursor on that item and then clicking the left mouse button. Otherwise, you can select a Main menu task by pressing and holding down the Alt key and then pressing the first letter of the task name (for example, Alt-F for File). You can also move from one Main menu task to another by pressing the left and right arrow keys.

Figure G.1
Turbo Pascal File Menu

The screen in Fig. G.1 shows what happens when you select File. The list of tasks (New, Open, Save, and so on), all subtasks associated with File, appears on a *pull-down menu*. A different pull-down menu appears for each Main menu task that you select. You can use your mouse to select a subtask from the pull-down menu, or you can move the highlight bar over a particular task (using the up and down arrow keys) and then press Enter. You also can select a task from a pull-down menu by typing in the capitalized letter for that task (for example, N for New) or by pressing the function keys shown on the right of the task (for example, F3 for Open).

The line at the bottom of the screen describes the task you have highlighted (New—Create a new file . . .) and lists other tasks you can select (for example, Press F1 for Help). The bottom line changes as you move from one portion of the Turbo Pascal environment to another.

The dark area in the middle of Fig. G.1 is the desktop area, where you will open the various windows used to create and test your Pascal programs.

On-Line Help

Through its on-line Help system, Turbo Pascal provides additional information about any menu task. If you want more information about a particular menu option, highlight that menu option (using your mouse or arrow keys) and then press F1. A Help window will pop up on the screen, displaying descriptive information about this operation. To exit the Help window and return to your current screen, select Cancel or press Esc (Escape).

Creating a New Program

To create a new Pascal program, you must begin with an empty Edit window on the desktop. To open a new window, select the New option from the File menu, as shown in Fig. G.1. Turbo Pascal 7.0 places you in an Edit window called NONAME00.PAS.

Once Turbo Pascal places you in the empty Edit window, you begin entering your program one line at a time. Press the Enter key after typing each program line, and use the arrow keys on the keyboard to position the blinking cursor anywhere on the screen. Correct typing errors by pressing the backspace key to erase all characters from the current cursor position back to the incorrect character, then entering the correct letters in their place. Figure G.2 shows a complete program in the Edit window NONAME00.PAS.

After your program is complete, place a formatted floppy disk in a floppy disk drive and save your program on the disk by selecting Save or by pressing the F2 key. Up until this point, your program has been assigned the name NONAME00.PAS by Turbo Pascal. Before saving your program with this name, Turbo Pascal gives you a chance to use a more meaningful name. For example, if you want to save your program as file HELLO on disk drive A, type A:HELLO.PAS when prompted by Turbo Pascal, as shown in Fig. G.3. The A: is the computer's disk drive designator, HELLO is the file name, and .PAS is an extension signifying to Turbo Pascal that this file contains Pascal source code. MS-DOS file names (for example, HELLO) may be any combination of

Figure G.2
Program Hello

Figure G.3
Saving Program as
HELLO.PAS

no more than eight letters, digits, or some special characters (no periods or spaces are allowed). If you fail to type a file extension, Turbo Pascal automatically adds the file extension .PAS. Now you are ready to save the file and return to the Main menu, which you do by selecting OK.

Compiling and Running a Program

To compile a program, select the Compile menu from the Main menu bar. Since you wish to compile your program, select the Compile option. Turbo Pascal will begin to compile the program displayed in the Edit window.

To run (or execute) the program from the Main menu after it has been compiled, select the Run menu. Since you want to run the program, select the Run option. Turbo Pascal begins executing the program. The Main menu is replaced briefly by a user screen containing the program output, and then the Main menu display returns. To review your program output, type Alt-F5 (that is, press and hold down the Alt key, then press the F5 key). The user screen containing the program output reappears and remains visible until you press any key on the keyboard, which returns you to the Main menu screen.

Viewing Program Output in Windows

When using Windows, you must insert the line

```
uses WinCrt;
```

as the second line of every program you write. This line causes a window with your program output to appear on the screen. Without this line, your program output will not be displayed.

Loading a File

To load a previously saved file into an Edit window, you must get Turbo Pascal to display an *Open a File* dialog box (Fig. G.4). Do this either through the File menu (select option Open) or by pressing function key F3. When the dialog box appears, either type the name of the file into the bar labeled Name or select the file name from the list shown under the label Files. If you do not have a mouse, press the Tab key to access the list of files, then use the up and down arrow keys to select the desired file.

Exiting Turbo Pascal

The File menu Exit option provides you with a way to leave Turbo Pascal and return to the operating system. If you choose the Exit option and have made changes to your program in the Edit window, but have forgotten to save your revised program, Turbo Pascal gives you one last chance to do so.

Figure G.4
Loading File HELLO.PAS
from Disk A

Reference Guide to Pascal Constructs

Construct	Page	Example of Use
Program heading	33	`program Guide (Input, Output, Infile, Outfile);`
Comment	51	`{`
		`  This program shows examples of`
		`  Pascal constructs.`
		`}`
Constant declaration	38	`const`
Integer	38	`   StringLength = 20;`
Character	38	`   Blank = ' ';`
String	38	`   School = 'Temple University';`
Real	38	`   DeansList = 3.5;`
		`   Probation = 1.0;`
Type declaration		`type`
Subrange	282	`   StudentIndex = 1..100;`
		`   StringIndex = 1..StringLength;`
Enumerated	287	`   College = (Business, Arts, Science, General);`
String	425	`   StringType = packed array [StringIndex] of Char;`
Record	465	`   StuData = record`
		`               Name : StringType;`
		`               GPA : Real;`
		`               InCollege: College`
		`            end; {StuData}`
Pointer	588	`   ClassPointer = ^Student;`
List node	595	`   Student = record`
		`               Info : StuData;          {data field}`
		`               Next : ClassPointer       {pointer}`
		`            end; {Student}`
Array	371	`   MajorArray = array [StudentIndex] of College;`
File	561	`   StuFile = file of StuData;`
Set	546	`   GradeSet = set of 'A'..'Z';`
Variable declaration	38	`var`
Record	465	`   CurStu : StuData;          {input - student data}`
Set	546	`   Grades : GradeSet;         {allowable grades}`
Text file	309	`   InFile : Text;             {input - text file}`

Construct	Page	Example of Use
Binary file	561	`OutFile : StuFile          {output - binary file}`
Pointer	595	`ClassList : ClassPointer;      {list of classes}`
Array	370	`Major : MajorArray;         {array of majors}`
Character	36	`NextCh : Char;            {input - character}`
Integer	35	`CountProb : Integer;            {counter}`
Function declaration	246	`function Member (NextCh : Char;`
Formal parameters		`                  TestSet : GradeSet) : Boolean;`
		`{Returns True only if NextCh is in TestSet}`
		`begin {Member}`
Boolean assignment	124	`  Member := NextCh in TestSet`
Set operator `in`	550	`end; {Member}`
Procedure declaration	231	`procedure PrintSet (InSet : GradeSet);`
		`{Displays set InSet}`
Local variable	220	`  var`
		`    NextCh : Char; {loop control variable}`
		`begin {PrintSet}`
`for` statement	191	`  for NextCh := 'A' to 'Z' do`
`if` statement with	129	`    if Member (NextCh, InSet) then`
function designator	247	`      Write (NextCh);`
`WriteLn` procedure	44	`  WriteLn`
End of procedure	231	`end; {PrintSet}`
Program body	31	`begin {Guide}`
`WriteLn` procedure	44	`  WriteLn ('Registration for ', School);`
Assignment	40	`  CountProb := 0;              {initialize counter}`
`with` statement	470	`  with CurStu do`
Compound statement	118	`    begin                 {define fields of CurStu}`
String assignment	424	`      Name := 'Jackson, Michael Bad';`
Display prompt	45	`      Write ('Enter GPA> ');`
`ReadLn` procedure	46	`      ReadLn (GPA);`
Enumerated assign	287	`      InCollege := Arts;`
Pointer assign	590	`      NextStu := nil`
		`    end; {with}`
`case` statement with	155	`case CurStu.InCollege of`
field selector as	154	`  Business : WriteLn ('Business major');`
case selector		`  Arts     : WriteLn ('Arts major');`
		`  Science  : WriteLn ('Science major');`
		`  General  : WriteLn ('General major')`
		`end; {case}`
Nested `if`	145	`if CurStu.GPA > DeansList then`
Embedded apostrophe	74	`  WriteLn ('   On the Dean''s List')`

Construct	Page	Example of Use
		```else if CurStu.GPA > Probation then```
		``` WriteLn ('Satisfactory progress')```
		```else```
		``` begin```
Format a string	426	``` WriteLn ('On Probation' :21);```
Increment counter	172	``` CountProb := CountProb + 1```
		``` end; {nested if}```
Array element assign	372	```Major [1] := CurStu.InCollege; {save in array}```
Set assign	547	```Grades := ['A'..'F', 'I', 'W'];```
Set union	550	```Grades := Grades + ['P', 'W'];```
Procedure call	101	```PrintSet (Grades);```
Print a set	554	
Open input file	316	```Reset (InFile);```
Repeat statement	197	```repeat```
File read	311	``` Read (InFile, NextCh); {get character}```
Function designator	247	``` if Member(NextCh, Grades) then```
		``` WriteLn ('Valid grade')```
End-of-line test	317	```until EOLN(InFile);```
ReadLn with text file	311	```ReadLn (InFile); {skip end of line}```
while statement with	172	```while not EOF(InFile) do```
end-of-file test	317	``` begin```
File Read	311	``` Read (InFile, NextCh);```
Echo print	69	``` Write (NextCh)```
		``` end; {while}```
Open output file	579	```Rewrite (OutFile);```
File buffer assign	580	```OutFile^ := CurStu; {save in file buffer}```
Put procedure	579	```Put (OutFile); {write buffer to file}```
Write to binary file	562	```Write (OutFile, CurStu); {write second copy}```
Reset binary file	577	```Reset (OutFile);```
Compare strings in		```if OutFile^.Name <> CurStu.Name then```
buffer and record	425	``` WriteLn ('File I/O error');```
Get procedure	577	```Get (OutFile); {get second copy}```
New procedure	590	```New (ClassList); {allocate list node}```
Assign node data	596	```ClassList^.Info := CurStu;```
Allocate second node	596	```New (ClassList^.Next); {connect nodes}```
Assign second node	598	```ClassList^.Next^.Info := OutFile^;```
List traversal	600	```while ClassList <> nil do```
		``` begin```
Display node data	601	``` WriteLn (ClassList^.Info.Name);```
Advance pointer	601	``` ClassList := ClassList^.Next```
		``` end {while}```
Program end	31	```end. {Guide}```

Answers to Odd-Numbered Self-Check Exercises

CHAPTER 1

Section 1.1
1. Software

Section 1.2
1. Cell 0: `75.625`
   Cell 2: `0.005`
   Cell 999: `75.62`
3. Bit, byte, memory cell, main memory, secondary memory

Section 1.3
1. Since computers don't think, they don't check the correctness of your thoughts. If there is a logic error, only you can determine whether the answer makes sense. It is better to catch errors prior to entering the program into the computer.

Section 1.4
1. Add A, B, and C. Store result in X.
   Divide Y by Z. Store result in X.
   Subtract B from C and then add A. Store result in D.
   Add 1 to Z. Store result in Z.

Section 1.5
1. Source program, compiler, editor

CHAPTER 2

Section 2.1
1. Problem requirements, analysis, design, implementation, testing, operation and maintenance

Section 2.2
1. Algorithm with refinements:
   1. Read the fabric size in square yards.
   2. Convert the fabric size to square meters.
      2.1 The fabric size in square meters is the result of dividing the fabric size in square yards by 1.196.
   3. Display the fabric size in square meters.

Section 2.3
1. Declaration section and program body.
3. Reserved words: `end, program, begin, const`
   Standard identifiers: `ReadLn`
   Valid identifiers: `ReadLn, Bill, Rate, Start, XYZ123, ThisIsALongOne`
   Invalid identifiers: `Sue's, 123XYZ, Y=Z, Prog#2, 'MaxScores'`

Section 2.4

1. a. 0.0103   1234500   123450
   b. 1.3E+3   1.2345E+2   4.26E-3
3. Because the value of pi will not change during program execution

Section 2.5

1. Enter two integers>
   M = 10
   N = 10
3. a. Valid, 8.5 is stored in R   f. Valid, digit character 5 is stored in C
   b. Valid, 10 is stored in I   g. Valid, letter I is stored in C
   c. Invalid   h. Valid, value of I is stored in R
   d. Invalid   i. Invalid
   e. Invalid   j. Valid, 10 plus value of I is stored in R

Section 2.6

1. {This is a comment?}
   (* How about this one -it seems like a comment- doesn't it *)
3. program Small (Input, Output);

```
   var
     X, Y, Z : Real;

   begin
     Y := 15.0;
     Z := -Y + 3.5;
     X := Y + Z;
     WriteLn (X, Y, Z)
   end.
```

The first statement says that the name of the program is Small. The reserved word var indicates that variable declarations follow. The next line declares and reserves space in memory for three variables (X, Y, Z) of type Real. The begin line indicates that executable code follows. The first assignment statement sets the variable Y to the value 15.0. The next statement sets the variable Z to negative Y plus 3.5, which is 11.5. The next statement displays the values of X, Y, and Z (3.5, 15.0, and -11.5, respectively). The last line indicates the end of the program.

Section 2.7

1. a. 22 div 7 = 3   7 div 22 = 0   22 mod 7 = 1   7 mod 22 = 7
   b. 16 div 15 = 1   15 div 16 = 0   16 mod 15 = 1   15 mod 16 = 15
   c. 23 div 3 = 7   3 div 23 = 0   23 mod 3 = 2   3 mod 23 = 3
   d. 16 div -4 = -4   -4 div 16 = 0   16 mod -4 = 0   -4 mod 16 = -4

3.

Value of last expression is 2

5. a. White is 2.5.   c. Orange is 0.   e. Lime is 2.
   b. Green is 1.0.   d. Blue is -3.0.   f. Purple is 0.6666....

Section 2.8
# denotes a blank space.
1. #-99#Bottles
   #-99#####-99
3. ####1#1#####1
   ###10#10###10
   ##100#100##100
   #1000#1000#1000

Section 2.9
1. WriteLn statements that display prompts (interactive) precede the associated ReadLn, while WriteLn statements that echo print (batch) follow the ReadLn.

CHAPTER 3

Section 3.1
1. Problem inputs: Hours : Real   {number of hours worked}
                   Rate : Real   {hourly rate of pay}
   Problem output: Gross : Real   {gross salary}
   Algorithm
      1. Read hours worked and rate of pay.
      2. Compute gross salary.
      3. Print gross salary.
3. The algorithm needs to read separately the number of hours to be paid at the normal hourly rate (RegHours) and hours to be paid at overtime rate (OTHours); the formula used to compute gross salary also would need to be modified.

Section 3.2
1. a. Sqrt(U + V) * Sqr(W)
   b. Y * Ln(X)
   c. Sqrt((X - Y) * Sqr(X - Y))
   d. Abs((X * Y) - (W / Z))

Section 3.3
1. The design phase

Section 3.4
1. The code for PrintM would have to be duplicated twice if the program did not use procedures.

Section 3.5
1. Procedure parameters are used to pass information between the separate modules of a program and between the main program and its modules. Parameters simplify the use of a procedure by many different calling procedures or other programs. Procedures with parameters are building blocks for constructing larger programs.

CHAPTER 4

Section 4.2

1. a. Incorrect—`and` has a higher precedence than `<`.
   b. Correct
3. a. `True`   b. `True`   c. `True`   d. `False`   e. `True`

Section 4.3

1. a. Not less
   b. Greater than

Section 4.4

1. `A23B, A1c`

Section 4.5

1. ```
{correct if statement}
if X > Y then
   begin
      X := X + 10.0;
      WriteLn ('X Bigger')
   end
else
   WriteLn ('X Smaller');
WriteLn ('Y is ', Y);
```
3. `Y` would be printed only when `X` is not greater than `Y`.
5. The `if` statement, expression, simple expression, term, factor, variable, statement, and assignment statement syntax diagrams would be used to validate this `if` statement.

**Section 4.6**

1. Step 4 Refinement (revised)
   4.1 Net gets `Gross`
   4.2 `if` there are union dues `then`
         Net gets `Gross - Dues`

3. Initial Algorithm for circular or square pizza:

   1. Read in the pizza's size, price, and shape.
   2. Compute the pizza's area.
   3. Compute the pizza's unit price.
   4. Display the unit price and area.

   Algorithm Refinements for Steps 2 and 3:

   Step 2 Refinement
     2.1 `if` shape is round `then`
         2.2 Compute area for pizza with diameter `Size`.
            2.2.1 Assign `Size / 2` to `Radius`.
            2.2.2 Assign `Pi * Radius * Radius` to `Area`.
       `else`
         2.3 Compute area for pizza with side `Size`.
            2.3.1 Assign `Size * Size` to `Area`.
   Step 3 Refinement
     3.1 Assign `Price / Area` to `UnitPrice`.
```

Area is not used by the first subproblem (Read data). It is computed in the second (Compute area) and is passed out so that the third subproblem (Compute unit price) can use it as an input for further computing. Area is an input to the fourth subproblem (Display results). Because Display writes the results to the screen, the value of Area is a program output (output for program user).

Section 4.7
1. Hours = 41, Rate = 2.25

Section 4.8
1.

Statement Part	Salary	Tax	*Effect*
	13500.00	?	
if Salary < 0.0			13500.00 < 0.00 is False.
else if Salary < 1500.00			13500.00 < 1500.00 is False.
else if Salary < 3000.00			13500.00 < 3000.00 is False.
else if Salary < 5000.00			13500.00 < 5000.00 is False.
else if Salary < 8000.00			13500.00 < 8000.00 is False.
else if Salary <= 15000.00			13500.00 <= 15000.00 is True.
Tax := (Salary - 8000.00)			Evaluates to 5500.00.
* 0.25			Evaluates to 1375.00.
+ 1425.00		2800.00	Tax is 2800.00.

3. a. True with and without short-circuit evaluation
   b. True with short-circuit evaluation; a division by zero error results without short-circuit evaluation.

Section 4.9
1. if X = 2 then
     WriteLn ('Snake Eyes!')
   else if (X = 7) or (X = 11) then
     WriteLn ('Win!');
3. Most of our examples in Section 4.8 contained nested if statements using conditions requiring the comparison of Real expressions, which are not valid as case selectors.

CHAPTER 5

Section 5.1

1. The loop will be executed three times.

   Output: 9
   81
   6561
   3

3. The loop will execute forever if the last statement in the loop body is omitted.

Section 5.2

1. 1
   5
   25
   125

3. Exponential, X raised to the Y power

Section 5.3

1. 0

3. Trace of program in Fig. 5.6:

Statement	InitBal	Balance	Bill	Effect
ReadLn (InitBal)	150.00	?	?	Enter start balance
Balance := InitBal;		150.00		Initialize Balance
while Balance >= 0.0 do				150.00 >= 0.0 is true
ReadLn (Bill);			25.00	Enter first bill
if Balance >= Bill then				150.00 >= 25.00 is true
WriteLn ('Issue check..				Pay the bill
Balance := Balance - Bill		125.00		Reduce Balance
while Balance >= 0.0 do				125.00 >= 0.0 is true
ReadLn (Bill)			30.00	Enter second bill
if Balance >= Bill then				125.00 >= 30.00 is true
WriteLn ('Issue check..				Pay the bill
Balance := Balance - Bill		95.00		Reduce Balance
while Balance >= 0.0 do				95.00 >= 0.0 is true
ReadLn (Bill)			50.00	Enter third bill
if Balance >= Bill then				95.00 >= 50.00 is true
WriteLn ('Issue check..				Pay the bill
Balance := Balance - Bill		45.00		Reduce Balance
while Balance >= 0.0 do				45.00 >= 0.0 is true
ReadLn (Bill)			75.00	Enter fourth bill
if Balance >= Bill then				45.00 >= 75.00 is false
WriteLn ('No check ...				Display Balance
Balance := Balance - Bill		-30.00		Reduce Balance
while Balance >= 0.0 do				-30.00 >= 0.0 is false, exit loop
WriteLn ('Insufficient ...')				Display final message

Section 5.4

1. This is necessary to ensure that the columns will line up. They can do so only if a column width is specified for every output value.

3. `program SumScores (Input, Output);`

```
{Accumulates the sum of exam scores}

   const
     Sentinel = -1;        {sentinel value}

   var
     Score,                {input - each exam score}
     Sum : Integer;        {output - sum of scores}
     SentRead: Boolean;    {flag to terminate loop}

  begin {SumScores}
    {Accumulate the sum.}
    Sum := 0;
    SentRead := False;
    WriteLn ('When done, enter ', Sentinel, ' to stop.');
    Write ('Enter the first score> ');
    ReadLn (Score);
    SentRead := (Score = Sentinel);
    while not SentRead do
      begin
        Sum := Sum + Score;
        Write ('Enter the next score> ');
        ReadLn (Score);
        SentRead := (Score = Sentinel)
      end; {while}

    {Display the sum.}
    WriteLn;
    WriteLn ('Sum of exam scores is ', Sum :1)
  end. {SumScores}
```

Section 5.5

1.

Program Statement	I	J	Effect
	?	?	
J := 10		10	Sets J to 10.
for I := 1 to 5 do	1		Initializes I to 1.
WriteLn (I, J)			Displays 1 and 10.
J := J - 2		8	Assigns 10 - 2 to J.
increment and test I	2		2 <= 5 is true.
WriteLn (I, J)			Displays 2 and 8.
J := J - 2		6	Assigns 8 - 2 to J.
increment and test I	3		3 <= 5 is true.
WriteLn (I, J)			Displays 3 and 6.
J := J - 2		4	Assigns 6 - 2 to J.
increment and test I	4		4 <= 5 is true.
WriteLn (I, J)			Displays 4 and 4.
J := J - 2		2	Assigns 4 - 2 to J.
increment and test I	5		5 <= 5 is true.
WriteLn (I, J)			Displays 5 and 2.
J := J - 2		0	Assigns 2 - 2 to J.
increment and test I	?		Exits loop.

3. a. `for Celsius := -10 to 10 do`
   b. `for Celsius := 100 downto 1 do`
   c. `for Celsius := 15 to 50 do`
   d. `for Celsius := 50 downto -75 do`

Section 5.6
1. a. `(X > Y) or (X = 15)`
   b. `(X > Y) and (Z <> 7.5)`
   c. `(X = 15) and ((Z <> 7.5) or (X > Y))`
   d. `not Flag and (X <> 15.7)`
   e. `Flag or (X > 8)`
3. A `repeat-until` loop may be used instead of a `while` loop when the loop body must be executed at least once.

Section 5.7
1. a.
```
*
**
***
****
*****
```
   b.
```
***
***
***
***
***
```

Section 5.8
1.
```
while Count <= N do
   begin
      WriteLn ('Count = ', Count);
      Sum := Sum + Count;
      Count := Count + 1;
      WriteLn ('Sum = ', Sum)
   end;
```

CHAPTER 6

Section 6.1
1. a. 321   b. 54321 is displayed.   c. 5
   d. M should be declared on the same level that procedure `Down` is called from, be it the main program or another procedure. It must be assignment compatible with integers.

Section 6.2
1.

Statement	X	Y	Z	Temp	*Effect*
`Shuffle (X, Y, Z);`	5	7	2	?	
`Temp := X;`				5	Temp gets 5 from X
`X := Y;`	7				X gets 7 from Y
`Y := Z;`		2			Y gets 2 from Z
`Z := Temp`			5		Z gets 5 from Temp

3. Inputs: W, X
   Outputs: Y, Z

Section 6.3

1.

Actual Parameter	Formal Parameter	Parameter Kind
M	A	Integer, value
MaxInt	B	Integer, value
Y	C	Real, variable
X	D	Real, variable
Next	E	Char, variable
35	A	Integer, value
M * 10	B	Integer, value
Y	C	Real, variable
X	D	Real, variable
Next	E	Char, variable

3. a. Type Real of Z does not correspond to type Integer of formal parameter X.
   b. Correct
   c. Correct
   d. Type Integer of M does not correspond to type Real of variable formal parameter A.
   e. 35.0 and 15.0 cannot correspond to variable parameters. Type Real of actual parameter X does not correspond with type Integer of formal parameter X.
   f. Correct
   g. Parameter names A and B have not been declared in the main program. Type Real of actual parameter X does not correspond with type Integer of formal parameter X.
   h. Correct
   i. Expressions (X + Y) and (Y - Z) cannot correspond to a variable parameter.
   j. Type Real of actual parameter X does not correspond with type Integer of formal parameter X.
   k. Four actual parameters are one too many for three formal parameters.
   l. Correct

Section 6.4

1. You is local to Proc1; therefore it can be referenced only within the block of Proc1, not outside.
   Because Proc1 is declared before Proc2
3. a. Parameter X is set to 5.5; global variable Y is set to 6.6; identifiers M, N, and You are undeclared.
   b. Global variables X and Y are set to 5.5 and 6.6, respectively; identifiers M, N, and You are undeclared.
5. Pi is a global constant. A is a global procedure. F is also a global procedure, but it cannot be called by procedures A or D, which are declared before it. The scope of parameter X and local variables B and C declared in procedure A is the block for A, including procedure D. The scope of procedure D is the block for A. This means it can be called only by A or by itself. The scope of parameter S and local constant Star is procedure D. The scope of parameters X and Y and local variable D declared in procedure F is the block for F.

Section 6.5

1. Functions allow us to simplify numeric computation, since they directly relate to the mathematical view of a function. Also, a well-written function avoids side effects, simplifying program verification.

3. a. Function `Hypot` squares its arguments and returns the square root of their sum as its value.
   b. `C := Hypot(A, B)`

Section 6.6
1. `ComputeSum` contains calls to `Write` and `ReadLn`.
3. Main program data area   `PrintSumAve` data area

Section 6.8
1. `Mystery(4, 3)` → `4 * Mystery(4, 2)` →
   `4 * (4 * Mystery(4, 1))` → `4 * (4 * (4))` = 64
   `Mystery` computes the value of M^N.

CHAPTER 7

Section 7.1
1. The result is `1000.0`. Cancellation error implies the number cannot be represented to this accuracy.

Section 7.2
1. a. `True and True` is `True`.
   b. `True or True` is `True`.
   c. `True and False` is `False`.
   d. `True or False` is `True`.

Section 7.3
1. ASCII values are shown.
   `65 < 97` is `True`.   `48 <> 0` is `True`.
   `65 <> 97` is `True`.   `48 <= 48` is `True`.
   `90 > 65` is `True`.   `51 <= 57` is `True`.
   `90 > 97` is `False`.   `57 <= 65` is `True`.

Section 7.4
1. a. `1`   b. `False`   c. `True`   d. `1`
3. `Ch := 'A';`
   `while Ch <= 'Z' do`
   `  begin`
   `    WriteLn (Ch, Ord(Ch));`
   `    Ch := Succ(Ch)`
   `  end;`

Section 7.5
1. The invalid subranges are `e`, `f`, `g`, `h`, and `i`.

Section 7.6
1. a. OK   c. OK
   b. Out of range   d. `J > 0`

  e. Invalid type   g. Invalid type
  f. OK

Section 7.7
1. a. 1   f. 5
   b. 4   g. Wednesday
   c. False   h. True
   d. Thursday   i. Undefined
   e. Invalid   j. 6

CHAPTER 8

Section 8.1
1. a. An airline reservation program would probably be best implemented as an interactive task, because booking an airplane seat is often done by seeing what's available and then reducing the list of possibilities to a single choice by asking the client about his or her preferences before actually booking the seat.
   b. The task of printing student transcripts could be done as a batch processing task, since the program input could reasonably be stored and the output printed without additional information from the program user.
3. a. N is 123, X is 3.145, C is '3'
   b. N is 123, X is 3.145, C is ' '
   c. N is 123, X is 3.145, C is 'X'
   d. N is 123, X is ?, C is '3'
   e. N is 5, X is 123.0, C is '3'
   f. N is 35, X is 3.145, C is '3'
   g. N is 35, X is 3.145, C is 'Z'
   h. N is 123, X is 3.145, C is 'Z'
5. The \<eoln\> characters indicate when a line should end and the next begin.

Section 8.2
1. InFile is the input file, the screen is the output file, and InFile is tested by function EOLN:

```
Reset (InFile);
while not EOLN(InFile) do
   begin
      Read (InFile, Next);
      Write (Next)
   end; {while}
```

Section 8.3
1. a. Trailing blanks after a name would be copied as part of the employee's name by procedure CopyLine and would not be encountered by the ReadLn statement in procedure ProcessEmp. Trailing blanks after a value read into Rate would cause CopyLine to read a blank name and would cause the error described next.
   b. Blank lines processed by CopyLine would have the effect of having no name printed if encountered by CopyLine and would potentially cause a run-time error if encountered by the ReadLn statement in ProcessEmp (if a name data line were encountered while looking for a numeric data value to read).

CHAPTER 9

Section 9.1
1. Specification, analysis, and design (to analyst); implementation (to librarian).

Section 9.2
1. Procedures are called by other modules, some of which the programmer may be unaware of. Changing procedure parameters would require changes to all programs that use the procedure.

Section 9.3
1.

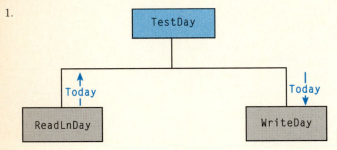

Section 9.4
1. Test data used during white box testing are designed to exercise every logic path within a given code segment or procedure. A procedure interface error would not be discovered until after the procedure has become part of a larger module or complete program and has been called at least once.

Section 9.5
1. a. {invariant:
```
      InRange = False and no N has been read satisfying
      the condition MinN <= N <= MaxN.
}
{assert:
  MinN <= N <= MaxN, or,
  MinN > MaxN and N is not defined.
}
```

   b. Add the following assertion after the `if-then-else` statement:

```
{assert:
  MinN <= MaxN and an in-range value for N has not been
  entered; or MinN > MaxN and it is not possible to
  enter a value of N in the interval MinN..MaxN.
}
```

3. The loop invariant must be true after each loop repetition. `Number > 0` would conflict with the assertion made following the loop that `Number` is 0.

Section 9.6
1. The user cannot override the code that is already within the system, while a computer programmer can create loopholes in that code to cover unscrupulous acts.

CHAPTER 10

Section 10.1

1.
```
type
    XArray = array [1..3] of Real;

var
  X : XArray;
  Y, X3 : Real;
```

3. Five memory cells are allocated for type `Char` data after the variable declaration.

5. a.
```
type
    RealArray = array [Boolean] of Real;

var
  N : RealArray;
```
   b.
```
type
    IntArray = array ['A'..'F'] of Integer;

var
  N : IntArray;
```
   c.
```
type
    BoolArray = array [Char] of Boolean;

var
  Flags : BoolArray;
```
   d. Invalid array
   e.
```
type
    RealArray = array [Char] of Real;

var
  X : RealArray;
```
   f. Invalid array
   g.
```
type
    Day = (Sun, Mon, Tue, Wed, Thu, Fri, Sat);
    RealArray = array [Day] of Real;

var
  Y : RealArray;
```

Section 10.2

1. The initial contents of array X are:

[1]	[2]	[3]	[4]	[5]	[6]	[7]	[8]
16.0	12.0	6.0	8.0	2.5	12.0	14.0	-54.5

Statement	*Effect*
`I := 3;`	Initializes array subscript I to 3.
`X[I] := X[I] + 10.0;`	Increases value in X[3] to 16.0.
`X[I - 1] := X[2 * I - 1];`	Assigns value in X[5], 2.5, to X[2].

```
X[I + 1] := X[2*I] + X[2*I + 1]      Assigns sum of values in X[6] and X[7] to X[4], 26.0.
for I := 5 to 7 do                   Shifts values up one array element. Sets X[5] to 12.0, X[6] to
   X[I] := X[I + 1];                 14.0, and X[7] to -54.5.
for I := 3 downto 1 do               Shifts values down one array element. Sets X[4] to 16.0, X[3] to
   X[I + 1] := X[I];                 2.5, and X[2] to 16.0.
```
The final contents of array X are:

[1]	[2]	[3]	[4]	[5]	[6]	[7]	[8]
16.0	16.0	2.5	16.0	12.0	14.0	-54.5	-54.5

Section 10.3

1. It is better to pass the entire array of data rather than individual elements if several elements of the array are being manipulated by a procedure.
3. I is equal to MaxSize if both arrays are the same; I is equal to 3 if the third elements do not match; I is equal to MaxSize if only the last elements do not match.

Section 10.4

1. The condition (ClassLength < ClassSize) in the while loop evaluates to False; therefore, the loop containing EnterInt is exited.
3. If (TempScore = Sentinel), we do not want the Sentinel value to be included in the array. If (ClassLength = ClassSize), the array is full, so there is no room to insert the next data value, even if it is valid.

Section 10.5

1. a. ClassLength is returned as the position of the match.
   b. The position of the first match is returned.
3. To sort in descending order, replace the > with a < in the comparison statement of function FindMin (Fig. 10.17). Also, rename FindMin to FindMax, FindMin's variable MinIndex to MaxIndex, and SelectSort's variable IndexOfMin to IndexOfMax.

Section 10.6

1. a. N * N times; O(N^2).
   b. N * 2 times; O(N).
   c. N + (N-1) + ⋯ + 2 + 1 times; O(N^2)

Section 10.7

1. Change ReadCode by adding a local Char variable InCode and replace the Read with:
```
begin
   Read (InCode);
   Code[InCode]:= NextLetter
end;
```

CHAPTER 11

Section 11.1

1.
```
   InString                  CurLength
   'The quick '                 10
   'The quick fox jumped'       20
   'The quick fox jumped    '   25
```
3. To compare two arrays of real numbers for equality, you must compare corresponding array elements individually, using a loop. You can use the operator = to compare two strings stored in packed arrays and having the same subscript type.

Section 11.2

1. The number of characters used to display a string is determined by its length
(e.g., `Company :CompLen`); consequently, only the characters actually read in
are displayed, not the blank padding.

Section 11.3

1. a. 20
   b. `WriteLn (Matrix[3,4])`
   c. 11
   d. Offset = 4 × (i - 1) + (j - 1)

Section 11.4

1. a. All the quarters for person 1.
      `Sales[1, Fall], Sales[1, Winter], Sales[1, Spring], Sales[1, Summer]`
   b. The `Spring` quarters for the first 5 people.
      `Sales[1, Spring], Sales[2, Spring], Sales[3, Spring], Sales[4, Spring], Sales[5, Spring]`
   c. The `Fall` quarter for the first 5 people, followed by the `Winter` quarter for
      the first 5 people, and so on.

Section 11.5

1. An array of this type can hold 420 elements (6 × 10 × 7):

```
type
   LetterRange = 'A'..'F';
   NumberRange = 1..10;
   Day = (Sun, Mon, Tue, Wed, Thu, Fri, Sat);
   AnArray = array [LetterRange, NumberRange, Day] of Real.
```

3. The array would be stored as follows:
```
[1, Main, Freshman]        {all elements for course 1}
   ...
[1, Main, Senior]
[1, Ambler, Freshman]
   ...
[1, Ambler, Senior]
   ...
   ...
[1, Montco, Freshman]
   ...
[1, Montco, Senior]
```
All elements for course 2.
```
   ...
```
All elements for course 50.

CHAPTER 12

Section 12.1

```
1. const
      StrLength = 20;
   type
      StringIndex = 1..StringLength;
      StringType = packed array [StringIndex] of Char;
      Part = record
```

```
        PartNum : Integer;
        Name : StringType;
        Quantity : Integer;
        Price : Real
      end; {Part}
```

Section 12.2
1. This program segment prints the statistics for `Exam1`, copies the contents of `Exam1` into `Exam2` (type `ExamStats`), modifies the `High` field of `Exam2`, and finally prints new statistics for `Exam2`.

Section 12.3
1. If `with` is used, we could refer to the record member `Second` directly, conflicting with the existing definition of `Second`.

Section 12.4
1. a. The letter `e`
   b. Invalid
   c. Invalid
   d. `Jones, Sally`
   e. Invalid
   f. The letter `A`
   g. Invalid
   h. Invalid

Section 12.5
1. `NewAddress` must be type `Address`.

Section 12.6
1. a. `Real` data type operators: `:= , +, -, *, /, = , <>, <, >, <= , >=`
      `Real` data type standard functions: `Abs, ArcTan, Cos, Exp, Ln, Round, Sin, Sqr, Sqrt, Trunc`

   b. `Char` data type operators: `:= , = , <>, <, >, <= , >=`
      `Char` data type standard functions: `Ord, Pred, Succ`

   c. `Boolean` data type operators: `:= , = , <>, <, >, <= , >= , not, or, and`
      `Boolean` data type standard functions: `Ord, Pred, Succ`
3. Initializes two data objects and checks whether their key values are the same. It displays the key values: `Jennie Moss*****Jackie Moss`.

Section 12.7
1. `Married`: 16 bytes
   `Divorced`: 6 bytes
   `Single`: 1 byte

CHAPTER 13

Section 13.1
1.

3. The output of the program is 4 3 2 2 3 4.

Section 13.2
1. The actual parameter in the recursive call `Reverse (N-1)` is an expression and must therefore correspond to a formal parameter that is a value parameter.

3.

			Result
`Multiply (5, 4)`	`M| 5`	`N| 4`	?
`Multiply (5, 3)`	`M| 5, 5`	`N| 4, 3`	?
`Multiply (5, 2)`	`M| 5, 5, 5`	`N| 4, 3, 2`	?
`Multiply (5, 1)`	`M| 5, 5, 5, 5`	`N| 4, 3, 2, 1`	?
`Return from (5, 1)`	`M| 5, 5, 5`	`N| 4, 3, 2`	5
`Return from (5, 2)`	`M| 5, 5`	`N| 4, 3`	10
`Return from (5, 3)`	`M| 5`	`N| 4`	15
`Return from (5, 4)`	`M|`	`N|`	20

Section 13.3
1. The output of the program: 3. Function `Puzzle` computes log (base 2) of N or the number of times N can be divided by 2.
3. The resulting Fibonacci number would be the next Fibonacci number in the series, that is, `Fibonacci(n)` = `Fibonacci(n+1)`. This results in the series 1, 2, 3, 5, 8, 13, 21, 34 ... as opposed to the original series 1, 1, 2, 3, 5, 8, 13, 21, 34....

Section 13.4
1. Trace of recursive function `Equal`:
   Call `Equal` with N = 3. X[3] <> Y[3], return false.
3. Function `Mystery` returns the largest value in an array.
   Trace of function `Mystery`:

   Call `Mystery` with N = 3.
      Call `Mystery` with N = 2.
         Call `Mystery` with N = 1.
            `Mystery := X [1]`; (1).
            Return from third call.
         `Mystery := X [2]`; (15).
         Return from second call.
      `Mystery := Temp`; (15).
      Return from first call. Answer is 15.

Section 13.5
1.

Call Number	`First`	`Last`	`Middle`
1	1	9	5
2	1	4	2
3	3	4	3
4	4	4	4

Thus the `Target` of 40 is found at index position 4.

Section 13.6
1. Problems generated from "Move three disks from peg B to peg A":
   1. Move two disks from peg B to peg C.
      1.1 Move one disk from peg B to peg A.
      1.2 Move disk 2 from peg B to peg C.
      1.3 Move one disk from peg A to peg C.
   2. Move disk 3 from peg B to peg A.

3. Move two disks from peg C to peg A.
   3.1 Move one disk from peg C to peg B.
   3.2 Move disk 2 from peg C to peg A.
   3.3 Move one disk from peg B to peg A.

Problems generated from "Move three disks from peg A to peg C":

1. Move two disks from peg A to peg B.
   1.1 Move one disk from peg A to peg C.
   1.2 Move disk 2 from peg A to peg B.
   1.3 Move one disk from peg C to peg B.
2. Move disk 3 from peg A to C.
3. Move two disks from peg B to C.
   3.1 Move one disk from peg B to peg A.
   3.2 Move disk 2 from peg B to peg C.
   3.3 Move one disk from peg A to peg C.

CHAPTER 14

Section 14.1
1. a. Valid: 1, 2, 3, 4, 5
   b. Valid: '1', '2', '3', '4', '5'
   c. Invalid
   d. Valid: '1', '3', 'A', 'B', 'C'
   e. Valid: 1, 10, 500, 501

Section 14.2
1. a. `[1, 3, 4, 5, 6, 7]`   g. `[1, 2, 3, 5, 7]`
   b. `[1, 2, 3, 5, 7]`   h. `[2]`
   c. `[1, 2, 3, 4, 5, 6, 7]`   i. `[]`
   d. `True`   j. `True`
   e. `True`   k. `False`
   f. `False`   l. `True`

CHAPTER 15

Section 15.1
1. In a binary file, 36 bytes are required to store six type `Real` numbers.

   In a text file, 4 bytes are required to store each `Real` number formatted with `:4:2`. If each number is followed by an `<eoln>`, there are 6 bytes per line or 36 bytes in total.

   There are no circumstances in which the storage capacity required to store six type `Real` numbers in a binary file will change. However, this is not true for the text file. The storage capacity will increase if any numbers require more than a field width of four. This will be the case for a real number larger than `9.99` or any negative number.

3. Assuming that six bytes are required for type `Real` and two bytes are required for type `Integer`, then 50 bytes are required to store one component of file `Books` (2 + 20 + 20 + 6 + 2).

Section 15.2
1. The program reads a collection of numbers from `Data` and writes each number less than fifty to `OutData` and displays it on the output screen with the message `'failed.'`

```
program Mystery (Data, OutData);
  type
    NumberType = file of Integer;
  var
    Data : NumberType;
    OutData : NumberType;
    Next : Integer;
begin
  Reset (Data);
  Rewrite (OutData);

  while not EOF(Data) do
    begin
      Read (Data, Next);
      if Next < 50 then
        begin
          Write (OutData, Next);
          WriteLn (Output, Next :2, ' failed')
        end {if}
    end {while}

end. {Mystery}
```

3.
```
type
    ScoreArray = array [1..5] of Integer;

    Student = record
                ID : Integer;
                Scores : ScoreArray
              end;

    StudentFile = File of Student;

var
  StuFile : StudentFile;
  NextStu : Student;
begin
  Reset (StuFile);
  while not EOF(StuFile) do
    begin
      Read (StuFile, NextStu);
      WriteLn (Output, NextStu, ID, NextStu, Scores[1])
    end; {while}
```

Section 15.3

1. The file types are the same, all records are in order by stock number in each file, and both files have a sentinel record at the end. The input files need not have the same number of records.

3. The merge would complete when the end of either file was reached, without transferring the remaining records in the other file.

Section 15.4

1.
```
program Double (InFile, OutFile);
  type
    NumberFile = file of Integer;
```

```
  var
    InFile, OutFile : NumberFile;

begin {Double}
  Reset (InFile);
  Rewrite (OutFile);
  while not EOF (InFile) do
    begin
      OutFile^ := 2 * InFile^;
      Put (OutFile);
      Get (InFile)
    end {while}
end. {Double}
```

CHAPTER 16

Section 16.1

1. a. The string `'CA'` is stored in the `Current` field of the record pointed to by `P`.
   b. The record pointed to by `Q` is copied into the record pointed to by `P`.
   c. Invalid, should be written as `P^.Current := 'HT'`
   d. Invalid, `P` cannot be assigned an integer
   e. Copies the `Volts` field of record `Q^` to record `P^`.
   f. Assigns `P` to point to the same record as pointer `Q`.
   g. Invalid, the `Current` field cannot be assigned an integer.
   h. Invalid, should be written as `Q := P` or `Q^ := P^`.

Section 16.2

1. The memory is not returned to the heap, so it is unavailable for other programs and/or operations that could use it.

Section 16.3

1. a. Assigns the `Link` field of the record pointed to by `R` to point to the same node as `P`. Node `Q^` is deleted from this new circular list of two nodes.
   b. Assigns the `Link` field of the record pointed to by `P` to point to the node pointed to by `R`. The list is unchanged.
   c. Assigns `P` to point to the record pointed to by `P`'s `Link` field (node `R^`). The original first list node is deleted from the list.
   d. Assigns the `Count` field of the record pointed to by `P` to the same value of the `Count` field of the record pointed to by `Q` (`P`'s `Count` field is assigned the value of `3`).
   e. Creates a new node and stores its address in the `Link` field of the record pointed to by `Q`. Initializes the fields of the newly created node to `'zzz'`, `0`, and `nil` for `AWord`, `Count`, and `Link`. Thus a new node is added to the end of the linked list.
   f. Assigns `nil` to the `Link` field of the record pointed to by `P`, thereby denoting that this node is the last (as well as the first) node in the list.
   g. Causes the `Link` field of the record pointed to by `P` to point to the same node as the `Link` field of the record pointed to by `Q`, `nil`.
   h. Copies the `AWord` field from the record pointed to by `R` to the `AWord` field that `P` points to, `'the'`.
   i. Assigns the `Link` field of the record pointed to by `R` to `nil` by following the chain of pointers starting from `P`. Node `Q^` is deleted.
   j. Traverses the list, incrementing the `Count` field of each node by one until all nodes have been processed.

Section 16.4

1. Operator `Insert` does indeed work properly for an empty list. The `nil` pointer gets stored in the `Link` field of the node being inserted by copying the old value of the list head (which was stored in `OldHead`) into the `Link` field.

3. It is easier to insert a new element at the head of the list because it is pointed to by `Head`, whereas there is no pointer to the end of the list.

   To insert at the end of a list, we would have to traverse the list starting at the head until we reach a `nil` pointer value in the `Link` field. We would then allocate a new node, initialize its data fields, connect it to the node whose `Link` field was `nil`, and store the `nil` pointer in the `Link` field of the newly created node.

   This is an O(N) operation because a traversal requires that we examine N nodes.

   To make the insertion at the end of a list an O(1) operation, we need to add a second pointer to the end of the list, say `Tail`, as a data field for a `LinkList` object.

CHAPTER 17

Section 17.1

1. `Pop` removes and returns the element from the top of the stack, providing that the stack is not empty. `Retrieve` returns the element at the top of the stack, providing that the stack is not empty, without affecting the state of the stack.

3. The necessary changes to the type declarations are:
   a. Add field `NumItems`, which should be type Integer.
   b. Add a new header for an operator that returns the value that `NumItems` contains.

   The necessary changes to the operators are:
   a. Initialize `NumItems` to zero in `Init`.
   b. Increment `NumItems` by one in `Push`.
   c. Decrement `NumItems` by one in `Pop`, only if the stack is nonempty.

Section 17.2

1. First expression:

Stack	OpenParen	CloseParen	Balanced
(			
({			
({[			
({	[	]	True
(	{	}	True
empty	(	)	True
(			
empty	(	)	True

Second expression:

Stack	OpenParen	CloseParen	Balanced
(			
({			
({[			
({	[	}	False

Section 17.3

1.

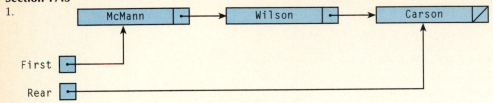

After insertion: Rear points to node following Carson.

After removal of McMann, First points to Wilson.

Customer McMann is the customer removed. There are three customers left.

3.
```
procedure RudeInsert (var Q : Queue; El : QueueData);
   var
      OldFront : QueuePointer;

begin {RudeInsert}
   if Q.Front = nil then
      begin {empty queue}
         New (Q.Front);
         Q.Rear := Q.Front
      end {empty queue}
   else
      begin {extend queue}
         OldFront := Q.Front; {Save old Front.}
         New (Q.Front);          {Allocate node for rude person.}
         Q.Front^.Link := OldFront {Connect to old queue.}
      end; {extend queue}

   Q.Front^.Info := El;
   Q.Size := Q.Size + 1
end; {RudeInsert}
```

Section 17.4

1. The first tree is a binary search tree whereas the second is not.

Inorder traversal of first tree:
    10, 15, 20, 40, 50, 55, 60
Inorder traversal of second tree:
    25, 30, 45, 40, 50, 55, 60

In the left subtree of the node containing 50, one would expect to find key values that are less than 50.

3. a.
```
        25
       /  \
     15    45
    /        \
  10          60
    \        /
     12    55
```

b.
```
        25
       /  \
     12    55
    /  \   /  \
  10   15 45   60
```

c.
```
        25
       /  \
     12    55
    /  \   /  \
  10   15 45   60
```

d.
```
     10
       \
        12
          \
           15
             \
              25
                \
                 45
                   \
                    55
                      \
                       60
```

Trees (b) and (c) are the most efficient to search.

The binary search trees in (b) and (c) are full binary search trees. Every node, except the leaves, has a left and a right subtree. Searching the tree is an O(log N) process.

For the binary search tree in (d), each node has an empty left subtree. Searching (d) is an O(N) process just as in searching a linked list with the same keys.

Section 17.5
1. `Init (MyTree);`
   Creates an empty binary search tree by setting the data member `Root` to `nil`.
   `Insert (MyTree, 3000, Success);`

Inserts 3000 into the binary search tree returning True in Success. This is the root since it is the first value inserted.

`Insert (MyTree, 2000, Success);`

Inserts 2000, in the left subtree of the node containing 3000, into the binary search tree returning True in Success.

`Insert (MyTree, 4000, Success);`

Inserts 4000, in the right subtree of the node containing 3000, into the binary search tree returning True in Success.

`Insert (MyTree, 5000, Success);`

Inserts 5000, in the right subtree of the node containing 4000, into the binary search tree returning True in Success.

`Insert (MyTree, 2500, Success);`

Inserts 2500, in the right subtree of the node containing 2000, into the binary search tree returning True in Success.

`Insert (MyTree, 6000, Success);`

Inserts 6000, in the right subtree of the node containing 5000, into the binary search tree returning True in Success.

`Search (MyTree, 2500, Success);`

Searches the binary search tree for the key value of 2500. Takes the left subtree of the node containing 3000 (since 2500 < 3000), and then the right subtree of the node containing 2000 (since 2500 > 2000). Success is True, indicating that the search key was found.

`Search (MyTree, 1500, Success);`

Searches the binary search tree for the key value of 1500. Takes the two left subtrees of the nodes containing 3000 and 2000, respectively. Success is False (since the left subtree of the node containing 2000 is nil), indicating that the search key was not found.

`Retrieve (MyTree, TreeData, Success);`

Searches the binary search tree for the key value of 6000 (value of TreeData). Searches the right subtrees of the nodes containing 3000, 4000, and 5000, respectively. Success is True, indicating that the key value was found, and returns this element of the tree in TreeData.

`Display (MyTree)`

Displays the binary search tree in key order.

The tree built by the sequence of insertions is:

```
          3000
         /    \
     2000      4000
         \         \
        2500       5000
                       \
                      6000
```

The values displayed are:

`2000, 2500, 3000, 4000, 5000, 6000`

Section 17.6

1. Excluding the pointer comparisons (testing for nil):
   a. With a target key of 50, two comparisons are necessary to find the target:

Key	Result	Subtree taken
40	40 < 50	Right
50	50 = 50	None

b. With a target key of 55, four comparisons are necessary to find the target:

Key	Result	Subtree taken
40	40 < 55	Right
50	50 < 55	Right
60	60 > 55	Left
55	55 = 55	None

c. With a target key of 10, three comparisons are necessary to find the target:

Key	Result	Subtree taken
40	40 > 10	Left
15	15 > 10	Left
10	10 = 10	None

d. With a target key of 65, three comparisons are necessary to determine that 65 is not present:

Key	Result	Subtree taken
40	40 < 65	Right
50	50 < 65	Right
60	60 < 65	None

e. With a target key of 52, four comparisons are necessary to determine that 52 is not present:

Key	Result	Subtree taken
40	40 < 52	Right
50	50 < 52	Right
60	60 > 52	Left
55	55 > 52	None

f. With a target key of 48, three comparisons are necessary to determine that 48 is not present:

Key	Result	Subtree taken
40	40 < 48	Right
50	50 > 48	None

3. There will be no left subtree for each node, only a right subtree. The Big-O notation for searching a tree like this is O(N).

Index

Note: A boldface page number indicates that the term is defined on that page.

ORDER FORM AND COUPON

The Dr. Pascal software can help you in learning Pascal and doing the exercises in this text. See Appendix F for a full description. To order, the information below can be mailed or telephoned to:

Visible Software, Box 949, Newark, DE 19715-0949 USA
Phone: (302) 455-9400

Please send the following software:

❏ Dr. Pascal interpreter for IBM-PC and compatibles ($39)
  Diskette size: ❏ 5.25″   ❏ 3.5″
❏ Dr. Pascal interpreter for Macintosh ($39)
❏ Extended Pascal Compiler for MS-DOS ($130)
❏ Public-domain programming tools ($10)
❏ Public-domain Pascal-S ($10)

Software total _____
Shipping & handling _____ $4.00 ($12 outside North America)
TOTAL _____
Order code: AW-1

Ship to:

Your name _____

Address _____

_____

City _____   State _____

Zip _____   Telephone _____

Payment method (U.S. currency):

❏ Check/money order
❏ VISA   ❏ MasterCard

Card # _____

Expiration date _____

Signature _____
(Add card name and address if different from "Ship to.")

Telephone orders must specify "Order code: AW-1" to qualify for the special $39 price.

A photocopy of this form is acceptable. For more information on Dr. Pascal see Appendix F.